NIXON

Expand your library with other titles from
Regnery History's featured collections

THE PRESIDENTS

Cleveland:
The Forgotten Conservative
by John M. Pafford

Coolidge:
An American Enigma
by Robert Sobel

Nixon:
A Life
by Jonathan Aitken

Reagan:
The Inside Story
by Edwin Meese III

THE GENERALS

Curtis LeMay:
Strategist and Tactician
by Warren Kozak

George S. Patton:
Blood, Guts, and Prayer
by Michael Keane

Hap Arnold:
Inventing the Air Force
by Bill Yenne

Omar Bradley:
General at War
by Jim DeFelice

COLD WAR CLASSICS

Operation Solo:
The FBI's Man in the Kremlin
by John Barron

The Venona Secrets:
The Definitive Exposé of Soviet
Espionage in America
by Herbert Romerstein and Eric Breindel

Witness
by Whittaker Chambers

CIVIL WAR

Backstage at the Lincoln Assassination:
The Untold Story of the Actors and
Stagehands at Ford's Theatre
by Thomas A. Bogar

Lee vs. McClellan:
The First Campaign
by Clayton R. Newell

Lincoln and Grant:
The Westerners Who Won the Civil War
by Edward H. Bonekemper III

The Real Custer:
From Boy General to Tragic Hero
by James S. Robbins

Look for these other collections by Regnery History

EARLY AMERICA & WORLD WAR II

www.RegneryHistory.com

NIXON

A Life

JONATHAN AITKEN

REGNERY
HISTORY

Regnery History™ is a trademark of Salem Communications Holding Corporation; Regnery® is a registered trademark of Salem Communications Holding Corporation

First published in Great Britain in 1993 by Weidenfeld & Nicolson.
First U.S. hardcover edition published 1994; ISBN 978-0-89526-489-3
First U.S. paperback published 1996; ISBN 978-0-89526-720-7
This paperback edition published 2015; ISBN 978-1-62157-405-7

The Library of Congress has cataloged the U.S. hardcover edition as follows

Aitken, Jonathan, 1942–
    Nixon—a life / Jonathan Aitken.
        p.   cm.
    Includes bibliographical references and index.
    ISBN 0-89526-489-7
    1. Nixon, Richard M. (Richard Milhous), 1913–
    2. Presidents—United States—Biography. I. Title.
    E856.A68   1993
    973.924'092—dc20
    [B]   94-5671
                                           CIP

Published in the United States by
Regnery History
An imprint of Regnery Publishing
A Division of Salem Media Group
300 New Jersey Ave NW
Washington, DC 20001
www.Regnery.com

Manufactured in the United States of America.

10 9 8 7 6 5 4 3 2 1

Books are available in quantity for promotional or premium use.
For information on discounts and terms, please visit our website:
www.Regnery.com.

Distributed to the trade by
Perseus Distribution
250 West 57th Street
New York, NY 10107

To Lolicia
Alexandra, Victoria, and William

CONTENTS

ACKNOWLEDGEMENTS

So many friends, helpers, and sources have made this book possible that it is somewhat invidious to single out only a few names for special acknowledgement. Nevertheless, a selection must be made so I begin by expressing my gratitude to the staffs of the principal public libraries and archives on which I relied heavily, notably the Nixon Presidential Materials Project at Alexandria, Virginia; the Nixon Pre-presidential Materials Project at Laguna Niguel, California; and the Richard Nixon Library and Birthplace Archives at Yorba Linda, California. I particularly thank Fred Klose and Diane S. Nixon, Federal Archivists at Laguna Niguel and John H. Taylor, Director of the Nixon Library, whose wise counsel and support at all stages of my researches was invaluable.

In tracing Nixon's footsteps during his childhood and youth I received exceptional help from his brother Edward C. Nixon; his Whittier College contemporary Hubert C. Perry; and his fiancée Ola Florence Welch Jobe. Their recollections, introductions, letters and papers proved to be hitherto unmined seams of biographer's gold. The same may be said of the generous assistance I received from several members of Nixon's long sisterhood of secretaries and personal assistants. They include Evlyn Dorn, his secretary at Wingert and Bewley 1937–40; Dorothy Cox Donnelly, his first secretary as a Congressman who worked for him 1947–60; Betty Lewis Walton, who worked with him on the Hiss case 1948–9; Loie Gaunt, who joined his Senate staff in 1951, remaining his personal archivist and book-keeper; Rose Mary Woods, his private secretary and confidante for nearly forty years; and Kathy O'Connor, his executive assistant today.

From 1947 onwards Nixon lived his life as a public figure and the source notes on each chapter tell their own story of my indebtedness to various interviewees, documents and records. Yet at every stage of Nixon's career I was helped by some outstanding mentors and interlocutors, among them: Patrick J. Hillings and Robert Finch on the congressional years 1947–52; Herbert Brownell, Vernon Walters and James D. Hughes on the Vice Presidency 1952–60; Len Garment, Tom Evans and Ray Price on the wilderness period 1961–8; H. R. Haldeman, John Ehrlichman, Charles E. Colson, Alexander M. Haig and Ron Ziegler on the Presidency 1969–74; Howard Baker,

Sam Dash, Elliot Richardson, G. Gordon Liddy, Len Colodny, Benjamin C. Bradlee and Richard Helms on Watergate; Jack Brennan, Frank Gannon, Diane Sawyer, Bob Abplanalp, Bebe Rebozo, John Taylor and Julie Nixon Eisenhower on Nixon's years of exile and renewal 1974–92. The greatest boon of all to this biography was to be allowed access to so many of Nixon's private papers, letters and diaries, as well as to be granted some sixty hours of interviews with the former President, whose good-natured patience I must at times have sorely tested.

On my own staff, a warm tribute is due to my two principal research assistants Alison Maitland and Sam Whipple, two US citizens resident in London, who lasted the course of my Nixon Marathon with professional dedication and tenacious enthusiasm. I am also grateful for individual items of research work to David Barbour, Helen Haislmaier, Ted Morgan, Jacqueline Williams and Lauri Halderman.

Writing such a *magnum opus* on top of an already heavy workload of parliamentary and business correspondence put severe pressure on the staff of my private office. My personal assistant Lynn Fox carried the brunt of these extra burdens with unfailing cheerfulness and exemplary efficiency. She was helped by Karen Seymour, Jill Denning and Alan Woods, Sarah Chalkley, whose typing of the final manuscript was a paragon of speed and accuracy, deserves a special word of thanks for her contribution.

At my publishers Weidenfeld and Nicolson I am grateful to Christopher Falkus, who commissioned this biography in 1988; to my ever-encouraging editor Ion Trewin; to his editorial assistant Catherine Lightfoot; and to my indefatigable copy-editor Lesley Baxter.

Completing a presidential biography of this magnitude is not unlike docking a liner. There are many hands on deck, but only the Captain-Author is responsible. I alone have steered the course and every judgement, opinion and decision in this book is my own.

Jonathan Aitken

PROLOGUE

'How does a British Member of Parliament come to be
writing a biography of Richard Nixon?'

I first met Richard Nixon in 1966 when I opened the door of a London flat and showed him into a meeting of 'exhausted volcanoes'. Disraeli's phrase was appropriate to describe the three participants: Sir Alec Douglas-Home, a defeated ex-Prime Minister; Selwyn Lloyd, an ex-Foreign Secretary; and Richard Nixon, an ex-Vice President. None of them had a political future, at least in the judgement of contemporary journalism.* So far as Nixon was concerned that judgement was resoundingly confirmed by a trawl through the press cuttings on his defeat in the 1962 election for the governorship of California. The logical conclusion from this research was that not only was Nixon finished, it was a thoroughly good thing that he was finished. He was a second-rate hack politician; a vindictive loser; in John F. Kennedy's phrase, he had 'no class'.

I reflected these views in a background paper prepared for the meeting. To my surprise, Alec Douglas-Home and Selwyn Lloyd were crushingly dismissive of my briefing note, which one of them described as 'complete tosh'. Patiently they explained to their embarrassed young researcher that the man who was coming to tea had a first-class brain, a profound understanding of international affairs,

---

* The judgement was wrong in all three cases. Douglas-Home again became Foreign Secretary 1970–74; Selwyn Lloyd was Speaker of the House of Commons 1970–76; Nixon was President of the United States 1969–74.

and a superb speaking ability. They added that General de Gaulle and Konrad Adenauer greatly admired him and that he would have made a far better President than Kennedy or Johnson. This encomium of Nixon was such heresy in 1966, particularly to a twenty-three-year-old Kennedy admirer, that I began to wonder if my employers had taken leave of their senses.

My anti-Nixon prejudices were shaken still further by listening to the foreign affairs discussion that took place between the three politicians. Alas, the notes of this meeting are lost, but I recall that the conversation centred mainly on Southeast Asia and that Nixon displayed a dazzling mastery of the politics, personalities and differing philosophies of that region. In particular, he made three judgements which look obvious with hindsight but which were prophetic in the mid-1960s. The first was that Japan was on its way to becoming an economic superpower and that if the West did not improve its political communications with Tokyo we would one day be outflanked in trade and aid policies. The second was that Vietnam would turn into a 'quagmire' unless the war ended quickly. The third was that China somehow had to be brought back into the family of nations and that Britain, with its diplomatic representation in the PRC, should act as a long-term bridge builder between Peking and Washington.

Nixon's authority in the foreign policy discussion was commanding, yet it was slightly diminished by his awkwardness of manner. He sounded phoney in the preliminary small talk; he was ludicrously clumsy when it came to putting sugar lumps into his tea with a pair of silver tongs; he kept looking at his watch in a series of surreptitious glances, and his responses to his hosts' far less interesting observations on the Asian scene ranged from the over-deferential to the overenthusiastic. This odd mixture left me puzzled.

It was the first of many contradictory Nixon experiences. I spent much of the late 1960s and early 1970s watching him from the vantage point of a foreign correspondent in Vietnam, in other parts of Southeast Asia, the Middle East, and the United States. Seen from such perspectives, he was by far the most fascinating figure on the world stage in that period, not only because of the power of the Presidency, but also because of the complexity of the President's character. Depending on whom one talked to, Nixon was a giant or an ogre; a peacemaker or a warmonger; a high achiever of soaring grandeur or a base conspirator of villainy most foul. In such polarised forms he wove himself into the fabric of public opinion in almost every part of the world.

Nine months after Nixon's resignation from the Presidency I had my second opportunity to meet him. 'It's like Elba here, but if you can come down and stay with us for a night, the Boss will see you for a fifteen-minute cup of coffee,' said the voice on the line from San Clemente.

The call was from Frank Gannon, a student friend of mine from Oxford days who had been a junior aide in the Nixon White House. He and Diane Sawyer,* another ex-aide from the White House press office, had travelled into exile with Nixon on 9 August 1974, and had become the leading members of the research team helping him on his memoirs. Their invitation was irresistible to a fledgling politician recently elected to the House of Commons. The next day I drove down from Los Angeles and presented myself for the appointment.

In the spring of 1975 Richard Nixon was at the nadir of his reputation. To say that he was in disgrace was an understatement. The bombardment of post-Watergate vilification from his political and media opponents had made him the most despised man in America. Conditioned by this atmosphere when I went into the office that, a few months earlier, had been called 'The Western White House', I almost expected to meet a monster complete with horns and a tail.

The fifteen-minute cup of coffee turned into a conversation lasting more than two hours. Nixon was gracious in his welcome, but nervous in his body language. He was in frail physical health (a Naval Medical Corps man brought him large pink pills at approximately thirty-minute intervals) yet his voice was resonant and strong. He seemed glad to have an overseas political visitor. As he embarked on a *tour d'horizon* of foreign policy developments in various parts of the globe it became clear that his grasp of the international scene was still formidable. He had a striking gift for tying all the threads of a long, analytical discourse neatly together in a precise and authoritative conclusion. As he talked, my mind went back to the 1966 meeting in London, and to those favourable judgements on Nixon by Alec Douglas-Home, Selwyn Lloyd—and at one remove by de Gaulle and Adenauer. The more I listened, I could only surmise that Nixon's ability to attract admiration from foreigners and abomination from his fellow countrymen must be yet another of those perplexing polarisations which always seemed to surround this extraordinary man.

As I was leaving, Nixon asked an unexpected question. 'Everyone who comes to see me these days gives me advice. Do you have any advice for me?' I managed to overcome my surprise enough to mutter something about how I hoped the day would come when he would again speak out in public on foreign affairs as interestingly as he had just been speaking in private. 'Unfortunately it looks as though

---

* Diane Sawyer is now a senior correspondent with ABC News.

the climate of opinion in the United States is not going to let you do that here for some time,' I stumbled on, 'but if you ever feel that you want to make your re-entry into public life on an international platform, I'd be glad to try and help you in any way I could in London.'

Nixon later took me up on this spur of the moment suggestion. His first post-resignation trip to a Western country was to Britain in 1978, and at his request I organised his programme.

The trip got off to a bad start when he arrived at Heathrow Airport. The Labour Government of the day had decided to give a pointed signal that his visit was unwelcome by sending no one to meet him. To make matters worse, one of his *bêtes noires*, the US Ambassador Kingman Brewster, did turn up at the airport apparently with the unusual diplomatic intention of snubbing a former President in person. When asked what role the embassy was playing in the visit, Brewster retorted, 'The minimum'. He taunted the ex-President about the notorious White House Enemies List,* on which his own name had appeared, adding as a parting shot, 'We have given you our bulletproof limousine—just in case you need protection from your enemies.'

Nixon did not enjoy this reception but the atmosphere improved when he walked out towards his car and was recognised by a group of about fifty construction workers. 'Bloody hell, it's Tricky Dicky', one of them shouted, apparently meaning it as a term of endearment since his next call was, 'Three cheers for the ex-Pres'. Hip hip hoorays rang out and the workers waved their hard hats in the air. 'Come and be Prime Minister, you wouldn't be no worse', was another friendly cry. Nixon waved back vigorously as though he was in the middle of an election campaign. 'Great, great', he enthused as he got into the car, beaming in my direction. 'You're a great advance man.' It took some effort to convince him that the demonstration had been entirely genuine and spontaneous.

As the former President's instantly appointed British advance man, I was at his side for virtually the entire four-day visit. The trip is described in detail in Chapter Twenty. It was a riveting experience, full of surprises, and new Nixons, at least to me. I saw at first hand a strategic Nixon engage in substantive foreign policy discussions with political leaders such as Margaret Thatcher, Christopher Soames, and Alec Douglas-Home; a convivial Nixon, singing word-perfect Gilbert and Sullivan duets with Harold Wilson; an intellectual Nixon, jousting with

---

* The White House Enemies List was a memorandum written in August 1971 by the Counsel to the President, John Dean, entitled 'Dealing With Our Political Enemies'. The document proposed that opponents of the Nixon administration be harassed by government agencies. It made a great stir when it was made public during the Watergate hearings.

university professors on philosophy; a literary Nixon, dissecting Disraeli with Robert Blake and Hobbes with Paul Johnson; a happy Nixon, relaxing over claret and political gossip at Marks Club; a kind Nixon, listening sympathetically to a sad tale from a Claridges Hotel waiter about his disabled child; and an eloquent Nixon, winning over hostile audiences with outstanding addresses to students at the Oxford Union, and to Members of Parliament at Westminster. What I did not see at the time was that the trip was excellent therapy for a still-ambitious elder statesman.

Within a year or two Nixon's reputation started to recover in the United States. However, he remained inordinately grateful for the modest trouble I had taken over the arrangements for his British visit, which he saw as something of a breakthrough on his road back to political respectability. Although it seemed unlikely that I could ever be useful to him again, nevertheless he took pains to nurture the relationship with letters, calls and invitations. The most memorable of these resulted in a honeymoon visit to San Clemente of the just married Mr. and Mrs. Aitken in November 1979. The attention to detail taken by the former President to ensure that his newly wedded guests had a magical time at the Nixon family home, La Casa Pacifica, revealed another unexpected dimension to his nature as a generous and touchingly romantic host.

On more routine occasions I became an intermittent caller at Nixon's New York office for talks on foreign policy issues. I was one of a number of young men he used as occasional sounding boards for his writings and speeches. From these encounters I formed a great respect for Nixon's industry and intellect. Gradually I came to the conclusion that his mind was not merely unusual, it had the seer's dimensions of foresight and insight. On the international scene he had a talent for thinking ahead, not just to the next move but to the next decade or generation. He had antennae which could pick on a small item and from it predict with intuitive accuracy some development of far deeper significance. This was a gift which enabled him to make judgements and interpretations which other foreign policy strategists reached much later. After seeing him do this many times I came to believe that there was a touch of the prophet within Richard Nixon on international issues. Such a view was unfashionable in the 1970s and early 1980s, but Nixon's special position as America's outstanding foreign policy strategist has now been widely recognised.

Small talk was always minimal in our discussions, which could be exhausting in their length and intensity. However, by contrast, I also found Nixon enjoyed relaxing over a meal and a good bottle of wine. As he unwound he could become an engaging, and sometimes fascinatingly personal, conversationalist. Although careful to protect his privacy, he could occasionally be careless in revealing glimpses of his intimacy. For in his upbeat or downbeat, Nixon was capable of disclosing many of the insecurities, vulnerabilities and animosities that lie below the surface on the darker side of his personality. However, on a more even conversational keel, the overriding impressions of his character are those of profundity, intensity, realism spiced with cynicism, a surprising generosity of spirit, and a visionary ability to see the big picture clearly.

Listening to Nixon over a long period is not unlike monitoring a complex radio transmitter that broadcasts on a variety of high and low frequencies, sometimes in code. The foreigner can pick up signals that may be missed by the domestic listening posts, and vice versa. One justification for this first non-American biography of Richard Nixon may be the fact that I have stayed tuned to one of his foreign wavelengths for long enough to have caught aspects of his career and character that some others may have missed.

Persuading Nixon to give his co-operation to this book was not easy. He has never before granted a writer over sixty hours of interviews, allowed extensive access to his private papers, and encouraged members of his family and inner circle of friends to talk. I believe that he did this for two reasons. The first was that a good relationship had existed between us for some fourteen years before I asked him if he would co-operate with this biography. The second may perhaps be found in the words of the great French writer and philosopher, André Malraux, used in the White House in 1972 when briefing Nixon on the eve of his historic visit to China, about Chairman Mao: 'Mr. President, you will meet a man who has had a fantastic destiny and who believes that he is acting out the last act of his lifetime. You may think he is talking to you but in truth he will be addressing Death.'[1]

Entering his ninth decade, Nixon undoubtedly thinks beyond death to the judgement of history—which is a long way from becoming final as far as he is concerned. To date the arguments towards it have mainly been conducted in the courtroom of American journalism. That forum has rarely been personally or politically fair to Nixon, nor he to its members. But its traditional atmosphere of mutual antagonism is fading fast, for Nixon has proved an enduring figure, who may well have almost as many books written about him as Napoleon before the historians' appeal court starts to form its verdict.

All I can hope for is that my book will be a useful contribution to the continuing evaluation of America's 37th President. I should make it clear that this is not an authorised biography. Nixon has neither read it nor exercised any sort of editorial control over it. He was generous, although occasionally nervous in his co-operation. He opened doors to his friends, yet was troubled by the number of interviews I conducted among his former enemies. He gave me access to many personal papers, but he still maintains a wall of privacy around himself and much of his archives. Yet, despite these inhibitions, which are par for the course with Nixon, I believe I reaped an exceptionally good harvest from our writer-subject relationship.

From new material comes new judgements. Some of them are harsh. This is certainly not a work of hagiography, even though many of my assessments swim against the stream of journalistic opinion in the United States. At the end of my long biographer's journey into the career and character of Richard Nixon, I found much more to like in the man, and to admire in the statesman, than I had anticipated.

In a life of enormous political turbulence, which stretches from the legacy of Yalta to the era of Yeltsin, Nixon's performance and experience are unique. The same overworked adjective may be applied to his formative years, his faults, his resilience, his resignation and his rehabilitation. Warts and all, he deserves to be portrayed on a grand canvas, for there are few, if any, historical characters of the twentieth century who have had such a remarkable political and personal life.

The last time I saw Richard Nixon I said to him at the end of my final interview, 'Mr. President, most people will, I hope, think that my book adds up to a full and fair biography, but you and I will know that it has failed.' 'What do you mean?' asked Nixon, visibly surprised. 'I mean, I have come to the conclusion that you are too complicated a character to be captured accurately by the pen of a mortal writer.'

'Aha!' he chuckled. 'Now I know you are really getting somewhere.'

Jonathan Aitken
Sandwich Bay, Kent
July 1992

ONE

BACKGROUND AND BOYHOOD

I. FRANK AND HANNAH

> His career was an extraordinary one but there is no need to make it
> seem more extraordinary than it really was. His point of departure,
> though low by the standards of nineteenth-century Prime Ministers,
> was neither as humble nor as alien as some people have believed. It
> is possible to overestimate the obstacles in his way and underestimate
> the assets he possessed.

These are the opening words of *Benjamin Disraeli* by Robert Blake. It was
Richard Nixon's favourite biography, and the passage is underlined in his heavily
annotated personal copy.[1] During his Presidency, Nixon went through a phase of
romantic self-identification with Disraeli, seeing many parallels between his own
career and that of the humbly born outsider who rose by force of intellect and
perseverance to become an outstanding but controversial Conservative leader in
Queen Victoria's England.

In his climb to 'the top of the greasy pole',[2] the story of Disraeli's youth was
clouded in apocrypha. Some of it he embellished himself, but much more was
invented by opponents. Perhaps it was this peculiar symmetry between himself

1

and Disraeli which caused Nixon to underline the book's opening paragraph. Certainly, he resented the mythology which sprang up in some early biographical accounts of his childhood, for he believed that these presented a caricature of his 'cruel' father, his 'cold' mother and the 'grinding poverty' of his upbringing.[3] The reality was rather more normal.

Richard Nixon was born in Yorba Linda, California on 9 January 1913, into a loving family with strong roots and sturdy independence of character on both sides. His father, Francis Anthony Nixon, always known as Frank, was an argumentative jack of all trades whose early character reflected the qualities of a rolling stone, a rough diamond and an erupting volcano. Born in Ohio on 3 December 1878, Frank had a miserable childhood. He grew up in rural poverty. His mother died of tuberculosis when he was eight, and his father remarried a woman who proved to be a harsh stepmother. Frank hated her so much that, at the age of thirteen, he ran away from home, taking his first job as a farmhand with wages of 25 cents a day, plus the right to fatten a calf on the farmer's pasture. When he sold the fatted calf, he spent the proceeds on a new outfit of clothes, quarrelled with the farmer and moved on to a new job. This set the pattern for Frank's nomadic life style for the next fourteen years.

To call Frank Nixon a rolling stone would be to underestimate both the restlessness of his soul and the velocity of his employment record. Among the jobs he is known to have had during his trek across the Midwestern states were: driver of an ox team; carpenter; sheep shearer; bricklayer; potato farmer; potter; house painter; glass-blower; tractor driver; barber; installer of some of the first hand-crank telephones; oilfield roustabout; steeplejack; electrical linesman and streetcar motorman. Later in life, Frank could move his son Richard to laughter with anecdotes from this saga of onward, if not upward, job mobility. It emerged from these stories that the cause of Frank's restlessness had nothing to do with the quality of his work, for he was skilful with his hands and reliable in his duties. A surviving employer's reference, dated 23 January 1900, signed H. A. Cramp, praises Frank Nixon for his work as a farm labourer, stating: 'He has no bad habits that I know of. He does not smoke tobacco or drink.... He does his work fully and well. He is a good man and you will make no mistake employing him.'[4]

In fact, employers did sometimes make a mistake if they took on Frank Nixon. He was a hard worker but he was too fond of arguing.

Although his education had been rudimentary, for he had quit school in sixth grade, he had a natural intelligence and he loved to express himself vigorously.

His Irish ancestry* had given him a quickness to wrath and when roused he had the belligerence of a warrior. Frank's heroes were the War of Independence General 'Mad Anthony Wayne',† from whom his middle name had been taken, and his grandfather George Nixon, who had been killed in action at the Battle of Gettysburg in 1863.[5] Any martial qualities Frank might have inherited manifested themselves in his combative nature. He was a fighter with words. Far from being a boss's man, his idea of a boss was someone who was there to be shouted at. Early in his employment wanderings, his natural belligerence earned him a reputation as a labour agitator. Soon after obtaining a job in 1905 as a streetcar motorman in Columbus, Ohio, Frank rebelled over the company's winter working conditions. These required the motormen or drivers to operate their trams from open vestibules, while the conductors rode inside stove-heated compartments. In the bitter Columbus winters there were many complaints of chilblains, colds and frozen limbs. One particularly bitter day, Frank organised a rally of motormen and won a mandate to demand protected vestibules and other improved winter conditions.

Then he went off to see a local political candidate, telling him, 'If you'll help us get legislation against the open vestibules, we motormen will help you get elected to the State Senate.'[6] The bargain was struck and, after several weeks of manoeuvring, both sides delivered. In spite of fierce opposition from the railway company, closed vestibules were introduced by law.

Frank's employers were far from enchanted by the extra expense necessitated by his leadership. He got the sack. However, by moving to Los Angeles, Frank was soon able to land another streetcar motorman's job and in 1907 he was to be found driving the trams on the Red Line, which ended at Whittier.

Whittier‡ was a Quaker town twenty-five miles east of Los Angeles, where social life centred on the Friends Church. Early in 1908, Frank Nixon, who was a devout Bible reader and worshipper even in his nomadic bachelor days, attended a Sunday service there. His roving eye picked out an attractive girl in the choir.

---

* The origins of the Nixon ancestry are lost in the mists of Irish genealogy. They were Ulster Protestants, originally from Fermanagh and South Tyrone, with later offshoots in Scotland and County Wexford. The first Nixon to come to America was James Nixon in the early years of the eighteenth century. He died in Delaware in 1773. He was Richard Nixon's great-great-grandfather.

† Mad Anthony Wayne' (1745–96) was a legendary soldier who had earned his nickname leading the most daring action of the War of Independence, the recapture of Stony Point (1779).

‡ Whittier was named after the anti-slavery Quaker poet John Greenleaf Whittier (1807-92), a staunch ally of the emancipationist William Lloyd Garrison.

Her name was Jane Milhous, and Frank managed to get an introduction and an invitation to accompany her to a St. Valentine's Day party organised by the Society of Friends. At the party, on 14 February 1908, he discovered that Jane had five sisters, one of whom, twenty-two-year-old Hannah Milhous, seemed to him even more attractive. At the end of a circumspect evening of conversation and taffy pulling,* Frank Nixon asked Hannah if he could walk home with her. 'I'd be delighted', she replied.[7] Thus, under the legendary influence of St. Valentine, their courtship began. As it advanced, the Milhous family were, at best, ambivalent about Hannah's new admirer. 'The Milhouses thought highly of the Milhouses',[8] was how one relative described their tribal complacency, which was ruffled by Frank with his bombastic arguments, his ungrammatical speech, and his fiery temperament. 'He was very unlike my birthright relatives,' wrote the Milhous novelist cousin Jessamyn West, 'who were quiet, subdued, inclined to see both sides of every question. Frank saw one side: his; and he was not bashful about letting you know what was wrong with your side.'[9]

Frank was always better at bashing than being bashful, and perhaps it was his exciting, bull-headed energy that first attracted Hannah, whose sisters recoiled and advised ending the romance. Objectively, their arguments sounded convincing. Frank had no prospects. He was not a Quaker. He had no educational background. His social standing was far below that of the middle-class Milhouses.[†] His noisy, anti-establishment political opinions jarred with the prevailing Republicanism of the Whittier community. His demonstrative behaviour, which sometimes included public physical embraces of Hannah, embarrassed her reserved relatives and offended their taste for privacy and restraint. Worst of all, Frank planned to marry Hannah quickly, taking her out of her college education and away from her close-knit family. When the engagement was announced the youngest Milhous sister, thirteen-year-old Olive, summarised her relatives' feelings when she scribbled on the trunk of the pepper tree in her father's back yard, 'Hannah is a bad girl.'[10]

---

* Taffy pulling is the equivalent of making candyfloss.

† The Milhous family were of German descent and were originally named Melhausen. In 1729 they emigrated to Pennsylvania via England and Ireland. In 1897, Richard Nixon's grandparents, Franklin and Almira Milhous, moved with their nine children from Butlerville, Indiana to Whittier, California. Franklin was a devout Quaker and a prosperous nurseryman. He died in 1919, having been one of the first major contributors to the endowments of the Whittier Friends Church and Whittier College. After his death the family was often called the 'Milhous Matriarchy' on account of the strong personalities of Almira Milhous and her six daughters.

Neither Frank nor Hannah took much notice of such objections. Hannah was attracted to Frank's good looks and muscular physique. He, in turn, saw beauty in her tranquil face, whose high cheekbones and intense, greenish-brown eyes fell away to the strange twirl of the Milhous ski-jump nose, which cartoonists loved to caricature when it was later inherited by her son Richard.

Yet it was more than physical attraction that drew the unlikely couple together. Frank's raw intelligence sparkled in communication with Hannah's well-stocked mind. Hannah's air of stained-glass-window serenity drew warmth from Frank's boisterous *joie de vivre*. Each brought new dimensions to the other as passion met privacy; education met energy; and vigour met vision. Hannah also had the inner strength to cope with the darker side of Frank's nature, which revealed itself in sporadic shouting, explosions of temper, and outbursts of vindictiveness.

Frank was certainly a challenge, yet for all his attractions, it is possible that Hannah might ultimately have bowed to family pressure if he had not touched a particular chord in her compassionate nature. In a perceptive comment Richard Nixon has highlighted what may have been the final motivation for Hannah to accept Frank's proposal of marriage:

> I think another thing that affected her was the fact that she felt he really needed her. I mean, my mother had such a heart and I think when she realized that this boy hadn't had a mother and hated his stepmother, and had never really had much of a chance in life—well that was it.[11]

On 25 June 1908, just four months after they had met, Frank Nixon and Hannah Milhous were married. Their first permanent matrimonial home was at Yorba Linda, an agricultural settlement thirty-five miles southeast of Los Angeles. Hannah's father, Franklin Milhous, had advanced $3,000 to his daughter and son-in-law in 1910*.[12] With this money they bought twelve acres of land and a $800 do-it-yourself house-building kit from Sears department store. Frank planted the land with lemon tree seedlings from Franklin Milhous's nursery and used his carpentry and bricklaying skills to assemble a one-storey timber-frame house, 700 square feet in size with double gables facing east. It was in the ground-floor bedroom of this house that Richard Nixon was born at 9.35 p.m. on 9

---

* $3,000 in 1910 would be equivalent to approximately $42,000 in 1990.

January 1913. His parents' joy at the safe arrival of a second son was tempered by their foreboding over the weather, an unprecedented cold spell with temperatures well below freezing. Frank had bought the property at Yorba Linda on the basis of an assurance from the real estate broker that the area was 'frost free'. The unexpected climatic discovery that lemon groves in Yorba Linda could be ruined by frost was to give the Nixons constant financial worries during their unsuccessful years as citrus farmers.

The new baby was named Richard after Richard the Lionheart, with Milhous as his middle name. Hannah's interest in European history caused her to name four of their five sons after early English Kings. They were: Harold, born 1909; Richard, born 1913; Francis Donald, born 1915 (named after Frank but always called Donald or Don); Arthur, born 1918; and Edward, born 1930. In spite of such monarchical names there was nothing royal about the Nixon residence. It consisted of one upstairs bedroom for the boys, one downstairs bedroom for the parents, a living room, kitchen, and outside privy. There were no modern conveniences; in 1913 the family were without electricity, running water, wireless set, refrigeration, telephone or motor car. Light was provided by oil lamps and heat by a wood-burning stove on which Hannah cooked all meals. The centrepiece of the house was a brick fireplace, the pride and joy of Frank's craftsmanship, which looms large in Richard's earliest memories:

> It was a marvelous fireplace which the old man built. It threw out a lot of heat, so we'd come down and sit around that fireplace and it seemed like it was a very big room and a very nice room. I guess what I remember most about that house though was talking. There was no television then. There was no radio. But we did talk evening after evening. And that's one of the reasons that I think I got an interest in politics very, very early because I can even remember my father berating my mother for having voted for Woodrow Wilson in 1916.[13]

This engaging picture of the future President of the United States sitting round the blazing hearth at the age of four, absorbing the issues of the 1916 presidential election, may have grown in the telling. But politics is a disease that can be caught young and it is interesting to note that throughout his career Richard Nixon had a fascination with Woodrow Wilson, quoting him more often than any other American statesman, and even moving what was thought to be Wilson's desk* into the Oval Office of the White House on the first day of his own Presidency in 1969. Moreover, the sheer magnitude of the military conflict engulfing Europe in those years meant that the First World War and Woodrow Wilson's role in it did make an impact on Richard's earliest consciousness. He remembers a visit to Yorba Linda from Frank's stepbrother, Lieutenant Hugh Nixon, in Navy uniform, telling dramatic tales of battles at sea. Another memory was of being allowed to touch a collection of spent shells and grenades brought back from the Western Front by Olive Milhous's husband, Uncle Oscar Marshburn. He also remembered accompanying his grandmother to the bedsides of horribly wounded soldiers in the Veterans Hospital at Sawtelle, West Los Angeles, but his most vivid impression was the coming of peace on 11 November 1918.

> The church bell rang, the big whistle at the packing house came on full blast, and everyone was enormously excited...I was then only five years old but I can remember it to this day. We went from Yorba Linda to Placentia where the American Legion had a parade, and I remember they had an effigy of the Kaiser hanging on one of the floats and I thought it was the real Kaiser they had hanging there![14]

Apart from the occasional dramatic episode to fire the boys' imagination, the First World War made little impact on the Nixon family. Frank had been exempted from the draft as the father of four young dependants, who were able to enjoy a healthy childhood in the then unspoilt countryside of southern California. Richard Nixon caught the flavour of the rural atmosphere around his boyhood home at the age of twelve in a school essay, 'Autobiography':

> One of the times of the year that I looked forward to was the time that the cover crop was sown and had reached its full height. Our neighbor boys, my brother and I, would go out and play games in it as it would be very tall and would make a fine place to hide. In front of our house was a holow [sic] with some tall trees in it. This made a fine place for a crazy house as we called it. We would make passages through it and holes for somebody to fall in. We would cover these holes over with sticks and brush so that they could not be seen. We would then let somebody walk through it. One day a young cousin,

---

* It was later discovered to have been the property of Henry Wilson, Vice President under President Ulysses S. Grant (1869–77).

Russ Harrison, and I climbed high in the holow. My oldest brother Harold got an axe and chopped down the tree. We stayed on it and it gave us quite a scare but we were not hurt.

On summer days when it was very hot we went in swimming in the irrigation ditch. Sometimes the boss would catch us. He said that he would put us in jail the next time he caught us, but we haven't been there yet![15]

Such happy memories of Yorba Linda are echoed by another writer who subsequently became famous, Jessamyn West. She grew up contemporaneously with her cousin Richard, living close to the Anaheim irrigation ditch only a few doors away from the Nixons. In several of her books and essays, West has vividly described the beauty of the area and its rural pleasures, calling her childhood 'the Midas time of my life'.[16]

There were no Midas touches in the Nixon household. The problem was not poverty, but cash flow. The ranch never fully recovered from the great freeze at the time of Richard's birth and the loss of the lemon trees meant a drop in income. Hannah went out to work, earning money as a packer in the local Sunkist Oranges factory. Frank contracted out his handyman's skills, plying his various trades as a carpenter, bricklayer, painter and tractor driver. The boys had to help with the farm chores, doing daily tasks of hoeing, weeding and watering in the lemon groves. Times were hard, but the family was a happy one. They always had enough to eat thanks to their large vegetable garden in the back yard, their fruit trees and their cow.

In his later years, President Richard Nixon liked to put a gloss on the hardships of life at Yorba Linda by citing a quote from President Dwight Eisenhower about his childhood in Abilene, Kansas. 'We were poor, but the glory of it was, we didn't know it.'[17]

In fact there were times when the boy Richard did resent the pressures of living on a low income. He has recalled how much he wanted to join the boy scout troop in Yorba Linda as his brother Harold had done, but 'the family budget simply wouldn't allow for another member of the family to be a scout even though the fee was very small—just the uniform and very small dues'.[18] He minded the fact that, of all the families in Yorba Linda, his parents alone could not afford to buy fireworks, even the small, 25-cent firecrackers for the Fourth of July celebrations. He has remembered Thanksgiving Dinners when the traditional fare of turkey had to be replaced by a cheaper chicken. He was bitterly disappointed when he was left behind as his parents set off on a train journey to Ohio in 1918, taking only Donald with them. It had to be explained to Richard that he was just over the five year old age limit for free travel, and even a half-price ticket could not be afforded.

> There were other ways we kept down our family budget. My father in addition to his many other skills had once worked in a barber shop. He used to cut our hair and while he did a pretty professional job I recall that his impatience in cutting the hair of four young boys would lead him to try and work too fast so that the hand clippers—there were no electric ones at that time—would get snarled into our hair with the inevitable discomfort which resulted. It was not until I was nine or ten years old that I went to the barber's shop for a haircut and I can still recall what a relief it was not to have to go through the ordeal of having my father cut my hair. My brothers incidentally unanimously agreed with me on this point.[19]

In or out of his makeshift barber's salon, Frank Nixon could be irascible. As a father he did not suffer foolish sons gladly. Yorba Linda residents of that period had many memories of times when 'shouting could be heard all through the neighborhood',[20] as Frank clashed with the boys, particularly Harold and Donald, who often goaded him to fury by their disobedience or by hollering back at him in an argument. Richard, however, showed early signs of diplomatic skill by managing to steer clear of most of these rumpuses. His technique, which he picked up from his mother, was to keep quiet until the storm had passed. Nevertheless, the effort required to avoid such scenes left its mark on him, for as he put it in a revealing line of his memoirs: 'Perhaps my own aversion to personal confrontations dates back to these early recollections.'[21]

In spite of his contrary nature, Frank was a loving father. His fiery temper would erupt without warning, but his bad moods blew away swiftly, and he was equally warm in showing and giving affection. Some neighbours, who may not have experienced the more private side of Frank the father, thought he was too harsh with his children, but Richard Nixon insists that this was wrong.

> My father had a pretty loud bark but his bite was far less severe because of the very hard life he had led. I imagine that he had received some pretty good lickings when he was a youngster. He was really very soft-hearted when it came to dealing out punishment to the boys. I always used to tell Don and even Harold, who was three years

older than me, that they made a mistake when they deliberately crossed him when he was in a bad temper. He would heat up pretty fast but he would cool off just as fast. Consequently I have no memory at all of his using his razor strap on me, and very few recollections of his resorting to its use even with my two brothers. Arthur was punished only once as I recall. This was the occasion when he was about six years of age, smoked cornsilk with some of the neighbors' children and my father found out about it. In that case all my father did was to send him to bed without his supper. He had an especially warm place in his heart for what was then my youngest brother.[22]

Hannah was a very different sort of parent and disciplinarian. She endured Frank's rages in stoical silence, disapproving of his threats and of his occasional executions with the razor strap. Hers was the still small voice of calm in the household and it was evidently effective, for when it came to punishments, the boys dreaded their mother's quiet lectures far more than their father's yelling. 'Tell her to give me a spanking. I just can't stand it to have her talk to me',[23] said little Arthur after the smoking episode, reflecting the view of all the Nixon boys that a private ticking-off from Hannah was far more of a deterrent than another volcanic eruption from Frank.

Hannah was a saintly mother, utterly dedicated to her faith and family. There was a touch of the mystic about her. Occasionally, her inner fires burned and she would talk with lyrical eloquence when explaining a passage from the Bible, or when describing the beautiful sunrises and sunsets she remembered from the harvest times of her childhood. More often, she had the quiet stillness of a nun, saying little in a low, sweet voice.

This enigmatic aspect of her personality was variously interpreted. Her youngest son, Edward, believes that his mother's silences were deceptive in the sense that she had formidable inner strength. 'She had a temper too, but controlled. She knew how to throttle my Dad if he was hurting one of us unintentionally... she was the great defender of hurt feelings in our family... she always looked beyond an action thinking in terms of consequences two or three moves ahead, but she often did not say much at the time because she had a proper sense of privacy.'[24]

Hannah's emphasis on privacy could seem curious to those outside the family. Many of her neighbours believed she had the Quaker virtue of 'peace at the center', detecting in her contemplative, almost fatalistic reserve a higher dimension of spiritual goodness. Others wondered whether she suppressed her emotions too much. Never a tactile mother, she gave few outward expressions of her affection. Yet she loved her sons in her own fashion, and as later events during times of illness showed, there were few limits to her maternal devotion.

Hannah was a character of still waters. How deep they ran was a matter for speculation among some of her contemporaries. Was she a 'Quaker Saint' as so many people called her? Or was she 'too good to be true', as others occasionally wondered?[25] Richard Nixon had no doubts. He adored his mother, giving an interesting insight into their relationship when responding to a question as to whether Hannah's sense of privacy made her seem a private person even to her sons:

> No one projected warmth and affection more than my mother did I think it could objectively be said that she loved everybody and everybody loved her. But she never indulged in the present day custom, which I find nauseating, of hugging and kissing her children or others for whom she had great affection. She was unsparing in her praise when we did well at school but never berated us when we might do badly. She believed only in positive incentives, never negative ones. Only one of those rather pathetic Freudian psychiatrists would suggest that her love of privacy made her private even from her sons. She could communicate far more than others could with a lot of sloppy talk and even more sloppy kissing and hugging—I can never remember her saying to any of us 'I love you'—she didn't have to![26]

Richard Nixon's relationships with his parents were complicated, but central to the formation of his character. On the negative side, it can be said that any boy would have found it difficult to have a secure filial rapport with Frank. 'All of us were kept on edge, concerned that Dad might explode and hurt someone with his tongue', recalled his youngest son, Ed. 'Boy, he could castigate us, but he loved us too.'[27] Such an erratic father must at times have been a heavy cross to bear, yet there was also an inspirational side to a parent with so much energy, such enjoyment of argument, and so many enthusiasms.

Hannah offered inspiration of a different kind. She started Richard on the high road to educational excellence. She gave him his noblest political ambition—the yearning to be a peacemaker. As long as she was alive she acted as a sheet anchor on his morality, and as a standard bearer for his idealism. In return, he loved her deeply, as so many of his later writings and actions have demonstrated. That her emotional response to her children was more cerebral than physical never consciously troubled her second son. Whatever 'pathetic Freudian psychiatrists' may make of a parent who did not kiss, hug, or say 'I love you', Richard was always intuitively confident of Hannah's maternal devotion. Perhaps the bond between mother and son was too deep for others to comprehend, but it was the strongest single influence on Richard Nixon's life.

II. THE SERIOUS SCHOOLBOY

One way in which both Frank and Hannah did demonstrate their love was in their willingness to make sacrifices for their children. As parents, they were dedicated to ensuring that their sons obtained the best possible education. At an early age they concentrated their efforts on Richard, as he showed most signs of being a talented and perhaps even a gifted child.

The making of the early mind of Richard Nixon owed most to his mother. If her marriage had not cut short her college education she would have become a teacher. She was a well-educated young woman, proficient in Greek, Latin, German and French, with a deep interest in European culture.

Hannah taught Richard to read before he went to infant school and awakened his interest in her own specialised areas of classics, languages, and history. By the age of five he had received a solid grounding in the three Rs and was an avid reader of children's encyclopaedias, history stories and adult periodicals.

Among the early volumes that captivated him were *Great Heroes of Early America; Greek Myths and Fables; The Wonderworld Children's Encyclopaedia;* the poems of James W. Riley; and the history stories of Inez N. McFee. As for publications, the Nixons took the *Los Angeles Times,* the *Saturday Evening Post,* and the *Ladies Home Journal.* Richard read them all and thirsted for more, so he regularly visited his Aunt Olive Marshburn to borrow her copies of the *National Geographic* magazine. This journal fired him with wanderlust. In later life, Richard Nixon often vividly described how he used to lie awake at night in the upstairs bedroom at Yorba Linda, listening to the train whistle from the nearby Santa Fe railroad, yearning to take a ride to the exotic locations he had read about in the *National Geographic.*

This international curiosity had its origins in Hannah's early teachings. She opened Richard's mind to European culture; started him off in French and German; introduced him to Shakespeare; and trained him to recite poetry. Hannah was, above all, a classicist. She believed that Latin was the fountainhead of language, and that the ancient historians and orators were the masters of clear expression. These nineteenth-century European disciplines left their mark on the little boy who was destined to become one of the twentieth century's most enduring American politicians. Under his mother's tutelage the classics cast a strong spell over Richard's childhood imagination. He remembers being 'fascinated by Roman and Greek mythology' and by the historical giants of that era such as Caesar, Cicero and Demosthenes.

> Curiously enough I never found the study of Latin to be as dull as most people did. Part of the reason was that I was fascinated by the Roman Heritage and being exposed to it in Latin as well as in English made an indelible impression on me...There is little doubt in my mind that the discipline I had to develop in studying Latin had a major effect on my later writing and speaking characteristics.[28]

Besides expanding Richard's mental curiosity and capabilities far beyond the horizons of the average five year old, Hannah drilled into him the importance of working hard in order to grow up to be somebody. A small clue to her aspirations for her second son was her attempt to stop the use of the nickname Dick as too frivolous, perhaps, for a future man of importance. 'By the way Miss George, please call my son Richard and never Dick. I named him Richard',[29] Hannah told his schoolteacher on the day he entered the first grade of Yorba Linda Elementary School in September 1919. Miss Mary George never forgot to comply with the request—one of the many reasons why this little boy was rather different from the others in her class. Her recollections of Richard Nixon's early progress are revealing:

> He was a very quiet, studious boy and kept mostly to himself... he was one of those rare individuals born with knowledge. He only had to be exposed or shown and he never forgot...he absorbed knowledge of any kind like a blotter.... in that year he read no less than thirty or forty books, maybe more, besides doing all of his other work.... He never had to work for knowledge at all. He was told something and he never forgot. He has a photographic mind, I think.[30]

Although this early assessment of Richard's ability by his first schoolmistress may be too flattering, nevertheless Miss George's reference to the photographic quality of his mind was perceptive. The phrase 'photographic memory' falls too easily from tongue and typewriter and is rarely accurate, but what can be said with certainty of Richard Nixon is that he was blessed with a highly retentive memory. For various reasons it has often suited him during his career to downplay or even to dissemble about this remarkable gift. Even today he prefers to brush aside discussion of this talent with the comment, 'My memory is very good only for a mundane reason—I worked at it.'[31] However he acquired it, there is little doubt that this capacity for remembering information of every description, from names, facts and figures to speeches and documents, was fundamental to his later political success.

Richard's first success came at the age of six, when Miss George decided he was too advanced in his learning skills to spend his next year in second grade like all the other children in his class, so she jump-promoted him from first to third grade with effect from September 1920. Although Yorba Linda Elementary was just a small village school with only four teachers, there was an interesting multiracial and international flavour to its intake of pupils due to the influx of outside workers after oil had been struck near the town in 1919. In addition to the Black and Mexican children, there was competition for top places in the class from a young Japanese girl, Yoneko Dobashi; from the sons of a Chinese family; and from the brightest offspring of the Quakers who were the largest element in the population, for Yorba Linda had been founded as an offshoot of the Whittier Friends community.

Richard beat the competition from his schoolmates and was consistently top of his class during his three years at Yorba Linda school from 1919 to 1922. His first year's report card, which survives in the family papers, awarded him an E (Excellent) in every subject except handwriting, for which he received a U (Unsatisfactory).

Also surviving in the archives are one or two of his early school exercise books. One of them consists mainly of famous speeches and poems, copied out with scrappy copperplate penmanship. There is Lincoln's Gettysburg Address: 'Four score and seven years ago our fathers brought forth upon this continent a new nation conceived in liberty and dedicated to the proposition that all men are created equal'; Mark Antony's Funeral Oration: 'Friends, Romans, Countrymen, lend me your ears'; Antony's speech on Brutus: 'This was the noblest Roman of them all'; Rudyard Kipling's Recessional: 'Lord God of Hosts be with us yet, lest we forget, lest we forget'; and many more. The school imposed these as handwriting tests, but Hannah made Richard learn them by heart. When he performed them, the effect was startling.

Virginia Shaw, who was two years senior to Richard in the school, is one of several witnesses of that period who have recorded, in 'Oral History' reminiscences, their amazement at how this tiny little Nixon boy could manage to recite

long extracts from Shakespeare and other poets. She recalls one particular dec-
lamation contest at the Friends Church when Richard, the youngest competitor,
was up against his brother Harold and other older children.

> We all learned poems. Harold learned one, I learned one, and my
> brother Gerald learned one and Richard was in on it. So was Mildred
> Dorsey and her older sister. We got up on the platform and said these
> pieces. Of course Harold and I were confident that we were going to
> win. But Richard won it and we were so jealous. We just really thought
> it was because he was so little and had such a long piece… I remem-
> ber all of us were very very envious that this little five-year-old could
> come in and recite this long poem.[32]

Richard's parents had every reason to be proud of him. This must have been
a spectacle to savour, the Yorba Linda equivalent of the Whig historian Thomas
Babington Macaulay holding the drawing rooms of nineteenth-century London
spellbound when, aged four, he recited the great soliloquies from *Hamlet*. But
unlike Macaulay, whose gifts of memory gave him great conceit at an early age,
Richard Nixon was never allowed to become bigheaded. The grind of the farm
chores, the shortage of family money, the sibling rivalry, and the disciplines of
the Quaker Church (once felicitously described as 'no pomp in any circumstance')
were all strong antidotes to excessive self-esteem.

The Friends Church in Yorba Linda was important in the upbringing of
Richard Nixon, who followed a regime of daily prayers and four services on Sundays. This discipline was initiated by Hannah, a devout birthright Quaker, but
Frank, who had been a practising Methodist before marriage, changed in 1909
to the Quaker faith and embraced it with the archetypal zeal of the convert. He
was a leader of the congregation at the Friends Church and became the Sunday
school teacher, largely because no one else could control a rowdy group of boys.
Frank rose to the challenge and was the most impassioned of pedagogues,
impressing on his swiftly quiescent class the connection between spiritual and
civic values. 'Frank was certainly ardent in his Sunday school teaching', remembered Jessamyn West. 'His cheeks flamed and his voice trembled.… All of us who
had been in his class had been convinced that Christians should be political and
that politics, if not Christian, should at least be ethical.'[33]

Frank earned a lot of respect in the town because of his good works at the
Sunday school. It was also widely noted how sharp young Richard was as a member of the class, participating enthusiastically with a wide range of political and

religious opinions of his own. He often seemed advanced for his age, both in his conversation and in his abilities. His early reading of the newspapers enabled him to talk like an adult about current events, particularly politics. Such precocious-ness was proudly noticed by his mother. 'Richard was very mature even when he was five or six years old. He was interested in things way beyond the usual grasp of a boy his age. He was thoughtful and serious. "He always carried such a weight." That's an expression we Quakers use for a person who doesn't take his responsi-bilities lightly.'[34]

Lightheartedness does not seem to have been a significant element in Rich-ard Nixon's childhood. He had his fun in his mind. He was frequently off on his own, reading books, thinking, daydreaming, exhibiting the characteristics of the loner that were to become so marked in his later life. He was never really one of the boys. 'He was a very solemn child and rarely ever smiled or laughed', recalled his first schoolteacher Miss George. 'I have no recollection of him playing with others in the playground, which undoubtedly he did...Like other youngsters in mild weather Richard always came barefoot. Every day he wore a freshly starched white shirt with a big black bow tie and knee pants. He always looked like his mother had scrubbed him from head to toe. The funny thing is, I can never remember him ever getting dirty.'[35]

The one person who could divert Richard from his inclination to dwell in his fastidious, rather introspective shell was his elder brother Harold, the extrovert of the family. Harold was a daredevil, a charmer, an outgoing risk-taker who loved danger, excitement, rough and tumble. Richard hero-worshipped his elder brother. Never agile himself, he found it difficult to match the pace set by Harold as they raced off together into scrapes and adventures. Their physical inequality was painfully apparent. Yorba Linda contemporaries have recalled the gutsiness of the smaller Nixon boy as he tumbled down, cut his knees, ran out of breath, yet never quit in his struggles to keep up with his stronger sibling. The first signs that Richard was going to be a great competitor and a great trier were displayed in his childhood relationship with Harold.

One other close relative who had a major impact on Richard was his grandmother, Almira Milhous. After the death of her husband, Franklin, in 1919 she became the matriarch of the family. She was by nature optimistic, gregarious and hospitable. She liked a good party and particularly enjoyed presiding over large family reunions at Christmas and Thanksgiving or on midsummer picnics. Her outer vitality was matched by an inner strength. She radiated energy but also serenity. Her fellow Quakers who understood her deep spirituality said she too had 'peace at the center',[36] but she had earthly passions too—for history, for poetry, for racial equality and especially for educating the young.

This last interest made her a good communicator with her thirty-two grandchildren. She wrote to them regularly, sending them inspirational rhymes and verses, often composed by herself, although with some irreverence for the traditional rules of scansion and metre. She was a keen student of English literature and something of an author and poet *manqué*. Having been a schoolteacher before her marriage, Almira had a good eye for the brightest child in the class and she quickly spotted that of all her descendants, Richard Nixon had the most talent for absorbing knowledge. She was the first person ever to say, 'That boy will one day be a leader.'[37] Although she tried to be careful not to single him out for privileged treatment at family gatherings, it was nevertheless noticed that Almira was 'especially attached to Richard'.[38] This was a well-reciprocated feeling. Richard felt that his grandmother set the standards for the whole family in terms of religious values and humanitarian ideals.

> She was deeply religious but not in a flamboyant exhibitionist way. She did not lecture her children and grandchildren and friends with high-minded moral lectures. She led by example rather than by rhetoric. But although she believed in the literal interpretation of the Bible she was tolerant of the views of others which might be different from her own. She had unlimited compassion for less fortunate people. I can hardly remember a time when we visited her home that she didn't have a tramp living in the barn. Nobody was ever turned away from her door. Her racial and religious tolerance was legendary. Like my mother, she corresponded regularly with Blacks who had worked for my grandfather when they lived in Indiana. She was proud of the fact that the Milhous family had provided refuge for escaped slaves during the Civil War.[39]

The Civil War, together with the pacifist and civil liberties lessons to be learned from it, loomed large in the conversation of Almira Milhous. Her idol was Abraham Lincoln, whom she virtually worshipped. On Richard's thirteenth birthday she gave him a Lincoln portrait, framed with two verses from Longfellow's *Psalm of Life* copied in her own handwriting.

> Lives of great men oft remind us
> We can make our lives sublime

And departing leave behind us
Footprints on the sands of time
Footprints that perhaps another
Sailing o'er life's stormy main
A forlorn and shipwrecked brother
Seeing may take heart again[40]

Almira's 'footprints on the sands of time' was the impact she made on the upbringing and education of her grandson Richard. At her knee he read her history books, imbibed her staunch Republicanism, and came to share her admiration for Ghandi, Lincoln and other peacemakers whose biographies she gave to him. Above all, Richard absorbed from his Quaker grandmother certain key values that stayed with him throughout his life. 'A passion for peace and a passion for privacy'[41] was his summary of his Milhous heritage. He could well have added 'a passion for hard work'.

Richard Nixon grew up to be an industrious as well as a clever boy. The old saying that genius is one per cent inspiration and ninety-nine per cent perspiration was applicable to him. He made the most of his talent by dedicated study. Surrounded by workaholics on both sides of his family, he had the virtue of application drilled into him from his earliest years. When he was ten, Grandmother Almira gave Richard an anthology, *Poems of Inspiration*, drawing his attention to the lines by Angela Morgan:

Work!
Thank God for the might of it
The ardor, the urge, the delight of it
Work that springs from the heart's desire
Setting the brain and the soul on fire[42]

III. THE STORE AND THE COW

Academic work was not the only form of labour to play an important part in Richard Nixon's boyhood and teenage years. When he was nine years old, his father abandoned the struggle to make the lemon ranch pay and, after borrowing $5,000, opened a service station and grocery store in East Whittier, fifteen miles north of Yorba Linda. It was the quintessential family business. Each member of the family had a role assigned to them, and even the youngest sons were expected to serve at the counter for three or four hours a day. Frank Nixon was a successful shopkeeper, who rarely missed a chance to air his views on politics to his customers.

Richard Nixon's formative years thus involved a daily round of work in the store, schoolwork, homework and extracurricular lessons in politics.* The routine was arduous, for the Nixons were always up and about doing their chores well before dawn. Hannah was the first on duty, baking her homemade pies and angel food cakes, which sold for 35 cents apiece, beginning at three o'clock in the morning. Richard was not far behind her. Every day he went with his father to the Los Angeles vegetable market at 4.30 a.m. to load up their truck with fresh produce which it was Richard's job to wash and display on the counter before catching the school bus at 8 a.m. When he came back from school in the afternoon he had other regular duties, such as doing the inventories, and spraying the premises with flykiller. His tasks were limited by the fact that he was clumsy. He dropped things and got tangled up with the simplest machinery. An early stint on the butcher's counter ended with him bleeding profusely into the hamburger mince, when he nearly chopped off the top of his finger with a meat cleaver. After the incident he was not allowed to touch knives or machinery again. Instead, he was assigned the role of waiting on customers while Don presided over the meat counter. Frank once joked: 'Don's got the salesman's personality. He can be President of a corporation. Dick's got the brains. He can be President of the United States.'[43]

Richard Nixon had a natural courtesy towards customers, particularly the downhearted ones. He seemed to have absorbed from his mother a certain empathy for despondent people. In later speeches, as a candidate for office, he could stir the crowds by describing his days in the store, when he had seen fear in the faces of unemployed fathers and worry in the eyes of mothers checking through the dimes and nickels in their purses to see if they had enough money to buy food for their families. This was no empty rhetoric. During the Depression years many people in Whittier were down on their luck, particularly the Mexicans. Hannah listened to their woes like a mother confessor, allowed them easy credit, and slipped free gifts of food into their shopping bags when times were particularly hard. Richard admired his mother for her sensitivity.

One small example of Hannah's kindness which made a great impression on him was her instinctive reaction at his 1923 school graduation ceremony when a Mexican boy, who had come bottom of the class, was required to be the last child to walk through the line amidst pejorative comments from his contemporaries.

---

* Nixon's childhood duties as a junior shopkeeper bear an intriguing similarity to the upbringing of Margaret Thatcher (British Prime Minister 1979–90) who was raised in a small, family grocery store in Grantham, Lincolnshire, working hard in both shop and school with after-hours tuition from her highly political father, Alderman Roberts.

Hannah took pity on the tearful nine year old, rushed forward to comfort him, and sent Richard round with some flowers to the Mexican family's home later in the day. There may be a clue from this episode to the little-known private generosity of Richard Nixon, who in later life so often sent flowers, gifts, and sensitive notes to friends in trouble.

In 1924 there was an incident in the Nixon Market involving a woman shoplifter which highlights Richard's own sensitivity towards a troubled individual and his pragmatism for solving problems. Concerned about a certain pattern of theft at the store, the Nixons kept watch and identified the culprit. She was an unhappy, middle-aged woman with young children. Hannah spoke to her quietly outside the store and she confessed in floods of tears that she had been stealing butter and other small items from the grocery counter for more than a year. The Nixons had a family conference and took outside advice. The sheriff's office urged them to press charges. Frank was in favour of prosecuting, but Richard put forward an alternative plan, which involved getting the shoplifter to pay back the $100 worth of goods she admitted stealing in weekly instalments of $5. Hannah supported her son. There was no prosecution, and the offender kept the bargain, forever grateful that public disgrace had been avoided. There had been quite an internal power struggle in the Nixon household over the handling of this case, in which Richard's voice had been the decisive one. 'My husband thought the woman would never pay us back,' recalled Hannah, 'but Richard was sure I had done the right thing. It took months and months, but eventually she paid us back every cent. Richard was right.'[44]

Frank Nixon was not often overruled by his family. He could be an impossibly stubborn man. One example of his blinkered approach was the sad story of the household cow.

Frank was an early Californian food faddist. He had an obsession that his family should drink only raw milk. As Richard remembers it: 'My father had a thing about raw milk. "Pasteurized milk!" he used to say. "What do they do, they take milk and they heat it up. It's all dirty and filthy because it's been heated and then they sell it to you."'[45] In his efforts to avoid what he called the 'new-fangled' pasteurised milk, Frank kept a cow, which he subsequently replaced with a family goat on the advice from some other local food faddist, who told him that raw goat's milk was even more healthy than cow's milk.

'The experiment did not last too long, fortunately', recalls Richard Nixon. 'The goat had a rather volatile temper which was only a shade less than my father's temper. Time after time it would kick over the bucket of milk until finally my father gave up in disgust, came into the house and said he was going to sell it or give it away.'[46]

Frank then went out and bought another family cow. She was sufficiently placid and productive to keep the Nixons well supplied with raw milk, but ultimately with terrible consequences. Up to about 1922 there were no health problems in the family apart from the usual crop of childhood mumps, measles and minor infections. Although Richard, aged three, had been involved in a nasty buggy accident,* which had required a number of stitches in his scalp (accounting for the unusual central parting of his hair for the rest of his life) he had made a swift and full recovery. After 1922 however, mysterious intimations of lung disease cast their shadow across the Nixon household.

The first to suffer was little Arthur, who became a sickly child for no obvious reason. One doctor thought his illness could be traced to intestinal weakness caused by eating mildewed grapes. Another diagnosis was a possible tubercular infection, but no one could be sure. Then Richard had a terrifying bout of undulant fever which caused him high temperatures for several days and a weight loss of 20 pounds. Undulant fever is generally thought to be linked to infected milk, but Frank either did not understand or did not heed the warnings. Next came Don, who developed a pulmonary shadow which cleared. Most serious was Harold who, when he was in seventh grade, collapsed with a serious lung haemorrhage. Tuberculosis was diagnosed.

With such serious harbingers of ill health knocking at their door, it might have been expected that Frank and Hannah, who had both seen premature deaths from TB in their families, would take all possible precautions to eradicate the source of infection. The cow was inevitably the prime suspect. But Frank remained obdurate. He believed in raw milk and insisted that the family kept on drinking it. As Richard Nixon has sorrowfully recorded: 'He refused to pay any attention to the doctor's warning that the cow ought to be tested for tuberculosis and for this our family paid a heavy price in the years ahead.'[47]

IV. THE FIRST LOSS

Richard Nixon attended five schools: Yorba Linda Elementary, East Whittier Grammar, Lindsay Grammar, Fullerton High and Whittier High. At East Whittier he was consistently top of his class, with straight As in all subjects, and had his first experience of debating as an eleven-year-old sixth grader. He was not a popular boy, regarded as prickly and aggressive—particularly by the girls, who nicknamed him 'Gloomy Gus'. He did not seem to like them much either. Almost

---

* Described in his memoirs as his 'first conscious memory'. Nixon was thrown out of the family horse-drawn trap when the horse went too fast round a corner. Although badly cut, he got up and ran after the buggy.

the only prank attributed to him in his schooldays was one in which he and a cousin filled their mouths with raw garlic cloves, then deliberately puffed the fumes over the girls in the class. Richard's punishment was to have to stay in and learn Kipling's poem, *If.* Around this time he was sufficiently worried by his unpopularity to go out and buy a copy of Dale Carnegie's *How to Win Friends and Influence People,* which he read aloud at home in the evening, discussing its recommendations with his parents.

In January 1925, Richard was taken away from East Whittier Grammar School and transferred to Lindsay so that he could take an intensive course in advanced piano lessons from one of Hannah's sisters, Aunt Jane Beeson, a professional music teacher. This move followed advice from his East Whittier teacher that he had great musical talent and required special coaching.

The musical career of Richard Nixon was brief but interesting. Towards the end of his six-month stay at Lindsay he had acquired sufficient competence from his daily lessons to give a solo recital in public, playing a Grieg piano sonata and Sinding's 'Rustle of Spring'. Later in his education at Whittier College he received intensive coaching from an established concert pianist, Margarethe Loman, who apparently shared Aunt Jane's view that Richard had the talent to become a professional musician. Loman introduced him to Brahms, Beethoven and Bach, bringing him up to the standard of being able to give at least one student concert performance of Brahms's Rhapsody in G minor.

Despite considerable encouragement from his teachers, Richard took an uncharacteristically dilettanteish attitude to his music. He practised sporadically. He dropped in and out of school orchestras, finally abandoning the violin because he felt foolish holding it under his chin. He never learned to read a score fluently, yet had a sufficiently good ear to memorise complex piano pieces. He later came to believe that this aspect of his musical education had been 'a major contribution to my apparently better than average memory... I was never adept at reading music, but I was very proficient in committing it to memory.'[48] Apart from this possible improvement to his powers of memory, music has made only a peripheral impact on the life of Richard Nixon. He enjoyed opera, sometimes relaxed to records of classical music and retained the ability to do occasional impromptu renderings of popular tunes as a party pianist. He has had some twinges of regret about his limited musical role:

> As I look back I sometimes regret that I did not go forward with my musical education... I believe I might have developed the ability to play concert piano, although that would have been a very high goal.

What would have particularly appealed to me would have been to explore the possibilities of being a composer...I believe I might have done best of all in expressing my inner feelings in music.... From a very early age one of my major ambitions was to conduct a symphony orchestra or to play a great organ. In this connection I envy Ted Heath* who was able to combine a successful political career with his outstanding musical talent.[49]

Away from Aunt Jane's music room in Lindsay, Richard's six-month sojourn with the Beesons was an unhappy time in his life. He was homesick, and the atmosphere was far stricter than in his parents' house. On the journey to Lindsay passing through the Tehachapi Mountains, he had seen snow at close quarters for the first time in his life. Feeling excited, he threw a few snowballs with his Beeson cousins Alden and Sheldon and exclaimed, 'By Golly, this is fun!'[50] only to be sternly admonished for using such a wicked expression. That was typical of the puritanical tone of the household, for Harold Beeson was a martinet, who found it necessary to whip his sons with a razor strap almost every day for minor breaches of his rules.

Richard, however, was never subjected to this fate, even when he committed exactly the same offences as Alden and Sheldon. On one occasion, after all three boys had annoyed Uncle Harold by stopping off for a few minutes to play at a neighbour's house on the way home from school, the two Beesons were taken off to the woodshed for a beating. Hearing their screams Richard could not bear it and burst in, saying that he deserved to be punished too. Uncle Harold replied: 'No, you're here as our guest and it's not my responsibility but your father's in the event that you do something that deserves any punishment.'[51]

Although his tuition at the piano from Aunt Jane went well and he enjoyed his two semesters at Lindsay Grammar School, Richard longed to return home and was delighted when the day came in June 1925 when his parents drove over from Whittier to bring him back. Little Arthur, aged seven, made the journey with them, and had evidently missed his older brother because in the car he asked whether he could have permission to give him a kiss as he had been away so long. The permission was granted.

As Richard Nixon remembered their reunion: 'When he got out of the car and saw me he ran to me...I remember how vital and cheerful he was...very shyly he said to me, "Would it be all right if I kissed you?" Our family has always had a

---

* Rt. Hon. Edward Heath, British Prime Minister, 1970–74.

very deep sense of privacy. Public demonstrations of affection seemed always to somewhat embarrass us. But I had been very close to Arthur through the seven years of his life and loved him deeply. He put his arms around me and kissed me on the cheek.'[52]

In July 1925 a mysterious sickness came over Arthur. At first it was diagnosed as indigestion, then influenza. Arthur's condition deteriorated. He lost his appetite, his breathing grew weak, he only wanted to sleep. Dr H. P. Wilson, the family doctor, became increasingly worried, called in another doctor and then a specialist. None of them came up with a clear diagnosis, let alone a cure. In desperation a lumbar puncture was made to tap Arthur's spinal fluid.

After that most painful of tests, Richard met his parents coming downstairs weeping. It was the first time he had seen either of them in tears. 'The doctors are afraid that the little darling is going to die', sobbed Frank.[53]

Soon after the spinal tap, Doctor Wilson said that there was no point continuing with Arthur's medicated liquid diet and that he could have anything he could be persuaded to eat. Hannah prepared one of his favourite dishes, tomato gravy on toast. Richard Nixon recalls how he and his mother took the meal upstairs. 'I remember going upstairs with my mother, and how much Arthur seemed to enjoy it. But then while it was still the middle of the day he said he was very sleepy and that he thought he should say his prayers, and he recited:

If I should die before I wake
I pray thee Lord my soul to take...
and then he went into a coma.'[54]

As the coma deepened, Harold, Richard and Don were sent away to stay with Aunt Carey Wildermuth in Fullerton so that their parents could devote their full attention to Arthur. After three days of anxious waiting, in which Richard prayed hard for his little brother, Aunt Carey woke him at midnight on 11 August with the dreaded news. Arthur was dead.

Richard was shattered. Of all the moments of sadness and despair in his life, including other deaths in the family and the loss of the Presidency, this one hit him hardest. He was numb with shock and grief. 'He sank into a deep impenetrable silence', said his mother.[55] 'For weeks after Arthur's funeral there was not a day that I did not think about him and cry',[56] he wrote in his memoirs. Nearly seventy years later, Richard Nixon still finds it impossible to talk about those days of bereavement, even to his surviving brother Edward.

I am not going to go into any psycho-self-analysis of my reactions after his [Arthur's] death…. Suffice it to say that it was the first sad moment in an otherwise very happy childhood. It had a dramatic emotional effect on all of us. We could not understand why one so young with such a compelling winning personality could be taken away from us so suddenly. There is no doubt that experiencing such an emotional ordeal at such an early age contributed to my sense of fatalism which, ironically, helped me to prepare for and overcome difficult crises in the years ahead.[57]

Hannah's sense of religious fatalism helped her to cope with the tragedy, for she convinced herself that Arthur's death was some mysterious manifestation of God's will. Frank's grief was more belligerent. First he argued with the doctors, blocking their request for a postmortem. The cause of death was therefore ambiguously certified as 'Encephalitis or Tubercular Meningitis'. Frank blamed himself and even started to believe that Arthur's loss was some sort of punishment from God. From that time onwards he never again allowed the Nixon Market or the service station to open on Sundays. He became fanatically religious, attending revivalist meetings in Los Angeles, and spreading their evangelical message back in Whittier. One member of the Quaker congregation at that time remembers him giving passionate public witness in church and shouting, 'We must have a reawakening! We've got to have a revival! We have got to get the people back to God!'[58]

Richard's reactions were quieter and more profound. He withdrew into his shell and worked even harder. His brother's death was the catalyst that accelerated his determination to make himself a great career. A few months after the tragedy he handed in his eighth-grade essay entitled 'Autobiography', which included this passage: 'My plans for the future if I could carry them out are to finish Whittier High School and College and then to take postgraduate work at Columbia University, New York. I would also like to visit Europe. I would like to study law and enter politics for an occupation so that I might be of some good to the people.'[59]

It was the first recorded indication that Richard Nixon, aged twelve, was dreaming of a career in politics.

V. HIGH SCHOOL POLITICIAN

Richard Nixon's career as a schoolboy politician did not get off to a good start. Academically he was a star, consistently coming top or near the top of his class in all subjects except for art and drawing, where he barely scraped through with passing grades. However, outside the classroom he was not a popular boy, partly as a result of his intense shyness and partly because he did not play sports. This last perceived failing was not his fault. From the age of ten Richard had been a sports nut in terms of his general enthusiasm, his ability to recall statistics from the sports pages of the *Los Angeles Times*, and his keenness for playing football. But to his intense disappointment his dreams of being a member of his school football squad were cut short on doctor's orders. After he had played only a handful of freshman games, a routine X-ray revealed a shadow on his lung. Given the family history of tubercular problems, this anxiety assumed panic proportions.

The doctors banned Richard from all sports activities. 'I had to turn in my [football] suit...it was one of the saddest days of my life',[60] was his description of the blow. The ban remained in force for five years, even after it eventually transpired that the shadow on his lung was not tuberculosis but scar tissue left over from a childhood bout of pneumonia.

To compensate for his absence from the sports field, Richard threw himself into an alternative competitive activity—debating. In the beginning, his father was his coach. At his first ever school debating contest, in 1923, ten-year-old Richard won the motion 'That it is more economical to rent a house than to buy one', using a how-to-outwit-the-landlord argument devised by Frank, who at one stage in the nomadic period of his life had apparently acquired some practical experience in this subject. The following year Richard again won the school contest with family help, proposing the motion 'That insects are more beneficial than harmful' getting specialist advice on insect pollenisation from his Milhous uncle Tim Timberlake, a leading entomologist at the University of Southern California.

Arriving at Fullerton High School in 1926, Richard won the School Public Speaking Competition at the end of his freshman year and thereafter became a regular member of the debating team. However, there were disappointments, one of which seemed so awful at the time that he temporarily abandoned debating completely. All that happened was that in one particular inter-school contest, Richard suffered from that classic affliction of the young debater, drying up completely on his feet. Losing the contest in this way was such a blow to his pride that he announced he was dropping out of the team for good. He recalled the event as 'a very painful episode...I lost my place sometime towards the end of my delivery and walked off the stage very humiliated...but the teacher drove by the store a day or two later, talked to my folks and to me about what had happened and urged me not to let it discourage me.'[61]

The teacher who was to give the future President of the United States his only formal lessons in public speaking was H. Lynn Sheller, Fullerton's Head of English. Sheller was critical of the florid style of oratory which prevailed in those days. He taught his pupils that the most effective method of public speaking was to be natural, to adopt a conversational tone, and to cut out artificial gestures. At first Richard had difficulty in accepting his advice. Either he tensed up and delivered his speeches in a wooden monotone, standing stiffly to attention with his hands clenched by his sides, or he reverted to elaborate phrases and gestures. But his teacher straightened him out in the end. 'Sheller used to say to me over and over again, "Remember, speaking is conversation. If you have an audience you may raise the level of your voice but don't shout at people. Talk to them. Converse with them." I have used, to the greatest extent possible, the conversation tone ever since.'[62]

Sheller's techniques evidently succeeded, for in the period 1926–9 Richard developed into an outstanding high school debater, regularly carrying off the top prizes in a range of school, state and regional championships. Sheller was a hard taskmaster, drilling his protégé into what became a lifelong discipline of ruthless self-preparation before a major speech. But he was not only a debate coach. Sheller also fuelled the Nixon mind with an imaginative introduction to the great works of English literature, including those by Dickens, the Brontës, Trollope, Gibbon and Shakespeare. Unusually for a schoolboy, Richard was always highly appreciative of good teachers, especially the toughest ones. After Sheller, his best pupil—teacher relationship was with Miss Jenny Levin of Whittier High, who taught American history. Miss Levin was a strict disciplinarian and a notoriously mean grader, eventually becoming so unpopular with parents, pupils and faculty that the school took all teaching assignments away from her, allowing her only to perform invigilation and administrative duties. Richard considered this treatment unfair, believing that Miss Levin had pushed him to a level of excellence in history that he would not otherwise have reached. 'I learned from her that those teachers who grade hardest are the best, just as those dentists that aren't afraid to hurt you to get the cavity cleaned up are the best.'[63]

With such a philosophy instilled into him both at home and at school, Richard pushed himself to the limit. He seems to have taken to heart another Longfellow verse sent to him by his grandmother Almira Milhous:

The heights of great men reached and kept
Were not attained by sudden flight

But they while their companions slept
Were toiling upward in the night[64]

Sleep was low on his agenda. Relatives would often see a light burning in his rooftop bedroom late at night and remark that Richard was still at his books. He learned to manage on as little as four hours' rest a night, for while he regularly burned the midnight oil on his homework, he still continued to rise at 4 a.m. each day to go to the market and buy the day's vegetables for the store.

This punishing routine did not affect his academic performance, for Richard Nixon's years of schooling ended in a blaze of glory. He was an honour student, the champion debater, the lead actor in the Latin play and he won the Harvard Club of California's annual award as 'the best all round student' in the state. After four consecutive years of straight A grades in Latin (a record which won him a special award) he excelled as a classical scholar who could fluently construe the poems of Virgil and the speeches of Cicero. He was a capable French student, familiar with the works of Rousseau, Voltaire and Moliére. He achieved a high level of competence in maths, physics and chemistry. Most important of all, he had an intellectual curiosity which took him off on his own voyages of discovery. He read voraciously far beyond the limits of the school syllabus, particularly in his favourite areas of history and literature. To the teachers who knew him best, he seemed to be capable of high intellectual achievement. Richard Nixon's own retrospective self-assessment is more prosaic: 'Perhaps the most important thing I learned in my high school and grade school years was to think, write and speak in an orderly and logical manner. I never became a very fast reader, but it is seldom that I have read something I did not understand. Putting it another way, I made up for any lack of natural genius by hard work, discipline, and a very competitive spirit.'[65]

This competitive spirit was nurtured by his sorrow over Arthur, and also by some of the taunts that had come his way from contemporaries. In a revealing interview more than half a century after his schooldays, Nixon told a friend how his determination to succeed had been sharpened by his early experiences of unpopularity:

> What starts the process really are laughs and slights and snubs when you are a kid. Sometimes it's because you're poor or Irish or Jewish or Catholic or ugly or simply that you are skinny. But if you are reasonably intelligent and if your anger is deep enough and strong enough you learn that you can change those attitudes by excellence,

personal gut performance, while those who have everything are sitting on their fat butts.[66]

Richard's reaction to these 'laughs, and slights, and snubs' was to fight back. His record proved that he usually fought successfully, but in his last months at high school he had to face two unexpectedly tough setbacks in the shape of a political and an academic disappointment.

The political disappointment consisted of losing the 1929 election for the presidency of the Whittier High School student body, after having entered this race as firm favourite. The school custom was that a teachers' committee selected two candidates and that the students then voted to choose between the pair of faculty nominees. Richard Nixon was one of the 'official' candidates, the other being his friend and classmate, Roy Newsome. In the Nixon v. Newsome contest, Richard was expected to win but before the final ballots were cast there was an unusual development.

To widespread surprise, a third, dark horse candidate, Bob Logue, was nominated without the backing of the teachers. A popular groundswell moved in his favour. Posters went up around the school on the day of the election: 'STOP, THINK, VOTE BOB LOGUE FOR STUDENT BODY PRESIDENT'. After a few hours of spirited campaigning, Logue won. His victory was initially ascribed to ballot rigging (Nixon declined to demand a recount despite evidence that one ballot box had been stuffed[67]) but the more probable cause was that Logue was perceived by the students as the more attractive and more stylish candidate. One Whittier High co-ed, Elizabeth Glover, summarised the general feeling: 'I think probably the main reason that Nixon lost was that Robert Logue was a football player and a basketball player and some of the people on the teams really got out and worked for him. He was a very nice person too…He was real popular with most students and had gone out for sports. I think the girls were interested in backing someone out for sports.'[68]

Although on the surface Richard took his defeat well, making every effort to pretend that he was unaffected, there is no doubt that deep down the election result hurt him. He retired from the fray not just to lick his wounds but to learn from them, making a painstaking analysis of the reasons for the student voting pattern. This post-election soul-searching, which became another lifelong habit, stood him in good stead. The Whittier High School poll in 1929 was the only election he was to lose for the next thirty-one years.

Richard Nixon's second major disappointment in the period 1929–30 was having to refuse a Harvard scholarship. When he had won the Harvard Club of

California's annual award as the state's 'best all round student', there came with it the offer of a scholarship to Harvard University. There was another similar, if more tentative, offer from Yale University. The Eastern establishment talent spotters had done their job well.

For a boy who had yearned in his 1925 autobiographical essay of 'going East'[69] for his university education, these potential scholarships were a dream come true. But there was a snag. Harvard and Yale were offering 'tuition scholarships', meaning that the tuition fees were free but that the scholar still had to pay all the costs of his living accommodation, travel and out of pocket expenses. In good times Frank would gladly have scraped together the necessary parental subsidy, for he was the most ardent advocate of a college education in the Eastern states, but times were hard. The Great Depression was shrinking the takings of the store, and the family savings were draining away fast because of the need to pay medical bills for Harold, whose early TB infection had reappeared with a vengeance. Anguished discussions took place, but at a time when Frank was already planning to sell some of his precious land around the store to pay the bills for Harold's sanatorium and nursing costs, there was no way additional funds could be found to send the second son across the continent to Harvard.

The decision must have been a bitter disappointment to Richard, but he never showed it. He faced up to the situation with the same wintry courage which he subsequently displayed in later reversals of fortune. For his higher education he would not be making the long journey across the continent to Harvard; he would be taking the short step from Whittier High to Whittier College. In later years he put his own gloss on the facts.

> I decided to go to Whittier.... my folks needed me. They needed me in the store. There was no way I could go. After all Harold was still sick and this was the time when the medical expenses were enormous. So I decided to stay home and I have no regrets...I was not disappointed because the idea of college was so exciting that nothing could have dimmed it for me.[70]

TWO

WHITTIER COLLEGE

I. 'A GUY APART'

In September 1930 Richard Nixon entered Whittier College. If he had any lingering feelings of disappointment at having missed out on his scholarship offers from Yale and Harvard, he suppressed them. Getting good grades was his priority. His transparent dedication to this goal was resented by some of his fellow students. 'In today's terms we kids would have called him a nerd', recalled Dolores Latrup. 'He was so serious. He never sat around talking or laughing like all the rest of us. He was a guy apart, either stuck into his books or rushing across the campus, forever going somewhere.'[1]

In fact the young Nixon was not entirely sure where he was going. He was full of contradictions and uncertainties. His contemporaries may have thought he was too studious, but his teachers felt he was spreading himself too thin. He divided his time between classes, sports, and a plethora of extracurricular activities. The football pitch; the dramatic society; the Glee Club; basketball games; weekend skiing trips; off-campus picnics; Gilbert and Sullivan operas; the debating team; the college orchestra and student politics, all won his participation and sometimes his passionate commitment. As he still had to do his shopkeeping duties at the family store, his schedule became impossibly crowded. Far from being aloof, he was a campus action-man in perpetual motion. He may have been

31

alone within himself, but at face value he was trying so hard on so many fronts that no one thought of him as lonely. He had certainly changed his high school persona, perhaps into the first of the many 'new Nixons'.

One of Nixon's earliest actions at college was to create an anti-establishment student society. Founded in 1887, Whittier was a Quaker institution which flourished in that fertile middle ground between strictness and tolerance. Although nonsectarian since 1916, its 400 students chafed under its anachronistic rules. These reflected the moral precepts of its trustees, who tended to be pillars of the local Friends Church. One of the restrictions was a ban on fraternities, which in the eyes of the egalitarian Quaker elders smacked too much of class distinction. Some of the better-off students had different ideas, and had manoeuvred around the ban by setting up a men's student society known as the Franklins. Its social élitism, symbolised by the members appearing in their group photograph wearing tuxedos, underlined what one college professor called 'this cleavage within the various classes of people living in the city of Whittier and even with the Quaker people'.[2]

Soon after arriving on campus, Nixon took stock of the Franklins and the resentment their activities created. Even as a seventeen-year-old freshman he had an instinctive feel for a political issue. With the help of a student friend, Dean Triggs, Nixon founded an alternative men's society called the Orthogonians. He invented its name; wrote its constitution; created its mascot—a wild boar; wrote the lyrics for its song; and dreamed up its symbol—'The 4 b's'. '"The 4 b's" stood for beans, brains, brawn and bowels', he has explained. 'The bowels were the guts for the football players; brains, we were all students; the brawn, we were going to be strong; the beans were the bean feeds we had every week. In those Depression years we didn't have meat so we had beans.'[3]

Much of the activity of the Orthogonians was devoted to being as different as possible from the Franklins, whom they viewed as an effete, rather snobbish lot. 'They were the haves and we were the have nots',[4] was Nixon's later characterisation of the two groups. The Orthogonians symbolised their proletarianism by having their group photographs taken wearing open-neck shirts to emphasise the contrast with the Franklins' tuxedos, but equally important was the muscular divide between those who played football and those who did not.

All the charter members of the Orthogonians were footballers. Nixon, having been cleared by his doctor of the suspected TB shadow on his lungs, was now sufficiently healthy to indulge his passion for this sport. At Whittier he came under the spell of a remarkable coach, 'Chief' Wallace Newman. 'I think I admired him and learned more from him than any man I have ever known aside from my father', wrote Nixon in his memoirs. 'He drilled into me a competitive spirit and the determination to come back after you have been knocked down or after you lose.'[5]

Nixon got plenty of practice at being knocked down or losing during his college football days. He was too small to be a good line player, weighing just 155 pounds compared to the team average of over 200 pounds. He was too slow a runner for the backfield. His inborn clumsiness made him inept when it came to catching or passing the ball. A further flaw was his chronic tendency to rush offside through overeagerness. With all these defects it was not surprising that he did not make the first team, even after four seasons of regular practice. He was a permanent fixture on the reserve bench, becoming the butt of much good-natured ribbing. One joke had the coach asking, 'Nixon, what would you have done on that play?' and getting the reply, 'Sir, I would've pulled the blanket up just a little tighter around my shoulders.'[6]

Such teasing of Nixon was good-natured because his team-mates liked him and were amazed by his tenacity on the pitch. 'I remember thinking, "Dick Nixon, I don't know why you do this but I admire your red-blooded intestinal fortitude to stay with it until the end of the season or the end comes otherwise"',[7] said Clint Harris, describing his impression of those gruelling practice sessions in which Chief Newman used his second-string players to create a wall of resistance into which the heavy forwards of the first team could practise their aggressive plays and battering-ram charges. 'Nixon and I were cannon fodder', recalled another member of the resistance wall, Gail Jobe. 'We were the two smallest guys on the squad but we learned how to hang in there and smash the big guys back. I'll say this for Nixon. He had plenty of guts when it came to taking a beating, getting up off the floor, and coming back fighting.'[8] Chief Newman agreed, describing Nixon as 'tenacious as the dickens. When he got hold of something he never let go.'[9]

Nixon never made the football team, even though he practised with the squad for four years most weekday afternoons from 4 p.m. to 7 p.m. However he has always regarded Chief Newman, a mixed-blood American Indian, as an almost mystic influence on his life, describing him as 'a fine coach but an even more talented moulder of character'.[10] He has credited the Chief for instilling into him the inspirational dream that, by hard work, training and preparation, even the greatest of victories could be achieved. When the team did lose Newman had a fall-back philosophy that also made its impact on Nixon. 'The Chief was always trying to inspire us to be self-sufficient, to be competitive, and…never to give up. You know in those days they used to say…in some of the so-called better schools, it isn't whether you win or lose but how you play the game that counts. And the

Chief said, "That's all fatuous nonsense. Of course how you play the game counts. You must always play fair. But it also counts whether you win or lose. You play to win. And if you don't win you kick yourself in the butt and be sure you don't make the same mistakes again." He drilled that into us, and I must say I was affected.'[11]

So affected, indeed, that Nixon relied heavily on the philosophy of Chief Newman throughout his political career. He even consulted his old coach in 1975 on how to fight back from the depression that engulfed him after his resignation from the Presidency. It was an important and lifelong influence.

II. STUDENT POLITICIAN

Nixon tried hard to become a team player in arenas other than football. By temperament he was still a loner rather than a joiner, yet at Whittier College he joined virtually everything in sight. Sometimes the rituals of joining jarred his soul. There were times when he wished he had never founded the Orthogonians, such as those evenings when the society held its 'knock n' boost' sessions. On these occasions, about twenty-five members would sit round a four-sided table called the Orthogonian Men's Square, and then, rising one after another, would either criticise (knock) or congratulate (boost) someone else who was present. Given the locker-room joviality of young male footballers, these knock n' boost sessions could become uncomfortably intimate, as Nixon recalled: 'It just really turned me off. I couldn't do it. I never knocked anyone, incidentally, at one. I could give someone a boost but what I didn't like was the fact that it was such an invasion of privacy…I could never do it.'[12]

Another Orthogonian ritual which turned Nixon off was the initiation ceremony. As a charter member he was exempt from the grisly series of tests designed to make applicants for new membership prove their manhood. But he still had to watch and participate. One of the worst tests involved going into a remote part of the woods around Whittier, digging up the corpse of a dead boar, and eating its raw meat on the spot. Since a wild boar (the society's mascot) was not an easy animal to find conveniently buried in the Californian countryside, the Orthogonians substituted the corpse of a dog, whose meat had been soaked in some foul-smelling chemical just to make it doubly appetising for the initiates—who were frequently sick during this part of the ceremony. Nixon loathed such aspects of campus life, but he made himself go through with them. One of his worst experiences was his own initiation to the Glee Club.

> I remember that when I was initiated into the Glee Club they had a
> rather crude kind of custom and that was you'd have first to take off

all your clothes. And they had a huge cake of ice there. You'd sit on the ice for a while and then they'd take a big paddle. You'd get up and they'd slap you over the rump to warm up. Well, by the time you'd gone through that a while you were pretty tired. And I got so tired I got pneumonia. I was knocked out for at least a week. My mother was out of her mind, my father thought we ought to sue them and so forth. I said, 'Forget it. Say nothing.' So I went back and we had a great time thereafter.[13]

These snapshots of Nixon's reluctant participation in such strange rituals raise the question: why did he do it? It can be argued that it would have been stranger if he had not participated. The hazings, bull sessions and demonstrations of manhood that went on at Whittier in the 1930s may seem weird to anyone who has never sampled college life in Middle America, but they are typical of fraternity house ceremonies that continue on many campuses to this day. Nixon wanted to be a member of the Glee Club primarily because it offered him the prospect of travelling all over the western states, as well as an opportunity to enjoy singing good music. The initiation ceremony was disagreeable but it was the price of the entry ticket. As things turned out, he had a lot of fun with the Glee Club, becoming its Master of Ceremonies, developing a fair baritone voice, and going on several long-distance singing trips.

He also had fun and fellowship from his general Orthogonian activities. On that basis, there is surely nothing unusual about Nixon's fairly common experience of disliking the initiation part of the package. Alternatively, it could be argued that, as a particularly sensitive teenager, it must have cost Nixon a superhuman effort of will to grin and bear such distasteful humiliations. But he did have a motive for swallowing almost anything, including stinking dog meat, in order to put himself across as the hail fellow well met (and well paddled), buddy-buddy type he so definitely was not. Nixon always learned from his mistakes. One of the first political mistakes in his life was to have lost the election for the presidency of the student body at Whittier High to Bob Logue in 1929. It hurt him more than he admitted, shaking his early dream of a political career. So he analysed that loss carefully, realising that he had been seen as unpopular, nonsporting, and not as one of the boys. Perhaps he was now overcompensating for his poor image as a schoolboy by overdoing his 'regular guy' act as a college student.

One Nixon contemporary who sat with him on the bench during many a football game and regularly sang with him in the Glee Club was Hubert Perry, son of the leading bank manager in Whittier, Herman Perry, who was later to prove an important benefactor and mentor in Nixon's early political career. Hubert Perry was one of the most perceptive student observers of the Nixon character and motivation:

> I don't think any of us were ever buddy buddy with Dick Nixon. We liked him, we respected him, but he was always a private person who didn't share confidences much. In a group he dominated yet basically he was shy. What he was really great on was asking questions. He would sit on the back of a bus on those Glee Club trips and talk about things in a world way beyond Whittier, putting his own ideas forward about international things or politics, and then always asking us what we thought. I remember once he said on the bus, 'You should never run for office from a city council base. If you're going to go for politics, don't hang about with local politics, go for the big time. What do you think?' Well, of course, none of us were thinking on those lines at all, but he obviously was...even at that early age there was always a political edge to his actions. Why did he keep coming out for football? I think Dick saw it as a chance to associate with people he had a lot of respect for. It gave him a chance to be one of the guys. He didn't have so many other social activities that gave him the entrée to people who could be useful to him.[14]

Whatever the reasons, Nixon was certainly adept at building himself a base in student politics. He became President of his freshman class; Sophomore representative on the student executive committee in his second year; and was elected Vice President of the student body in his third year by 267 votes to 73.

At the beginning of his fourth year he declared his candidature for the student body presidency. Initially the contest was presented as a straight fight between the Franklins and the Orthogonians, the principal alternative candidate being Dick Thomson of the Franklins. The key to winning the election, however, lay not with these two student societies but with the off-campus vote and the women's dormitories vote. Nixon appealed to both constituencies with his campaign platform, whose centrepiece was a pledge to get student body dances allowed on the campus. Coming from a candidate who was known to be too shy and too flat-footed to enjoy dancing himself, the move was pure opportunism, an early example of Nixon's ability to ambush an opponent with his feel for an emerging issue.

The old Quaker establishment of Whittier disapproved of many harmless pleasures in life, and dancing was still on their banned list. It was hardly surprising that twentieth-century students should be chafing under such old-fashioned restrictions. Nixon's promise to negotiate an ending of the dancing ban attracted support from the uncommitted voters while also persuading many Franklins into his lobby. By comparison, Dick Thomson's principal campaign pledge—to work for a new student union building—fell on deaf ears. The climax of the election was a debate in front of the entire student body in the Poets' Theater. It was Nixon's first debate where a political position was at stake. He prepared his speech meticulously and won the election by a landslide. Analysing his defeat, Thomson said afterwards, 'His issue had student appeal and I guess mine was a little too practical. It was the silver-tongued orator up against a babbling idiot. Even if he didn't say anything it sounded good.'[15]

Delivering the promise on dances turned out to be a problem. Nixon's first proposals received a flat rejection from the College President, Dr. Walter Dexter. That should have been the end of the matter, but Nixon then made an appeal to the Trustees, arguing that the students were going to dance anyway and that it would surely be better for their moral welfare if they danced on campus under supervision, rather than in the speakeasies of Los Angeles, where they might be exposed to more serious temptations. One member of the Whittier faculty, Professor Paul Smith, was amazed at Nixon's cheek in going over the head of the College President with such an argument: 'Think of the nerve of this lad, appearing before the august body of the Board of Trustees at Whittier College in a plea of no dancing on that campus which the Quakers didn't look fondly upon at all. That was a rule from the time the College was founded. It took a lot of guts and nerve and crust, I think, to do that. But he did it and convinced the board that they really ought to modify their policy.'[16]

In his submission to the Trustees, Nixon cunningly proposed a face-saving compromise. He did not request the Members of the Board to give their formal approval for student dances. Instead, he simply asked them to allocate $200 a year to rent the nearby Whittier Women's Club building for large social functions of the student body. This was a formula which enabled the hardline Quakers to turn a blind eye on the issue of what happened at these 'large social functions'. Nixon got his $200 budget allocation. With the tacit approval of the Trustees, he spent it on the successful organisation of eight ballroom dances during the last six months of his presidential year.

Away from the dance floor, Nixon had one other triumph as an organiser of student social events. He was elected Rally Chairman, a role whose principal function was laying on a huge campus bonfire the night before the annual Armistice Day football match between Whittier and Occidental College. The Rally committee spent weeks gathering wood from every available source and built a heap some thirty feet high. It had somehow become a student custom that the *pièce de résistance* was to top the heap of firewood with an outdoor privy. This presented Nixon with an unusual challenge. 'Up until the year I was Rally Chairman I was informed that they had only had two-hole outhouses. We all determined that we were going to outdo our predecessors and someway find a three-holer.'[17] In the week before the Armistice Day match, Nixon and his team scoured the surrounding countryside in their efforts to locate a triple latrine outhouse. Eventually their efforts were rewarded when, to their great delight, they discovered a *four*-hole outdoor privy on a ranch near Downey, some eight miles away. It was a difficult nocturnal mission for Nixon and his collaborators to enter this outhouse, disconnect it from its sewer lines and silently remove it. If the *Washington Post* had been around to report the event, they might have headlined it 'Break-in by Whittier College plumbers', but this 1933 de-plumbing operation did not leak.

There were some students who thought that Nixon's exploits of derring-do and *joie de vivre* were phoney. One classmate said of his enthusiasm, 'I used to wonder if it was wholly genuine...how much was simulated for the benefit of all present.'[18]

But this was a minority view. All available evidence suggests that Nixon's drive and energy made him a popular student leader. He even got a consistently favourable press from the *Quaker Campus* and from the Whittier College yearbook, *Acropolis,* whose 1934 edition profiled Nixon on its front page with the concluding judgement: 'After one of the most successful years the college has ever witnessed we stop to reminisce and come to the realization that much of the success was due to the efforts of this very gentleman. Always progressive and with a liberal attitude he has led us through the year with flying colors.'[19]

III. PERFORMING AND THINKING

Drama and debate were the activities in which Nixon's colours flew highest. During his schooldays, he had made one disastrous appearance on stage when his performance in the Whittier High Latin play was greeted with boos and catcalls. After such a début it might have been thought that he would be reluctant to tread the boards again. Nixon felt differently, possibly because at the back of his mind he had the notion that acquiring the skills of the actor could be a useful complement to the skills of the politician. True to form, he was therefore determined to learn from his previous mistakes and to turn himself into a competent stage player. Equally true to form, he succeeded, despite his apparent disadvantage of a somewhat jerky style of movement and a wooden manner of speaking.

Nixon's stage career began with the job that is traditionally regarded as the lowest form of theatrical life—assistant stage manager. He was the ASM for productions of two Gilbert and Sullivan operas, *HMS Pinafore* and *The Pirates of Penzance*. Thereafter, he successfully auditioned for a number of character parts in straight plays. He was the dithering Mr. Inglesby in Booth Tarkington's *The Trysting Place*; an old Scottish miner in *The Price of Coal* and a comic in George M. Cohan's *The Tavern*. Nixon's big break as a student actor came when he was chosen to play the lead as Thomas Greenleaf, the English innkeeper in John Drinkwater's *Bird in the Hand*. This is an exceptionally long part, with a two-page soliloquy in the middle of the second act. Nixon's retentive memory was already something of a college legend, and the producer, Professor Albert Upton, cast him in the starring role because no one else who auditioned for it had the capacity to remember so many lines. The part, however, needed more than a good memory because Nixon had to speak with an English accent, walk with an old man's shuffle, and break down in floods of tears. Eventually he mastered all these histrionic skills. 'The finest dramatic performance yet witnessed at Whittier College', said the *Quaker Campus* in its review, adding that Nixon had 'carried his part with exceptional skill. His interpretation of a difficult character was accompanied with finesse seldom displayed by amateurs.'[20]

Albert Upton was even more laudatory of his pupil, saying that Nixon 'was one of our first successful actors...I wouldn't have been surprised if after college he had gone on to New York or Hollywood looking for a job as an actor.'[21]

Much as he enjoyed the stage, the thought of a career on Broadway or in Hollywood never entered Nixon's head. He was becoming far too serious about issues of substance as his career as a college debater soon showed.

Whittier College took debating seriously. It entered its team for national and regional speaking competitions; set aside a 'debaters only' room in the library; and appointed a full-time coach, Dr. Eugene Knox. Knox believed content to be the all-important element in a speech, with delivery coming a poor second. Under his tuition, research, more research, and still more research was the order of the day. Nixon enjoyed the discipline and the intellectual exercise. He discovered that his initially firm views on a particular resolution could be totally reversed as a result of the profound study on which his coach insisted.

Gradually, he developed a methodology of approaching an issue without being inhibited by preconceived notions, digging deeply into both sides of the

subject, making detailed notes of facts, quotes, pros and cons on yellow pads as
he went along, and then finally reaching a conclusion. It was a technique which
stayed with him into his White House years.

As a regular member of Whittier's four-man debating team, Nixon was
required to master the annual topic which had been selected for competition
debates in universities all over the country. In 1931 the subject was 'Free Trade
versus Protectionism'. The next year it was whether or not to cancel the Inter-
Allied war debts. Nixon believes that his lifelong dedication to internationalism
and to free trade date from those debates:

> In those debates we always had to be prepared to argue both sides.
> But in the process of my studying, in the research, I became a com-
> mitted free trader. I remained so ever since. I certainly became an
> internationalist. I was thoroughly convinced that the Inter-Allied
> war debts should be cancelled not simply because the Allies had taken
> far greater losses than we had, but because in terms of our own eco-
> nomic progress it was essential to get their economies back on solid
> footing. So when people see my support of foreign aid and interna-
> tional co-operation a lot of it may go right back to that.[22]

These early stirrings of Nixon the internationalist were augmented by his
wide reading and by visits to the campus by international speakers such as that
of an overseas lecturer on China in 1934. However, the main stimulation of
Nixon's intellect derived, as it had in high school, from his unusually good rapport
with certain teachers.

Nixon majored in constitutional history at Whittier College and his most
important Professor was Dr. Paul S. Smith, from whom he took courses in British
and American civilisation; the United States Constitution; international relations
and law.

A birthright Quaker, Smith had obtained his PhD in American History from
the University of Wisconsin and was regarded as both liberal and progressive in
the Whittier environment. Smith taught his pupils that history was much more
than a chronicle of past events. It could be the basis for analysis, criticism, and
the understanding of the tides of politics. An inspiring lecturer who usually spoke
without notes, his nickname was 'Mouthwatering Smith' on account of his tendency to get so carried away with enthusiasm that he dribbled while reading aloud
to his class. 'What he particularly inspired in all of us was a passion for books',
recalls Nixon. 'I remember he used to get some fine books, such as Sir Esme

Wingfield Stratford's *History of British Civilisation*, which he had assigned to the course. He'd open it up and read a passage on architecture or something and his mouth would water. We used to say, "Don't sit in the front of Paul Smith's classes because maybe it will get on you." As his mouth watered he'd say, "Isn't that wonderful? Isn't that wonderful?" But it made you want to read the book.'[23]

Sixty years after the young Nixon had first sat in the classes of 'Mouthwatering Smith', this author interviewed the retired historian at his home in Whittier. Taking down volume after volume from his bookshelves, reading out selected passages with his mouth visibly watering just as it had done before his 1930s students, Paul Smith enthusiastically described the early educational influences that had shaped the mind and character of his most famous pupil.

> Now look here at this shelf, these are the books that I taught Nixon—histories, biographies, great classics of learning and scholarship. The autobiography of Robert La Follette ... *Lincoln* by Nicolay and Hay ... Teggerts's *Theory of History* ... Gibbon's *Decline and Fall* ... The collected speeches of William Jennings Bryan. Do you know what runs through them all? They are books that are as much moralistic as historical. They are solid, substantial histories, but they give a good fundamental training in moral values as well as historical values. Whatever the bad things are that Nixon has done in his life, never forget that he took in these great moral teachings. That's why there is so much good in that man ... sometimes the good side of him has been subsumed by political ambition. I could see that might be going to happen but also I have always known that he is two guys in one and that the decent, Quaker, moral side has been there all the time, sometimes creating great tension: Do you know what I think is happening to him now. ... Listen to this: Morrison on John Quincy Adams, 'The greatest chapter in his life came after he was defeated in his election as President.' That may well be the verdict on Richard Nixon.

Asked to expand on his view that Nixon was 'two guys in one', Dr. Paul Smith commented:

> Nixon was an efficient manager of his time but he sliced himself into so many pieces that he became a split personality. He was as busy in the classroom as he was in the extracurricular activities. He was

cautious and he was a risk taker. He was an ambitious political operator and a quiet, diligent Quaker. He was an introvert trying to be an
extrovert. He was a slow thinker but a fast mover, sometimes too fast
for his own good. I wanted him to stay on one activity more than he
did. He didn't give each subject the reflection it deserved. When it
came to examinations, he answered the questions well but with the
minimum of decoration. You couldn't fault his answers, but he lacked
the flourishes that appeal to academicians, so his papers always
seemed too brief.

But when you went back and read them you saw he hadn't left
anything out and that he had got to the heart of the matter, so you
had to give him the top grade. Nevertheless, I always felt he was
spreading himself too thin because of his other ambitions...I spotted
his ambition early because of his absence from the library. Dick
Nixon was out on the football pitch every afternoon at 4 p.m. when
he should really have been at his books. And when he wasn't out at
football he was always rushing around to the next whatever-it-was.
He had a terrific variety of interests and the only rhyme or reason
behind them was that he wanted to run things. His father pushed
him too hard. I didn't like his father. He was a man who bore grudges,
but he was the one that fired up that boy with an innate leadership
impulse and he was the one who gave Richard Nixon the taste for
liberalism which has been so underrated in his political career.[24]

Richard Nixon responded well to the contagious enthusiasm of his history
professor. The two men met and corresponded for many years despite Smith's
fidelity to liberal causes and his disapproval of some of Nixon's campaigns. Nixon
has described Smith as 'the greatest intellectual inspiration of my early years',[25] a
well-deserved epitaph for a remarkable teacher.

Paul Smith, who went on to be President of the College, was only one star
in the galaxy of teaching talent that had somehow found its way to the small
Whittier campus during the early 1930s. There were other lecturers holding
doctorates from Harvard, Columbia, Yale and the University of Southern California. The English professor, Dr. Albert Upton, was one of Nixon's favourites.
Nicknamed 'The Owl' on account of his thick, bifocal spectacles, Upton was an
agnostic—an even rarer species than a liberal on a Quaker campus—who
inspired Nixon into a wide range of reading far beyond the boundaries of his
courses and subjects. 'Nothing was sacred to him and he stimulated us by his

outspoken unorthodoxy',[26] was Nixon's judgement of the teacher who introduced him to the wider realms of philosophy, prose, drama and poetry.

'The Owl' was a maverick who loved to shock. A vignette from a later period, which illustrates Upton's style, occurred during 1955 in the days immediately after President Eisenhower had suffered a massive heart attack. Vice President Nixon, as the man a heartbeat away from the Presidency, was suddenly the focus of intense media speculation and a CBS television news crew came down to Whittier College to interview some of his old teachers. The interviews were filmed in the college President's office, which had a painting of Nixon hanging on one of its walls. When Upton entered the room, instead of walking towards the cameras as expected, he went over to the picture, got down on his hands and knees and prostrated himself before Nixon's portrait with three Islamic salaams. The CBS newsmen's eyes almost popped out of their heads as they watched this solemn performance, which apparently confirmed their worst suspicions of what really went on in Nixon loyalist circles. Getting up from the floor, Upton came over and shook hands with the TV producer as if nothing had happened. Only after several deadpan answers to the newsmen's questions did Upton acknowledge that he had been pulling their legs.

Albert Upton was nobody's loyalist. At one of his first tutorial encounters with Nixon, in 1931, he told the prim young Quaker to stop reading the Bible for religion and to enjoy it as literature, adding that he should start with the Book of Ecclesiastes as this was the greatest novel ever written.[27] This was the point of departure for a long journey into philosophy and literature. Under his Professor's guidance, Nixon read Hobbes; Locke; Hume; Dover Wilson's commentaries on Shakespeare; Will Durrant's *Mansions of Philosophy*; Bacon's essays; Kant; Villon; Darwin; Voltaire; Balzac; de Tocqueville, and Rousseau.[28]

As the increasingly iconoclastic Nixon–Upton agenda progressed, the author who seems to have caught their joint imaginations most was Tolstoy:

> One summer Upton said to me, 'Look you've got to broaden your education. You ought to read Tolstoy.' So that summer I read virtually everything that Tolstoy had written. *War and Peace*; *Resurrection* (my favorite); *Anna Karenina*; *Possession*, and some of the philosophical treatises. I became, frankly, a Tolstoyan, which was very easy to do because nobody can read Tolstoy without being deeply moved.... Tolstoyan in my case meant a belief in the individual and his importance, a belief in freedom, but particularly a passion for peace.[29]

IV. HIDDEN DEPTHS

There were many indications during his college years that Nixon's new Tolstoyan 'passion for peace' had not developed into the more personal area of peace for himself. There was an unsatisfied restlessness in him, which showed itself most visibly in his habit of overextending his schedule. He always seemed to be rushing hither and thither on campus in order to fulfil an impossibly heavy load of commitments. Under these pressures he could sometimes be moved to angry overreaction. There was an episode during his last year when he became so indignant over an unfavourable article in the *Los Angeles Times* about the Whittier College football team, that he led six car loads of students on a protest visit to the *Times* building. They wandered aimlessly around the fourth floor of the editorial department before being ushered out without receiving the apology Nixon had been demanding.[30]

On the academic front, Nixon's steady application was matched by a somewhat unsteady ferment of intellectual confusion. He had come a long way from the simple certainties of his Quaker upbringing, although he did not yet know where his cerebral travels were taking him. As a student he was highly intelligent but not truly intellectual in the sense that he lived off ideas rather than for ideas. He could analyse, scrutinise, and synthesise a subject but he had not yet developed his own originality of thought. However, he was quick to admire the original thinking of others. He had a laudable readiness to jettison old nostrums and to welcome uncomfortable new ideas. A healthy scepticism, even cynicism, mingled in his brain with romanticism, traces of Quaker fundamentalism, and a yearning for creativity. He was a student of great potential, but his intellect and his beliefs were in a state of some turmoil.

His home life, although solid and loving, did not provide much in the way of navigational assistance when he was searching for clear stars to steer by on his early intellectual journeys. Great strains and stresses had developed in the family as his elder brother Harold's TB grew worse.

His mother, secure in the fundamentals of her Quaker faith, grew worried about Richard's new ideas and sternly admonished him not to be led astray by college professors who were too liberal in their views.[31] His father was all over the place with new arguments of his own about religion, current events and politics. Frank Nixon was by temperament a populist Republican in so far as those terms were not mutually exclusive in the 1930s. However, his voting habits had been erratic during Richard's early years. Frank had voted for the Democrat Woodrow Wilson in 1916, and for the Republican Warren Gamaliel Harding in 1920. In 1924 he had again deserted the Republican ticket, believing that Bob La Follette, the Progressive party's presidential candidate, and the Democrats would do more for the working man and the small farmer, while the Republicans were too much under the thumb of big business and the big eastern banks. In 1928 and 1932 Frank Nixon voted for Herbert Hoover, apparently largely on the single issue of Hoover's prohibitionism, which, as a strict dry, he strongly supported. By the mid-1930s, however, Frank was enamoured of the Democrat Franklin Roosevelt, and voted for FDR in his second term in 1936.

These shifting loyalties were accompanied by much ardent discussion at home, and there can be little doubt that the young Richard Nixon, far from growing up as a hardline right winger, scarcely knew whether he was liberal or conservative, Republican or Democrat. Dr. Paul Smith probably summed up this ambivalent situation accurately when he described Nixon at Whittier College as 'a liberal in a conservative sort of way'.[32]

Although the politics of the Nixon household may well have had their phases of leaning towards liberalism, the underlying family philosophy remained resolutely conservative. The Nixons maintained their good habits of work, thrift, honesty and prayer. They were ambitious for their children, with Frank a loud champion of the American Dream. By self-discipline and application, anyone in the United States could achieve anything he repeatedly told his sons, adding the rider that the supreme effort of hard work must be made in the educational years. Frank pointed with pride to the example of his brother Ernest Nixon, who had not run away at thirteen; who had stuck it out with stepmother, school and college, and who had ended up as a university professor at Penn State as a result of his persistence.

This family parable was well understood by Richard, who revered his Uncle Ernest and who for a time seriously considered following his footsteps into the academic world. Richard knew that he had to achieve good results at Whittier if he was to move on to postgraduate education and he worked relentlessly towards that goal. By the summer of 1934 he had achieved it.

In May 1934 Nixon read a notice on the college bulletin board which was to change his life. It was a printed announcement saying that the Duke University School of Law was offering twenty-five scholarships at $250 each for the academic year 1934–5. The money was deliberately tempting, for Duke was a new and heavily endowed university in North Carolina seeking to build up the prestige of its law school to the same level as other more established Eastern colleges. Nixon did his research. He contacted a recent Whittier graduate, Ray Cook, who had gone to the Duke School of Religion, and who gave him 'rave notices' on the excellence of the university. Further enquiries established that the new Dean of the

Duke Law School, Justin Miller, had previously been the highly regarded Dean at the University of Southern California.

Nixon was told that Miller's motivation for his move was to create a university better than the Ivy League colleges. Reassured by this, Nixon sent in his application to Duke, backed up by several letters of recommendation from his college professors. These emphasised his excellent grades; his debating and other extracurricular successes; his good character; his graduation result (which was a disappointment, since he only came third in his class of eighty-five students), and his outstanding year as President of the Student Body. The most glowing endorsement came from the President of Whittier College, Dr. Walter Dexter, who wrote, 'I cannot recommend him too highly because I believe that Nixon will become one of America's great if not important leaders.'[33] It was a tribute that evidently impressed the Duke University selectors, for Richard Nixon won his scholarship.

Although Dr. Dexter's comment about Nixon's potential for leadership was prescient, even as early as 1934 there were contemporary observers who would have added that his character also contained a dimension of strangeness. There was nothing negative to put a finger on. However, it was noticeable that the 'Best Man on Campus' had no best friend. Richard Nixon's human touch was uncertain. Underneath his 'regular guy' facade there was something unusual. He had plenty of amicable acquaintances sharing mutual interests with him, but no disinterested friendships. No one outside his family could really claim to know him. He remained an enigma to his team-mates in debate and football. Even his steady girlfriend, Ola Florence Welch, said, 'Most of the time I just couldn't figure him out.'[34]

To suggest that, in his student days, Nixon was widely seen as a man of mystery would be an exaggeration, yet he was increasingly perceived as a perplexing character. His debating partner Kenny Ball described Nixon at the end of his Whittier days as well as anyone: 'a guy with many sides to him. Insecure in one-on-one conversations but totally sure of himself when debating in front of an audience. Complicated but pretending to be ordinary. I liked him, spent a lot of time with him, but couldn't get to know him. He buried a lot of himself below the surface. It wasn't difficult to see that he had hidden depths.'[35]

THREE

SPIRITUALITY, SADNESS, AND ROMANCE

I. CHILDHOOD FAITH

Richard Nixon was a deeply spiritual young man. This will seem a surprising assertion to those familiar with the dark side of his character as revealed by the White House tapes. Yet whatever may have happened to him at the time of Watergate, new evidence suggests that Nixon's intensely private religious beliefs have long been an important dimension in his life. Indeed it can be argued that the complexity of his character becomes more comprehensible once there is some knowledge of the well-documented spiritual struggle with which he wrestled in his youth.

In the course of some preliminary correspondence with the author about this biography, Richard Nixon wrote: 'The impact of my Quaker heritage on my personality has been underestimated.'[1] Starting from that clue, it has proved possible to trace the map of Nixon's youthful spirituality through three distinct phases. First there was the Quaker influence of his family during his childhood and adolescence. Second, there was the traumatic effect of the death of a brother. Thirdly came a troubling period in his life as a college student aged twenty to twenty-one when his faith was shaken by doubts. These doubts surfaced in an emotionally searing collection of religious essays which are the most revealing of all Nixon's early writings.

Long before her second son became politically important, Hannah's mystic piety had earned her the label of 'a Quaker saint' among her Whittier neighbours. However, there was nothing ostentatious about either her deeds of compassion or her strict practices of religious observance, for she had an almost obsessive desire for privacy in spiritual matters. She took literally St. Matthew's injunction, 'When thou prayest, pray in secret',[2] shutting herself in her closet for her frequent daily intercessions. Within her home she insisted on a period of silent grace before each meal, usually followed by prayer and Bible readings afterwards. On Sundays she took her sons to four services—morning prayer, evening prayer, Sunday school, and Christian endeavour classes. On the Milhous side of the family, Richard had still deeper Quaker roots. His great-grandmother, Elizabeth Milhous, whom he remembers well as a small boy, was a famous preacher in demand at meeting houses and churches all over the United States on account of the legendary fervour of her sermons. Richard tells how, on one occasion, she was so carried away relating the miracle of the loaves and fishes that she threw her lunch pack of sardine sandwiches over the congregation! Elizabeth's daughter-in-law, Almira Milhous, was another strong influence, instructing her family with Bible stories, prayers and religious poems. Grandmother Almira, who always wore the white ribbon of the Women's Christian Temperance Union and used the Quaker plain speech ('Hast thou done thy homework? Is this book thine?'), believed in the literal interpretation of the Bible. She instilled this fundamentalist faith into all her thirty-two grandchildren.

How much of this religious activity rubbed off on Richard? All the indications are that he absorbed and obeyed the Quaker teachings with profound commitment. During his childhood, it was recalled how he said his prayers with unusual intensity: 'He'd clasp his little hands, and close his eyes, and you could just feel it. He was really praying instead of just saying his prayers',[3] remembered Elizabeth Guptill, a hired help who lived in with the Nixons from 1918 to 1924. Later on, he manifested his faith by giving witness and by leading extensive prayers in the East Whittier Friends Church. Such public performances were the tip of a much deeper religious feeling. Richard acquired from his mother the same protective shield of privacy which made it difficult, if not impossible, for him to talk to anyone about his spiritual dimension. Yet it was noticed that he had open and sensitive channels to religious emotions. 'Dick was very sensitive to atmospherics. He always knew when there was, as we Quakers say, a disturbing presence about'[4] said Tom Bewley, a family friend and fellow churchgoer who was later to invite the twenty-five-year-old Richard to join his Whittier law partnership. Bewley was one of several contemporaries who thought that Richard, during his formative years, experienced the acknowledged Quaker states of grace such as 'having the spirit'; 'standing squarely in the light'; and 'peace at the center'. He also believed that Richard obeyed 'one of the most fundamental tenets of Quakerism—that you are first honest with yourself'.[5]

Certainly the tenets of Quakerism had a strong hold on the young Nixon's behaviour and beliefs, so much so that he completely accepted strict biblical fundamentalism until he was nineteen years old. As he wrote in an essay dated 9 October 1933, 'The infallibility and literal correctness of the Bible, the miracles, even the whale story, all these I accepted as facts when I entered college.'[6]

II. THE LEGACY OF THE LOST BROTHERS

Nixon's simple faith was tested in his teenage years by the early deaths of two brothers, Arthur and Harold. When the trauma of family bereavement involves the premature loss of a loved sibling there can be times when those left behind to mourn have doubts about the nature or even the existence of the Deity. With his sensitive and thoughtful mind, it would be surprising if Nixon had not experienced such moments of despair. However, this is speculation. All that is known is that the deep sadness that swept over him in the two tragedies had a profound impact on the formation of his character.

As has been recorded in an earlier chapter, Arthur's sudden death in 1925 at the age of seven devastated Richard. At the time, he tried to suppress his grief by hiding his tears from his parents, although he poignantly recorded in his memoirs, published fifty-three years after the event: 'For weeks after Arthur's funeral there was not a day that I did not think about him and cry.'[7]

Far from losing their faith, the Nixons intensified their religiosity in the months after Arthur's death. Frank was tormented by the thought that God had taken his beloved Arthur away as a sign of displeasure or punishment. He vowed never again to open the store on Sundays and took solace from the revivalist movement that was sweeping through Southern California in the mid-1920s. Every evening he gathered his family around their mahogany Gil Filan wireless set and tuned in to the sermons from the celebrity preachers of the day. His favourites were the Reverend 'Fighting Bob' Shuler, whose Blue Ridge drawl commanded by far the largest radio following; Billy Sunday, whose theme was 'Oh Lord, save us from Hellfire'; and 'Sister Aimee' Semple McPherson, whose followers had contributed sufficient funds to build the 5,000-seat Angeles Temple and other shrines to her movement. Stirred by the emotional outpourings of these evangelists, the Nixons began attending revival crusades and rallies on a regular basis. Hannah's instinct for religious privacy soon caused her to limit

her involvement to being a radio listener. Frank, by contrast, wanted to participate to the full. Once a week or so he took his sons to hear either 'Sister Aimée'
at the Angeles Temple or 'Fighting Bob' at Trinity Methodist Church.

One evening in the summer of 1926, Frank and Richard went to worship at
a rally led by the most forceful figure among California's new wave of evangelical
orators, Paul Rader, head of the World Wide Gospel movement. Emotions of the
spirit were evidently running high that evening, for at Rader's command 'Come
Forward for Christ!' the shy and reserved Richard Nixon rose up from his seat
and dedicated his life anew to God.

'We joined hundreds of others that night,' he later told the Reverend Billy
Graham, 'in making our personal commitments to Christ and Christian service.'[8]
This conversion to Born-again Christianity was Richard's most public reaction
to the death of Arthur. Privately he assuaged his grief with the therapy of hard
work, apparently with a new purposefulness. 'I think it was Arthur's passing that
first stirred within Richard a determination to help make up for our loss by making us very proud of him', his mother said later. 'Now his need to succeed became
even stronger.'[9]

One other pointer to the depth of Nixon's sense of loss can be found in a
moving, 1,500-word eulogy which he wrote five years after the bereavement.
Arriving at Whittier College in 1930, his first academic assignment was a freshman English essay. He chose as his topic, 'My Brother, Arthur R. Nixon'. Using
the literary device of describing a family photograph, he recounted his memories
of Arthur, including the story of his last prayer: 'If I should die before I wake, I
pray thee Lord my soul to take.' The essay concluded with Nixon's explanation of
why the photograph meant so much to him: 'There is a growing tendency among
college students to let their childhood beliefs be forgotten. Especially we find this
true when we speak of the Divine Creator and His plans for us. I thought that I
would also become that way, but I find that it is impossible for me to do so…when
I am tired and worried, and am almost ready to quit trying to live as I should, I
look up and see the picture of a little boy with sparkling eyes, and curly hair; I
remember the childlike prayer; I pray that it may prove true for me as it did for
my brother Arthur.'[10]

By the time Nixon wrote his eulogy on Arthur, the shadow of death was again
closing in on the family. His eldest brother Harold had been sowing too many
wild oats for Frank and Hannah's taste during his teenage years in Whittier, so
he was sent away to the strictly evangelical Mount Herman School in Massachusetts. The winter fogs of Cape Cod were the worst possible climate for a boy with
a history of tubercular infection. Harold coughed and lost weight so severely that

the school sent him home to California. Richard met him at Pasadena station and was shocked by his appearance. 'He was painfully thin and he'd grown a moustache. He cut a fine figure but I knew something was wrong.'[11] Tuberculosis was soon diagnosed, setting in train a long period of anguish, expense, and sacrifice for all members of the family.

The financial costs, huge though they became, were unnecessary. Only a few miles away from Whittier was the Los Angeles County Hospital with TB wards which had a high reputation for expert medical treatment. The hospital was administered by the State of California, and free to all patients. Frank, however, disliked socialised medicine on principle. He decided it was his duty as a citizen and taxpayer to have nothing to do with the state hospital service on the grounds that it would be taking charity. For this determination to maintain the purest standards of free-market ideology, Frank and his family paid a heavy price. Instead of going for treatment to the Los Angeles County Hospital, Harold was installed in an expensive, private institution, the Hillcrest Sanatorium. He recovered sufficiently from his haemorrhage to be well enough to win the heart of one of the nurses there, to whom he became engaged. He was moved on to another private sanatorium in Antelope Valley. Then it became apparent that his treatment would be a long haul and that the best place for him would be at one of the clinics in the high, dry air of the Arizona mountains. The medical bills were already ticking away expensively and with no end in sight. Frank held a family conference and decided to sell off some of the land around the store. With the proceeds, Harold was moved first to a sanatorium in Tucson and then to an even higher, 5,000-foot altitude in Prescott, where Dr. John Flynn, a renowned TB specialist, presided over a hospital full of First World War veterans who had contracted TB as a result of being gassed. Frank was upset by Dr. Flynn's fees, accused him of running 'a fat cat lunger clinic' and wanted to move Harold again, but this was impossible for his left lung had collapsed and he was now bedridden. Hannah stepped in and took charge.

At a cost of $25 a month she rented a four-bedroomed house in Pinecrest, an enclave on the edge of Prescott which was regarded almost as a leper colony, full of incurable TB patients struggling to breathe more easily in the mountain air. In order to be able to pay the expenses, Hannah took in three other TB victims as lodgers. Richard Nixon remembered them as two youths, Leslie from a town in the Midwest; Larry from the East; and a third man, 'The Major', a Canadian who had been gassed in the trenches of Flanders. Richard was a regular visitor to his mother's TB nursing home at Prescott. He stayed there for two summers, sharing in the difficult and sometimes disgusting conditions under which she had to work. In those pre-antibiotic days, there was no cure except fresh air for TB victims, most of whom required intensive nursing as they gasped for breath, coughing up large quantities of blood and sputum.

'It was my mother's finest hour', he recalled. 'She loved and cared for each one of those three patients as if they were her own sons...They were all bedridden patients except for The Major who now and then could be ambulatory. My mother alone, with no help whatever, took care of them all in that little house she had rented. She did the cooking, did the cleaning, took them trays, took care of their laundry, gave them their bed baths, carried their bedpans, gave them their alcohol rubs—everything that in those days a nurse would do for a patient, she did by herself... and they all died.'[12]

To see a mother coping with such strain in primitive conditions (the Pinecrest house had no modern conveniences and only one wood-burning stove for cooking, heating and sterilising), amidst a prevailing atmosphere of despondency, would have been a distressing experience for any son. It is hardly surprising that Richard carried those memories with him into his White House years.

'He never let us forget his mother had to scrub bedpans',[13] remembered a member of Nixon's White House Staff. On one of the rare public occasions when Nixon let himself go emotionally, in his last speech as President two hours before his resignation on 9 August 1974, he described Hannah with tears welling up in his eyes:

> Nobody will ever write a book, probably, about my mother: well, I guess all of you would say this about your mother. My mother was a saint. And I think of her, two boys dying of tuberculosis, nursing four* others in order that she could take care of my older brother for three years in Arizona, and seeing each of them die, and when they died it was like one of her own. Yes, she will have no books written about her. But she was a saint.[14]

One consequence of Hannah's saintly commitment to nursing Harold was that it involved long family separations. Frank responded well to the crisis, doing his utmost to fill the gap left by Hannah, both at home, where he did most of the family cooking, and in the store, where he took on her cake-baking and pie-making operations. There were many pressures on this all-male household, but the three remaining Nixons, Frank, Dick and Don, were bonded together in

---

* Nixon had forgotten that Hannah only had three other patients.

adversity and helped each other through Hannah's three-year absence from home.

About once every six weeks, Frank would strap a huge, thirty-gallon gasoline tank onto the back of the family car (gas was 13 cents a gallon cheaper in California than it was in Arizona) and make the 750-mile journey from Whittier to Prescott. It was hard driving, most of it on unmade roads, and the one-way trip took around fifteen hours. In summer it was too hot to travel, so during their long vacation the boys moved to Prescott, staying in a back bedroom of Hannah's cabin, while the patients slept out of doors on a screened porch in order to get the maximum amount of fresh, desert night air into their lungs as Dr. Flynn had prescribed.

Such close proximity to Harold, Leslie, Larry and The Major brought obvious risks of infection even though precautions were taken. Dick seems to have become fatalistic about his chances, buoyed up at certain times by Hannah's faith that she would not catch the disease, but according to his Whittier College girlfriend, Ola Florence Welch, he also had pessimistic moods in which he expected to become infected. 'He thought he would get it too', she said. 'He said he was worried about what he called his "paper lungs".'[15]

In spite of the difficulties of life within the Pinecrest TB community, Nixon managed to make a good life for himself in and around the town of Prescott, working at various jobs which included chicken slaughtering, corn cutting and swimming pool cleaning.

> I had very little time for reading in Prescott, but I would not for one
> moment suggest that my spirits were low there. The summer jobs
> brought in some much-needed money for the family budget and
> except for wringing the necks of chickens, or worse still chopping
> them off, I enjoyed the work. Prescott also provided opportunities
> for hikes in the mountains, for picnics, and swimming...it was one
> of the most delightful towns I have ever been in.[16]

Prescott had once been the capital of a booming gold-mining district, but this era had long since passed and the only revival of it was a big summer rodeo festival called 'Frontier Days', which had a fairground area labelled 'The Slippery Gulch Carnival'. Nixon had several jobs at Slippery Gulch during the summers of 1928 and 1929. His most successful role was that of a fairground barker on a stall which he named 'Dick's Wheel of Fortune'. His task was to entice punters to buy numbers on a roulette-type wheel for 10 cents a time. He must have been good at it, since

'Dick's Wheel of Fortune' became the best money-making concession in the entire fairground. His most unlikely gambler was Grandmother Almira, aged eighty-one, who was persuaded by her fast-talking grandson to forget her Quaker principles and to place the one and only bet of her life at Slippery Gulch. With true beginner's luck, her number came up and she won a large ham.

Harold's luck, however, was steadily running out. His chances of survival were probably low in any event, but he tilted the odds against himself by reckless behaviour during the intermittent periods when he was well enough to walk. Even when he was bedridden, he managed to lead a complicated emotional life, falling in love with another Pinecrest TB patient, eighteen-year-old Jessie Lynch, and becoming so jealous of her contacts with other male patients in the lunger community that he rigged up a home-made wiretapping device for listening in to her telephone calls.

Harold might well have ended his days at Prescott had it not been for an unexpected event. Hannah became pregnant, aged forty-five. Frank was astonished, declaring, 'The doctor doesn't know what he is talking about!'[17] But the doctor was right and the whole family had to return to California so that Hannah could be safely delivered of her new baby, Edward, who was born in May 1930 in Whittier Hospital.

After his return home, Harold threw medical caution to the winds. He took a part-time job fumigating citrus trees, despite the obvious risks to his diseased lungs of working amidst chemical fumes. He rushed round town, wild as ever and still chasing girls. 'He was a headstrong, devil-may-care Irishman who at every turn did the opposite of what his doctor and parents told him to do', said one neighbour.[18]

Dick watched his elder brother thinning and weakening with mounting sadness. He did not blame Harold for ignoring the doctor's orders to stay in bed, for he understood his vital urge to try to lead what was left of his life in as normal a way as possible. Frank evidently understood it too. In February1933, when Harold was in a very fragile state, he asked his father if he could get a trailer and take him on a sightseeing trip through the San Bernadino mountains and over into the Mojave desert. Instead of calming Harold down and persuading him to rest, Frank jumped at the idea, hired a trailer and set off with his eldest son in the direction of the mountains, saying they would return in about a month's time. Within three days they were back. Harold had suffered another severe haemorrhage and was only semiconscious. Miraculously he rallied well during the next few days, then weakened again. Richard Nixon recalled the story of his brother's last twenty-four hours:

On March 6th Harold asked me to drive him up to Whittier. He had
seen an ad in the newspaper for a new kind of electric cake mixer. He
wanted to be sure that we had a good present for my mother on her
birthday which was March 7th. He barely had the strength to walk
with me into the hardware store. We picked out a cake mixer. I think
the cost was about $10. We had it wrapped as a birthday present and
brought it home. The next morning I was in the bathroom, the only
one with a lavatory, which was right off the bedroom in which he was
confined. I was shaving around 8 o'clock in the morning before going
on to College. When I was about half through, he called me and asked
me if I would hurry; that he didn't feel well and wanted to rest. Before
I left he said that I ought to give the present to mother that night when
I returned from school.

About three hours later I was studying in the library. One of the
assistant librarians came over to me and said that I should come
home. I knew of course what had happened. When I arrived home I
saw the hearse out in front of the house. My mother and father were
both crying uncontrollably as the undertaker wheeled his body into
the hearse and drove away to the funeral parlor.[19]

Tears for Harold flowed in torrents from all the family. The prolonged agony
of his illness made his death less of a shock than Arthur's had been, but the final
blow hurt just as deeply. In the immediate aftermath of the tragedy, Frank and
Hannah were so overcome that Dick, now the eldest son, had to take on some of the
administrative responsibilities such as notifying relatives, escorting mourners to
visit the body at the White–Emerson Funeral Parlor, and making the arrangements
for the burial service. His most poignant responsibility came the evening after
Harold's death, when he took out the cake mixer and gave it to Hannah, explaining
that it was Harold's birthday present to her. Hannah was totally overwhelmed,
vowing never again to celebrate her birthday. She stuck to this pledge, banning all
parties or presents for the rest of her life. Instead, she marked every March 7th by
making a pilgrimage to Harold's and Arthur's graves to leave flowers. Amidst her
sobbings, Dick remembered that his own last exchange of words with Harold that
morning had ended just as he was leaving for the library with his brother requesting
him 'to ask Mother to come in'. What had happened next, Dick asked.

She said he had asked her to put her arms around him and hold him
very close. Harold was not a particularly religious boy but he said to

my mother, 'This is the last time I shall see you until we meet in Heaven', and then he died.[20]

Nixon prefers not to talk about the impact on him of the deaths of two of his brothers. His younger brother Ed, who was only three when Harold died, has recalled how he once asked Dick in middle age to describe their lost siblings.

> He just couldn't do it. He broke down completely, walked out of the room. We apologized to each other afterwards. I think he just decided to sink those tragedies deep in his mind and never to talk about them again. That's his way and I respect it.[21]

Ed Nixon and other members of the family believe that the fraternal tragedies somehow strengthened the character of the eldest survivor. They feel that when Richard buried Arthur and Harold, he also buried a part of his own natural feelings, particularly that warmer and more joyous part which his brothers brought out in him. As for Frank and Hannah, having lost the two sons they most loved, they concentrated their affection on the surviving son they most respected. This increased parental interest in Dick intensified his ambition to a still higher plane. He was now working not just for himself but to make up to his parents for the bereavements they had suffered. This was Hannah's judgement:

> From that time on it seemed that Richard was trying to be three sons in one, striving even harder than before to make up to his father and me for our loss.... unconsciously, too, I think that Richard may have felt a kind of guilt that Harold and Arthur were dead and that he was alive.[22]

Richard Nixon in later life has downplayed the long-term effects on his own development of Harold's struggle: 'I can't in all honesty say that the close contact with TB and the family sacrifices during Harold's ordeal scarred my life or affected me permanently in a detrimental way. It was a difficult time, but we fought the battle because we thought it was worth fighting. We never gave up hope that Harold might recover.'[23]

Hoping against hope and fighting against seemingly impossible odds is a Nixon family characteristic that first emerged during the dark days of Harold's illness. Instead of depressing Richard or his family, the experience uplifted them, and brought them closer together. 'It was a battle in which each of us in his way played a part', he recalls. 'Eventually it was lost, but we had no regrets whatever for the sacrifices we had to make in fighting it.'[24]

Until Harold's illness, Richard was not often thought of as a fighter, more a fastidious, somewhat aloof child who worked hard at his books in solitude. As long as he remained the second son, he was still something of a mother's boy, safely cocooned in the embrace of his extended Quaker family. He was good at winning academic prizes from judges or schoolmasters; he was a dutiful worker in the store; but when it came to life's more difficult races, he had missed out at high school football on doctor's orders; he had failed in his only open electoral contest; he had only managed to come third in his class; and he was full of worries and insecurities about his personal popularity.

The toughness, the cutting edge, and the drive that later personified his political career had not yet made their appearance. For all his application to his studies, there was a suspicion of weakness in his schoolboy character; for he could be accused of failing to fight his corner with sufficient zest and of seeking the palm without the dust.

Any such assessment of Nixon's temperament was soon to prove fleeting and false. The turning point was Harold's death. Immediately after the funeral, Richard went into a period of lonely withdrawal, marked by long, catatonic silences. When his mourning was over, he emerged as a new and much changed eldest son. From that time on he was always in the arena, always competing fiercely, always fighting. Whether this was due to some teenage personality metamorphosis, or a direct legacy of his involvement in Harold's struggle we shall never know, but it was a different Richard Nixon who returned to the scene at Whittier College.

III. 'WHAT CAN I BELIEVE?'

At Whittier, Nixon's perceptive contemporaries did not see him as the 'regular guy' he tried so hard to be, despite this run of successes, which reached its peak in 1933/4, a year after his elder brother's death. The more he achieved the more they recognised that there was something unusual, perhaps even strange, about their student body President, champion college debater, and winner of the Harvard Club prize for the 'outstanding all-round student in the state'.

'There is no excellent beauty that hath not some strangeness in the proportion', wrote Francis Bacon. It is true of both body and mind. Nixon's strangeness was to be found in his developing intellect. He had begun to use his professors and their curriculum merely as the point of departure for his private intellectual travels. The most extraordinary of these voyages of discovery began when he attended a series of lectures by Dr. J. Herschel Coffin on 'The Philosophy of Christian Reconstruction'. Until he began the preparatory reading for it, Nixon could accurately be described as a devout Quaker with unshaken fundamentalist beliefs. Now he was shaken to the core. While most Whittier students must have regarded the course merely as an interesting academic exercise designed to give them a grounding in theology, philosophy, and the theory of evolution, Nixon's involvement was at a far deeper level. He concentrated on it with such intensity that he was whirled into a vortex of emotional and mental self-agonising.

Between October 1933 and April 1934, while going through what could well be called his first crisis, Nixon wrote twelve essays under the general title 'What Can I Believe?' These are the account of his journey into religious doubt and changing belief, described in a passionate and highly personal tone.

Nixon's first essay poses a series of rhetorical questions such as: 'What can I do with religion?', 'Where am I heading for?' Early on he describes where he has come from:

> My parents, 'fundamental Quakers', had ground into me, with the aid of the church, all the fundamental ideas in their strictest interpretation. The infallibility of the Bible [sic], the miracles, even the whale story, all these I accepted as facts when I entered college four years ago. Even then I could not forget the admonition to not be misled by college professors who might be a little too liberal in their views! Many of those childhood ideas have been destroyed but there are some which I cannot bring myself to drop. To me the greatness of the universe is too much for man to explain. I still believe that God is the Creator, the first cause of all that exists...I am no longer a 'seven day-er'! In declaring that God created the world, I am only acknowledging that my own mind is not capable of explaining it any other way...My education has taught me that the Bible, like all other books, is a work of man and consequently has man-made mistakes. Now I desire to find a suitable explanation of man's and the universe's creation, an explanation that will fit not only with my idea of God but also with what my mind tells me is right. I want to know why I am here in order that I may better find my place in life.[25]

After two well-researched but predictable essays on the theory of evolution and Christian philosophy, Nixon next tackled the subject of the relationship between personality, social consciousness, morality and spirituality. Apparently inspired by Dr. Coffin's lectures, he wrote hundreds of words on the flow of energies between these four interrelated aspects of human mentality and ended up explaining his thesis by drawing a chart depicting his vision of higher energy.

Nixon's mysterious jottings, which are re-created below, should not perhaps be taken too seriously, for at first glance they merely reflect the confusion admitted in Nixon's opening essay, when he stated that his methods and hypotheses would be illogical: '...Certainly any system of ideas would be better than this absurd collection of science, religion and philosophy that I now have'.[26] But one clear point emerges from his charts and writings. In the strange private struggle with himself to redefine his faith in the context of the doubts created by his scientific and philosophical readings, Nixon was stumbling towards a conclusion hinted at by the arrows on the flow chart, and explained more clearly by the next essay, dated 29 November 1933, entitled 'More About The Soul'.

> I have always believed that the soul and even the mind were separate entities. I am now wavering about the mind and I am also not so sure about the soul! I cannot see why the soul would lose any of its spiritual significance if we say that it emerges from self-conscious mental life. The soul is the culmination of the development of a being, the highest level to which that being can aspire...The soul is that part of us which enables us to understand God's works...It is the spiritual part of personality. It flows into beauty as soon as personality realizes its highest aims.[27]

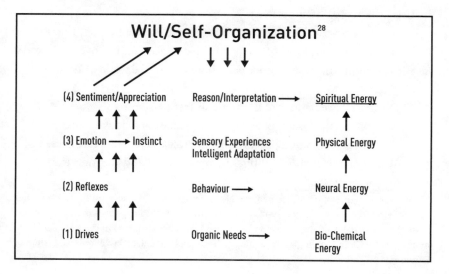

Will/Self-Organization[28]

(4) Sentiment/Appreciation	Reason/Interpretation ⟶	Spiritual Energy
(3) Emotion ⟶ Instinct	Sensory Experiences Intelligent Adaptation	Physical Energy
(2) Reflexes	Behaviour ⟶	Neural Energy
(1) Drives	Organic Needs ⟶	Bio-Chemical Energy

By January 1934, after essays on topics such as 'Where does moral authority come from?' and 'What is Spirituality?', Nixon set out what might be called an interim report on his crisis of faith under the heading 'What Can I Believe?—The Half Way Mark.'

> My beliefs are shattered, but in their place a new philosophy has been built. Some of the fragments of my own religion have proved useful in building this new philosophy.... my religious thinking, as can be seen, has been revolutionized, but I believe that a process of enlightenment and purification has taken place at the same time. As I see myself now, I am still a thorough believer in God as the creator of all things. I believe in the philosophy of Christ and I have learned to more thoroughly understand and appreciate it. I have gained an immeasurable amount of tolerance, because I have learned that men make mistakes because they are striving for something better.[29]

In his next four essays, Nixon dealt with definitions of God; comparative religion; and various concepts of Biblical teachings. In one passage he developed his view that the Resurrection story is a myth. 'It is not necessary to show that Jesus rose from the dead on the third day and then lived on earth for forty days with his disciples before ascending into heaven. The important fact is that Jesus lived and taught a life so perfect that he continued to live and grow after his death in the hearts of men. It may be true that the Resurrection story is a myth, but symbolically it teaches the great lesson that men who achieve the highest values in their lives may gain immortality.'[*]

On a more practical level, Nixon's imagination was captured by the work of Christ as peacemaker. Most of the penultimate essay is given over to Nixon's idealistic view of what Jesus's peace plan should be for the world of 1934:

> Disarm all the nations of the world as fast as is humanly possible. Re-establish the League of Nations. Repeal the obnoxious features of the Versailles Treaty, especially the war guilt and reparations clause. Work for the eventual abolishment of tariffs and immigration

---

[*] It may say something for the originality of Nixon's mind that this theory of the Resurrection put forward by an unknown twenty-one-year-old student in 1934 appears remarkably similar to the controversial doctrine expounded fifty-two years later to uproar in the Anglican community by the Church of England's leading radical theologian, Dr. David Jenkins, Bishop of Durham.

restrictions... The first step in reorganizing the international field is to bring the religion of Jesus in all its power and simplicity to all the nations of the earth... world friendship can be attained; war can be abolished; but men must first get a renewed vision of the religion and kingdom of Jesus.[30]

How to put Jesus's principles into practice is the theme of Nixon's final essay, which ends with this personal conclusion:

I have as my ideal the life of Jesus. I know that the social system which he suggested would be a great boon to the world. I believe that his system of values is unsurpassed. It shall be my purpose in life, therefore, to follow the religion of Jesus as well as I can. I feel that I must apply his principles to whatever profession I may find myself attached. What Do I Believe? My answer to this question could have been better called 'What shall I do with the religion of Jesus?' For to me this intellectual log has proved to be a gradual evolution towards an understanding of the religion of Jesus. My greatest desire is that I may now apply this understanding to my life.[31]

These 'What Can I Believe' essays are by any standards an extraordinary display of self-analysis from a student who was twenty years old at the beginning of the course. They have laid buried in Nixon's private papers for sixty years, but still today they give the impression of a soul on fire, illustrating not only Nixon's capacity for hard work and deep thinking, but also the ardour of his spiritual commitment at that age. One obvious question that arises from them is: 'What happened to all that burning spirituality?' The answer may be stranger than anything written in the essays themselves. Having bared his soul in these compositions, Nixon subsequently changed course and kept his spiritual beliefs private. Unlike most American politicians, he developed an aversion to mentioning God or religion throughout his public career. He has been just as taciturn on the subject in his interviews and reminiscences. He has acknowledged that Dr. Herschel Coffin's teachings and the essays that resulted from them were a seminal event in his life. Beyond that he has given no further clues on the development of his beliefs other than to say: 'Mine is a different kind of religious faith, intensely personal, intensely private.'[32]

It would be a mistake to draw the conclusion from his silence on religion that somewhere along the line after he left college Nixon either lost his faith or massively downgraded its importance in his life. Throughout his life, as will be seen, he has remained a practising Christian. He was a dutiful attender of chapel at Duke University; he was a Sunday school teacher in his twenties; he read his Bible daily during his war service in the South Pacific; he discussed with his mother the possibility of becoming a Quaker minister; just before the Checkers broadcast in 1952 he sat with his head in his hands saying, 'God, thy will be done, not mine'; on election day 1960 he went off alone to pray in the Roman Catholic Chapel of San Juan Capistrano, California; during his wilderness years period 1963–7 he worshipped regularly at the Marble Collegiate Church of New York, where the Reverend Norman Vincent Peale counselled him; he developed a spiritual friendship with the Reverend Dr. Billy Graham 1967–8; he was the first President to hold Sunday services in the White House; he said silent prayers in the Lincoln sitting room on the eve of major presidential journeys; in the middle of the Watergate crisis in 1973 he told Haldeman and Ehrlichman of his daily intercessions to God for guidance; and he knelt to pray with Henry Kissinger on the eve of his resignation from the Presidency on 9 August 1974. And yet it can be speculated that he may have had more than his share of struggles with periods of doubt and darkness.

Returning to Nixon at the age of twenty-one, his 'What Can I Believe?' essays shed light on one aspect of the emerging character of the future 37th President of the United States. An Anglican Archbishop who read the essays in 1990 at the request of this author without any clue to the identity of the original writer made an intriguing comment: 'Whoever wrote this was already at an advanced level of spirituality which could not have remained static within him. He must either have risen very much higher or fallen very much lower, quite possibly both, but such strong spiritual roots would never have died and must have been very important to him.'[33]

IV. A BROKEN ENGAGEMENT

Nixon's spiritual crisis did not prevent him from having a great romance during his college years, finding happiness with one serious girlfriend, Ola Florence Welch, the daughter of the Whittier police chief. The couple were together for six years from 1929 to 1935, building a deep but sometimes turbulent relationship. They went steady, fell in love, and were engaged to be married.

The romance started after an embarrassing failure for both parties in public. Ola Florence Welch and Richard Nixon first met as contemporaries in Whittier High School. In their early years as classmates there was no rapport and some antipathy between them. At the time of the student body presidential election in

March 1929, Ola Florence remembered writing in her diary, 'Oh how I hate Richard Nixon'[34] and being glad to vote for his rival. Bob Logue. However, this negative impression melted a few weeks later when she was selected to play the leading lady in a production of *The Aeneid*. Her leading man was Richard Nixon. They were cast in the roles of Dido and Aeneas on account of their classical, rather than their theatrical, talents. The play was put on by the Latin Club to mark the 2,000th anniversary of Virgil's birth. Nixon was the top Latin scholar at Whittier High and Ola Florence Welch, also an A-grade student, was not far behind him. The producer of the play was a school classics master far more interested in coaching his pupils to perfection with their lines than directing their movements as performers on stage. The result was not all right on the night; it was a disaster.

The plot of *The Aeneid* reaches its climax when Aeneas declares his love for Dido, embraces her tenderly, then they both throw themselves onto a funeral pyre. This was too much for Nixon, partly because of his natural inhibitions against displaying so much affection, even on a stage, and partly because such dramatic style as he had was agonisingly cramped by having to wear silver boots three sizes too small. He tiptoed delicately around his heroine, managing only the most simpering of kisses before tugging awkwardly at her toga as they slithered towards the flaming bier. The audience of teenagers, restless from an already long evening of Virgil, erupted in catcalls, whistles and raucous laughter. 'I was never so embarrassed in my whole life',[35] was Ola Florence's recollection, while Nixon remembers the evening as 'sheer torture'[36] which left him with a lifelong horror of wearing boots.

As soon as the stars came offstage, with one or two boos ringing in their ears, Nixon had some plans of his own. 'He never said a word about the play but he insisted that I must come and meet his folks immediately', recalls Ola Florence. 'He wouldn't even let me take my make-up off. But that was the first moment when I realized he liked me.'[37] Dick liked Ola Florence a lot. He tried to explain why in his first love letter, written shortly after the play opened on 2 May 1929. However, he begins with an apology for having reacted badly to some postmortem criticisms of his acting made by the school's drama coach, Miss Miller. These had caused him to storm out in a rage, leaving his leading lady behind.

> Dear Ola Florence,
>
> I wish to apologize for the caddish way I acted Saturday evening. I certainly wish now I could have kept my temper in my pocket instead of losing it and acting angry out there on stage, especially when Miss Miller made her criticism. I know I should have taken her

criticism in a kindly spirit but aw heck I can't help it! I don't want to excuse myself but...please don't think I'm that way all the time.

You know I've tried to figure out why I'm so cracked about you. These are the reasons. You are not a boy chaser. You use your brains to good purposes. You never show your anger to anyone. You are talented in other lines besides studying (dramatist, music, etc.) and most of all, 'You are just you.' That's the only way I can put it.

Love from,

Dick Nixon[38]

Ola Florence Welch had beauty as well as brains. Photographs of the period portray her as statuesque and sultry, with high cheekbones and deep-set doe eyes. She had character, too, one Milhous cousin describing her as 'a damn strong woman'[39] and the Whittier College *Acropolis* magazine praising her for having 'the dignity of a true lady'.[40] Nixon was entranced, dating her steadily throughout their last year of high school and four years of college. In those Depression times there was not much money in anyone's pocket to spend on dates. For 10 cents a ticket they went to the occasional movie such as *All Quiet on the Western Front*; shared milk shakes; or even more occasionally went out for a hamburger. But their most frequent activities together cost nothing, such as going to the beach, playing miniature golf, walking in the mountains and visiting each other's families. Ola Florence was warmly welcomed by the Nixons. 'I have nothing but good memories of his folks. They were so nice to me, especially Mrs. Nixon who was such a kind, gentle lady but at the same time with quite an iron hand inside her velvet glove. I went with them on all kinds of family outings, picnics, trips to the desert. Once I remember spending a week with them down at Laguna in the house of a Milhous aunt...we had many good times.'[41]

The Nixon hospitality was only partly reciprocated. From the beginning, Ola Florence's mother disapproved of her daughter's steady boyfriend, possibly because a grocer's son was not her idea of a future son-in-law. However, Captain Welch, the former Sheriff of Cochise County who became Police Chief of Whittier, thought better of Richard and they enjoyed many long conversations together. Welch, Nixon recalls, 'was a very well-read man, particularly interested in psychiatry. He used to talk to the two of us about Jung and Freud, the subconscious and the unconscious, the id and the ego etcetera. I never took psychology in college but I learned to read about it because of the influence of the man we called Captain Welch.'[42]

Anyone who spends time with Richard Nixon is sooner or later tempted to indulge in a little amateur psychology, and Ola Florence Welch was no exception:

> Of course I thought Dick was wonderful...so strong, so clever, so articulate. He wrote me notes which I just couldn't believe, they had such beautiful words and thoughts. I admired his intellectual ability. I always thought he would achieve something extraordinary in life, like becoming Chief Justice of the Supreme Court, at least that's what we dreamed about at the time...yet deep down he had this insecure side to him. I remember how unsure of himself Dick always was before he debated...how he wouldn't let me help him improve his dancing...and how when he ran against Dick Thomson for student body president he was really down, absolutely sure that he wasn't going to win. Then when he won he went up and changed for a time and became so different. He suddenly started dating other girls and I was left thinking maybe now he's President he's changed. He wants someone else...but then he wrote me letters that were so apologetic they would probably fascinate a psychologist. He was a real enigma...Anyway we made up after that and then we started going together really seriously.[43]

The increasing seriousness of the romance won approbation from the Nixon parents but it incurred the wrath of Ola Florence's mother. Mrs. Welch developed a sharp dislike for her daughter's suitor. 'She just couldn't stand Dick. She wouldn't speak to him when he came to the house', recalled Ola Florence's younger sister, Dorothy. 'I didn't like him either. He was a real pill. I think what really put me and my mother off him was that he was so disloyal to my sister. He two-timed her. Sometimes he would take her to parties and then go home with someone else so my mother had to come out and pick Ola Florence up. Mothers don't like that.'[44]

Dorothy Welch had a talent for palmistry and other forms of second sight which stayed with her into old age. As a teenager she read Dick Nixon's hand at Christmas 1932. 'I got quite a shock', she recalled. 'What I saw in his palm was a path of incredibly brilliant success and then the most terrible black cloud like a disaster or an accident or something. I told him what I read but in a toned-down version because he was such a serious sort of a guy that the full version would have made him distraught. He wouldn't have known how to cope with it. But I did tell

Ola Florence exactly what I'd seen.* "If you stick with him you'll have real nasty trouble one day", I said. She didn't take the slightest bit of notice. By that stage she was besotted with him."[45]

On 10 June 1933 Dick and Ola Florence agreed to get married. The moment of decision came after the wedding party of their college friends Helen Bewley and Julian Hathaway in Santa Fe Springs. Confirmation that the date was an extra special one is to be found in a coded entry in Nixon's handwriting in Ola Florence's 1933 Whittier College Year Book. Alongside all the customary signatures and compliments she collected from her classmates, Dick wrote a full-page essay praising her many qualities ('You are a really splendid student even if you are a girl...you can sure play the piano...you are fair on the typewriter...you are a splendid letter writer...you will make a good schoolteacher') and ending mysteriously:

> Now that I have done my duty to the others I shall tell you what I really think if they will close their eyes. You will notice what everybody else says to you about sweetness, etc. etc. Multiply that by as much as you can, and you can get my opinion. Add to that *11.30 Saturday night June 10th,* multiplied several other times, subtract what you think of me and there you are.
>   Dick

And Ola Florence recalled: 'Everything about that night was so beautiful— the flowers, the music, the atmosphere. Dick was really moved. He became soft and tender and told me how much he loved me. He had never said that before. After the service was over we sat and talked for hours. It was more an understanding that we were engaged, although without definite arrangements to get married, but from then on we made quite serious plans for it.'[46] Their most serious plan was saving for a wedding ring. They each regularly put aside some of the pocket money they earned from their respective part-time jobs, his in the store, hers in the college treasurer's office. 'Whenever we had a date and there was some change left over, Dick would pass me a quarter, a dime, or whatever it was, saying "that's for the ring".... and I kept it faithfully.'[47]

One of Dick's attractions was his generosity. Unlike other young men, he never allowed Ola Florence to pay towards the cost of their dates. He lent her his

---

* Ola Florence Welch Jobe confirmed her sister's palm-reading story to the author in September 1991.

car. From time to time he gave her corsages of flowers and presents such as the cedarwood box of cosmetics he brought back from one of his trips to Harold in Prescott. But the couple had their problems, too, quarrelling quite frequently. Dick could be mean and moody. Sometimes he would break off communication for days, refusing to return Ola Florence's calls. When she needed a shoulder to cry on at such times, she would go and see Dick's parents. They approved of the impending match and usually took their future daughter-in-law's side in these tiffs. Frank would get angry at his son's lack of chivalry. 'He'll hang himself if he's not careful',[48] Ola Florence remembers Frank shouting.

Another less personal cause of friction was that the couple were at opposite ends of the political spectrum. 'We were strong Democrats and a very political family—probably more so than his', recalled Ola Florence. 'I admired Roosevelt while he really hated him. In those days I think Dick's strongest political belief, which he got from his father, was that you shouldn't rely on the Government for any sort of help. I didn't agree with that.' Their arguments could get heated, even bitter. 'We had a stormy relationship, more stormy than most.... sometimes he'd be harsh and I'd cry. Then we'd make up.'[49]

Despite such ups and downs, the relationship strengthened. Ola Florence shared to the full in Dick's happiness when the news came through in May 1934 that he had won a scholarship to Duke University Law School. 'The night he found out, oh we had fun that night', she recalled. 'He was not only fun, he was joyous abandoned—the only time I remember him that way. He said it was the best thing that ever happened to him. We rode around in his car and just celebrated.'[50]

The scholarship meant a separation, in their case one which could be summarised by those ambivalent lines: 'Absence makes the heart grow fonder/of whom let absent lovers ponder.' Nixon was initially homesick at Duke. He poured out his feelings of loneliness and inadequacy in a spate of correspondence, beginning each letter 'Dear Blue Eyes'.

'Nothing mushy.... simple boy and girl kind of writing.... but they were real love letters', was how they seemed to Ola Florence.[51] She sent him a big basket of fruit for Thanksgiving and was touched by the warmth of his response. Nixon seemed to appreciate her more now that he was far away. Their engagement was a firm commitment in his mind, less so in hers. Back in Whittier she did not lack admirers and she gradually became intrigued by the attentions of Gail Jobe, another college contemporary with whom she had a brief flirtation during one of the periods when Nixon was dating other girls. Jobe was good looking and well off. He laughed and liked dancing more than his absent rival had ever done. His family's ranching background appealed to Mrs. Welch. Ola Florence, although always a morally circumspect girl in accordance with the strict conventions of those times, was becoming a footloose fiancée.

When Nixon returned from Duke in the summer of 1935 he found himself facing competition, and he did not like it. 'I'm an emotional person, warm, outgoing and in those days I enjoyed the lighthearted side of life, things like dancing all evening and, well, just being a bit silly', explained Ola Florence.[52] By contrast, Nixon seemed a bit heavy, weighed down by his studies. One day he started telling her about the Duke Law School lectures on torts. Ola Florence made a joke about how she would learn to cook torts, and earned herself the rebuke, 'You're going to have to learn something about law terms now.'[53]

The break-up came later that summer. Nixon called one afternoon to announce he was coming over, but Ola Florence said no, that wouldn't be convenient. Pressed for an explanation, she replied that Gail Jobe was in her parents' living room. Nixon exploded. 'He was really furious. He shouted, "If I never see you again it will be too soon", and then slammed down the phone on me. I'll never forget that', recalled Ola Florence.[54]

Nixon did not mean what he had said. He put on a brave face and behaved as if Gail Jobe did not exist, coming round to the house the next day, still talking about marriage plans. He became more possessive, while Ola Florence grew more elusive. Although it was evident that the relationship was going sour, Nixon did not give up. After he returned to Duke he continued to send her weekly letters, all of them on the assumption that their marriage was still on. In December 1935, Ola Florence wrote to him ending the romance, telling him of her new plan to marry Gail Jobe and sending back the money saved towards the ring. Nixon still did not concede defeat. In the early weeks of 1936 he kept up a plaintive correspondence, displaying a confused emotional state.

'Strange to say, I write to you not to pour forth a heart filled with love but only because I wish to write a letter to a girl and you seem to be the only one around right at the moment', was the unconvincing start of his letter of 15 January 1936. 'You see it's impossible to get rid of a bad penny and when a person is worth even less than that the impossibility becomes complete...I realize now that I lost my chance with you about this time last year and don't think I'm trying to get it back because I know you are happier now.'

After more in this 'don't cry for me Argentina' literary style, he suddenly came off his high horse: 'This is a bunch of tripe isn't it? Please don't believe that I'm trying to be sentimental but I must tell you that you meant more to me than anyone. Don't answer but remember your promise—an invitation to your wedding.'[55]

In spite of this valedictory note, Nixon persisted in writing to Ola Florence, who replied only to ask him to stop. Her request produced another 'final' letter, this time expressed in clearer and more moving terms:

> February 2nd, 1936
>> Dear Ola Florence,
>> Finally I have become wise! And although I regret having embarrassed you with my letters, I don't regret the feeling I've had towards you for the past year.
>> In the year and a half I've been at Duke, I've realized more than ever the perfection, the splendor, the grandeur of my mother's character. Incapable of selfishness she is to me a supreme ideal. And you have taken your place with her in my heart—as an example for which all men should strive.
>> Old memories are slowly fading away. New ones are taking their place. But I shall always remember the kindness, the beauty, the loveliness that was, that is, and shall for ever be Ola Florence Welch.
>> Your friend,
>> Richard Nixon[56]

For Nixon to have bracketed Ola Florence Welch with his mother in this rare declaration of love is a most telling indicator of the depth of his feelings. He continued to express them in further 'final' correspondence. 'His letters went on arriving right up to two weeks before our wedding', recalled Ola Florence. 'My mother used to tell me not to open them, but I think I did, even though I felt I couldn't reply.'[57] At the eleventh hour, Nixon accepted that he had loved and lost. He sent Mr. and Mrs. Gail Jobe a gracious letter of good wishes for their future happiness, and a silver-plate hors d'oeuvres tray as a wedding present.

There can be little doubt that Nixon was deeply hurt by these events. He had revealed himself as a sensitive and vulnerable young man to whom rejection must have been agonisingly painful. His pride as well as his heart was wounded. Yet on the surface he gave no impression that anything was wrong. He confided in no one. He never mentioned Ola Florence to his new friends at Duke. To his old friends at Whittier, who were puzzled by the breakup of what many of them had regarded as a 'great couple', he said nothing. His family, who respected his privacy, had to be content with the most insouciant and implausible indications of his true feelings. It was a desperately sad moment in his life and he faced it entirely alone.

The impact of Ola Florence Welch on Nixon's private persona is too deep a subject for those who are not psychologists. It should, however, be recorded that at least one of his relatives believes that this early débâcle in the romantic life of the young Nixon could be the key to that deep-seated inability to trust which later proved so damaging to the political life of President Nixon.[58]

The same train of thought was followed by Bryce Harlow, one of Nixon's oldest friends and White House aides. He occasionally expressed the view that Nixon's character must have been affected by being deeply wounded when he was young 'by somebody in his family or maybe by a girl'.[59] But such theories are speculation. In the factual story of Nixon's life, Ola Florence Welch's importance is that she was his first great love. She gave him his first experience of both passion and rejection. He took the rejection hard, but recovered well. After his first flush of hopeless letter-writing, he coped by burying the hurt within himself; then by working even harder, striving more mightily, and preparing still more intensively for whatever the next battle might be. It was to prove the classic pattern of Richard Nixon's reaction to any kind of defeat or disappointment.

FOUR

DUKE UNIVERSITY

I. THE LONER WITH AN IRON BUTT

Duke University was initially an unnerving experience for Nixon. His under-graduate successes at Whittier had made him a big fish in a small pond, but the postgraduate challenges of Duke left him feeling more like a fish out of water, gasping for survival in the face of fierce competition, the like of which he had never encountered.

A few days after his arrival on campus, Nixon learned that his law course was labelled 'the meat grinder'. The origin of the nickname lay in the competitive-ness of the scholarship programme which, in the eyes of the students, was designed to pulverise all but the best and brightest. There were forty-five graduates in Nixon's class from all over the United States, thirty-two of them members of Phi Beta Kappa (an élite society of scholarship), twenty-five of them with scholar-ships. Yet only twelve of these scholarships would be renewed on a competitive basis in the following year, no matter how good the grades of the near-misses might be. This was a far tougher interpretation of the renewal terms indicated in Nixon's original letter from Duke, which had misleadingly referred in vague terms to the need for maintaining 'at least a B average'.

Once he realised the full implications of the faster track on which he now found himself, Nixon became despondent. He wrote 'sad letters' to Ola Florence

Welch back in California. 'He sounded like he was scared of the competition and close to quitting two or three times', she recalled.[1]

Money was the root of his insecurity. His $250-a-year scholarship was vital to him, for his finances were fragile. He was struggling to make ends meet by borrowing $35 per month from his father towards his living expenses and by taking a $30-a-month clerk's job in the university library provided by the National Youth Administration—a New Deal agency. Even so, his budget was precarious and only balanced because of dollar bill gifts of $5, $10 and $20, which arrived intermittently in the mail from Aunt Edith, Grandmother Almira and other relatives.

In addition to his financial worries, Nixon was beset by doubts about his own intellectual competence. Part of the trouble was that he was overawed by his first impressions of his new university. The tobacco fortune of its chief benefactor, James Buchanan Duke, had been devoted to re-creating Oxford in North Carolina, complete with a 'Brideshead Revisited' atmosphere of dreaming spires, castellated turrets, stained glass windows, tudor gothic quadrangles, and a star-studded faculty of unusual academics.

The law school epitomised Duke's drive to create a centre of educational excellence. The Dean, Justin Miller, had been given the resources to create a southern rival to the law schools of Yale and Harvard. Supported by a policy of cheque-book jurisprudence, Miller recruited some of the top legal teaching talent in the United States by offering salaries of up to $12,000 per annum. This was an amazing sum for an academic in those days, equivalent to a 1990's salary of $130,000. Lured by this gold of academe, twelve full professors, most of them with national or international reputations, were on the staff of Duke Law School by 1934, teaching just over one hundred students.

On Nixon's first day of lectures at Duke, an Olympian tone was set by Dr. Bryan Bolich, a former Oxford Rhodes scholar, who opened his property law class with a homily about the dispensability of lawyers in the depths of the Depression. 'Well ladies and gentlemen, I have a little advice to you before we start this course', he said. 'Marry for money and practice law for love.'[2]

Nixon was struck by this early signal that finding a good job after graduation might prove a tough assignment. His confidence was further shaken by his initial contacts with some of his more gifted teachers. Professor David Cavers, who had been first in his class at Harvard Law School, taught Current Decisions and criticised an early Nixon essay with the words, 'You've got constipation in writing. You've got to let it flow out more easily.'[3]

The Professor of Torts, Douglas B. Maggs, described by the official historian of the law school as 'a high-spirited scholar who enjoyed intellectual combat',[4] specialised in making students perform under stress by shouting at them with difficult, even insulting questions amidst much pounding of his desk. Nixon found Maggs 'a volatile, hot tempered, brilliant teacher... at times bombastic'.[5] A fellow classmate described the experience as being 'like Christian Martyrs facing the lions. Maggs would reduce you to a shambles in class. He'd make you look like an idiot.'[6]

Although he was never an idiot, Nixon felt inadequate in the face of all this pressure. 'I've almost decided that I don't like this law business. No fooling. I'm getting almost disgusted', he wrote in a letter to Ola Florence Welch on 14 January 1935, signing himself, 'Your studious but dull student —Dick'.[7]

The studiousness was enforced by fear. 'The faculty was very tough on us', Nixon recalled. 'They pulled no punches. They deliberately wanted to scare us, and they were right. You either worked harder or you quit. One evening late, I guess it was around 11.30 p.m., I was working in the library, studying. Bill Adelson, a big hulking fellow who later became a lawyer in Maryland, came by and he says, "Nixon, what's the matter? You look a little worried." I said, "Gee Bill, I'm scared... all these guys and this course is so hard.... don't know if I'm ever going to keep this scholarship." This was just before the mid-year exams. He looked at me with his cynical look. "Don't worry Nixon. You're gonna do all right. You know what it takes to learn the law. An iron butt. You've got one."'[8]

Bill Adelson was right in his prediction. When those examination results came through, Nixon's burning of the midnight oil had paid off, for he was placed third in his class with marks of 81.6 per cent and an A rating. It was a result that boosted his fragile self-esteem.

'A men make the professors, B men make the judges, C men make the money', was one of the sayings of the law school.[9] With his straight A grades in all subjects, Nixon had proved he could compete with the best students in the country. He had abandoned his Whittier College habit of spreading himself too thin over a multiplicity of interests. He was learning that the long, hard road of single-minded concentration paid the highest dividends. At Duke, Nixon discovered what Dr. Benjamin Jowett, Master of Balliol College, Oxford, once felicitously described as 'that sense of power, real or imaginary, which comes from long steady working'.[10] It was a power which intensified and made permanent in him the spirit of the loner. Forty-five years after he left Duke, Nixon made a revealing reference to his law school experiences during an interview in the

Oval Office of the White House with Theodore H. White, author of *The Making of the President* books.

Nixon had just been re-elected for his second term and was explaining how he was determined to ensure that his time as President was not wasted by unnecessary diversions such as receiving oral briefings. 'My disposition is to see that the President's time is not frittered away', he told White. 'I've found a way to do it. I'm a reader not a buller. Most of the boys at law school had long bull sessions about their cases. I studied my cases alone.'[11]

Nixon's avoidance of legal bull sessions with his fellow students was partly due to physical separation. On his income he could not afford to room in the campus dormitories. During his first six months at Duke, he lived on the outskirts of the town at 814 Sixth Street, a house that was otherwise occupied by a group of Methodist theological students. These future ministers of God had proved expert at paring the requirements of Mammon down to the bone by finding the cheapest billet in the area. The price of one dollar a day for full board and lodging suited Nixon's purse, but his concentration was disturbed by his fellow lodgers' habit of talking religion until the small hours of the morning.[12]

Finding it difficult to cohabit with these chattering clerics, Nixon moved out to an abandoned tool shed in woods near the campus. He was discovered there by a maintenance man, Mr. R. Blackman, who found Nixon studying in the eight by twelve-foot shack. Its furnishings consisted of a bed, a table and chair, but no stove. The only protection against the cold was an improvised walling of corrugated cardboard. Blackman thought, 'This boy must want an education real bad',[13] and did not report his discovery of the tool shed squatter to the college authorities.

Nixon the lonely, impecunious student enduring the snow and ice of a North Carolina winter in an unheated tool shed can be made to seem like a character from the pages of a Charles Dickens novel. Yet his life style was not entirely uncharacteristic of the difficulties faced by students of slender means during the years of the Great Depression. Nixon endured harsher conditions than most, but they sharpened his fighting spirit. He was young, resilient, and oblivious to creature comforts. He cared little about his clothes and even less about his food. His contemporaries recall him as a thin, gangling youth, invariably dressed in the same purple sweater and patched, grey flannel trousers. If he ate at all during the day, his meal consisted of the cheapest available snack in the coffee shop, often just a Milky Way chocolate bar. In the evenings he had supper in the Duke union, sitting at the 'shysters' table', reserved for law students, alongside the 'quacks' table' of the medical students. He is remembered for wolfing down his soup at double-quick speed and rushing back halfway through the meal to the library, working there until midnight or later in pursuit of those crucial A grades which would guarantee the future of his scholarship.

II. WHIPPOORWILL MANOR

Early in 1935, Nixon formed a friendship with a student who was brighter and poorer than himself. This was Bill Perdue, a brilliant academic performer who had come top of the class in the mid-year exams and who scraped along the bottom financially by supplementing his scholarship with the commissions he intermittently earned as a door-to-door Bible salesman. In later life Perdue achieved distinction as a corporate lawyer and as a codebreaker, still revered in the secret world for his wartime service as the US liaison officer who analysed the output of intelligence from Britain's legendary decoding of the German Enigma device.

At Duke, Perdue was the student Nixon most admired for brain power. The two young men competed fiercely inside the classroom and collaborated closely outside it. At first their relationship was one of economic necessity. They came together in order to share a tiny room two miles away from the campus that suited their tiny budgets. However, Perdue was not just a convenient room-mate. He was the prototype of the intellectual sparring partner that Nixon, later in his life, found that he needed to have around him in order to do his best creative thinking. Henry Kissinger was the most famous of these cerebral companions, but there were many others in different phases of Nixon's life.

In the summer of 1935, Nixon and Perdue improved both the quality of their accommodation and the quality of their intellectual joustings by moving into a section of a house owned by a widow on the edge of Duke Forest. They grandly nicknamed their lodgings 'Whippoorwill Manor'. It consisted of a large room with two brass double beds. Perdue and Nixon slept in one, taking in two new lodging partners, Frederick Albrink and Lyman Brownfield, to occupy the other. Albrink and Brownfield were scholarship boys from Ohio. As their final graduation results were to show, they had the brains to compete on equal terms with their new room-mates.

Conditions at Whippoorwill Manor were primitive, for there was no electricity, no inside plumbing and the only heat came from an old-fashioned iron stove. 'In the middle of the winter we'd each stuff paper into it the night before we went to bed', recalled Nixon. 'We crawled in at midnight, never before then. The first one up in the morning would light the fire so that it heated up the room, took the chill off. Then we would get into our clothes and walk the mile and a half that it took to get back to the campus. We shaved over at the men's room at the campus and took our showers later in the day. It was inconvenient, but worth it for $5 a month each.'[14]

Although the law course remained tough, Nixon and his room-mates managed to find some outlets for low-cost recreation. Sports came top of their list. They played handball almost every day and were regular spectators of the football games in Duke Stadium. Tickets for the big matches were issued free to all students and could be sold for a useful profit to the public. Nixon alone of the Whippoorwill Manor quartet was too keen a fan ever to sell his ticket.

In the evenings there was not much to do for those on a low budget. The students' union ran a Saturday night cinema with the entry price of a nickel, and Nixon is remembered enjoying *Henry VIII* starring Charles Laughton; *The Thirty-Nine Steps; Mutiny on the Bounty,* and other black-and-white movies of that era—early examples of Nixon's love of historical and adventure films. Dance music at the Duke Union was of an exceptionally high standard in the mid-1930s. Two of Nixon's student contemporaries were Les Brown and Johnny Long, later to become nationally famous bandleaders. Their rival groups performed regularly and Nixon loved to go and hear them play. 'I can see Dick now, standing on the edge of the lobby smiling and tap-tapping his feet to the beat of Les Brown', recalled Fred Albrink. 'But I don't think he ever danced or went out with a girl. It wasn't that Dick was allergic to the opposite sex. He liked girls, as all of us did, but we just didn't have any money and on that basis dates were mighty rare.'[15]

One place where inexpensive dates could be organised was at the university swimming pool. Entry was restricted in the evenings to married students and members of the faculty with their wives, although many single students found their way round the rule by signing in with their date as a married couple. 'Old Dick would never agree to do that. I guess he was kinda prudish about signing on as Mr. and Mrs. Nixon', remembered Albrink.[16]

Almost the only occasions when Nixon let himself go were the end of term parties. These required careful preparation in the dry state of North Carolina. Lyman Brownfield owned a clapped-out 1926 Packard, christened *Corpus Juris* by the Whippoorwill room-mates, which had to be driven over the Virginia border to obtain a supply of liquor. 'These parties were really blasts', recalled Nixon. 'After all, none of us, including myself, would have a drink at all for months, and then all of a sudden we were confronted with an opportunity to relax, let our hair down and "hang one on". Most of us would end up with terrible hangovers the following day, vowing that we would never take a drink again.'[17]

On the morning after one of these parties, Bill Perdue stumbled out of bed at Whippoorwill Manor announcing that he felt as if he had been 'drug through

hell and beat over the head with a shit bag'.[18] Nixon was shocked by such a colourful Southern expression. According to his contemporaries, no expletive stronger
than the occasional 'Goddamn' or 'Dammit' was ever heard to pass his lips. His
mother's Quaker example was still having a strong influence on him, as he indicated in a paragraph of self-portraiture written in a letter to Ola Florence Welch
in January 1936:

> Let me tell you about the nuttiest of the nutty Nixons. He remains a
> stolid bachelor and I think his hair is beginning to thin out. He
> doesn't smoke, he drinks very little, he swears less and he is as crazy
> as ever. He still thinks an awful lot of his mother.[19]

Nixon did not often yield to life's temptations during his time at Duke. He
briefly developed a taste for playing bridge, but abandoned the game after three
months when he realised that his hours at the card table were reducing his hours
in the library. Almost his only deviation from the path of rectitude was the story
of 'Nixon's first break-in', as it was melodramatically labelled thirty-eight years
later during the era of Watergate.

The incident took place at the end of Nixon's second year. Like many of the
students in his class, he was on tenterhooks about his grades. These were not
posted on the Law School noticeboard on the expected day. Upset by the delays
Nixon, Perdue and Albrink were passing the Dean's office late in the evening
when they noticed that the transom above the door had been left open, although
the door itself was locked. On impulse, the trio decided to get in and look at the
grades, rationalising their action by telling each other that the results were not
secret and that the Dean had slipped up by forgetting to publish them on time.[20]

Perdue, the smallest of the three, was hoisted onto the shoulders of Nixon
and Albrink and climbed through the open transom. Once inside he let his collaborators in and together they found the records in the top drawer of the Dean's
desk. Nixon was disappointed to discover that he had slipped to fourth place in
the class, with a mark of 74.2 per cent, although he was relieved that this was still
good enough to guarantee his scholarship.

After noting their grades, the Whippoorwill Manor invaders replaced the
list and returned to the common room undiscovered. None of them regarded
their spur of the moment prank as a big deal. 'What the heck! All we did was look
at the grades. We didn't take anything or change anything', was Fred Albrink's
later assessment of the affair. 'We weren't running any big risk. Nobody was in
the building and if by any chance we had been caught, I think it would have been

treated as a low level matter of curiosity espionage. They could hardly have expelled their three top students in one go for that!'[21]

Nixon had no guilty conscience about the incident, since he himself revealed the story to his first biographer, Bela Kornitzer, in 1959. The episode was motivated by nothing more sinister than a degree of impatient recklessness and did not deserve the high moral indignation subsequently heaped on it by some of Nixon's critics. So far as he was concerned, it was an out of character piece of foolishness which, had it been discovered, might have cost him a reprimand and the glowing references he was later to receive from his professors.

Aside from this 'break-in', Nixon rarely strayed from the disciplines of his Quaker upbringing during his law school years. Every Sunday he went either to a Quaker service at the Friends Church in Raleigh or attended the university chapel. Nixon was impressed by the splendour of Duke's Chapel's ecclesiastical architecture, which had been modelled on parts of Canterbury Cathedral, with soaring transepts, a 290-foot nave, pews for 1,500, and a glorious panoply of seventy-seven stained glass windows. The sermons, however, disappointed him. The two regular preachers at the Duke University Chapel in the 1930s were a Quaker and a Methodist. 'I cannot recall in those three years any occasion when either of those ministers addressed the subject of race relations', said Nixon, who was troubled by the segregation all around him. 'We had virtually no contact whatever with Negroes...The only time I really saw them was when we would go downtown in Durham on occasion late in the day. The tobacco factories would be having a change of shift. Pouring out of the factories like a black smoke from a furnace came the thousands of Negroes who worked there. They walked down one side of the street and we were on the other. There were no incidents and no one really seemed to think of them as individuals. They were just a mass of people living their life as a race completely apart from the rest of us.'[22]

With a heritage of Quaker tolerance on race that ran back to his roots at Yorba Linda, and beyond that to the safe refuge provided by his Milhous ancestors on the underground railway for runaway slaves during the Civil War, it was not surprising that Nixon should have felt uncomfortable in the segregationist South. To his credit, he spoke up and said so. He told his classmates of his experiences at his home, where Negroes sometimes joined the family for lunch, and at Whittier College, where he had established a friendship with William Brock, the black football player he had made a charter member of the Orthogonians. These revelations seemed almost perverse to his Southern contemporaries, some of whom refused to discuss race relations with him. Nixon's convictions were well remembered. 'He was shocked and disturbed at the prevalent North Carolina treatment of the Negro population as an inferior group', recalled one Duke contemporary. 'He looked upon the issue…as a moral issue and condemned it very strongly as such, but did not realize the problems that confronted the people of the South in regard to the Negro.'[23]

Nixon's stand on the race question was only one of the reasons why he was viewed by his contemporaries as a rather moralistic young man. 'The only time I went to church was when Dick urged me to come with him', recalled Albrink. 'He wasn't trying to proselytize or convert me. He was a believer who put his faith into practice. That was the fundamental explanation for his views on the race question and for his general good behavior.'[24]

There was still a lot of Hannah Nixon in her son Richard the law student. He was particularly remembered for his treatment of Fred Cady, a student crippled by polio. Day after day, Cady used to wait on his crutches at the law school entrance until his friend Nixon arrived to carry him up the steep steps and into the lecture hall. Another kindness was to Charles Rhyne, a classmate who was hospitalised for several months with a poisoned arm. Every evening Nixon went to Rhyne's bedside and read over to him his notes on the day's lectures. These small acts of compassion to Rhyne and Cady were part of a wider behaviour pattern towards contemporaries in trouble or down on their luck, which have filtered on to the oral history records, tending to confirm Fred Albrink's general characterisation of Nixon at Duke as 'a thoroughly decent guy with no flaws in his character that we could see'.[25]

III. DISAPPOINTMENTS ON THE ROAD TO GRADUATION

Nixon was also remembered by his Duke contemporaries for his ability to argue, although his discussions tended to concentrate on law and history rather than on contemporary politics. 'The War Between the States', as Bill Perdue and other Southerners insisted on calling it, was the most divisive topic. Nixon had arrived at Duke believing that Grant was the best general produced on either side in the Civil War, but after debating the merits of every battle for two and a half years with Perdue, he recalled: 'I was almost convinced that Ulysses S. Grant would be lucky to be about fourth behind Robert E. Lee, Joseph E. Johnston and Stonewall Jackson.'[26]

Although more topical issues such as FDR's abortive plan to pack the Supreme Court and the extensions of the New Deal inevitably started arguments among the students, after a long day's stint in the library they were often too tired to inject real passion into their conversations. Nixon was no exception to the general student disinterest in politics, and none of his room-mates spotted him as a future politician. Even when he was elected President of the law school Bar Association in his final year, his success was attributed not to political skill but to his academic and forensic talents. 'The factor that swung the election for Nixon was genuine respect for his scholarship', said Lyman Brownfield.[27]

Nixon's few political memories from his time at Duke included listening on the radio to President Roosevelt's famous fireside chats. 'They were very effective', he recalled. 'FDR had a buoyant characteristic in his voice, a sense of optimism.... it was that buoyancy, that optimism which people needed to feel in the depths of the Depression.'[28]

Rather surprisingly, however, a royal voice over the airwaves in 1936 made a greater impact on Nixon. 'The broadcast that I remember far more than the fireside chats was the time that King Edward VIII, afterwards the Duke of Windsor, gave his famous speech saying he was going to abdicate. I remember we all sat and heard it on the radio, and Douglas Maggs, the Professor of Torts who was so tough and seemed to be the one that had no sentiment at all, afterwards just said over and over again, "Wasn't that a magnificent thing? Wasn't that a magnificent thing?"'[29]

Nixon got on well with the faculty, extracting the maximum value from the law school's advantageously low pupil–professor ratio. He formed some of his best relationships with his teachers, including those who had appeared so forbidding at first encounter. Douglas Maggs, who had seemed bombastic in the freshman torts class, came to respect Nixon for his ability to argue the finer technical points of a well-researched case. The respect was mutual, for in the second year, when Maggs taught a course in constitutional law, Nixon found him 'inspirational' for his vision of the great role the law could play in shaping the social and economic development of America through Supreme Court decisions. Another inspirational influence was Professor Lon L. Fuller who taught jurisprudence, a course which Nixon believed gave him a global vision of the law 'which went far beyond the British–American tradition and was international in scope'.[30] A third important teacher was Professor David Cavers. He had initially criticised Nixon for intellectual constipation, but grew to regard him as one of the university's outstanding students. He published several Nixon essays in the *Duke Law Review* and mailed one to Supreme Court Justice Robert H. Jackson, who wrote back a letter of commendation.

Nixon was extremely proud of this letter, which thirty-five years later was to be the trigger for his most successful appointment to the Supreme Court. It came up by chance during a discussion in the Oval Office during October 1971. Nixon was considering the vacancy left by the retirement of Justice Hugo Black and, on the advice of John Mitchell, had all but settled on the choice of Senator Howard Baker.

However, White House Special Counsel Richard E. Moore urged the President to consider Assistant General William Rehnquist. Nixon's first reaction was dismissive, saying, 'But he's only the Assistant Attorney General.' Nevertheless Moore pressed on, emphasising Rehnquist's intellectual qualifications, and making the point that he had served for two years as law clerk to Justice Jackson. This caught Nixon's attention: 'Jackson! The only good judge Roosevelt ever appointed. He wrote me a letter once congratulating me on one of my essays in the *Duke Law Review*'. He immediately took a new interest in Moore's advocacy of Rehnquist. The subsequent discussion led to the choice of the nominee, who later became Chief Justice of the Supreme Court, William H. Rehnquist.[31]

Outside the classroom, one of Nixon's main preoccupations was saving up enough money to go on interstate travels. He earned extra cash by varnishing books in the law library at 30 cents an hour, mimeographing research papers, and clearing tables in the coffee shop. This drudgery produced the desired financial results, for Nixon made several long-distance trips to cities like Boston, Baltimore (where he developed a lifelong fondness for the local delicacy of Maryland crab cakes) and New York. His first visit to the Big Apple, with Bill Perdue and his brother Don Nixon over Christmas 1935, left him 'enormously impressed'. The highlights of his five-day trip included a low-cost Christmas dinner at Schraffts on Fifth Avenue; a long walk around the Wall Street area, during which he gazed up at the skyscrapers for so long that he got a crick in his neck; and picking up last-minute returned tickets from the box offices of theatres at bargain prices. Over that period Nixon saw four Broadway plays, including *Tobacco Road, What Price Glory* and *Front Page*. He was exhilarated by his first visit to the Metropolitan Opera, sitting through two consecutive performances of Ponchielli's *La Gioconda,* coming back with welts on his knees because the cheapest seats in the top row had been too closely jammed together for his 5ft 11in frame.[32]

During this first trip to New York, Nixon got the better of a brush with a street-corner con man. He and his brother Don were standing by Perdue's car when a man came up with a large box containing what appeared to be a fine fox fur piece. The man, who claimed to be a delivery porter for Saks department store, showed the Nixon boys a bill for $150 and said that by mistake the store had duplicated the order. As a result he was at liberty to sell it at a cut-price rate. 'We stood there rather open mouthed,' recalled Nixon, 'thinking how much it would mean to buy a fur piece for my mother, who because of the difficult financial

straits of the family had not bought even a new coat for ten years.... the man first
told us that he would take $100 for it. We told him that was too much. Then he
began to come down: $75; $60; $50...'[33] At this moment Bill Perdue walked up
and denounced the fur as 'a pretty shoddy piece of merchandise', but offered the
opinion that it might just be worth $10. The trickster grew nervous, apparently
fearing that Perdue might be a plainclothes detective, and clinched the deal
quickly when the Nixon boys each produced their $5 bills. Hannah Nixon got her
Christmas present and wore the fur proudly for many years, showing it off to
journalists during the 1960 presidential election campaign as an example of her
son's kindness.

With financial help from his family, Nixon managed to get home to California for two visits during his years at Duke. On one occasion Nixon was helping
out at the family store when on the spur of the moment he was persuaded to join
an informal political gathering of some fifteen young people of voting age in a
friend's barn near Whittier. As Nixon recalled: 'Sitting there in the middle was a
young person who was running for Congress. He was smoking a pipe. He was a
professor or lecturer at Pomona College. It was Jerry Voorhis. I remember how
impressed I was. He was highly idealistic...He impressed me. He impressed
everyone else there and if I had voted in 1936, which I did not, I would have voted
for him.'[34]

This first Nixon–Voorhis meeting seemed without significance, although
ten years later they would contest the same congressional seat. Nixon's sole preoccupation at that time was the degree that would lead to a good job. During his
third year at Duke he was putting out feelers towards big law firms, and over the
Christmas vacation of 1936 he made his second visit to New York, this time for
job hunting rather than sightseeing purposes. Accompanied by Bill Perdue and
another classmate, Harlan Leathers, Nixon stayed in a YMCA hostel and did the
rounds of the top law partnerships in the city. The experience brought out some
of his worst insecurities: 'I knew that these firms were virtually closed shops which
hired only from the establishment élite of the Ivy League law schools, but I thought
it would be worth a try', he recalled. 'I must have looked pretty scruffy sitting in
those plush, polished mahogany and leather reception rooms in my one good
suit.'[35] In fact, he did not get quite the cold shoulder he had feared. At Sullivan
and Cromwell he was formally interviewed for the best part of an hour by a panel
of senior partners including John Foster Dulles. He was given an even better
reception at Donovan, Leisure, Newton and Lombard. Mr. Lombard conducted
the first interview and was sufficiently taken with Nixon to introduce him to Mr.
Leisure and the head of the firm, the legendary 'Wild Bill' Donovan. However,

Nixon returned to Duke empty handed, unlike his travelling companions Perdue and Leathers, who both got good jobs.

About a month later Donovan, Leisure did write to ask if Nixon would be interested in a further interview, but he responded negatively, for he was having second thoughts despite the temptation of an $1,800-a-year starting salary. 'I was not sure that I wanted to get bogged down in one of those huge New York law firms',[36] he wrote afterwards, although at the time his friends recall that he was sore at having been passed over. One form of secure employment which did attract Nixon was working for the Federal Bureau of Investigation. The FBI had sent a head-hunting team to Duke in the spring of 1937 and, after an interview, the recruiters encouraged him to file a formal job application. Nixon sought advice from his teachers. Professor Lon Fuller told him that he was 'too good a man'[37] to enroll as one of J. Edgar Hoover's G-men, but Nixon thought differently, saying later, 'The FBI looked very good to a young lawyer wanting work that year.'[38] Dean Horack, the new head of the law school, supported Nixon's FBI application. In a personal letter to Hoover, Horack commended Nixon as 'one of the finest young men I have ever had in my classes. He is a superior student, alert, aggressive, a fine speaker and one who can do an exceptionally good piece of research when called upon to do so.'[39]

In spite of this recommendation, Nixon never received a job offer from the FBI. The mystery of his apparent rejection was solved some twenty-five years later when Nixon met J. Edgar Hoover socially at a party in the Washington home of Mrs. Alice Roosevelt Longworth. On hearing that his bureau had missed out on recruiting the aspiring G-man who had instead gone on to become the Vice President of the United States, Hoover checked the files and discovered that Nixon's name had been approved as a special agent, but that his letter of appointment had been cancelled just before mailing because of an unexpected cut in the FBI's 1937 budget appropriation for new recruits. Since this part of the story was unknown to Nixon at the time, he was discouraged and decided to revert to his job-seeking activities on the New York circuit of law firms. Dean Horack, who knew of Nixon's long-term political ambitions, gave different advice. Nixon recalls Horack telling him: 'Don't go to New York. If you're interested in politics, go home. Practice law at home. You may not get as much money but that's the only way if you want to do anything in the political arena.'[40]

As a result Nixon asked his family to sound out job possibilities with law firms in Southern California. Nixon did not, however, take his eye off his main objective of ending up with a first-class academic record. The competition was getting tougher, the 'meat grinder' reducing the size of the class to only twenty-six of the original forty-five students on his course. The faster pace quickened his competitive instincts. He was desperately keen to achieve membership of the Order of the Coif, Duke's highest distinction, awarded only to the top three in the graduating class. The race was a fierce one, but by small fractions of a percentage point the laurels went to Whippoorwill Manor, those top three places going in order to Bill Perdue, Fred Albrink and Richard Nixon—with Lyman Brownfield close behind in fifth place.

Graduation came in June 1937. Nixon's cup was running over. One manifestation of his happiness occurred at the Senior Beer Bust, an evening picnic for the faculty and the senior class. Nixon amazed everyone by getting up on a table and delivering a comic turn of a speech on 'insecurity', complete with hilarious mimicry which had the entire audience rolling around with laughter. Since his classmates had previously thought him to be somewhat lacking in humour, the emergence of Nixon as a court jester who could keep the table in a roar came as a big surprise. This unexpected talent for carefully scripted comedy was to show up on several occasions during Nixon's later political career.

An additional cause of Nixon's rejoicing in graduation week was the presence of his family. Frank had crammed Hannah, Don, Edward and Grandmother Almira Milhous into a small Chevrolet Sedan, driving them 3,000 miles across the continent from Whittier to see the ceremonies. It was a time of deep emotion for all the Nixons. 'I can't tell you how proud we felt, sitting there in the Page auditorium in that sea of black gowns', recalled Ed Nixon. 'Dick was the first member of our family ever to go to law school, ever to go to a nationally famous university, ever to get a top flight postgraduate education. For my father, who had quit school when he was thirteen, it was one of the high peaks of his life. My mother felt the same way but for a different reason. She thought the day belonged to her mother whose dream was coming true because as a grandmother she had done so much to encourage Dick and he was now fulfilling her highest expectations.'[41]

Richard shared the view that the day belonged to his eighty-eight-year-old grandmother. He could hardly believe how she had found the stamina to make the trip and to tour the sights of the campus with such animated vigour. He had always felt a special bond with this remarkable family matriarch. Throughout his educational years she had encouraged him with her poems and letters; inspired him with her example and teachings; and supported him with financial and other presents. An indication of his feelings is shown by a letter Nixon sent his grandmother in December 1936. 'At this Christmas season I should like to be sending you a gift which would really express my love for you—but it will probably be several years before I reach such a high financial level—if ever', he wrote, explaining that instead of a present he was sending her 'this Christmas note'. He told her how proud he was of being a member of her extended family. 'You will never know how much I've appreciated your remembrances', he continued. 'Sometimes—in our spare moments, some of us indulge in reminiscing sessions here at school— and the boys are amazed at the remarkable person I describe as my Quaker Grandmother. I myself share their respect. Your loving Grandson, Richard Milhous Nixon'.[42]

The homely Quaker grandmother in her shawl and sturdy black boots; the ambitious graduate in gown and mortarboard; the presentation of the law school's highest award; the backdrop of ivy-clad walls and stone-carved crests; the soaring cathedral spire; the tears of pride in the eyes of Frank and Hannah—all made an evocative combination of symbols and signposts that marked the ending of Richard Nixon's formal education.

He had already travelled far from the lemon ranch at Yorba Linda, yet he was still close to his family roots and Quaker heritage. He was laden with academic prizes, but the graduation day book that pleased him most was Canon Farrer's *Life of Christ*, a leather-bound 1899 edition given by his grandmother. The award of the Order of the Coif should have been the perfect entry ticket to one of the the big East-coast law firms, but he had opted for a small-town legal practice close to home.

The ideals, insecurities and ambitions which could explain the complex make-up of Nixon at the age of twenty-five were largely hidden, even from his close friends and relatives. However, one clue to his secret thinking emerged early in the journey home. Soon after piling into his father's overcrowded Chevrolet for the long drive back to California, he persuaded his family to make a major detour to Washington DC, which none of them had ever visited before. The highlight of their visit to the nation's capital was listening to a debate in the House of Representatives. It was a dull afternoon, dominated by a longwinded speech from Congressman John Stephen McGrority of California, but Nixon was entranced. Only about fifteen members of the House were present, among them Jerry Voorhis, the Nixon family's local Congressman whose office had supplied their gallery tickets, but the whole spectacle of the legislature at work clearly caught Richard's imagination. At that time his political dreams were supposedly on the back burner, for his immediate priorities were to pass the California Bar exam and then to find a job in a local law firm. Nevertheless, as he continued on his homeward journey after Washington, in Nixon's inner soul there must have been an echo of the words his hero Woodrow Wilson used to describe his feelings at the time of his matriculation from the University of Virginia Law School in 1879: 'The profession I had chosen was politics; the profession I entered was the law. I entered the one because I thought it would lead to the other.'[43]

FIVE

LAW, LOVE, AND MARRIAGE

I. WINGERT AND BEWLEY

Nixon's transition from law student to lawyer was not easy. Arriving back from Whittier in June 1937 he was brought down to earth by discovering that most of the papers for the California Bar examination were based on the state code which the Duke syllabus had barely touched on. Moreover, the standard was high, for the previous year's results showed that only 46 per cent of the candidates had passed and that most of those failing were from colleges outside the state. Writing to Helen Kendall, Dean Horack's secretary at Duke Law School, on 3 July 1937, Nixon set out his fears:

> I found that the Bar exam cram course began in March and that I could only get two months of the five-month course. However.... thought I might as well make a stab at it in September anyway since I have little else to do and then if I fail it I can take it again in March. I seriously doubt if I can get up the stuff in good enough shape in two months but I'm going to try. Tell Dean Horack therefore that the 1st Duke graduate to take the California Bar has a darn good chance to fail it the 1st time he takes it.[1]

The possibility of failure preyed heavily on Nixon's mind as he battled against the clock and a debilitating bout of flu on his preparations for the exam. He withdrew from all normal social and family life, finding sanctuary in Grandmother Almira's house at Whittier, where he worked alone for up to sixteen hours a day, memorising the California code. Almost the only interruptions came at meal times, when Almira brought him up trays of his favourite dish—finely chopped beef on toast—with whispered messages that she and Hannah had been 'thinking of thee'—a Milhous euphemism for 'praying for you'. On a less celestial level, Dean Horack sent his old pupil a robust message of good cheer:

> Dear Nixon,
>   Don't worry about the Bar exams for they will have to flunk all
> of them if they don't let you by.[2]

Nixon's studies were focused on the William Burby review course. Burby, the Professor of Torts at the University of Southern California Law School, had devised a cramming method used by over 90 per cent of candidates, which required intensive study of the California law reports. Nixon had access to these at the library of Wingert and Bewley, Whittier's leading law firm, whose senior partner, Tom Bewley, had been a college classmate of Hannah Nixon. She had approached him in April 1937 to ask if there could be any chance of an opening in the firm for her son. Her timing was fortunate because the two partners were thinking of recruiting a young lawyer to help them with the increasing flow of business and had already seen one candidate for the post. Impressed by what they heard about Richard Nixon's academic achievements at Duke they agreed to interview him after his graduation.

Nixon came in to Wingert and Bewley a few days after his return to Whittier in June 1937. The firm's only employee, the partners' Canadian-born secretary, Mrs. Evlyn Dorn, remembers him on that first morning as 'very punctual, very correct, and neatly dressed in a blue serge suit. He looked the part.'[3] There was a fifteen-minute delay over the appointment because a client took up more time than expected, so Nixon waited, 'getting rather nervous'[4] before being shown in to see Jeff Wingert and Tom Bewley. They had already checked him out with some of his old college professors, such as Dr. Paul Smith, so they needed only a twenty-minute discussion before making him an offer. Nixon was invited to join the firm as an associate with a salary of $50 a month for the first two months; $75 for the next two months; and $100 for the following two months. Thereafter he would be given an appropriate annual salary. He was also promised an early partnership in the firm if everything proved satisfactory.[5]

Although Nixon was somewhat underwhelmed at the prospect of earning only $450 in his first six months of employment,[*] he had no serious hesitation about signing on. For the rest of the summer he did part of his studying for the Bar exam in the Wingert and Bewley library. Evlyn Dorn recalled him 'coming in regularly to look up cases in the California law reports. I remember one day I saw him taking down every single volume and dusting them all for us.'[6]

In his final months as a law student, Nixon was occasionally taken into court by Tom Bewley, who recalled him making voluminous notes and even timing the speeches of the attorneys with a stopwatch. However, these professional preparations seemed superfluous, for immediately after he had sat the Bar exam in September, Nixon convinced himself that he had failed. He thought he had performed badly in the papers on Corporation Law and Evidence, and that he had made a mess of the questions in the Equity paper relating to the use of injunctions in labour disputes.[7] He had nightmares that his answers would be marked down due to the illegibility of his handwriting. These fears grew until the day the results arrived. Nixon recalled the scene at his home in Whittier:

> The scuttlebut was that if you had passed you received a notice in a small envelope; if you had failed it would be a big manila envelope with all the papers necessary for applying to take it again. The days and weeks passed before we finally got the results. I had been going each day to the mailbox, but on this particular day my mother had got there before me. She came in with tears coming down her cheeks because I had told her about the large and small envelope and she handed me a brown manila envelope. It wasn't very big, but it wasn't small … I did not want her to see my distress if it turned out that I had failed, so I walked into the bathroom, shut the door and opened the envelope. I had passed! As I came out everybody cheered. Happy as I was, I think my mother and father were even happier, especially my father who was overjoyed because his ambition, which he had not been able to realize for himself, had now been achieved through one of his sons. If we had been a drinking family, we'd have had a drink, but as it was, we celebrated in milk.[8]

---

[*] By comparison, Patricia Ryan, his future wife, was making $1,800 per annum in 1937 as a first-year schoolteacher.

Soon after the celebrations, Nixon was writing to Dean Horack, telling him of his impending admission to the California Bar:

> November 9th is the day when we are sworn in—up at San Francisco before the Supreme Court. After that I shall be with the firm of Wingert and Bewley, Bank of America Building, Whittier. They have already assigned a couple of motions to me—to be made before the LA Superior Court just as soon as I'm sworn in. So you see they're breaking me in fast.[9]

As it happened, Nixon was broken in rather too fast, for his very first case—one of the motions he had proudly mentioned in his letter to Dean Horack—ended in a welter of recriminations, allegations of professional misconduct, and a costly malpractice lawsuit. Nixon's brief, which he initially handled just six days after being sworn in as a member of the California Bar, was at first instance a simple action in the Los Angeles Municipal Court on behalf of Wingert and Bewley's client, Miss Marie Schee, who was seeking to recover a $2,000 debt owed to her by an uncle. The uncle, Mr. Otto Schuer, owned a house said to be worth $6,500. Nixon won the necessary court order in November 1937 compelling Schuer to repay his niece by disposing of the house in an execution sale. When the house came up for sale by the court marshal on 29 June 1938, Tom Bewley was ill and unable either to instruct his young associate, or to arrange for a conference with the client. Nixon was thus sent into court singularly ill-prepared. Somewhat naïvely he covered up for the shortcomings of his brief by asking the opposition's lawyer, David Schwartz, for advice. Schwartz advised Nixon to put in a bid for the house equal to the full amount of his client's debt. This was a mistake, for it transpired that there were two outstanding liens on the property. Nixon should have checked on this before putting in the bid on behalf of his client, although this error of omission was primarily the responsibility of Tom Bewley, who accepted the blame. 'If there was anyone who caused the mistake it was me', Bewley said later of Nixon's handling of the case. 'He got caught in the backwash...I always felt he was unjustly criticized.'[10]

The backwash became complicated, vindictive and expensive. Instead of recovering her debt, Miss Schee found herself owning a house which had a negative value on account of the liens. Bewley made matters worse by putting up the property for sale again but at too low a price, with the result that Miss Schee lost everything. Five years of bitter malpractice lawsuits followed in which Nixon was called upon to defend himself under hostile cross-examination from Miss Schee's new lawyer. In the end, after losing two appeals, the enraged Miss Schee had to be content with an out-of-court settlement of $4,800. Nixon, although accused by the opposing attorney of misconduct, had nothing much to reproach himself for apart from a degree of inexperience which should have been corrected by a more vigilant senior partner. Nixon's reaction to the affair did, however, illuminate one negative aspect in his character, namely an intransigent reluctance to apologise for an error. As Tom Bewley put it: 'He was terribly upset about this case...and he was more upset not because he did anything, but because I said, well, we've made a mistake and we'll have to pay for it.'[11]

Despite the hiccup over the Schee case, Nixon's career as a Whittier lawyer made steady, if mundane, progress. His desk diaries for 1938 and 1939 show the expanding scope and nature of his practice. His professional appointments were related to matters such as estate tax negotiations; will draftings; certifications of various documents for small corporations; divorce petition filings; preparing defaults; and oil drilling company registrations. It was the typical routine of a small-town California lawyer in that period, but he evidently performed well, joining the partnership early in 1939, some eighteen months after he had entered the firm. 'I was on my way to becoming a young pillar of the community in which I had grown up. It was an interesting experience to return home as the young professional man. I had become a grown-up and to people I met for the first time I was no longer Frank and Hannah Nixon's son—I was Mr. Nixon, the new partner in Wingert and Bewley', was how he later proudly recorded the elevation to his new status.[12]

The partnership also improved his financial status. Nixon's early tax returns record him as making $1,480 in 1938; $2,978 in 1939 and $3,971 in 1940.[13] However, some of the work that came his way was uncongenial to him. Friends of that period remember how emotionally wound up he could become over divorce suits, angrily describing one defendant as 'a bitch on wheels',[14] and after another case, ruminating sadly at a private dinner, 'Goddamn it, why couldn't they get back together?'[15] In an interview with the Washington columnist Stewart Alsop when Vice President, Nixon described another aspect of his distaste for matrimonial disputes: 'I had a divorce to handle and this good-looking girl, beautiful really, began talking to me about her intimate marriage problems...I turned fifteen colors of the rainbow. I suppose I came from a family too unmodern really. Any kind of personal confession is embarrassing to me personally'[16]

With or without divorce cases, the business was too slow at Wingert and Bewley for Nixon's ambitious tastes. In an effort to increase the firm's activities, he opened a new branch office in the nearby town of La Habra, but although it brought in a few new clients and provided him with contacts which were to prove useful to him politically at a later stage, it was of marginal value financially. The same was true of Nixon's role as Deputy City Attorney for the town of Whittier. He successfully prosecuted a few minor law breakers and built up a reputation as an aggressive courtroom attorney who could 'take hold of a cantankerous witness and shake him like a dog',[17] but it was mostly dull work and Nixon was often bored.

II. BUSINESSMAN AND COMMUNITY LEADER

With time on his hands, Nixon eased his feelings of professional frustration by participating in community affairs and venturing into business. He was approached by two enterprising local citizens, Ralph Ober and Don Brings, who had developed the idea of freezing fresh orange juice in plyfilm bags and selling it nationwide. With a small amount of sugar added, plus a touch of gelatine, they contended that the juice, if quick-frozen, would last indefinitely and when defrosted would taste as fresh as the original juice. Nixon formed a corporation for them called Citrifrost, and was selected as President. They proceeded to sell stock but soon ran into difficulties. 'I experienced my first, and I trust my last, failure in business', Nixon recalled. 'Our product was good, the market was there, but we were doomed to fail for reasons beyond our control'. The plyfilm in which the orange juice was packed became a scarce commodity as demand for it grew. With no plyfilm, Citrifrost was doomed to failure, and eventually had to file for bankruptcy. Nixon felt a great responsibility to the stockholders. 'My only consolation was the fact that their investments were small, they had a pretty good run for their money, and the cause of the failure was not bad management but events far beyond their control.'[18]

The Citrifrost débâcle distressed Nixon far more than this brief account suggests. It was a serious financial blow to him for he lost most of his own savings in the collapse, having taken a personal stake in the company of $1,000. Even worse, he felt under siege so far as his reputation was concerned when other local investors began complaining semi-publicly about their losses. Evlyn Dorn recalled an incident which illustrates the depth of Nixon's anxieties on this score:

> One afternoon, just as I was leaving the office, Dick said 'Can I talk to you privately?' This was so unlike him, and he looked so distraught that I managed to get a neighbor to pick up my daughter from school and I got into his Chevrolet. He drove to the car park of the Friends

Church and then we sat there for over an hour as he poured out his heart to me about all the things that were going wrong with Citrifrost. He was so unhappy! He even said he felt he should leave Whittier and go and start a career in New York. I think what had almost upset him most was that one of the shareholders, a Dr. Charlton, had complained to Mr. Herman Perry, the Manager of the Bank of America, instead of coming to him direct. One way and another he was really miserable.[19]

Nixon's misery deepened as the Citrifrost problems increased. Although the company took some good orders, it was not able to fulfil them because of the technical delivery problems. On one occasion, a consignment of frozen orange juice was shipped to New York only to break in transit, causing 'a horrible sticky mess'[20] first in the railroad car and later in the profit and loss account. Another drama came when the company had problems meeting its small payroll, and two disgruntled employees filed a lawsuit against the Citrifrost directors. The case was scheduled for 4 December 1940, but was settled just before the hearing, when the officers of the company, including Nixon, paid the outstanding wages out of their own pockets.

At the time of these crises, Nixon fought to save the operation with an intensity that went far beyond the call of duty of an ordinary company lawyer. He recruited the services of his father, Frank, who worked at the Citrifrost plant for several weeks without pay. He contributed his own legal and professional services free of charge, then his own money (more than $700 in personal cash advances to the company over and above his original investment) and finally even his own manual labour. 'He worked like a dog. He was out there cutting oranges and squeezing oranges day and night', recalled Tom Bewley.[21]

After the bankruptcy, Nixon was particularly upset by the plight of the small investors who had contributed about two-thirds of the company's paid-up capital of $10,000. Many of these were family friends, classmates and teachers, including his old college tutor, Dr. Herschel Coffin. Nixon anguished for those he felt had been personally hurt by their losses. According to Dr. Paul Smith, 'Years after the whole business had been forgotten by most people, I know for a fact that Dick came round offering to pay one or two friends' losses from his own pocket. There was absolutely no need for him to do that. It seemed like a pretty honorable thing for him to do.'[22]

Although Nixon was severely criticised by some of the investors for his part in the Citrifrost affair, it is difficult to see what more he could have done to improve the fortunes of this speculative venture. He shared in the risk, and made a great personal effort to pull the company round. Perhaps he should never have permitted himself to become the front man of such an enterprise operating at the then limits of citrus-freezing technology. Yet some allowance should surely be made for the fact that, at the age of twenty-six, he was still on the learning curve of business and legal life. On the record of anyone who was not destined to be President of the United States (an office in which no past mistake, however small, is ever wholly forgotten) the Citrifrost story would have been no more than a minor error of youthful judgement. Even so, it left its scars on Nixon, who never again accepted an executive position in a corporation, despite many attractive offers.

The Citrifrost saga did not, however, have an adverse effect on Nixon's general standing in Whittier community affairs. Between 1937 and 1940 he became President of the Whittier College Alumni Association; President of the Whittier 20–30 Club (a young businessmen's group); President of the Duke Alumni Association; President of the Orange County Association of Cities; Chairman of the La Habra Kiwanis Club; and Program Chairman of the Junior Chamber of Commerce. He was invited to join the Board of Trustees of Whittier College, a distinguished group which included Mrs. Herbert Hoover, wife of the former President. Despite being the youngest member of the board, Nixon evidently made his mark, for by 1941 there were moves afoot to make him President of the Trustees until Pearl Harbor intervened.

All these multifarious community activities had their advantages. Nixon found his contacts in the local clubs useful for bringing in new business to Wingert and Bewley. He enjoyed the political manoeuvring that brought him four presidencies and two chairmanships. He relished taking on speaking engagements on the Lions—Kiwanis—Elks—Rotary Club circuit in Southern California. He even developed a standard speech, 'Nine Young Men', which was an attack on President Franklin Roosevelt's plan to pack the New Deal-thwarting Supreme Court of 'Nine Old Men'. As an added attraction to his speaking skills, Nixon knew most of the service clubs' musical rituals well enough to pound the piano as an accompanist for the traditional singsongs at the beginning and end of their functions.

The game plan that lay behind Nixon's drive to establish himself as a community leader was obscure to his contemporaries, but clear to some of the older figures in the Whittier hierarchy. They saw in Nixon an able political comer striving to make his mark. Tom Bewley had been Nixon's earliest benefactor, taking him into the law firm, appointing him Deputy City Attorney, and giving him the lion's share of the town's public legal work. This platform gave him a useful start, but now there emerged an even more helpful political benefactor in the shape of Herman Perry.

III. HERMAN PERRY

Herman Perry was the high-principled son of a Quaker minister who, for more than twenty years, held the post of Manager at the Whittier branch of the Bank of America. He was the town's leading banker, tough on overdrafts, but with a flair for making good loans to small companies with interests all over Southern California. Although banking was his profession, Perry's real passion was politics. At one time in his life he had thought of running for Congress, but by the late 1930s such ambitions had faded and his political activity was confined to being the Chairman and leading figure in the Republican Party of Whittier.

Herman Perry first spotted Nixon as a talented high school debater. He had monitored the younger man's progress ever since, and now had him literally right under his eye since the Wingert and Bewley office was on one of the lower floors of the Bank of America building. Perry liked the look and sound of Nixon, the fledgling politician. He gave him every encouragement and much tuition on the ways of local politics. It was due to Perry's patronage that Nixon received a steady flow of speaking invitations and became a leading light of the Young Republicans, soon adding the presidency of that organisation to the growing number of presidential offices he seemed to be collecting.

Nixon's relationship with Herman Perry was to prove a crucial one in his quest for elected office. The years 1937–41 were the period when Perry acted as his tutor and mentor. Few tangible results emerged from the friendship at this stage, although in 1940 Perry did prepare the ground for Nixon to win the nomination for a safe seat in the California State Assembly. The vacancy failed to materialise, but Herman Perry's preliminary manoeuvres over this episode confirmed his growing bond with Nixon. His son Hubert Perry recalls that the relationship was 'that of a father towards an adopted son. He saw in Dick the chance to live through him and to do some of the things he had longed to do himself. He began living vicariously through Dick Nixon.'[23]

Every rising politician needs a patron, and as the later chapters of the story show, Nixon was undoubtedly fortunate in the emergence of Herman Perry in this role. Yet Perry could not have exercised his patronage successfully unless Nixon had possessed both the talent and image to become a political winner. Among those who heard him speak, there were few doubts about the Nixon talent. But the Nixon image seemed more problematical. This intense, introspective, somewhat humourless young man needed to lighten his touch, and to soften his outlook. As the grey heads of the Whittier Republican Party mulled over the Nixon possibilities, they said to one another what wise old political activists all over the world are apt to say about intense, ambitious, bachelor politicians: 'He needs a wife.'[24]

IV. PATRICIA RYAN

On the night of 16 January 1938, Richard Nixon fell in love at first sight. He was so smitten that he threw all his usual caution to the winds. On the evening of his first meeting with the young woman who had captivated him, he asked her for a date, was rebuffed, then blurted out: 'You may not believe this but I am going to marry you some day.'[25]

As the opening to a turbulent romance, culminating in a marriage lasting for over fifty years, the story of the initial encounter between the future 37th President of the United States and his First Lady was the stuff of which novels are made. The hero was the dark, brooding attorney Dick Nixon, indulging in his hobby of amateur theatricals by auditioning for a part in the Whittier Community Players production of *The Dark Tower*, a mystery melodrama by Alexander Woollcott and George S. Kaufman. Also auditioning, much more reluctantly, was the heroine Patricia Ryan, a twenty-six-year-old schoolteacher with strikingly attractive features and a glorious cascade of golden-red hair. At the insistence of her school supervisor, Pat was reading for the part of Daphne, 'a tall, dark, sullen beauty of twenty, wearing a dress of great chic and an air of permanent resentment'.[26] Dick was trying out for the part of Barry, 'a faintly collegiate, eager blushing youth'.[27] As soon as he set eyes on his potential co-star, the earth moved for him. 'I found I could not take my eyes away from her. For me it was a case of love at first sight.'[28]

It was a long time before Dick's passion was reciprocated. 'I'm too busy',[29] was Pat's cool response when he asked her for a date on the night of the audition. Although sufficiently flattered by his instant forecast of marriage to report it to her flatmates when she came home,[30] Pat stayed cool for the early months of their acquaintanceship. She was a cautious, self-reliant young woman with an aura of inner reserve as a result of her difficult upbringing.

Born in a miner's shack in the frontier copper town of Ely, Nevada on 16 March 1912, she was christened Thelma Catherine. Her father, Will Ryan, was a wandering Irish prospector, volatile in his temper and unsuccessful in his work. Her mother was a German immigrant widow, Kate Halberstadt Bender, who had five children, two of them from her first marriage. A year after Thelma's birth Will Ryan moved with his family to Artesia, California, a poor farming community of around 400 people, twenty miles southwest of Los Angeles. Life on their Artesia smallholding was a harsh struggle for the Ryans, far closer to poverty than anything experienced by the Nixons on the Yorba Linda lemon ranch. The harshness was made worse by the violence of Will's temper, and the frequent explosions between her mother and father left their mark on their youngest child. In a revealing passage of her filial biography, *Pat Nixon, The Untold Story,* Julie Nixon Eisenhower wrote in 1986:

> My mother has resolutely buried the unpleasant memories of her childhood. Only once did she admit to me her father's temper and confrontations with Kate. Then firmly, so that I would know she was speaking her final words on the subject, she said: 'I detest temper. I detest scenes. I just can't be that way. I saw it with my father.' She paused for a moment and then added, 'And so to avoid scenes or unhappiness, I suppose I accommodated to others.'[31]

Thelma did not have much time in which to accommodate to her mother, for Kate Ryan died of cancer in January 1926. Bedridden for the last months of her illness, she was nursed by her thirteen-year-old daughter, who also had to take on all the cooking and house cleaning. Traumatic though the experience must have been, Thelma remained composed, even at the funeral. She never showed her feelings to her friends, who regarded her as a 'tremendously disciplined person'.[32] Throughout her early teens, Thelma continued that self-discipline, combining the roles of schoolgirl, housewife and mother, running the Ryan home for her father and brothers on top of her workload at Excelsior High School. Although it was noticed that she quite often fell asleep in her class as a result of tiredness from the household chores, Thelma achieved good grades, a place on the debating team, and membership of the honor society in recognition of her academic and other achievements. But before she graduated the shadows of death were again looming over the family. In 1928 Will Ryan was diagnosed as having tuberculosis. Thelma nursed him through his terminal illness, washing out the sputum cups and sterilising the dishes just as Hannah Nixon had been doing for Harold and her other TB patients in Prescott.

After Will Ryan died in May 1930, Thelma changed her name to Patricia or Pat (because she had been born on St. Patrick's Day) and enrolled in Fullerton Junior College, three miles from Yorba Linda. She studied there for a year before jumping at a chance to travel East to stay with two aunts, one in New York, one in Connecticut. Her New York aunt, Kate Ryan, was a seventy-seven-year-old nun in charge of the X-ray unit at the Seton Sisters of Charity Hospital in the Bronx. Pat lived in the nun's residence next door to the hospital, went on a course which qualified her to work as an X-ray technician, and worked intensively with the TB patients. 'My six months there were perhaps the most haunting of my life',[33] was how she recalled the experience. The intensity was mutual, for the dying patients worshipped the beautiful, red-headed radiologist technician they called 'The White Sister', who seemed so young, vital and utterly fearless about catching the dreaded disease.

After two years in New York, Pat had saved up enough money to return to Southern California and resume her education. She worked her way through college doing part-time work as a bank clerk and as a salesgirl at Bullocks, the fashionable Los Angeles department store. Her earning power was occasionally boosted by her beauty, which helped her to win some lucrative assignments as a demonstrator of cosmetics, and to be hired by Hollywood studios as a movie extra at $6.50 a day (a handsome sum for 1937). Her film career was limited to crowd scenes, except for a one-line speaking part in MGM's *Becky Sharp*, which ended up on the cutting-room floor. All this helped to pay her bills at USC, from which she graduated with honours in June 1937. She won a BA and a diploma which qualified her to teach commercial subjects—typing, book-keeping, business principles—in secondary school. In September she began her first teaching job with a salary of $1,800 a year ('a fabulous sum', she called it[34]) at Whittier Union High School. She was in her second semester there when she first met Richard Nixon at the Whittier Community Players audition on the night of 16 January 1938.

Pat's formative years had been hard and often unhappy, but greatly to her credit. Yet she blocked out many of her earliest experiences and rarely talked about herself, not even to her close friends or favourite dates. She was a difficult person to get to know. At least one admirer evidently felt frustrated by her reserve, for he sent her a note after their date: 'I was just struck with the thought that I knew so damn little about you after being at your feet for a whole lovely evening.'[35]

It took much more than one evening to get to know Patricia Ryan. Her eventual husband Richard Nixon has recalled with astonishment how little he knew about his wife's past life at the time of their marriage. 'Pat never told me, she never talked about what she had done, where she had been, what she had been through. It was always about the future, never about the past... she never had told me about some of her family problems, the tragedy of her mother who died when she was about nine or her father who died when she was sixteen.'[36]

Pat's reluctance to discuss her early life seems odd, if not extraordinary. It suggests that the future Mr. and Mrs. Nixon must have had some communication problems in their courtship, which indeed they did.

The old saying, that in most romances there is one who loves and one who turns the cheek, would have applied to the early stages of Dick and Pat's relationship. He was the ardent pursuer. She was the reluctant turner-away of the cheek. She was polite, friendly, and to some extent intrigued by his attentions, but she remained resolutely unwilling to become involved. Anyone less persistent than Richard Nixon would soon have become discouraged by her lack of enthusiasm. During and for many months after their theatrical cooperation in *The Dark Tower*, he repeatedly asked her for dates and was usually turned down. She refused to spend any time with him at weekends, which she regarded as sacred, normally escaping to Los Angeles to get away from the confining atmosphere of Whittier. During the week she saw him only when she had nothing better to do. To overcome her indifference, he began turning up unannounced at the apartment she shared with Margaret O'Grady. He took her for walks and drives in the countryside around Whittier, which she appreciated, but in a detached way. There was one particular walk they enjoyed in the hills towards La Habra. It struck quite a chord, at least in his imagination, for he sent her a love letter about it when he had walked the route again on his own.

> Miss Pat:
>
> I took *the* walk tonight and it was swell because you were there all the time. Why?—because a star fell right in front of me, the wind blowing thru the tops of the palms making that strangely restless rustling, a train whistle sounded just as I got to the bridge. The Dipper was turned upside down right over where your house should be and was pouring down on you all the good things I've wished looking up at it in the past.
>
> And because there was no moon the sky was full of stars—every one filled with good wishes for you.
>
> Yes—I know I'm crazy and that this is old stuff and that I don't take hints, but you see, Miss Pat, I like you![37]

Dick was impervious to her hints. She had tried pretending not to be at home when he called, ignoring his knocking at her door, and on one occasion fixing for Margaret O'Grady to go out on a date with him in her place. He spent that particular evening talking incessantly about his feelings for Pat. Eventually this pressure, which included proposals of marriage, became too much. On one of his unscheduled visits she asked him to leave, telling him that she could not reciprocate his feelings. It was a painful scene which should have ended the relationship, but a few days later Dick was manoeuvring for a comeback, writing to her:

> Dear Patricia:
>
> Please forgive me for acting like a sorehead when you gently ushered me out the other night. You must have thought I was trying to put on the attitude that I really didn't give a darn—i.e., school boy bluff!
>
> ....May I say now what I should have said then: I appreciated immeasurably those little rides and chats with you. I hope that you survived them without too much mental worry over the problem 'what shall I do to get rid of him before he falls.'
>
> (And that isn't said in a sarcastic way either)—and may I tell you now what I really thought of you? You see I too live in a world of make believe—especially in this love business. And sometimes I fear I don't know when I'm serious and when not! But I can honestly say that Patricia is one fine girl, that I like her immensely, and that though she isn't going to give me a chance to propose to her for fear of hurting me! And though she insulted my ego just a bit by not being quite frank at times, I still remember her as combining the best traits of the Irish and the square-heads [the Germans].
>
> Yours,
> Dick[38]

In the face of such blandishments, Pat's resolve never to see him again crumbled. Her daughter described the situation: 'She decided to continue dating but with the understanding that there would be no declarations of love or proposals of marriage.'[39] At first Dick was allowed back into her life in the role of a glorified chauffeur. He drove her into Los Angeles on Friday evenings, filled his own lonely weekends in Whittier by doing out of hours legal work and teaching a Sunday school class in the Friends Church, then returned to pick her up in the city on Sunday nights. 'He chased her but she was a little rat',[40] was how one friend described this phase of their relationship in which Dick appeared to be the backmarker in her string of beaux. But his persistence paid off, and with the help of a dog, a dentist, and some double-dating, the romance gradually gathered momentum.

The dog was King, a big, red Irish setter. A gun dog who had grown gun-shy, he had been given away to Dick by his previous master who was about to put him down because he had become useless for hunting. Pat fell for King long before she fell for his owner, recalled Nixon, 'partly I suppose because of her half-Irish background and also because of her love for animals generally, which I shared. We would often take King with us to the beach and run with him on the sand.'[41]

The dentist was Dr. 'Killer' Sheel of Los Angeles. His professional skills helped the romance along after Pat confessed to Dick that she could not bear one aspect of his appearance—a gold-rimmed cap on his front tooth which dated back to a basketball accident at Duke. 'Without Pat's insistence I would probably not have had this dental work done', recalled Nixon. 'But having porcelain rather than gold in the front of the mouth might have been one of those decisive factors which made a difference between victory and defeat...she had an obsession about good dentistry.'[42]

The dentist had been recommended and given his nickname by Curtis Counts, a young executive with the Douglas Aircraft Corporation who was dating Virginia Shugart, Pat's best friend at USC. From early 1939 onwards, Curt, Virginia, Dick and Pat became a regular double-dating foursome. 'I'd say that in the beginning theirs was a much more indecisive courtship than ours,' recalled Virginia Shugart, 'but Dick was very much the pursuer, totally determined to win her over, and in the end his fighting quality came through.'[43]

An illuminating anecdote about Dick's determination in this period was told by a Whittier contemporary, Kenny Ball. He was a regular ice-skater at the local rink and was surprised to see Dick Nixon suddenly turning up for practice. 'I'd known Dick all through college and he'd never been known to put on a pair of skates, so as soon as I saw him I said "What the heck's up?" He was the worst ice-skater in the world, I've never seen anyone fall over more often or more painfully. After about three afternoons of practice he wasn't getting any better, in fact he was getting worse. I remember him flying out of control and hitting his face on the ice so hard that he was all covered in blood. I picked him up and asked him, "Dick, why do you keep doing this?" His answer was, "I've got a great date to go ice-skating with on Saturday and I *must* be able to keep up with her." I didn't know till years later that he was talking about Pat.'[44]

Keeping up with Pat gradually became easier. They went out more and more often, and Dick's confidence blossomed. 'In our group he was always the one who gave the lead, told the jokes, made things happen', recalled Virginia Shugart.[45] Their double dates took them regularly to the Hollywood Bowl, the Long Acres race track, the Hines ice rink, football games, the movies, and the occasional restaurant. 'Dick was the planner, and sometimes his plans were quite crazy', recalled Curtis Counts.* 'One night he insisted we went to Topsy's in East Los Angeles, which we thought was a wild place because they had striptease dancers there. Dick made us all dress up in way-out clothes for the occasion. He put on his mother's racoon coat, which made him look extraordinary. The entrance fee that night was $3 because the stripteaser was Betty Roland—the famous blonde bombshell. She came on strong, taking off her clothes and swinging her fanny all over the place, until some guy in the front seat touched her butt with a lighted cigarette. The whole place blew apart. I'll never forget how much we all laughed, including Dick.'[46]

In their quieter moments, Pat and Dick went for more and more of those long walks with King, particularly on San Clemente beach, which became their favourite courting place. Pat spent a lot of time with the Nixon family, listening to Frank's political opinions, helping Hannah bake her pies and looking after nine-year-old Ed, who remembered her as a happy, laughing companion with whom he loved to play games on the sands.[47]

By the end of 1939, Pat's hesitations were melting away. She thought she was in love with Dick, although still not as deeply as he was with her. On 16 January 1940 he wrote her a touching letter to mark the anniversary of their first meeting:

> As I look out the windows at the clouds with the sun trying to break through, I'm thinking of how much you've meant to me the past two years. Do you remember that funny guy who asked you to go to a 20–30 ladies night just about two years ago? Well you know that though he still may be funny—he's changed since then. But you may not know—dear one—that he gets the same thrill when you say you'll go someplace with him that he did when you said one time that he could take you for a ride in his car!
>
> And did you know that he still looks out the windows towards wherever you are and sends you the best he has in love, admiration, respect and 'Best of Luck'?
>
> And when the winds blow and the rains fall and the sun shines through the clouds, as it is now, he still resolves as he did then, that nothing so fine ever happened to him or anyone else as falling in love with Thee—my dearest heart.

---

* Curtis Counts and Virginia Shugart were married in 1940.

Love,
Dick[48]

Eight weeks later, in mid-March 1940, he drove her in his Oldsmobile to Dana Point, an ocean promontory overlooking San Clemente beach. It was a particularly beautiful evening, and as the sun slipped beneath the horizon, he proposed and was accepted. The couple's feelings were described by their daughter Julie: 'Sitting in an open car in the starlight with the sound of the waves breaking below she [Pat] knew that she was in love. She loved Dick's romantic nature which had brought them to Dana Point and his visions of a great future. But even as she consented she was not sure she wanted to marry. She was twenty-eight years old and had been independent for a long time. My father, in winning his beloved at last, was elated.'[49]

Dick insisted that they should go immediately to Whittier to break the good news to his parents. This was something of a miscalculation as the Nixons were already asleep and had to be woken up to be told of the engagement. As Pat later recounted the story, Frank and Hannah's somnolent reactions 'broke the romantic spell of the evening'.[50] Pat's relatives seemed equally underwhelmed, her half-sister Neva Bender saying, 'What are you marrying him for? He's too quiet.'[51] When the news got around Whittier there was some sneering among mothers with unmarried daughters that the eligible junior partner of Wingert and Bewley had been caught by a fiancée who was socially beneath him. 'Some people felt that he should have been going with a girl from, you know, a better family', recalled Judith Wingert. 'Whittier was very much like this. Somebody from Whittier and a better family, one that didn't work.'[52]

Richard Nixon had no such reservations. He joyfully bought a diamond engagement ring for $324. 'She was earning far more than I was and when we finally decided to take the big step I think she contributed as much to the cost of the engagement and wedding rings as I did', he recalled.[53] The next step was getting a marriage licence. When completing the formalities on the eve of the wedding, the bridegroom discovered he did not know his bride's real name, for Pat had never mentioned that she was born Thelma Catherine. It was just another of those curious omissions, like the couple's mutual inability to discuss the bereavements they had each suffered in their early years, which suggested that the communication problems of their courtship might endure into their marriage. Or, as their daughter Julie Nixon Eisenhower put it, 'Both were shy and both would find it difficult in the years ahead to break through their reserve and discuss their deepest feelings.'[54]

V. MARRIAGE AND THE OPA

Richard Nixon and Patricia Ryan were married on Friday, 21 June 1940 at the Mission Inn, Riverside. This convention hotel, located on the edge of the desert some thirty miles east of Los Angeles, was a favourite venue for Californian weddings on account of its rococo-style decor, which included Italian frescoes, French stained glass windows, Chinese wallpaper and Belgian wood panelling.

The ceremony was held in the Presidential Suite, not on account of some astrological foresight into the bridegroom's political future, but because it was the smallest and least expensive suitable room the hotel could offer. The invitations were limited to fifteen guests, most of whom were immediate family members, headed by ninety-one-year-old Grandmother Almira Milhous wearing her favourite red velvet dress. The few non-relatives present included Virginia and Curtis Counts, who remembered the occasion as 'a very small wedding but joyously happy with an organist playing Pat and Dick's favorite songs. It was a private family affair.'[55] So private, indeed, that some members of the large Milhous clan felt offended at not having been invited. The reasons for having such modest nuptials were partly religious and partly economical. Pat was an agnostic (yet another surprise to her husband to be) and refused to countenance a church service. She also felt unable to ask her brothers to bear the cost of a large reception and was too proud to allow Dick to contribute to the expenses. 'We both had so many relatives that we thought a church wedding would present just too many problems for everyone concerned', was how he later explained it. 'We knew that if we gave invitations to a wedding it would have to include not only our relatives but many of our friends. They would all assume they would have to bring gifts, and frankly in that period, just before World War II when the Great Depression was still gnawing at the economic vitals of the country, we didn't want people to feel obligated to buy us wedding presents.'[56]

Nevertheless, they received two memorable wedding presents which they have used throughout their married life. Pat's brothers, Bill and Tom Ryan, presented them with a full set of Rosepoint sterling silver cutlery, while from Frank and Hannah came a dinner collection of porcelain dishes decorated in a bracelet pattern they knew Pat admired. Not a single piece of this set, which serves twelve, has been broken in fifty-one years and fifteen house moves of the Nixon marriage.

The honeymoon was spent in Mexico and at $178 'for two weeks, portal to portal' as Nixon has recalled, it was great value for money. 'We probably got more out of our wedding trip while spending less than any couple in history.'[57]

This remarkably economical budgeting was achieved partly because the couple had loaded up their car with canned foods before departure. In spite of this careful gastronomic planning, each meal turned out to be a menu surprise, because some of the younger guests at the reception thought it would be a good joke to remove all the labels on the cans. This meant that the newlyweds were often eating grapefruit slices for lunch or chili con carne for breakfast. 'But that added to the fun of the trip', said Nixon.[58]

The experiences of the honeymoon included going to a bull fight in Mexico City (the couple left in disgust after three *corridas*); visiting the great pyramids; and staying in the ancient mountain city of Puebla. Sightseeing was their main activity, much of it centred on ancient monuments and ecclesiastical buildings. 'We seldom went by one of the churches or cathedrals without stopping in and sitting for a moment of silence', recalled Nixon. 'Even in the anticlerical Mexico of that period, the churches were usually the cleanest and most attractive places to visit.'[59] Mexico's anti-Americanism was also a feature of the trip. When the Nixons attended a concert by the Mexican Symphony Orchestra they were startled when a number by the US composer Aaron Copland was roundly booed by the audience.[60]

Returning to California, Dick and Pat felt they had enjoyed a magical honeymoon and agreed that for the future they must save up to do as much travelling as they could. With a joint income of just over $4,900 a year, they were comfortably off for a young couple in 1940, and they showed it in the mobility of their lifestyle. During the first summer of their marriage, 'we splurged a bit and rented an apartment in Long Beach', recalled Nixon. 'Then we found an apartment over a garage in La Habra Heights and lived in it for three or four months. Finally we found another apartment, a duplex on Beverly Boulevard, which was each time a step upwards. We had many good times going out with old friends like Jack and Helene Drown and particularly with Pat's brothers and others that she had known at USC…it was a period when we really enjoyed life to the full.'[61]

Both Nixons had an explorer's streak in them, and in the first year of their marriage they were often on the move. They made long trips to British Columbia, and Yosemite Park, as well as many short trips around Arizona, Indiana, and California. On their first wedding anniversary, 21 June 1941, the Nixons sailed on an ocean cruise. They had spent most of their savings on booking a trip on the *Ulua*, an 8,000-ton liner making a Caribbean voyage from New Orleans to Panama and back, with stops in Havana and Costa Rica. Unfortunately their cabin, the cheapest berth on the ship, was next to the engine room and Dick had a bad time suffering from seasickness made worse by oil fumes. Even so there were nights when he seemed to be the life and soul of the passengers' parties. As Pat wrote in her diary, describing a vice-versa dinner when the men and women in their group exchanged clothes for the evening: 'Many laughs getting together costumes, trying stuff on etc. Dick and I had a party for the gang first in the palm court. Then we paraded to the music room where the rest of the passengers roared at the costumes. Dick as a Grecian lady, draped costume—sheet, turban, brooch, bosom etc.'[62]

On the homeward journey, the news came over the ship's radio that Germany had invaded Russia. If World War II still seemed far away, six months later it came dramatically closer. On Sunday 7 December 1941, Dick and Pat drove into Los Angeles to see a movie. Just before the end of the programme there was an announcement that all servicemen should report immediately to their units. As they came out of the theatre, the evening paper was on sale with the huge head-lines 'JAPS BOMB PEARL HARBOR'. 'We're at war, mister', said the newsboy as he sold Nixon a copy.[63]

Towards the end of 1941, Pat and Dick had already been taking decisions influenced by the war in Europe. Once it became clear that the seat in the California state legislature, which Nixon had been angling for in 1940, was definitely not going to be vacated, his mind turned to other career opportunities. Both Nixons wanted to spend some time outside California, Pat because she was restless, Dick because he was ambitious. Out of the blue an opportunity to move to Wash-ington came up. It arrived in the form of a letter from David Ginsberg, General Counsel of the Office of Price Administration. The OPA was a new Washington bureaucracy, brought into existence by Executive Order in August 1941 with a remit to fight the threats of inflation and consumer shortages being caused by the war. Attorneys were urgently needed to be the OPA's legal staff who would draw up the planned regulations for rationing and price control. Nixon's name had been put forward by two of his former Duke Law School tutors, Professors David Cav-ers and Douglas Maggs. On the basis of these recommendations, together with an interview with one of Ginsberg's assistants in San Francisco, Nixon was hired as a civil servant grade P-3 at $3,200 a year. The salary was $700 a year less than he had been earning at Wingert and Bewley and $1,400 less than the salaries of two of his Duke classmates, who had also been recruited by the OPA. The discrimina-tion rankled. 'I found that others with lesser academic records and not as much legal experience had come in as P-4s, a step higher, and some even as P-5s, at $4,600 a year', he wrote in his memoirs thirty-eight years later.[64]

Starting work as a P-3 in January 1942, Nixon was one of 177 junior lawyers in the OPA. He was assigned to the tyre rationing division, where he showed considerable skill in explaining and refining the complex regulations which had suddenly been imposed on the motor industry.

'My major responsibility was to help the staff reply to the thousands of inquiries that came in from tire dealers across the country as well as from the general public', he recalled. 'I became a good letter writer and learned how to dictate letters, which served me well once I became a Congressman and in my later years in public life. I always considered that a letter, even to a non-VIP, was very important to the individual who received it...in addition I perhaps rendered some service by co-ordinating the rationing regulations which were really a mess because they were being brought together so hurriedly to deal with the crisis that no one had anticipated would be so momentous.'[65]

Nixon's role in handling his corner of the rationing crisis soon earned him the respect of his superiors. Five weeks after arriving at OPA he reported that he had cleared his section's huge arrears of correspondence. 'Wires are being answered the day they are received. There is no backlog of letters', he wrote in a memo to his boss. 'Letters are being answered two days after receipt.'[66] On 14 February Nixon was recommended for promotion to be head of the interpretation unit, a P–5 post carrying a salary of $4,600 a year. The pay rise did not arrive, but he was given most of the responsibilities anyway, for in March 1942 he was 'designated informally' as 'acting Chief of Interpretations sub-branch of the Rubber Branch'.[67]

Nixon was a good bureaucrat but he never accepted the ethos of the bureaucracy. Halfway through his eight months at OPA, he complained to a senior colleague about his low pay and grading as a P–3. 'Build a little staff. Request two or three people to assist you, and then we can raise you to a P–5', he was advised. 'But I don't need a staff.' 'Then you won't get a promotion', came the reply.[68] Such experiences filled Nixon with a lifelong cynicism towards government bureaucrats, some of whom 'became obsessed with their power', he noted, 'and seemed to delight in kicking people around, particularly those in the private sector'.[69] He also observed 'the mediocrity of so many civil servants...angling for something and anxious not to miss the bandwagon'.[70]

In addition to these general criticisms, there was one specific connection between the experiences of OPA civil servant Nixon in the 1940s and the White House policies of President Nixon in the 1970s.

'Years later, when many were clamoring for us to ration gasoline during the period of the Yom Kippur War and the Arab Oil Embargo, I resisted those efforts to the hilt because of my experience in OPA', he recalled. 'I ordered a stop to the whole process and the disbanding of the rationing unit which had already hired over 1,000 people in anticipation of the opportunity to impose rationing on the public...I knew from my experience with many of the government bureaucrats with whom I came into contact with the OPA that these people believed in a controlled economy. They just did not like the private enterprise system. While to me rationing was a necessary evil, to them it was a heaven-sent opportunity to increase the size and power of government at the expense of the private sector.'[71]

With views such as these, it was unlikely that Nixon would stay long at OPA, and in April 1942 he applied to join the Navy. This was not a straightforward decision. As an OPA civil servant it would have been easy for him to obtain a deferment and as a birthright Quaker he was entitled to complete exemption as a conscientious objector. His parents hoped he would take this route, but he felt strongly that it was his duty to volunteer for military service. Pat agreed with him no less strongly, saying afterwards, 'I would have felt mighty uncomfortable if Dick hadn't done his part.'[72]

His application was accepted, and he received orders to report to the Navy's Officer Candidate School at Quonset Point, Rhode Island, on 17 August. Shortly before leaving for OCS Quonset, he took Pat for a long weekend to Cape Porpoise, Maine. This beautiful stretch of the New England coastline was almost completely deserted as a result of the wartime petrol rationing. The Nixons were the only guests in their small, clapboard hotel, and they relished the unexpected bonus of such solitude and privacy. The combination of long walks along the coast to the nearby town of Kennebunkport; fresh lobster dinners at a dollar a serving in the Porpoise Restaurant; and so much idyllic peacefulness all added up to a memorable vacation. On their last day they bought a painting of Cape Porpoise showing a small, open boat beached on the curving coastline. Pat hung the picture in the bedroom of every private home in which they subsequently lived, explaining to her daughters, 'I loved it because we were so happy there.'[73]

Happiness had clearly blessed the Nixon marriage, sweeping away the doubts and hesitations of their courtship. Although they were not a demonstrative couple in public, the strength of their love was obvious to their friends and is still obvious to anyone reading their letters half a century later. A few days after he had left her behind in Washington to go to Quonset, Pat wrote to him following up on a nocturnal phone conversation:

> It's two o'clock but I just had to write to you to say *how very much I love you*! It was clear all over again when talking to you on the phone. Also want to say that I hope I said nothing to worry you—when you are working so hard etc. it would be awful to add to the load. In talking with you tonight it was the first time I really felt it was you.[74]

Dick felt the separation equally keenly. 'I may not say much when I'm with you—*but all of me loves you all of the time*',[75] he wrote longingly to her. After his first weekend leave from the training school, which they spent together in New York, he said in his next letter: 'This weekend was wonderful. Coming back I looked at myself in the window and thought how very lucky I was to have you. I certainly am not the Romeo type and you are so beautiful! I was proud of you every minute I was with you…'[76]

Such marital bliss was idyllic, but it was to suffer a long interruption. The cause was Richard Nixon's war in the South Pacific.

SIX

WAR

I. LIEUTENANT (J.G.)

Richard Nixon's three and a half years' service in the US Navy were important to the formation of his character. The war took him 6,000 miles from home to a South Pacific environment that was far removed from the life style of a small-town lawyer in Quaker Whittier. Although he saw little direct combat he experienced danger and discomfort, his mettle was toughened, his language was coarsened and his card-playing skills were improved. These developments were balanced by some deeper dimensions of the Nixon personality that emerged during his long months of isolation. He expanded his intellectual horizons; developed qualities of leadership; and found an ability to express, at least on paper, his emotional and romantic feelings. When he returned to civilian life he was altogether a stronger and more rounded individual.

Arriving at OCS Quonset in the heat of August 1942, Nixon sweated his way through the basics of drill and discipline and was put on a course of aviation indoctrination training. His introduction to the martial arts came when he was issued with the standard Colt 45 revolver and told to go out on a range and learn to shoot. This was the first time Nixon had ever held a gun. Clumsy as ever, he fired ten shots at the target and missed with every one.[1] He did better at written subjects such as strategy; naval courts and boards; and service policy; but found it difficult to wrestle with the intricacies of navigation and seamanship. For the first time in his life he was nowhere near the top of his class, eventually coming 96th out of 750.

OCS Quonset was a high-speed military factory for converting professionally qualified civilians into immediate naval officers. The course lasted eight weeks and was full of lawyers, bankers, architects, and business executives. Among those in Nixon's class to achieve prominence in later life were a Detroit businessman, G. Mennen 'Soapy' Williams, who later became Governor of Michigan, and a young Washington attorney, William Pierce Rogers. Nixon and Rogers hardly knew each other as officer candidates, but their careers were later to intertwine as friends, colleagues, and national political figures during many important periods in the next thirty-three years.

Nixon's closest friend at Quonset was Desales Harrison, a Coca-Cola executive from Chattanooga, Tennessee. He was the oldest man in the class, so eager to serve his country that he had persuaded the Navy to waive the usual recruiting age limits. Harrison had an unusual problem. He simply could not learn the knack of making up his bunk with the required hospital corners. Each morning he got bawled out for his bed-making incompetence by the chief petty officers, until Nixon came to his rescue and made it for him every day. It was one of those small but characteristic acts of personal kindness that continually surface in the story of his life.

In October, Nixon passed out of Quonset with the qualifications of a ground aviation officer. His professional status as a lawyer enabled him to skip the usual rank of ensign, so he emerged as a fully fledged, if instant, lieutenant (junior grade).[2]

Lieutenant (J.G.) Nixon was offered a legal desk job in Washington but, wanting sea duty, he applied for 'Ships and Stations'. In response to this request, the Pentagon moved in its usual mysterious ways and assigned Nixon to Ottumwa, Iowa, where there were neither ships nor stations. The Navy were building a pilot training airfield in the agricultural heartlands of this Midwestern state, and in a sublime piece of miscasting, Nixon was appointed to a role in the construction operation which required considerable technical expertise. He expressed his own surprise in a letter to his parents dated 1 November 1942.

> Dear Folks,
>   Well here I am, standing a 24-hour Navy Watch in the middle of Iowa!

They have appointed me communications officer of the Base, and
I have spent a lot of time working on the telephone, teletype, crash
alarm and public address systems which are still in the Blue Print
stage.… All in all it's probably a good experience and after all the boys
must be trained. There are only three carriers left so here I am.[3]

Nixon's limitations as a communications systems expert were quickly
noticed, and he was moved to the more suitable appointment of administrative
assistant to the commanding officer. One of his first tasks in this role was to set
up the officers' club, writing its constitution and securing its finances by install-
ing a number of slot machines in the mess.[4]

He had not joined the Navy to be an administrator, however, and he soon
chafed at these deskbound duties. The only memorable experience of his six
months at Ottumwa was his first ride in an aeroplane. This came about by chance
when a Navy pilot, hearing that Nixon had never been airborne, offered him a
trip to Des Moines in a two-seater biplane. 'I had a heck of a time putting on the
straps, the harness and so on which you had to wear,' recalled Nixon, 'but I got it
on and I remember what a thrill it was for the plane to rise up there and then float
out over the cornfields.'[5]

Unfortunately, the thrill did not last long for he was promptly airsick, a
problem which was to trouble him for several more years of his military and
political life.

In spite of the welcome company of Pat, who found herself a bank clerk's job
in Ottumwa, Nixon was restless. He wrote to his former instructor at Quonset
Point, Commander D.S. Harrison, asking for help in obtaining a posting to Air
Combat Intelligence (ACI). Harrison responded by writing to a senior ACI officer
on 5 December 1942:

> Sir,
>
> I have a letter from Lieut (J.G.) Richard Nixon—Quonset 4. He
> is now in Ottumwa, Iowa—legal officer and crying his heart out to
> get into ACI. If you run short of (J.G. s) he is a good one. Class stand-
> ing in Quonset was 96 in Class of 750. Young, no children, and *wants*
> ACI. Has he gone too far to be redeemed?[6]

Although he was eventually offered a job in Air Combat Intelligence, Nixon
found a faster route to redemption from Ottumwa on his own. In December 1942

he saw an announcement on the mess noticeboard stating that officers who were twenty-nine years old or younger could obtain immediate assignments for sea duty. Without telling his CO (an omission which caused a major explosion of wrath), Nixon applied, and was given a posting to Noumea, New Caledonia.

With Pat's full support he was glad to be moving 'up the line' towards the centre of America's war effort in the Pacific. 'It wasn't a move I made because I was a real brave fella. It was just simply an innate inner feeling that it was vitally important to be where the action was. Not to show your courage but because you had to be there. I felt that if I didn't get where the action was I would not have done my duty.'[7]

The tensions between Nixon's response to the call of duty and the Quaker ideals of pacifism became painfully apparent when he said goodbye to his family. The farewell scenes at Union Station in Los Angeles were agonising, as Evlyn Dorn recalled:

> A little group of us met for breakfast to see Dick off. It included his Grandmother Almira Milhous, Mr. & Mrs. Nixon, Donald and his wife Clara Jane, some uncles and aunts, Pat, and his youngest brother Eddie. Everyone tried so hard at breakfast to be merry, but the conversation ran out and then as we walked to the train it was so sad. Frank Nixon started to sob and really everyone got upset, although Mrs. Nixon just stood up straight and strong. The last thing that happened was that Dick pointed to Eddie, who was only thirteen at the time, and said in a very powerful voice, 'Eddie, *YOU* take care of your mother!' and then the train pulled out.[8]

Two days later, on 31 May 1943, Nixon sailed from San Francisco for the South Pacific on the SS *President Monroe,* a requisitioned liner designed for 250 cruise passengers but now crammed with 3,000 servicemen. The seventeen-day voyage was a misery for him on account of his chronic seasickness. He never managed to finish a full meal and his fellow officers ran a regular sweepstake on how many minutes he would last at the ship's dining table.

Arriving in New Caledonia, Nixon was disappointed at not being assigned to an aircraft carrier. Instead, he was appointed an assistant operations officer on the Noumea airstrip for South Pacific Combat Air Transport Command (SCAT). It was a humdrum but essential role. He was in charge of a small detachment of enlisted men who had the task of loading and unloading combat supplies into aircraft. They also had the responsibility for evacuating the wounded—'sitters and Utters' as the wheelchair and stretcher case patients were called. In addition, Nixon had many routine administrative duties which ranged from censoring his men's mail to making up the passenger and cargo manifests on the departing and arriving aircraft.

SCAT was the island-hopping military transport airline for US forces in the South Pacific. Its four squadrons of DC3s operated over enemy territory often in extreme weather conditions with inadequate navigation equipment. Several times in his period of duty at Noumea, Nixon had to stay up all through the night on the airstrip anxiously awaiting the return of a missing aircraft, hoping against hope that the pilots, most of whom he knew, had only been delayed and would make a late arrival. His vigils were often in vain. SCAT'S losses soon earned it the ghoulish nickname 'Murder Incorporated'.

In January 1944 Nixon and his fifteen-strong detachment moved further up the line via Guadalcanal and Vella Lavella to Bougainville in the Solomon Islands. The airfield was in striking distance of the important Japanese airbase at Rabaul and their bombers attacked frequently. Nixon's first month at Bougainville was hazardous, with heavy bombardment from air raids on fourteen consecutive nights. 'One night it was pretty close ... we heard this plane. It had come in very low. We heard the bombs dropping as they came down the runway', he recalled. 'We dived out of our tent into the foxhole. As soon as we got out we saw that our whole tent had been sprayed with bullets. It was a close one.'[9] Near misses seemed to be almost routine in the Solomons. After another air raid, Nixon counted thirty-five bomb craters within a hundred feet of the bunker he and six of his men were sharing. But it was part of the culture to take a laid-back attitude to such experiences, and in any case there was just too much work to spend time on worrying.

One memorably busy day in the Bougainville life of Lieutenant Nixon would feature in the speeches of his 1946 congressional campaign. Early on the morning of 25 January 1944, he received a secret radio message from US Navy headquarters at Guadalcanal telling him that thirty C47S carrying 135,000 pounds of rocket bombs would be arriving at Bougainville by 10 a.m. Nixon and his detachment (depleted to a strength of nine by malaria) were given what at first seemed the almost superhuman task of unloading the bombs from the cargo planes and transferring them to the combat aircraft in time for a night air raid against Rabaul.

After that the C47S had to be reloaded with 'sitters and litters', the casualties of the Japanese attack the previous evening. One officer estimated the job could take thirty men twelve hours. Nixon took off his shirt, worked nonstop alongside his nine-man crew in the hot sun, successfully accomplishing the whole operation in less than six hours. After the work was done, Nixon organised an evening barbecue for his team as a mark of appreciation. As *Navy* magazine subsequently reported: 'This was a typical example and one which earned [Nixon] the respect and devotion of his enlisted men who were not unused to seeing officers watch them labor.'[10]

The episode confirms Nixon's wartime reputation for having a good rapport with his platoon. He seemed to have been instinctively aware of the old military maxim, 'The US serviceman is easy to lead but difficult to order around', for he made a point of living, eating, and working alongside his men. He shared their discomforts, jollied them along with pep talks reminiscent of his football days on the bench at Whittier College, and led from the front by personal example.

He had a remarkably diverse group in his squad, including a Pole from Buffalo; an Irishman from New Jersey; a farm boy from Nebraska; a Mexican from Los Angeles; a Kentucky ridge runner; a super-tough Texan and an American Indian. 'They talked rough, they worked hard, they were intensely patriotic and I learned to respect them and to like them', said Nixon. 'They illustrated one of the great lessons of the war, that when the chips were down, Americans of all creeds, classes and ranks worked together as a team.'[11]

Nixon's good feelings about his detachment were reciprocated, for long after the war several of the men who had served under him told different reporters, apparently quite spontaneously, that Nixon reminded them of Mr. Roberts, a folkloric wartime character of the US Navy immortalised in a 1955 movie of that name. Mr. Roberts, as the screen character played by Henry Fonda, was legendary for his good humour, his can-do spirit of improvisation and his affable personal charm. Such a likeable and popular human persona has not often been attributed to Nixon.

These favourable wartime impressions of his comradeship and leadership highlight a somewhat neglected aspect of Nixon, namely his ability to strike a chord in the minds and even in the affections of ordinary, working-class Americans. Those enlisted men who responded so well to Lieutenant Nixon were the first examples of the phenomenon that was later to emerge as 'the silent majority' in the political career of President Nixon. Such followers, whether on the wartime airstrips of the Solomon Islands or in the peacetime factories of smokestack America, came to revere Nixon largely because they saw in him a smarter and more successful reflection of themselves. To many working people he looked and sounded like 'one of us', even though he had the brains and vision of 'one of them'.

This rapport between blue-collar America and Richard Nixon was an important ingredient in his rise to power. The superficial warts which later caused some commentators to underestimate Nixon the candidate, such as his occasional lapses into bad taste, pugnacity, and awkward behaviour, were the very indicators that proved to the masses that Nixon the individual had not lost touch with his roots. For all his uncommon ability, he was still a kindred spirit to the common people. He had shared in their backgrounds; he supported their aspirations; he was at one with their patriotism. This perception of Nixon, and the mutual bond that flowed from it, first emerged during his tour of duty in the South Pacific.

II. THE GREEN ISLAND GAMBLER

In April 1944 Nixon took part in the invasion of Green Island, an enemy stronghold occupied by about 1,000 Japanese troops. He arrived in a seaplane just after the US Marines and the New Zealand Infantry had gone in.

One of his first tasks was to evacuate the wounded from the beaches. To his surprise he found another US Navy Lieutenant commanding a SCAT detachment doing exactly the same job. 'Who are you?' asked Nixon. 'Jim Stewart—I'm supposed to be the officer in charge of SCAT on Green Island', was the reply. Laughing over the administrative bungle that had resulted in two identical sets of orders being issued from Admiral Halsey's HQ, Stewart established that his rival's commission predated his own by two months and declared, 'OK, Nixon, I guess you're the officer in charge.'[12]

From this inauspicious beginning there developed an interesting friendship. Lieutenant James B. Stewart was at the opposite end of America's geographical and social spectrum from Richard Nixon. A well-heeled New Yorker in his late twenties, whose prewar bachelor life style had revolved around the Social Register, debutante parties and champagne dinners at Manhattan's fashionable Stork Club, Stewart was a life-enhancing companion with a highly developed sense of humour. This was useful for keeping up the SCAT teams' spirits during the early days of the occupation of Green Island, for they had some grim moments as they struggled alongside the Seabees to build and operate the airstrip under Japanese air raids. Nixon recalls one searing experience when a damaged B29 attempted to make a forced landing:

> The B29 had its undercarriage shot off. It was dusk at the time, almost dark, and we all cheered as the pilot made a belly landing, but then as the crippled plane wobbled down the strip with controls out of commission it swerved and crashed head on into a bulldozer. The carnage was terrible. We rushed over. I had a marvelous corpsman, an Indian boy, who went right in through the flames and saved a

couple of badly burned survivors. I got one body out and I can remember his face to this day. He was so young and I looked at his hand and saw his wedding ring, with just a single gold band.... I was glad that I wasn't the commanding officer that had to write to his wife.[13]

The days of carnage on Green Island soon came to an end as the New Zealand Division under the command of General Barraclough mopped up the last Japanese stragglers. Thereafter, the most dangerous attackers were giant centipedes.

However, the airstrip kept busy with SCAT movements, so there was always work to do. Off duty, Nixon increased his popularity by creating a fun catering establishment on the base which became known as 'Nick's Snack Shack'. This was a beer and hamburger stand which Nixon set up with the help of the cooks of the 22nd Seabee Battalion. Some of the skills he had acquired during his short stint at the butchery counter of the family store in Whittier came in handy at the Snack Shack, but Nixon's real talent was scrounging, trading or just plain 'liberating' the food and drink for the stand, which he gave away free to men of all ranks, particularly to the returning flight crews.

'It meant so much', recalled Air Force fighter pilot Chandler Worley. 'Just a few minutes' relaxation, good sandwiches, and the coldest pineapple juice in the islands'.[14] Nick's Snack Shack was a good works operation which made life a little more pleasant for many servicemen on Green Island, and also acted as an antidote for boredom, a common problem on the island. In Nixon's case this was further alleviated by conversation, reading, correspondence and poker.

Good conversation was sometimes hard to come by in the outlying islands of the South Pacific, but Nixon was lucky to have such a congenial and intelligent companion as Jim Stewart. From their first meeting at the invasion beach head they had taken to one another. Their friendship ripened first through shared misfortunes and later in shared luxury. The misfortunes included air raids, bad reactions to insect bites, a common fungus infection and a tent which kept blowing away in the night. The luxury came when the enterprising Stewart bribed the CO of the Seabees, with a 'liberated' consignment of 6,000 bottles of beer, into replacing the tent with a custom-built cabin complete with plywood flooring, copper-lined walls, a private water tank and scenic views overlooking the ocean.

This was the cushiest billet on Green Island and it was not surprising that Lieutenants Nixon and Stewart spent a good many of their off-duty hours enjoying the comparative comforts of their centipede-proof lodging. As Jim Stewart recalled:

We used to sit on our veranda looking out over the edge of the cliffs towards California talking about anything and everything under the sun.... My strongest impression of Nick at that time was that he was an absolutely straight arrow and a true Quaker. He didn't smoke. He didn't drink. He told me he hadn't slept with anyone in his life except Pat. He spent a lot of time reading his Bible, a Quaker Bible with poems in the middle. He was outstandingly intelligent. He had a good sense of humor in a kinda buried sort of a way. I got the impression that he was very interested in the future of his country, and that he had some strong views on the America that he wanted to live in after the war...I agreed with him on that and on many other things, particularly with his thinking on the conduct of the war in the Pacific. He was very anti-MacArthur, who he felt was prolonging the hostilities through personal vanity.... we also talked a lot about the law and opportunities for lawyers, but I never got the impression he was interested in a political career.[15]

Although Nixon established a level of conversational intimacy with Jim Stewart which was probably deeper than he had enjoyed with any other individual up to that time outside his family, it is interesting that he held back from any revelations about his political ambitions. This was an early example of Nixon's lifelong tendency to compartmentalise his friendships so tightly that even the closest of intimates are sometimes puzzlingly excluded from matters of mutual interest.

Whatever he may have omitted from his conversations with Jim Stewart, Nixon's wartime reading habits certainly leave the impression of a young man keenly interested in contemporary politics. Throughout his service in the South Pacific he was disappointed by the shortage of good reading material. Yet if he could not find the books to emulate the literary habits of Winston Churchill, who spent his afternoons as a subaltern with the British Army in India devouring Gibbon and Macaulay in his tent, Nixon at least partly solved his problem by following the example of the young Theodore Roosevelt, who always took a reading notebook with him into the jungle.

Nixon in his off-duty hours read anything and everything he could lay his hands on, from detective stories to the Bible. However, his staple literary diet was a steady flow of old newspapers and magazines such as *Time, Life, Colliers, Harpers, The Red Book,* the *Saturday Evening Post,* and occasional copies of the *New York Times.* His habit was to take detailed notes on any article or subject that caught his interest, sometimes in exercise books, but more often or small scraps of brown, service-issue writing paper. Many of these annotations have survived and make fascinating reading half a century later because they so clearly reveal the mind of an interesting politician in the making. Lieutenant Nixon the note-taker was always on the hunt for the striking phrase, the elegant quotation and the paragraph that dances with felicity of expression. He was an avid collector of facts and arguments, usually marshalled in carefully numbered lists which can be seen as the harbingers of his later speaking style in which he so often used the 'Point one, Point two, Point three, etc.' approach to presenting an issue. Above all, the Nixon notes from the South Pacific reveal a mind surging with intellectual curiosity on a wide variety of subjects and issues, often of international importance.

For example, on 14 September 1943, Nixon's reading notes included the headings 'The Malta Story'; 'Herbert Morrison'; 'German Atrocities'; and 'On Peace'. Under 'The Malta Story' he took down various military and air raid statistics, '400 bombing raids in 400 days', and concluded, 'Countries can't be reduced by bombing if military holds up and if civilian morale is up or is not allowed to interfere.' On 'Herbert Morrison', Nixon seemed to find an affinity with the career of the British Labour Cabinet Minister. 'Cockney of Brooklyn—Father a cop—hard work—grade school education—much reading—good debater', and went on to summarise details of his career and political philosophy, quoting a Morrisonian speech in favour of state nationalisation: 'Useless to try and preserve private enterprise in areas in which it is systematically stifled by combines and price fixing agreements. Public enterprise should take over here and also in the "natural monopolies"'.

In the midst of these political reflections, Nixon copied out a quotation from Henry James: 'For a man to pretend to understand women is bad manners. For him really to understand them is bad morals.' He also noted with astonishment, 'Head waiter at El Morocco earns 40 G's a year!!!' Then he went on to 'German Atrocities', enumerating a list of horror stories, including several from the Russian Front, among them the complete destruction of Tolstoy's village, the desecration of churches and the massacres of civilians. 'Attempt to put Russians back in Dark Age', concludes Nixon. 'Result—Russians hate Germans, as such'.

After interspersing a line from Tennyson—'The most virtuous hearts have a touch of hell's own fire in them'—Nixon's notes briefly tackled the subject of 'On Peace'. He was impressed by a speech from the deposed Czechoslovak leader Eduard Beneš who argued for a postwar federation of Europe provided 'France must not be overlooked as was Russia after the war'. Nixon then scribbled, 'There are some good Germans—but must destroy Military clique—must re-educate Germany'. Under a subheading, 'What am I fighting for?' Nixon answered his own question: 'Simple things, privilege of choosing friends, creeds, papers, radio programmes, etc.—the vote'.

On another day's pages of note-taking, dated 6 June 1943, Nixon was at his most international. He summarised some medical statistics on the mortality of children in Finland, and made a list of the Koranic punishments upheld by King Abdul Aziz of Saudi Arabia. Under the heading 'China' he annotated a Pearl Buck article from *Life* magazine, adding his own conclusion: 'Undemocratic forces at Work. Censorship, Corruption (with US Monetary gifts). Lack of spirit in troops and people. Chiang not to blame—US is for insufficient help.... Chinese army full of dissension'.

From China, Nixon's notes moved to the Middle East, where he tackled the subject of Zionism and Palestine. He observed, 'We must have international not national viewpoint', and recorded some fears that a Zionist Palestine might turn out to be a weak country which would embarrass Jews in the US by its divisions and create a dual allegiance. 'Pal[estine] should be a state where Ch[ristians]—Jews—Moh[ammedans] could live together freely' was his final point.

Nixon's day of reading apparently ended with an article on Ben Hecht from whom he took down the quotation: 'There is nothing more troublesome to genius as success. It substitutes press notices for dreams and cocktail parties for the pursuit of beauty. Fame is a sort of mummy case in which the creative talents of yesterday lie in state.'[16]

It would be tedious and perhaps misleading to record more extensive extracts from these materials, for it is not always clear which of the words written down are Nixon's own opinions and which are merely a digest of the original writer's views. Yet these jottings highlight the quality of an intensely active mind, shining its torch across a broad canvas of subjects. Nixon's notes combine the curiosity of an energetic journalist with the more academic approach of a college professor. His researches on international issues are usually the most thorough and give many hints of the far-sightedness that eventually surfaced in the thought processes of Nixon the statesman. Even without a clue to the identity of the note-taker, this private anthology of quotes, facts and ideas is impressive. There can have been few, if any, military men in the South Pacific who spent their off-duty hours preparing for their future civilian careers with such diligence. It is difficult to resist the conclusion that Nixon the politician rose faster and went further than anyone else because even in his days as a serviceman he was training his mind to work harder and to think more deeply than any other prospective candidate for political office.

Another new dimension of Nixon that developed during the Navy years was his fluency as a letter writer. He had never before been much of a correspondent, but in the Solomon Islands he became prolific on paper, mailing regularly to relatives, old classmates, and former professors. An interesting letter of the period, dated 1 September 1943, was to Dean Horack at Duke University Law School. After summarising some chatty details of his life as a naval officer ('My work is about as far removed from law as is anarchy but at least I'm picking up some practical information about aviation'), Nixon explains that he is writing to present an idea which has come up in his conversations with other lawyers turned servicemen who are worried about their futures in civilian life after the war.

> There is another problem which concerns us and one about which state and local Bar associations might do something constructive. After two to four years away from the law we will need a refresher course—covering not only the new law that has been made but also the regular courses. It is amazing how much we have forgotten already and in another year it will be still worse. It would seem that well-heeled Bar associations like that in California could well undertake to finance classes at certain centers; the co-operation of the law schools and the older lawyers would undoubtedly be certain. With the hue and cry already being raised for government aid and control in the field of postwar job finding, I believe that professional associations might well set the pace in establishing a policy of 'taking care of their own'. As suggested you have probably already gone into this matter so I simply throw out the idea for what it is worth.[17]

Nixon's letters from the South Pacific were both sentimental and practical. When the news of Almira Milhous's death on 23 July 1943 reached him on Noumea, he was much moved and he wrote home many times expressing his love for his ninety-three-year-old Grandmother, saying to more than one cousin that he felt he would never be able to bear revisiting her house in Whittier. His brother Ed was another regular recipient of letters from the Solomon Islands. In an effort to inspire the slowest reader of the family to take more of an interest in his books, Nixon made him an offer: 'I'll give you 10 cents for every ten pages you read.' The incentive worked, for when he returned from the war, big brother paid up $300 to Ed, who by then was reading fluently.[18]

The most touching correspondence of all was with Pat. 'I wrote letters to her every day of the fourteen months I was out there, numbering them all, and Pat wrote to me every day numbering them all', he recalls.[19]

Many of these letters survive in the family papers, but the privacy threshold of both Nixons is still far too high for them to allow publication. However, after a chance glimpse into the private files, this author can record that the Dick and Pat wartime correspondence is a deeply romantic one—warm, humorous, touching in the minutiae of its details and always very loving. 'Please say it [I love you] always—because I always look for that first...you are the only one for me, it's been that way from the first', he wrote to her in August 1943.[20] Their letters are full of physical longings. A flavour of these was conveyed in a poem he copied out in his spindly handwriting from some magazine and sent to Pat. After headlining it 'Materialist—Eva Byron' Nixon wrote:

> Oh, I can hear your voice my love
> Though wide the sea between us lies
> And I can sit alone and look
> Deep in your eyes.
> I feel your touch upon my hand
> Across the half of all creation
> Because, my darling, I possess
> Imagination.
> In dreams I have you with me, love
> Quite charming and ethereal
> But, oh, I much prefer you more
> Material.[21]

These lines may not be great poetry but they convey a message of yearning likely to appeal to any separated couple.

Richard Nixon the lovelorn romantic husband is not a character who ever seems to have made an appearance in the numerous media profiles and portrayals of Nixon the politician. Yet both he and his wife exist vividly as warm, attractive and sensitive human beings in the poems and prose of their billets-doux from the South Pacific. Anyone reading that correspondence would hesitate for an eternity before accepting some of the stereotype labels such as 'Plastic Pat', 'Clockwork Dick' or 'loveless marriage' that journalists have stamped on the Nixons over the years.

Although Nixon has recalled that getting the mail from home was much the most important thing in his life as a naval officer,[22] some of his fellow officers could be forgiven for taking the view that an even higher priority on his agenda was poker. It was not a game he had played until he joined the Navy, but after learning the basics he studied and played it with an intensity that bordered on the obsessional. His introduction to the card table had come from Jim Stewart, who had located the regular Green Island poker game within days of the invasion. Nixon came and watched for a couple of evenings and asked his friend thoughtfully, 'Jim, is there any sure way to win at poker?' 'Hell, Nick, if there was I'd be sitting in Brazil with five million bucks in the bank,' replied Stewart, 'but I do have a theory which might just work for a guy who has your kind of iron discipline.'[23]

The theory was one of maximum caution. It required a player to turn in his cards in four hands out of every five and only to stay in the game if he felt confident he held the best cards. It was a tedious strategy, but one which evidently appealed to Nixon's instincts. 'We played two-handed poker on our own without money for a week until he knew all the various plays. Soon his game became tops. His secret was that he simply never raised until he was convinced he had been dealt the best hand', recalls Stewart.[24]

Long before he sat down at his first poker game, Nixon was a man who liked to hold his cards close to his chest in every sense. He was cautious and calculating by temperament. He brought these qualities with him to the South Pacific and it would be wrong to suggest that his developing skills at poker created any new dimensions in his character. Nixon played to win and he was remarkably successful in this objective. 'I know for a fact he sent home $6,800 from Green Island,' says Jim Stewart, 'and I dare say he stashed away quite a bit more after that.' This was a large sum in the 1940s (equivalent to approximately $45,000 in 1990s money) and it was to provide much of the initial expenses for Nixon's first congressional election race two years later. Winning was made easier in the South Pacific for the man who could stay cool, calm and collected. In an atmosphere where overexcitement at the card table was often artificially induced by alcohol, by competitive male machismo, or by the exuberant relief of those returning from successful combat missions, the man who, in Kipling's phrase, 'could keep his head, while all around were losing theirs', often scooped the pot. This seems to have been the foundation for Nixon's poker-playing success. He was a quiet, steady winner of small sums. 'He always seemed to end up a game somewhere between $30 and $60 ahead. That didn't look like showy winnings, but when you multiplied it day after day, I'd say he did all right', was the verdict of one of his fellow players, Lester Wroble.[25]

Another more prophetic assessment came from James Udall. 'Nick was as good a poker player as, if not better than, anyone we had ever seen. He played a quiet game but wasn't afraid of taking chances. He wasn't afraid of running a bluff. Sometimes the stakes were pretty big, but Nick had daring and a flair for knowing what to do. We watched him closely and made the prophecy that he would succeed in whatever civilian career he chose.'[26]

Nixon himself believed that his skills at poker were exaggerated. 'The technique in my case was to play it very close to the vest. I knew when to get out of a pot. I didn't stick around when I didn't have the cards. I didn't bluff very often. I just bluffed enough so that when I really had the cards people stayed in.'[27]

Sometimes he had his coups. James Udall recalled a night when Nixon bluffed a senior officer out of $1,500 with a pair of deuces. His own most dramatic memory concerned a five-card stud poker game on Bougainville when he drew a hand which the text books say is a 650,000:1 chance:

> I drew the ace of diamonds down, and then in exact order came the Queen of Diamonds, the Jack of Diamonds, the ten of Diamonds—a royal flush. Four of them showing. Well I played it pretty well. There were pairs—a couple of the other fellows had pairs and instead of raising, I just sort of checked, or stayed in or called until there was a pretty big pot... when I finally got to the ten I didn't make any gesture whatever to show my excitement, but after the other fellows had raised one another then I did bet the maximum. Unfortunately I had established my credibility too well on the small pots. Nobody called me, so I raked in the chips, a pretty good pot. And then although you should never let people see your card unless they call you I flipped over my ace and everybody yelled. They never saw anything like it.[28]

Much has been written about the impact of those long hours at the poker games on Nixon's personality in later life. This is a doubtful area of speculation, if only because so many of the characteristics, such as self-discipline and restraint, that helped to make Nixon a winner at the card table, pre-dated his initiation to poker. However, Nixon was to admit in a 1978 interview to one particular asset picked up from his gaming experiences, which later benefited his role as an international statesman.

One of the problems in dealing with great leaders abroad, particularly those that are adversaries, is the almost insatiable tendency of American politicians to want to put everything out on the table. Their inability is to know when to bluff, when to call, and above everything else how to be unpredictable. Unpredictability is the greatest asset or weapon a leader of a major country can have. Unless he is unpredictable he's going to find that he loses a great deal of his power.[29]

III. COMING HOME

By the time he had become an ace poker player, the most predictable ambition in Richard Nixon, which he had in common with every other serviceman in the South Pacific, was his desire to go home. He had no specific plans, but an indication that politics was not far from his mind came when Harold Stassen, the young Governor of Minnesota and a rising star in the Republican Party, toured the Solomon Islands in February 1944. Nixon had hitherto shown a typical serviceman's disdain for visiting firemen, once even refusing a dinner invitation from his CO to meet the world-famous aviator Charles Lindbergh because of a prior engagement to play poker. On this occasion Nixon went out of his way to meet Stassen and to talk politics with him, confiding to the Governor his ambition to run for Congress. Stassen promised that if Nixon could secure a congressional nomination, then he would come over to California and support his campaign.

In the summer of 1944, Nixon was ordered to Alameda, California. One of his last conversations on Green Island was with Jim Stewart, who jokingly advised him to watch his newly acquired vocabulary of bad language when he got home.[30] The final formality of his service on the Solomon Islands came when Nixon was handed an official letter of commendation for his service in SCAT signed by Vice Admiral J.H. Newton, Commander of the South Pacific Area, 'for meritorious and efficient duty'. The citation continued: 'He displayed sound judgement and initiative in organizing the South Pacific Combat Air Transport Command at both Bougainville and Green Island. He established the efficient liaison which made possible the immediate supply by air of vital material and key personnel and the prompt evacuation of battle casualties from these stations to rear areas. His able leadership, tireless efforts and devotion to duty were in keeping with the highest traditions of the US Naval Service.'[31] With this testimonial in his pocket, Nixon flew home from the South Pacific on a USAF turbo C54 on 3 August 1944.

During the sixteen-hour flight from Guadalcanal to Hawaii, the atmosphere was euphoric. Nixon threw his usual card-playing caution to the winds and started betting fairly heavily on gin rummy. He had never seen the game before and learned it in the air 'at a considerable price.... I enjoyed it but got so tired of play-ing it that I have never played it since'.[32]

One other memory he retained of that homeward journey was a midnight refuelling stop on Wake Island. Accompanied by an aircraft mechanic, Nixon stretched his legs by strolling around the airfield and suddenly came across a wartime cemetery. The sight of its white crosses, row upon row, moved him deeply and sent him into a rumination about the human cost of war and the folly of sacrificing young lives for worthless bits of ground. He recalled the scene elo-quently in a speech delivered some eighteen months later to an audience in South Pasadena:

> It was one of those rare nights in the South Pacific, a soft full moon,
> not as warm as usual, just the whisper of a breeze in the air. When
> we reached the cemetery at the top of a little rise we stopped in silence
> at the lonesome beauty before us. No lawn, no monuments, the sim-
> plicity of white crosses in the white sand. I read the names—all of
> America was there, from New York, California, the Midwest. As we
> returned to the plane we did not talk. I thought of this fact. Why did
> those men have to die in this desert island? Why did they rush that
> deadly beach? Not because of the love of fighting; not to pull chest-
> nuts out of the fire for England and Russia; not to save American
> investments overseas; but for the great cause for which we Americans
> have always fought, for the maintenance of human freedom through-
> out the world, and for the building of a new world which would not
> know the horror of war.[33]

After landing at Hawaii, Nixon went by ship to San Diego where he was reunited with Pat. She had travelled down from San Francisco in a four-hour flight on a United Airlines DC3. His fifteen months absence had made both their hearts grow fonder. 'I vividly remember the time she came off that plane', Nixon recalled. 'She was wearing a red dress, which is my favorite color incidentally for her, and I was standing behind the airport fence. She ran towards the fence and I got through the gate some way and ran to her.... when she saw me her eyes lit up and she ran about fifty yards at breakneck speed and threw her arms around me.... That was one of the few times when we weren't concerned about showing a little public affection. We usually never did before—or after.'[34]

Soon after his reunion with Pat, Nixon went back to Whittier, where his parents had organised a homecoming lunch party for some thirty friends and relatives. Towards the end of the meal a small incident took place which indicated that Lieutenant Nixon had shed some of the good Quaker disciplines he had learned in the local Sunday school. As Jim Stewart told the story: 'One of his cousins, apparently an "armchair general", knew everything and was holding forth. Nick listened with growing resentment, for he knew that the cousin probably had seen combat only on the screen of the town movie. Then all of a sudden, without realizing all of what he was saying, he leaned across the table and slapped down the old fellow in language that we used only when the going was really tough. This stopped the conversation abruptly. The guests were amazed.'[35]

These manifestations of a new Nixon who embraced his wife in public and bawled out a relative in sailor's language were little more than a part of the process of getting shore bearings. It was not long before Nixon was his old buttoned-up self again. In his first posting to Alameda, California, he was First Lieutenant of Fleet Air Wing Eight, a mundane role. Nixon described his duties as those of a 'head janitor' who had to keep the base clean under the eagle eye of an exceptionally strict commanding officer, Captain Peter Boyle, who was in the habit of leaving imperious notes for his subordinates such as: 'Lieutenant Nixon, you will soon be a J.G. again if the heads [toilets] are not white by tomorrow morning'; 'Lieutenant Nixon, has my desk been dusted today?'[36]

After four months of coping with this martinet and his fetish for cleanliness, Nixon was glad to move on. He was ordered first to the Pentagon where he did a course on war contracts, living in a dormitory at Georgetown University. Then he was assigned as a legal officer to a series of Navy appointments in Philadelphia, Baltimore, New York and Middle River, Maryland. His job was to negotiate contract termination arrangements with various defence equipment suppliers such as Glenn L. Martin and Bell Aircraft. He performed well, saving the taxpayer millions of dollars; getting promoted to Lieutenant Commander on 3 October 1945; and receiving a letter of commendation from the Secretary of the Navy for 'meritorious service, tireless effort, and devotion to duty'.[37]

From this period, two historical events stood out in Nixon's memory. The first was the death of Franklin Delano Roosevelt on 12 April 1945. Dick and Pat were dining at Bookbinders Restaurant in Philadelphia. 'We were kind of splurging that night, eating lobster,' he recalled, 'when our waiter came up to us, crying, practically sobbing as he said to me, "Have you heard the news? President Roosevelt has just died." That's how we heard it.'[38]

The other major news story of 1945 was Japan's surrender. Nixon heard about it over the radio on the afternoon of 14 August 1945 when working on Navy contracts in a Defense Department office in New York. He abandoned his duties for the day and took Pat down to join the cheering crowds in Times Square. They both enjoyed the festive atmosphere of the VJ Day celebrations, talking excitedly about how soon they could return to civilian life. But the day ended with 'a personal disaster' when Nixon discovered, on returning to their small $90-a-month apartment on West 93rd Street, that he had been pickpocketed. His wallet and over three months' pay had been stolen.

This knock to the Nixon finances somewhat dampened his enthusiasm for rushing off into a new job in civvy street. For the moment, he was content to be receiving the steady salary of a lieutenant commander as he worked away on the final phase of his contract settlement duties in Little River, Maryland. Politics had rather faded from his agenda. Earlier in the year, while stationed in Alameda, he had made one or two well-received speeches on the Southern Californian Rotary Club circuit about his experiences in the Solomon Islands. He had also renewed his contacts with some of his influential Republican friends in and around Whittier. But having cast these few crumbs of political bread upon the waters, there were no discernible returns. Suddenly all this changed when Nixon received a telegram followed by a letter asking if he would be interested in running for Congress.

SEVEN

ELECTION TO CONGRESS

I. THE COMMITTEE OF 100

The letter that launched Nixon on his political career was from his old mentor in Whittier, Herman Perry:

> October 3rd, 1945
>
> Dear Dick,
>   I am writing you this short note to ask if you would like to be a candidate for Congress on the Republican ticket in 1946.
>   Jerry Voorhis expects to run—registration is about 5050. The Republicans are gaining.
>   Please airmail me your reply if you are interested.
>   Yours very truly
>   H.L. Perry
>   P. S. Are you a registered voter in California?[1]

Not surprisingly, when this letter first arrived at his small rented apartment in Middle River, Maryland, he and Pat spent the next two days in a state of excitement, 'talking about the novel, heady idea of serving in Washington'.[2]

However, their initial enthusiasm soon gave way to serious doubts. Voorhis was a wealthy and well-entrenched, five-term Congressman. Nixon was an unknown naval officer stationed 3,000 miles from California with no obvious political assets. The political battle for a seat in Congress would involve almost a year of primaries and full-time campaigning. The Nixons had no rich backers and only $10,000 of personal savings, which had been earmarked for the down-payment on their first home—an important priority now that Pat was pregnant. Although the path of prudence pointed towards a regretful refusal of Herman Perry's offer, the Nixons were an unusually adventurous young couple. Each argued the other into abandoning the path of caution. The challenge brought out the gipsy streak in Pat, who pointed out that the baby would not be born for another four months and that owning a house was not necessarily all that impor-tant. Richard professed to be more hesitant, but in an early example of his lifelong tendency to take advice from those who would guide him to the destination he had already chosen, he travelled up to New York to consult his wartime compan-ion from Green Island, Jimmy Stewart.

Stewart had no doubts. 'Get out there and run, there's no downside to this', he advised. 'But what if I run and lose?' asked Nixon. 'Well, you want to be a lawyer. There's no better advertisement for your future practice than running for Congress—even unsuccessfully', retorted Stewart. 'But I could lose all my life savings', was the next objection. 'C'mon Nick. I know where those savings came from. What's happened to those six thousand bucks you won at poker? If I know you, you've added to them by now. You made your money by gambling, you should be ready to risk it again to win a bigger pot either in politics or in the law.'[3] Stew-art reinforced his advice by giving Nixon his first campaign contribution—a cheque for $100. The message evidently went home, for the following day Dick told Pat:

> Look, if we lose we won't have any money. I won't have a job. We'll have a little baby and not much else. But we're not starting off with a lot in any event and we won't be much worse off for losing. And if I lose, I'll always have the option of picking up my law practice in Whittier or even going to LA to open up an office. They say running for Congress is good publicity for a lawyer. Let's do it.[4]

Having taken the decision, Nixon responded positively to Herman Perry, expressing his surprise and delight at being considered for the nomination. He confirmed that he was still a registered Republican at his parents' Whittier address, having voted for Dewey in the last presidential election by absentee ballot from the South Pacific. Nixon's letter continued:

> I feel very strongly that Jerry Voorhis can be beaten and I'd welcome the opportunity to take a crack at him. An aggressive, vigorous campaign on the platform *of practical* Liberalism should be the antidote the people have been looking for to take the place of Voorhis's particular brand of New Deal idealism. My brief experience in Washington with the bureaucrats and my 3½ years in the Navy have given me a pretty good idea what a mess things are in Washington. I think it would be possible to tear Voorhis to pieces on any number of issues and to present a possible program in opposition which would appeal to voters who have been on the fence during the past 12 years but who have voted for Voorhis because he seemed to offer them the most. I also feel that his lack of a military record won't help him particularly since most of the boys will be home and voting by November. You can be sure that I'll do everything possible to win if the party gives me the chance to run. I am sure I can hold my own with Voorhis on the speaking platform and without meaning to toot my horn I believe I have the fight, spirit and background which can beat him.[5]

Nixon's horn-tooting owed more to youthful enthusiasm than to a professional appraisal of the electoral prospects. More expert observers, including senior politicians from both major parties, regarded California's 12th District as a safe seat for Jerry Voorhis. Incorporating most of the eastern end of Los Angeles County, the District's 205,000-strong electorate was spread over five principal towns—San Marino, Whittier, Pomona, Alhambra and South Pasadena—and the large swathes of agricultural territory between them. Blue-collar workers and farm labourers were the two largest identifiable groups of voters. Their record of rock-solid support for Voorhis was the main reason why the seat was listed as the Democrat's third most secure congressional stronghold in the entire country.

At the outset of the Republicans' selection process, several senior names were under consideration, including those of Dr. Walter Dexter, the former President of Whittier College, and General George S. 'Blood and Guts' Patton Jnr., whose home was in the District. However, for differing reasons, they soon faded out of the running. Herman Perry then persuaded Roy O. Day, the Chairman of the 12th District Republicans, to give Nixon an inside track. He was invited to fly out to California on an expenses-paid basis to appear before the Committee of 100, an influential group of Republican small businessmen who were acting as a screening panel under Day's chairmanship. Nixon had three meetings with various members of this Committee. The first was at a $1 a plate testimonial dinner organised by Herman Perry for known supporters at the Bell Ranch in Whittier, which Nixon afterwards described as 'like preaching to the choir'.[6] The second was at a small, private lunch hosted by Frank Jorgensen, a key leader of the San Marino contingent on the Committee, held in the Los Angeles University Club the following day. The third and only public meeting with the six other aspiring candidates present took place on the evening of 2 November in South Pasadena.

At all three meetings, Nixon made a favourable impression. Appearing in his naval uniform (the only suit he then possessed), he radiated commitment and energy. At the University Club lunch, one of the most important guests was McIntyre Faries, a South Pasadena lawyer who, in addition to his local credentials, was Vice Chairman of the Republican National Committee's executive committee. Faries had some experience of appraising congressional candidates, but had never seen anyone as impressive as Nixon. 'I said to myself, "Here's a man who's really on the ball." He had a lot of brains, and a lot of fight in him,' recalled Faries. 'Perhaps there was a bit too much of the boy debater in some of his answers to us, but we could see that he was a comer. We all wanted him, so the talk at lunch soon turned away from Nixon towards Voorhis and how to beat him. There wasn't much talk of money. We concentrated on how we could get the voters of the 12th District to swing over to the Republicans.'[7]

Nixon developed this theme when he faced the full meeting of the Committee of 100 the following day. Called to speak last of the candidates, he delivered a brief address, putting over the political message which his audience most wanted to hear. Nixon opened by saying that there were two options for the future of the American system: 'One, advocated by the New Deal, is government control in regulating our lives. The other calls for individual freedom and all that initiative can produce.' After a dramatic pause he crescendoed: 'I hold with the latter viewpoint.... Returning veterans, and I have talked to many of them in the foxholes, will not be satisfied with a dole or a government handout. They want a respectable job in private industry where they will be recognized for what they produce or they want the opportunity to start their own businesses.' In his peroration he pledged that if selected: 'I will be prepared to put on an aggressive and vigorous campaign on a platform of practical liberalism and with your help I feel very strongly that the present incumbent can be defeated.'[8]

Although the meeting had no decision-making powers on the choice of nominee, most members of the Committee of 100 present were under no doubt as to which of the candidates under audition had come off best. Roy Day in particular seemed delighted by Nixon's good showing, for he kept walking round the room saying repeatedly: 'This man is saleable merchandise.'[9] The final selection of a candidate was to be made at a full meeting of 12th District Republicans on 28 November, but two weeks ahead of this date, Roy Day was writing ('strictly off the record as I am still Chairman of the Committee') to Nixon, now back in Maryland, with good news:

> Everything is shaping up fine in the 12th District and I feel very safe in telling you that it looks like a landslide for you at our meeting on the 28th. There have been several meetings held informally over in San Marino, Alhambra and South Pasadena and they are going for you all the way. The Pomona delegation will nominate Gist as per schedule then move to make the vote unanimous for you immediately after the first ballot as Gist has about five votes and no more. Of course the Whittier boys and girls will come in solidly behind you.
>
> Frankly Dick we feel we have SOMETHING and SOMEBODY to sell to this district now and we are going to do our very best to close the deal.[10]

The deal was duly closed very much in line with Day's forecast. Seventy-seven members of the Committee attended the final meeting and on the first ballot Nixon received sixty-three votes, with his nearest competitor, Captain Sam Gist, a furniture dealer from Pomona, scoring twelve. The meeting then voted to make the selection unanimous. Roy Day rushed out to telephone Nixon, even though it was 2 a.m. in Maryland, and shouted jubilantly: 'Dick, Dick, the nomination's yours!'[11]

Ten minutes later, Herman Perry called in an equally exultant mood and Nixon tactfully dissembled an equally surprised and delighted reaction. After these conversations, Pat and Dick were too excited to go back to sleep, so they talked until dawn about the coming election and the changes it could make to their lives.

Within hours of his selection, Nixon went into overdrive, preparing himself for the coming battle with Voorhis. There was no immediate pressure on him to do this since the election was eleven months away and he had several more weeks of contract settlement work ahead of him in Washington before he could hope to obtain his discharge from the Navy. But Nixon's political ardour was inflamed. With that single-mindedness that came to characterise all his campaigns, he devoted every available moment of his spare time to studying the potential issues and strategies. His reconnaissance included visits to Capitol Hill, where he had introductions to various Republican Congressmen. One particularly useful piece of advice was offered by Representative Charles Halleck from Indiana who, in colourful language, told Nixon: 'Jerry's just a damn socialist, not because he's a bad guy but because he doesn't know any better. You can beat him on his record because if the people back home knew the damnfool nonsense he talks they'd throw him out on his ass!'[12]

Steered in this direction, Nixon spent days and nights researching Voorhis's votes and speeches. Soon he was writing to Herman Perry setting out a plan.

> There can be no question about Jerry Voorhis's voting record. Despite his magazine articles and his speeches, he consistently votes with the most radical element of the New Deal group. He is definitely lined up with Congressman Vito Marcantonio of New York, Hook of Michigan and Helen Douglas of Hollywood, whose political views are not open to doubt. As to his record of achievement it can clearly be established that in his four terms he has never yet been able to pass even one of the bills or amendments which he has personally sponsored and he has introduced more per session than any other member according to his Republican colleagues.
>
> On the other hand, all agree that he is honest, conscientious and able. His difficulty seems to be the attempts to speak on every subject which comes up and consequently fails to concentrate on the issues which are important. All seem to agree, however, that our Campaign should not be directed *against* Jerry Voorhis. They say we should concentrate on selling the Republican candidate to the district and not even mention Jerry's name. He is very popular and a personal attack would backfire.[13]

Nixon's assessment of his opponent was a fair one. Jerry Voorhis did enjoy a high level of personal popularity in the 12th District on account of his transparent sincerity. Son of the chairman and principal shareholder of the Nash Motor Company, Voorhis went to Yale, where he graduated with honours and membership of Phi Beta Kappa. In his student days, he became a Christian Socialist, and from then on his life was largely dedicated to the ideals of what was known as 'the social gospel'. He ran an orphanage in Wyoming; did missionary work for the YMCA in the slums of Germany; and married a fellow social worker. He gave away most of his family inheritance when he founded and endowed the Voorhis School for Boys, a home for runaways, located ten miles north of Whittier. During the Depression years, Voorhis taught at his boys' home; did part-time academic work as an economics lecturer on various Californian campuses; and began to dabble in politics. He was initially a registered Socialist, then moved to becoming a New Deal Democrat. Active on the picket lines and in organising workers cooperatives, he became a significant figure in the EPIC (End Poverty in California) movement led by Upton Sinclair, influential novelist and Utopian Socialist who had been the Democratic candidate for the state governorship in 1934. As the Great Depression deepened, Voorhis, in 1936, became the Democrats' congressional candidate for the 12th District, winning the seat from an unpopular Republican on the coat tails of Franklin Roosevelt and the New Deal.

In the House of Representatives, Jerry Voorhis cut a curious figure. Academic in mind and altruistic in spirit, he proved ineffective as a legislator. Not only did he find the horse trading and the hard bargaining of congressional life uncongenial, he came across as too prolix a speaker and too woolly a thinker. Away from the floor and the committees he wrote *Out of Debt, Out of Danger* and two other largely unread books on his pet subject of monetary reform. He was modest to the point of crankiness, insisting on the deletion of the traditional prefix 'Hon.' before his name in the Congressional Record in order to save paper. Conscientious in attendance, and unwavering in his support for virtually all left-of-centre causes, some of his liberal colleagues thought of him as 'a political saint'.[14] A more realistic judgement came from the columnist Drew Pearson, who described Voorhis as: 'so kindly and altruistic that he often defeats his own purposes'.[15]

Despite his ineffectiveness in Washington, Voorhis still looked a formidable opponent back in his home district. He had served his constituents well for nine years, successfully defending his seat in four elections with majorities ranging from 35,000 votes in 1938 to 14,000 in 1944. His gentle, pipe-smoking approachability, his manifest honesty, and his earnest seriousness all made him an attractive candidate.

One of his skills was presenting a series of subtly different images to his varied electorate. 'Jerry knew how to empathize with the voters in a poor area like Maravilla Park', recalled McIntyre Faries. 'Sometimes you'd see him squatting on the kerb in a slouch hat and sandals, whittling at a stick and puffing his pipe as he sat around talking to second-generation Mexicans about their welfare problems. A couple of hours later he could dress up nicely in his best suit and be addressing the Rotary Club about trends in business.'[16]

Nixon had witnessed something of this multi-faceted voter appeal when, as a law student, he had been so impressed by Voorhis's idealism during their only previous encounter at a barn meeting in the summer of 1935. Yet, for all his good personal rapport with the electorate, Voorhis was politically vulnerable. His greatest weakness was that he was out of step with the political and economic thinking of the majority of his voters. He was still caught in a time warp of enthusiasm for socialist planning and state interventionism. Such a philosophy had appealed to the electorate in the depths of the Depression, but it had become an anachronism. In Southern California, the postwar 1940s were a time of impatience against government controls, centralised bureaucracy, and Washington-induced shortages. Voorhis was therefore at risk as an unreconstructed New Dealer in a constituency which no longer supported the New Deal.

Additionally, Voorhis had never found it necessary to master the techniques of the professional politician. Lulled into complacency by a succession of mediocre opponents, he had never been required to defend his record in a vigorous election campaign. For all his sincerity, he was a verbose and often rambling public speaker. He was weak when it came to putting across a clear political message and he took little or no interest in the mechanics of vote-getting.

By contrast, in December 1945, his unknown opponent, Richard Nixon, was immersed in the most professional of preparations. Hunched over his yellow legal pads, he worked long into the nights, studying the Congressional Record, planning, scheming, and drafting the speeches which were to make him the most formidable challenger that Jerry Voorhis ever faced.

II. THE CHALLENGER

Nixon's first electioneering problem was recognition, for he was virtually unknown in the 12th District outside his home town of Whittier. Overcoming this disadvantage was not an easy task. There was little press interest in the campaign as the primaries would not be taking place until June. The difficulty evidently worried him for, on 2 December 1945, only three days after winning the Republican nomination, he was writing to Herman Perry with his suggestions:

> I'm working up some speeches for Service Clubs, women's organizations, etc. I have also outlined a talk which I believe could go over in the churches.... I'd like the opportunity to speak for every group possible throughout the district. Those speeches will be non-political

and could be used for several months until the campaign begins to get underway.[17]

Herman Perry duly swung into action and arranged a heavy speaking schedule for Nixon on the lunch- and dining-club circuit starting soon after he achieved his release from the Navy and returned to Whittier in mid-January 1946. The handwritten texts of these early, non-political speeches survive in Nixon's private files, often providing, as one reads them today, revealing insights into his fundamental political beliefs.

One of Nixon's first and most interesting pre-campaign speeches, entitled 'The Challenge to Democracy', was delivered early in 1946 to the Kiwanis of Pomona.* It was uncharacteristic of the usual light fare for lunch club addresses, consisting of a deeply serious historical analysis of the Soviet threat to American democratic values. Nixon began on a bloodcurdling note: 'The history of Russia is a tragic story of war, starvation, torture, rape, murder and slavery. They have never in all their history known as we Americans have the peaceful existence of neighboring states side by side with established boundaries. To them all foreigners are potential enemies. They have never known what it means to live in freedom. They have always been ruled by dictators.'

The audience was then taken through a grisly and highly detailed catalogue of the crimes of Russia's rulers starting in 1240 with Batu, the grandson of Genghis Khan; to Ivan the Terrible ('a sadist who by 1544 had conquered 168 peoples, created the secret police, killed his own son with his bare hands and had hundreds of priests and religious leaders boiled and roasted alive in Moscow's squares'); and on to Peter the Great; Catherine the Great; Alexander II; Lenin; Trotsky and Stalin. As far as the post-revolutionary Soviet leaders were concerned, Nixon was harshly critical of their domestic cruelties; of their collectivisation of the farms that had led to three million deaths from starvation in the Ukraine alone; and of their brutal suppression of all dissent and democracy. When he turned to the international dimension of Soviet policy and the appropriate American response to it, Nixon's 1946 vision was remarkably prophetic.

> Russia has now grabbed Estonia, Latvia, Lithuania, Eastern Poland, parts of Finland, Czechoslovakia and Romania. The Soviets do not need these parts of Europe... now the Soviet Government is strong and firmly entrenched, but it is weak in the light of history because

---

* The Kiwanis are an altruistic, small businessman's organisation, similar to Rotary, with a strong commitment to local community service.

it has set itself against the surge of mankind towards freedom and democracy.

So what have we to offer? We should not hesitate to help democratic elements in the states controlled by Soviet puppet governments. But we must not attack Russia on the grounds that it may attack us. This would reduce us to a moral level not far below theirs. Man cannot murder by becoming a murderer. We must use means that conform to the highest moral standards. The most legitimate use of force on earth is to gain time to permit the growth of moral ideas. But at some point we must stop Soviet imperialism. We must use our economic, political and military power... we owe it to the world to hold the line for the growth of democratic ideals, to show how well our own democracy works here and to sell our ideas to the rest of the world and to the Russian people.[18]

This is a speech of considerable historical interest. Delivered when Nixon was an unknown, unelected, and internationally inexperienced young candidate, it illuminates some of the qualities that were to make him a world statesman.

Only Nixon (two words which are frequently juxtaposed in the story of his career) would have devoted so much thought and historical study to the preparation of a major foreign policy address for such a minor audience.

Only Nixon, among congressional candidates in the 1940s, had the long-range vision to foresee that the Soviet Empire would eventually crumble, provided America used the restraining influence of its military power 'to gain time to permit the growth of moral ideas'.

Only Nixon had both the intellectual prescience to think out such a policy and the political persistence to put it into effect.

Nixon's detractors have sometimes portrayed the anti-Communist stance in his early career as pure political expediency. This speech goes a long way to refute such a theory, for it illustrates the depth of his anti-Communist commitment. It also demonstrates the far-sightedness of his foreign policy judgement. What Nixon predicted in the 1940s did occur by the 1990s. His scenario came true partly, perhaps largely, because he was around to make it come true. In his fifty-year career as prophet, politician, President and foreign policy pundit, Nixon has been America's leading and most consistent advocate for holding the line against Soviet expansionism. The policy started and succeeded on his watch. The first sign that he was interested in watch-keeping came in this address to the Kiwanis of Pomona in the spring of 1946.

The 'Challenge to Democracy' was one of several major topics Nixon tackled in his early tours of the 12th District's lunch- and supper-club circuit. Others included a talk on veterans' rights and a remarkably accurate forecast of the trends in aviation, television, and computers, entitled 'America's New Frontiers'.

The meticulous details of the scripts for these addresses, impressive even when read today, were enhanced when delivered by Nixon. Using his talent for committing a prepared text to memory, he would give the entire speech without notes. The effect this had on an audience was electrifying. Hubert Perry, Herman Perry's son, remembers being swept along in the general enthusiasm for the new candidate: 'I've never seen people rally around any political figure like they rallied round Dick Nixon in those early days. After hearing his speeches we couldn't wait for him to have a crack at Voorhis.'[19]

In the build-up to the primary of 4 June, Nixon developed a standard speech known to insiders as 'The Bougainville'. In it he told the story of the men in his SCAT detachment on Bougainville Island ('a typical melting-pot crew…ordinary guys from all over America'). Describing each man with a vivid word-portrait, he recounted their exploits on the day in January 1944 when they had unloaded and reloaded a squadron of combat aircraft in record time. Then he detailed the privations they were each facing in civilian life. Red Hussey of New Jersey could not find a place in school; Tex Massingill from Texas could not buy a truck; Bill James in Nebraska could not get a permit for the materials to build his own house—and so on. All these hardships were attributed to the red tape and bottlenecks created by 'Washington Bureaucrats'. It was a theme which struck a chord with the small businessmen and tradesmen in his audiences, who were having many of the same problems with their own supplies and government permissions. The speech was also good for Nixon's image, for it subtly portrayed him as a hardworking, courageous, can-do type, who had shared the burdens of war with his men in an unusually egalitarian style for a naval officer.

In addition to speech-making, Nixon worked hard at coffee morning appearances, house meetings, and literature distribution—all important activities in the pre-television age of electioneering. Yet his organisation was amateurish and his living arrangements were uncomfortable. He had rented an 'atrociously furnished'[20] house from a local barber whose main disadvantage was that it overlooked a mink farm. The baby minks screeched all night, disturbing the candidate's sleep and speech-writing. His campaign office was hardly any better. It was a long-unoccupied storeroom in Whittier. Its only furniture consisted of two chairs and a sofa contributed by his mother; a typewriter borrowed from his old law partnership; and a throw rug tossed onto the bare floorboards by his brother, Don.

By far the hardest campaign worker was the candidate's wife. Pat was a tower of strength in those days, accompanying her husband to all functions, often exhibiting a personal warmth and charm which Nixon himself found hard to display. She put in long hours mimeographing and mailing letters to supporters despite being heavily pregnant. In addition to being chief secretary, she was also chief critic, giving 'thoughtful and sometimes quite persistent critiques of my performance after house meetings',[21] as Nixon recalls. Pat was also responsible for the campaign's first major publicity breakthrough, for when she gave birth to Tricia on 21 February 1946, virtually every newspaper in the district carried a family photograph with a somewhat presumptuous comment from the proud father: 'She is the only boss I recognize. Patricia is a lucky girl. She will grow up in the finest state in the Union in the greatest country on earth...and when the time comes she will register and vote Republican.'[22]

Tricia's arrival in the world brought another unexpected bonus to the Nixon campaign. Like many Congressmen of the period, Voorhis followed the practice of having his staff monitor all birth announcements in the local press and sending the new parents a congratulatory note with a government booklet entitled 'Baby Care'. Nixon replied politely, referring briefly to his challenge. Voorhis then wrote back to his opponent: 'Yes, I have heard one or two rumors that you were a candidate for Congress from the 12th District.... I am hoping after I am able to get home that we can arrange to have some joint meetings where both of us can speak. They could either be in the form of formal debates or occasions where both of us would make addresses, whichever you might prefer.'[23]

This was an offer which ultimately proved fatal to Voorhis's political career. Why he made it in this way is a mystery. Every incumbent knows that a debate with a contender usually presents a potential risk. Yet here was Voorhis unilaterally offering his unknown opponent a precious debating opportunity before the campaign had even begun. It seems fair to assume that Voorhis was suffering from overconfidence, possibly on account of his disdain for the quality of the previous Republican challengers in the 12th District.

The results of the June primary should have put the Voorhis camp on the alert. Under the California electoral rules, both candidates cross-filed and ran on the Democratic and Republican tickets. While Voorhis had failed to visit his district, detained by legislative pressures in Washington, he still managed to score what looked like a convincing win, outpolling his challenger by a decisive margin of 7,000 votes. Nixon's initial reaction was despondency, but after a careful analysis of the percentages his morale quickly recovered. They contained a quite different message, indicating that Voorhis's share of the vote had fallen from the 60 per cent he had won in the 1944 primary to 53.5 per cent.

'All we need is a win complex and we'll take him in November',[24] was Nixon's comment to Roy Day and he followed this up with a circular letter to all Republican workers: 'In receiving 53.5 per cent of the total vote cast, Voorhis made the weakest showing he has made in *either* a final or a primary campaign since 1936.... the results of the primary election definitely indicate we can win in November. We have, however, a real job cut out for us because, as you know, Mr. Voorhis has been endorsed by the National Political Action Committee.'[25]

This revelation of Voorhis's endorsement by the National Political Action Committee was a red rag to the Republican bulls, for the initials PAC struck fear in the minds of many conservative Americans. The trade union leaders of the CIO had formed a Political Action Committee in 1944 to back the election of Franklin Roosevelt, and subsequently this PAC had become associated with excessive union power, Socialism, bossism and Communist infiltration. FDR had himself contributed to the myth of the PAC's sinister influence by frequently telling Democratic leaders to 'clear it with Sydney'—a reference to Sidney Hillman, the aggressive union leader and PAC Chairman. Roosevelt haters thus came to see the CIO's PAC as a fountain of power and patronage which was polluted by extreme socialists, Communists and fellow travellers. Although these groups were undoubtedly active in the CIO-PAC, there was always a clear majority of anti-Communists on the committee, and on the committee of its sister organisation, the non-union National Citizens Political Action Committee (NCPAC). However, these distinctions were blurred in the minds of many Republicans, who simply saw both PACs as a combined den of left-wing political iniquity.

Jerry Voorhis's relationship with the PAC was a complex one. He had been endorsed by the CIO-PAC in 1944, but subsequently became unpopular with its hard leftists because of his frequent criticism of the Soviet Union and his personal antipathy towards Communism. This had manifested itself in his work as a member of the House Un-American Activities Committee and in his support for various anti-Communist bills. By 1946 the CIO-PAC had ostentatiously refused to endorse Voorhis's candidature, a denial of support which caused him little distress. On the other hand, Voorhis had no quarrel with the National Citizens Political Action Committee, a milder coalition of non-union progressives with noticeably less Communist influence. For their part, the NCPAC were well disposed towards Voorhis and did endorse him in 1946. However, the fine distinction between the different PACs and their endorsement dates were to cut little ice with

Nixon and his supporters who were determined to make every effort to paint Voorhis as a candidate who was tarnished and compromised by his PAC backers.

Up to this moment in the Republican campaign, money had been something of a problem. Although Nixon had displayed a cool bravado about his ability to help with the costs at the beginning of the contest, saying somewhat disingenuously in his initial letter to Herman Perry: 'With Pat working I have been able to put aside some cash in the last few years so I'd be able to stand the financial expense that a campaign would entail',[26] by June a cashflow crisis was looming. Far too high a percentage of the Nixons' life savings had already gone into the party coffers, and this was certainly worrying Pat. Charles Cooper, a staunch Republican supporter who later succeeded Roy Day as GOP 12th District Chairman, was the first to hear her tale of woe. As he remembered it: 'One morning Pat came into my office almost in tears. She said they were running out of money for the campaign and did not think they could finish it unless they could get more money…we got hold of the right people and raised the money in a hurry.'[27]

Before Charles Cooper and others came to the rescue, Nixon himself had made at least one abortive attempt to solve his campaign's financial problems. This had started as an unusual joint-initiative by Nixon and his fellow Republican candidate from the 15th Congressional District, Don Jackson. Nixon's account of the incident is pure Marx brothers comedy.

> Jackson called me one day and said, 'Dick, you got money problems, I got money problems. I've just had a very interesting letter from one of my constituents. He's been following you and me and he believes that we're the young people of the future. He has got a scheme, he says, where he can finance our whole campaign.' I said, 'Well, I don't know', but Jackson said, 'He lives in a very good area of the district. He must have the dough.' So I drove over one day and Jackson and I went to call on this fellow at about six o'clock at night. He lived in a gated lot in Beverly Hills, a big house on perhaps two acres. It reminded me of the house in the film *Sunset Boulevard*. It was rather run-down. It looked like another era. We knocked on the door. A butler came to the door, bowed, and let us in. It had that musty smell and feel of great wealth that had sort of fallen on bad days. We met the man. He was wearing, I remember, a very handsome smoking-jacket. He was very proper. He shook our hands when we came in and took us into a big library. I remember there were books on all

sides, very impressive, and we sat in front of an open fire and he began to tell us how he was going to finance our campaigns.

Unfortunately, we found out within a few minutes that he was a funny-money man. He thought that if you just printed enough money and distributed it to enough people then that would mean the economy would get going and that things would be settled from then on out. My eyes rolled at Jackson. I was already fighting one funny-money man in Voorhis and now here was a worse one. But the guy went on and on about this scheme and he said: 'If you two fellows will push this I am sure the word would get around and I and others like myself will make contributions to your campaign.'

Just as he was going into this and getting more and more enthusiastic and I was stealing a look at Jackson and Jackson at me, wondering how we were going to get out of there—in walked the butler. He had a 45 pistol. He pointed it at this guy and he said to me as he turned to us, he says, 'Young Fellows, do you know who this fellow is? Don't you have a thing to do with this son-of-a-bitch. He's no good. He's murdered two wives already.' And he waved the pistol around in our direction too and we began to sweat. And this fellow said, 'George, quiet down now, quiet down now.' He said, 'Oh, no, no. You know what you did. You poisoned the first one and the second one, you made her take an enema and kept the enema going until it burst her belly.' And, my God, we wondered what all this was about. The man said, 'George, don't do this.' And so finally, Jackson and I sort of gradually eased up, keeping our eye on him, backing out of the room. And then we said, 'Maybe we'll see you another time and we should talk.' We both got out of the room. We got out of the door and we were both perspiring on a very cool evening and Jackson said, 'I think we need a drink.' And I said, 'Fine, let's go to your place.' He says, 'Oh, no. Let's go to a bar.' I said, 'To a bar? I wouldn't think of going to a bar during a campaign, not in the 12th District.' He said, 'Well, in the 15th District we campaign in bars.' So we went to the closest bar and we both had a double scotch.[28]

The need for such adventurous ways of making money soon receded, for once Nixon had rung the alarm bell on Voorhis's PAC endorsement he began to be seen as a winner and the Republican contributions rolled in. Some of the cash was spent ingeniously. 25,000 red thimbles were purchased and distributed, each bearing the inscription, 'Nixon for Congress—Put the Needle in the PAC'. More conventionally the budget was devoted to advertising, mailshots, and occasional payments to hired workers. However, the Republican campaign was far less well funded than the Democrats'. During the primaries, Nixon had no paid workers at all, whereas Voorhis had at least a dozen professional staff. This imbalance grew as the battle intensified. In the month before polling day, Voorhis had twenty-five paid workers in the city of Alhambra alone, whereas Nixon had none. The two most expensive professional helpers available to Nixon, who each earned a fee of only $500 for the entire campaign, were Bill Arnold, a former journalist turned publicity manager; and Murray Chotiner, a Los Angeles lawyer who had built up something of a feared reputation for managing Republican political events. Although Chotiner later became an influential figure in Nixon's political career, his role in the 12th District during 1946 was limited, for he was usually occupied elsewhere in California managing the re-election campaign of Senator William Knowland. However, Chotiner did give Nixon two valuable pieces of advice. The first was to seize with enthusiasm Voorhis's unsolicited offer of a debate between the candidates. The second was that Nixon should devote a significant amount of time visiting newspapers in the district.

'As a result, I called in on every local newspaper office, however small, usually spending several hours talking with the publisher, the editor, the reporters and sometimes even the printers', recalls Nixon.[29]

It was a technique which resulted in a media honeymoon for him. By the end of the contest, twenty-six out of the thirty newspapers serving the district had endorsed Nixon, including the powerful *Los Angeles Times*. The political editor of the *Times,* Kyle Palmer, initially looked on the Republican challenge in the 12th District as a hopeless cause because of Voorhis's strength and popularity as incumbent. However, after meeting Nixon in mid-campaign, he and the *Times'* proprietor, Norman Chandler, changed their minds.

'My first impression of Nixon was that here was a serious, determined, some-what gawky young fellow who was out on a sort of giant killer operation...but it wasn't too long after he settled down that we began to realize that we had an extraordinary man on our hands', recalls Palmer.

Norman Chandler was equally positive: 'After Nixon departed, I told Mr. Palmer, "This young fellow makes sense. He looks like a comer. He has a lot of fight and fire. Let's support him."'[30]

Although, with the help of increasingly sympathetic press coverage, the Republican campaign was beginning to gather momentum, most contemporary observers agree that the turning point was the first Nixon–Voorhis debate, which took place in September against the background of a rising political temperature on the PAC issue. In the first week of September, Nixon's campaign headquarters placed an advertisement in many local newspapers. The text, written by Bill Arnold, ran: 'A vote for Nixon is a vote for impartial representation in Congress for all the people of the 12th District with no favoritism for any faction, pressure group, special interest or individual. A vote for Nixon is a vote against the Communist-dominated PAC with its gigantic slush fund. Elect Nixon—World War II Veteran—Your Congressman.'[31]

In his own speeches at this time, Nixon took a similar line, fiercely attacking the PAC and 'the radical doctrines fostered by this and other extreme left-wing elements that are seeking to eliminate representation of all the people from the American form of government'.[32] However, before launching such verbal onslaughts, Nixon was always careful to include a neatly worded disavowal insisting he was not attacking Voorhis's personal motives or integrity. Voorhis did not take this lying down. On 11 September he issued his own advertisement, totally denying that he had the CIO–PAC endorsement and rejecting the charge that he was in any way associated with Communists. The Nixon camp promptly issued a statement saying that it would shortly produce proof of Voorhis's PAC endorsement and thus the support of a 'Communist-dominated' organisation. The stage was set for an exciting clash of issues, candidates, and evidence at the debate scheduled for two days ahead.

III. THE DEBATES—'RABBITS AND RADICALS'

Friday 13 September was an unlucky day for Jerry Voorhis. Nixon had prepared meticulously, withdrawing from two full days of campaigning in order to rehearse. He seemed to be brimming with confidence to the 1,000-strong audience crammed into the South Pasadena Junior High School auditorium, giving prepared statements and answers to questions in a direct and convincing manner. By contrast, Voorhis was on the defensive. In his prepared statement he gave a rambling presentation of his views on monetary policy; on the activities of the Congressional Post War Planning Committee, of which he was a member; and on the relationship between the legislature and the executive branch. In the question period he appeared to be severely hampered by the three-minute time limitation on answers. As the independent chairman of the meeting, Paul Bullock later put it: 'His answers seemed fuzzy or incomplete or uncertain, whereas Nixon was always ready with a quick and acceptable response.'[33]

The climax of the debate came when Voorhis again denied the CIO–PAC endorsement and demanded the proof of its existence that the Republicans had been promising. This was the moment that Nixon had been waiting for. Using his theatrical talent to the full, he strode across the stage holding aloft a piece of paper as if he was King Arthur bearing Excalibur. 'Here is the proof!' he thundered. Voorhis was completely thrown by such a strong demonstration of confidence on the part of his opponent. He looked and sounded off balance as he read the document. Although correct in his certainty that the CIO–PAC had refused to endorse him, Voorhis had forgotten (or perhaps had never known) that a political committee of the National Citizens PAC had earlier in the year recommended his endorsement. The piece of paper which Nixon had so dramatically thrust into Voorhis's hand was indeed a genuine internal NC–PAC bulletin confirming that he had been so endorsed.

Visibly flustered, Voorhis could only mumble that the support seemed to have come from a different PAC. Nixon pounced mercilessly on this accurate but feeble rebuttal. He read out to the audience the names of the many individuals who served on the committees of both organisations, scornfully asserting that the two PACs were to all intents and purposes identical. Voorhis's protestations that NC–PAC and CIO–PAC really were two different organisations became drowned by boos and catcalls from the increasingly boisterous audience.

By the end of the evening it was clear that Nixon had scored a great victory over his opponent. Pressing home his advantage, he challenged Voorhis to further debates and four of these were held at different locations during the final weeks of the campaign, attracting total audiences of over 7,000. In these contests, Nixon had two attacking themes—'Radicals' and 'Rabbits'.

The charge that Voorhis was a radical in a progressive's clothing was a further exploitation of the PAC endorsement issue. In effect, Nixon was making a somewhat dubious claim of guilt by association, which Voorhis should have been able to rebut by detailing his own independent and predominantly anti-Communist record in Congress. Instead, Voorhis floundered badly, sending off a telegram to the NC–PAC asking for their endorsement to be withdrawn. Nixon swooped delightedly on this misguided tactic, telling an overflowing debate audience in Whittier ten days before polling day that Congressman Voorhis's voting record had 'earned him the endorsement whether he wanted it or not'.[34]

By this time Nixon was really enjoying himself. Ridicule, often a killer when used against a long-standing incumbent, was his next weapon. Nixon's research had revealed that while Voorhis had introduced 132 public bills in Congress in the previous four years, the only one to become law had been a bill transferring the control of rabbits from one federal department to another. In the ensuing hilarity, he dubbed Voorhis 'The Rabbit Representative', claiming that voters of the 12th District would have to become rabbits in order to get effective representation. Such a specious charge offered Voorhis his opportunity to get even. He could have drawn attention to his hard-working record as a legislator and listed the numerous amendments and joint resolutions for which he had been responsible. More importantly, by stepping out of Nixon's artificially selected four-year period, he could have cited the Voorhis Act of 1940, which had set up a compulsory register for Communists and had been highly unpopular with the American Communist Party. This alone might have thwarted Nixon's charges. However, when it came to fending off Nixon's attacks, Voorhis had lost his political touch.

Although the debates were a triumph for Nixon, the two subjects of 'Rabbits' and 'Radicals', much though they had amused the audiences, were not the decisive issues in the campaign. To win the 12th District, Nixon had to convince approximately 10,000 predominantly blue-collar workers, who were natural Democrats, that they should switch sides and vote Republican. He was always conscious that Voorhis's previous challengers had failed largely because their appeal had been too narrowly and conservatively based. So, despite all the rhetorical flourishes which so delighted his original backers in the Committee of 100, Nixon actually spent most of his time campaigning in 1946 as a centrist and a moderate. As he had said in his original reply to Herman Perry, it was 'an aggressive, vigorous campaign on a platform of practical liberalism' that would beat Voorhis, and it was just such a programme that he sold to the floating voters. The words 'practical liberalism' in Nixon's lexicon meant more or less any non-New Deal policies that might work. He could be flexible to the point of political chameleonism, sometimes asking small groups what they wanted in their Congressman and then agreeing as far as possible with what had been requested if it could be made to square with his basic philosophy of strength abroad, and fewer controls at home.

One issue that he did exploit consistently was the need for new labour legislation to curb the growing national problem of walkouts, wildcat strikes, and irresponsible industrial strife that was then plaguing the economy. Yet he simultaneously managed to sound sympathetic to protecting individual workers' rights, agreeing to support legislation that would allow farm labourers to form trade unions and to engage in free collective bargaining.

Nixon's most telling theme was his presentation of the Republican national slogan 'Had enough?' California was suffering particularly badly from meat shortages, empty clothing stores, gasoline rationing, black markets, acute housing problems and a plethora of bureaucratic controls emanating from Washington. By hammering away at these basic grievances, Nixon struck hard at the fundamental issue that transcended established voting loyalties.

Nixon's day-to-day campaigning was also an essential ingredient in his success. Although he could and did put on oratorical firework displays both in the Voorhis debates and in some of his major set speeches, they were not his usual method of communication with the voters. The broadcasting media were also of little relevance, for in 1946 television sets were a rarity, and the radio wavebands were too broad in California to make an impact on individual congressional districts. In those days the only sure way for a candidate to reach the electorate was by personal speech-making. This suited Nixon well. Those who have followed his career closely during the last half century agreed that he has always been at his best when talking to smaller groups and audiences. In comparison with his tendency to freeze before television cameras or to sound artificial when addressing mass rallies, Nixon on the stump, or before a private audience, comes across as a much more thoughtful and attractive politician. He visibly relaxes, enjoys taking questions, and gradually warms up both emotionally and intellectually as he develops an empathy with those present. The first manifestation of this process was apparent to those who watched Nixon campaigning in 1946. He went round speaking to as many as ten or twelve groups a day, and usually left behind him a favourable impression. In an electorate of just over 200,000 voters, word of mouth is a potent force, and so it proved in the 12th District.

IV. VICTORY—WITH QUESTIONS AFTERWARDS

Two weeks before polling day, a groundswell of support was running so strongly for Nixon that some of Voorhis's closest supporters were warning of a major upset. However, since opinion polling was still in its infancy and had not yet reached Southern California, it was impossible to confirm Nixon's trend towards victory. Yet the surge could be felt and the increasingly confident Republicans pulled out all the stops. They put on extra rallies; stepped up the electioneering parades; and plastered the district with posters and billboards. Some of the enthusiasm may have led to misbehaviour by a small minority of right-wing zealots. Months after the result, there were complaints from a handful of voters who claimed to have received anonymous phone calls asking, 'Did you know that Jerry Voorhis was a Communist?', or saying, 'I just wanted you to know that Jerry Voorhis is a Communist.'[35] The suggestion that these calls were orchestrated dirty tricks has always been denied, and has remained unproved. It is extremely doubtful that they made any impact on the result, but the existence of such rumours only confirms that the campaign was being fiercely fought right to the end.

When election day came on 4 November 1946, it ended in glorious victory. Nixon won with a convincing majority of 15,000, capturing 57 per cent of the vote to Voorhis's 43 per cent out of 114,321 ballots cast. He carried every polling area in the district with only three exceptions, even winning in Voorhis's home town of San Dimas by 491–401. The Nixons were jubilant as they toured the district after the result had been announced, celebrating with one group of supporters after another until finally ending up in the early hours at the home of their closest friends, Jack and Helene Drown. Helene produced an expensive bottle of vintage wine which the Congressman-elect politely refused after the long night of revelry. Helene then suggested: 'Let's save it for the day when we'll be able to crack it over the mantle of the White House.'[36]

The Drowns were not the only loyal supporters who believed they had taken part in launching a political career that would lead to the Presidency. Such hyperbole continued for several days, particularly at an official, victory stag party organised by the Committee of 100 in the Huntingdon Hotel, Pasadena. Several of the toasts and speeches contained flattering references to the presidential prospects of the new Congressman-elect. However, Nixon himself was more interested in the party than the Presidency on that occasion, letting himself go with rare abandon. As he later recalled: 'As the evening wore on and we all got boisterous, I repaired to the piano in the room and began pounding out songs for group singing. Unexpectedly a couple of the fellows decided to relieve Frank Jorgensen of his pants, a project in which everyone joined. I flinch now even as I recount the story of how we tossed Frank's pants on a high chandelier and of the hoots and guffaws of all of us there as Frank leapt up again and again to rescue his trousers. Victory celebrations in later years were more contained.'[37]

Nixon's enjoyment of his success was unalloyed. The immediate press coverage of the election was favourable. *Time* reported on how clean the fight for the 12th District had been, praising Nixon for having 'politely avoided personal attacks on his opponent'.[38] Even the displaced Voorhis recorded a pleasant handover meeting with Nixon and referred to the hope that they had parted as 'personal friends'.[39] Such civility in defeat was not to last, and some weeks later Voorhis began making oblique but apparently pejorative references to certain aspects of his opponent's campaign. Such inferences, later fuelled by largely unsubstantiated allegations of campaign irregularities, came to form the basis for many subsequent assaults on Nixon's moral and financial integrity.

Criticism of the campaign has, for the most part, been tainted by hindsight. Herbert Parmet, biographer of Eisenhower, Kennedy and Nixon, concluded that: 'Except for Nixon's subsequent reputation, what happened in California's Twelfth [District] would have been indistinguishable from campaigning across the country to elect the Eightieth Congress.'[40] That it did not remain indistinguishable was largely due to the Democratic Party's remorse at the unexpected toppling of a liberal icon and its regret over the meteoric rise of the new Republican hero who won the seat. Such circumstances made the Nixon–Voorhis campaign fertile ground for revisionism, and it is perhaps understandable that what began as a reaction of the whispering defeated has been so distorted.

There are three main elements to the allegations of dirty campaigning: financial improprieties, a vicious smear campaign, and dirty tricks. On the first charge, it has been claimed that Nixon was the pawn of big business interests who provided lavish funding for his election expenses and manipulated his propaganda. The original source of this suggestion was Jerry Voorhis writing in the first draft of his memoirs, *Confessions of a Congressman*: 'There was a lot of material...I had in documentary form for weeks which would have shown how the Bank of America, the big utilities, the major oil companies, were resolved to beat me. I never used it.'[41]

Such charges were, and remain, vague and unconvincing and it is interesting that Voorhis never published the words quoted. However it is to this theme that Nixon's detractors subsequently returned in their efforts to uncover financial irregularity. There are certain factors worth outlining in this context. The Republican campaign budget for the 12th District was never large as a result of the decision not to spend money on radio advertising. Estimates of the expenditure have been variously calculated by journalists over the years as being in the $24,000–35,000 range, and there is no reason to doubt Nixon's own figure of $37,500[42] since it is higher than anyone else's. It is still not large for an electorate of 205,000 as it works out at less than 20 cents per voter. There was nothing sinister about the sources of this money, which came initially from the members of the Committee of 100 and later from local Republican supporters. In his memoirs, Nixon identified his early backers as being, 'typical representatives of the Southern Californian middle class: an auto dealer, a bank manager, a printing salesman, an insurance salesman, and a furniture dealer'.[43] The only banker on the Committee of 100 was Herman Perry, a small-town branch manager, who hardly conforms to Voorhis's Bank of America paymaster myth. His son Hubert firmly believes that Herman Perry contributed limited sums of his personal money, and never the Bank of America's.[44] Nixon himself contributed some $4,000 to the campaign coffers, which he could ill afford and for which he was eventually reimbursed.

It was not until after the June primaries, and particularly after the first debate with Voorhis, when Nixon's chances of winning had noticeably improved, that campaign funds began to look healthier. If there were any oil or utility company donations at this time, none of them were over $500[45] and even taken collectively they could not have amounted to a sizeable percentage of the funding for the Republican National Committee paid $12,000 towards Nixon's total budget of $37,500—a remarkably generous allocation for what at the outset had been regarded as an unwinnable seat. The responsibility for this decision can be traced to former President Herbert Hoover, still 'The Chief' of the GOP, who heard of Nixon's prowess during a September vacation, and was so impressed, having seen him in action, that he ordered the diversion of extra funds from the Republican National coffers.

The funding arrangements for Nixon's first campaign reveal none of the skeletons speculatively exhumed with hindsight. Compared to the personally wealthy and politically well-connected Voorhis, Nixon only had shoestring campaign finances which grew to adequate but far from lavish levels. There is no evidence that favours were ever asked for, or granted, in return for Republican contributions. Indeed, there are old men living around Whittier and Alhambra who still complain about Nixon's lack of generosity to his supporters in the form of government contracts, appointments and political favours.[46]

The second count of dirty campaigning relates to the 'Communist smears' made against Voorhis. To put these in context, it is worth recalling what the word 'Communist' was generally understood to mean in the political vocabulary of 1946. At that time there was little anti-Russian hostility in the United States and the term 'Communist' did not imply that an individual so labelled might be controlled by the Soviet Union. Communism was an imprecise term of political abuse and primarily meant believing a doctrine of pure Socialism. The equivalent label today might be 'left winger' or 'hard leftist'. Communism did not gain its connotations of treachery and espionage until the Hiss case of 1948 and the McCarthy era of the 1950s.

Nevertheless, one of the most consistent themes used by Republican candidates was the failure of the Democrats to combat the Communist menace. Nixon's use of this tactic was by no means extraordinary. Given this background it was fair game for Nixon and his supporters to charge that the PACs were Communist-dominated organisations since many of their most vociferous members were indeed left wingers and members of the Communist Party. There is no suggestion that Nixon ever directly labelled Voorhis a Communist, indeed he was careful to avoid this. In his memoirs he wrote: 'I thought then and still think that the endorsement was a legitimate issue to raise.'[47] Nixon was successful in associating Voorhis's name with the PAC and thus with Communism, while Voorhis failed to defend himself against the charges—something that his record of anti-Communism should have made easy.

As far as the anonymous telephone calls are concerned, Nixon has always denied any knowledge of them at the time, and voiced strong disapproval of such methods if, indeed, they were used. The evidence of these calls is of doubtful provenance, for they were never raised by an actual recipient, and only emerged as an issue some months after polling day. It was obvious to the entire Nixon camp quite how great a task they faced in their efforts to unseat Voorhis, and it is conceivable that a few such unauthorised calls were made. In any case, underhand tactics were certainly not limited to one side. Early on in the campaign, Pat Nixon was distraught to find that the Nixon headquarters had been broken into and that hundreds of expensive campaign leaflets had been stolen.[48] It was a loss that the Nixon camp could ill afford.

On 4 November 1946 such highly charged analyses of the minutiae of Nixon's campaign ethics were not merely academic, they were non-existent. Although Nixon himself still believes that his 1946 campaign was 'very gentlemanly',[49] what was remembered was its apparently seamier, and less representative side. In view of the panoramic sweep of the political career to follow, it is all too easy to overlook that, as clear underdogs, Richard and Pat Nixon had staked their life savings and their immediate future on the outside chance of a seat in Congress. That they succeeded was as well deserved as it was unpredictable. Nixon personally considers the 1946 election his most glorious moment: 'Pat and I were happier on November 6, 1946, than we were ever to be again in my political career.'[50]

EIGHT

FRESHMAN CONGRESSMAN

I. THE INDUSTRIOUS APPRENTICE

'**G**o along to get along' was the first piece of advice Nixon received after being sworn in as a Congressman on 2 January 1947. It came to him from his close friend and mentor. Representative John Phillips, and he took it. 'Established members of the House told me and other Freshmen to be seen and not heard', he recalled. 'It was not a period when youthful Congressmen came to Washington to tear up the pea patch. So I followed that advice, I served my district, did my homework and didn't make a lot of speeches in the House.'[1]

In his early weeks on Capitol Hill, Nixon concentrated on serving his constituents. He made a point of answering every incoming letter from the 12th District by the next mail and of returning all telephone calls on the same day. Frequently this practice required him to stay late in his office, making good use of the three-hour time difference between Washington and California. He also pioneered *Under the Capitol Dome,* one of the first congressional newsletters to an electorate. His attention to these constituency chores was, however, secondary to the political finesse Nixon displayed when it came to ingratiating himself with the Republican leadership of the historic 80th Congress. Swept back into power after fourteen years of Democrat majorities, the GOP bosses were searching for talent to spearhead their long-awaited counter-revolution against New Deal legislation. Nixon was soon identified as a comer with all the right credentials. He had youth, debating skills, legal qualifications and sound conservative views. He also had his own home-grown supporters club in the shape of The Chowder and Marching Society, a group of fifteen junior Republican Congressmen who met over supper on Wednesday evenings for strategy discussions and mutual lobbying. Nixon's role as a co-founder and moving spirit in this small power bloc bore more than a passing resemblance to his activities with the Orthogonians of Whittier College sixteen years earlier.

Although it was agreeable to be well liked by his contemporaries, it was much more important for Nixon to be well seen by his elders. He was helped towards this goal by letters of recommendation from Herman Perry and other influential Californians to the House Speaker, Joe Martin, who soon became Nixon's political patron. Martin selected him during his first seven months as a Congressman for plum assignments on three high-profile committees. Education and Labor gave him his basic expertise in US domestic legislation; the House Committee on Un-American Activities took him into the spotlight of the anti-Communist controversy; and the Herter Committee enabled him to gain his first experience in foreign affairs.

Nixon had lobbied hard for the junior Republican seat on the Education and Labor Committee, anticipating that reform of the labour laws would become the hottest item on the national political agenda. He was right. No other single problem, including rationing, inflation, anti-Communism or relations with the Soviet Union, was as divisive an issue in 1947 as sorting out the labour unions.

Feeling was building up in the country that the New Deal's National Labor Relations Act (the Wagner Act) had granted the unions too many powers and privileges, which were steadily being abused. Responding to this pressure, the newly elected Republican majority in Congress determined to end these excesses by outlawing the closed shop and creating a new legislative framework for the rights of organised labour. The task of reform was given to the Education and Labor Committee, which held extensive hearings and drafted the Taft-Hartley Bill. This was the most controversial legislation of the Truman era, denounced by its opponents for opening the door to slave labour and lauded by its supporters as the harbinger of a new dawn in harmonious industrial relations. So long and fiercely did the fires of partisanship rage around Taft-Hartley that, for the next two decades, a Congressman or Senator's vote on the bill was regarded as the litmus test of whether he was pro or anti organised labour.

Nixon had secured his membership of the Education and Labor Committee on the expectation that he would be staunchly conservative, but when it came to the legislative details of Taft-Hartley, he displayed an enlightened centrism. There was too much of the son of Frank Nixon in him to start voting with the Republican hawks for punitive curbs on the legitimate rights of union members. Yet he was hostile to the New Deal legislation, which he felt was discriminating both to the public interest and to the individual interests of workers. Early in the Taft-Hartley hearings, Nixon achieved national press coverage when he travelled to Scranton, Pennsylvania on a fact-finding visit to coal miners and their families. He claimed, on the strength of this one-man, grass-roots survey, that what the American worker really wanted was freedom from union domination and the opportunity to avoid having to obey the union bosses' orders to strike. As he reported back to the Committee: 'We must never forget that the man who suffers most from strikes is not the employer or the consumer but the man who is forced to go on strike—the member of the union himself. I am confident that we will find a great deal of support among union members for a sane, fair, workable national labor policy which will reduce industrial strife to a minimum.'[2]

Nixon made a more important contribution to Taft-Hartley than his junior freshman status would normally have permitted. Making the most of his legalistic skill at drafting amendments, he was able to ensure that the Bill incorporated his moderate views. The legislation reached its final stages in the House amidst bitter opposition on the floor from the Democratic minority and angry demonstrations on the streets from organised labour. In an eloquent speech, Nixon compared the Bill to Magna Carta. Conjuring up the image of King John at Runnymede, he declared that Congress was passing a comparable 'Bill of Rights' destined to reduce the power of 'the barons of organized labor'.[3] Even if his English history was the wrong way round, Nixon was right to see the Taft-Hartley Bill as a watershed. Its main provisions outlawed the closed shop, prohibited secondary picketing, and established an eighty-day cooling off period, ushering in a period of relative tranquillity in American industrial relations. Once the Bill had passed by 308 votes to 107, Nixon entered his own analysis of the legislation in the Congressional Record. Thousands of copies of this cogent summary, entitled 'The Truth about the New Labor Law', were reprinted and widely distributed by Republican Congressmen as a standard defence of the Act. Nixon had made his first mark.

It was as the two most junior members of the Education and Labor Committee that Richard M. Nixon and John F. Kennedy met for the first time. Their later relationship has been immortalised in Kennedy's epithet on his rival in the presidential election of 1960, 'No class'.[4] But in 1947, a more accurate description (to Kennedy's disadvantage) would have been 'No competition'. Among their peers in the 80th Congress, the thirty-four-year-old Nixon was seen as the comer—a hard worker, a team player, and an effective speaker. By contrast, the twenty-nine-year-old Kennedy was regarded as a lightweight with a squeaky Boston twang who owed his Massachusetts seat in the House to his father's money. Notorious for his philandering and conspicuous for his unexplained absences, he was easy to underestimate. Nixon, however, did not make this mistake. From their early encounters on the Committee, he quickly came to appreciate Kennedy's considerable qualities as an intelligent and charismatic political operator. 'We sat at opposite sides of that Committee like a pair of unmatched bookends', recalled Nixon.

> He had drawn the last straw on the Democratic side and I drew the last straw for the Republicans. So, in the hearings, by the time the questioning came to us, virtually all the good questions had been asked. But we were both pretty sharp and he would come up with some good questions, and I usually did and, consequently, we'd get together in our offices from time to time and discuss how we could do well the next hearing around. Of course, we differed on that Act. He, coming from a heavily pro-labor district, voted against Taft-Hartley…but we had other things in common. He was very intelligent. However, I sensed that he was very shy, frankly as I was. I rather thought we were alike in that respect. We were very different in many ways, but he had a very great sense of privacy and he concealed his emotions. I think that's one of the reasons perhaps we hit it off rather well. I remember one night, for example, that Eunice Kennedy, his older sister who was not married then, had a dinner at her house. He was there and I was there and we talked far, far into the night, mainly about foreign policy where Kennedy and I saw the world pretty much alike. He was anti-Communist. I was anti-Communist. He was for foreign aid under proper circumstances, as I was. He was for reciprocal trade, and I was. Yes, we had a lot of things in common.[5]

The early Nixon–Kennedy collaboration extended to making arrangements for the first Nixon–Kennedy debate. This took place not, as is widely believed, during the 1960 presidential election campaign before an audience of 70 million television viewers, but on 1 April 1947 at McKeesport, Pennsylvania, in front of 150 small businessmen. As a personal favour to the local congressman, who had been asked by his chamber of commerce to organise a debate on Taft-Hartley,

Kennedy and Nixon travelled to northern Pennsylvania and spent three hours arguing the political positions on the Bill they had so often rehearsed at the Education and Labor Committee. Nixon remembered the debate as 'very friendly and gentlemanly',[6] and believed that he had the better of the evening largely because the McKeesport Chamber of Commerce audience contained few, if any, blue-collar workers or trade unionists. After the debate the two Congressmen travelled back to Washington on the night train, sharing a sleeping compartment. As Nixon recalled:

> We drew for who got the upper berth and who got the lower berth and I won—one of the few times I did against him! I took the lower berth, but it didn't make a lot of difference because all night long we talked about our experiences in the past, but particularly about the world, and where we were going—all that sort of thing. I recall telling him about my having been stationed at Vella Lavella and we found that his PT boat had put in there at the same time and we reminisced about whether we might have met on that occasion. We each assumed we did.

Although Nixon and Kennedy were never intimate, these and many other anecdotes suggest that as young politicians they had a far better relationship than later accounts have assumed. Nixon's private archives for the 1947–60 period contain two books inscribed 'To Dick from his friend John F. Kennedy';* several friendly notes; and an invitation to Kennedy's wedding to Jacqueline Lee Bouvier. There were other indications of more personal trust. In August 1947, when Nixon was departing with the Herter Committee to Europe, Kennedy apparently thought his Californian colleague might be glad of some female company in Paris. So he supplied Nixon with the telephone numbers of three suitable young ladies in that city, one of which was the number of his sister. 'I don't think Mr. Nixon even took the numbers away with him. He was far too embarrassed', recalled his secretary, Dorothy Cox.[7]

By the time Nixon was running for the Senate in 1950, Kennedy evidently had even more confidence in his future rival, for he personally delivered a $1,000 campaign contribution from his father Joseph P. Kennedy to help Nixon in his race against Helen Gahagan Douglas. It was unusual, to say the least, for a Democratic Congressman to act as the delivery man of family funds designed to bring

---

* The books were *Profiles in Courage* and *Why England Slept*.

about the defeat of a Democratic senatorial candidate, yet the early Nixon–Kennedy relationship apparently took these unconventional arrangements in their stride.

A later incident which gives an insight into Nixon's feelings about the relationship took place in November 1954. Kennedy, by this time the thirty-seven-year-old junior Senator from Massachusetts, was in Bethesda Naval Hospital recovering from a perilous spinal fusion operation. Nixon, who two years earlier had been elected Vice President, came to the hospital with the intention of making a brief visit to cheer up the patient. By chance he arrived soon after Kennedy had taken a dramatic change for the worse. Severe postoperative complications had developed, leading to adrenal failure. Kennedy was believed to be dying. His family were summoned and a priest was rushed in to administer the last rites. Nixon witnessed part of this drama. When he came out of the hospital he was emotionally shattered. He slumped into his car alongside his Secret Service agent Rex Scouten, saying over and over again through his tears, 'That poor young man is going to die. Poor brave Jack is going to die. Oh God, don't let him die!'[8]

A second hospital visit also produced an effusive letter from Jacqueline Kennedy. 'If you could only know the load you took off his mind', she wrote. 'He has been feeling so much better since then and I can never thank you enough for being so kind and generous and thoughtful...I don't think there is anyone in the world he thinks more highly of than he does you...and this is just another proof of how incredible you are.'[9]

A further example of Nixon's kindness to Kennedy in the aftermath of his illness was that he offered to ease his convalescence by allowing him to share the vice-presidential office suite adjacent to the floor of the Senate, thus saving him from having to rush all the way from his senatorial office every time a vote was called. 'When you return, I want you to know that my formal office will be available for you to use anytime you have to stay near the Floor', Nixon wrote to Kennedy in February 1955. 'I think you will find it very convenient to handle your appointments or any other business which you have to take care of when you find it necessary to attend a session.'[10]

These exchanges suggest that the Nixon–Kennedy relationship in the 1950s was warmer than was generally appreciated before it chilled into the intense rivalry of the 1960 presidential campaign. In the 1940s, however, it would have seemed fanciful to suggest that Kennedy would ever be a serious competitor against Nixon for high office. During their early years together in Washington there was no contest as to which of the two future Presidents was the better

Congressman. The contrast between them could be compared to Hogarth's etchings of the idle and industrious apprentices. Kennedy, for all his natural advantages, was seen as a dilettante. Nixon, despite his rough edges, was regarded as a diligent parliamentarian.

Nixon's growing reputation for diligence was responsible for his next two appointments—to the House Committee on Un-American Activities (always known by the acronym HUAC) and to the Herter Committee on Foreign Aid. It was unusual in those days for a freshman to be assigned to more than one congressional committee. Nixon had plenty to do on Education and Labor and it was therefore surprising when, in February, the Speaker, Joe Martin, asked him to take a seat on HUAC as well. Far from being pleased by this invitation, however, Nixon fussed and fretted before reaching a decision.

II. HUAC AND THE MAIDEN SPEECH

HUAC had an appalling record. Originally established in 1938 to guard against Nazi infiltration and more generalised foreign subversion, it had deteriorated into a refuge for congressional primitives whose overweening desire to catch headlines gave them too many Red-baiting prejudices and too few scruples about smearing the reputation of innocent witnesses. The prospects for improving HUAC's reputation in the new session of Congress were poor, for its surviving members were a motley collection of unsound mediocrities and uncontrollable bigots. They included such characters as 'Lightnin' John Rankin of Mississippi, who had denounced the integration of Black soldiers in the US Army for being the cause of minor military reverses during the Second World War; John Wood of Georgia, a prominent member of the Ku Klux Klan, who had called for an inquiry into the possibility of subversive links between the Kremlin and the manufacturers of 'Kreml' hair tonic; and the Chairman, J. Parnell Thomas of New Jersey, an erratic exhibitionist whose future plans for the Committee included transparent publicity stunts such as an investigation into the Communist leanings of Hollywood film stars. It was hardly surprising that for days after receiving Speaker Martin's invitation, Nixon was to be found pacing up and down his office, asking colleagues whether they thought HUAC was the political kiss of death.[11]

Although Nixon had good cause to fear being tarnished by an association with HUAC's old guard, his nose for an emerging political issue scented an opportunity which he knew should not be rejected out of hand. Nixon realised that Middle America was becoming frightened by the deepening chill of the Cold

War and by the mounting evidence of foreign subversion. These anxieties were present long before the notorious Senator Joseph McCarthy burst onto the scene with such venom in 1950. Events in the mid-1940s had provided several signals indicating that a major Soviet programme of espionage and infiltration was being pursued throughout the West.

In February 1946 the Canadian Government arrested a network of twenty-two people charged with illegally passing information to Soviet agents. The existence of this spy ring had been revealed by Igor Gouzenko, a cipher clerk working at the Russian Embassy in Ottawa who defected with a mass of incriminating files which conclusively proved the existence of a massive espionage structure in the West. Gouzenko's information on the activities of the KGB and other Soviet intelligence organisations led either directly or indirectly to the arrest and subsequent conviction of eleven Communist agents in the United States and many more overseas. President Harry S. Truman was disturbed both by advice he received from the FBI and by the outside pressures of public opinion. In early 1947 he issued Executive Order 9835, which required every federal government employee to be positively vetted.

Against this background of rising national concern on the anti-Communist issue, Nixon could see that a responsible new member of HUAC might be able to capture favourable media attention, and perhaps some glittering political prizes. So when Speaker Martin pressed him to act as a new broom on HUAC, telling him 'We need a young lawyer on that committee to smarten it up',[12] Nixon overcame his doubts and accepted the assignment.

Nixon's first day on the Committee, 6 February 1947, brought him into startling contact with his first Soviet agent. Gerhard Eisler was an Austrian-born professional Communist revolutionary who had been trained by the Soviet Secret Police, the OGPU, at the Lenin Institute in Moscow. He had been under investigation by the FBI and HUAC for some months, suspected of having been the controller of undercover agents and the principal link between the Comintern and the Communist Party of the USA. The most damaging testimony against Eisler came from his sister, Ruth Fischer, who had long ago renounced her previous loyalties to the Communist Party of Austria. After emigrating to the USA she became a Harvard academic and author of the acclaimed work, *Stalin and German Communism*.[13] Fischer, who was also a HUAC witness on the same day, denounced her brother as a spy and dangerous terrorist, giving the Committee details of the sabotage and subversion operations he had carried out on behalf of his Soviet masters in Germany, China and Spain. When Gerhard Eisler himself was called to give evidence, pandemonium broke out when he refused to take the stand unless he was first permitted to make an opening statement. The Chairman, J. Parnell Thomas, agreed to the statement but insisted that Eisler must take the oath and answer questions first. Eisler erupted with an angry declaration that he was a political prisoner who would do no such thing. A screaming match between Eisler and Chairman Thomas ensued, ending after fifteen minutes with the witness being cited for contempt of Congress and taken away by immigration officers, who were already detaining him for passport fraud. Some weeks later Eisler jumped bail and fled to East Germany, where he was given a hero's welcome and a professorship at the University of Leipzig.

Nixon was astonished by the Fischer–Eisler performances at HUAC, saying later, 'This was the first time I had brought home to me the character of the Communist Party and the threat which it presented to the country. It was the beginning of my education in this field.'[14] Such an initiation to HUAC strengthened Nixon's instinctive feeling that concern about Communist subversion would become a big issue. He therefore jettisoned his plans to make his maiden speech on labour relations. Instead, his first speech on the floor of the House introduced a motion to declare Eisler in contempt of Congress for his refusal to testify before HUAC.

Nixon was called to speak on 18 February 1947, when the House of Representatives was full. He made the most of his opportunity, beginning in a low key by examining the view that Eisler might be 'a political prisoner, a harmless refugee whom this Committee is persecuting because of his political belief', then going through the evidence of Eisler's 'criminal acts against the United States' and ending up denouncing him as 'an arrogant, defiant, enemy of our government'.[15]

A maiden speech to a packed national legislature is a formidable test for any politician. Success in this perilous field is rare. It requires a skilful tightrope walk ideally combining the becoming modesty of a parliamentary virgin with tantalising glimpses of expertise and hints of a more flamboyant taste for high political adventure. Nixon evidently steered this course skilfully, having devoted several days of intensive preparation to his performance. *Newsweek* reported that his eleven-minute speech was 'deeply impressive', delivered 'in calm measured tones and with an intense sincerity' and with 'a quality of steel behind the voice'.[16] He was off to a good start, with the House voting to accept his motion with only one vote against it. The sole dissenter, who was to become a symbolic bogeyman in Nixon's election to the Senate three years later, was Congressman Vito Marcantonio of New York.

During his first few months on HUAC, Nixon played a cautious role. He took part in the unedifying hearings on Communist influence in Hollywood, but was noticeably more circumspect than his other colleagues, for the record does not reveal a single instance of scaremongering, name-calling or exaggeration by him. When it came to the hearings on a bill to outlaw the Communist Party, Nixon was a realist.

He opposed making the CP illegal, insisting that such legislation would merely drive the activists underground. It was his advocacy that turned the Committee around to a surprise 5–3 majority in favour of rejecting the bill. Having thus inflicted a defeat on the right wingers, he initiated a compromise of his own. Working in harness with Congressman Karl Mundt of South Dakota, Nixon prepared the first piece of legislation ever to emerge from HUAC. The Mundt–Nixon Bill was intended to bring the CP out into the open, providing for the registration of all CP members, and requiring a statement of the source of all printed or broadcast materials issued by acknowledged Communist Front organisations. Introducing this Bill, Nixon said, 'There is too much loose talk and confusion on the Communist issue. By passing this Bill the Congress of the United States will go on record as to just what is subversive about Communism in the United States... It will once and for all spike many of the loose charges about organizations being Communist Fronts because they happen to advocate some of the same policies which the Communists support.'[17]

The Mundt–Nixon Bill passed the House by a vote of 319–58. Although it died a death of filibustering in the Senate, it did much to enhance the reputation of its principal author, and to revive the fortunes of HUAC. In what is generally agreed to be the most scholarly study of HUAC in this period, Dr. Robert K. Carr, Dartmouth Professor of law and political science, concluded: 'It is not hard to overpraise Nixon, for he brought to the Committee enthusiasm, a willingness to work hard, ability as a lawyer and a reasonable detachment and sense of fairness, qualities that have been rare among Committee members.'[18]

Published in 1951, before Nixon emerged as a vice-presidential candidate, before he entered the demonology of the liberal establishment, and before his early political career became the subject of so much revisionism, Carr's view is likely to have greater objectivity than later commentators' views. Nixon was able to inject into the Committee a modicum of sanity and moderation, something it had lacked before, and would lose forever, under the influence of McCarthyism.

In his work on HUAC, Nixon acted as a bridge builder between the prejudices of the Republican right and common sense political realism. Even the

Committee's 'good ole boys' from the Deep South felt that they had some rapport with Nixon, for he was adroit in persuading his colleagues to avoid some of the excesses and absurdities that had occurred on HUAC in previous sessions of Congress. A close analysis of the record suggests that Nixon sometimes used the voice of a conservative yet always retained the mind of a centrist. It was a technique which was to serve him well in his much later efforts to heal wounds in the Republican Party at a national level.

III. THE HERTER COMMITTEE

One of the first foreign policy issues to confront the young Congressman Nixon was the controversy over foreign aid to Greece and Turkey. This was a troublesome question for many Republicans, whose isolationist-minded constituents were suspicious of President Truman's call for massive military and economic assistance to these beleaguered countries. As part of the lobbying exercise for his policy, Truman invited selected Congressmen to the White House and Nixon's turn came on 2 July 1947. It was his first visit to the Oval Office, which he noted was 'a big pleasant room...with no gadgets'. Nixon, whose relationship with Truman was soon to become turbulent, was on that day impressed by the President's 'hominess, democratic attitude, and sincerity'.[19] He was also sympathetic to the President's appeal for bipartisan co-operation on the issue of European rehabilitation. His researches fifteen years earlier in the Whittier College library, preparing for student debates on foreign aid, had taught him that an internationalist approach could well be in the best long-term interest of the United States, so in spite of some criticism from his supporters back in the 12th District, Nixon endorsed the Truman doctrine and voted for the Greek and Turkish aid programme.

Four weeks after his meeting with the President, Nixon was 'the most surprised and pleased person in Washington',[20] when on Monday 30 July he picked up his morning newspaper and read that he had been selected by Speaker Joe Martin to be one of the nineteen members of a select committee headed by Congressman Christian Herter of Massachusetts. The Committee's task was to visit Europe and report on the proposals for the massive aid plan which had been put forward by the Secretary of State, George C. Marshall, in a commencement address at Harvard in June. At the time of this announcement, reactions to the Marshall Plan were mixed and it was by no means a foregone conclusion that Congress would support these far-sighted proposals with the massive funding they required. The Herter Committee was required to make its report to the

House before the crucial vote was taken, thus casting the members of the Committee in an exceptionally influential role on one of the most fateful decisions of the twentieth century.

With so much at stake for the future of Europe, the Congressmen chosen to serve on Herter were a handpicked yet representative élite. Speaker Martin had tried to select a team which would be seen as a cross-section of the House, but according to the Washington columnists, Joseph and Stewart Alsop, he had also avoided 'good time Charlies, professional baby kissers, or incorrigible victims of the terrible oratory habit ... he wanted only men who would work'.[21]

The Committee consisted of eleven Republicans and eight Democrats, representing fifteen different committees and covering every part of the political spectrum from dewy-eyed internationalism to hard-nosed isolationism. Nixon was one of only two freshmen on the Committee, and its youngest member.

Nixon's euphoria over his appointment was not entirely shared either by his wife or by his constituents. Pat, who was already suffering from pangs of loneliness caused by her husband's long hours in the Capitol, was distressed when she realised that she would be left alone with two-year-old Tricia for almost the whole six weeks of the summer vacation. From the 12th District, a group of Nixon's strongest supporters and financial contributors wrote him a letter warning that he would be subjected to 'a skillful orientation program by the State Department and to no less skillfully prepared European propaganda'. After attacking the whole concept of the Marshall Plan, the letter concluded with a pointed reminder that 1948 would be an election year and that it was Nixon's duty to get rid of all the hangover philosophies of the New Deal by securing the election of a Republican President. 'This can be done provided the Republican members of Congress are wise enough to refuse to be drawn into support of a dangerously unworkable and profoundly inflationary foreign policy and, provided further, that the Democrats do not succeed in so dividing our Party by bipartisan internationalism that there is no longer any way to tell who is a Republican.'[22]

Nixon did not escape from such pressures by crossing the Atlantic, for he soon discovered that some members of the Herter Committee were even more suspicious of the Marshall Plan than his California supporters. During the voyage to Europe on the *Queen Mary,* Nixon shared a cabin with Tom Jenkins, an Ohio Congressman of twenty-two years' seniority. Jenkins was one of the great characters of the House, a dyed-in-the-wool isolationist and supporter of the America First Movement who had even voted against the United States entering the war after Pearl Harbor. Nixon found it 'a real education to get to know this man who had been in Congress since I was twelve years old'.[23] The cabin-mates struck up a good relationship which survived their differences of opinion over the daily on-board briefings the Committee received from the then unknown State Department official, Charles Bohlen, and the eminent Harvard historian, Professor William Y. Elliott.*

In spite of the excellence of those briefings, Nixon, Jenkins and the other members of the Herter Committee were not prepared for the scenes which greeted them on their arrival in Europe. The contrast between the luxurious comfort of the *Queen Mary* and the desolation of the ruined docks and housing estates in bomb-ravaged Southampton was the first impression to be recorded in Nixon's voluminous notes. It was followed by an observation from his train journey to London: 'Railway right of way completely cut up into little gardens—people doing everything possible to feed themselves—making use of every available piece of ground.'

During the next six weeks of his travels all over the continent, Nixon set a pattern of reportage worthy of any professional journalist. His notebooks, card jottings and more formal summaries, dictated at the end of a day's events, tell a story full of poignant eye-witness details, feline observations of personalities, narrow statistical facts and broad judgemental conclusions. Reading through these materials nearly half a century later, they can be seen as the first overseas tutorial notes in the career of Nixon, the lifelong foreign affairs student.

On the British leg of the tour, Nixon and his colleagues had tea at Number 10 Downing Street with the Prime Minister, Clement Attlee, followed by a more substantive meeting with the Foreign Secretary, Ernest Bevin ('Falstaffian—tough—humorous—hand shakes as he talks—one eye out, but a CO—the balance wheel of the Labour Party', said Nixon's handwritten scribbles). Other encounters with top figures in the Labour Government, such as the Food Minister, John Strachey, and the Chancellor of the Exchequer, Sir Stafford Cripps, left Nixon with the feeling that the Government was getting tired and might not be willing to follow a sufficiently austere and radical programme which should combine longer hours at work in key export industries with added incentives for the workers. 'Labour Government will go out of power some time next Spring', he predicted.†

---

* Charles Eustis Bohlen (1904–74): acted as interpreter and adviser to President Roosevelt at the Tehran and Yalta Conferences, and to President Truman at the Potsdam Conference. Attended the San Francisco and Dumbarton Oaks Conferences. Ambassador to the Soviet Union (1953–7), the Philippines (1957–9) and Paris (1962–8). William Yandell Elliott (1896–1979): Professor of history and government at Harvard University and author of several books on political science. Staff director for the Herter Committee.

† Nixon was wrong. The Labour Government survived a General Election in 1950, finally losing to the Conservatives in 1951.

Away from the confines of Westminster and Whitehall, Nixon talked to dock workers, farmers and shopkeepers. He thought the British were exhausted by their diet ('worse off now from the standpoint of rations than they were before the war'), but that their spirit, their belief in individual freedom and their traditions would see them through. 'There is no chance the British will ever vote Communist regardless of how low their fortunes may sink', was his political overview.

Nixon's emotions, which had only been superficially touched by his rather depressing impressions of Britain, were far more deeply stirred when he came face to face with the devastation of Germany. He toured the ruins of Munich, Dresden and Hamburg ('great gaunt skeletons') and was shaken by Berlin ('just block after block, mile after mile of charred desolation. It hardly seemed possible that three million people could still be living amidst the rubble, but there they were.') Soon he was focusing on the problems of disease and malnutrition. Amidst the rubble of Essen he broke away from the official party and went down to some cellars where he and another Congressman explored a rabbit warren of tiny, 9ft by 12ft underground caves, each one packed with six or more starving people, huddled together in appalling conditions. Nixon knew from his own family experiences that many of the children coughing noisily in these damp conditions were likely to be suffering from tuberculosis. He asked to visit the nearest children's hospital and was shown a shed full of 200 young TB patients ('They called it a hospital, but it was a great long barn with very little heat or light').

Then he asked what was being done to fight the malnutrition problems and was taken first to some children's soup kitchens and on to a miners' feeding station. As he recorded: 'We went to a mine in Essen in the middle of the afternoon and they happened to be handing out an incentive ration which would allow the miners to have additional strength to do the work essential to Germany's recovery. It consisted of a thin soup with no meat, with cucumbers thrown in on the top. I suppose that a hungry man could have eaten it... however, we noted that great numbers of them were not touching it. I walked up to a young, red-headed boy of fourteen who looked as if he could eat anything. I asked him why he was not eating his soup. He replied that he was going to save it and take it home that night so that members of his family would be able to water it down and spread it among them... in the soup kitchens we noted the same situation. Little tots of six, eight and ten were refusing to eat the rations they received and carefully took them home so that their mothers would be able to water it down and divide it among other members of the family.'

Nixon records many other incidents, such as his glimpse of German prisoners coming back from Russia ('walking skeletons of what they had been') and an approach made to him in the ruins of the Reichstag by 'small, thin-faced German boys attempting to sell us the medals their fathers had won during the war'. But the dominant political theme of his notes is the necessity of feeding the German workforce. Amidst complex statistical calculations of how much aid would be required to provide miners and factory workers with an adequate number of calories per day, Nixon concluded that getting food aid to the Germans was a moral and physical priority of the highest order.

The same necessity could be seen in at least three of the neighbouring war-ravaged countries he visited on forays from Germany. As he wrote on leaving Berlin for the last time: 'The simple unvarnished fact is that hunger is stalking over the continent of Europe and that the people simply do not have enough to eat which will enable them to do the hard work which is necessary to get the factories back into peacetime production capacity.' He concluded: 'There is marked hunger and malnutrition on a universal scale. This is the case even with the United States aid. Without United States aid, and if United States aid is discontinued this winter, there is no question but that thousands of Germans will die of starvation.'[24]

Although the humanitarian problems initially affected Nixon most deeply, he also showed an early capacity for making shrewd long-term political judgements on the countries he visited. In Paris he diagnosed that the French people were 'suffering virtually from a national nervous breakdown'; and that de Gaulle would eventually come to power,* although in the short term 'he has no program for France and too often acts upon impulse'. Nixon also noted, with underlining, a French deputy's observation that de Gaulle 'in political matters thinks he has a direct telephone line with God'.

In France, Italy and Greece, Nixon made a point of meeting with Communist leaders at both national and local levels, despite State Department objections that he was wasting the Committee's time. Nixon nevertheless persisted with such appointments because he was determined to understand the thinking and motivation of CP members. He gained useful insights into their philosophy from a series of meetings with Italian Communist leaders, such as Giuseppe Di Vittorio, the boss of the major trades unions; Amadeo Terricini, the President of the Chamber of Deputies; and Palmiro Togliatti, the CP Chairman. After a fierce personal debate with Di Vittorio in which the Italian savaged US foreign policy, Nixon was struck by the fact that his opponent had used phrases and political expressions that were virtually identical to those spoken to him by the Communist leader of

---

* De Gaulle was elected President in 1958 after a decade in retirement.

the miners' union in Britain, Arthur Lewis Horner, and by provincial Communist union chiefs in France. After comparing his notes from these different encounters, Nixon wrote, 'This indicates definitely that Communists throughout the world owe their loyalty, not to the countries in which they live and reside, but to Russia.'[25]

Nixon and his subcommittee spent three weeks studying conditions in Italy, which he felt was 'a battleground...because the Communists have chosen this country as one of their most clever and well-financed operations against the forces of democracy'.[26]

One of the most dramatic moments of the trip occurred in Trieste on 17 September. Nixon looked out of his hotel window and saw a parade passing by. Five hundred marchers were singing the 'Internationale', waving red flags, and 'raising their hands in the clenched fist salute of Moscow. They were young, vigorous, and full of fight.'[27] He quickly found himself an Italian interpreter and followed the parade, which erupted into violence when a grenade was thrown to disperse a small gaggle of anti-Communist opponents who were attempting to block the road. A boy's head was blown off by the explosion and Nixon saw the headless torso pouring blood into the gutter as the crowd screamed and gesticulated. More bombs were thrown and fusillades of gunfire were exchanged between police and rioters. Nixon saw an elderly woman killed when she got in the way of a demonstrator fleeing from the police. ('He was one of the Communists...a big man running like a college fullback going through the line...he hit the old woman head on and knocked her halfway across the street against the curb where she lay motionless.'[28] By the end of the evening, five people had been killed and seventy-five wounded in the fighting. Nixon's eyewitness account of these events made a great impact when he reported to the full Committee, which agreed with his conclusion that 'what was happening in Trieste would soon be re-enacted throughout Western Europe unless America helped to restore stability and prosperity'.[29]

Nixon's subcommittee, chaired by his *Queen Mary* cabin-mate, Congressman Tom Jenkins, had so many excitements and covered so much territory that the rest of their Herter colleagues nicknamed them 'The Jenkins Raiders'. The 'Raiders' were cheered for ten minutes at an emotional performance of Puccini's *Tosca* at the reopening of La Scala Opera House in Milan, and booed by an angry crowd of mourners at a Communist funeral in Venice. They flew in a doorless C47 on a nerve-racking flight to a tiny airstrip in the Greek mountains where the Communist guerrillas were making regular attacks on village communities. The local mayor introduced the members of the subcommittee to a girl whose left breast had been cut off by terrorists because she had refused to betray her brother, who was an anti-Communist leader in the area. The Congressmen, including Nixon, were so moved by this story that they emptied their wallets in a whip-round for the victim.

At another flashpoint, the border area near Trieste, 2,000 Yugoslav troops threatened to invade at 3 a.m. while the Congressmen slept nearby. Lieutenant Oaks of the US Army and his small peacekeeping platoon of twelve men with two machine guns faced the aggressors resolutely, insisting that they would fight to the death in order to stop the invasion. The Yugoslavs backed down. Nixon arrived on the scene soon after to see for himself what had occurred. In notes he took in pencil immediately after this episode, he reflected on Lieutenant Oaks's courageous stand. His conclusion was one that would become the mainstay of his foreign policy thinking. 'One basic rule with Communists—never bluff unless you are prepared to carry through, because they will test you every time.'[30]

The Herter Committee was Nixon's first and perhaps most formative encounter with foreign policy. His unusual but disciplined style of work set a pattern he was to follow on many subsequent overseas missions. Nixon liked to start work early with a personal briefing from an embassy desk officer or specialist, and then to make his own schedule of one-on-one meetings. He learned to avoid embassy cocktail parties and dinners with members of the élite in a foreign capital. He placed high value on talks with political leaders, and was no less interested in establishing his own contacts with ordinary people at all levels of society. He would spend hours walking around shopping centres, residential areas and factories in order to talk directly to workers and their families. His notebooks are filled up with quotations from labourers, housewives, taxi drivers, nurses and stockbrokers. It was almost as though arrival on foreign soil transformed Nixon's solitary personality into a gregarious enthusiasm for dialogue with strangers.

This style provided Nixon with many moving experiences. In Europe, his emotions were seared by the horrific scenes he encountered. Like other hitherto hard-boiled Congressmen on the Committee, there were occasions when he was moved to tears and to giving away his own money, food or articles of clothing to the starving victims of the war. What was characteristic of Nixon, however, was that, powerful though they were, he always tempered his emotional reactions with his realism and intellect. He gathered feelings and impressions by day, and analysed them by night to draw from them their lessons for the future.

In 1947, it was obvious that Europe urgently needed humanitarian assistance. It was a starving continent, needing to be fed. Nixon saw that the Communists were exploiting the desperate conditions to advance their own interests. He had met Communist leaders face to face and was impressed, if concerned, by their determination and strength. It was a respect that Nixon would never lose. By comparison, he saw that the democratic leaders of Europe were weak, unable to resuscitate their countries and so secure their freedom. The United States could not itself defend Europe. Only by providing military protection and long-term aid, and allowing European leaders to decide for themselves how such aid should be used, could the US inspire the Europeans with the confidence that would allow freedom and democracy to take root. He realised further that by doing what was good for European prosperity and independence, the US would be contributing most to its own security. In helping others, it would be helping itself. He saw that the United States had a mission that was both humanitarian and strategic.

Nixon had departed for Europe with the sirens of isolationism ringing in his ears, urging America to come home, luring it, he now believed, towards the rocks. If the isolationists won control of American foreign policy, not only would Europe suffer, but the US would abandon its responsibilities and betray its own security. The US could only perform its mission if it played a truly internationalist role, which was both interested and beneficent and which recognised a community of international interests.

In later years, Nixon was fond of quoting from his book *Six Crises*: 'A man who has never lost himself in a cause bigger than himself has missed one of life's mountaintop experiences. Only in losing himself does he find himself.'[31]

In Europe, in 1947, Nixon found a cause much greater than himself which he has pursued ever since: the cause of keeping the world's peace through internationalist American leadership.

IV. RE-ELECTED UNOPPOSED

Back in America after his travels, Nixon set about securing the massive aid which he and his colleagues on the Herter Committee had unanimously agreed was necessary to save Europe from the twin evils of starvation and Communism. In the 12th District, polls showed that his constituents were still resolutely opposed to the Marshall Plan by a margin of 3:1. Nixon realised that he had arrived at that classic politician's crossroads, so well described by Edmund Burke in his address to the electors of Bristol, when he had to decide whether to follow the dictates of his own conscience or yield to the views of his electorate. Nixon did not hesitate, and set out on a speech-making campaign to explain his position. One initially sceptical constituent in those audiences was Hubert Perry: 'We were all against him at first, but he was so darn convincing and he made the scene in Europe come alive so vividly that by the time he'd finished most of us agreed with him and were right behind him all the way on the Marshall Plan vote.'[32] Perry's reactions were characteristic of the 12th District as a whole, for Nixon received almost universally favourable editorial endorsement from the local newspapers supporting his position on Herter. By December 1947, when the House of Representatives voted by 313 to 82 votes in favour of the Marshall Plan, polls showed that he was considerably more popular in the 12th District than he had been at the time of his victory over Jerry Voorhis.

Once the international excitements of the Herter Committee and the Marshall Plan votes were over, Nixon returned to the domestic work of HUAC and especially to the local affairs of the 12th District, for 1948 was the first year in which he would be seeking re-election. In fact, he had no need to worry about his chances, for his well-reported activities had given him the image of an unbeatable and non-partisan incumbent. The Democrats were so demoralised that they had difficulty in finding a candidate to put up against him. When it came to the primaries, Nixon cross-filed, in accordance with standard Californian practice. Unopposed in the Republican race, he ran in the June Democratic primary against the party's official nominee, an obscure thirty-one-year-old lawyer and one-time Voorhis aide, Stephen Zetterberg. Nixon trounced Zetterberg by 21, 411 votes to 16,808, a resounding victory which meant he was the unopposed candidate of both parties who could safely relax and forget about the formal congressional general election scheduled for November.

Although Nixon's first two years as a Congressman could hardly have been more successful, he had at the back of his mind a nagging anxiety about his future. The 80th Congress had been unusual, particularly for Nixon, who had been offered so many opportunities although still in his first term. The huge GOP majority; the determination to eliminate the New Deal; the appetite for counter-revolutionary legislation; the creation of new committees with specialist agendas; the adversarial relationship with the White House which had led to Truman calling it 'The Do Nothing Congress' (a perverse label because, in fact, it did so much to annoy the President); and the benevolent patronage of Speaker Martin; these were all one-off factors that had worked to Nixon's advantage. His fear was that such good times might end in the 81st or subsequent Congresses, and that he would find his talents suffocated by the seniority system that normally kept young legislators firmly in their places.

One close unofficial aide to Nixon in this period was Pat Hillings, a twenty-two-year-old USC law graduate and Chairman of the Young Republicans in Los Angeles County, who gave up much of his spare time to act as an unpaid Californian assistant to 'The Boss', as Nixon's staff were beginning to call him. Hillings, who eventually succeeded Nixon as the Republican Congressman for the 12th

District, often listened to Nixon ruminating on his future at this time and concluded: 'Dick was getting restless and impatient even at this early stage. He knew it could take years and years to go through the seniority system in the House. In his mind he had decided to move either up or out. He was quite ready to leave Congress and go into law practice, but what he was really looking for was a big play or a big gamble that would move him up into the Senate as soon as possible.'[33]

The big play that came Nixon's way was the Hiss case.

NINE

THE HISS CASE

I. THE BEGINNING OF A CAUSE CÉLÈBRE

The Hiss case was a five-star political and espionage thriller which transformed the career of Congressman Richard Nixon. In the eyes of his Republican supporters he emerged from it as a national hero, a spycatcher extraordinary, and a fearless exposer of a White House cover-up. These reputations were soon to catapult him into the Senate and the Vice Presidency. Yet his success was a two-edged sword, for the Hiss case also transformed Nixon into a *bête noire* of the liberal establishment, thus triggering a profound polarisation of opinion on his character. In the aftermath of the drama it would be hard to judge which was the more astonishing: the impact of the Hiss case on Nixon's career, or the story of his role in the case itself.

The story began, so far as Nixon was concerned, on 31 July 1948 when HUAC heard testimony from Elizabeth Bentley, dubbed by the press 'The Red Spy Queen'. She told the Committee that she had been a courier for a Communist spy ring inside the US Government, and that she had reported these facts to Department of Justice officials who had apparently taken no action. She identified several past and present government officials as Communist agents, the best known of whom was Harry Dexter White,* an assistant secretary of the Treasury in the Roosevelt and Truman administrations.

Various members of HUAC, with Nixon to the fore, immediately attacked the Department of Justice for its inactivity, but since Bentley's evidence was largely hearsay, the criticism could not be sustained without further corroboration. Nixon was the leader of the HUAC members who instructed the Committee's Chief Investigator, Robert Stripling, to start an immediate search for witnesses who could support Bentley's story. Stripling found and served a subpoena on Whittaker Chambers, a former member of the Communist underground who had since renounced the Communist Party and had become a senior editor of *Time* magazine.

Nixon's first impressions of Whittaker Chambers when he took the stand before the Committee on 3 August were uncomplimentary: 'I could hardly believe that this was our witness…he was probably the most unkempt and dishevelled person I had ever seen. Everything about him seemed to be wrinkled and unpressed. It would be hard to imagine a more unimpressive or unprepossessing figure than Chambers made on that hot August morning.'[1]

Mumbling in an almost inaudible voice (the microphone had broken down) Chambers told the story of his personal road to Damascus. With a tearful and almost mystical fervour, he spoke of how he had come to hate Communism. Confessing to having been the dues collector for a Communist group whose primary objective was to infiltrate the Government, he corroborated Bentley's story by identifying six previously named, low-level Government employees as members of his network. The surprise of the day came when Chambers added a new and much more senior name, that of Alger Hiss.

Alger Hiss was such a well-known figure in the New Deal foreign policy élite that this totally unexpected allegation against him seemed at first hearing to be another example of a HUAC session soaring into the stratosphere of unreliable rumour. Members of the Committee did not immediately seize on the charge for most of them felt that Chambers was cutting such a poor figure as a witness. Although the press picked up the story the next day with headlines such as '*TIME* EDITOR CHARGES CARNEGIE ENDOWMENT HEAD WAS

---

* Harry Dexter White (1892–1948) led the American delegation to the 1944 Bretton Woods Conference which set up the international monetary system after the Second World War, creating the International Monetary Fund and the World Bank. White became the first director of the IMF in 1946. It was White's sudden death from a heart attack, days after he testified to HUAC in August 1948, that saved him from facing further investigation.

SOVIET AGENT',[2] the matter might well have died a natural death if Hiss had issued a swift denial and left it that.

Instead, it was Hiss himself who set in motion the events that led to his downfall. With what in hindsight seems foolhardy daring, he sent a telegram to HUAC asking for an opportunity to come before the Committee and testify under oath. His request was granted and on 5 August he took the stand. Had it not been for Nixon, his daring might have paid off.

The contrast between Hiss and Chambers as witnesses could not have been more striking or more to Hiss's advantage. Alger Hiss symbolised all that was best and brightest in the upper-class, liberal establishment of the New Deal era. On the surface, his career was a story of steadily upward progressions from golden youth to middle-age *gravitas* and statesmanship. 'No lark more blithe than he',[3] had been the citation in his high school yearbook, and Hiss had rapidly fulfilled his early promise with milestones such as President of the Student Council at Johns Hopkins University in Baltimore; Editor of the *Harvard Law Review* at the Harvard Law School from which he graduated *summa cum laude*; and Clerk to Supreme Court Justice Oliver Wendell Holmes. After four years practising with private law firms in Boston and New York, Hiss was attracted to Washington by the challenge of the New Deal and in 1933 he joined the Agricultural Adjustment Administration.

After a stint as counsel on a Senate committee investigating the munitions industry, he worked in the Solicitor General's office, before finding his *métier* in the State Department. He quickly rose to become the executive assistant to the Assistant Secretary of State, and was later appointed Director of the Office of Special Political Affairs. While at the State Department, he acted as one of Roosevelt's advisers at the Yalta Conference, responsible for drafting the President's principal position paper prior to that historic summit.

After Yalta, Hiss made such a valuable contribution to the early international planning meetings for the setting up of the United Nations that, on President Roosevelt's personal instructions, he was appointed temporary Secretary General of the San Francisco Conference at which the UN Charter was drafted. He was widely tipped, with Soviet support, for the post of permanent UN Secretary General. When he did not get that appointment he left the State Department to become President of the Carnegie Endowment for International Peace, a prestigious foundation whose Chairman was John Foster Dulles. It seemed a fitting culmination for such an illustrious career.

As he took the witness stand on 5 August, Hiss cut an impressive figure. Tall and handsome with youthful looks that belied his forty-four years, he gave a performance that was persuasive, patrician, and supremely confident. He read from a text which he had prepared with the help of Dean Acheson, who was then acting Secretary of State. He categorically denied all of Chambers' charges. He insisted that he had never known or met Chambers. When one Congressman pointed out that Chambers had been testifying under oath when he said he knew Hiss, Hiss retorted 'I also know that I am testifying under those same laws to the direct contrary.'[4]

Hiss's testimony ended in a burst of applause from the spectators, many of whom were his personal friends. He also won congratulatory handshakes from several members of HUAC and from journalists on the press bench. Outside the committee room, the tide was running strongly in his favour. While Hiss was on the stand, President Truman had given a White House press conference in which he denounced HUAC's activities as a 'red herring' and said that the hearings were doing 'irreparable harm to certain persons, seriously impairing the morale of federal employees and undermining public confidence in the Government'.[5] He also issued a directive which prohibited executive agencies from giving information concerning a federal employee's loyalty to congressional committees. This compelled the Committee to carry out its own independent investigation without co-operation from the FBI and departmental security offices, which made its task immeasurably harder and pitted it against the Administration.

The media seemed to take their line from the President, judging from the hostile tone of reporters' questions. The Committee was flooded with telegrams and messages of support for Hiss from a number of influential people, including Mrs. Eleanor Roosevelt, the Dean of the Stanford Law School, several Senators, and the acting Secretary of State.

All this pressure threw the Committee into a panic by the time they reassembled after the lunch interval. With an election in the offing, none of the Congressmen wanted to undergo an assault from the President and the press who were both already highly critical of HUAC's past performance. They felt they were vulnerable for having allowed Chambers to give such damaging testimony against Hiss without first having verified his story. Confusion reigned. Karl Mundt said that HUAC must quickly find some other issue to divert attention from the Hiss–Chambers affair. Edward Hebert argued that the Committee should wash its hands of the case completely and turn it over to the Attorney General to discover who was telling the truth. 'We've been had. We're ruined,' was the cry of one Congressman reflecting the prevailing view, which was to abandon the whole case that very afternoon.[6]

It was in the midst of all this defeatism that Nixon made his fateful intervention. He alone took the high ground. He supported a strategy of hanging tough and continuing the investigation. He appealed to his fellow Congressmen to take the Hiss case one further stage in the interests of rescuing their own reputations. Handing the investigation over to the Department of Justice would, he argued, 'be a public confession that we are incompetent and even reckless'.[7] Moreover, since Chambers had testified that he had reported his charges against Hiss to the authorities four times already without further official action, a fifth request from HUAC would be unlikely to cause them to pursue it fully. The Committee had started its inquiry. It should see it through to the end. With heads beginning to nod in agreement, Nixon emphasised the opportunity that had been presented to them. The testimonies of Hiss and Chambers were diametrically opposed. One must therefore be lying. HUAC had an obligation to expose the liar, and in so doing it would be carrying out the public duty it had been set up to perform. As Nixon described his reasoning:

> I argued that while it would be virtually impossible to prove that Hiss was or was not a Communist—for that would simply be his word against Chambers'—we should always be able to establish by corroborative testimony whether or not the two men had known each other. If Hiss were lying about not knowing Chambers, then he might also be lying about whether or not he was a Communist. And if that were the case the charges were so serious—in view of the vitally important and sensitive positions Hiss had held—that we had an obligation running to the very security of the nation to dig out the truth.[8]

Nixon's motivations for this argument have been much analysed. His gut instincts, his personal prejudices, and his keen powers of legalistic observation were central to his stand. But did he, as some historians have alleged, have an inside track of secret knowledge about Hiss's involvement in the Communist underground? Was Nixon playing his cards so confidently because they came from a stacked deck?

As far as his instincts were concerned, Nixon's first reaction was one of sympathy for the underdog. He felt that Chambers' poor presentation and shabby appearance were secondary to his transparent sincerity. Moreover, Nixon had an intuitive mistrust of the man from Harvard who was too smooth, too well connected and too clever by half. As he recalled his first impressions: 'Hiss was good looking, suave, sophisticated, Ivy League dressed, Ivy League manner. He was everything that an elegant Washington executive should be in the New Deal era... with his clipped words and his very professional way of answering questions, a very careful way.'[9]

In the lunch interval, Nixon discussed his distaste for Hiss with his secretary Dorothy Cox. She supported her boss's opinion. She has recalled thinking that Hiss was 'wonderfully handsome but untrustworthy'. She told Nixon, 'There is something about him that just doesn't ring true. He has such cold eyes.'[10]

The Committee's investigator, Robert Stripling, believed that at this early stage Nixon was motivated by instant personal antipathy for the witness. 'Nixon had set his hat for Hiss. It was a personal thing', Stripling said later. 'He was no more concerned whether Hiss was [a Communist] than a billy goat.'[11]

Whatever prejudices Nixon may have had, he reinforced them by focusing on a curious pattern of ambiguity in the testimony. He noticed that Hiss had never given a categoric and unequivocal denial to the suggestion that he knew Chambers. Every one of his answers had been qualified by such phrases as 'to the best of my recollection', or 'as far as I know'. When asked if he had ever met Chambers, Hiss stated with conviction '*the name* [author's italics] means absolutely nothing to me', admitting a little later that he 'would not want to take oath that I have never seen' Chambers without having first seen him in the flesh.[12]

The hedging by Hiss was barely perceptible but Nixon's experience as a courtroom lawyer had given him a nose for when a witness was lying, and he persuaded the other members of HUAC that this continual flow of careful qualification cast doubt on Hiss's truthfulness.

Turning to the arcane but intriguing question of whether Nixon's instincts about the testimony were fortified by a prior knowledge of Hiss's Communist connections, this 'stacked deck' theory depends on the view taken of a triangular relationship that came to exist between Nixon, an FBI agent named Ed Hummel, and a Catholic Priest, Father John Cronin.

HUAC was in fact a latecomer with its interest in Hiss. Several parts of the executive branch had been watching him with mounting concern for some time, especially the FBI. For Chambers had not been lying when he claimed to have briefed the authorities about Hiss's participation in the Communist underground. As early as September 1939, he had told Adolfe Berle, the Assistant Secretary of State in charge of security at the State Department, about an espionage network that had infiltrated the Government. He named Hiss as being among those involved. From that year onwards, Hiss had fallen under increasing suspicion. In

1940, French authorities had warned Ambassador William Bullitt that Hiss was a Soviet spy. In 1943, information from a Soviet defector to the American embassy in Paris had reinforced that warning.[13] In 1945, the evidence against Hiss was strengthened with the defection of Igor Gouzenko, a Soviet cipher clerk in Canada. He claimed that there was a Soviet spy in the State Department, whose description matched Hiss's. The information was thought important enough by Mackenzie King, the Canadian Prime Minister, for him to come in person to tell President Truman about this infiltration of the American Government. Gouzenko's claims were corroborated later that year when Elizabeth Bentley defected and gave the FBI information which suggested that Hiss was a Soviet agent.

As the evidence against Hiss built up, the Government's investigations of him intensified. He was first confronted by his State Department superiors in 1942 and apparently satisfied their questions. In 1945, the State Department's office of security wrote a report on Hiss which found the evidence against him to be inconclusive, but by 1946 the same office had changed its opinion and recommended that his employment with the State Department be terminated. Meanwhile, the FBI had been carrying out inquiries of its own. By December 1945, it had enough information to convince the Attorney General to authorise it to keep Hiss under surveillance and to tap his telephones. Clearly, well before the HUAC hearings in 1948, there was a lot of information within the Government which would have told anyone privy to it that Hiss was not telling the whole truth when he testified on 5 August.

One of those who knew about the information against Hiss was Father John Cronin, a respected Catholic academic who had made a study for the hierarchy of his church on the problems of domestic Communism. Cronin was aided in his research by information supplied to him by an FBI agent, Ed Hummel, who was working on the Hiss investigation.

There is no doubt that Nixon knew Cronin well, and that he later met Hummel and indirectly benefited from FBI leaks on the case. But the timing of these exchanges of information is crucial. According to Nixon, 'I did not meet Hummel or discuss the case with Cronin until *after* we had broken the case by getting Hiss to admit that he knew Chambers on August 17th and again on August 25th.'[14] He also stated, in *Six Crises*, that when Chambers testified, 'It was the first time I had ever heard of either Alger or Donald Hiss.'[15] In a 1990 interview with this author, Cronin gave qualified support to Nixon's claim. 'The stacked deck remark was unfair. Nixon might have read something about Hiss in my reports, I don't know whether he did or not, but we didn't discuss the case until after Hiss had made his public denial. From then on I worked with Nixon a lot and gave him everything I had on Hiss. He needed that help. He was very unsure of himself at the beginning.'[16]

Aside from the above statements, it seems inconceivable that if Nixon did possess information incriminating Hiss, he would have allowed Hiss's testimony on 5 August to go unchallenged. For by remaining silent he allowed Hiss to persuade the audience of his innocence, an impression it took twenty days of intensive investigation and questioning by Nixon to erase. To have held a stacked deck of cards and not to have played any of them at the critical moment on 5 August, either in public or in executive session with the Committee, seems improbable. The theory that at this stage he was running on an inside track of secret knowledge about Hiss does not appear convincing.

Despite Nixon's advocacy, HUAC very nearly decided not to pursue the case any further after Hiss's first appearance. Several members of the Committee were nervous and only came round reluctantly because they were convinced that they would have a better chance of preserving their own reputations if they could demonstrate that one or other of the two witnesses had been lying. Which one, most of them did not seem to care. Eventually the members of HUAC agreed to create a special subcommittee under Nixon's chairmanship to question Chambers further. Nixon therefore won his first battle of the Hiss case but he soon found that he had left himself in an exposed and vulnerable position.

II. IN HOT PURSUIT

Within hours of this decision, Nixon began to feel the heat. He had gone out on a limb in the face of fierce opposition from the President, the Administration, the press, and the vast majority of his colleagues in Congress.

The consensus believed that Chambers was lying, and that HUAC had discredited itself. Nixon, for the first time in his life, was under heavy and hostile bombardment from cartoons, editorials, hate mail and pejorative comments from congressional colleagues. However, far from wilting under the strain, Nixon not only stood firm but positively revelled under the pressure. As Dorothy Cox recalled, 'He was living on the exhilaration of it. You could see his adrenalin flowing. In spite of all the attacks, he seemed to love the challenge. He worked unbelievably hard, staying up in the office all through the night preparing himself.'[17]

On the morning of Saturday 7 August, Nixon's preparations began to bear fruit as the subcommittee consisting of himself, McDowell and Hebert, took evidence in a New York courthouse from Whittaker Chambers. Nixon had drawn up a list of all the kinds of things that one friend would be likely to know about another and his questions were aimed at draining Chambers' memory dry. The strategy worked, for Chambers poured out a flood of detailed and intimate recollections about Hiss in the 1930s.

Chambers said he had stayed on several occasions with Alger and Priscilla Hiss, sometimes for as long as a week. He described the three houses Hiss had lived in during the years of their friendship; his taste in food; his favourite lines from Shakespeare; the nicknames he and his wife used for each other; the location of the kennel where they would put their cocker spaniel when they went to the eastern shore of Maryland on holiday. He told them that Hiss had owned a Ford Roadster, which he had given to the Communist Party after he bought a new Plymouth. He remembered, in particular, that the Ford had hand-operated windscreen wipers—he had driven it himself one rainy night. Asked about hobbies, Chambers said that Hiss was a keen birdwatcher and that he remembered Hiss's excitement one morning when, out on the Potomac, he had seen a prothonotary warbler, a particularly rare species. At the end of two and a half hours of exhaustive questioning, Nixon asked:

'Would you be prepared to submit to a lie detector test on this testimony?'

'Yes if necessary.'

'You have that much confidence?'

'I am telling the truth', Chambers calmly replied.[18]

Although the session ended with the subcommittee 'dazzled by detail',[19] as Robert Stripling put it, the Congressmen began to worry on reflection that Chambers' memory had been too good to be true. Even Nixon had yet to be completely convinced, while the wider membership of HUAC was 'more confused than helped'[20] by the subcommittee's report on their first session.

As for the media, the *Washington Post's* editorial was characteristic of the general hostility as it denounced the state of the Hiss case as 'an absurd and indeed shameful impasse...as things stand it is the Committee which is subject to the most serious indictment of all.'[21]

The next ten days were a critical period for Nixon's reputation. Immense pressure was building up on HUAC to drop the case. Nixon felt this pressure personally from the stakeout of reporters who besieged the doors of his congressional office; from the adverse comments of his fellow Republicans in the House dining room; and from the wave of press criticism. Self-doubt began to haunt him. As soon as the transcript of the New York hearings became available, Nixon studied it with an intensity that kept him in his office throughout the night. He then decided he must ask Chambers even more questions. Evading the crush of journalists by climbing out of his window through to the next-door office of

Congressman Don Jackson,[22] Nixon secretly left the Capitol and drove alone for two hours through the sultry August heat to Westminster, Maryland, where he found his quarry working out in the fields.

For the next two hours Nixon again interrogated Chambers as they sat in rocking chairs on the shaded porch of his old farmhouse, drinking from a pitcher of lemonade brought in by his wife Esther, a strikingly dark woman. The questions, as Nixon bluntly told his host, were to convince himself that Chambers really had known Hiss intimately, and that he was not just concocting a false story out of personal animus. Although Nixon did not mention it, one of the many rumours that had been spread about Chambers was that he was a homosexual whose motives for attacking Hiss were those of a spurned lover.

Chambers came across to Nixon more like a fatalistic saint than a jealous sinner. Once again the plenitude of detail he remembered from his encounters with Alger and Priscilla Hiss was overwhelming. He also captivated Nixon by the quality of his intellect and the depth of his sincerity. Both impressions were correct. Chambers was a scholar-poet whose theological essays and translations of avant-garde German novels had won renown. His conversion from Communism to anti-Communism was so sincere that it bordered on religious mysticism.

Chambers looked back on his friendship with Hiss not in anger, but in sadness, believing that America faced a life-and-death battle between Communism and freedom, and that his former associate was a mere pawn in this wider struggle. The personality clash between Hiss and himself was largely irrelevant. 'This is what you must get the country to realize', he told Nixon.[23] Asked point blank whether he had any hidden grudge as motive for what he was doing to Hiss, Chambers gazed out over the rolling Maryland hills in silence for a long time before replying, 'Certainly I wouldn't have a motive which would involve destroying my own career.'[24]

Chambers listed with melancholic fatalism the potential penalties he faced from his accusation of Hiss: disgrace; dismissal from his $25,000-a-year job as a senior editor at *Time*; a perjury charge; and the loss of the personal privacy he cherished. Nixon became increasingly convinced that the personal vendetta theory did not stand up. The only logical explanation for Chambers' behaviour was that he was risking everything because he felt it his duty to warn the nation of the Communist conspiracy.

In the final minutes of his visit to the farm, Nixon made a passing reference to the coincidence that he and Chambers both happened to be Quakers. Chambers recalled that Mrs. Hiss had been a Quaker too. Then his eyes lit up as he snapped his fingers and said, 'That reminds me of something. Priscilla often used the plain speech in talking to Alger at home.'[25]

This was the moment when Chambers fully established his credibility with Nixon, who wrote afterwards, 'From my own family I knew how unlikely it would be for anyone but a close friend to know such an intimate detail. Of course it was still possible that he could have learned it from someone, but the way he blurted it out convinced me that he was telling the truth.'[26]

Nixon's personal conversion to believing in Whittaker Chambers' story was important, but he was a long way from persuading others to follow suit. He decided to test his own judgement by taking advice from three wise men. Returning to Washington he first sought out William Pierce Rogers, a highly regarded thirty-five-year-old District Attorney from New York who was a protégé of Governor Tom Dewey. Rogers was serving as Counsel to the Senate subcommittee which had also been investigating Elizabeth Bentley's allegations. Rogers therefore had some familiarity with the spy ring story, even though his committee had not yet taken evidence from Whittaker Chambers.

Bill Rogers had been in the same class as Nixon at the Navy's Officer Candidate School, Quonset, in 1942, but they had not known each other there. When they met, in effect for the first time on 10 August 1948, Rogers was impressed by the intense young Congressman. 'Dick Nixon struck me as an exceptionally high-minded individual', he has recalled. 'He was very uncertain and rather humble in his approach. He didn't appear to have a fixed position on Hiss. I remember him saying, "We may have made a horrible mistake here. We may have smeared an innocent man." There was no doubt in my mind that he was quite ready to admit that HUAC had made a mistake. He wanted advice on what was the right and fair thing to do.'[27]

Rogers sat down in Nixon's office and read the transcript of Chambers' evidence to the subcommittee in New York on 7 August. 'As I studied it, it became clear to me that Chambers was telling the truth', he recalled. 'I was an experienced prosecutor and I knew that no one would make up such a story with such a wealth of small details and hope to get away with it. So I reassured Congressman Nixon, and told him "press on".'[28]

Nixon was grateful for Rogers' reassurance. It was the beginning of a complex relationship that went through many phases and shades of trust, ultimately ending in acrimony because of tensions created by Henry Kissinger during the White House years. However, in August 1948, Rogers' confident endorsement of Chambers was the message Nixon most wanted to hear.

The second wise man to whom Nixon turned for advice was Bert Andrews, the Washington bureau chief of the *New York Herald Tribune*. Andrews had just won the Pulitzer Prize for a series of articles, 'Washington Witch Hunt', which had been critical both of HUAC and of the shoddy practices within the State Department's loyalty probe system. He had also recommended Hiss to John Foster Dulles for the presidency of the Carnegie Endowment. In spite of these apparent sympathies for Hiss, Nixon felt Andrews was an ideal outside adviser, for he was known as a scrupulously impartial journalist. Nixon asked Andrews to look at the evidence as a devil's advocate and to join him on a second visit to Chambers' farm.

Bert Andrews gave Chambers a third-degree grilling, opening up with a barrage of hostile questions. Was he a chronic drunk? Had he ever been in a mental institution? Was he a homosexual? Every allegation was answered to the questioner's satisfaction* although the replies were sometimes punctuated with such long silences that Andrews thought Chambers had gone into a trance. After a three-hour session, Andrews 'was almost beside himself with excitement… convinced that Chambers was telling the truth'.[29]

The third and most important figure consulted by Nixon during the week 9–16 August was John Foster Dulles. Nixon had learned from Congressman Charles Kersten that Dulles was on the verge of making a statement in support of Hiss. Such a position would have been entirely logical for Dulles, who as Chairman of the Board of the Carnegie Endowment, was Hiss's employer. Dulles was also the principal foreign policy adviser (and Secretary of State designate) to the 1948 Republican presidential candidate, Governor Tom Dewey. The potential for embarrassment to both Dulles and the Dewey campaign from the Hiss case was considerable. Dulles therefore had every motive for using his meeting with Nixon as an occasion for persuading the young freshman Congressman to back off. When Nixon, accompanied by Congressman Kersten, arrived for his appointment at the Roosevelt Hotel in New York, he found not only John Foster Dulles, but also his brother Allen Dulles, who had been a wartime agent in Switzerland for the Office of Strategic Services and who later became Director of the CIA. Had they advised Nixon to abandon his investigation of Hiss and Chambers' testimonies in the best interests of the Party, such a recommendation would have been difficult, if not impossible, to resist.

---

* Chambers did, in fact, lie about his homosexuality to Nixon and Andrews. Later, realising that Hiss's defence lawyers might use evidence of his homosexuality to discredit his testimony, he voluntarily submitted to the FBI a memorandum confessing his past homosexuality and answered the FBI's questions about it.

Nixon was nervous but made his presentation effectively and then handed over the transcripts of the 7 August hearings. He sat quietly on a sofa as the reading session took place. Outside in the corridor, Nixon could hear the confident bustle of a presidential campaign headquarters in full swing. Inside the room the atmosphere seemed to him to be getting quieter and quieter with the silence punctuated only by an occasional exclamation as one of the readers came across some particularly striking passage. After they had finished, John Foster Dulles stood up and paced back and forth in front of the fireplace. 'There's no question about it', he said. 'It's almost impossible to believe but Chambers knows Hiss.'[30]

Nixon asked if he should go ahead with the HUAC investigation. 'In view of the facts Chambers had testified to,' replied John Foster Dulles, 'you'd be derelict in your duty if you did not see the case through to conclusion.'[31]

Nixon was much impressed by Dulles' complete disregard for the potential embarrassment to himself that such advice made likely. For his part, Dulles seemed to be much impressed by the serious diligence of the young Congressman. It was the beginning of the close Nixon–Dulles relationship that was later to become so important in Nixon's years as Vice President and emerging foreign affairs statesman.

Fortified by Dulles's approval and the similar advice he had received from Rogers and Andrews, Nixon intensified his contacts with Chambers, running a virtual shuttle service between Washington and the Westminster farm. Robert Stripling was taken up for a meeting. Although he came away a believer, he made the prophetic utterance: 'I don't think Chambers has yet told us the whole story, he is holding something back.'[32]

Frank and Hannah Nixon, who had retired and moved to a smallholding near York, Pennsylvania, were also taken on the pilgrimage to Chambers after expressing some doubts. 'Richard why don't you drop the case? No one else thinks Hiss is guilty', was Hannah's maternal advice when she saw that her son was so obsessed with the drama that he could not eat his meals. 'Mother, I think Hiss is lying. Until I know the truth I've got to stick it out',[33] was Nixon's reply, which he followed up by driving his parents over the state border into Maryland so that they could give their verdict on Chambers. It was favourable.

In addition to submitting himself to further questioning from Andrews and Stripling, Chambers made a secret, early-morning visit to Nixon's office in Washington in a scene which nearly developed into a French farce according to Dorothy Cox:

Whittaker Chambers was in the inside office talking to the boss when
Mary Spargo of the *Washington Post* turned up in the outer office
wanting to ask some questions. Then who should arrive but Donald
Hiss, Alger Hiss's brother, followed by a horde of reporters. We were
besieged! Eventually I got the press around my desk and pretended
to get their advice on how to work our new Robotype typewriter.
While they were distracted, the boss smuggled Chambers out the
back way through Don Jackson's office.[34]

The Hiss camp evidently got some wind of Nixon's clandestine meetings
with Chambers, for when Alger Hiss appeared before the HUAC subcommittee
in Washington on the morning of 16 August, he accused Nixon of spending the
weekend 'at Mr. Chambers' farm in New Jersey'.

Nixon: That is quite incorrect.
Hiss: It is incorrect?
Nixon: Yes sir, I can say as you did a moment ago that I have never
     spent the night with Mr. Chambers.[35]

This is the first recorded example of Nixon's willingness to be economical
with the truth and it was not to be the last time that he sacrificed his honesty in
an effort to keep embarrassing information from being revealed. Nevertheless, it
was a mere pecadillo of evasion when compared to the massive perjury that Hiss
proceeded to perpetrate. Insisting that he had never known or met Chambers,
Hiss grew more and more shaken as the questions took him through every detail
of the testimony. For most members of the Committee, the exchange that clinched
the case arose over bird-watching. Nixon casually asked Hiss whether he had any
hobbies, and was given the answer tennis and amateur ornithology. Congressman
McDowell then asked, 'Did you ever see a prothonotary warbler?' Hiss virtually
lit up with excitement:

Hiss: I have right here on the Potomac. Do you know that place?
Nixon: Have you ever seen one?
Hiss (to McDowell) : Did you see it in the same place?
McDowell: I saw one in Arlington.
Hiss: They come back and nest in those swamps. Beautiful yellow
     head, a gorgeous bird.[36]

There was a stunned silence as the impact of this exchange went home. 'I quickly asked another question lest Hiss realize what had happened',[37] wrote Nixon afterwards, and the records shows him pounding away with an inquisition on cars, maids, vacations and apartments. Although the detailed answers impressively matched Chambers' evidence, Nixon could have saved his breath. From the moment of the warbler, Hiss had lost most of his credibility as a witness.

Hiss himself seemed to have sensed that his story was wearing thin earlier in the questioning, for before he was asked about his ornithology and in a theatrical volte-face, he suddenly interrupted Nixon's cross-examination and announced that he had just remembered the name of a man who had stayed with him and who had done many of the things that Chambers claimed to have done. However, Hiss said he could not reveal the name of this new character in the story on the grounds that it might be leaked back to Chambers, who would then incorporate it into his perjurious tale. This was too much for Congressman Hébert, who said bluntly to Hiss, 'Either you or Mr. Chambers is lying.' Hiss coolly replied, 'This is certainly true.' Hébert came back, 'And whichever one of you is lying is the greatest actor that America has ever produced.'[38]

After a short recess, Hiss declared that he had now decided to reveal the name of the mystery man, saying 'The name of the man I brought in—and he may have no relation to this whole nightmare—is a man named George Crosley.'[39]

For the next two hours Hiss led HUAC off on a completely false trail about George Crosley, the man who never was. At the beginning of this part of his evidence, Hiss claimed that he scarcely knew 'Mr. Crosley' but under questioning he revealed that he had allowed this grubby freelance journalist to stay in his home as a guest, to sublet a section of his apartment, and to borrow his car. Nixon took Hiss through a physical catalogue of 'Crosley's' appearance, which was remarkably similar to that of Chambers, right down to his bad teeth. Questioned about 'Mrs. Crosley's' appearance, Hiss replied that she was 'strikingly dark'. As Nixon later recalled: 'From that moment on, although I did not say anything about it or give any indication by my conduct, I knew that the case had been broken. I was the only member of the Committee who had ever seen Mrs. Chambers and I knew that she fitted Hiss's description perfectly. Now I was sure that Hiss had known Chambers. Whether or not he had known him as George Crosley was the only question that remained to be answered.'[40] The answer was not long in coming.

III. THE CASE IS BROKEN

The Committee ended its 16 August session by deciding to schedule a confrontation between Hiss and Chambers on 25 August. Almost immediately afterwards, Nixon began to worry that this nine-day delay might give Hiss time to build his deception into a more convincing form. So at 2.00 a.m. in the morning of 17 August, Nixon called Stripling and instructed him to summon both Hiss and Chambers before the subcommittee in New York City that very afternoon.

The confrontation took place at 5.30 p.m. in suite 1400 of the Commodore Hotel at Grand Central Station in Manhattan. A mix-up by Chambers nearly ruined the drama. As Nixon was rushing out of the House of Representatives office building on his way to Union Station to catch the afternoon train to New York, he literally bumped into Chambers, who had got the information wrong and thought he was supposed to come to Washington for the meeting. Nixon bundled his star witness into the cab with him, marvelling at how close the confrontation had come to never taking place that day.[41]

When Hiss arrived at the Commodore Hotel he was irritable, getting involved in some verbal skirmishing with Nixon about how long he would have to delay his dinner appointment at the Harvard Club. When the subcommittee had formally convened, Hiss was seated in the witness chair about seven feet away from the table behind which sat the subcommittee members plus Stripling and his staff of four investigators. The Committee was in executive session and the press and public were absent.

Nixon asked for Chambers to be brought in. Hiss did not move a muscle as his accuser entered, but just stared at the curtained window. Nixon then told both men to stand and face each other. They were no more than four or five feet apart.

'Mr. Hiss,' said Nixon, 'the man standing over there is Whittaker Chambers, I ask you now if you have ever known that man before?'[42]

Instead of replying directly, Hiss started an elaborate charade. He made Chambers say some words of self-identification. He asked him to read from a magazine. He questioned the Committee about whether the voice had been the same the last time Chambers had testified. He told him to open his mouth as wide as possible. He pretended to study Chambers' teeth and asked detailed questions about the accuser's dentistry. Nixon struggled to keep a straight face during this performance and finally asked: 'Mr. Hiss, do you feel you would have to have the dentist tell you just what he did to the teeth before you could tell anything about this man?'[43]

Hiss earnestly insisted that he did, and continued to protest that he could not be sure that the Chambers of 1948 was the man he had spoken of as Crosley in his previous testimony. He asked Chambers if he had ever used the name Crosley. Chambers said that he had not.

Then he asked him whether he had lived in his apartment in Washington. Chambers said that he had. Hiss acted as if dumbfounded by the contradiction and asked: 'Would you tell me how you reconcile your negative answers with this affirmative answer?'

Chambers softly replied, 'Very easily Alger, I was a Communist and you were a Communist.'

A moment or two later Hiss inexplicably abandoned his pretence.

> Hiss: Mr. Chairman, I don't need to ask Mr. Whittaker Chambers
>   any more questions. I am now perfectly prepared to identify this
>   man as George Crosley....C-R-O-S-L-E-Y.
> Nixon: You are sure of the one *S*?
> Hiss: That is my recollection. I have a rather good visual memory and
>   my recollection of his spelling of his name is C-R-O-S-L-E-Y.

Nixon was amazed but elated. A few minutes earlier Hiss's 'visual memory' had been so bad that he insisted on consulting dental charts before he could be sure of Chambers' identity. Now he was so emphatic about his identification that when asked if he was absolutely certain he said 'If he had lost both his eyes and taken his nose off, I would be sure.'

Chambers was then asked whether he could make a positive identification of Hiss as the Communist he had known so well. He answered 'Positive identification'. Hearing these words, Hiss suddenly shot out of his chair. Nixon thought Hiss was going to hit Chambers as he moved towards him, shaking his fist and shouting, 'May I say...that I would like to invite Mr. Whittaker Chambers to make those same statements out of the presence of this Committee without their being privileged for suit for libel. I challenge you to do it and I hope you will do it damned quickly.'[44]

Nixon lowered the temperature by resuming a line of questioning about Hiss's generosity with cars, apartments and hospitality to Chambers/Crosley and asked why this apparent closeness had not been matched by the slightest curiosity about Chambers' background, writings and political views. Hiss continued to bluff, but even his close friend Charles Dollard, who was present, saw that the game was up, writing afterwards, 'Alger behaved very badly, was very irritable...both McDowell and Nixon were trying to be fair.'[45]

What stood out through all the theatricals was that Hiss had quite clearly been lying to the press, the public and HUAC when, at his first self-requested appearance before the Committee, he had so brazenly insisted that he had no idea who his accuser was even when shown photographs of Chambers. Nixon realised that Hiss was from now on a broken reed, musing afterwards about his own 'sense of shock and sadness that a man like Hiss could have fallen so low...it is not a pleasant picture to see a whole brilliant career destroyed before your eyes'.[46] At the time, however, Nixon's mood was upbeat. The 17 August sessions drew to a close with Hiss cornered, unable to cover the naked exposure of his mendacity except by the occasional fig leaf of anger and sarcasm.

'Mr. Hiss, that is all. Thank you very much', said Chairman Thomas finally.

'I don't reciprocate', replied Hiss.

'Italicize that in the record', Thomas ordered.

'I wish you would', snapped Hiss in response.[47]

As Hiss stalked out of the room, the members of the subcommittee and Whittaker Chambers remained seated for a long moment of silence. It was broken by Robert Stripling, hamming up his Texas drawl as he asked, 'How-are-ya Mistah Crawz-li?'[48] For the first time in the Hiss case, Richard Nixon, along with everyone else present, had a good laugh.

Nixon did not allow himself to relax for long. Although he had now persuaded the Committee that Hiss had been lying, his last and most important task was to repeat the feat for the public and the press. Nixon therefore spent the seven days before the public confrontation between Hiss and Chambers, scheduled for 25 August, preparing himself with such vehemence that even his wife was later to describe his commitment as 'an absorption that was almost frightening'.[49] One of the reasons for his sleepless nights and ceaseless rehearsals was that the session would be the first televised congressional hearing in history.

As Nixon began the Committee's cross-examination of Hiss on 25 August, the atmosphere was somewhere between a sauna and a bullfight. About 700 people had crammed into the caucus room of the House Office building and the steamy August heat was made even more sweltering by the television arclights. Hiss, the wounded bull, floundered badly throughout the five hours that the Committee spent questioning him. It was the cumulative effect of Nixon's detailed cross-examination which sank him as his previous testimony began to haunt him.

Chambers had originally told the Committee on 5 August that Hiss had owned a Ford Roadster, which he had donated to the Communist Party once he had bought a new Plymouth. When questioned about the same Ford on 16 August, Hiss had said that he had moved apartments in 1935 and, because the leases on his new and old apartments had overlapped, he had sublet his old apartment to Crosley for the time remaining on its lease. He recalled giving the Ford to Crosley along with the apartment, because he had already bought his new Plymouth and so no longer needed the Ford.

In the public hearing on 25 August, Nixon's and the Committee staff's hard work paid dividends. They had established that Hiss's lease on his old apartment had expired on 28 June 1935. They had found the certificate of title assigning a new Plymouth to Hiss on 7 September 1935. They had also found the transfer certificate for the Ford, showing that it had been transferred to a William Rosen on 23 July 1936.* So at the time the lease expired, Hiss did not own the Plymouth, and therefore the Ford could not have been his second car. Also, Hiss could not have given the Ford to Chambers as part of the sublease of his old apartment (that is, prior to 28 June 1935) because, according to his signature on the transfer certificate, he still owned the Ford in July 1936.

Hiss sought to obfuscate the details of the evidence by qualifications and legalisms. He had a clash of class warfare with Nixon, who had sought to correct the witness's comment on a point of law. 'I am familiar with the law', said Hiss grandly. 'I attended Harvard Law School. I believe yours was Whittier.' At this piece of condescension Nixon 'turned red and blue and red again', according to Robert Stripling. 'You could see the hackles on his back, practically pushing his coat up. It irritated Mr. Nixon no end that Mr. Hiss had harpooned him real good.'[50]

Hiss's arrogance did not last long. Flailing desperately, he tried a different tack. He insisted that any differences between his and Chambers' conflicting stories were irrelevant because the only real issue was whether or not he was a Communist. Nixon pounced on that one, declaring: 'The issue in this hearing today is whether or not Mr. Hiss or Mr. Chambers had committed perjury before the Committee as well as whether Mr. Hiss is a Communist.'[51]

Hiss then tried to fudge, claiming that he could not remember the exact sequence of events. His claims rang hollow and seemed ridiculous when he was confronted with the photostat of the certificate of transfer for the Ford. Hiss complained that he could not be certain that the signature on the document was his own signature. 'Could you be sure if you saw the original document?' asked

---

* When Rosen testified before the Committee, he declined to answer questions about the Ford and about whether he knew Alger Hiss on the grounds that his answers would tend to incriminate him.

Congressman Mundt. 'I could be surer', replied Hiss absurdly, to the laughter of the crowd.[52] Hiss's friends began to shake their heads sadly.

Hiss again brought up the importance of the dental work to explain his initial reluctance to identify Chambers as Crosley. Nixon, the matador, took the chance to put in a brutal stab:

> Nixon: You even asked the name of his dentist and wanted to consult with his dentist before you made the identification positive. My question may sound facetious but I am just wondering: Didn't you ever see Crosley with his mouth closed?
>
> Hiss: The striking thing in my recollection about Crosley was not when he had his mouth shut but when he had his mouth open.[53]

The audience, already restless at Hiss's evasions, burst into derisive laughter. Chairman Thomas called for order and said to Hiss: 'If you have got any very humorous remarks in the way of answers, call me out later on and give them to me because I always like a good laugh, but let's not have any more laughing in here if we can possibly avoid it.'

Hiss angrily retorted, 'I understood the laughter to be at the question, not at the answer, Mr. Chairman. Maybe you or Mr. Nixon would like to withdraw to tell your jokes.'[54]

Hiss's testimony ended with him reading a statement which contained a rather pompous (though impressive) recital of thirty-four names of famous people with whom he had worked, suggesting that they should all be consulted about his loyalty. He even went as far as to claim that the allegations against him had been made in order 'to discredit recent great achievements of this country in which I was privileged to participate'[55]—a veiled reference to his connection with FDR at Yalta.

This line of what Nixon called 'innocence by association' cut no ice with the Committee or the audience and soon afterwards Hiss left the stand. Gone was the applause and the crowd of well-wishers which had greeted him after his first appearance before the Committee. Now he picked his way through the crowd in lonely friendlessness, accompanied only by his attorney. James Reston of the *New York Times,* who knew Hiss well enough to have been one of his supporters for the Carnegie Endowment presidency, caught the mood when he reported that Hiss had always answered Nixon's questions 'with a caution which angered members of the Committee and in the opinion even of his friends, hurt his case'.[56]

Whittaker Chambers took the stand immediately after Hiss, and his answers seemed refreshingly straightforward in comparison with his predecessor's dodging and weaving. Asked for his reaction to Hiss's evidence, Chambers said simply, 'Mr. Hiss is lying.'

The Committee members questioned him for an hour and forty minutes, less than one third of the time devoted to their interrogation of Hiss. The climax of the cross-examination came when Nixon asked Chambers whether he had some secret agenda of hatred for Hiss.

> Nixon: Mr. Chambers, can you search your memory now to see what motive you can have for accusing Mr. Hiss of being a Communist at the present time?
> Chambers: What motive I can have?
> Nixon: Yes. I mean, do you—is there any grudge that you have against Mr. Hiss over anything that he has done to you?
> Chambers: The story has spread that in testifying against Mr. Hiss I am working out some old grudge, or motives of revenge or hatred. I do not hate Mr. Hiss. We were close friends, but we are caught in a tragedy of history. Mr. Hiss represents the concealed enemy against which we are all fighting, and I am fighting. I have testified against him with remorse and pity, but in a moment of history in which this Nation now stands, so help me God, I could not do otherwise.[57]

Soon after this exchange, which Nixon afterwards described as 'the high point of the hearings both as history and as drama',[58] HUAC adjourned. The public's mind was made up. Various Gallup Polls indicated that between 70 and 80 per cent of Americans approved of HUAC's investigation and were now convinced that Hiss was guilty of perjury.

Among the dissenting voices was the *New York Times,* which declared in an editorial that, 'The Committee has not proceeded in a manner that commanded confidence',[59] but Nixon could safely disregard such criticism. By his determination to investigate Chambers' allegations against Hiss, he had won acclaim from his once disapproving congressional colleagues and in the country at large he acquired the status of a hero. Even inside the Truman White House, the climate was changing in Nixon's favour, for on 27 August, presidential aide George Elsey, sought and obtained the President's authority for the Justice Department to start its own perjury investigation into the Hiss case.[60]

Nixon was therefore right in his later judgement. 'The case was broken on the 17th in the Commodore. The 25th we wrapped it up publicly.' But there were far too many loose ends for him to start resting on his laurels.

IV. THE SOVIET SPY

Nixon and HUAC never saw Hiss again after 25 August 1948, but Nixon's involvement with the case was far from over. The various hearings already held had shown without doubt that Hiss had known Chambers, and Hiss had failed to explain convincingly why he had failed to recognise pictures of Chambers in his first appearance on 5 August. On other details of their relationship, Hiss had lied and misled. The Committee had succeeded in establishing Chambers' veracity on one count. But what of his more serious allegation that Hiss was a Communist? The most startling development of the Hiss case was still to come. Again, Hiss would unwittingly cause his own downfall and Nixon would play a central role in ensuring that justice was done.

The prelude to Hiss's final undoing was his own rash challenge to Chambers to repeat his allegation that Hiss was a Communist where he would not be protected against a libel action by congressional immunity. Two days after the public confrontation, Chambers appeared on the television programme 'Meet the Press'. The first question came from a reporter from the *Washington Post*: 'Are you willing to say now that Alger Hiss is or ever was a Communist?'

'Alger Hiss was a Communist and may be now', replied Chambers, adding for good measure, 'I do not think Mr. Hiss will sue me for slander or libel.' For a month it looked as though Chambers was correct, for Hiss took no action, to the dismay of his supporters. Finally he was goaded into action by press criticism. 'Mr. Hiss himself has created a situation in which he is obliged to put up or shut up', said an editorial in the *Washington Post*,[61] the paper that had hitherto been Hiss's strongest supporter. The *New York Daily News* made the same point more bluntly by asking: 'Well Alger, where's that suit?'[62]

In the face of such comments, Hiss had little choice but to act and on 27 September he sued Chambers for $50,000 damages, later raising his claim to $75,000. Watching these events from the sidelines, Nixon feared for Chambers, because he did not believe that Chambers had corroborative evidence of the kind necessary to prove his allegations in court. Hiss was probably thinking on similar lines, for in commencing his legal action he must have assumed that if Chambers had possessed any such proof, he would have produced it during the Committee hearings.

During the next two months, while the lawyers for Hiss and Chambers were exchanging written pleadings, Nixon travelled all over the country giving dozens of speeches. Because he had already won both the Democratic and Republican primaries in his own District, he had no need to trouble himself with further personal campaigning. Instead, as the Congressman with the highest profile of the year, he was a major audience attraction with his standard address on the Hiss case. Speaking invitations flooded into his office, and in accepting many of them Nixon began to build his national network of contacts, friends and returnable favours as he criss-crossed the country supporting Republican candidates for the House and Senate.

The results of the 1948 election were a blow for Nixon and his Party. Contrary to most forecasts, Truman beat Dewey and brought in a Democratic Congress on his coat tails. This unexpected victory made the outlook for the next phase of the Hiss case look bleak from Nixon's point of view. With the Democrats firmly in charge of the Administration and of the House committees, the odds were that the Justice Department would not indict Hiss and that HUAC itself would be marginalised, if not dissolved. As for the libel suit, this too seemed to be moving in Hiss's favour, partly because of Chambers' apparent lack of hard evidence and partly because the action had been set down for trial in Hiss's home town of Baltimore, where the jury might be expected to believe their native son.

On 17 November the tide turned dramatically against Hiss. As part of the normal pre-trial procedures for the libel case, Chambers had travelled to Baltimore to make a deposition in the offices of Hiss's attorneys. On 4 November he was asked the crucial question, whether he had any documents he had received from Hiss or which might bear Hiss's handwriting. Hiss must have wished in retrospect that no such question had ever been asked. During the next week and a half, before the deposition was reconvened, Chambers visited his nephew in New York, with whom he had left some papers for safe keeping. In one of the many bizarre events of this infamous case, his nephew took him to the shaft of an unused dumb waiter where he had sashed his papers. He brought out a dusty envelope whose contents would ultimately send Alger Hiss to prison.

When the deposition reconvened on 17 November, Chambers was asked whether he had found any materials he had received from Hiss. Chambers calmly took a pile of documents out of his coat pocket and tossed them onto the lawyer's table. 'Only these', he said. 'Alger Hiss gave me these when we worked together in the Communist conspiracy.'[63]

'Only these' turned out to be sixty-five sheets containing typewritten copies and summaries of secret State Department documents and four sheets of handwritten notes, also of secret State Department documents. All the documents fell within the period of 5 January—1 April 1938. Their subject matter consisted broadly of political and military affairs, in particular concerning the war between Japan and China, events in Central Europe, the Spanish Civil War, and even the Royal Navy's shipbuilding plans.

The handwriting was Hiss's and it was later proved that Hiss's typewriter had been used to type the other pages. Chambers explained to the stunned lawyers that he had kept the documents as an insurance policy against attempts he feared would be made after his defection to blackmail or kill him. He spoke of a meeting he had had in 1937 in Brooklyn with Hiss and Colonel Boris Bykov, the KGB's *rezident,* or spymaster. Bykov had asked Hiss to steal documents from the State Department and Hiss had agreed. Every week or ten days, Chambers would collect from Hiss a briefcase full of documents, which he would have photographed before he gave them back to Hiss to return to the State Department. The typed documents, Chambers explained, were documents which Hiss could only risk removing for one night. What the lawyers saw before them were Priscilla Hiss's typed copies and summaries, which would be forwarded to Moscow. Occasionally Hiss would come across a document which he could not remove from his office at all, in which case he would make handwritten notes. The four sheets of handwriting were examples of such notes.

This testimony sent the Baltimore libel lawyers into orbit. They contacted the Justice Department in Washington, which immediately despatched the chief of its Criminal Division to take charge of this amazing escalation of the case. He impounded the papers and obtained a court order enforcing secrecy on everyone concerned. Chambers and his lawyers assumed that it would only be a matter of days before the Justice Department brought the case to a Grand Jury and indicted Hiss on espionage charges.

Two weeks passed. Nothing happened. Then, on 1 December, a story appeared in the *Washington Daily News* saying that because of a lack of evidence the Justice Department had decided to drop the case against Hiss. Another article reported that a perjury charge was being considered against Chambers.

That same day, a young lawyer who had been present for Chambers' explosive pre-trial revelations, Nicholas Vazzana, came to tell Nixon about the existence of the new papers proving that Hiss was a spy. He expressed his fears that, in spite of the new evidence, the Justice Department was planning to indict Chambers for perjury on the grounds that he had lied about never having been involved in espionage himself.

Nixon heard this news when he was within hours of departing on a cruise with Pat to Panama. They had not had a holiday together for three years. The Voorhis campaign and the Herter Committee had resulted in the cancellation of their summer travel plans in 1946 and 1947. The August excitements of the Hiss case had postponed their 1948 vacation once already. Would the latest developments mean a cancellation for the third year running? The conflict between his obligation to his wife and his urge to stay close to the scene of the action in the Hiss case made Nixon unusually bad tempered. He reacted to Vazzana's report with fury. Part of his anger was directed at Chambers, who had clearly deceived him and HUAC by withholding crucial evidence which could have made the Committee's hearings even more productive and dramatic. 'I felt confused, surprised and disappointed that Chambers, who had seemed so truthful and for whom I and many others had risked so much, should have been holding out on me all this time', he explained later. 'I felt that somehow he had not trusted me and had let me down.'[64]

His reaction at the time was not nearly so cool. Nixon erupted into an incandescent rage. 'He cussed me out real good',[65] recalled Stripling, who tried to persuade him to make an immediate journey to Chambers at the Westminster farm.

'I'm so goddamned sick and tired of this case I don't want to hear any more about it and I'm going to Panama. And the hell with it, and you, and the whole damned business', roared Nixon,[66] cooling down sufficiently to change his mind later with bad grace. 'Goddamn it, if it'll shut your mouth, I'll go',[67] he finally declared.

Nixon and Stripling visited Chambers that afternoon, finding him at his most enigmatic as he insisted that the court order for secrecy made it impossible for him to disclose any information about the new developments in the case. Nixon nevertheless pressed him hard and extracted confirmation that 'a bombshell' of new evidence had indeed been deposited at the Baltimore pretrial hearing. When the visitors voiced their criticism of Chambers' folly for not having presented this new material to HUAC in the first place, Chambers hinted that he might have a second bombshell up his sleeve and asked mysterious questions about whether the Committee had access to highly skilled photographic technicians.

'Well what do you think he's got?' Nixon asked Stripling as they drove back to Washington empty handed. 'I don't know what he has,' replied Stripling, 'but whatever he has it'll blow the dome off the Capitol. Certainly you're not going to Panama now?'

'I don't think he's got a damned thing. I'm going right ahead with my plans',[68] retorted Nixon, afterwards admitting that he had really wanted to remain on the spot but that he could not face breaking the news to Pat that their thrice-postponed vacation was off.

Just before embarking on the cruise ship on the morning of 2 December, Nixon left instructions for Stripling to serve a blanket subpoena on Chambers which would compel him to produce all the remaining evidence he had. With the Nixons on the high seas, two HUAC investigators arrived at the Westminster farm later that night. Chambers agreed to co-operate, and in a scene of high melodrama, led the investigators out into the moonlit vegetable garden. Explaining that he had felt the need for a secure hiding place away from the house, Chambers headed for his pumpkin patch. There he fumbled about for a moment, then lifted off the severed top from a large, hollowed-out pumpkin shell and took out five rolls of film wrapped in wax paper. 'I think this is what you are looking for', he told the bewildered men from HUAC.[69]

Bewilderment turned to sensation the following day when, in a photographic darkroom. Stripling and his team discovered that the rolls of film were copies of fifty-eight pages of confidential State Department documents, several of them top secret despatches, with three summaries in Hiss's handwriting. The documents contained information concerning a proposed trade agreement between the United States and Germany, and military and political issues to do with the war between China and Japan, both items of profound interest to the Soviet Union in the 1930s. For the first time, the HUAC investigators could see what their counterparts in the libel case had known since Chambers had produced his first store of documents: Alger Hiss's real crime had been far more serious than simple perjury. This was the biggest espionage case in the history of the State Department, and perhaps the United States.

Oblivious of the new dimensions to the drama, Nixon was dining at the captain's table on the evening of 3 December when the purser brought in a radio telegram from Stripling:

SECOND BOMBSHELL OBTAINED BY SUBPOENA 1.00 AM
FRIDAY. CASE CLINCHED. INFORMATION AMAZING. HEAT
IS ON FROM PRESS AND OTHER PLACES. IMMEDIATE ACTION
APPEARS NECESSARY. CAN YOU POSSIBLY GET BACK?

'Here we go again!' cried Pat, throwing up her hands in disappointment as Nixon read out the wire to the assembled company.

Andrews also sent a telegram:

DOCUMENTS INCREDIBLY HOT. LINK TO HISS SEEMS CER-
TAIN. LINK TO OTHERS INEVITABLE... MY LIBERAL

FRIENDS DON'T LOVE ME NO MORE. NOR YOU. BUT FACTS
ARE FACTS AND THESE ARE DYNAMITE...LOVE TO PAT.
VACATION-SPOILER ANDREWS.[70]

Nixon radioed Stripling to make arrangements to get him off the boat, which
was nearing Cuba. Stripling, in turn, contacted James Forrestal, the Secretary of
Defense, who personally ordered the US Coastguard and the US Air Force to
furnish Nixon with transportation. The Coastguard in Miami sent a seaplane
which made a mid-ocean rendezvous with the cruise ship, returning with Nixon
to Florida and a waiting crowd of newspaper men. Asked for his comments on
'The Pumpkin Papers', Nixon was completely in the dark. 'What are you talking
about. Is this a joke?'[71] he responded nervously as the press outlined the midnight
drama of the vegetable garden. The pumpkin story sounded too crazy to be true,
even by the cloak and dagger standards of Whittaker Chambers. As he strapped
himself into the bucket seat of a US Air Force Transport DC3 that had been
assigned to fly him to Washington, Nixon was plagued by new doubts. 'Oh, my
God, we really have a lulu on our hands this time',[72] he said gloomily.

Returning to Washington on 5 December, the true nature of the 'lulu'
became apparent to Nixon. He was in a precarious predicament. The Pumpkin
Papers, which Nixon studied in detail the moment he got back to the Capitol,
were amazing evidence of espionage on a grand scale. However, HUAC could
not bring a prosecution itself. Nixon had to rely on the Justice Department to
do so, and he knew that it had had similar documents (the ones Chambers had
produced at his deposition) for two and a half weeks but were apparently intent
on prosecuting Chambers for perjury on the grounds that he had lied in denying that he had been involved in espionage. With the Grand Jury which was
investigating the case due to expire on 15 December, Nixon was in a battle
against the Administration, against Hiss's team of prestigious lawyers and
most importantly against time, but he had one major weapon: the films of the
Pumpkin Papers.

Nixon's strategy was to keep the films from the Justice Department while
at the same time publicising the case against Hiss in an effort to keep the Administration from covering up Hiss's apparent guilt and to embarrass the Justice
Department into prosecuting Hiss not Chambers. As he described the issue at
one of his press conferences: 'We have learned from unimpeachable sources that
the Justice Department now plans to indict Chambers for perjury...if Chambers
is indicted first, Hiss and the others will go free because the witness against them
will have been discredited as a perjurer.'[73]

Nixon soon found himself in the midst of a media circus and a constitutional power struggle for physical possession of the Pumpkin Papers. Nixon's first salvo came with a press conference on 6 December which produced dramatic pictures of the young Congressman with Stripling, studying the film through a magnifying glass like an American Sherlock Holmes with his trusty Watson by his side. The press conference was followed by near calamity. One of the photographers had casually asked, 'What's the emulsion figure on these films?' explaining that this number would confirm the year of manufacture. Stripling checked with Eastman Kodak, who told him that the films had been made in 1945, not in 1937, when Chambers had claimed to have bought them. Nixon was horror-struck by the news which suggested that Chambers had been a diabolical liar. After a moment of shocked silence, Nixon lashed out in fury. 'Oh my God, this is the end of my political career', he cried, cursing Stripling and his staff. Reaching Chambers on the phone, Nixon demanded an explanation. After a long silence, Chambers replied in a despairing voice: 'I can't understand it. God must be against me'.

'You'd better have a better answer than that', snapped Nixon. 'The subcommittee's coming to New York tonight and we want to see you at the Commodore Hotel at 9.00 and you'd better be there.'[74]

Slamming down the receiver, Nixon despondently called a press conference for what he said would be 'the biggest crow-eating performance in the history of Capitol Hill'.[75]

Chambers, even more distraught, was making preparations for a suicide attempt, which would have ended the case against Hiss altogether. Five minutes before the humiliating announcement was due to be made, Eastman Kodak called back to say they had made a mistake. The film had been manufactured in 1937. Stripling gave a Texan war-whoop, leapt onto the couch, then grabbed Nixon and waltzed him round his office as he shouted the good tidings. As the emotional temperature cooled, Nixon said quietly, 'Poor Chambers. Nobody ever believes him at first.'[76] Then he went out to the waiting reporters and calmly told them that the Committee was thoroughly checking every aspect of the case, and it could now be confirmed that the dates of the microfilm's manufacture corroborated Chambers' testimony.*

This drama now over, Nixon went the same night to New York to hold a hearing where Chambers repeated the account he had given to Hiss's defence lawyers on 17 November of how Hiss had given him State Department documents. For the next few days, HUAC held a series of hearings and press conferences

---

* Chambers later made an unsuccessful suicide attempt, despite having been reassured on this point. It may be wondered how Nixon's future might have been affected had he succeeded.

designed to corroborate Chambers' tale and to keep the pressure on the Department of Justice to indict Hiss. On 7 December, the Committee heard testimony from Sumner Welles, who had been Under Secretary of State from 1939 to 1945, and John Peurifoy, a State Department security officer. They told the Committee that the documents were highly prejudicial to national security, so much so that they recommended that they still not be published, ten years after they had been written.

Meanwhile, Nixon was engaged in a bitter struggle with the Administration. The Department of Justice badly wanted to get the original films from the Pumpkin Papers for use as evidence. Nixon refused to relinquish them until he was sure that they would not be used to indict Chambers. The first round of this fight was held when Nixon arrived in New York on the evening of 6 December. Nixon would not yield to the Justice officials' demand that he hand over the films, and a temporary compromise was reached whereby he agreed to provide them with copies of the enlargements taken from the films. Nixon explained his behaviour to the press: the White House and its Justice Department, he told them, could no longer be trusted to deal with the matter. What the case now required was 'a special prosecutor'.[77]

One week later, Nixon, who had been served with a court order to appear with the films, strode up the steps to the court house in New York, a briefcase clutched firmly in his hands. Again he refused to hand them over. A ferocious courtroom clash broke out with the US attorney in charge of the case. Nixon argued that he had obeyed the order by bringing the material to court. However, he was acting as the representative of an independent and separate branch of government, and in this capacity he would not surrender the films because they were the property of the House of Representatives until released by Congress. After heady argument about these somewhat dubious new constitutional principles, which Nixon had more or less invented on his feet, the US attorney was forced to accept a compromise whereby Nixon would produce the original films to the FBI not the Department of Justice.

It was an agile feat of brinkmanship, which displayed Nixon's determination not to be intimidated by the Administration. Nixon's defiance had brought him into direct confrontation with the President. In the privacy of the Oval Office, President Harry S. Truman read the Hiss files and exploded, 'The son-of-a-bitch. He betrayed his country.'[78] In public, however, he played political hardball and attacked HUAC. In an uncharacteristic display of double standards, he repeated his denunciation of the hearings as a 'red herring'. Nixon retaliated with a declaration that an indictment of Chambers would be 'a Department of Justice whitewash which would give the greatest encouragement to the Communist conspiracy in this country'.[79]

At the end of the day, the evidence confronting Hiss and his inability to answer it convincingly swung the Grand Jury's decision. The FBI had compared samples that Hiss had supplied of typing done on his typewriter with the documents Chambers had produced. The print was identical. Hiss produced laughter from the Grand Jury when his only counter to this damning evidence was, 'Until the day I die, I shall wonder how Whittaker Chambers got into my house to use my typewriter.'[80]

On 15 December 1948, the Grand Jury voted to indict Alger Hiss on two counts of perjury: count one for denying that he had passed confidential State Department documents to Whittaker Chambers; count two for denying that he knew Whittaker Chambers. Espionage charges were time-barred by the statute of limitations.

V. THE LEGACY

Once Hiss had been indicted, Nixon's direct involvement in the case ceased, but he remained active on the touchlines as the drama continued through two highly publicised trials. The first ended in a hung jury, the inconclusive vote going 8 to 4 in favour of conviction. Nixon was dismayed by the result and became a vociferous member of the Republican chorus claiming that the trial judge had been biased in the defendant's favour. On 21 January 1950, at the end of the retrial under a different judge, the jury found Hiss guilty on both counts of perjury. Nixon learned of the result in a telephone call to his Washington office, where at 2.00 p.m on a Saturday afternoon he was in the middle of dictating to his secretary Betty Lewis.

'He put down the phone, gave a little whoop, and punched the wall with the palm of his hand', was her recollection of his joyous reaction.[81]

Back in the courtroom, Hiss was sentenced to five years imprisonment. His appeals failed and he served forty-four months in Lewisberg State Penitentiary. After his release, he sank into obscurity, working as a stationery salesman in New York, a role from which he was occasionally exhumed into temporary media prominence during bouts of anti-Nixon hysteria, particularly at the time of Watergate.

As for Whittaker Chambers, he had an unhappy personal life until his death in 1961, living as something of a recluse, often reviled for his past notoriety as an informer. The publication of his book *Witness* in 1952 brought him some respect and eventually acclaim from the conservative right. In 1984 he was posthumously awarded the Congressional Medal of Freedom by President Ronald Reagan.

Nixon's legacy was more complex. The immediate effect of the case was to bring him national fame and following. 'The first time I thought he was made of the stuff from which destiny creates heroes was when he came to Los Angeles soon after Hiss had been found guilty', recalled Bob Finch, then a twenty-three-year-old graduate of California's Occidental College. 'He was speaking to a big Jewish convention, which was not a sympathetic audience for him. But he held them spellbound as he took them right through the twists and turns of the Hiss case. It was a *tour de force* which had them on their feet cheering. From that moment on I knew he was going to be a major player.'[82]

Bob Finch, who was destined to play a major part of his own in Nixon's future career, recalled a reaction which was widely shared among Republicans and in a much wider section of the community. For there was a deeper presentiment of 'Cometh the hour, cometh the man' towards Nixon in this period. Many Americans were growing increasingly anxious about Communist subversion at home, because they were so worried by the threat from Communist expansion abroad. The testing of the first Soviet atom bomb; the victory of Mao Tse-tung in China; and the spread of Stalinist tyranny across Eastern Europe created the background for what historian David Caute called 'The Great Fear' within the United States. Circumstances presented Nixon with the opportunity to make his name as the sentinel safeguarding America from Communist penetration. He seized it boldly and throughout the case luck remained on his side, from his first hunch about Hiss's mendacity on 5 August 1948 to his last-minute reprieve from the 'crow eating' press conference on 7 December. It was more than chance, however, that allowed Nixon to conclude the case so triumphantly.

Winston Churchill once said that the most formidable politicians are those who know 'how to make their own weather' and by that definition Nixon had indeed shown a talent for political climate control. In the light of later events at Watergate it was perhaps ironic that the thirty-five-year-old Congressman should have made his reputation as a fighter against cover-ups, a role which was just as crucial to his success as his determination to unmask Communist treachery. But there were no such ironies in 1948. These perceptions were the principal ingredients of the rocket fuel which propelled Nixon on his meteoric rise from freshman Congressman to Vice President within four years.

In Washington there were shadows as well as sunlight over Nixon's new reputation, for the acclaim from his supporters was soon to be followed by denunciations from his detractors. The first manifestation of this phenomenon was a social reaction by upper-class liberals, furious with Nixon for committing the unpardonable sin of proving a gentleman a liar. Then came a political reaction. When Hiss first testified, many leading Democrats flocked to his side, making their support for him public. They thus became pawns in Hiss's strategy of 'innocence by association'. When this strategy collapsed with the jury's verdict, those same Democrats were anxious to avoid the appearance of guilt by association. So rather than blaming Hiss, some of them attacked Nixon. He was amazed by such reactions, which scarred his attitudes towards certain types of opponent for the rest of his career. Forty years after the Hiss case, he spoke to this author about an incident from that period which had clearly left its mark on him.

> I recall being at a dinner party at Virginia Bacon's house in Washington. She was one of the great hostesses and Paul Porter was there, a good liberal Democrat. This was right after the Pumpkin Papers had come out and someone was needling Porter a little because they knew he had been strongly pro-Hiss. He was being pressed to admit that the Committee had done a good job in exposing this. And Porter got angry and replied, 'No! I think the Un-American Activities Committee Hearings have been a disaster. I don't care whether Hiss or Chambers is lying. These hearings should be stopped because they are detrimental to the country in the way they cast reflections on Roosevelt's foreign policy.'
>
> Well, there you had it. That was perhaps typical, typical of people in the foreign service, typical of people closely associated with Harvard and other great universities. They couldn't bear to find one of their own like Hiss being involved in this kind of thing. They considered the Hiss case as being an attack on the whole élite establishment, an attack on the foreign service, an attack on those who were for the UN, and even an attack on Roosevelt's foreign policy. Those attitudes were all crap, but that was what I had to fight against.[83]

Such liberal attitudes towards the Hiss affair would later be amplified when the impact of the case was hijacked and perverted by Senator Joseph McCarthy. For a few weeks after Hiss was convicted, McCarthy made his notorious speech in Wheeling, West Virginia, whipping up in generalised and wildly exaggerated form the fears which Nixon had proved to be justified in one specific case of treachery.

As part of the reaction to McCarthyism, a myth grew up in certain quarters that Hiss had been wrongly convicted and that Nixon was to blame for ruining an innocent man. Hiss did his utmost to perpetrate that myth. He persistently denied ever having been a Soviet spy and made several unsuccessful attempts to have his conviction overturned. During the next four decades he and some misguided journalistic followers continued to protest against the jury's verdict with much writing about conspiracies, stolen typewriters, perjured witnesses and other exculpatory theories. These are the real red herrings of the saga. For Hiss could come up with no plausible explanation for the fact that the samples of typing which he admitted had been done by him or his wife, were proved to have been written on the same Woodstock machine that had typed the documents produced by Chambers.

Moreover, the dwindling band of conspiracy theorists received a terminal blow to their arguments when the revelation of certain Moscow intelligence archives in the 1980s provided the ultimate confirmation that Hiss had been a Soviet agent. One of the most persuasive statements on the subject came from Oleg Gordievsky, the former KGB station chief in London who defected to the West in 1985. In his book, written with Christopher Andrew, *KGB: The Inside Story of its Foreign Operations from Lenin to Gorbachev*[84] Gordievsky cites a wealth of detail corroborating Hiss's role. 'There is absolutely no doubt about it. I have studied the files myself. Hiss and White* were two of the KGB's most important agents in the entire history of foreign espionage',[85] he has stated.

The legacy of Alger Hiss on Nixon's long-term thinking and attitudes was a mixed one. On the credit side, the case completed his education on the nature of Communism. His experiences on the Herter Committee had shown him its international face. Hiss showed him the threat it posed domestically. Having had his eyes opened to its danger, Nixon's determination to counter Communist expansion would never falter for the rest of his career.

On the debit side, the case caused a sharp deterioration in Nixon's relationship with the media. He has always believed that the trouble started when he proved so many columnists and editors to have been wrong about Hiss.

---

* Mention of Harry Dexter White is a reminder that the same evidence that uncovered Hiss also uncovered a number of other spies. Nixon was aware of this evidence but made no further effort to continue his role as a spycatcher or to prolong his membership of HUAC. Once he had got Hiss, he distanced himself from the generalised scaremongering on Communist subversion and was privately dismayed by the unprofessionalism of McCarthy's broad brush smears.

Up to the Hiss case it seemed to me that I had a very good career and a relatively non-controversial career. Everybody likes to be kind of non-controversial. You don't like to get up in the morning and see a Herblock cartoon showing you climbing out of a sewer—and he had worse on occasion with me. You don't like your family to see it because children grow up and those images become seared into their brains and in their minds and in their souls. And so after the Hiss case, it left a great mark on all of us because what happened there was that many people in the media never forgave me...they felt in some way that I was attacking their whole way of life, what they stood for and so forth. I don't mean they were Communists. They probably disapproved, if they thought he was guilty at all, of what Hiss had been charged with at least, but on the other hand they just didn't like the idea of somebody coming along and demonstrating that there was some Communist infiltration in the Government.[86]

This is a revealing, but questionable piece of self-diagnosis. Like many outwardly tough figures in public life, Nixon can be hypersensitive to attacks that affect members of his family. This is an understandable reflex action, but not if a journalistic pinprick is reciprocated by a permanent grudge. Part of Nixon's post-Hiss problem with the press was that he always had a longer memory than his critics. He found it difficult to forgive or forget the personal aspersions that he felt had hurt members of his family, or perhaps himself.

Alongside the press and Nixon's new category of people to be distrusted after the Hiss case, came the Hiss types—members of the New Deal ruling class who had been to Ivy League universities; who appeared in the social register; and who had demonstrated an aloof scepticism about the dangers of Communist subversion. When he became President two decades later, Nixon still frequently referred to 'Hiss types', the general inference being that they survived in the federal bureaucracy and were adversaries of whom to beware.

Nixon's ability to remain angry with individuals whose opinions on the Hiss case differed from his own says much about the depth of his political passion at that time. There was a great deal of moral indignation in the young Nixon, surprising perhaps for a man who in later life was so often to be described by his critics as amoral. A little less zeal might well have served his interests better in the aftermath of the case. Perhaps he needed someone to remind him that he had won a great battle and that he would be wise to follow Winston Churchill's advice, 'In victory—magnanimity'. Instead, he continued to fulminate against his real or imaginary enemies in the press and in the Washington establishment. It was round one of a long fight. Although some of the fulminations were to develop into obsessions, they should be seen in the context of a high risk drama, in which Nixon was ultimately proved generally fair and gloriously right.

There can be no gainsaying the fundamental facts that resound to his credit. He alone fought the cover-up in the early stages by persisting with HUAC's investigation of Chambers' evidence. He alone did not falter in the face of press and presidential pressure. He alone battled against the Justice Department which, as late as December 1948, wanted to drop the whole case. To help him in this struggle against the combined forces of the White House, the Administration and Hiss's prestigious defence lawyers, he had only the HUAC staff, namely Stripling and five other investigators, none of whom were lawyers. Without Nixon's determination, the Truman administration would have turned a blind eye to the allegations of Communist espionage and subversion by Alger Hiss. Painful though his exposure of the case was, suppression of it would have been infinitely worse for America's national interest. The jailing of Hiss as an individual was relatively unimportant but the unmasking of Hiss as a Soviet activist within the US Government marked a watershed in postwar history. For once the case had been proven by due process of law, the public's awareness of the Soviet Union's long-term intentions towards the United States was significantly raised. This new awareness was an important factor in strengthening America's resolve never to be defeated by Communism on either the international or the domestic front.

One observer of these events who well understood the wider implications of Hiss's conviction was the man destined to be America's next President, Dwight D. Eisenhower. As a trustee of the Carnegie Endowment he had followed the unfolding events with close attention, initially believing that Hiss was being unfairly treated. As Nixon persisted, Eisenhower changed his mind. When the two men met in 1951 in their respective roles of Senator and army general, Eisenhower made a remark which could be regarded both as the epitaph on the Hiss case and as the overture for Nixon's future political prospects: 'The thing that most impressed me was that you not only got Hiss, but you got him fairly.'[87]

TEN

THE SENATE ELECTION

I. THE PRIMARIES

The 1950 Senate race in California between Richard Nixon and Helen Gahagan Douglas has passed into legend as a melodrama of political mud-slinging. It was an election that had mixed results for Nixon. He became the junior Senator for California at the age of thirty-seven and established himself as one of the rising stars of the Republican Party. Yet his success was tempered by allegations that he had conducted a dirty campaign and by the nickname he acquired of 'Tricky Dick'. Both the reputation and the soubriquet were to haunt him for the rest of his career. But was this infamy deserved? Was his behaviour really as bad as it was later claimed? As with so many electioneering controversies, the myths and the realities are blurred, for the evidence against Nixon seems insufficient to justify the censorious verdicts that have been handed down by some journalistic judges.

Surveying his prospects in the aftermath of the Hiss case, Nixon had little hesitation in deciding to contest the Senate seat held by Sheridan Downey. Downey's term was ending in 1951 and although he was a popular, two-term Democratic incumbent, his 150,000 majority was by no means impregnable in a state which had undergone major demographic changes. Moreover, there were strong rumours that, for health reasons, he was not intending to run again.

Nixon went through all the motions of consulting carefully with friends, supporters and knowledgeable outsiders. Most of his backers in the 12th District, led by Herman Perry, advised him not to jeopardise his safe seat in the House of Representatives by entering a Senate race where success looked highly uncertain. Others were more sanguine about his chances. 'He could whip Abraham Lincoln if necessary in the Senate fight',[1] said Roy Day in response to Herman Perry's pessimism.

Nixon let the argument roll back and forth for several months, outwardly keeping his options open while inwardly becoming increasingly convinced that he should take the plunge. He had three powerful allies in helping him to reach this decision. The first was the march of events. Throughout 1949–50 the chill of the Cold War was deepening. In Eastern Europe and in the Far East, free nations were crumbling under Communist domination. The Western alliance was increasingly troubled by fear of espionage. The conviction of Alger Hiss on 21 January 1950 was followed on 3 February by the atomic scientist Klaus Fuchs's confession to the British authorities that he had been passing Anglo-American nuclear secrets to the Russians from 1943 to 1947. Nine US citizens, including Ethel and Julius Rosenberg, were later arrested in connection with this atomic spy ring.

The mood of anxiety deepened with the advent of a raucous new voice in politics. Senator Joseph McCarthy of Wisconsin had made a speech on 9 February 1950 in Wheeling, West Virginia, in which he claimed to have uncovered a network of Communist spies operating throughout the federal government. This was the beginning of an unscrupulous scaremongering campaign designed to prey on the growing fears of Middle America. Although McCarthy's rantings were based on exaggerated suspicions rather than factual evidence, he did not lack either followers or imitators. A strong anti-Communist stance became almost de rigueur among candidates for office, Democrats as well as Republicans. Nixon's expertise on the subject made him look far more credible than many of his political contemporaries who came belatedly, noisily and sometimes irresponsibly to this issue. He was the experienced professional in a pack of wild amateurs, gaining in stature as the public's mounting concern about subversion was matched with growing respect for the one politician who had so visibly fought to expose it in the Hiss case.

Nixon rode the crest of this wave with a series of well-publicised speeches, of which the most important was a two-hour special address delivered to the House of Representatives on 26 January 1950 entitled 'The Lessons of the Hiss Case'. This contained a critical analysis of the lethargy and 'politics as usual' thinking which Nixon claimed had characterised the Truman administration's cover-up. It also set out an agenda for action, including more backing for the FBI; an extension of the statute of limitations on espionage cases from three to ten years; and an improvement on the vetting system for federal government employees. Reprints of the speech were circulated on a massive scale to voters in California and to newspaper editors, most of whom published long extracts. It could hardly have been a better opening for a Senate campaign.

Pat was the second ally, proving, as she had in 1946, a decisive supporter of the high risk strategy. For most of 1949 Nixon was advised by many well-meaning friends and relatives to limit the horizons of his ambitions; to be patient; to stay a Congressman and rise quietly through the seniority system to a position of influence in the House. He was also approached with business offers which would have made him independently wealthy. One came from his now-prosperous Uncle Ernest Nixon, who wanted his nephew to leave politics and become the managing partner in a chain of Pennsylvania potato farms. None of these options appealed to Pat. Contrary to the myth that she was fed up with the life of politics because of its disruptions to the life of the family, she was in fact the strongest supporter of Nixon's own urge to advance. As her daughter, Julie Nixon Eisenhower, wrote later, 'In the midst of the negative voices, he had one vitally important backer who believed he could and should win, Pat Nixon.'[2] His wife's support must have been music to Nixon's ear because it was in harmony with the tune he was hearing from his third ally, his own inner voice.

Never much of an enthusiast for the path of caution, Nixon privately calculated that he had reached his peak in the House and that he must strike out for the Senate while his star was in the ascendant. The national results of the 1948 election had left him in a position which he knew would soon become frustrating, and which had turned him overnight into a junior member of the minority party, 'a "comer" with no place to go'.[3] Above all, his instinctive judgement told Nixon that he could win the Senate seat, even though he knew that there were many imponderables, especially the unknown voter loyalties in northern and central California, where he had no base of support. Commenting retrospectively on his calculations at that time, Nixon has said, 'Looking back I think the risks were much greater than I believed, but at age thirty-six one can be a dreamer.'[4]

Towards the end of 1949 his dreams hardened into definite ambition and on 3 November Nixon announced his candidacy for the Republican nomination, promising 500 cheering supporters in Pomona that he would put on 'a fighting, rocking, socking campaign'.[5] In fact, most of the rocking, socking, and other more aggressive activities were provided during the early months of the campaign, not by Nixon but by the Democrats, who embarked on a subplot of internecine feuding worthy of the Borgias. Playing the part of Lucrezia was Helen Gahagan Douglas, a colourful and combative left-of-centre Congresswoman from California's 14th District who, a month earlier, had announced her intention to overthrow the incumbent, Sheridan Downey. Douglas's campaign against her fellow Democrat was bitter and personalised. She attacked Downey as 'a part-time Senator'[6] and her rhetoric was full of aggressive allegations about his absenteeism; his poor legislative record and his subservience to big business interests. The invective was reciprocated and Downey traded blows with Douglas for five months, accusing her of political ignorance, fiscal irresponsibility and left-wing extremism. Douglas retaliated with new claims about the Senator's unethical dependence on California oil money and widened her attack to include his Democratic conservative fund raisers. Eventually Downey could stand the pressure no longer and on 28 March, as he entered hospital for an ulcer operation, he issued a withdrawal statement saying that he was no longer fit enough for 'waging a personal and militant campaign against the vicious and unethical propaganda' of his woman challenger.[7]

Instead of seeking to heal the wounds at this turning point in her race, Douglas ridiculed his claim of ill health as 'a cheap gimmick',[8] thus ensuring that the Senator would remain her enemy. Nixon watched these developments from the sidelines in Washington with private jubilation. He shrewdly displayed some personal solicitude towards Sheridan Downey, visiting him in hospital during his convalescence and issuing a statement wishing the Senator 'a complete and speedy recovery'.[9] Meanwhile, back in California, the Democratic feuding was sharply deteriorating into civil war as Manchester Boddy, the conservative publisher of the *Los Angeles Daily News,* entered the fray as Douglas's new opponent for the primary. Boddy was a spoiler rather than a serious candidate, but as befitted a newspaper proprietor, his campaign was always in the headlines. Downey's supporters flocked to join his colours as Boddy presented himself as the true keeper of the Democratic faith. In this role he attacked Douglas with unprecedented venom, charging that she and her supporters constituted 'a statewide conspiracy on the part of a small subversive clique of red-hots to capture through stealth and cunning the nerve centers of our Democratic party'.[10]

These opening shots fired by the Boddy forces set the tone for the whole campaign. The 'red-hots' label stuck and worse name-calling followed, most of it from fellow Democrats. Douglas was pilloried in the language of Boddy's wilder supporters as 'a Russia Firstie', 'a nigger lover', 'a bleeding heart liberal' and 'a playmate in the mire of Communism'. There were many associations made between Douglas and the colours red and pink. She was variously described in newspaper stories as 'the darling of the Hollywood parlor pinks', 'a pinko', 'the red queen' and 'the pink lady'. There were also many vicious anti-Semitic taunts, based on the fact that Douglas's Jewish husband, the actor Melvyn Douglas, had changed his name from Hesselberg.[11]

None of these smears had anything to do with Nixon, who watched in grateful silence as his opponents carved themselves into pieces. The unkindest cut of all came from Senator Downey, who rose from his hospital bed to deliver a brutal anti-Douglas speech over statewide radio on 22 May 1950. 'As one who seeks only the welfare of the state and its people, it is my opinion that Mrs. Douglas does not have the fundamental ability and qualifications for a United States Senator...She has shown no inclination, in fact no ability to dig in and do the hard and tedious work required to prepare legislation and push it through Congress', he said.[12]

Having questioned Douglas's very fitness to serve, Downey went on to do further damage to his political successor's standing within her own party by reminding the Democrats how disloyal she had been to the President. 'She wept in total collapse when Harry Truman was finally nominated over Henry Wallace', said Downey, harking back to the 1944 Democratic Convention and making the point that Douglas had failed to support Truman in his greatest hours of need. 'Mrs. Douglas gave comfort to the Soviet tyranny by voting against aid to both Greece and Turkey. She voted against the President in a crisis when he most needed her support and most fully deserved her confidence', he added.[13]

All this was grist to Nixon's political mill. He was campaigning hard in the primaries, making more than 600 speeches in sixteen weeks, mainly to small audiences in small towns. He had no problem elevating himself to a position of centrist rectitude above the Boddy–Douglas scrimmage. His standard speech included praise for Sheridan Downey; reminders of his own role as a staunch anti-Communist fighter; and a general setting out of his stall with moderate domestic policies designed to capture the traditional Democratic voters from the farms, factories and big cities. These were sound tactics in a primary race where all candidates cross-filed and stood in each other's party contests. When the results were announced on 6 June, Douglas had scored less than 50 per cent of the Democratic vote while Nixon took 22 per cent of it, as well as winning the GOP nomination with a resounding 70 per cent total. In the popular vote, with over 2.5 million ballots cast, Nixon led Douglas by 42 to 35 per cent. This was an encouraging victory in a state where registered Democrats outnumbered Republicans by a 3–2 margin, particularly since Boddy's conservative, anti-Douglas votes were thought likely to switch to Nixon in the final contest.

II. TRICKY DICK

The battle lines for the general election were now clearly drawn and Nixon was delighted to be on his own in a fight to the finish with Helen Gahagan Douglas. He regarded her as an electrifying political personality but with a capacity to repel as well as attract support. He had carefully analysed her voting record, which in his view exemplified the great left–right divide on the national security issues that were concerning the voters.

Douglas was an exotic character. Born in 1900 into a wealthy family, she had disobeyed her parents by going from private New York schools and Barnard College* on to the stage, where she swiftly achieved stardom, first on Broadway, then as an international prima donna in light opera, and finally in Hollywood movies. Voted one of the ten most beautiful women in America, she married one of her leading men, Melvyn Douglas, and together they achieved another form of stardom as Hollywood's most charismatic political couple. Queen of the social milieu which in a later era became known as 'Radical Chic', Helen Douglas was a dedicated liberal activist for many New Deal causes. Befriended by Eleanor and Franklin Roosevelt, she emerged as a significant national figure in the Democratic Party and was appointed to the Presidential Advisory Committee of the National Youth Administration—the New Deal programme that had helped fund the young Richard Nixon working his way through college as a Duke Library assistant. In 1944, at FDR's urging, she became a candidate for Congress and served the 14th District of California for three terms.

As a member of the House of Representatives, Douglas made both friends and enemies in abundance. Her allies were the unabashed New Deal liberals. She and Jerry Voorhis had been soul mates in the 79th Congress and although the policies they espoused were out of fashion by 1950, Douglas and a handful of surviving radicals still held the left-wing flame aloft. Their positions were considered out of the Democratic mainstream, so much so that the corridor of the House building where she and other members of this group had their offices was known to other members of her party as 'Red Gulch'.[14]

The personal animosity that Douglas aroused was not just the product of her controversial views. On the whole, the House Republicans were merely her opponents. Her enemies were her fellow Democrats. Male jealousy of this aggressive and successful female outsider may well have played its part in creating this situation, but Douglas herself contributed to it, for there was an element of righteousness in her speeches, and haughtiness in the way she dealt with her colleagues.

---

* Barnard College is the New York women's college affiliated with Columbia University.

Nixon himself had not fully appreciated the degree of Democratic resentment until one afternoon when Congressman John F. Kennedy came into his office. 'Dick,' he said, 'I know you're in for a pretty rough campaign, and my father wanted to help out.' He handed over an envelope containing $1,000 in cash. 'I obviously can't endorse you,' Kennedy continued, 'but it isn't going to break my heart if you can turn the Senate's loss into Hollywood's gain.'[15] After thanking his benefactor, Nixon came back into the office showing the money to his aide Pat Hillings and saying over and over again, 'Isn't this something! Isn't this just something!'[16]

All campaign contributions, even from as unexpected a source as the Kennedy family, were welcome. Senate races were usually expensive, especially in a huge state like California. Nixon's total campaign costs have been variously estimated at figures between $350,000[17] and $1.6 million,[18] while his own calculations assessed the bill at $750,000.[19] One of the key factors contributing to such high costs was that 1950 was a watershed year in which the art of American electioneering was in transition. The age of open-air hustings, torchlight parades and handwritten precinct voting sheets was being replaced by an era of television and modern communications. The Democrats were quicker than the Republicans to exploit the opportunities offered by the new technologies. In the early stages of the Californian Senate race, Helen Douglas had the electronic edge. With the help of a campaign organisation well funded by the big labour unions, Douglas had pre-booked large quantities of radio and television time and moved across the state in her personal helicopter. Nixon, by comparison, was touring in a second-hand, wood-panelled station wagon equipped with antique loudspeakers. His media efforts were initially confined to visiting newspaper editors in the same way as he had done in his 1946 campaign against Voorhis. Hesitant about using television, which at that time had reached less than a third of California's homes, he put out only one major campaign commercial. This was a five-minute broadcast whose climax was a human interest sequence of the Nixon family having a singsong. To the tune of 'Merrily We Roll Along', the refrain was supposed to be 'Off we go to Washington, Washington, Washington. Off we go to Washington— Vote for Nixon!' All went well in the rehearsals. But when the broadcast was going out live, two-year-old Julie, who was clasping a toy bunny, mixed up her political loyalties as it came to the punchline. 'Vote for Bunny!' she sang out loud and clear, to the mortification of the producers.[20]

Such amateur efforts at political communication were necessary because Nixon faced huge problems in bringing out the voters despite the advantages of the national recognition that had come to him in the wake of the Hiss case.

The major hurdle was the size of the constituency. By 1950 California was already the second most populous state of the Union. Its seven million voters were distributed over a geographical area roughly equivalent to unified Germany, Belgium and the Netherlands. Many of them were newcomers. Since the end of the war in 1945, more than three million Americans had moved into the West Coast state, prompting the Governor's office to describe the inflow as the largest voluntary migration of peoples in the history of the world. Such a demographic shift made California almost *terra incognita* for political pundits. It was impossible to make accurate forecasts with such a large and scattered electorate. Faced with this Herculean task, Nixon picked as his campaign manager one of the most effective professional strategists of the period—Murray Chotiner.

In the mythology surrounding Nixon's early political career, Murray Chotiner has been portrayed as a Svengali-like evil genius whose manipulation of his boss was the cause of a descent into 'dirty' electioneering. This is largely a misrepresentation, for in every campaign Nixon was always his own chief decision-maker. He frequently disregarded Chotiner's advice, particularly when it came to deciding which issues should be exploited. However, Chotiner did bring one new and controversial diversion to the election. He could be described as the father of negative campaigning, for he believed in the theory that electorates vote against politicians rather than for them. In pursuance of this theory he believed it was his job to discredit the opposition as much as possible. Such an approach, now accepted as standard practice in many US election campaigns, was novel in 1950.

With his sallow skin and pudgy appearance, Chotiner would never have won a beauty contest, although he enjoyed considerable success with the ladies. He could be charming and humorous but he did not suffer fools gladly, and his abrasive tongue made him many enemies. Like Helen Douglas, he had the ability both to repel and attract. Some Nixon supporters found him obnoxious, while others adored him. What united them all was a genuine respect for Chotiner's sheer professionalism, particularly his meticulous scheduling, and his innovative organisational methods. Without his drive, the disparate geographical and political factions in California's GOP could have fragmented into the chaotic in-fighting that characterised the Democrats' campaign. Instead, Chotiner welded the Republicans into a co-ordinated team which continually upstaged and outmanoeuvred the opposition. Nixon himself was well aware of the debt he owed his master tactician, describing Chotiner as 'the most capable campaign technician I have ever known. His management of the 1950 campaign was truly textbook in character. He left nothing to chance and saw to every detail and nuance…Murray did not let any constituency go unnoticed. Every newspaper and radio station received his attention. No opportunity passed for him to make political news with a handout or statement. He covered everything from local finances to organizing rallies and running advertisements. He was in short a consummate and extraordinarily skilful politician in the best sense of that word.'[21]

For all their good rapport and mutual dependency, Chotiner and Nixon disagreed for a time on the central theme of the campaign. Chotiner favoured a more domestic slant towards localised issues but Nixon was determined to keep the spotlight on the menace of international Communism. Just as he had done before the Voorhis campaign, Nixon spent many hours researching into his opponents' speeches and voting records. These revealed a rich harvest of potential embarrassments for a candidate seeking support from a worried California electorate which was visibly swinging away from the liberal corner. In addition to her opposition to military aid for Greece and Turkey (the key plank in the Truman doctrine for Communist containment), Douglas had voted against establishing and funding HUAC; against the Selective Service Act of 1948, which had strengthened America's military preparedness; against loyalty checks for federal government employees; and against clauses in the Security Bill of 1949 which permitted the heads of key national defence agencies to discharge government workers found by the FBI to be poor security risks. In his general election campaign Nixon regularly invoked this litany of votes as evidence for the claim that his opponent was not to be trusted on vital national security issues. He supplemented his attack with quotations from Douglas's more injudicious speeches, of which his prime examples were her praise of Soviet 'sincerity' at Yalta and the opening line of her 'My Democratic Credo' address to the House of Representatives: 'I think we all know that Communism is no real threat to the democratic institutions of our country.'[22]

Throughout the election, Douglas never attempted to deny Nixon's charges. However, they put her on the defensive, particularly when the start of the Korean War added an element of panic to the voters' concerns about national security. As Soviet-trained North Korean troops poured over the 38th parallel in the late summer of 1950, Nixon's earlier warnings of the dangers of Communist aggression made him look like a prophet. In his speeches he rammed home the message that Communists could start hot wars as well as cold ones, while red, white and blue billboards symbolised his stand with their message 'RICHARD NIXON— ON GUARD FOR AMERICA'.

Goaded by the success of the Republican propaganda, the Douglas camp made a fatal miscalculation and started to attack Nixon personally for being soft on Communism. This was folly of a high order. Not only did it shift the election debate on to ground favourable to the Republicans, it was also the one issue on which Nixon's credentials were invulnerable. Apparently unaware of the pitfalls of her strategy, Douglas struck out with a campaign leaflet printed on yellow paper that read: 'THE BIG LIE! Hitler invented it. Stalin perfected it. Nixon uses it…LET'S LOOK AT THE RECORD…YOU pick the Congressman the Kremlin loves! Compare the voting records of Richard NIXON and Helen Gahagan DOUGLAS with the vital bills that concerned KOREA. Compare their votes with those of Vito MARCANTONIO, American Labor Party (Pro Communist) Congressman.'

The abstruse argument about whose votes in the House of Representatives had coincided with those of the notorious Congressman Marcantonio of New York had first surfaced during the primaries, when one of Manchester Boddy's supporters, Rex Whittemore, a former Commander of the American Legion, issued a statement advising all veterans not to support Douglas because she had voted four times with Marcantonio against further funding for HUAC.[23] Marcantonio, who stood defiantly on the extreme left of the political spectrum, was widely regarded as being a Communist in everything but name. He could be relied on to vote the CP line on every possible occasion and had surfaced in Nixon's demonology after being the only Congressman in the entire House of Representatives to vote against the contempt citation of Gerhardt Eisler. Against this background the suggestion in Douglas's 'yellow sheet' (as it became known) that Nixon and Marcantonio were fellow travellers was patently absurd. The yellow sheet was soon proved full of errors. Far from voting against aid to Korea, Nixon had merely withheld his support for three weeks as part of a successful manoeuvre to get the bill strengthened by the inclusion of additional aid to Formosa. As for another charge that he had promoted Communism by voting with Marcantonio to cut European aid in half, Nixon had simply preferred a one-year bill with a strengthened renewal provision over a two-year bill with no renewal clauses. With Douglas's distortions falling apart as a result of the Republican rebuttal, Chotiner exulted over the 'yellow sheet', which he regarded as a turning point in the campaign, saying, 'She made the fatal mistake of attacking our strength instead of attacking our weaknesses.'[24]

Although he was safely ahead in the polls, Nixon was sufficiently stung by the yellow sheet's comparisons of himself to Hitler, Stalin and Marcantonio that he too entered the black propaganda war. In mid-September he put out a flyer headlined 'Douglas-Marcantonio Voting Record'. Beginning with a statement, 'Many persons have requested a comparison of the voting records of Congresswoman

Helen Douglas and the notorious Communist party-liner Congressman Vito Marcantonio of New York', the leaflet claimed that on 354 occasions the two of them had voted in the same lobby. After setting out the voting statistics together with detailed dates and references, the leaflet referred to the 'Douglas-Marcantonio axis' and continued, 'After studying the voting comparison between Mrs. Douglas and Marcantonio, is it any wonder that the Communist line newspaper the *Daily People's World* in its lead editorial on 31 January 1950 labelled Congressman Nixon as "The Man to Beat" in this Senate race and that the Communist newspaper the New York *Daily Worker* in the issue of July 1947 selected Mrs. Douglas along with Marcantonio as "One of the Heroes of the 80th Congress"?'[25] This broadside delighted Nixon supporters and made a big impact on voters throughout the state as campaign manager Murray Chotiner increased the original print order from 50,000 to 500,000 copies.[26] The leaflet became known as 'the pink sheet' because the paper on which it was published had a pinkish tinge, a choice which Chotiner later praised as a good early example of the influence of colour on a political campaign.

Whatever the merits or demerits of its aesthetic appeal, the actual content of the pink sheet was misleading. The so-called 'Douglas–Marcantonio axis' was an illusion. Nixon himself had voted with Marcantonio 112 times, which was unsurprising considering that most of the 354 votes were minor and often procedural. Only seventy-six of the votes listed were major 'roll calls'. Of these, Douglas and Marcantonio voted together fifty-three times in line with the Democratic party whip, sometimes supported by Republicans. Looking at the remaining twenty-three votes in which Douglas defied her party, most of them were liberal stands on domestic measures such as housing, rent and price controls. The only issues on which she was out on a limb with Marcantonio were the Greek–Turkish Aid Bill; the Mundt–Nixon Bill and its successor the McCarran Internal Security Bill, where she had voted to support President Truman's veto. On ten key roll-call votes she had been in the opposite lobby from the New York Congressman. Douglas was certainly independent in temperament and left-wing by inclination, but she did not deserve the pink sheet's unscrupulous tarnishing of her as a neo-Communist clone of Marcantonio.

After the salvoes had been exchanged between the yellow and pink sheets, the last weeks of the campaign deteriorated into a downward spiral of name calling. Sometimes it seemed that they were equally offensive, countering one good smear with another, but the record suggests that Douglas was the worst offender. Her response to the pink sheet was to issue a series of newspaper advertisements headlined 'THOU SHALT NOT BEAR FALSE WITNESS', which returned to the baseless charge that Nixon was a fellow traveller. Accusing Nixon of 'blind stupidity on foreign policy', the text claimed that he had given 'aid and comfort to the Communists' and that on every key vote in the House of Representatives he had 'stood with party liner Marcantonio against America in its fight to defeat Communism'.[27] Even wilder calumnies were to follow. In a series of increasingly hysterical speeches, Douglas said she 'despised Communism, Naziism and Nixonism',[28] and linked Nixon to Mussolini's fascists by saying his supporters were 'a backwash of young men in dark shirts'.[29] She also falsely claimed that he had secretly invited Senator McCarthy to come and campaign for him; alleged that he was 'conspiring to sell the welfare of the American people down the river of fear and hysteria for personal ambition'[30] and repeatedly denounced Nixon as 'a pipsqueak...and a peewee who is trying to scare people into voting for him'. In a famous gibe, which was to endure as a political albatross around Nixon's neck for the rest of his career, she dubbed him 'Tricky Dick'.[31]

Nixon was not one to take these insults lying down, particularly as Pat was getting upset by the personalisation of the attacks. He denounced the 'false witness' advertisements as 'sacrilegious', and ridiculed Douglas in the heat of at least one whistle-stop speech as 'pink right down to her underwear'.[32] In a radio broadcast delivered on 18 September, Nixon went for his opponent's jugular:

> If she had her way, the Communist conspiracy in the United States would never have been exposed and Alger Hiss, instead of being a convicted perjurer, would still be influencing the foreign policy of the United States...If she had her way, our troops in Korea would have been even less well prepared than they are...I want to point out one very significant thing about all of the votes I have mentioned. These were not party line votes. My opponent did not vote as a Democrat. She did not vote as a Republican...it just so happens that my opponent is a member of a small clique which joins the notorious Communist party-liner Vito Marcantonio of New York in voting time after time against measures that are for the security of this country.[33]

Although Nixon was unfair in his exaggeration of Douglas's links with the bogeyman Marcantonio, there were other exploitable campaign issues on which he exercised restraint. Early in the primaries he disassociated himself from Senator McCarthy's generalised charges of Communist infiltration, saying at a press conference on 15 April 1950 that only the CP was helped by them.[34] 'Wild unsubstantiated charges of disloyalty,' declared Nixon, 'could very well render a disservice to the security of our nation.'[35] When Dr. Robert Oppenheimer, the Chief Scientist on the Manhattan Project,* was accused by a committee of the California Senate of being a Communist, Nixon condemned the allegations, saying, 'I have complete confidence in Dr. Oppenheimer.'[36] Later in the campaign, the Republicans were embarrassed to receive the fervent backing of the Christian Nationalist Crusade, whose leader, Gerald L. K. Smith, urged California's voters to 'Help Richard Nixon get rid of the Jew Communists', and 'Do not send to the Senate the wife of a Jew.' Nixon swiftly repudiated the CNC in a strong statement which won praise from the Anti-Defamation League. In it he pointed out that his own Quaker faith made him totally opposed to all racial or religious discrimination, a valid claim which was personified by the presence of the Jewish Murray Chotiner as his campaign manager.

Chotiner himself had to be reined in by Nixon from some of his more aggressive propaganda techniques. On one occasion, when the candidate discovered his manager checking the proofs of another anti-Douglas leaflet set in bold red type, Nixon ordered a colour change and had the prints done in blue. He vetoed some news releases drafted by his press aide, Bill Arnold, warning him 'not to be ungallant' to a woman opponent.[37] However, such examples of restraint were rare. Nixon undoubtedly did take liberties with Douglas's record. His concentration on national security and her alleged weakness in the face of Communism, to the exclusion of almost all other issues, is hard to defend. Yet it should be remembered that he was constantly responding in kind to outrageous charges that had been levelled against him by his opponent. If there were times when he counterattacked too fiercely, it can be said that the provocation was great and that Helen Douglas's own record of virtuous electioneering behaviour was small. If there had been a contest as to which candidate had the cleaner hands in this unsavoury campaign, victory would have gone on points to Richard Nixon. But they were almost as bad as each other.

III. HAPPY DAYS ARE HERE AGAIN

Six weeks before polling day, Douglas's support was haemorrhaging badly and many Democrats were changing sides, among them the young Ronald Reagan and his girlfriend, Nancy Davis. They had started out as Hollywood supporters of their friend Helen, but by mid-campaign they were holding fund-raising parties for Nixon.[38] With Congressman John F. Kennedy vacationing in California during the fall but remaining conspicuously absent from the Democratic campaign, the

---

* The Manhattan Project was the Allies' wartime effort to develop the first atom bomb.

only current or future President to support Douglas was Harry S. Truman, who badly wanted to see Nixon beaten. He made a 'non-political' visit to San Francisco in October, but foreseeing defeat, changed his campaigning plans and sent a shoal of big-name Democrats, headed by Vice President Alben Barkley, into the fray with endorsements for Douglas. This tactic misfired. Nixon was able to exploit Californians' well-known dislike of outsiders, telling them how to vote by ridiculing Truman's surrogates as 'the foreign legion'; 'carpet baggers' and 'cows mooing in at milking time'.[39] To add to Douglas's woes, one of the visiting firemen, Attorney General J. Howard McGrath, made the tactical error of claiming that the prosecution of Alger Hiss should be credited to the Justice Department rather than to Nixon and HUAC. That was untrue and gave Nixon a golden opportunity to play the Hiss card in the closing stages of the campaign. On 19 October he gave a long radio address retelling the story of the Hiss case in great detail and rebutting McGrath's speech point by point.

Viewed from a distance of over four decades, it seems likely that by this stage in the election, the voters of California might have been getting tired of Nixon's constant banging of the anti-Communist drum. There were some in his camp who at the time evidently felt this way. Murray Chotiner strongly advised the candidate to lay off his role as a spycatcher and to concentrate on domestic issues. This was a sound tactical recommendation. Douglas had taken up unpopular positions supporting the Truman administration's proposals for federal control of California's offshore oil and gas resources; and for federal laws restricting free irrigation water supply to farms of 160 acres or less. She also favoured the complex Brannan plan for agricultural subsidies to certain crops. On all these questions Nixon, as a supporter of states' rights and a free marketeer, was much more in tune with the wishes of the voters than his opponent. He made his stance clear enough, but his speeches on these populist issues took second place to his unrelenting rhetoric on the Communist menace. There are usually many more votes in local bread and butter subjects than in long-distance warnings about foreign policy, but Nixon disregarded his supporters' urgings to change tactics, sincere in his deep conviction that America needed a much stronger posture of military preparedness abroad and domestic vigilance at home in order to contain the threat of international Communism. By the end of the campaign he sounded positively defiant towards his own backers as he began a standard passage in his stump speech: 'I have been advised not to talk about Communism, but I'm going to tell the people of California the truth.'[40] Such defiance looked like prescience when, with less than a week to go to polling day, China entered the Korean War. With Chinese Communist troops pouring across the Yalu river into Korea, the US forces were on the verge of one of the bloodiest retreats in modern history. Nixon publicly demanded that Douglas should state her position on the admission of Red China to the United Nations. Although known to favour full diplomatic recognition of Peking, Douglas equivocated and finally refused to answer. 'This is the last straw', declared Nixon. 'I know that my opponent was committed to the State Department policy of appeasement towards Communism in the Far East, but I never dreamed she would stick to it even after we were attacked.'[41] This parthian shot went home. Douglas's already weakened support crumbled still further in the days before voting, as the dramatic events of the Korean War unfolded.

Despite some encouraging Gallup Polls, Nixon spent election day in a state of high nervous tension, so worried about his chances of defeat that he was unable to eat the getting-away-from-it-all picnic which Pat had prepared for him. As he sat shivering on a chilly Los Angeles beach on 6 November alone with his wife, anxiously awaiting the electorate's judgement, the one thing that did not worry him was that aspect of the campaign that has subsequently been of greatest preoccupation to journalists and commentators—its dirt. Nixon knew that the battle had been a rough one. He had fought hard, neither asking nor yielding quarter. He felt that he had run on the issues, not the personalities. He believed, with justification, that his opponent's campaign rhetoric had been more offensive than his own. But the strongest reason for Nixon's oblivion to the later charges of dirty campaigning was that he believed he had fought within the boundaries of the prevailing electioneering conventions in those turbulent times. In 1950 the curtain had not yet come down on the age of the open-air hustings and the savagely aggressive oratory that characterised it. Even the greatest politicians still used language that would soon be regarded as outrageously offensive. In an election on the other side of the Atlantic, Winston Churchill had recently accused his wartime colleague Clement Attlee of 'Gestapo tactics', while the Labour Government's Minister of Health, Nye Bevan, had denounced his Conservative party opponents as 'lower than vermin'. Throughout the English-speaking world, election orators put on their kid gloves with the advent of the television cameras. Some of the words used by both Nixon and Douglas in 1950 read badly now; but they reflected the rhetorical standard of their day. It is a disservice to wrench that election too far out of its historical niche and to apply contemporary judgement to yesteryear's oratorical excesses.*

---

* For many years much has been made of an apology Nixon supposedly gave in an off-the-record conversation about the conduct of the Senate Election campaign, with the British journalist David Astor (Editor of the *Observer*): 'I'm sorry about that episode. I was a very young man.' David Astor himself has no recollection of this much vaunted retraction which is quoted by

Such philosophical reflections were on nobody's mind as the votes were being counted. When the results were announced late at night on 6 November, Richard Nixon had defeated Helen Gahagan Douglas by 680,000 votes out of 3.7 million ballots cast, a staggering margin of 59 per cent to 40 per cent. It was the largest majority achieved by any Senate winner in that year and by any standards a remarkable personal victory. As he spent the night of the election moving triumphantly from one celebration party to another, Nixon pounded out 'Happy Days are Here Again' on every available piano and basked in the flood of congratulations. One of the first telegrams to reach him came from Sheridan Downey: 'Please accept my congratulations on your notable victory and my best wishes and regards.'[43]

Two weeks later Downey announced that he would resign on 30 November, thus allowing Nixon to be appointed as his replacement with an immediate seniority advantage over other incoming freshman Senators. At the age of thirty-seven, he had become a member of the world's most important legislative body, the United States Senate.

---

other biographers.[42] It would certainly have been uncharacteristic of Nixon, who is not noted for giving political apologies.

ELEVEN

SENATOR AND VICE-PRESIDENTIAL CANDIDATE

I. RISING STAR

W ithin months of his election to the Senate, Nixon emerged as a fancied runner in the 1952 vice-presidential stakes. The process by which this was achieved was mysterious even to himself. The political variables of the time were so unpredictable that there could be no such thing as a game plan for winning the second spot on the ticket. Yet for all his disclaimers of interest in presidential politics, Nixon took on a speech-making schedule which was a clear signpost to where his ambitions were heading. During the first six months of 1951 he criss-crossed the country in almost perpetual motion, fulfilling more than four engagements each week and visiting twenty-five states. This frenetic programme consolidated Nixon's network of allies among party officials; raised his national profile; and established his reputation as a crowd puller. The measure of his growing prominence may be gauged from his activities on the anniversary weekend of Lincoln's birthday, when he was the keynote speaker at a chain of Republican rallies, attracting audiences of 2,100 in Philadelphia; 750 in Louisville; 600 in Grand Rapids; and 1,000 in St. Paul. No other national figure in the GOP was making a comparable impact on the party loyalists at that time.

Nixon's appeal had several ingredients. His celebrity as the spycatcher of Hiss was still a draw but was becoming secondary to his new importance as the rising star of the West. As the youngest and most spectacular Republican victor in the 1950 election when the GOP had gained five Senate and twenty-eight House seats, he had come to personify his party's prospects for revival. His zestful enjoyment of the battle came as a tonic to a party that had been badly demoralised by the loss of the 1948 presidential election. His willingness to slash at the Democrats with the language of the political slaughterhouse delighted the faithful. It was an era of angry exaggeration in Republican oratory, and Nixon was at the forefront of the offensive. There was plenty to attack in the accident-prone Truman administration. The plethora of financial scandals that oozed to the surface; the humiliation of US troops in the Korean War; the pomposity of Dean Acheson as Secretary of State; the weakness of US foreign policy; and the ineptitude of Truman's dismissal of General MacArthur as Commander in Korea were perfect targets for opposition invective. Nixon pounded them all mercilessly, often blasting the administration for being 'soft on Communism'. In one characteristic speech in June 1951 to the National Young Republican convention in Boston, he slammed the State Department for 'the whining, whimpering, grovelling attitude of our diplomatic representatives', and accused the White House of refusing 'time and time again to recognize the existence of the fifth column in this country and to take effective action to clean subversives out of the administrative branch of our Government'.[1]

Such rhetoric exhilarated the converted, but it also infuriated the antagonistic and offended the agnostic. In Washington, opinions on the youngest member of the Senate grew increasingly polarised. At one Georgetown cocktail party, Averell Harriman, a leading Democrat and an administration official,* walked out when Nixon arrived, declaring angrily, 'I will not break bread with that man.'[2] Some of his fellow Republicans also found certain aspects of Nixon disagreeable, Senator Robert Taft on one occasion describing him as 'a little man in a big hurry', with 'a mean and vindictive streak in him'.[3] Even to his admirers there was a perplexing contrast between Nixon's aggressive stridency on the public platform and the gentler side of his private character. This was perceived by those working for him in his Senate office, where his team of three young aides and nine secretaries saw 'The Boss' or 'Himself as a sensitive and intellectually profound individual whose only faults as an employer were his occasional bursts of bad temper

---

* Averell Harriman (1891–1986) had been Ambassador to the Soviet Union (1943–6) and to Britain (1946), and Secretary of Commerce (1947–8). He was at this time Director of the Mutual Security Agency (1951–3). He was later elected Governor of New York (1955–8). Returning to foreign policy, he acted as Assistant Secretary of State for Far Eastern Affairs under Kennedy (1961–3), and was appointed by Johnson to lead the US delegation to the Paris peace talks on Vietnam (1968–9).

caused by overwork. Dorothy Cox, who had become his appointments secretary, particularly remembers his consideration for both staff and constituents. 'He was always so polite. He always noticed people's appearances, saying things like, "My, you look nice today. That's a fine dress", sometimes even asking, "How much did it cost?"' She recalls many kindnesses to staffers with personal problems and his dutiful but somewhat awkward attendances at secretaries' birthday parties, where he usually cut the cake on his desk, distributed the ice-cream and read out a specially composed poem.

To visitors from California he was elaborately courteous, even when under pressure. Cox remembers an evening when a Mexican couple arrived unexpectedly in the outer office, bursting to express their gratitude to the senator who had secured an immigration permit for their son. 'Oh, Dorothy, do I have to see them?' groaned Nixon, who was visibly tired and immersed in the preparation of a speech. 'I really think you should', advised Cox. After a ten-minute meeting and greeting session the Mexicans happily departed and Nixon said quietly, 'Thank you for bringing them in, Dorothy. I'm glad you made me see them. Don't ever let us forget that the world is hungry for little bits of human kindness.'[4]

The private Nixon emphasising compassion as an important part of his personal philosophy juxtaposes uncomfortably with his public persona as a ruthless, Red-baiting, Democrat hater. However, all those closest to him in his Senate days are insistent that behind the outer shell of political toughness lay a heart as soft as his mother's. 'Of all the millions of words written about him, none have emphasized his considerable kindness', says Rose Mary Woods, Nixon's long-time personal secretary. 'He's never been given any credit for being a kind person, partly because he's too shy to show it.'[5]

Rose Mary Woods, who was to become the lynch pin of Nixon's professional life for the next quarter of a century, joined him late in 1950. Her Irish grandfather had come to America at the turn of the century as a stowaway, 'borrowing' the name Woods from a ship's captain in order to bluff his way past the US immigration authorities. Rose Woods had been brought up in Sebring, Ohio, and after working there as a secretary in a pottery company she gravitated to Washington and a typist's job on the Herter Committee. She first noticed Congressman Nixon when it was her task to sort out the expenses of the Committee members, several of whom submitted their claims in chaotic form. By contrast, Nixon's expenses were not only neat and punctiliously documented with receipts accounting for the last cent, but also significantly lower than anyone else's.

When Nixon was looking for a secretary just after his election to the Senate, Woods came in for an interview and was impressed by her future employer. 'I remember being particularly taken by the fact that he didn't ask what my religion was. That was unusual in the Washington of those days and even more unusual to someone of my Catholic background because I had grown up in a town where the Ku Klux Klan burned crosses on our lawn on Easter Day. Yet here he was, a Quaker and a Republican, not asking a single question about religion or about my political loyalties, which were pretty vague at that time.'[6]

Once Rose Woods gave her personal loyalty to Richard Nixon, it was as constant as the Northern Star. She was intelligent, literate, and clam-like in her discretion. Technically superb, she possessed the high-speed skills of shorthand and typing necessary to keep up with her boss's often frantic and always demanding schedule. She fully merited that hackneyed but occasionally apposite label 'the perfect secretary'. One of the reasons why Woods struck up such a good rapport with her boss was that their characters were similar. Disciplined in her emotions yet passionate in her convictions, Woods was intuitive, protective and obsessive about privacy. She derived an important spiritual dimension in her life from her Catholicism. Like Nixon she was the product of Irish ancestry diluted by a union of opposites. Her mixture of what she describes as 'my father's temper' and 'my mother's cool head'[7] matches Nixon's combination of his mother's tact and his father's fire.

Rose Mary Woods' professional dedication to the career of the young Senator was soon reinforced by a personal friendship with Pat Nixon. The two women grew to trust one another implicitly. Their shared Irish heritage was part of their bond, but so too was their joint commitment to the mountainous workload of the office. Even with the statutory allowance of $75,000 a year, which enabled him to employ nine stenographers, there were many weeks when Nixon's unanswered mail piled up like snowdrifts. Pat often sweated away alongside Rose Woods and the rest of the secretariat on evenings and weekends to clear this backlog. When the political temperature rose on issues such as the MacArthur dismissal, the snowdrifts could become an avalanche. Pat worked fourteen-hour days as an unpaid volunteer to help the office cope with the 600 telegrams and 30,000 letters that came in on this subject alone.[8]

Although there were many pressures of work and enforced absences in this period of Nixon's career, his family life was a happy one. Pat's regular correspondence with her best friend Helene Drown reflected the contentment in the Nixon home. The only shadows were some nagging health worries. In the summer of 1951 Nixon began to be afflicted by back and neck pains, a problem which was worsened, if not caused, by too much stress and travelling. Soon after moving into a new home on the corner of Tilden Street in Spring Valley, northwest

Washington, Pat wrote on 4 September 1951 to Helene Drown, 'We are pleased with the house, the decorating and the neighbors. What a luxury to have s-p-a-c-e. The children have nice playmates; they have never been as happy as here with their space to dig, their Sears-Roebuck swimming pool, their gym with swings etc...but Dick is more tired than I have ever seen him. The doctor told him that he would have to get away and also take it easier.'[9]

The doctor who gave him this advice was Dr. Arnold A. Hutschnecker, a New York internist specialising in psychosomatic medicine. Hutschnecker was the author of *The Will to Live,* a best-seller which had been serialised in the *Reader's Digest.* Nixon read the book, and came to Hutschnecker's consulting rooms at 829 Park Avenue in September 1951.

'He came to see me because he thought he was suffering from tension,' recalled Hutschnecker. 'This was showing in his neck and back pains, and of course I could pick up that he did have this tension and that the root cause of it was his drive, his ambition, his insecurities, and his tendency to overwork. But I told him that he did not have a medical problem. As a physician I could do nothing for him because there was absolutely nothing wrong with his mental or physical health. However, as a friend, which is what I believe I became to him, I think I helped him quite a lot just by sensible non-medical advice.'[10]

The friendship between the Senator from California and the German-born specialist in psychosomatic medicine became a strong one. 'Right from the beginning we struck up a rapport', said Hutschnecker. 'He related to me very trustingly. We talked a lot about his family, but also about his drives, his hopes, his ideals. There was a great openness between us. More than any other subject we talked about peace. I am a pacifist and he wanted to use politics to become a peacemaker. We talked man to man...I was so, so careful not to give him the feeling that he was being analyzed. And it was true. I never analyzed him. But naturally I did form my own private theories about him. In a nutshell these were that he felt he owed everything to his mother—his superior intellect, his success, and his ideals. The driving force of his life was that he wanted to prove to his mother that he was a good boy. He could not be a loser because that would mean he was letting his mother down.'

Nixon rarely came to Dr. Hutschnecker's consulting rooms. 'We usually met privately whenever he was in New York. He would call up very early in the morning and say, "Can you come over for coffee", and I would drop almost everything to do that', recalled Hutschnecker. 'At the beginning of our relationship I remember going to his suite in the Waldorf, and I heard him singing so happily in the shower. And I said to myself, "Aha, my treatment is working." But the truth was

I never really gave him much treatment. It was not a professional relationship. I never sent him a bill. As an immigrant from Nazi Germany I felt I wanted to give something back to this wonderful country, and in helping Nixon I felt I was helping someone who was powerful in government. I was just a friend. Nixon felt he could confide in me, trust me, and get some simple advice from me on how to relax and keep fit.'[11]

As with so many of Nixon's relationships, the bond of trust was broken as a result of press comments. Hutschnecker went on helping him throughout his years as Vice President and up to 1968. However, ten days after Nixon had been elected President, the Washington columnist Drew Pearson published a sensational story about the President-elect's 'psychiatric problems'.[12] The only fact in this account was the connection with Hutschnecker. He was described as a Park Avenue psychiatrist and was quoted as saying that he had treated Nixon 'for strictly medical problems'.[13] 'This was a complete fabrication,' claimed Hutschnecker, 'but after a lot of even wilder rumors and stories about how I was "Nixon's shrink", he could never get rid of that and I could never get rid of that, so I only ever saw him again on two occasions.'[14]

Back in 1951, there was no such media interest in Nixon's visits to a doctor, so Hutschnecker's advice was accepted. Nixon slowed his schedule and most uncharacteristically took four vacations in six months. The first, alone with Pat, was a glorious, ten-day visit to Sea Island, Georgia in November 1951, where they bicycled for five miles every morning, swam, shared golf lessons and for almost the last time in their lives went completely unrecognised. 'It was a real rest for Dick, but not long enough', wrote Pat to Helene Drown,[15] a view which was evidently shared by worried colleagues in the Senate. 'Dick is on the verge of a physical breakdown. We're all concerned about him',[16] Florida's Senator, George Smathers, was telling friends some three weeks later, as he organised a therapeutic trip to the sun in his home state. One of the people Smathers asked to help out was his high school classmate Charles 'Bebe' Rebozo, a Miami businessman who arranged for Nixon to have treatment from a local osteopath and took him on cruises in his boat. Nixon started to unwind and was appreciative of Rebozo's quiet and unassuming solicitude for his welfare. It was the beginning of a deep and unusual relationship.

Bebe Rebozo was an unlikely character to become Richard Nixon's best friend. His grandparents were Canary Island fishermen who had arrived in Cuba on a sailing ship in 1856. His parents emigrated from Havana to Florida at the turn of the century and got married in Tampa. They had nine children of whom Bebe was the youngest, born in 1912. The Spanish-speaking family grew up on the wrong side of the tracks, always struggling to make ends meet on the meagre wages Rebozo senior earned as a cigar maker. Bebe's formal education at Miami High School ended when he was seventeen, but he put himself through night school to do a business course. After a spell as a Pan Am airline steward, he started to wheel and deal in boats, real estate, and anything else that would make him a profit. By 1951 he was a prosperous entrepreneur, wealthy enough to own a large beachside home and a motor launch on which he took the tense Senator Nixon for suntanning trips around Miami Bay.

Rebozo possessed several qualities that appealed to his guest. A self-made man, he had a natural generosity of spirit; an absolute discretion when it came to respecting confidences; a warm sense of humour; and an intuitive sixth sense which enabled him to empathise with difficult people. Nixon somehow tuned in to that empathy, and immediately felt comfortable with his host. His feelings were not immediately reciprocated. According to George Smathers, Rebozo wrote to complain that his visitor had been a bore. 'Don't ever send another dull fellow like that down here again', said Bebe in a letter to his old friend George. 'He doesn't drink whisky; he doesn't chase women; he doesn't even play golf.'[17]

Rebozo's recollection of his first encounter with Nixon was more favourable. 'He was a completely different kind of person from other political types* I had met. He had a depth and a genuineness about him which didn't come through because of his shyness, but I saw it. I knew that he would return and that we would become friends. I can't explain why, except to say that it was perhaps the attraction of opposites. He's a kind of genius. I just muddle through.'[18]

The good times with Rebozo in early December were followed by a long Christmas break with Pat and the children, then, in April 1952, by a two-week vacation in Hawaii. Pat and Dick shared this trip with Jack and Helene Drown who remember how carefree Nixon became as he swam, laughed, danced and even acquired some skill at doing the hula. The contemporary letters which survive with descriptions of these holidays belie the stereotype portrait of Nixon the buttoned-up workaholic who could never relax.[19]

The months of troubled medical symptoms which surrounded these vacations had a lasting effect on Nixon's life as it was the period in which he had learned to pace himself. Every leading public figure needs to discover how to

---

* Rebozo knew a surprisingly wide range of 'political types' through his connection with his Miami High School classmate, Senator George Smathers. They included John F. Kennedy, Lyndon B. Johnson, Governor Claude Kirk of Florida, Senators Stuart Symington of Missouri, Russell Long of Louisiana, and Richard Russell of Georgia. All of them were entertained by the hospitable and easy-going Bebe, but only Nixon became his friend.

balance the supply of physical energy with the demands of political ambition. Nixon, who had not been away for a proper vacation since his honeymoon, was wise enough to heed the danger signals in 1951–2 and to benefit from them. Dr. Hutschnecker had advised him that he needed regular breaks in the sunshine to bring him back into tune with the primal harmony of his California childhood. Nixon seems to have accepted this recommendation in both his senatorial and presidential years if the frequency of his trips to the sun at Key Biscayne and San Clemente are anything to go by. In 1952 he returned from the Hawaii vacation with fully recharged batteries which helped him to compose and deliver the address which changed the course of his political career.

II. IKE CHOOSES NIXON

Although Nixon's energetic speech-making had made him a favourite among the grassroots workers in the Republican heartlands, he was still an unknown quantity to the paladins of the Republican establishment. They were confident of victory in 1952, but were in disarray on the choices for the first and second spots on the national ticket. One of the king-makers was Governor Thomas E. Dewey of New York, the defeated but still respected GOP presidential candidate of 1948. Dewey was sufficiently intrigued by Nixon's potential to invite him to make the principal address at the New York State Republican Party's annual $100 a plate fund-raising dinner at the Waldorf Astoria Hotel on 8 May 1952. This was one of the most prestigious annual events in the political calendar, providing the keynote speaker with a national radio audience as well as a platform from which to capture the hearts and wallets of the GOP's most influential backers.

Fully appreciating the opportunity that had been offered to him, Nixon sweated over his address in one of those bouts of monastic seclusion that preceded all his ground-breaking speeches. The preparations resulted in a *tour de force* that was his entry ticket into presidential politics. 'That was a terrific speech. Promise me you won't lose your zeal. Promise me you won't get fat. Promise me you'll keep your fighting spirit—and you can be President one day',[20] enthused Dewey as Nixon sat down with the Waldorf audience erupting round him in cheers. He had spoken without a note for precisely the twenty-nine and a half minutes requested by the radio networks, combining a clever dissection of the Truman administration's failings in Korea with his own internationalist prescription for a new foreign policy that would contain Communist aggression in Europe and the Far East. This was the perfect message for the audience. In an age when many of the old Republican warhorses in the Senate hardly seemed to know that the world was round, the New York establishment was over the moon to discover this intelligent young Californian who wrote his own speeches; had an enlightened international outlook; possessed a good war record; was a sound domestic conservative; and knew how to deliver electoral success in the new heartlands of political power on the West Coast.[21]

After the dinner, Dewey took Nixon to his suite at the Roosevelt Hotel for a one-on-one talk about the vice-presidential nomination and promised his help. Nixon's private response to this offer of patronage was to say that he would be 'greatly honored', while in public he professed that he 'couldn't believe Governor Dewey was serious'.[22]

In fact, Nixon had been making detailed financial and political provisions for national office ever since his victory over Helen Gahagan Douglas. Within days of that result he had given his blessing to the setting up of a fund designed to pay the expenses of the next political moves in his career. This was the arrangement that was to become known as 'The Fund' and which was destined to explode into one of the most dramatic personal controversies in the history of presidential campaigning.

Looking back on The Fund crisis, it appears as an unreal episode, a piece of pure political theatre deserving the Shakespearean title 'Much Ado about Nothing'. Certainly, the opening scenes of the plot were almost tedious in their lack of ill-intent.

The central figure in The Fund saga, after Nixon himself, was a fifty-two-year-old Pasadena lawyer, Dana C. Smith. He and a group of Nixon's oldest supporters in Southern California had discussed the prospects of their new Senator-elect in November 1950 and came to the conclusion that help would be needed to finance certain routine political expenses which were not covered by the statutory government allowances. There was nothing unusual in such a plan. The legislature's restrictions on taxpayer-funded expenses were tightly drawn in those days. A Senator was limited to one government-paid round trip per session between his home state and Washington. The free mail franking privilege could not be used on political or personal communications. The annual office expense allowance of $75,000 was not allowed to be diverted into campaigning or advertising expenditure. Many elected representatives therefore needed, and regularly received, non-government funding from their supporters for items such as travel expenses; printing of political materials; buying radio air time and providing the postage costs of mail shots, political circulars or Christmas cards. Nixon himself, along with many congressional colleagues, had been receiving such assistance on an *ad hoc* basis for some years. For example, his trips to the 12th District at the time of the Herter Committee and Marshall Plan votes had been paid for not by the taxpayer but by Republican supporters such as Herman Perry and his friends. This was routine political practice in the 1940s and 1950s.

Dana Smith, who had been the finance chairman for Nixon's Senate campaign was a cautious attorney of unquestioned integrity. Immediately after his post-election conversations on the subject, Smith set up a political expenses trust fund with its own bank account and began asking selected Republicans if they would give it their support. The first contribution arrived on, 15 November 1950, one week after the defeat of Helen Gahagan Douglas.

The conditions Smith laid down for The Fund were intended to make it embarrassment-proof. Contributions were only solicited from 'people who have supported Dick from the start' and were limited to a maximum of $500 a head in order that 'it can never be charged that anyone is contributing so much as to think he is entitled to special favors'.[23] Nobody would draw any salary or personal benefit from The Fund. It would be administered by Smith himself in accordance with agreed guidelines. The budget for 1951, drawn up by Smith on 28 December 1950, estimated an income from contributions of $21,000. This would be spent on predictable political expenses, of which the most important items were $7,500 for radio advertising and $5,700 on mailings, including the postage costs of 20,000 Christmas cards to Senate campaign workers.

Nixon approved these arrangements in principle, seeing them as legal and commonplace. He regarded The Fund as the financial base for what Murray Chotiner called 'a permanent campaign'[24] and was disappointed when the contributions did not flow in at the expected rate. One of the ironies of The Fund is that it was a financial failure. Instead of bringing in $20,000–25,000 a year, Dana Smith only managed to raise $18,000 over two years. Despite sending out several hundred letters to potential donors, only seventy-six contributions were ever received at an average of $240 per head.

At the time when The Fund was set up, no one involved dreamt of the firestorm that was to rage around it some two years later. In those early days, the real importance of The Fund was that it gave Nixon the financial self-confidence to get out on the road and establish his national political credentials. He no longer had to worry about his ability to pay air fares, hotel bills, long-distance telephone calls and other political expenses. His rivals on the presidential and vice-presidential campaign trail either had similar funds of their own, as Governor Adlai Stevenson did, or were wealthy men in their own right, like Senator William Knowland. Nixon was now supported by Dana Smith's Fund arrangements and was the better and more secure politician because of them.

The field of contenders for the Republican presidential nomination in 1952 was led by a front runner, Senator Robert Taft; a non-runner, General Dwight D. Eisenhower; and a compromise candidate, Governor Earl Warren of California. Nixon backed the right horse early. He had first met Eisenhower at the Bohemian Grove* in the summer of 1950, when they were both visitors to Cave Man Camp as the lunch guests of Herbert Hoover. Later that day, Ike had delivered a short address to the lakeside audience. Nixon, unlike some of the Republican heavy-weights present, was impressed both by the content of the speech—a visionary endorsement of NATO—and by the charismatic appeal of Eisenhower's personal mystique.[25] Some nine months later the two met again. Nixon, who was in Geneva for a World Health Organisation conference, visited Paris to call on Eisenhower, who by this time had taken up his appointment as Supreme Commander of NATO. They talked alone for forty-five minutes, both knowing but neither mentioning that mutual friends had urged them to get together for a discussion on presidential election possibilities. Eisenhower, ostensibly aloof from domestic politics, charmed Nixon. He had evidently done his homework for the meeting, for he quoted from recent speeches by the young Californian Senator. This was also the time when he delighted his guest by citing the latest book on the Hiss case and commented, 'The thing that most impressed me was that you not only got Hiss, but you got him fairly.'[26]

The geniality of the encounter did not prevent Nixon from making a shrewd assessment of Eisenhower the potential colleague. In a series of telling observations he noted the contrast between Ike's warm smile and icy blue eyes, commenting that 'beneath his captivating personal appearance was a lot of finely tempered hard steel'.[27] He was also somewhat sceptical of Eisenhower's naïve optimism about Europe's immediate prospects for recovery, which had characterised the foreign policy part of their conversation. However, these reservations were minor in comparison to Nixon's intuitive feeling that Eisenhower was an electable winner. He thought that the General's military charisma and his skilful handling of the NATO allies could be swords that would turn into highly effective ploughshares if Ike emerged as a presidential candidate determined to cultivate an electoral consensus among domestic voters. 'I came away convinced that he should be the next President', wrote Nixon afterwards. 'I also decided that if he ran for the nomination I would do everything I could to help him get it.'[28]

---

* The Bohemian Grove is The Bohemian Club of San Francisco's annual summer retreat. It is regarded as one of America's most prestigious gatherings, at which top industrialists, bankers and national politicians gather in the Californian Redwoods in the atmosphere of a boys' summer camp, to hear concerts, lectures, and political speeches.

The instant mutual appreciation between Nixon and Eisenhower at that Paris meeting was founded in their mutual political interests. They both needed each other, although Nixon's needs were far greater for he had nowhere else to go. His ambitions for the second spot on the Republican ticket were certain to be dashed if either Taft or Warren won the nomination. Quite apart from the personal coolness in his relationships with these two contenders, Nixon realised that a Governor of California was never going to share the ticket with a junior Senator from the same state. He also knew that Taft's choice of a running mate was almost certain to fall on his close friend Senator William Knowland, the senior Senator from California.

Although these doors were closed to Nixon, Eisenhower's was already half open. If Ike was going to fight for the nomination, he needed an influential Californian to help him unlock that state's vital convention votes which would initially be pledged to its favourite son, Governor Earl Warren. He also needed a running mate who would balance the ticket in terms of age, geography and acceptability to the GOP's conservative activists. Nixon fitted these specifications perfectly. To some members of the Eisenhower camp his selection as vice-presidential nominee was obvious, provided certain question marks could be eliminated. Was he too young and brash? Was he too extreme as a Red baiter? Was he sound on foreign affairs? These hesitations were dispersed by a series of meetings and speeches, of which the most important was his address to the New York State Republican Dinner in May 1952. A month after Nixon's New York success his new patron, Governor Thomas E. Dewey, arranged a meeting with Eisenhower's inner circle at the Mayflower Hotel in Washington. Several of Ike's most trusted advisers were there, among them General Lucius Clay and Herbert Brownell, the eminent New York attorney who had just returned from Paris, where he had been asked by Eisenhower to take charge of the operation to deliver the votes at the convention. 'We saw Nixon to size him up and to get his help in the delegate hunt', recalled Brownell. 'There was no specific talk about the Vice Presidency. It wasn't in our power to make suggestions along those lines. But I had been thinking about Nixon as the General's running mate ever since the dinner at the Waldorf. I remember Dewey saying to me that night, "We've found our man for Vice President." I had agreed. It was just such a natural fit for the ticket. Seeing Nixon at closer quarters confirmed my view. He had an outstandingly good, quick mind. He was certainly up to the job.'[29]

Always at his best discussing issues of substance with small groups of intelligent questioners, there is little doubt that Nixon passed his test in the Mayflower Hotel with flying colours. He would have had no difficulty in convincing

Eisenhower's men of his centrist views on foreign policy and of his ability to hold the right wing of the GOP in the aftermath of a Taft defeat at the convention. Although there was no understanding about the Vice Presidency at the Mayflower meeting, Nixon nevertheless came away from the discussion with a clear idea of what he had to do to further his own and Eisenhower's position. Both Taft and Warren should be undermined.

In the run-up to the Republican convention in July, Nixon manoeuvred to achieve these objectives. He loosened Warren's stranglehold on the California delegates by sending out 23,000 questionnaires to party workers asking for their opinion on 'the strongest candidate the Republicans could nominate for President'. The returns from this ingenious exercise in private polling showed that Eisenhower was far ahead. Warren, whose hopes were based on a deadlocked convention, was understandably furious. He had only just won the California primary, establishing himself as the state's clear choice for presidential nominee. His fury intensified when Nixon lobbied the California delegates on the train going to the Chicago convention, telling them that Eisenhower was heading for victory and they had better abandon their loyalty to a favourite son while there was still a chance to get a good price for California's support. These tactics, which included hints of a Nixon for Vice President deal, divided the delegation and weakened Warren's power base.

As for Senator Robert Taft, Nixon paid elaborate lip service to the qualities of 'Mr. Republican', as he was known, but then simultaneously did his utmost to diminish the Ohio Senator's chances of holding on to his delegates. Nixon's technique was to move round the convention telling the conservative loyalists how sad it was that Taft was so utterly unelectable. This propaganda campaign struck home because it was true. The saintly Taft was revered by the right-wing faithful but the cold austerity of his campaigning style severely limited his appeal.

Taft may have been unelectable, but he had the inside track on the Republican nomination. Bitter divisions between different wings of the party had led to the awkward result that many a Southern state had sent two rival delegations to Chicago, one committed to Taft, one to Eisenhower. Two delegations from the same state could not both be recognised. Thus the race for the nomination degenerated into a fight over the contested delegates. Taft held the ace. He controlled the credentials committee which ruled on which delegations could be seated. Eisenhower's supporters, however, played a trump card in the form of the 'Fair Play' amendment. This called for jurisdiction over the contested delegations to be removed from the credentials committee and given over to the vote of uncontested delegates from other states, where Eisenhower was confident of having a majority.

The nomination therefore hinged on the success of the 'Fair Play' amendment. Nixon spoke at a crucial moment to the California delegation, opposing Senator Knowland's proposal that the delegation split its votes on the issue in half in order to bring about the deadlocked convention that would serve Warren's interests best. Nixon's intervention was decisive. The Californians were freed to vote according to their consciences. They overwhelmingly favoured the amendment by 62 votes to 8 and it passed in the convention by 658 votes to 548. With his delegates from the South duly installed, Ike swept to a first ballot victory Nixon had played a useful part in delivering his nomination.

Although by this time the newspapers were printing rumours about an 'Ike–Dick' ticket, Nixon was enough of a realist to know that there were a multitude of slips between cup and lip. The principal uncertainty was that Eisenhower's views on the choice of a running mate were unknown—even to Eisenhower himself. On the night of his nomination, Ike dined in his suite in the Blackstone Hotel alone with Herbert Brownell. 'General, who do you want as Vice President?' asked Brownell at a late stage in the meal. 'Gee, I don't know!' replied Eisenhower. 'I thought the convention decided that.'[30]

The surprised Brownell explained that the nominee had the power to choose his running mate. The equally surprised Eisenhower said 'Gee!' and 'I don't know' a few more times, then picked up a piece of paper and wrote six names on it. 'Unfortunately I've lost that bit of paper' recalled Herbert Brownell, 'but I do remember that they were all obvious names and that Nixon's was among them. I asked Eisenhower whether he had a preference. He said no, everyone on the list was equally acceptable to him. Then he asked me for my view. I said: "I think that if you say nothing, Nixon is likely to be the choice of the party." Then Ike said, "I'd like you to call a meeting of the heads of the delegations that supported me and get their recommendation."'[31]

While Brownell was making the overnight arrangements for this unusual vice-presidential selection meeting, Nixon was having to handle a no less unusual problem of his own. Fierce resistance to his nomination was coming from an improbable source—Pat. During the day, she had become unnerved by the vice-presidential rumours. Still scarred by the memories of the bitter Senate campaign, she dug in her toes and rebelled against the prospects of another election. For her, the intrusive effects of the Vice Presidency on family life seemed too high a price. An all-night argument between husband and wife took place. At 4 a.m. on the morning of 11 July, Nixon called up Murray Chotiner. 'What are you doing?' he asked. 'Sleeping', was the reply. Putting on his dressing gown and slippers, Chotiner was brought in to reinforce his boss's case. 'What do you think?' Nixon asked as he arrived in the suite. 'If this thing is offered to me, do you think I should take it?' 'I could tell that Pat had been talking against it', recalled Chotiner, who proceeded to deliver a homily largely for Mrs. Nixon's benefit on the merits of going onwards and upwards in politics:

> Dick, you're a junior senator from California and you will always be a junior Senator from California. Bill Knowland is young and he's healthy, and unless something should happen to him, you will always be second man in California. The junior Senator from California doesn't amount to anything. There comes a time when you have to go up or out. Suppose you're the candidate and we lose? You're still the junior Senator and haven't lost anything. If you win and are elected Vice President and at the end of four years you become all washed up, you could open a law office in Whittier and have all the business in town. Any man who quits political life as Vice President as young as you are in years certainly hasn't lost a thing.[32]

None of this special pleading can have seemed entirely convincing to Pat Nixon, whose desire to avoid yet another round of electioneering was hardly likely to have been placated by the prospects of a return to the Whittier from which she had made such efforts to escape. The argument went on until dawn until Pat wearily gave in, saying, 'I guess I can make it through another campaign.'[33]

Later that morning the leaders of the GOP assembled in Herbert Brownell's suite to hold their debate on the vice-presidential nomination. 'It reminded me of a ward committee in Philadelphia discussing the selection of a candidate for alderman',[34] was how Sherman Adams described the atmosphere, which soon became that of the traditional, smoke-filled room as cigars were lit up and coats taken off. Approximately thirty senior Republicans attended, among them seven governors, five senators, several RNC committee men, and a small group of Eisenhower's cronies.* Brownell chaired the meeting, opening the proceedings by giving an assurance that 'No deals had been done', and asking all those who considered themselves as candidates for nomination to leave the room. Nobody did.

---

* According to Herbert Brownell's recollection, the Governors were Fine of Pennsylvania; Langley of Washington State; Beardsley of Iowa; Duff of Pennsylvania; Thornton of Colorado; Driscoll of New Jersey and John Lodge of Connecticut. The Senators were Smith of New Jersey; Wisdom of Louisiana; Tuttle of Georgia; Carlsen of Kansas and Cabot Lodge of Connecticut. Others present included Arthur Summerfield and Russell Sprague from the RNC; Sherman Adams, Lucius Clay, Roy Roberts and Thomas E. Dewey.

As Brownell recalled the discussion:

> I didn't reveal that I had Eisenhower's list in my pocket, I just asked
> for views. Senator Alexander Smith of New Jersey opened up by say-
> ing it would be a great idea to have an Eisenhower–Taft ticket.
> Sprague, the RNC representative from New York, killed that one
> stone dead by saying that not even Ike could carry New York with
> Taft. Then someone suggested Senator Knowland, but that didn't go
> down at all well because Knowland had been Earl Warren's campaign
> manager, and there was a lot of hostility towards the Warren camp
> for refusing to let the nomination vote for Eisenhower go unanimous.
> Then several more names were tossed around but none had any real
> support, which was just as well since Ike wouldn't have known most
> of them from a brick wall. There was quite a pause until Dewey spoke
> up. He was strongly for Nixon and gave all the reasons why he was
> such a good fit on the ticket with Eisenhower. Nixon's youth and Ike's
> seniority; the Navy and the Army; West coast and East coast; the Hiss
> case; great campaigner and speaker—by the time Dewey had finished
> everyone seemed to be convinced that Nixon was the right choice.
> There wasn't a lot of discussion after that. I called for a show of hands
> and it was unanimous. I reported to Eisenhower and he immediately
> gave his OK. That was it.[35]

Compared to the modern methods of in-depth screening for vice-presidential candidates, the 1952 selection procedures in Brownell's hotel suite seem
perfunctory. The discussions about Nixon were superficial and exclusively political. Nobody seemed interested in his character, his private life, his finances, or
his personal suitability for an office 'one heart beat away from the Presidency'.
This reflected the attitudes of an era in which the press were less intrusive and
the public more trusting. It was also a comment on the status of the Vice Presidency, whose first incumbent, John Adams (Vice President 1789–96) had
described the role as 'the most insignificant that ever the invention of man con-
trived or his imagination conceived'.[36]

This perception of the vacuity of the office had lasted well into the twentieth
century. Charles G. Dawes (Vice President 1924–8), Calvin Coolidge's Vice
President, told the world that he had only two duties, to listen to the Senators
giving speeches and to read the morning papers for news of the President's health.
A blunter and more recent incumbent, Vice President John Nance Garner of Texas

(Vice President 1932–40), had declared that his job 'ain't worth a pitcher of warm spit'. By the standards of most of his predecessors, Nixon was an outstandingly well-qualified nominee, yet in personal terms he was almost completely unknown to those who had picked him.

A few days after the convention, Herbert Brownell had a sporting encounter with Nixon. It brought home Brownell's own ignorance about the style of the running mate he had championed. After an office meeting in New York to discuss campaign strategy the two men went to watch a baseball game. 'Someone hit a home run', recalled Brownell. 'Nixon jumped up, stood on a chair and yelled his head off, waving his arms about and screaming as if he was a high school kid. This was in my own box at Yankee Stadium, and frankly I was embarrassed to put it mildly. I could hardly believe that a man who was a Senator and a vice-presidential candidate could be so raw and brash.'[37]

An earlier glimpse of the generation gap that existed between the styles of the brash Nixon and the more sedate Eisenhower circle was shown in the minutes after the vice-presidential nomination had been decided. Nixon heard the news in his Chicago hotel room. He had been taking a nap in his underwear when the bedside telephone rang. On the line was Herbert Brownell from Eisenhower's suite. 'We picked you', were his magic opening words. 'The General asked if you would come see him right away', he continued. 'That is, assuming you want it!'

Nixon certainly did want it. Although he needed a shower, a shave and some clean clothes, he put speed before elegance and dashed over to Eisenhower's hotel in his crumpled suit feeling 'hot, sleepy and grubby'.[38] Coming face to face with the General, Nixon's opening words were the cheery salutation 'Congratulations Chief!' In a further attempt at convention *bonhomie* he made an awkward attempt to put his arm around the shoulder of his running mate. Eisenhower froze, visibly displeased. 'It was the first hint that beneath the engaging, disarmingly wide smile, Eisenhower was reserved and protocol conscious',[39] Nixon said afterwards, adding that he was 'taken aback by the formality' as Ike delivered a rather stilted sermon on the need for the campaign to be a crusade for ideals. 'Will you join me in such a campaign?' Eisenhower eventually asked. 'I would be proud and happy to', responded Nixon.

Totally unaware that her husband had crossed the threshold of history in the Eisenhower suite, Pat Nixon was relaxing over a late lunch in the Stock Yard Inn with Murray Chotiner's wife and Helene Drown. Pat had somehow come away from the night of argument with the impression that no clear decisions had been made on her husband's future and that in any event the vice-presidential nomination was extremely unlikely to be offered. This illusion was shattered when a news bulletin interrupted the restaurant's screening of a B-movie with the flash, 'Ike chooses Nixon'.[40] As in the familiar cliché, Pat's jaw dropped with astonishment, so much so that a lump of her sandwich fell from her mouth onto the table. 'Oh honey, you're going to be in the history books now', enthused Helene Drown as they ran back into the Convention Hall, where they were submerged in a mêlée of excited delegates babbling about Senator Nixon without realising that his wife was in their midst.

Soon after Pat finally reached the platform, the formal announcement was made to the convention that Nixon was to be Eisenhower's running mate. The delegates cheered themselves hoarse but one visitor to the press box, Clare Boothe Luce, was surprised by 'shouts of rage and disbelief'[41] from some of the journalists standing near her.

After Eisenhower's acceptance speech, Nixon came to the rostrum for his big moment as the new vice-presidential nominee. His opening line, 'Haven't we got a wonderful candidate for President of the United States?' was well pitched to catch the euphoric mood of the convention. He followed it with a fulsome tribute to Taft ('one of the really great Senators, one of the greatest legislative leaders in the history of America…let's be sure that Senator Bob Taft is Chairman of the Majority Policy Committee after next January') which drew even longer and louder cheers than the ovation for Eisenhower.[42] This passage in his speech was a shrewd act of healing by Nixon. It was appreciated as balm to the wounds of Taft's supporters and was personally approved in advance by Eisenhower. However, a few of Ike's closest supporters took umbrage at Nixon's encomium of the defeated rival. 'You have to remember that some of Ike's personal friends knew nothing about politics and had never been near a convention in their lives', recalled Herbert Brownell. 'They considered Eisenhower close to God or even somewhat above him. Listening to Nixon praising Taft was for them like hearing a sermon from a blasphemer.'[43]

Nixon, who was himself quite willing to deify Eisenhower, had no inkling that his speech had caused offence. Nevertheless, his 'blasphemy', and his consequent fall from grace among Ike's inner circle of guardian angels, was to cause a serious problem for him in the coming campaign.

III. THE FUND CRISIS

Returning to Washington after the convention, the Nixons soon realised that life would never be the same again. Their Tilden Street home was under siege by reporters and photographers, some of whom had upset the children by bursting into their bedroom with flashbulbs popping. Telegrams and letters poured in by the sackful, among them a handwritten note from a 1947 House of Representatives classmate:

> Dear Dick,
>
> I was tremendously pleased that the convention selected you for VP. I was always convinced that you would move ahead to the top—but I never thought it would come this quickly. You were an ideal selection and will bring to the ticket a good deal of strength.
>
> Please give my best to your wife and all kinds of good luck to you.
> Cordially
> Jack Kennedy[44]

Another who came to pay court to the new celebrities was a glamorous young photojournalist for the *Washington Times-Herald*, Jacqueline Lee Bouvier, who had still to meet her future husband. Her street vigil was eventually rewarded by an impromptu interview with four-year-old Julie Nixon, who responded when asked by the future First Lady, 'Do you play with Democrats?', 'What's a Democrat?'[45]

Flaying Democrats was Nixon's task for the election. The occupant of the number two spot on the ticket is often cast as opposition hit man, a role well suited to both Nixon's talent and Eisenhower's inclination. Eisenhower knew that he would look best as a presidential candidate if he could maintain his symbolic magic as a hero and overlord, high above the squabbles of the campaigning farmyard. But to preserve this lofty eminence, Ike needed a fighting cock. Someone had to be left down there scavenging the mess of Washington scandals made by the Truman administration. Someone had to be goading the Democratic nominee, Governor Adlai Stevenson. Someone had to be picking at the sores of the Democratic Party. Nixon undertook these tasks with relish.

Kicking off his campaign with what he called 'a shakedown cruise'[46] in the shape of a four-day speech-making tour of New England in early September, Nixon's rhetoric immediately went into high gear. He dubbed Stevenson 'Sidesaddle Adlai…and like all sidesaddle riders his feet stick out well to the left'.[47] He slammed the Democrats for riding on 'a four-headed monster of Korea, Communism, corruption and control'.[48] Following press exposure of widespread bribery among White House staffers and the dismissal of 166 Internal Revenue Service officials for tax favours, Nixon made one of the strongest themes in his speech the need to clean out the Augean stables of Democratic Party corruption. Calling the Truman government the 'scandal a day' administration, he charged that for every corruption case that had surfaced 'there are ten which have not yet been uncovered', and added that respect for public servants in Washington 'can only be restored by a thorough housecleaning of the sticky-fingered crew now contaminating the national capital'. In Maine he told audiences that he would make 'Communist subversion and corruption the theme of every speech from now until the election', adding for good measure, 'If the record itself smears, let it smear. If the dry rot of corruption and Communism which has eaten deep into our body politic during the last seven years can only be chopped out with a hatchet, then let's call for a hatchet.'[49]

Nixon's hatchet-man campaigning style caused pain to his opponents and pleasure to his Republican supporters in almost equal measure. 'I am filled with superlatives in regard to your visit here', wrote Christian Herter after the swing through New England.[50] It was a common reaction among the GOP faithful, who recognised in Nixon, as did the growing crowds of all political persuasions, an exciting stump speaker. But while the actor in him honed and sharpened his attack lines to maximum effect, the statesman in him varied the pace so that every speech also contained thoughtful passages on the international situation, the importance of NATO and other wider issues. The multilayered nature of his intellect was reflected in the light and dark shading of his speech-making. It would not have been possible for Nixon to win plaudits from the likes of Christian Herter, *Newsweek's* Stewart Alsop, and other perceptive observers of the New England campaign tour if his speeches had consisted entirely of Democrat bashing, and it is an oversimplification of old newspaper headlines to suggest that they ever did.

As the campaign progressed, it became clear that the Democrats were getting rattled by the Republican ticket's presentation of themselves as the team who would clean up America's political corruption. Even Eisenhower had started calling in his speeches for an end to 'shady and shoddy government', promising to drive out of Washington the 'crooks and cronies' who had been responsible for the 'cancerous conditions of dishonesty'.[51] With so much sanctimonious rhetoric filling the air, it was inevitable that the Democrats would soon retaliate. The backlash came with the surfacing of The Fund crisis as a counterattack whose main purpose was to cast Nixon in the role of the venal villain.

The first warning that the spotlight of controversy might be moving to Nixon's personal finances came after a 'Meet the Press' television interview on 14 September. One of the interviewers, the Washington political columnist Peter Edson, took Nixon aside after the programme and asked, 'Senator, what is this "fund" we hear about? There is a rumor to the effect that you have a supplementary salary of $20,000 a year contributed by a hundred Californian businessmen. What is it about?'[52] 'He didn't attempt to duck the question in any way',[53] reported Edson, who was impressed by Nixon's straightforward account of the expenses-only nature of the fund and by Nixon immediately giving him the telephone number of Dana Smith as the best source for further details. Over the next few days several journalists called Smith and were given full answers to their questions. Most of them either downplayed or ignored the story, but on 18 September the pro-Democrat *New York Post* filled its front page with screaming headlines: 'SECRET NIXON FUND! SECRET RICH MEN'S TRUST FUND KEEPS NIXON IN STYLE FAR BEYOND HIS SALARY!' In keeping with the tabloid's political bias, the story was luridly written and manifestly unfair. The fund was not 'secret'; there was no 'millionaires' club devoted exclusively to the financial comfort of Senator Nixon', whose life style had certainly not prospered 'far beyond his salary'. Riding through Nevada on board his campaign train, 'The Nixon Special', the vice-presidential candidate felt he could afford to ignore such a transparently partisan smear. He conferred with his immediate advisers, particularly Bill Rogers, who said after hearing all the details, 'I don't see anything to worry about. There is nothing illegal, unethical or embarrassing about this fund. If your opponents try to make something out of it they will never get anywhere on the merits.'[54]

This sanguine view was soon shattered by noisy demands for Nixon's resignation from the ticket. Some of these were from predictable sources such as the chairman of the Democratic National Committee and the *Washington Post,* but much more disturbing was an editorial in the *New York Herald Tribune* of 20 September which said that Nixon should offer to withdraw from the ticket and leave the decision on his fate to 'General Eisenhower's unsurpassed fairness of mind'. Nixon was stunned when he read this editorial, partly because the *Herald Tribune* was normally the staunchest of Republican supporters in the press, but more because he assumed that the Trib's establishment-minded editor would never have taken such a line unless it reflected Eisenhower's personal attitude to the growing crisis.

In fact, Eisenhower was having trouble making up his own mind what to do. His initial response was robust, saying to his campaign manager Sherman Adams as the news broke, 'Well, if Nixon has to resign we can't possibly win.'[55] That was the right reflex action. If Ike had been forced to dump Nixon on the grounds that his own choice of running mate was as corrupt as the 'crooks and cronies' he had been lambasting in his speeches attacking the Democrats, then the Republican bandwagon, which in September was rolling comfortably ahead in the polls by 51 to 42 per cent, would have come to an embarrassing halt.

However, Eisenhower's instant political reflexes were not shared by his largely non-political entourage. Several of the General's old comrades had disliked Nixon from the time of his convention tribute to Taft. Now their dislike deepened into a small but influential 'Dump Nixon' movement on board the 'Look Ahead Neighbor Special', Eisenhower's campaign train. They spread their message first to the accompanying reporters, who were only too pleased to write the story, and then to Eisenhower himself, who began to waver. Instead of issuing a statement expressing confidence in his running mate, Ike remained damagingly silent. Eventually, after hearing that the political correpondents on his train had voted 40–2 in favour of throwing Nixon off the ticket, Eisenhower decided he should try to calm the situation. He only succeeded in making matters considerably worse: 'I don't care if you fellows are forty to two. I'm taking my time on this', he told the reporters in a relaxed press briefing over a beer in his lounge compartment. 'Nothing's decided, contrary to your idea that this is a set-up for a whitewash for Nixon.' After repeating his personal conviction that his running mate was an honest man, Ike said that Nixon would still have to prove it to fair-minded people, and added, 'Of what avail is it to carry on this crusade against this business of what has been going on in Washington if we, ourselves, aren't as clean as a hound's tooth?'[56] The colourful phrase made headlines across the country, causing great dismay on the vice-presidential train where Nixon said the reports made him 'feel like the little boy caught with jam on his face'.[57]

With his own morale plummeting, Nixon was grateful to be thrown a lifeline from Senator Robert Taft, who declared he could see no reason why a Senator should not accept gifts from his friends or constituents in order to pay expenses which were not paid by the government. It was a generous gesture from the man whose presidential prospects Nixon had done much to thwart, but Taft, whose nicknames included 'Mr. Integrity' and 'Mr. Republican', at least had the political experience to know that dozens of Congressmen and Senators had similar funds at their disposal. Some of these colleagues spoke up and defended Nixon. One of them was Congressman Oakley Hunter of California's 9th, Fresno, District, who admitted to a political expenses fund of his own. In an angry speech to the Humboldt County Republican Committee, Hunter described the criticism of the Nixon fund as 'pure hogwash and poppycock…a deliberate political smear cooked up to offset Republican charges of crooks, commies and cronies in government'.[58] He declared he would 'repudiate Eisenhower and resign from the Republican Party' if Nixon was removed from the ticket. Unfortunately for Nixon, such voices were lost in the growing clamour for his resignation. His chances of survival began to look slim. The press were behaving like a lynch mob with more and more editorials demanding dismissal. Even when it was revealed that the Democratic nominee Governor Adlai Stevenson had a similar political expenses fund* of his own, reporters did not go after him with critical stories or even hard questions. Nixon was understandably aggrieved by what he regarded as appalling double standards. He became still further distressed when the crowds began turning against him. In Oregon he was booed; coins were thrown at his car; and his rallies were besieged by Democrats rattling collecting tins labelled 'Nickels for poor Nixon', or holding up placards with messages such as, 'Pat, what are you going to do with the bribe money?'[60]

Pat was standing firm under all this pressure with rather better fortitude than her husband. She was furious at the unfairness of it all. 'Not only isn't the fund illegal,' she said, 'but you know how you bent over backwards to keep it public and to make sure that every cent was accounted for.'[61] When Nixon privately discussed the option of resignation with her, Pat emphatically told him not to think of it, arguing that unless he fought to defend his honour he would leave a stain not only on his own life but on that of his daughters too. Fired up by this counsel, Nixon began fighting back against his tormentors, scoring well against hecklers with several effective punchlines which were later to appear in the 'Checkers' speech.

Although Nixon sensed that the tide was beginning to turn on the campaign trail, the silence from Eisenhower remained unnerving. The failure of the two candidates to speak directly to one another during the first eight days of The Fund crisis was initially explicable by the difficulties in communicating between two mobile trains, but such an excuse wore thin and the impression grew that Ike was freezing out his running mate. By the evening of 21 September, as the 'Nixon Special' pulled into Portland, Oregon, the strain was becoming unbearable. Finally, at around 10 p.m., Eisenhower called. After some initial pleasantries, the General delivered the astonishing message that he had decided to remain indecisive. 'I have come to the conclusion,' he told Nixon, 'that you are the one who has to decide what to do. After all, you've got a big following in the country, and if the impression got around that you got off the ticket because I forced you off, it is going to be very bad. On the other hand, if I issue a statement now backing you up, in effect people will accuse me of condoning wrongdoing.' There was a long pause, eventually broken by Eisenhower, who continued, 'I don't want to be in the position of condemning an innocent man. I think you ought to go on

---

* Stevenson's fund was worth $146,000 and had been used in payment for such expenses as the Governor's dues to private clubs; hiring the orchestra at a party for his son; and the mysterious budget entry 'bowling costumes for girls'.[59]

to a nationwide television program and tell them everything there is to tell, everything you can remember since the day you entered public life. Tell them about any money you have ever received.'

'General,' asked Nixon, 'do you think after the television program that an announcement could then be made one way or the other?' Ike vacillated. 'I am hoping that no announcement would be necessary at all,' he replied, 'but maybe after the program we could tell what ought to be done.' Nixon lost his cool. 'There comes a time in matters like this when you've either got to shit or get off the pot', he blurted out, irritating Ike not by his language but by his insubordination. 'The great trouble here is the indecision', Nixon added, as a chill spread over the telephone wires. The conversation petered out soon afterwards, Eisenhower ending it with the lukewarm exhortation, 'Keep your chin up.'[62] This was difficult advice to follow in the circumstances. Nixon was to be left on his own to stake his career on a single television broadcast. His chances of survival seemed almost hopeless, particularly after Dewey called from New York to tell Nixon that the pressure for him to get off the ticket could only be halted if the public response to the broadcast was favourable by a margin of 90 to 10.

Nixon was understandably demoralised by this extraordinary 90–10 advice from his former patron. Deeply depressed, he was on the verge of quitting, but two forces seem to have put new heart into him—the power of prayer and the anger of his wife.

The identifiable sources of prayer that inspired Nixon at this time were from his own Quaker community and from the Carmelite Nuns at Long Beach. From his mother came a report that many of her relatives and neighbours in Whittier 'were thinking of you'—the familiar Hannah Nixon euphemism for 'praying for you'. The same message was delivered by Tom Bewley, his former law partner and a devout Quaker, who flew up to Portland to tell Nixon that the Friends Church in Whittier had been holding a special prayer session on his behalf. Nixon was touched by this news and immediately made an unscheduled and private visit to the morning service of the First Friends Church in Portland. According to Bewley, Nixon came back from this service 'a changed man', grabbing his former partner's hand and saying, 'I'm not worried any more.'[63] Meanwhile, on a different denominational track, Helene Drown telephoned a friend who was a Sister of the Carmelite Order of Nuns at Long Beach and returned with the news that the nuns were saying a special mass for him. 'Dick was really lifted up when I told him', recalled Drown. 'I know it made a huge difference to him. He wrote and told me so the day after the broadcast.'[64]

In search of further, non-divine guidance, Nixon went to his wife and again asked whether she thought he should resign. Pat blazed at him without a second's hesitation: 'We both know what you have to do, Dick. You have to fight it all the way to the end, no matter what happens!' Years afterwards, Nixon told his daughter Julie that these words were what he 'desperately' needed to hear. 'From that time on I never had any doubt but that I would fight the thing through to the finish, win or lose.'[65]

IV. THE CHECKERS BROADCAST

Nixon's weapons for his televised fight to the finish were surprise, preparation, and his instinctive feel for the symbols and phrases which would win support from Middle America. Surprise was easy, as never before in the history of presidential elections had there been an event like The Fund crisis broadcast. Once the Republican National Committee had been persuaded to pay the $75,000 bill for thirty minutes of nationwide television, a huge viewing audience was guaranteed, provided the newspapers kept the story on their front pages until transmission time. There was never any doubt that the press would oblige in this respect. Every hour reporters were flying in like vultures to join Nixon's beleaguered campaign headquarters, which had moved down to Los Angeles. 'They are here so as to have front row seats for the hanging', joked press aide Jim Bassett to Nixon,[66] who stubbornly resisted the pressure to give the journalists any advance indication of what he was going to say in his broadcast, thus magnifying the suspense and the editorial build-up.

Would he or wouldn't he offer to resign from the ticket? It was not only the press corps who were hounding Nixon for a preview of his big decision. Back on the Eisenhower train there was anger because Sherman Adams had been unable to get any advance information on the contents of the broadcast despite several calls to Murray Chotiner. This lack of co-operation intensified the friction between the two staffs. The feeling grew stronger among Ike's men that Nixon must be persuaded to do the decent thing and resign. Senator William Knowland had even been summoned from Hawaii to stand by as an alternative vice-presidential candidate. Although most members of the Republican National Committee strongly opposed such a change, Eisenhower was leaning towards dumping Nixon. His view of the problem was unclear, but he seemed to be increasingly convinced by his personal friends that The Fund crisis had grown into too much of a distraction from the clean up 'crusade' which he had promised the electorate. As the 'Look Ahead Neighbor Special' arrived in Cleveland, Ohio, on the afternoon of 23 September, Ike called a meeting of his senior advisers to review the situation. After listening quietly to the opinions of those present, Eisenhower at last moved decisively. He instructed one of his aides, Congressman Leonard Hall, to call Thomas E. Dewey, who was in turn asked to reach Nixon and convince him that it was his duty to resign from the ticket at the end of his broadcast.

Entrusted with this task, Dewey eventually got through to Nixon in his hotel suite approximately an hour before he was due to go down to the studio. Dewey came quickly to the point. 'There has just been a meeting of all Eisenhower's top advisers,' he said, 'and they have asked me to tell you that it is their opinion that at the conclusion of the broadcast tonight you should submit your resignation to Eisenhower.' Nixon was dumbfounded. He had prepared his speech on the basis that the public reaction to his broadcast would decide his fate. Now he was apparently getting an order from Eisenhower to commit political suicide on live television. With cold politeness Nixon refused, telling Dewey, 'It's kind of late for them to pass on this recommendation to me now. I've already prepared my remarks and it would be very difficult for me to change them now.' After pressing Nixon to reconsider without success, Dewey tried an unorthodox, almost surrealistic approach: 'I've got another suggestion as to how you can follow this up and come out of it all the hero rather than the goat', he continued. 'What you might do is announce that you're resigning from the Senate as well. Then, in the special election which will have to be called for the Senate, you can run again and vindicate yourself by winning the biggest plurality in history.'[67] Nixon thought the world was going mad around him when he heard this bizarre proposal. He kept silent on the telephone. Eventually Dewey said, 'Well, what shall I tell them you are going to do?' Nixon lost his temper. 'Just tell them I haven't the slightest idea what I'm going to do, and if they want to find out they'd better listen to the broadcast. And tell them I know something about politics too!' he shouted as he slammed down the receiver, ordering everyone out of his suite so that he could sit alone for the next thirty minutes, contemplating his options.[68]

Although shaken by Dewey's call, Nixon did not change his carefully prepared speech. He had too many aces up his sleeve to consider shooting himself at the card table. He knew he could disprove the basic charge against him of personally benefiting from an improper fund by revealing two impressive reports that had been prepared since the controversy erupted. One was a set of accounts audited by Price Waterhouse, which showed that every cent on the fund had been spent on legitimate political expenses. The other was an opinion from the respected law firm of Gibson, Dunn, and Crutcher, which unequivocally declared that there was nothing illegal or unethical about the fund. As for the underlying accusation that his life style had been enriched through the fund, he decided to knock this charge on the head by doing a personal financial striptease. Pat had at first objected to this plan for laying bare the details of their private finances. 'Why do we have to tell people how little we have and how much we owe? Aren't we entitled to have at least some privacy?' she cried when, on the plane coming down from Portland, she had first seen his draft speech notes. Nixon could only reply that political life was like living in a fish bowl and that he had to use all the facts to assure the success of the broadcast.[69]

In addition to presenting the financial and legal facts, Nixon knew that he must also appeal to his audience's emotions. Such an appeal would mean a descent into a style of folksy corniness which could either stick in the gullet or pluck at the heartstrings. Pitching his speech at the right emotional level was therefore his greatest challenge. For the first, but by no means the last, time in his career, Nixon decided to ignore the élite and to target his words at that mass audience which many years later he would describe as the silent majority. He was encouraged to reach out in this direction by the knowledge that some of his punchlines had already played well with the crowds on the stump. References to Pat's cloth coat; his refusal to put his wife on the Senate staff payroll as the Democratic vice-presidential nominee had; and his description of himself as someone who was 'not a quitter' were all well-tested applause winners from the campaign trail. Everything now depended on whether Nixon could generate an even stronger response from America's living rooms.

Arriving in the television studio, Nixon was overwhelmed by a loss of nerve. Five minutes before the broadcast, he buried his head in his hands, making a prayer which he apparently thought went unanswered. With three minutes to air time, sitting just off camera, he turned to Pat and said in a voice breaking with emotion, 'I just don't think I can go through with this one.' 'Of course you can', Pat said in a matter-of-fact voice, taking his hand and leading him back on to the set.[70] Nixon was behind a small table, his only prop some four pages of speech notes to which he occasionally referred. Pat sat on a divan a few feet away from him, making the perfect picture of a loyal wife backing her husband in his hour of crisis.

'My fellow Americans,' he began, 'I come before you tonight as a candidate for the Vice Presidency and as a man whose honesty and integrity have been questioned.' Gradually his faltering nervousness fell away as he explained why he wanted to tell his side of the story. 'I am sure that you have read the charge and that you've heard it that I, Senator Nixon, took $18,000 from a group of my supporters. Now was that wrong? It isn't a question of whether it was legal or illegal;

that isn't enough. The question is: was it morally wrong? I say it was morally wrong if any of that $18,000 went to me for my personal use. I say it was morally wrong if it was secretly given and secretly handled. And I say it was morally wrong if any of the contributors got special favours for the contributions they made.'

With growing confidence in his voice, Nixon demolished the moral anxieties raised in his rhetorical questions with an account of how the fund was spent exclusively on political expenses, citing the lawyers' and auditors' reports. Then he changed gear, answering another rhetorical question, 'Is there a possibility that you feathered your own nest?', by saying, 'So what I am now going to do—and this is unprecedented in the history of American politics—is to give this television and radio audience a complete financial history: everything I've earned; everything I've spent; everything I owe.' The item-isation of the Nixon family finances took about six minutes of air time. His inventory listed not only major items such as their house in Washington, 'which cost $41,000 and on which we owe $20,000', but got right down to their smallest assets and liabilities, which included 'a 1950 Oldsmobile car'; 'our furniture'; and 'no stocks and bonds of any type'. Income and outgoings were listed in similar detail, as were their debts, which included the mortgage on the house in Washington; a $4,500 bank overdraft; a $3,000 loan from his parents ('and the interest on that loan I pay regularly because it's part of the savings they made through the years when they were working so hard'); and finally a $500 loan on his life insurance. 'Well that's about it', he concluded, 'That's what we have and that's what we owe. It isn't very much but Pat and I have the satisfaction that every dime that we've got is honestly ours. I should say this, that Pat doesn't have a mink coat. But she does have a respectable cloth coat. And I always tell her that she'd look good in anything.' Pausing for a second, Nixon changed gear again to deliver in a voice breaking with emotion the passage that would for ever give the speech its name, its fame, and its notoriety.

'One thing I probably should tell you, because if I don't "they'll" probably be saying this about me too: we did get something—a gift—after the election. A man down in Texas heard Pat mention on the radio the fact that our two youngsters would like to have a dog. And believe it or not, the day before we left on this campaign trip we got a message from Union Station in Baltimore saying they had a package for us. We went down to get it. You know what it was?

'It was a little cocker spaniel dog in a crate that he sent all the way from Texas. Black-and-white spotted. And our little girl—Tricia, the six year old—named it Checkers. And you know, the kids love that dog and I just want to say right now that, regardless of what "they" say about it, we're going to keep it.'

Coming out of this bathos, Nixon switched into a cunning attack on the Democratic ticket of Stevenson and Sparkman. 'I believe it's fine that a man like Governor Stevenson, who inherited a fortune from his father, can run for President. But I also feel that it's essential in this country of ours that a man of modest means can also run for President. You remember what Abraham Lincoln said, "God must have loved the common people—he made so many of them."'

Having established himself as the representative of the common people, Nixon then suggested some courses of conduct for his wealthy opponents. Governor Stevenson should give the public all the details of his political fund: names, amounts and favours. Senator Sparkman, who had his wife on the Senate payroll, should come clean with all his outside sources of income. Both Democrats must 'make a complete statement as to their financial history. If they don't, it will be an admission that they have something to hide.'

At these words, Eisenhower, who was watching the speech in Cleveland, stabbed his pencil into his notepad so hard that it snapped. Ike was appalled at the prospect of full financial disclosure, particularly since his candidature had long been handsomely bankrolled by wealthy friends. Meanwhile on the screen Nixon was moving even more confidently through the final phases of his speech. After a passing reference to the Hiss case as the source of all smears against him, he assured the viewers that he was 'not a quitter'. ('No, and you never have been!' Hannah Nixon shouted to her television set in Whittier in an uncharacteristic moment of vehemence.) Then he switched into a eulogy for Eisenhower, which he linked to an appeal for support for himself. 'I would do nothing that would harm the possibilities of Dwight Eisenhower to become President of the United States. And for that reason I am submitting to the Republican National Committee tonight, through this broadcast, the decision which is theirs to make. Let them decide whether my position on the ticket will help or hurt. And I am going to ask you to help them decide. Wire and write the Republican National Committee whether you think I should stay on or get off.'

Amidst frantic time-up signals from the producer, Nixon rose from behind his desk and moved towards the cameras. His body language was radiating defiance as he ad libbed his way to a fist-clenched peroration. 'Regardless of what happens I am going to continue this fight. I am going to campaign up and down America until we drive the crooks, and the Communists, and those who defend them out of Washington.'

With his voice cracking and the screen fading, Nixon took another step towards the cameras and changed tack from the fight against Communism to the greatness of Eisenhower. 'Remember folks, Eisenhower is a great man…believe me…he is a great man', he was saying. The producer waved still more frantically. 'Wire and write the National Committee…wire and write…' were Nixon's last audible words in the final seconds of emotional and televisual confusion.[71] Then the screen went blank, and the verdict was in the hands of the public.

V. THE PUBLIC REACTS

The effect of the 'Checkers' broadcast was extraordinary. Although the black-and-white production was primitive by today's standards, and although parts of the speech look maudlin in cold print, Nixon touched the hearts of Middle America. One of the first to realise this was Bill Rogers, who in faltering spirits had accompanied the Nixons to the studio. 'But when at the end of the program I saw that all the cameramen were crying,' he recalled, 'I realized that the broadcast had turned defeat into victory and that a new chapter in political mass communication had been written.'[72]

No such lofty thoughts were passing through the mind of Richard Nixon. Drenched in perspiration, he came off the set in a mood of black despair. He was devastated when he realised that he had been cut off the air just before giving the address of where to wire or write to the Republican National Committee. 'I was a failure…I loused it up…it was a flop', he mumbled to Rogers. 'Let's get out of here and get a fast one. I need it.'[73] As he got into the car he slumped into the back seat, then, seeing a large Irish setter barking on the pavement, he gloomily joked to Pat, 'Well, we made a hit in the dog world, anyway.'[74]

His spirits started to lift when he returned to the Ambassador Hotel, where a crowd had gathered to cheer him. Someone shouted, 'The telephones are going crazy; everybody's in your corner!' Within minutes a torrent of calls and telegrams began surging in.[75] Ironically, Nixon's forgetfulness in not telling the audience where to send their wires enlarged the billowing wave of favourable communication as the viewers jammed switchboards, telephone lines and Western Union offices in their frantic efforts to make contact with anything that sounded Republican.

The magnitude of Nixon's success was quickly apparent. The TV networks announced a record-breaking audience of 58 million—a figure that was not surpassed until the first Nixon–Kennedy debate in 1960. Every Republican office in the country reported being inundated with messages of support, while the Republican National Committee had never seen anything like it, receiving at their Washington headquarters alone over 160,000 telegrams and 250,000 letters, backing Nixon by a margin of 350 to 1.

Amidst the tumult of enthusiasm, there were some sour notes. In the Roosevelt Hotel in New York, Dewey, Brownell and General Lucius Clay watched the broadcast together. 'Dewey was furious that Nixon had disobeyed his orders', recalled Brownell. 'He was mad and Clay was angry too. He kept saying "Sophomoric!" and "Sugary sweet!" in disgust.' However Brownell himself thought the broadcast was 'brilliant…a ten strike',[76] and Clay came round to the same view after going into the hotel lobby and seeing with amazement how the clerks and the elevator boys were crying.

Whatever might be the views of Generals and Governors on the taste of the 'Checkers' broadcast, there was no gainsaying the fact that Nixon had unlocked the emotions of 'the folks' of America. They were for him in their hundreds of thousands, and to judge by the tone of their calls and wires, they had given their hearts as well as their votes.

Yet for all this good news there was only one vote that counted and that was Eisenhower's. Watching the television in Cleveland, he had his own personal indications of how successfully Nixon had turned the tide. By the end of the broadcast his wife Mamie was weeping. Tears were also in the eyes of some of his most hard-boiled companions, among them Bill Robinson, the Vice President of the *New York Herald Tribune,* who had hitherto been Nixon's most vocal opponent. Robinson's volte-face was the first of many that night. Even the military and corporate figures in Ike's entourage, who found the emotional tone of the broadcast distasteful, had to admit that Nixon had scored a triumph. In any case the General could hardly ignore the voice of the people, which was making itself heard loud and clear. In the auditorium below Eisenhower's suite the large audience which had been listening to the speech on a radio relay began chanting, 'We want Nixon! We want Nixon!'

Eisenhower came down to this cheering crowd and told them 'I have been a warrior and I like courage. Tonight I saw an example of courage. I have seen brave men in tough situations. I have never seen anyone come through in better fashion than Senator Nixon did tonight.' Yet, later in his remarks, he also said that one thirty-minute television presentation was not enough to settle all the issues and that he was asking Nixon to come and see him the next day for a face-to-face talk, so that he could 'complete the formulation of my personal decision'.[77]

Back in Los Angeles, the euphoria in the candidate's hotel suite turned to anger when Nixon received the wire service report from Cleveland, which merely quoted Eisenhower as saying that one speech was not enough: 'What more can he possibly want from me? I'm not going to crawl on my hands and knees to him', declared Nixon. In a fit of temper he dictated a curt letter of resignation to Rose

Woods. She typed it. 'But I knew the Boss too well to even think of sending it', she recalled. 'And sure enough he sent Murray Chotiner over to tear it up. Murray was really angry, saying that Eisenhower deserved to lose both the Boss and the election, but that was only heat of the moment talk.'[78]

Eisenhower's apparent equivocation after the broadcast was partly due to a misunderstanding and partly due to a degree of personal pique. In fact Ike had sent Nixon a generously worded telegram within minutes of the speech ending, but this got lost in the torrent of incoming messages. Yet even in his wire of congratulation, Eisenhower subtly made the point that he was the one who would decide his running mate's future, not the Republican National Committee, hence the request that Nixon should meet him the following day in Wheeling, West Virginia, before any formal announcement could be made.

Nixon at first decided to defy Eisenhower and huffily sent off a telegram saying that he would be resuming his campaign tour and would only be available for a meeting in Washington in five days' time. However wiser counsels prevailed, particularly when intermediaries explained to Nixon that Ike only wanted to be seen to make the decision himself for protocol reasons and that the substantive issues had all been determined by the broadcast. This was indeed the case. However much Eisenhower might wish to remain aloof from the Republican National Committee, he could not ignore their 107–0 straw poll recommending that Nixon should stay on the ticket, any more than he could overlook the tidal wave of popular support for Nixon, which had now swollen to over four million favourable letters and telegrams. So, in the words of his speech writer Emmet John Hughes, Eisenhower 'in effect shrugged and nodded' and Nixon, once he knew Ike had given his nod, flew to Wheeling where the running mates staged a happy reunion. 'You're my boy', beamed the General, bounding up the aircraft steps to greet the man he had almost decided to throw off the ticket three days earlier, then they drove together to what was almost a coronation ceremony at Wheeling Stadium. To a cheering crowd of over 6,000, Ike read out two telegrams, one from the Republican National Committee announcing their 107 unanimous votes of support and declaring 'America has taken Dick Nixon to its heart'; the other from Hannah Nixon, sent five days earlier, which read:

> Dear General,
>   I am trusting that the absolute truth may come out concerning this attack on Richard. When it does, I am sure you will be guided aright in your decision to place implicit faith in his integrity and honesty.

Best wishes from one who has known Richard longer than anyone, his mother,
Hannah Nixon

Amidst all the outpourings of emotion over the maternal telegram, Nixon
came to the microphone and told the crowd, 'This is probably the greatest
moment of my life.'[79] After he sat down to another wild ovation, one of the first
to come up and offer congratulations was Senator William Knowland, now his
ex-replacement as vice-presidential nominee. Suddenly it was all too much for
Nixon. His pent-up emotions burst out of him and he fell on Knowland's broad
shoulders weeping tears of joy and relief. The drama was over.

Later that night, Nixon sat down and wrote the first of many thank-you notes
to those who had helped him through the crisis. It was to Helene Drown, who
three days earlier had invoked the prayers of the Carmelite Sisters at Long Beach:

Helene,
Tell the sisters they must have been praying for me last night. 5
minutes before it started I didn't think I could do it. Then I sat down,
put my head in my hands and prayed 'God—Thy will be done *not
mine.*"
Well I guess they came through for me.
Dick Nixon[80]

VI. ELECTED VICE PRESIDENT

The Shakespearean saga of The Fund crisis, which began as 'Much Ado about
Nothing', did not quite finish as 'All's Well That Ends Well'. That may have been
the superficial impression and it was undoubtedly the short-term result, but there
were deeper changes and more lasting scars left for ever on Nixon and his family.
What really hurt them was the public questioning of the financial integrity that
had been the cornerstone of their lives. From his earliest days as a boy shopkeeper
in the family store, Nixon had taken pride in his parents' unsullied reputation for
fair trading and Quaker probity in all business dealings. He himself had followed
the same path of rectitude. In matters of money he had always been scrupulously
careful. Whether it was looking after student funds at Whittier College; acting
for clients as a young lawyer; fighting to save and even personally repay the shareholders' losses at Citrifrost; accounting for his expenses down to the last cent as
a Congressman on foreign trips; insisting on splitting vacation hotel bills on a
precise 50–50 basis with wealthy friends like the Drowns; or living modestly

within his income as a budget-conscious father of a young family—in all these and many other respects the record suggests that the thirty-nine-year-old Richard Nixon was a man of financial honesty. If he had a weak spot in his economic armour it was naïveté not venality. The worst criticism that can be levelled at him over The Fund arrangements is that perhaps he should have initially insisted on even tighter safeguards than those imposed by Dana C. Smith. Yet any such extra safeguards would have been purely cosmetic, for the truth of the matter was that The Fund did operate as an entirely straightforward political expenses trust. Its donors neither received nor expected favours, while Nixon gained neither cash nor personal benefits. By all the known ethical rules of American political financing, The Fund was clean.

Yet even though he had won the moral argument and saved his career with the 'Checkers' speech, Nixon was enough of a realist to know that his reputation would forever be tarnished by the fire he had been through. No stranger in 1952 to political smears, Nixon was, deep down, appalled by the sheer unfairness of this new and unexpected dimension of a financial smear. 'I was deeply dispirited by much of the reaction to the fund...I regarded what had been done to me as character assassination', he wrote later.[81] Pat felt it even more keenly, and a part of her never recovered from the trauma of The Fund controversy. 'Do we have to talk about this? It kills me ...' was her response in 1978 when her filial biographer, Julie Nixon Eisenhower, tried to ask questions on the subject, abandoning the attempt when she saw the pain in her mother's eyes.[82]

Pat was not alone in her travail. Nixon's parents had been badly wounded, too, by the loss of privacy and reputation, Hannah saying afterwards, 'I didn't think I could take it but I drew courage from my faith',[83] while even the proud and combative Frank had been reduced to bouts of weeping as the smears surfaced.[84] With such negative emotions unleashed in the family, it was inevitable that there should come a souring of their previous enjoyment of the life of politics. Nixon himself, always quick to wrath when his nearest and dearest are being made to suffer, began to change in ways which at best reflected a feeling of 'never glad confident morning again'[85] and at worst foreshadowed the emergence of a new and darker side to his character. If one had to pinpoint a time when the optimistic young politician began to be consumed from within by strange fires of anger, that moment would be the aftermath of The Fund crisis.

As a crisis it was now politically irrelevant. On the election stage the last few weeks of the campaign were going superbly well for the Republicans. After holding out the promise of ending the war with his 'I will go to Korea' speech,

Eisenhower and all the candidates on his coat tails were cruising towards victory. Nixon was drawing ever larger and more adulatory crowds. In the eyes of the party faithful he was not merely vindicated and secure on the ticket; he was almost a candidate for canonisation. Yet his enemies were growing too. The 'Checkers' speech had been loved by the man in the street but loathed by the men on the press bench. It had delighted conservative Republicans but disgusted liberal Democrats. Perhaps sensing this, Nixon allowed his private venom to spill out into his speeches and press relations. His campaign rhetoric, often politically tough, now started to get personally vicious. He called Stevenson 'a weakling, a waster, a small caliber Truman' who had been installed as Governor of Illinois by a political organisation infected with 'mobsters, gangsters, and remnants of the Old Capone gang'.[86] In a speech at Texarkana on 27 October he told the audience: 'What we need in Washington is a President who instead of covering up, cleans up', going on to describe Truman, Stevenson and Acheson as 'traitors to the high principles in which many of the nation's Democrats believe'.[87] Three days later he described the Democratic nominee as 'Adlai the appeaser...who got a PhD degree from Acheson's College of Cowardly Containment'.[88] In his memoirs, Nixon made a rare apology for these excesses, saying, 'I regret the intensity of those attacks.'[89]

There was also a new edge of bitterness in Nixon's relationship with the press. Prior to September 1952 he had cultivated journalists, making himself agreeable and accessible to reporters in the manner of all rising politicians. Post 'Checkers', he withdrew from the press corps and sometimes nakedly displayed his animosity: 'Fuck 'em, we don't need them', he is remembered snarling in the direction of newsmen who were late for a campaign bus[90] and this pattern of contempt showed up on several occasions. 'By the end of the '52 campaign he had utterly no use for the press', said his own press secretary, Jim Bassett,[91] describing a feeling which was to a considerable extent mutual. The 'Checkers' speech had badly wrong-footed the pundits. They had come to bury Nixon and after his triumph they could not bear to praise him.

Some writers made their dislike clear by sneering at the tone of the broadcast. Others strove to prove they had been right all along by publishing an amazing series of rumours, lies and even forgeries purporting to justify corruption stories, which turned out to be totally untrue. The Washington columnist Drew Pearson was the worst offender. In one of his reports he alleged that Nixon had falsely sworn to a low property valuation on his house in order to claim a tax exemption. It turned out to be a valid claim by an unrelated Richard Nixon. In another column, Pearson asserted that as a Senator, Nixon had taken a $52,000-a-year bribe from the oil industry. The letter on which this claim was based was a forgery. There were several such calumnies and although all were disproved, the cumulative effect of them left Nixon with the feeling that although he had won the battle of The Fund crisis, he had lost the war to uphold his financial and personal honour. That never ceased to hurt him.

In the closing stages of the campaign, these strains began to tell on Nixon. He was outwardly too much on the offensive in his attacks on the Democrats because inwardly he was too much on the defensive about the press. He was also overtired. Two days before the election he spoke at a rally at the American Legion stadium in Hollywood. Because it was Hallowe'en night, many families had better tricks or treats than listening to political speeches, so the auditorium was only half full. When Nixon saw the empty seats he exploded with rage at his advance man, Pat Hillings. 'Goddamn you! Goddamn you! How the hell could you embarrass me like this', bawled Nixon, who seemed to Hillings to be close to violence. 'You could lose us the election by this, Goddamn you.'[92]

A less sensitive politician than Richard Nixon might have held on to his temper and rolled with the punches that came his way after The Fund crisis. After all, he had won and won big. The landslide of telegrams after the 'Checkers' speech was followed by an even bigger landslide of votes at the election, when Eisenhower won the Presidency by 34 million votes to Stevenson's 27 million—a margin of 55 per cent to 44 per cent.

Inaugurated on 20 January 1953, Richard Nixon was the second-youngest Vice President in the history of the Republic. Unknown freshman Congressman at thirty-three. Re-elected unopposed at thirty-five. National celebrity as a result of the Hiss case at thirty-six. United States Senator at thirty-seven. Now Vice President eleven days after his fortieth birthday. If one searches for historical parallels to Nixon's meteoric progress as an elected representative, only William Pitt the Younger, British Prime Minister in 1783 at twenty-four, and John F. Kennedy, President of the United States in 1961 at forty-three, could be said to have ascended faster.

Nixon rejoiced in his hour of glory, but he was not quite the fulfilled and happy man he should have been. The person who may have sensed this most deeply was his mother. A few hours after he had taken the oath of office, she took her son aside and gave him a small, handwritten note. Its message was Hannah's way of reminding the new Vice President that he needed to find that spiritual 'Peace at the center' which to her was more important than all the temporal power now coming into his hands. It read:

To Richard:

You have gone far, and we are proud of you always—I know that you will keep your relationship with your Maker as it should be, for after all, that, as you must know, is the most important thing in this life.

With love,
Mother[93]

Nixon has kept the letter in his wallet ever since.

TWELVE

THE VICE-PRESIDENTIAL YEARS 1953–1956

I. JOURNEY TO THE FAR EAST

Richard Nixon transformed the office of Vice President. At the time of his swearing in on 20 January 1953, he was taking on a job which was notorious for its insignificance. Eight years later, when he temporarily departed from the stage of national politics after his defeat in the 1960 presidential election, Nixon left behind him a Vice Presidency that had become the second most powerful office in the United States.

The reshaping of the Vice Presidency was initially to the credit of Dwight D. Eisenhower, whose military career had taught him the importance of training up a good subordinate. 'Dick, I don't want a Vice President who will be a figurehead. I want a man who will be a member of the team. And I want him to be able to step into the Presidency smoothly in case anything happens to me',[1] Ike had said to his running mate at the time of their nominations in Chicago in August 1952.

Arriving at the White House five months later, the President was as good as his word. From the beginning Nixon was accorded his proper status in the Administration, attending all meetings of the National Security Council and the Cabinet, chairing them whenever the President was absent. At one NSC meeting, in March 1953, Eisenhower asked him: 'Dick, what are you going to do this summer?' 'Anything you say, Mr. President', replied Nixon. 'Well, I think you should take a trip to the Far East. Take Pat along.'[2]

Behind this apparently casual suggestion lay the President's serious concern that the United States was ignoring the emerging nations of Asia. Truman had neglected them and Ike acknowledged his own lack of expertise in the area. Nixon was being asked to fill a gap in American foreign policy. He seized his chance.

Nixon's preparations for his Far East tour were influenced by his natural orientation towards the Pacific. His Californian outlook; his early education alongside Asian children; and his wartime service in the Solomon Islands were factors which stimulated his curiosity in the region. Ahead of the Washington foreign policy establishment of the day, he foresaw that the emerging political and economic power centres of Asia were likely to be more important to the long-term interests of the United States than the old chancelleries of Europe. However, for the purposes of his first vice-presidential mission overseas, Nixon was somewhat dependent on the European colonial powers, since eleven of the nineteen countries on his itinerary were still ruled or heavily influenced by France and Britain. Neither nation seemed particularly enthusiastic about an American leader's tour of their Far East spheres of influence. Paris was initially obstructive over Nixon's arrangements to visit 'The Associated States of French Indo-China', as Vietnam, Laos and Cambodia were still called, while the British diplomatic cable traffic reeked of condescension about his proposed journey to eight of Her Majesty's colonies and dominions. 'We must hope that the President's goodwill intention in sending Senator [sic] Nixon will not backfire…his record of Vice President has on the whole been rather better than might have been feared…but we must hope that he will be tactful…is he leaving his spaniel behind?' were among the initial lofty exchanges between the British Embassy in Washington and the Foreign Office in London.[3]

Even the circular telegram sent from Whitehall to all Britain's Far East missions on the eve of the Vice President's departure on 5 October seemed to damn him with faint praise. 'Nixon is a young man who has probably climbed rather higher, rather faster than his intrinsic merits justify', ran this Olympian judgement. 'He has picked up some quite good as well as some very bad ideas in the past. He is young enough and just intelligent enough to stand a fair chance of getting them sorted out…It is therefore quite possible that time and trouble spent on getting the right ideas into Nixon's head may later bear fruit in reducing congressional obstruction to an international US foreign policy. It might not, but it is worth trying.'[4]

It is interesting to notice how quickly Nixon's reputation was revised upwards by Britain's diplomats as his tour progressed. On 27 October from Kuala Lumpur in Malaya, the High Commissioner, Field Marshal Sir Gerald Templer, sent a dispatch to the Foreign Secretary, Sir Anthony Eden, describing the Vice President as: 'an extremely nice man in every way. He has got charming manners and in fact he was the very reverse of everything one had expected after reading press reports of the American Elections. He is easy in his conversations and got on extremely well with the many Asians that he met…I was really very impressed with Nixon indeed. He seemed to me potentially to be a much bigger man than Adlai Stevenson, who as you know stayed with us a few years ago.'[5]

A week later, in Singapore, Nixon made a similarly favourable impression during a three-hour meeting with Malcolm MacDonald, Britain's Commissioner General for Southeast Asia and son of the former Prime Minister, Ramsay Mac-Donald.

'I was agreeably impressed by Mr. Nixon's general knowledge of the situation in Southeast Asia, of the mood susceptibilities and aspirations of the Asian nations and of broad Asian problems', reported MacDonald. 'He seemed to me to have exactly the right approach to the Asians and their difficulties and to have very sensible views on the policies which we in the West should pursue towards them.'

One of the most interesting passages in the British envoy's despatch concerned Nixon's attitude towards China, which had evidently taken on a more positive dimension from the negative hostility he had expressed in his 1950 and 1952 election speeches. In his conversation with MacDonald, the Vice President acknowledged that Chiang Kai-shek was a fading force and that many of the men around him were discredited. He asked questions about the chances of weaning the Chinese government in Peking away from their dependence on and loyalty to the Russians. MacDonald suggested some long-term ways to achieve this, including joint moves towards maintaining the Korean peace settlement. He urged Nixon to keep a lookout for chances to get on to better terms with the Chinese. The dispatch continued: 'Mr. Nixon said that he too agreed that if the Chinese became more reasonable about the Korean political talks, we should seek to help them further. It might be possible to contemplate their entry into the United Nations Organisation, although American public opinion would make this difficult. He personally was not unsympathetic to the general notion. Perhaps the first thing, before any political concessions were made to Peking, would be to try and improve trade with China.'[6] This 1953 report was the first intimation of Nixon's open-minded thinking on China, which ultimately manifested itself with his historic presidential mission to Peking in 1972.

On the French Indo-China sector of his tour, Nixon displayed further political prescience. After a six-day visit, which took in Cambodia, Laos, Saigon and Hanoi as well as forays to the battlefields, he became pessimistic about the French army's chances of defeating the Vietminh guerrillas. Nixon diagnosed that the fundamental weakness of the military situation was the French commander's attitude of colonial superiority towards the Vietnamese troops under his command. He surprised his hosts by insisting on dividing his time equally in the field between the Vietnamese soldiers' tents and the French officers' mess. He sampled their respective menus of monkey stew and *boeuf a la Bourguignonne* washed down with Algerian red wine—gastronomic symbols of a divided culture and loyalty, which Nixon thought was deteriorating into enmity as a result of the offensive disdain the French showed for their Vietnamese comrades.

Although in public Nixon was supportive of the French stand against the Communist insurgents, he privately noted his fears that their resistance could collapse. He also recorded his view that Ho Chi Minh seemed to be 'far more appealing as a popular leader'[7] than any of the non-Communist alternatives. He flew out of Hanoi depressed by his conclusion that 'the French, if not losing the war, did not know how to win it'.[8]

Winning greater friendship and understanding for the United States was the main purpose of the tour, and in this intangible area of international relations Nixon appeared to do well. Most of the capitals on his itinerary had never been visited by an American President or Vice President. In an age before the term 'goodwill mission' had become a diplomatic cliché, a trip at this level was a significant event. Nixon's speeches, appearances, and private conversations often had the result of enlarging the area of confidence between the US and the host country. In Tokyo, for example, he and Pat were the Emperor's first state guests since World War II. Acknowledging that it had been a mistake for the US to have insisted on Japanese disarmament after the war, Nixon floated the idea of Japanese rearmament, which at the time was anathema to many Americans, whose memories of the war in the Pacific were still fresh. This trial balloon, which had been cleared in advance with Secretary of State John Foster Dulles, made international and domestic headlines. The domestic coverage led to Nixon being cheered by vast crowds wherever he went in Japan with the refrain 'Niku-san! Niku-san!'

On the wider public-relations side of the tour, both Nixons were innovators. Pat pleased her hosts with surprise requests to visit hospitals, orphanages, and schools. The Vice President had his own ideas for improving his understanding of Asia. He used one of his two Secret Service agents, Rex Scouten, as an unofficial advance man for setting up offbeat schedules that were apparently beyond the imagination of the State Department. 'Nixon sent me on ahead of the party with instructions to fill up any of his spare time with side trips', recalled Scouten. 'He wanted to go up country to meet real people, to sit and talk with villagers and to get away from the cocktail party set that our embassies were so keen to stick to.'[9]

This emphasis on improvised scheduling followed the pattern Nixon had set during his travels with the Herter Committee in 1947. At every destination he sought encounters with ordinary citizens. Inevitably a good many of these meetings must have been brief and superficial, yet Nixon's diligent notes are full of the *vox populi* side of his tour. Sometimes this could bring him into contact with the unusual. In India, where he had a chilly meeting with Nehru, the highlight of his visit was a talk with Rajagopalachari, a mystic contemporary of Gandhi. 'Rajiji', as he was known to his followers, received the Vice President in Madras sitting on a straw mat clad only in a *dhoti* loincloth and sandals. For an afternoon they discussed the spiritual life, particularly reincarnation and predestination. Nixon filled three pages of notes recording what the sage had told him, claiming in his memoirs thirty-six years later that the afternoon 'had such a dramatic effect on me that I used many of his thoughts in my speeches over the next several years'.[10]

Political rather than spiritual leaders were Nixon's standard fare during his ten-week odyssey. He met many remarkable figures, some of them in the twilight of their careers, others who remained on the international stage long enough to make their contributions to Nixon's Presidency sixteen years later. Chiang Kai-shek; Robert Menzies, Sukarno; Nehru and Syngman Rhee were among the first category. The Shah of Iran; Ayub Khan; Prince Souvanna Phouma; Lee Kwan-yew and U Thant were in the second. All of them added to Nixon's growing store of geopolitical knowledge and understanding.

The only country in which Nixon had a substantive diplomatic mission to perform was Korea. He arrived in Seoul bearing a private letter from Eisenhower to President Syngman Rhee. It requested specific assurances that Rhee would not jeopardise the Korean partition settlement by embarking on further military hostilities. Nixon had the task of extracting firm promises to that effect from the Korean leader. Rhee was difficult and evasive. All he would say was: 'I pledge to you that before I take any unilateral action at any time I shall inform President Eisenhower first.'[11] As this was a long way from the promise required, Nixon had a serious problem on his hands. He pressed hard to achieve his objective throughout two meetings, much of which were taken up with the seventy-eight-year-old Korean leader giving a tutorial to the forty-year-old Vice President on the virtues of being unpredictable when dealing with Communists. However, finally Rhee conceded and promised that he would not attack the North on his own. When

Nixon returned to Washington he convinced Eisenhower that Rhee's word could be relied on and that the US could now extend economic and military aid to South Korea.[12] The mission had been successfully accomplished.

After seventy days of travelling, the Vice President and his party returned to Washington on 14 December. They were exhausted. Sleeplessness, illness, insect bites and other travelling hazards had all taken their toll. As Pat Nixon recalled: 'It was the toughest trip we ever made. The conditions were hard on us. Dick had lost ten pounds from dysentery and in those days before air conditioning he had to shake the damp out of his pants every night. We were so glad to be home.'[13]

Arriving at National Airport on 14 December, Nixon drove straight to the White House, where he and Pat had coffee with the Eisenhowers in their private quarters. The following day, the President sent him an uncharacteristically effusive, handwritten letter:

> Dear Dick,
>
> Proud as I am of the record you—and Pat—established on your recent visit to a number of Asian countries, yet I must say I'm glad to have you home.
>
> We, by which I mean all the principal figures in the Administration, have missed your wise counsel, your energetic support, and your exemplary dedication to the service of the country.
>
> On the purely personal side it was fine to see you both looking so well after the rigors of a trip that must have taxed the strength of even such young and vigorous people as yourselves. I look forward to some quiet opportunity when I can hear a real recital of your adventures and accomplishments.
>
> With warm personal regards,
> Sincerely,
> Dwight D. Eisenhower[14]

Eisenhower had good reason to be pleased with his Vice President, for the tour had added both to Nixon's and the Administration's lustre. The favourable US press coverage reflected this, as did the public response to a network TV broadcast Nixon made on 23 December, reporting to the nation on his travels. A few days earlier he had reported to the National Security Council, giving a two-hour briefing, whose highlight was a pessimistic warning about the vulnerability of French Indo-China. His timing was uncanny, for while he was speaking, the news came through to the NSC that Ho Chi Minh's Communist guerrillas had launched a major offensive against French positions in Vietnam. When Nixon concluded his *tour d'horizon,* President Eisenhower, Secretary of State Dulles and all the members of the Council rose from their seats and applauded him. It was later said that this address marked a turning point in Nixon's career, making him from that moment on 'a respected participant in the nation's foreign policy councils'.[15]

II. THE GO-BETWEEN

On the domestic front, Nixon was the Administration's bridge builder between the Executive and Congress. He also played a high profile role as the deputy leader and chief campaigner of the Republican Party. These tasks were unusual for a Vice President. They devolved upon Nixon because there was no one else who could do them. Eisenhower's Cabinet was heavily weighted with politically inexperienced businessmen. Some of them were good departmental administrators, but they could be naive when it came to legislative affairs or the presentation of their policies. The President himself viewed party politics with distaste. He had little time and even less affection for the GOP activists who had put him in the White House. There was thus a political vacuum at the top of the administration which Nixon filled—not always with success.

Nixon's relations with Congress started well. He ensured the safe passage of Eisenhower's first tax programme, which without some clever wheeling and dealing in the Vice President's office would have been torn to shreds by the House Ways and Means Committee. He had several other legislative successes on Capitol Hill, but his biggest problem was Senator Joe McCarthy.

The junior Senator from Wisconsin had become a painful thorn in the Administration's side. During 1953 and 1954, McCarthy continued the pattern he had set with his speech at Wheeling, West Virginia in 1950, making wild allegations on the 'Reds under the bed' theme, and frequently demanding full-scale congressional investigations to prove his point. For a long time the American public believed him. A Gallup Poll in January 1954 recorded that 50 per cent of all voters and 62 per cent of Republican voters had a favourable view of McCarthy, while only 29 per cent disapproved of his activities. His support was even stronger amongst the Republican members of the House and Senate. Although Eisenhower and the predominantly liberal White House staff looked askance at McCarthy's activities, there was nothing much they could do in the face of so much congressional sympathy. Nixon, whose anti-Communist credentials were strong, was given the unenviable task of mediating between the pro- and anti-McCarthy factions.

This was a no-win position, and Nixon soon became an unpopular go-between. Part of the problem lay in his own ambivalent attitudes, for Nixon was mixed up in his approach to the cause, the man, and his methods. He approved of the general objective to unmask Communist sympathisers working for the Government. He found the Wisconsin Senator 'sincere' and 'personally likeable'[16], but he despaired of McCarthy's impulsive methods of championing the anti-Communist cause with publicity-seeking exaggerations and smears.

In the early months of 1953, Nixon found himself spending a lot of time heading off McCarthyite troubles. He worked behind the scenes to cool down Senate opposition to various presidential nominees whom McCarthy had fingered. He managed to block a full-scale congressional investigation into the loyalty of the CIA, which McCarthy demanded on the grounds that one of Langley's bright young men, William Bundy, had made a contribution to the Alger Hiss defence fund while studying at Harvard. However Nixon's skills as a mediator proved useless when McCarthy started to attack Eisenhower's beloved Army.

McCarthy's pursuit of the left-wing Army dentist Dr. Irving Peress (who had received several promotions despite the fact that he had refused to sign an oath of loyalty) and his performance at the subsequent Army–McCarthy hearings was a shameful saga. Eisenhower grew more and more furious as McCarthy became more and more vicious. However, public opinion was not on the side of the Army at the outset of the battle, which was why Ike did most of his indignant fuming in private. Even at the halfway point in the drama, the polls reflected no more than a deepening polarisation on the issue of whether McCarthy was on the right track. Nixon the go-between failed to lower the temperature, while Nixon the politician became increasingly disturbed at the impact of the Peress affair on the upcoming 1954 congressional elections. With the Democrats in full cry over the widening split in the GOP, Eisenhower decided that the slayer of Hiss was the right man in the Administration to go on television and slay McCarthy. Nixon knew that his broadcast 'would be as important as any I'd ever made from the point of view of the party and the country'.[17] Isolating himself in a Washington hotel for four days, his intensive preparations included listening to many suggestions from Eisenhower, whose emotions were running high, particularly after being accused of personal weakness towards McCarthyism by Adlai Stevenson. Influenced in this partisan direction, Nixon's eventual speech, delivered on 13 March to 10 million viewers, was far rougher on the Democrats than on McCarthy. He attacked Truman, Stevenson, Acheson and other figures from the previous administration, delivering one particularly low blow as he compared

Republican and Democrat handling of foreign policy with these words: 'Incidentally, in mentioning Secretary Dulles, isn't it wonderful that finally we have a
Secretary of State who isn't taken in by the Communists?'[18] Some Democrats never
forgave Nixon for this statement, which they rightly felt impugned Acheson's
honour.

Moving to domestic Communism, Nixon attacked McCarthy by implication
although not by name when he said: 'Men who have in the past done effective
work exposing Communists in this country have by reckless talk and questionable methods made themselves the issue rather than the cause they believe in so
deeply.'[19]

He developed this theme with a vivid image: 'Now I can imagine that some
of you listening will say, "Well, why all of this hullabaloo about being fair when
you're dealing with a gang of traitors?" As a matter of fact, I've heard people say
they're a bunch of rats. What we ought to do is go out and shoot 'em. Well, I'll
agree that they're a bunch of rats, but just remember this, when you go out to shoot
rats, you have to shoot straight, because when you shoot wildly it not only means
that the rat may get away more easily, you make it easier on the rat.'[20]

The mixed metaphors about Democrats, rats and Communists produced
mixed results. Eisenhower called his Vice President with enthusiastic congratulations, saying, 'I want you to know that I think you did a magnificent job.'[21] Stevenson fulminated with a rage which was to surface in many subsequent campaign
speeches. McCarthy was contemptuous, declaring himself 'sick and tired' of 'the
constant yack-yacking from that prick Nixon'.[22] Nixon himself felt that his 13
March speech marked 'the beginning of the end' of the McCarthy drama.[23]

To those who knew him best, McCarthy appeared to have been inwardly
shaken by the 'rats' attack even though he was outwardly noisier than ever. He
entered on a phase of erratic personal behaviour which manifested itself in drinking bouts and even wilder smears. His performance at the Army–McCarthy
televised hearings, between April and June, so appalled the public that his Gallup
Poll support was massively reversed. Reflecting the nation's mood, his fellow
Senators voted to condemn McCarthy for bringing the Senate into disrepute.

On 3 December, the morning after this vote of censure was passed, by sixty-
seven votes to twenty-two, Eisenhower chortled to his Vice President, 'McCarthyism is now McCarthywasm.'[24] Ike was right. Despite a short-term show of bravado,
McCarthy never recovered either his political prestige or his personal equilibrium.
After lurching into alcoholism, he died in June 1957 aged only forty-eight, a
discredited figure. One of the strangest, saddest, and most bitter chapters in
American history was over.

Nixon was a loser rather than a beneficiary from the McCarthy era. Although his star had risen in the cause of anti-Communism, it became tarnished as public opinion turned against those who over-zealously hunted subversives in the government. The 1954 congressional elections reflected this change of mood and also a change in the national perception of Richard Nixon.

During the 1954 campaign, the Democrats made a conscious decision to attack Nixon. This was partly because he was the only available target. Eisenhower had decided to remain above the battle, Taft had died, and there were no other national standard bearers for the GOP cause. Nixon thus assumed the mantle of chief campaigner. By the time the polls closed on 2 November, he had travelled 26,000 miles in six weeks; visited ninety-five cities in thirty states; and made speeches on behalf of 186 House, Senate, and Gubernatorial candidates. He saw two main issues in the election—the economy and McCarthy. The economy was a vote loser, because the winding down of the Korean War had caused a mini-recession. Nixon had urged the cabinet to take some well-publicised steps to stimulate economic activity, but found his arguments thwarted by the fiscal conservatives advising Eisenhower. 'I said quite bluntly to them that whatever the big business people in the East and the financial analysts in Wall Street might think, out in the country there were great numbers of ordinary people who felt that a recession was in progress', he recalled. 'I said we had to take this into account or we could find ourselves in real trouble at the polls.'[25]

This warning on behalf of Middle America was ignored, so Nixon went out to campaign against a background of rising unemployment and closing businesses. To divert attention from the economy, his standard speech consisted of what became known as the 'K-1, C-3' formula—Korea, Communism, Corruption, Controls. This was an all-out onslaught on the Democrats, particularly the Americans for Democratic Action (ADA). Slamming what he called 'the Truman—Stevenson—ADA left wing'[26] for its Socialist and even neo-Communist tendencies in extravagant language was a good formula for delighting the GOP faithful. It was a bad formula for enhancing Nixon's wider political reputation. His anti-Communist rhetoric had become too shrill for many of his listeners. At best he sounded as though he was playing yesterday's tune, and in his worst moments he seemed to be questioning the patriotism of his opponents. They were not slow to return his fire. Adlai Stevenson, in particular, kept shooting with a fusillade of barbed quips. The Republican Party, he declared, had 'as many wings as a boarding house chicken' and was 'as confused as a blind dog in a meathouse' over McCarthy.[27] As for Nixon, he was on 'an ill will tour' representing 'McCarthyism in a white collar'.[28] 'The President smiles while the Vice President smears.'[29]

The liberal press, led by the *Washington Post* and its cartoonist Herblock, lambasted the Vice President for the tone of his 1954 campaign speeches almost as roughly as did Stevenson. The sharpness of the criticism upset Nixon, so much so that in September he thought seriously of leaving the political arena: 'My heart wasn't really in the battle. For the first time I realized how much the agony of The Fund crisis had stripped the fun and excitement of campaigning from me. . . . I resented being constantly vilified as a demagogue or a liar or as the sewer dwelling denizen of the Herblock cartoons. As the attacks became more personal, I sometimes wondered where party loyalty left off and masochism began. The girls were reaching an impressionable age, and neither Pat nor I wanted their father to be the bad guy of American politics'.[30]

These forebodings apparently crystallised into a decision to quit. On the flight back to Washington on 2 November he handed his aide Murray Chotiner the handwritten notes of his election eve broadcast. 'Here's my last campaign speech, Murray', said Nixon. 'You might like to keep it as a souvenir. It's the last one, because after this I am through with politics.'[31]

This plan was soon shelved, partly because the election results were considerably better than had been expected. Although the Democrats had regained overall control of Congress, the Republicans lost only sixteen seats in the House and two in the Senate. This was noticeably less than the average mid-term losses for the party in power. West of the Mississippi, where Nixon had done most of his campaigning, the GOP broke even on House seats and gained one Senate seat. There was hope for the future here, for the West was the fastest growing region of the country. These crumbs of comfort buoyed up Nixon's spirits. Moreover, his willingness to go out on his own to battle against the Democrats earned him almost enough bouquets from his party to neutralise the brickbats thrown at him by the liberal press. The election postmortems on Nixon were therefore a bewildering mixture of praise and condemnation, cheers and sneers.

The analyst whose views counted most was Dwight Eisenhower, but he was curiously ambivalent. During the election Ike had urged Dick on, exhorting him to lay into Stevenson and sending little notes of encouragement and congratulation from the Denver White House to the campaign trail. After the battle was over, Eisenhower privately criticised Nixon for using tactics so offensive to the Democrats that working with them in Congress would be made more difficult. One of Ike's favourite grumbles to his cronies was that Dick had not matured enough.

Caught in the crossfire between all this contradictory comment from President, press, and party bosses, Nixon ended 1954 feeling rather like that over-advised centurion in Macaulay's *Lays of Ancient Rome* to whom

> Those behind cried 'Forward!'
> And those before cried 'Back!'[32]

The inherent dichotomy of his role was troubling him. He had done well as a presidential understudy abroad but at home the partisan stridency of his campaign speeches had undermined the statesman's image to which he aspired. Like several Vice Presidents before and after him, Richard Nixon was uncertain of his role.

III. A HEARTBEAT AWAY

In the weeks following the 1954 election, Nixon went through one of his periodic bouts of despondency. In late November of that year he talked over his future with his wife, and together they reached a decision that he should retire from politics when his term as Vice President ended in 1956. The rationale for this improbable change of course can be attributed to an inner unhappiness on the part of both Nixons at this time. Richard Nixon was unhappy because he was insecure in his relationship with the White House. Ike took the credit for everything that went well; Dick was the whipping boy when anything went wrong. This unfair division of the spoils (as the Nixon camp perceived it) was exacerbated by suspicions of a growing coolness between President and Vice President. There was nothing concrete, as yet, for Nixon to complain about. But hard as he tried he could not bridge the twenty-two-year age gap with his boss, nor could he manage to achieve acceptance from Eisenhower's inner circle of cronies. This was a matter of atmospherics rather than specifics, but Nixon's sensitive ear detected that there were too many wrong notes in the Dick and Ike mood music. It made him uneasy—rightly so, as later events were to show.

On the distaff side, Pat Nixon was unhappy because of her yearning for normal family life, a goal that she had discovered was incompatible with national office. With two small children and no resident help in the house, her dual roles of motherhood and Mrs. Vice President were often in conflict. Affected by the frequent separations from husband or daughters; by the gawping tourists outside their Tilden Street home; and by the relentless inquisitiveness of the media, Pat longed for that peace which the world of politics cannot give. The more private life style of a successful lawyer, which Murray Chotiner had dangled before her at the Chicago convention as the lot of an ex-Vice President, seemed attractive in comparison to the vagaries of a public career that was now so entirely dependent on the whim of the White House. Her daughter Julie Nixon Eisenhower later explained Pat Nixon's contribution to the 1954 family dialogue on retiring from politics. 'The nub of what she was saying was that although she still believed my father had much to give the country, she chafed at an existence in which they were not in control and in which their relationship with their boss, Dwight David Eisenhower, remained so delicate and tenuous.'[33]

Nixon was chafing too, even scribbling himself a memorandum headed 'Reasons to get out'. This divided his reasons into 'Personal' and 'Political'. Top of the personal reasons was 'Wife—(columns, personal, staff hurts)'. His political reasons were:

1. Politicians must be able not to take issues to heart—fight and forget—twist and turn—1 live each one—and hard ones.
2. Don't like social life, the prestige.
3. Some convince selves [they are] indispensable—but not the case.
4. Therefore—no reason to stay in—unless—you
   (a) Enjoy it—personal
   (b) Need the job (economic, money)
   (c) Job needs you[34]

The job nearly needed Richard Nixon in the most dramatic of all circumstances on 24 September 1955. He was spending a quiet Saturday afternoon at home with nothing more pressing to do than reading the national baseball batting averages, when a call came through from the White House. 'The President has had a coronary', said the voice of Press Secretary Jim Hagerty.[35] Nixon was so shocked that his long pause made Hagerty think that the line had been disconnected. Eventually the Vice President recovered himself enough to babble some medical folklore about how easy it was for doctors to misdiagnose indigestion as a heart attack. Hagerty replied that the doctors were sure of their diagnosis. Eisenhower had been stricken at 2.30 a.m. while staying in his mother-in-law's home at Denver, Colorado, and had been taken to Fitzsimmons Army Hospital. The public announcement of the President's coronary would be made in half an hour. 'Let me know where you can be reached at all times', were Hagerty's last words before hanging up.[36]

Shaken to the core, Nixon was so overcome by the confused jumble of thoughts which surged through his mind that he forgot to break the news to Pat.

Instead, he sat alone in his living room for ten minutes then telephoned his old friend Bill Rogers. He remembered Rogers' good judgement and public relations skills during the Hiss case and The Fund crisis. Both as a personal ally and as the Acting Attorney General of the United States (Herbert Brownell, the Attorney General, was abroad on vacation), Rogers would be the best possible adviser on how to handle the delicate position in which Nixon now found himself.

Rogers came over immediately. His first suggestion was that Nixon should avoid saying anything to the press, who were beginning to gather in Tilden Street. Dodging the reporters by leaving from a side door, Nixon escaped to the Rogers' home in Bethesda, Maryland, where he spent the night. Soon after arriving, he wanted to know what the Vice President's legal position was when a President was incapacitated. 'What does the Constitution say?' he asked Rogers. 'I'm sorry, I don't have the vaguest idea', was the embarrassed reply from the Acting Attorney General. Rogers started to look for a copy of the Constitution. He could not find one on his own shelves, and frantic search amongst his son's schoolbooks produced no results. He picked up the phone, saying he would call and have one sent over.

'For God's sake don't do that', exclaimed Nixon, ever the cautious politician. 'If it ever gets out that the Vice President and the Attorney General don't know what the Constitution says, we'd look like a couple of complete idiots.'[37]

Eventually Rogers did locate a copy of the Constitution, after remembering that it was printed as the annual frontispiece to the *Farmer's Almanack*. However, the text was not much use, for the Founding Fathers had never thought of the situation that now confronted the Government of the United States.

The non-legal advice Rogers offered his overnight guest must have been good, for during the days and weeks following Eisenhower's coronary, Nixon acted with impeccable tact and rectitude. Even his severest critics have conceded that there is nothing negative to be said about his conduct in this period. This was no small achievement, considering that he had to steer through a series of minefields, any one of which could easily have blown up in his face. His immediate difficulties included an uproar of speculation in the media; a power struggle amongst White House aides; and some awkward decisions on how to govern the country while Eisenhower lay incapacitated.

'The crisis was how to walk on eggs and not break them', was how Nixon described his situation. 'My problem, what I had to do, was to provide leadership without appearing to lead.'[38] Guided by Bill Rogers, Nixon spent the first hours of the crisis telephoning members of the Cabinet and developing the strategy of 'business as usual'. The general agreement that there would be no jealousies or struggles for dominance was, however, somewhat dented by the return to Washington of Eisenhower's principal aide, Governor Sherman Adams, whose first words on arrival at the White House were, 'It's quite a surprise to come back here and suddenly find yourself the President.'[39] Despite this inauspicious beginning, Nixon handled Adams with sensitivity, attributing the aide's prima donna-like behaviour and his possessive control of presidential access to his personal friendship with Eisenhower.

Internally, Nixon showed wisdom by striving to cool all personal frictions in the power vacuum and by coaxing the Cabinet into genuine unity. Externally he was a paragon of loyalty, both in his anodyne statements to the press and in his determined refusal to engage in any jockeying for position among aspirants for the newly perceived vacancy in the 1956 Republican presidential nomination. Determined not to pull rank, he made a point of calling on Cabinet members in their own offices; of working from his own rooms in the Senate rather than establishing an official presence at the White House; and of never sitting in the President's chair at meetings. When he presided over the Cabinet and the NSC, as he had always done in Ike's absence, Nixon was careful to act as a moderator rather than as the new man in charge. Nixon won high praise for this cautious *primus inter pares* approach, which later was compared favourably with the unseemly jostling for power by Secretary of State Alexander Haig and others in the aftermath of President Reagan's shooting in 1981. At the end of the Cabinet meeting on 30 September 1955, Secretary of State Dulles paid a formal tribute to the Vice President, saying: 'I realize that you have been under a very heavy burden during these past few days and I know I express the opinion of everybody here that you have conducted yourself superbly.'[40]

Even adversaries paid similar compliments. One long-standing Nixon antagonist, the journalist and White House speech writer Emmet John Hughes, described the Vice President in the post-heart attack period as 'poised and restrained…a man close to great power *not* being presumptuously or prematurely assertive. This discreetly empty time was surely his finest official hour.'[41]

The implications of his 'finest official hour' caused Nixon to rethink his earlier decision to quit politics. The truth was that he loved the pressure of great events. The crisis improved his standing with the Republican Party and increased his stature with the public. Departing from the stage of presidential politics when so much was going in his favour would be like kicking over the card table when holding the aces. Accordingly, he shelved his plans to return to the law, explaining his change of mind to the journalist Earl Mazo: 'Once you get into this great stream of history you can't get out. You can drown. Or you can be pulled ashore by the tide. But it is awfully hard to get out when you are in the middle of the stream—if it is intended that you stay there.[42]

Ironically it was Nixon's enhanced status in the stream of history as a possible President-in-waiting that caused his adversaries to make known their intention that he should not stay where he was. Back in Denver, Eisenhower was making a good recovery, returning to full duties at the White House on 11 November. Surprisingly he did not send Nixon a letter of thanks for his exemplary conduct during the seven-week interregnum. This was odd because Ike had in the past been generous with his personal notes of appreciation and had told his staff how impressed he was by the Vice President's steady performance. However, Eisenhower also knew that his illness had opened up a Pandora's box of questions about the succession, and about Nixon.

The early betting among President watchers was that Ike would not be well enough to run again. However, if the odds changed and he did win a second term, then the speculation about his mortality meant that the Vice Presidency would be perceived as a far more important office. Was Richard Nixon the man for the job? Several of Eisenhower's closest cronies thought not, and it was their hostility that triggered off the curious 'Dump Nixon' episode of 1955–6.

IV. DUMP NIXON

Nixon had performed well in his first three years as Vice President. He had developed an expertise in foreign policy as a result of his studious attendance at meetings of the National Security Council, his growing political friendship with Dulles, and his two long overseas tours. In domestic affairs he had worked hard to maintain a good relationship between the Administration and Congress. He had consolidated his position as campaigner-in-chief of the Republican Party. He had shed some of his reputation for partisan abrasiveness by displaying *gravitas* during the heart attack crisis. Above all he had been resolutely loyal to the President. If there was any justice in politics, Nixon should have had no trouble in retaining his Number Two slot on the national ticket.

It is therefore easy to imagine how upset Nixon must have been when Eisenhower unexpectedly indicated that it might be better for him not to continue as Vice President. This thunderbolt fell on 26 December 1955. Nixon had been asked to drop by the White House for a post-Christmas talk. Ike said he was about to go on a trip to Florida, where he intended to discuss his own and Nixon's future with his closest friends. The first item on the agenda was should he run again for President? Nixon, who saw that it was in his own and the GOP's best interests to keep Eisenhower in place, argued strongly for maintaining the status quo. Ike seemed to accept this advice, then switched to a new and more disturbing tack.

Meandering through his thoughts on the next election, the President said he was disappointed that Nixon's popularity had not risen 'as high as he had hoped it would'.[43] He referred to some Gallup Polls which put Stevenson well ahead of Nixon. Then came the blow. In Nixon's words, Eisenhower 'wondered whether I ought to run for Vice President again or whether I might do better to accept a Cabinet post instead. He said that a Cabinet position such as Secretary for Defense would give me the kind of administrative experience, so important for a President, that the Vice Presidency did not offer.'[44]

Nixon could hardly believe his ears when he heard this proposal, which had its genesis in a confused muddle of skulduggery and naïveté. The skulduggery came from Sherman Adams and a clique of White House insiders, who were so determined to throw Nixon off the ticket that they had even briefed Ike with outdated polls falsely exaggerating the Vice President's unpopularity.[45] The naïveté was Eisenhower's. Apparently sincere in his view that Nixon would benefit from the experience of running a large Government department, he did not see that such a move would be perceived as a public demotion. The political reality was that no Vice President could step down and accept a Cabinet post without giving the appearance of having been dumped.

Eisenhower should quickly have recognised that the suggestion he made in his 26 December meeting with Nixon would not work, and that his only choice was between backing or sacking his Vice President. Instead he retreated into indecision. During the months of January and February, Ike casually brought up the option of a Cabinet job in five or six private conversations with Nixon, who developed a stock response: 'If you believe your own candidacy and your Administration would be better served with me off the ticket, you tell me what you want me to do and I'll do it. I want to do what is best for you.'[46] Ike then had his own standard reply, which consisted of praising Nixon's services to the Administration and saying, 'No, I think we've got to do what's best for you.'[47] This stilted routine of 'After you, Mr. President—no, no, after *you*, Mr. Vice President' sounds ludicrous in retrospect but at the time it was agonising for Nixon. All he could do was hang in there and hope for the best. His ordeal was made worse by Eisenhower's 26 February press conference, at which he announced his intention to seek a second term as President. When questioned about his running mate, Ike declared that his admiration for the Vice President was 'unbounded,'[48] but that a decision on a Nixon second term would have to wait until the Republican National Convention. According to his appointments secretary Dorothy Cox, Nixon was 'dreadfully wounded and hurt'[49] by the President's public refusal to endorse him. She and other staffers saw at first hand the impact of Eisenhower's equivocation on Nixon's pride. It was one of the darkest periods of his Vice Presidency, as 'Dump Nixon' stories flooded into the press and hostile rumours spread round Washington.

This campaign did, however, offend Eisenhower's sense of decency. At a press conference on 7 March he angrily answered a reporter asking about a leak in *Newsweek* about Nixon being downgraded into the Cabinet: 'I will promise you this much: if anyone ever has the effrontery to come in and urge me to dump somebody that, I respect as I do Vice President Nixon, there will be more commotion around my office than you have noticed yet.' After this step forward Eisenhower then took two steps backwards, as he continued explaining to the journalists: 'I have not presumed to tell the Vice President what he should do with his own future...The only thing I have asked him to do is to chart out his own course and tell me what he would like to do...I am not going to be pushed into corners here and say what I would do in a hypothetical question that involves about five ifs.'[50]

The President's indecision was almost final. As the ambiguous phrase 'chart out his own course' made headlines, Nixon sank into a personal depression. He knew better than anyone that the notion of a Vice President mapping out his own career strategy independently from the President was absurd. He therefore interpreted Ike's message as a clear notice to get off the ticket, and acted accordingly. On 9 March, Nixon drafted a press statement that he would not be a candidate in 1956. He told several friends that he would be calling a press conference to make the announcement later that day.

When this news reached Len Hall, the Republican National Committee Chairman, he rushed to the Capitol with Jerry Persons, one of Nixon's few admirers on the White House staff. Together they persuaded the Vice President not to issue a retirement statement, on the grounds that it would make him look like a quitter and split the GOP wide open. An even more influential voice from the 'don't quit' corner was Pat Nixon. A few weeks earlier she had been in favour of her husband leaving politics—but on his own terms. Now that Eisenhower was, as she saw it, behaving unfairly, the Irish fighter in Pat came to the fore. She rallied Nixon's flagging spirits and urged him to stand his ground. 'No one is going to push us off the ticket', she told Helene Drown.[51] Pat's support came at a pivotal moment, just as it had in The Fund crisis. Nixon tore up his retirement statement. Silently he hung on to the Vice Presidency by his fingertips while press speculation about his future mounted.

Eisenhower's intentions towards his Vice President in the early months of 1956 were perplexing, to put it mildly. He was surrounded by hawks and doves on the 'Dump Nixon' issue. The hawks, led by Sherman Adams, Lucius Clay and Milton Eisenhower, disliked Nixon personally and were convinced that he would be a drag on the ticket. Although there was little evidence to support such a view of the ticket's electoral appeal, Ike listened to the hawks and leant in their direction to the extent of thinking aloud about a new political strategy which would give a lower priority to both Nixon and the GOP.

Eisenhower liked the idea of being a President above party. He was groping in his mind for a new consensus which would embrace the uncommitted, the middle of the road, and the Democrats. He even talked briefly about running as a Democrat, or as head of a new party, or without any party label at all. Nixon had no place in this political Utopia. He was too confrontational, too partisan, too much of a conviction politician on issues that were going out of fashion, such as anti-Communism. When Ike ruminated in private about how Nixon was 'immature', had not 'grown' or was not 'presidential timber',[52] what he partly meant was that Nixon lacked the right credentials to fit in with these dreams of a new political consensus.

Nixon's supporters, the doves in the dumping discussion, were party political realists. They had no time for this moonshine about a brave new world in which Republicans would meld with Democrats in one great, harmonious alliance under Ike's command. They had plenty of time for Nixon as the hardest-working GOP leader in the country. In one heated discussion of the Vice Presidency at a private White House dinner party in March 1956, the thoughts of many Republican supporters were harshly voiced by Charlie Jones, the President of Richfield Oil. 'Ike, what in the hell does a man have to do to get your support?' asked Jones, leaning across the table as he addressed his old friend the President. 'Dick Nixon has done everything you asked him to do. He has taken on the hard jobs that many of your other associates have run away from. For you not to support him now would be the most ungrateful thing that I can possibly think of.'[53]

Eisenhower was not ungrateful to Nixon. Although full of the military man's ingrained mistrust for professional politicians, he saw his Vice President as one of the best and brightest products of the species. He recognised the younger man's talent and achievements on behalf of the Administration. He thought Nixon might well make a good President one day, provided he broadened out. The offer of a Cabinet post was therefore not a ploy by which an unsatisfactory subordinate could be gracefully eased off the ticket. Eisenhower, with the mind of a great general, saw Nixon as a highly promising staff officer who needed experience of his own command in the field before becoming a candidate for the highest level of leadership. This would have been good military thinking if the candidate had been a brigadier but it was political suicide for a Vice President. Unfortunately for Nixon, Ike was blind to this simple fact of life. He claimed in his memoirs that he had not realised the difficulties of the Vice President's position until he read Nixon's account of the period in *Six Crises*.[54] Such myopia caused Eisenhower to handle the problem he had himself created with an insensitive, almost cruel, touch of man management. It was entirely understandable that Nixon's feelings should have been bruised at this time as Ike continued to hum and haw about his Vice President's future.

Nixon was rescued from his agony by the electorate. On 13 March, New Hampshire went to the polls in the first primary of the 1956 election. Eisenhower won comfortably for the Republicans with 56,000 votes. However, the big surprise of the night was that nearly 23,000 voters had written in Nixon's name on the ballot paper. Although Eisenhower did not move immediately to endorse Nixon, his comments about the Vice President at White House press conferences became noticeably more friendly. On 25 April Ike was asked by a reporter whether Nixon had yet charted his own course. 'Well he hasn't reported back in the terms in which I used the expression...no', answered the President.

'When I heard about this exchange', explained Nixon later, 'I knew the time had come to act. The more I thought about it, the more I was convinced that I could not get off the ticket without hurting Eisenhower more than helping him.'[55] The next day, 26 April, he saw the President and told him in direct terms that after weighing all the options he had come to the conclusion that he wanted to run again as Vice President.

Ike's indecision was over. Even if he had wanted to prolong Nixon's agony, it would have been extremely difficult to do so in the light of the New Hampshire write-in and a subsequent surge of support for the existing ticket on the Republican National Committee. Eisenhower therefore bowed to the inevitable. He called his press secretary into the Oval Office and instructed him to take Nixon out to the White House press corps to make the announcement. 'And you can tell them that I'm delighted by the news', he added.[56]

The press conference went well, and appeared to settle the matter once and for all. In fact this was not quite the case. A rearguard action to stop Nixon was fought by Harold Stassen, the former Minnesota Governor and unsuccessful presidential candidate who had retained a White House role as adviser to Eisenhower on disarmament. Stassen was widely regarded as a political clown, but he still retained some clout. When he called a press conference on 23 July to declare his support for Massachusetts Governor, Christian Herter, as an alternative Republican vice-presidential candidate, Nixon had to take the challenge seriously. For if Stassen's manoeuvre resulted in the nomination for Vice President once again being perceived as up for grabs, Nixon knew he might yet be toppled at the convention by any one of several aspirants who were waiting in the wings with hopes of a *putsch*.

For a few days the 'Stop Nixon' bandwagon did start to roll, at least to a small extent in Eastern establishment circles. The President was away in Panama, and his absence gave Stassen and other anti-Nixon White House aides the chance to feed the *New York Times* with rumours that the Herter for Vice President initiative had Ike's tacit acquiescence.[57] If such thoughts were ever in Ike's mind, they were short-lived, for by the time he returned from Panama he found that the GOP had rallied behind Nixon. 180 out of 203 Republican Congressmen had signed a letter endorsing the Vice President, a timely demonstration of support organised by Nixon's old friend, Representative Pat Hillings. The delegate count and private polls among GOP voters confirmed the same strong pro-Nixon trend. Eisenhower saw at once that any further ambivalence on his part about the Vice Presidency could be damaging to his own re-election prospects. He therefore acted decisively behind the scenes.

Christian Herter, enticed by the prospects of a future senior appointment at the State Department, was quickly persuaded to drop out of the running and was lined up to propose Nixon for the nomination at the convention.* Stassen was also brought into line by White House arm-twisting and reluctantly agreed to second Nixon. This made the convention proceedings a foregone conclusion, and Nixon was renominated as vice-presidential candidate by 1,323 votes to 1. He had survived.

V. RE-ELECTION

Nixon's delight at his renomination was clouded by the terminal illness of his seventy-eight-year-old father and later by the venom of the Democrats during the election campaign.

Frank's life had been hanging by a thread during the convention. On the day of the ballot for Vice President, Nixon received a message that his father's abdominal artery had ruptured and that death was imminent. Cancelling all appointments, he flew down from San Francisco and rushed to Whittier Hospital, where his father was struggling for breath in an oxygen tent. The old man rallied at the

---

* Herter became Under Secretary of State in 1957 and succeeded Dulles as Secretary of State in 1959.

sight of his son, and gave him his last piece of political advice: 'You get back there, Dick, and don't let that Stassen pull any more last-minute funny business on you.'[58] Nixon did not follow these instructions immediately, staying with the family and watching his renomination on television. This final defeat of the 'Dump Nixon' movement revived Frank's spirits a little, but a few days later he was sinking again. On 4 September Nixon was back at his father's bedside. Frank was reluctant to drink his evening mug of warm milk, until his son lovingly augmented it with a jiggle of Kahlua coffee liqueur. It was one of the few times in his life that Frank had tasted alcohol. 'My, that was good, what was it?' he asked as he sank content-edly back on the pillow. 'Just a tonic', came the filial reply. 'Now get a good night's sleep and I'll see you in the morning.' 'Good night Dick, but I don't think I'll be here in the morning', whispered Frank. They were his last words, for he died in his sleep that night.[59]

It was a peaceful ending to a father-son relationship which had been full of ups and downs, always transcended by strong mutual love and respect. To outsid-ers, Frank Nixon could seem a rough old fellow—noisy, opinionated, and aggres-sive. To Richard he was a loving parent with a warm heart and a keen intelligence, who had exercised a formative influence over his family. That influence was not always beneficial. Frank created deep insecurities in his sons because of the unpredictability of his temper and the mean streak in his character. Too often he bore grudges towards those he imagined to be his adversaries and too easily he hurt feelings among those whom he loved. These behaviour patterns may have contributed to the psychological complexities that were later to appear in his famous second son. Richard himself has never acknowledged such a possibility, preferring to emphasise the inspirational side of Frank's sharp edges. Nixon has always believed that it was his father's legacy of mental toughness and resilience of character that gave him the strength to come through the many tests of fire in his own political career.

Soon after his father's funeral, the 1956 presidential election campaign got into full swing. Nixon needed plenty of resilience to endure it, because from day one the Democrats made him the prime target of their attack. Eisenhower was at the peak of his national popularity, so there was little mileage for the opposition in going after the President. The Democratic nominee, again Governor Adlai Stevenson, therefore concentrated his fire on the Vice President, making Nixon's qualifications for the White House in the event of Ike's death a central theme of his campaign speeches. In Michigan on 17 October, Stevenson described the Vice Presidency as 'this nation's life insurance policy', claiming that with Nixon on the ticket the nation would 'go for four years uninsured'. He continued in even sharper vein: 'There is no man who can safely say he knows where the Vice President stands. This is a man of many masks. Who can say they have seen his real face?'[60]

Nixon, who had been urged by Eisenhower not to indulge in personal attacks on his opponents, made no response. This uncharacteristic silence drove Stevenson wild. He claimed that Nixon had 'put away his switchblade and now assumes the aspect of an Eagle Scout…this man has no standard of truth but convenience and no standard of morality except what will serve his interest in an election.' In the same speech he described 'Nixonland' as 'a land of slander and scare, the land of sly innuendo, the poison pen, the anonymous phone call, and hustling, pushing, shoving; the land of smash and grab and anything to win.'[61]

Nixon could afford to ignore this inflammatory language. The Republican ticket was well ahead in the polls, and the lead was consolidated by two international crises which caused voters to rally round the President in even larger numbers. The Hungarian revolution erupted on 23 October. Its brutal suppression by the Soviet troops shocked the American people. Nixon caught their mood when he called Khrushchev 'The Butcher of Budapest', a label that made headlines around the world.

On 5 November, the day before the election, the Suez crisis reached its zenith with British and French paratroopers landing in Egypt in support of the Israeli attack to recover the canal, which had been nationalised by Egypt's President Nasser. Nixon at the time was a vocal critic of the Anglo–French military intervention. He gave his full backing to the Eisenhower–Dulles policy of pressurising the British and French governments to withdraw their troops before the canal zone was secured, a move which ultimately gave victory to Nasser. Nixon subsequently said that the episode constituted 'perhaps my most serious misjudgement of a foreign policy situation'.[62]

He amplified this comment in an interesting letter about the Suez Crisis written to the British parliamentarian Julian Amery in 1987:

> If I may resort to a British understatement, the role of the United States in handling that crisis was not an admirable one. The serious mistakes the United States has made in handling the Iran-Contra flap pales into insignificance compared to the mistakes we made in handling the Suez crisis.
>
> I saw it first hand as Eisenhower's Vice President. It couldn't have come at a worse time. Eisenhower was running for re-election on a platform of peace and prosperity. Just a few days before, the United States had joined other countries in condemning Khrushchev for his

ruthless suppression of the Hungarian freedom fighters. We forced
the British and French to abandon their efforts to punish Nasser for
his expropriation of the Suez canal. In our public statements we
virtually put the British and French in the same category as the
Soviets in unjustifiably resorting to force to achieve their foreign
policy objectives.

Years later, after he had left office, I talked with Eisenhower about
Suez. He told me that it was his major foreign policy mistake. He
gritted his teeth as he remarked, 'Why couldn't the British and the
French have done it more quickly?' He went on to observe that our
action in saving Nasser at Suez didn't help as far as the Middle East
was concerned. Nasser became even more anti-West and anti-US.
We agreed that the worst fall-out from Suez was that it weakened the
will of our best allies, Britain and France, to play a major role in the
Mid East or in other areas outside of Europe.[63]

In the final analysis neither Suez nor Stevenson had much impact on the 1956
election result. The voters had made up their mind to support the Eisenhower–
Nixon ticket which carried forty-one of the forty-eight states and won 57 per cent
of the popular vote. Despite the frantic efforts of the Democrats to portray Nixon
as the most dangerous and controversial Vice President in the history of the
Republic, there was no evidence to suggest that he had been a drag on the ticket,
for the plurality over Stevenson had been twice as high as in 1952. Nixon's journey
to a second term had been a bumpy one, but he had shown courage and tenacity
in surviving it. He could now look forward with far greater confidence to his next
four years as Vice President of the United States.

THIRTEEN

THE VICE-PRESIDENTIAL YEARS 1956–1960

I. HEIR APPARENT

Nixon grew in stature during his second term as Vice President. Within months of the election there was a feeling that the Eisenhower era was fading and that Nixon represented the rising generation that would take its place. This perception was partly due to problems of age and ill health within the Administration. Dulles, although still dominant as Secretary of State, was in and out of hospital, gradually dying of cancer. Eisenhower seemed slower to take decisions now that he was in his late sixties. One political journalist described this period of his Presidency as 'the time of the great postponement'.[1]

Nixon, by contrast, was young, at forty-four, and full of energy. He continued to enhance the Vice Presidency by vigorous activity, particularly in foreign policy matters. Much of his expertise in this field was derived from his growing friendship with Dulles, whose home he visited regularly for cocktails and dinner. Wives were sometimes included in these evenings, although social talk was limited. Pat Nixon and Eleanor Dulles could be left on their own for hours, waiting patiently while their husbands sat in the next room enjoying their interminable one-on-one seminars. The political intimacy of these Dulles–Nixon discussions on geopolitical strategies and concepts may well have laid the foundation for the later Nixon–Kissinger relationship. Nixon discovered that he needed an intellectual partnership with a mind of similar complexity to his own in order to formulate his long-term foreign policy plans. His sessions as Dulles's pupil set the pattern that he followed later as Kissinger's mentor.

Dulles encouraged Nixon to develop his role as a global Vice President. In his eight years of office under Eisenhower, Nixon carried out ten official missions overseas, covering fifty-eight countries, and totalling 159,232 miles travelled.[2] The first trip in his second term took place in February 1957, when he set off on a month-long tour of eight African countries. Although the goodwill side of the trip was successful, Nixon was appalled by the low calibre of some of the State Department diplomats he encountered at US embassies. On his return he demanded, and got, a major shake-up of American diplomatic representation in Africa. At one stop on his tour he decided that remedial action could not even wait until he was back in Washington. At the US Embassy in Ethiopia the entire vice-presidential party was dumbfounded by the lamentable performance of the Ambassador, which culminated in an embarrassing dinner for Emperor Haile Selassie. The day after the dinner, Nixon spoke to his new military aide, Major Don Hughes, who had been assigned to him for the trip: 'He asked me if I could transmit a message to the State Department without using State Department facilities', recalled Hughes. 'When I said "yes sir", he handed me a personal message for the Under Secretary of State. The essence of it was a harsh critique of our embassy in Ethiopia, ending in a recommendation that the Ambassador had got to go. When I sent the Vice President's signal to Washington using Air Force back channels I thought to myself: "This guy is tough." He saw the problem and moved fast to sort it out. He was angry but he wasn't in a temper. He simply recognized that the United States wasn't being adequately represented and he wanted it all changed. I respected him for that.'[3]

Nixon also won respect on his African tour from a less friendly American observer—Martin Luther King. The young civil rights activist was an unofficial guest of President Kwame Nkrumah at the independence ceremonies for Ghana. Nixon, the official representative of the United States, found himself upstaged by King, who gave a press conference attacking segregation in the American South and urging the Vice President to come and study the violent situation there. Nixon subsequently had a long, private talk with King in Ghana and they arranged to meet in Washington to discuss ways of making progress on civil rights.

Nixon was spiritually and intellectually committed to the civil rights cause, a label which in the 1950s meant Negro rights.* His Quaker heritage, his friendship

---

* 'Negro' was the politically correct term in the 1950s.

with the Black footballer Bill Brock at Whittier, and the outspoken views on racial equality which he had proclaimed to his Southern classmates at Duke Law School, were early signposts along a political road on which he never faltered. When Martin Luther King followed up on the Ghana encounter by visiting the Vice President's office in Washington with his fellow campaigner, the Reverend Ralph Abernathy, in April 1957, he was surprised by the strength of Nixon's commitment to ensuring the passage of antidiscrimination legislation. The Administration's 1957 Civil Rights Bill was the first law of its kind to be proposed since Reconstruction, but the Senate gradually emasculated it by amendments. Even the amended legislation was in danger of being killed off by an unholy alliance of those Black leaders, who thought the Bill was now too weak, and the Southern Democrats, who had never wanted it in the first place. King argued that the Bill was worth saving even in its enfeebled form, because it would at least encourage many more Negroes to register as voters. Nixon agreed, and fought hard, in meetings with many legislative leaders to save it. His effort succeeded, for after a long struggle, the Bill was passed by Congress on 29 August. The following day Martin Luther King wrote to Nixon in fulsome terms: 'Let me say how deeply grateful we are to you for your assiduous labor and dauntless courage in seeking to make the Civil Rights Bill a reality. This has impressed people all across the country, both Negro and white. This is certainly an expression of your devotion to the highest mandates of the moral law. It is also an expression of your political wisdom.'[4]

Nixon's political wisdom was further recognised in February 1958, when Eisenhower sent him a letter setting out the terms on which power should devolve to the Vice President in the event of presidential illness.

The chain of events leading up to the letter began on the afternoon of 25 November 1957. Nixon was summoned urgently to the White House. On his arrival, Sherman Adams told him: 'The President has suffered a stroke.' 'How serious is his condition?' asked Nixon. 'We'll know more in the morning', replied Adams. 'Right now he's more confused and disoriented than anything else. It will take a few days before the doctors can assess the damage. This is a terribly, terribly difficult thing to handle.' He added ominously, 'You may be President in twenty-four hours.'[5]

In terms of its political implications, Eisenhower's 1957 stroke was more worrying than his 1954 heart attack. The stroke came at a time of considerable international tension. The Soviets had put their first Sputnik into orbit four weeks earlier, a triumph which had triggered an orgy of national self-doubt and recrimination about America's military and technological capabilities. Domestic public opinion, which had been solidly sympathetic to the physical problems of Ike's coronary three years earlier, was far more critical once it became known that the President's mental powers had been adversely affected by his cerebral occlusion. Ike himself was deeply depressed, particularly by the impairment to his speech. Like many stroke victims, his early symptoms included jumbling up words, getting confused, and consequently sounding as though he was talking gibberish. 'This is the end,' he said when he first heard the diagnosis. 'Mamie and I are farmers from now on.'[6]

Nixon once again demonstrated a safe pair of hands during this period of the Chief of State's second major incapacity. His first task as Vice President was to reassure a jittery press corps and nation. This he did well, giving his first ever White House press conference with calm authority. The *New York Times* caught the atmosphere with its lead story headlined 'NIXON NOW SPEAKS FOR WHITE HOUSE'. The report, by James Reston, praised the Vice President for the 'skill and confidence' with which he had answered questions, and continued, 'This was clearly a more assured young man than the Nixon of twenty-six months ago who stayed in the background at Denver while Governor Adams presided over the Administration during the early weeks of the President's heart attack. Nixon even looks different. He seems to have lost a little weight. His hair is cut closer on the sides and on top. His speech is more vivid and articulate and his manner more patient and courteous.'[7]

Although his previous dress rehearsal for handling a presidential illness led Nixon to stick in public to the line of 'business as usual' and 'The President is not considering resigning',[8] the reality behind the scenes was rather different. With uncertainty mounting, Nixon had to take on a far greater range of presidential duties. These included presiding over US defence policy changes in preparation for what was expected to be a critical NATO summit in mid-December, when he was slated to substitute for Eisenhower. 'My responsibilities and prerogatives were more clearly defined and understood, and my actions more readily accepted. The eggs upon which I had to tread had harder shells', was how Nixon later described his situation.[9]

Many newspaper editorials at this time recommended that Eisenhower should resign. This advice may well have been good therapy for the stricken President. At first Ike got mad, talking defiantly of 'dying with my boots on'.[10] Then he fought back, struggling to sort out his word blockage problems and insisting on resuming his duties. In fact, his stroke had been a mild one and his determination to take up the reins again, including travelling to the NATO meeting in Paris, was responsible for a swift and remarkable recovery.

As the crisis passed and Nixon's prospects for an immediate succession ebbed, there was a feeling that some contingency plan was needed in case Eisenhower had another, even more serious, illness. Accordingly, Ike himself drafted a letter to Nixon setting out the procedures by which presidential executive authority would be transferred. The essence of this personal agreement was that the President and Vice President should on their own jointly decide whether or not Eisenhower was capable of fulfilling his duties. However, if Eisenhower was incapable of making or expressing such a decision then Nixon, acting alone after appropriate consultations, should exercise the new authority conferred on him by the letter and assume the role of acting-President.

This document, although legally only a personal letter between two individuals, was remarkable for two reasons. First, it was the harbinger of the 25th Amendment to the US Constitution of 1967,* filling the power vacuum that would exist in the event of a President's incapacity to govern.

Secondly, the letter was a great compliment to Nixon. Eisenhower could easily have proposed other interim procedures of a more collegiate nature, such as some sort of regency by a committee of senior Cabinet officers. Yet the arrangements he actually recommended were highly personal. They required a level of mutual trust which had not always characterised the Dick and Ike relationship. In signing and publishing the letter, Eisenhower was therefore proclaiming a new era of confidence in Nixon, who was now annointed as the President's heir apparent.

II. FACING DEATH IN CARACAS

As heir apparent, Nixon started the year of 1958 intending to give more priority to domestic assignments. Although foreign policy remained his first love, he was conscious of the need to strengthen his political base, particularly with the mid-term congressional elections coming up. So when it was first mooted, in early January, that he should make an official visit to South America, Nixon turned down the invitation. He thought it would be an irrelevant diversion from his political agenda, and in any case too boring. In fact it turned out to be the most exciting foreign journey of his life—nearly fatally so.

After some arm-twisting by Dulles and the State Department, Nixon reluctantly agreed to make a seventeen-day South American tour in May. His itinerary

---

* The 25th Amendment trusts the Vice President less than Eisenhower did. Under it, the decision on whether the President is capable of discharging his duties is given to the Vice President and a majority of either 'the principal officers of the executive departments' or 'such other body as Congress may by law provide'.

would cover eight countries but had no agenda of major diplomatic substance, and no initiatives or aid packages for him to announce. The only clear purpose of the trip, apart from generally dispensing US goodwill, was to attend the inauguration of the new President of Argentina, Arturo Frondizi.

During his pre-departure briefings, Nixon was warned by the CIA that he might encounter anti-American demonstrations in two or three of the capitals on his route. But the warning was a low key part of a more general briefing about the youth of Latin American's simmering dislike of their rich Yankee neighbour for the support it gave to dictators, for exploiting their economic resources and for a whole host of other 'imperialist crimes'. There were no intimations of violence.

In most of the countries he visited, Nixon encountered little or no trouble. Colombia, Ecuador, Bolivia and Paraguay gave him a friendly welcome. In Montevideo he was booed by a handful of student hecklers. This prompted him to take a typical initiative. He insisted on coming to the National University campus, where he held an unscheduled question and answer session at the law school, said to be the hotbed of discontent. At the end of the session he was loudly cheered with chants of 'Long Live American and Uruguayan friendship.'[11]

In Buenos Aires Nixon missed the principal engagement of his tour—the swearing-in of President Frondizi. It did not appear to bother the Argentinians, who had eccentrically started the inauguration ceremonies five minutes early, despite the absence of both the American and the Russian delegations. Nixon arrived halfway through the event in his top hat and tails, having been caught in a mammoth traffic jam along with many other dignitaries. Later in the day he addressed a workers' picnic and had another impromptu session with students, who gave him almost as good a reception as he had received at the National University of Uruguay Law School.

In Peru the atmosphere of the trip began to turn sour. Nixon felt the tension on arrival at Lima airport, and grew more uneasy as President Manuel Prado and his ministers entertained the vice-presidential party to a sumptuous formal luncheon served on gold plates. Contrasting the scene in the President's dining room with the abject poverty he had seen on the streets, Nixon felt the lunch was 'almost obscene in its richness and waste'.[12] His forebodings increased as street demonstrations later in the day grew more menacing. So hostile did the crowds become that Nixon had to consider cancelling a scheduled visit to Lima's famous University of San Marcos, the oldest seat of learning in the western hemisphere (founded 1551), where Communist agitators were said to be whipping up a frenzy of anti-American hatred among the students. No Peruvian official would take responsibility for recommending cancellation, although privately many of them dropped dark hints on the dangers of going ahead with the programme. Nixon finally asked the US Ambassador, Theodore Achilles, for his advice: 'From a personal standpoint you should make a decision not to go. But from the standpoint of the United States, I will have to say that your failing to go may lead to some very detrimental publicity reactions throughout the hemisphere', was the response.[13]

After a sleepless night, Nixon left his decision to the last moment—then went. Arriving at the gates of San Marcos University accompanied only by his interpreter, Colonel Vernon Walters, and one secret service agent, Jack Sherwood, Nixon marched to the edge of a roaring crowd of students, which he attempted to address. One of the students listening to the opening speech was heard by Walters to say: 'El gringo tiene cojones' ('The Yankee has balls'),[14] but the vast majority had no such respect. Spit, stones, and finally rocks started to fly, one of them breaking Sherwood's front tooth. 'Let's get out of here', Nixon ordered. 'But move back slowly, facing them.' Reaching the safety of the car, a convertible, Nixon stood up shouting at the crowd as he drove away, 'Cowards! You are cowards! You are afraid of the truth! You are the worst kind of cowards!'[15] The episode, which was followed by a more dignified press conference, made Nixon a hero with the majority of patriotic Peruvians and with the US reporters covering the trip. But the Lima violence was a mere curtain-raiser to the terrifying scenes of mayhem that Nixon had to face in the final country on his itinerary, Venezuela.

Arriving in Caracas on the morning of 13 May, Nixon was greeted by a large airport crowd screaming obscenities. Coming down the aircraft steps he took Pat's arm and led her along the red carpet towards the terminal building. As they approached the entrance an army band struck up 'The Star Spangled Banner'. The Nixons came to attention, while the crowd erupted into a renewed frenzy of booing and catcalling which lasted all the way through the American and Venezuelan national anthems. Even worse was to come. As the official party moved inside the terminal, another jeering mob on the upper-floor balconies began spitting down on them. Within seconds a cascade of expectorant was landing on Nixon's blue suit and Pat's red dress, staining them with suppurating tobacco-brown splotches. There was no escape from this torment other than to run away from it, but vice-presidential dignity would not permit any such panic-stricken flight, so the Nixons walked steadily through the gauntlet of flying spittle with their heads held high, until they reached their car at the other side of the terminal. It must have taken a heroic exercise of self-control for the couple to endure this appalling experience with no outward sign of emotion. Inwardly they were at boiling point. As Nixon wrote later, 'One must experience the sensation to realize why spitting in a person's face is the most infuriating insult ever conceived by man.'[16]

In a phalanx of limousines, appropriately rented from a local funeral parlour, the shaken vice-presidential party was driven to downtown Caracas, where even more vicious mobs were waiting for them. Waving Nazi swastikas and posters portraying Nixon as a long-toothed Dracula, large gangs of demonstrators rushed out of the side streets attempting to ambush the motorcade, shouting 'Muerte à Nixon!' ('Death to Nixon'). To Earl Mazo, reporting on the visit for the *New York Herald Tribune,* it was 'like a scene from the French Revolution'.[17] Nixon himself thought it was 'like an Indian raid in an old western movie'.[18] The bad guys were certainly on the rampage, attacking the cars with rocks, iron pipes, clubs and even their bare fists. One large stone struck the windshield, spraying all the occupants in Nixon's car with glass splinters. Some of these hit the Venezuelan Foreign Minister in the eye, and he began to bleed heavily. Colonel Vernon Walters was also cut about the face. The escort of Venezuelan motorcycle police mysteriously vanished. The crowd surged up to the car, seized its bumpers, and began rocking it back and forth, slower and higher on each rotation. Nixon remembered old television pictures of mobs overturning cars and setting them on fire. He thought he was going to die.* The same thought evidently occurred to the two Secret Service agents protecting him, who drew their guns, one saying, 'Let's get some of these sons-of-bitches', the other explaining afterwards: 'I figured we were goners and I was determined to get six of those bastards before they got us.'[20] Nixon ordered his agents to put their guns away. Remaining 'very calm and very composed', he told them, 'You don't shoot unless I tell you to do so.'[21] He was cool enough to calculate that once a gun went off the crowd would go berserk and kill them all.

In the back-up limousines, the threats to life and safety were almost as dangerous. As far away as car number nine Rose Woods was injured by flying glass and left choking on tear-gas fumes. In car number two Pat Nixon was under heavy pounding from stones and missiles. Her escort, Major Don Hughes, the Vice President's military aide, described the scene: 'The mobs were coming at us; even now I can still remember the wild hatred on their faces. I saw this rock being slung, getting bigger and bigger as it came at us, finally smashing into the glass. The Venezuelan Foreign Minister's wife was sobbing in panic, but Pat was as calm

---

* Nixon never forgot those with whom he had shared this moment of mortal peril. Thirty-three years later, on the eve of Vernon Walters' retirement in 1991 from the post of US Ambassador to the Federal Republic of Germany, Nixon wrote to him, 'You and I have faced death together and that gives us a special bond.'[19]

under fire as any man I ever saw, touching her hostess on the shoulder and saying in a soft, kind voice, "We'll be all right. We'll be all right."[22]

Against all the apparent odds, this optimistic prediction came true. Nixon's life was saved by the unexpected arrival of the press truck which pulled out to the front of the motorcade and acted as a bulldozer, clearing a path through the mob. Nixon's driver followed in the truck's wake, steadily picking up speed, as did the other official cars. The party had been trapped for twelve terrifying minutes. It had seemed more like a lifetime.

The Venezuelan motorcyle policemen reappeared and started leading the motorcade towards the Vice President's next scheduled engagement, a wreath-laying ceremony at the Panteon Plaza. Nixon had a wiser idea, and gave orders to his party to drive to the safety of the US Embassy. It was the second life-saving move of the morning. Later investigations revealed that the hostile crowd waiting at the Pantheon included two groups heavily armed with weapons and Molotov cocktails. If Nixon had gone to the wreath-laying ceremony his assassination would have been a near-certainty.

Back in the safety of the US Embassy Nixon was visited by the leaders of the military junta, who arrived to offer their formal apologies. According to Don Hughes, Nixon deliberately kept them waiting for three-quarters of an hour. 'When he finally appeared he was in a cold fury. He gave them the most godaw-ful dressing down, telling them that they had abused their freedom and their responsibilities, and so on. They took it like a bunch of whipped puppies.'[23]

In public, Nixon was far more magnanimous. To the press, who gave him a standing ovation, he declared, 'No patriotic Venezuelan would have torn down his country's flag as the mob did to the Venezuelan flag and also to ours. I don't feel it at all as a personal offense. If anything, the future relations of the United States and Venezuela will be better than ever. As far as I'm concerned, the incident is closed.'[24]

That last prediction might just have come true, if Eisenhower had not over-reacted to the crisis. Back in Washington, the President was uncharacteristically displaying noticeably less coolness under pressure than the Vice President. Alarmed by the reports he had received of the scenes in Caracas, Eisenhower ordered two companies of the Marines and two companies of the 101st Airborne Division to move to forward bases two hours' flying time from Caracas. This was called 'Operation Poor Richard', later described as 'a purely precautionary mea-sure' in case the Vice President needed to be rescued. In Venezuela, and through-out South America, it was reported as an imminent invasion by the trigger-happy Yankee imperialists.

Nixon was appalled. Calm had by evening returned to Caracas and in the privacy of the US Embassy he exploded in fury at such foolishly provocative US action. He was particularly angry because he had not been consulted by the White House. This omission was later explained by the fact that all telephone and radio frequencies from Venezuela had been jammed for several hours, probably as an act of sabotage by the leaders of what was later discovered to be a full-scale assassination plot. Due to the communications blackout Ike's precautionary measures had gone too far.

Whatever long-term damage might have been done to US–Latin American relations by the reaction to these military manoeuvres, the drama did nothing but short term good to Nixon's public relations back home. Returning to Washington, he was given a hero's welcome by a 15,000 airport crowd led by the President, the entire Cabinet and about half the members of Congress. Praise flooded in from all sides as he and Pat were universally acclaimed for their courage. For weeks afterwards they could not go anywhere in public without people standing up to applaud them. Nixon's popularity soared to an all-time high. Inevitably the adulation could not last, but for two or three months he was seen as a Titan—and as the next President of the United States. His political rivals for that office looked minnows by comparison as he surged ahead of them all in the Gallup Polls. Across the country people chuckled at the topical political joke: 'Have you heard the latest? Jack Kennedy is demanding equal time in Venezuela!'

III. THE DÉBÂCLE OF 1958

Nixon's presidential prospects, which appeared glowing in the aftermath of his return from Caracas in May, looked jaded by November. The cause of this deterioration was the debacle of the 1958 mid-term elections.

Nixon had been strongly advised to take a back seat in this campaign. The electoral prospects were poor; the economy was in a downward spiral; GOP infighting was rife; and Eisenhower, whose popularity rating that summer had fallen below fifty per cent for the first time, had again decided to stay aloof from the battle. There were plenty of good reasons and excuses for Nixon to take the same line. As Tom Dewey had counselled him, 'I know that all those old party wheelhorses will tell you stories that will pluck your heartstrings, but you're toying with your chance to be President. Don't do it, Dick. You've already done enough, and 1960 is what counts now.'[25] Nixon ignored that advice, even though he knew 1958 would be a bad year and that his own prestige as a vote-getter would be damaged if he spearheaded an unsuccessful campaign. An underestimated feature of Nixon the party politician has always been his sense of *noblesse oblige*, in some ways a stronger though more hidden element in his character than the 'compulsive campaigner' side which his opponents and critics have preferred to highlight. Nixon cared deeply for the GOP, rather in the manner of a grown-up child who continuously loves a fractious parent. By this stage in his career Nixon had outgrown the Republican Party. Yet he could not forget that he had once been its golden boy, even its prodigal son. Made by it (after Hiss) and saved by it (during The Fund and Dump Nixon crises), it was not in his character to desert it because the going was tough. Nixon really minded about the GOP's policies and performance as a national party. He was genuinely interested in its personalities, from old wheelhorses to young comers. He may also have calculated that he would need them and their power bases again one day, for like his hero Disraeli, he had a fine instinct for the rises and falls in the currency exchange of political favours. Besieged by the requests for his presence on the campaign trail that Dewey had predicted, Nixon felt obliged to help. He set off on a six-week electioneering schedule covering twenty-five states.

Despite these efforts to give strong Republican leadership to the campaign, the 1958 election result was demoralising. It ended in a much worse defeat than even the pessimists were expecting. Some of Nixon's difficulties were due to his feeling that the Administration was losing its grip on political issues. The Vice President had ideas of his own on how to pull out of the 1958 recession; how to strengthen US foreign policy and how to beat the Democrats. Only on the last topic was he allowed to break his loyal silence, but when on the campaign trail he slammed a contentious foreign policy statement from the Democratic Advisory Council by calling it 'the same defensive, defeatist, fuzzy-headed thinking which contributed to the loss of China and led to the Korean War',[26] Eisenhower in effect publicly rebuked his Vice President. At a White House press conference on 15 October, the President responded to a questioner asking for a comment on Nixon's speech: 'Foreign policy ought to be kept out of partisan debate...America's best interests in the world will be best served if we do not indulge in this kind of thing.'[27] The remark made headlines, which Eisenhower subsequently tried to minimise by sending Nixon a telegram claiming that his words had been misunderstood.

This incident was one of the worst Nixon-Eisenhower upheavals, although on this occasion Nixon was strong enough to obtain a retraction from his boss: 'I was hurt and angered by what I considered to be such a devious course on the part of the President,' recalled Nixon. 'His telegram was hardly sufficient to repair the damage that had been done to me.'[28] In this mood, Nixon telephoned Dulles to say that unless he got 'a public statement of support from the President, I may just have to make a statement about how you and the President wanted me to carry on this attack'.[29] This threat to reveal how Eisenhower and Dulles had themselves asked Nixon to make a strong rebuttal of the Democrats' original critique of the Administration's foreign policy produced the desired result. Two days later, Eisenhower issued a statement supporting Nixon. The episode was closed but it left a sour aftertaste and was symptomatic of the Republican troubles in the campaign.

When the results came through on 4 November, they were a disaster for the GOP. The Democrats gained thirteen seats in the Senate, bringing their total up to sixty-two against thirty-four for the Republicans. In the House they gained seats, thus outnumbering the Republicans by 292 to 153. They also picked up two new governorships, giving them control of thirty-four out of the forty-eight state houses. This landslide gave the Democrats so much power that they were to control the government of the United States for the next ten years.

In the postmortems Nixon was easily cast as the scapegoat. To rub salt in the wound, his two most probable challengers for the 1960 GOP presidential nomination, Nelson Rockefeller and Barry Goldwater, had enjoyed excellent personal victories in their home states. Their stars were on the ascendant. Nixon's was on the wane. It was one of the lowest points of his career thus far, with many commentators writing him off. Nixon knew better. As he said in a prescient post-election interview, 'The one sure thing about politics is that what goes up comes down, and what goes down often comes up.'[30]

IV. MAKING FRIENDS IN BRITAIN

Nixon turned to the international stage to revive his fortunes. Late in November 1958, he travelled to Britain to represent the United States at the dedication service of the American Memorial Chapel in St. Paul's Cathedral. It was an emotive occasion with important political and diplomatic overtones. Nixon could not have handled the visit better.

The chapel was a beautiful shrine in the north transept of St. Paul's built with farthings, halfpennies and pennies collected from the children of Britain as their generation's contribution to honour American servicemen killed in action while stationed in the United Kingdom during World War II. To many on both sides of the Atlantic the chapel also symbolised the finest hour of Anglo–American co-operation. However, the Special Relationship was in a shaky state following the Suez crisis of 1956. The British political establishment was less sure of Washington than at any time in the previous twenty-five years. It was also uneasy about Nixon, still widely expected to become the next US President. That unease was reflected in several unflattering articles and profiles published by Fleet Street's newspapers on the eve of the Vice President's arrival.

Although Nixon was in Britain for just three days, he gave what the *New Yorker* described as 'a dazzling exposition of not putting a foot wrong'.[31] He had only a walk-on part at St. Paul's, where the ceremony was so moving that the television and radio coverage brought tears to millions of eyes in both countries. The service perfectly combined the temporal splendours of British pageantry with the spiritual emotions of American sacrifice, running from Cranmer's liturgy and the State Trumpeters, to 'The Battle Hymn of the Republic' and 'Taps' from a US Marine bugler. The *New York Times* caught the grandeur of the occasion: 'No man of imagination can go through a ceremony like a dedication of the American Memorial Chapel in St. Paul's without being deeply impressed...There he was, Richard Milhous Nixon from Yorba Linda, Calif, standing next to a Queen whose throne has existed for more than a thousand years on a site where Christians have worshipped for thirteen and a half centuries.'[32]

On the political front, Nixon did much to repair the fragile structure of Anglo-American relations. He delivered two major speeches, to the English-speaking Union at the Guildhall and to the Pilgrims' annual luncheon at the Savoy. He struck the right notes of reassurance, pleasantly surprising his hosts by a favourable analysis of Britain's colonial achievements in countries he had visited. At the ESU banquet he delivered an eloquent plea for improved aid to the Third World, calling for 'a great offensive against the evils of poverty, disease and misery in the undeveloped areas of the world on a scale far greater than any the American people or Congress have ever yet dared to contemplate.' The arch anti-Communist (as Nixon had been billed by the international press) ended by telling his audience that they should speak less of the threat of Communism and more of the promise of freedom. 'We should adopt as our primary objective not the defeat of Communism but the victory of plenty over want; of health over disease; and of freedom over tyranny...No people in the world today should be forced to choose between bread and freedom.'[33]

The speech won golden opinions, noticeably from the Leader of the Labour Opposition, Hugh Gaitskell, who declared Nixon was 'brilliant' and that he deserved 'extravagant praise'.[34] The same level of panegyric was maintained by the Conservative Foreign Secretary, Selwyn Lloyd, who summarised his private talks with the Vice President:

> After Dulles's ponderous evasions, Nixon's incisive frankness was
> a great relief. He has a first class mind backed up by a masterly

understanding of the world scene...The President's deputy does
not appear to be, as was sometimes feared, a kind of political ogre
without principle or integrity, but a rather tough politician who
possesses common sense as well as formidable energy, charm and
lively intelligence...if he succeeds Eisenhower the world has nothing to worry about. He may well be a considerable improvement![35]

Nixon moved in royal as well as political circles during his trip, hosting a
Thanksgiving dinner for The Queen at the US Embassy residence in London on
27 November. He had an animated conversation with the Monarch about what
makes a good literary style, sending her as a present the next day *The Art of Read-
able Writing* by Rudolf Flesch. However, he felt uncomfortable all evening as a
result of having forgotten to pack a black tie dinner suit. This mistake was discovered only forty-five minutes before The Queen was due to arrive. Nixon's
military aide, Don Hughes, has recalled how he rectified the situation.

We were frantic. I tried our staff, the embassy staff, and the Scotland
Yard team. No one had a suit likely to fit The Boss. It was getting to
desperation point, so I stood in the hallway of Winfield House sizing
up each American guest as they came in. Eventually some poor guy
arrived looking forward to his dinner with The Queen who was the
right build. With only a few minutes to go, I persuaded him to lend
The Boss his suit and have dinner alone in his shirt upstairs...Then
I told those who were in on the secret to keep it *en famille,* away from
the newspapers...Unfortunately Nixon ruined that part of the strategy. Just about the first thing he said to The Queen as she came
through the hall, in the hearing of reporters, was: 'I'm afraid this isn't
my suit.'[36]

As a result, this trivial story received almost as much media attention as the
more important aspects of the visit.

The two final highlights of Nixon's trip were his appearance at the Oxford
Union and his valedictory press conference. At Oxford Nixon was given a respectful but at times hostile grilling by the students. He found the question and answer
session 'quite an intellectual exercise'[37] but enjoyed himself—as he usually does
in such encounters with the thoughtful young. He evidently filed the occasion
away in his memory as a good experience, for twenty years later he chose the
Oxford Union as the venue for his re-entry to the arena of international affairs,

accepting an invitation from the students as his first post-resignation overseas engagement in 1978.

Nixon had a still greater success with the question and answer session at his final press conference. The British journalists of that era were unaccustomed to world leaders who duelled with reporters on the record, and after their initial surprise at the sharp tone of the American correspondents' interrogation they joined in the questioning with gusto. 'Nixon made an extraordinary impression. I never saw anything like it before or since', said Robert Carvel, the Political Editor of the *London Evening Standard*. 'At the end of ninety minutes of watching this man hit every single one of their questions to the boundary, three hundred and fifty hard-boiled reporters from all over the world rose to their feet and gave him a standing ovation!'[38]

Subsequent press comment confirmed the good impression. The British papers were admiring in their summaries, from the *Manchester Guardian*, who called the visit 'an unqualified success',[39] to the *Daily Telegraph*, who described the Vice President as 'a frank and engaging character who in passing by has done a great deal to cement the Anglo-American alliance'.[40] Both at home and abroad the trip also cemented Nixon's image as an internationally experienced politician of presidential calibre. The US press mirrored the favourable British judgement. 'Richard Nixon who arrived billed as an uncouth political adventurer in the political jungles departed trailing clouds of statesmanship and esteem', reported Drew Middleton in the *New York Times*.[41]

Amidst all this mutual admiration, Nixon established some lasting British friendships, mainly with Conservatives such as Selwyn Lloyd, Lord Home, and Christopher Soames. It was also the beginning of his enduring rapport with the British. Six weeks after the St. Paul's service, Nixon corresponded with William S. White, congratulating him on a pro-British article written for the *New York Times*. 'I've often heard the President say: "The British can be very difficult where negotiations are concerned, but when you are in a fight I don't know of anybody I would rather have on my side,"' wrote Nixon. 'I don't imagine I am any more of an Anglophile than you are, but you can't help but admire the real quality our British friends display when you get a chance to know them.'[42]

V. THE KITCHEN DEBATE

Of all Nixon's overseas visits as Vice President, the one which made most impact on his strategic thinking was the journey to the Soviet Union in 1959.

At the time, the results of the trip seemed largely ephemeral. The famous 'Kitchen Debate' with Nikita Khrushchev gave Nixon a public relations triumph and a boost to his prospects in the forthcoming US presidential election. Aside from this short-term domestic impact, there were few other immediately discernible consequences, since the diplomatic achievements of the visit were negligible and the Cold War grew steadily colder in the ensuing years.

However, looked at from a longer perspective, it is clear that Nixon's contribution to history as the President who started the sea change in the nature of the US-Soviet relationship had its origin in his first mission to Moscow. It was characteristic of Nixon that, while his previous studies of the Soviet Union had led him to many of the conclusions that would become the premises of his later diplomacy, it was in a personal investigation of the nation, its people and their leader that he grasped the practical significance of his theorising. The lessons he learned in 1959 were put into operation when he became President and it can be argued that we are still seeing their effect today.

The official reason for Nixon's 1959 visit was to give the United States senior representation at the first ever American trade exhibition to be held in Moscow. This could easily have turned out to be a superficial chore of vice-presidential flag waving. Both the United States Information Agency, which was responsible for publicising the exhibition, and the Kremlin, which wanted a diplomatic trailer for the anticipated follow-up visit by Khrushchev to America, had low expectations for the mission so far as issues of substance were concerned.

Nixon thought differently. After securing Eisenhower's approval for the trip, he spent nearly six months preparing himself with an intensity of study unequalled since his days before the California Bar exams. He received classified briefings from the CIA and the State Department; he conferred with domestic and foreign leaders who had met Khrushchev, including Foster Dulles, Harold Macmillan, Hubert Humphrey, and Konrad Adenauer; he took lessons in the Russian language, memorising phonetic phrases and proverbs ; he absorbed a long reading list of history books and biographies; and he held meetings with a wide variety of Soviet experts and visitors. These included the former US Ambassador to Moscow, Chip Bohlen; Whittaker Chambers; Turner Catledge of the *New York Times*; the columnist Walter Lippmann and Professor William Y. Elliott of Harvard. Elliott recommended a book on foreign policy and nuclear weapons by one of his most brilliant pupils. He urged Nixon to meet the young author, telling the Vice President how much he would 'enjoy the range and quickness of his mind'.[43] As it happened the meeting did not take place for some years, but the recommendation was significant, for this was the first time Nixon had ever heard of Henry Kissinger.

By the time of his departure from Washington, Nixon was superbly briefed, having committed to memory papers on 132 topics that he felt the Soviets might bring up. He arrived in Moscow at 2.50 p.m. on 23 July, scoring an immediate public relations coup by breaking the world air speed record between the two capitals. The credit for this was due to Howard Hughes. The reclusive aviation tycoon had called Nixon personally a month earlier to urge that the vice-presidential party should travel in one of the United States Air Force's new 707 Superjets. Hughes had argued that the aircraft was far more advanced than anything the Soviets could build and that it would make a great impression on them. 'As we taxied in past rows of old, two-engine TU-104 jet transports on Moscow's runway, I was glad that I had taken Hughes's advice', recalled Nixon.[44]

Although the weather in Moscow was warm, the diplomatic temperature was chilly. Nixon was greeted correctly by Deputy Premier Kozlov and a handful of senior officials, but the usual symbols of welcome such as crowds, bands, guards of honour and the playing of national anthems were conspicuously absent. The atmosphere of unfriendliness was heightened by the drive in from the airport along empty streets from which all pedestrians and other cars had been cleared. The cause of this *froideur*, as the US Ambassador Llewellyn 'Tommy' Thompson explained, was that the Soviets were angry with the US Congress for passing the Captive Nations resolution a few days earlier. This resolution, a popular annual event since 1950 with the ethnic minorities in many congressional districts, was a strongly worded attack on the suppression of rights and freedoms by 'Communist imperialism' in twenty-four subjugated countries of Eastern Europe.

When Nixon met Khrushchev for what was supposed to be a purely protocol welcome in the Kremlin, the Soviet leader wasted no time in getting tough. As soon as the photographers were out of the room, he started shouting abusively about the Captive Nations resolution, telling Nixon that he could not understand why Congress had taken such action on the eve of an important state visit. 'It reminds me of a saying among our Russian peasants, that "people should not go to the toilet where they eat"', bellowed Khrushchev, red-faced with anger. 'This resolution stinks. It stinks like fresh horse shit, and nothing smells worse than that!'

Nixon remembered from his briefing papers that Khrushchev had once worked as a swineherd, and from his own childhood in the California countryside that pig manure had an overpoweringly unpleasant stench. He hit back in the manner of a college debater. 'I am afraid that the Chairman is mistaken. There is something that smells worse than horse shit—and that is pig shit.'[45]

Apparently impressed by such expertise in farmyard odours, Khrushchev had the grace to laugh, telling Nixon, 'You are right there!'[46] and temporarily dropping the subject. This earthy exchange appeared to unlock in both men a chemistry of combative showmanship. When they arrived at the American exhibition, Khrushchev began playing to the gallery as soon as he saw the television cameras. He asked Nixon how long America had existed, and was told 150 years.* 'We have existed not quite forty-two years, and in another seven years we will be on the same level as America', retorted the Russian. 'When we catch you up, in passing you by, we will wave to you', he boasted, turning around to wave goodbye to an imaginary American. 'Then if you wish we can stop and say: Please follow up.'[48]

This was the beginning of a morning of Capitalist versus Communist theatricals. As the two leaders progressed round the exhibition they traded keen debating points and gestures to the crowd. Nixon was the more restrained, keeping to the line that America was a great country because of free competition and the free exchange of ideas. Khrushchev, aggressive and rude in his tone, accused his guest of ignorance ('You don't know anything about Communism except fear of it') and kept needling Nixon for being a slick and manipulative lawyer in comparison with his own 'honest' background as a simple peasant and mine worker.

During these exchanges, some of which were recorded by the cameras at RCA's colour television stand in the exhibition, Nixon was coming off worst. His politeness was giving the impression of weakness. Khrushchev seemed to sense he had his visitor on the run, for he became increasingly cocky and hectoring in manner.

The tide turned when the VIP party reached the exhibit which *Pravda* had labelled 'The Taj Mahal'. This was a model American home, complete with the typical furnishings and labour-saving devices that an average US family might own. Representing the builders, All-State Properties Inc., was a twenty-nine-year-old New York public relations executive, William Safire,[†] who ingeniously manoeuvred the group into prime position on his stand. The debating got tougher. 'You are a lawyer for Capitalism and I am a lawyer for Communism', said Khrush-

---

* Nixon had this wrong. America had existed for 180 years. This slip of the tongue was corrected in his memoirs.[47]

† Bill Safire was so impressed by Nixon's performance that he soon afterwards offered his services to the Vice President for the 1960 election campaign. He later became an unpaid member of Nixon's speech-writing team in the 1965–8 period, and in this role joined the White House staff in 1969 as a Special Assistant to the President. In 1975 he published *Before the Fall*, one of the most illuminating accounts of the Nixon White House. He is now a renowned columnist for the *New York Times*.

chev. 'Let's compete.' 'The way you dominate the conversation you would make a good lawyer yourself,' replied Nixon. 'If you were in the United States Senate you would be accused of filibustering. You do all the talking and don't let anyone else talk. To us, diversity, the right to choose, the fact that we have one thousand builders building one thousand different houses, is the most important thing. We don't have one decision made at the top by one government official. This is the difference.'[49]

By this time the leaders had arrived in the model kitchen, which Nixon said was typical of a steelworker's home. Khrushchev pooh-poohed the labour-saving devices such as the washing machine: 'These are merely gadgets. They are not needed in life. They have no useful purpose.' With a young aide, Leonid Brezhnev, standing beside him, he announced that the Soviet Union was full of peasants who could afford the $14,000 that the model home cost, but who nevertheless preferred to let the State spend their money on rockets—which in any case were far better than American rockets. 'Isn't it better to be talking about the relative merits of our washing machines than of the relative strength of our rockets? Isn't this the kind of competition you want?' Nixon asked. 'Yes,' was the reply, 'but your generals say, "We want to compete in rockets. We can beat you."'[50]

The protagonists were circling one another like verbal prize fighters, with much jabbing of fingers. As arguments were thrown back and forth with passion, Nixon more than held his own. In the eyes of the American observers present, he won a clear victory on points, not least because unlike his host he never lost his cool. 'Watching Nixon in that kitchen, I felt damn proud to be an American', recalled Don Kendall,* the President of Pepsi-Cola International, whose stand was another feature of the Moscow exhibition. 'He stood toe to toe with Khrushchev and really dished it out to him.'[52] Safire had similar feelings: 'Nixon was superb…cornball though it sounds he made me feel proud of my country.'[53] A journalistic witness of the scene, the Russian-speaking Harrison Salisbury of the *New York Times* was almost as complimentary : 'Nixon couldn't have done it better. He won the debate, and that shook up the Russians.'[54] But another contributor from the *New York Times* took a more jaundiced view: 'While all this was

---

* Don Kendall became a lifelong Nixon friend and financial backer. He was on the verge of being fired from his job of President of Pepsi-Cola International (in 1959 a relatively small company with sales of $120 million) for having wasted too much money and time on Pepsi's investment in the Moscow exhibition. However, after Nixon and Khrushchev had been photographed drinking Pepsi together on the stand, the corporation's directors were so delighted with the impact on their sales (their advertising slogan 'Be Sociable, have a Pepsi' was given the twist 'Khrushchev Learns to be Sociable') that Kendall survived and was eventually promoted to the chairmanship of Pepsico. He liked to say, 'I owe my career to Nixon and the Kitchen Debate.'[51]

going on,' wrote columnist James Reston, 'Ambassador Thompson and Milton Eisenhower were standing by wondering whatever became of diplomacy and why didn't someone pull a plug on the whole thing.' However, Reston also reported that although the kitchen debate was 'a disaster in terms of conventional diplomacy, Mr. Khrushchev was still smiling at the end. He had a good time. He had an argument with another politician today and an audience to go with it and naturally this was a politician's idea of fun.'[55]

The kitchen debate was not Nixon's idea of fun, for he thought he had lost to an unfair opponent, whom he afterwards described as 'a bare-knuckled slugger who had gouged, kneed and kicked'.[56] However, he had a plan to get even. In the diplomatic exchanges before the visit, the Kremlin had agreed to allow Nixon to make one live television and radio broadcast and to have the full text of his formal speech opening the exhibition reprinted in *Pravda* and *Izvestia*. These were unprecedented opportunities for a Western leader to communicate with the Soviet public and Nixon was determined to make the most of them. When he opened the exhibition he rebutted the Russian propaganda that the American model home was no more typical of a US worker's house than the Taj Mahal or Buckingham Palace were typical of average houses in India or Britain. He reeled off statistics showing that America's 44 million families owned 56 million cars, 50 million TV sets and 143 million radio sets. Thirty-one million of these families owned their own homes, and 25 million of them were houses or apartments larger than the model home in the exhibition. The figures, he said, showed that 'the United States, the world's largest capitalist country, has from the standpoint of distribution of wealth come closest to the ideal of prosperity for all in a classless society'.[57]

Although Khrushchev started bouncing up and down in the front row of the audience shouting, 'Nyet! Nyet!', Nixon, in possession of the microphone, overrode him, going on to emphasise that the material prosperity of America was secondary to its political and personal freedoms: 'To us, progress without freedom is like potatoes without fat... We are free to criticize our Government and our President... We live and travel where we please without travel permits, internal passports or police regulations. We also travel freely abroad.'

Nixon ended by reverting to his theme of peaceful competition:

> Let us extend this competition to include the spiritual as well as the
> material aspects of our civilization. Let us compete not in how to take
> lives but in how to save them. Let us work for victory, not in war but

for the victory of plenty over poverty, of health over disease, of understanding over ignorance, wherever they exist in the world... The last half of the twentieth century can be the darkest or the brightest page in the history of civilization. The decision is in our hands to make.'[58]

At the American Embassy reception afterwards, Nixon was told that his speech had ensured that the visit would go down 'as a major diplomatic triumph'.[59] This was a wild exaggeration so far as the Kremlin's leaders were concerned, but the speech certainly made an impact with the public, as did Nixon's even more important radio and television address on the eve of his departure.

This thirty-minute broadcast was one of the most effective performances of Nixon's career, and he spent two nights without sleep preparing for it. He began by talking to the viewers about his favourable impression of their beautiful country and their friendly people who shared Americans' desire for peace. Then he attacked *Pravda* for writing lies about his visit, going on to propose that there should be a US–Soviet agreement to allow a free flow of newspapers, magazines and reporting between the two countries. Free communication should be matched by the people's freedom to choose the economic and political system they preferred. 'We believe that you and all other peoples on this earth should have the right to choose the kind of economic or political system which best fits your particular problems without any foreign intervention', was his conclusion.[60]

Audience reaction to Nixon's broadcast was almost unknown at the time, although Western embassies reported favourably on it. However, nearly thirty years afterwards, a prominent Soviet civil engineer, Boris Armanov, gave an interesting response to the question about whether he remembered the 1959 Nixon visit.

Remember it? I never forgot it. We sat round my mother's big old radio set listening and then we argued about his talk and his speech about America to the exhibition for months afterwards. We knew he must be speaking the truth because of a small thing. There was a story on the front page of *Pravda* saying that Nixon had tried to bribe a man in the crowd at a market to come and hear him speak. This was a ridiculous charge. If anything, an ordinary Russian man would have tried to bribe an American official to be allowed to come and hear the US Vice President speaking, not the other way round! So nobody believed a word of the *Pravda* story anyway, but then on the radio Nixon got really mad about it and he actually accused *Pravda* of being untruthful! When he said that, we knew he was uncensored, speaking from the heart. So then we really listened to him, and afterwards we argued and argued about why the Americans had so much freedom, so much money, and all these truthful newspapers which he offered in exchange for *Pravda*. It was the first time many of my generation had ever even considered that the West might have some things in their society which might be good for our society, or that freedom of the press might be right for the Soviet Union. I know it sounds silly, but you can't imagine how brainwashed we were at school and university…There was something about Nixon's voice, too. It sounded so young, so strong. It was the voice of a working man…Mind you, not everyone thought the same way. My grandmother said, 'Don't trust him'…But most of us were fascinated by this American with his strength and openness. Do you know who brought *glasnost* to Moscow? Richard Nixon! It's a joke of course, but there's just a bit of truth in it; in fact there was a lot of truth in it if you think about what Nixon was saying and what life was like for us at the time of Stalin, Malenkov and Khrushchev.[61]

Whatever impact Nixon had on the Soviet Union, it was less important than the impact his private talks with Khrushchev had on him. No American leader had ever before had so much exposure at close quarters to a Soviet leader. The two principals were in face-to-face dialogue with each other for nearly twenty hours in the first four days of the visit. Yet there was no sign throughout these talks that the Soviets were interested in mutual co-operation, peaceful compromise or improved understanding. From beginning to end Khrushchev came across as a ruthless, domineering bully who was utterly determined to outsmart, outpace and if necessary outgun the West. His public aggression at the kitchen debate continued through a series of private lunches and dinners. He exuded confidence about the inevitability of Communism's victory and Capitalism's defeat. He kept up a stream of boasting about the military strength of his forces and the destructive power of Soviet armaments. Even his jokes had a warlike edge. 'A pessimist is a General who says it will only take six atomic bombs to wipe out Britain', he told Nixon. 'An optimist is one who says it will need nine or ten.'[62]

In the middle of one five-hour lunch at Khrushchev's summer dacha outside Moscow, there was an illuminating moment when Milton Eisenhower tried to stem the flow of Russian militaristic threats with a personal statement about

America's desire for peace. He spoke with emotion of his brother's fifty-year record of service to his country, ending by saying that he was hoping and praying for a miracle in the final year and a half of the Eisenhower administration—'a miracle that something can be done to ensure that no war will ever happen again in the world'.[63]

All the Americans present were impressed by this burst of heartfelt idealism. Nixon had watched Khrushchev closely. 'During this very moving statement, his small eyes remained impassive and steely cold', he recalled. 'It was clear that he was contemptuous of such feelings, interpreting them merely as a display of American weakness.'[64]

Impressions such as these left their mark on Nixon. He had travelled to Moscow with an open mind about the opportunities for civilised dialogue and future negotiations between the superpowers on the basis of mutual interests and understanding. He returned convinced that no such dialogue or negotiation could succeed unless the United States first established a position of strength. He had seen at first hand that the Soviet leadership's belief in the supremacy and the eventual triumph of Communism was so strong that the US would only achieve results in the fields of diplomacy and disarmament after raising its military guard, increasing its economic advantage, and strengthening its political will.

Learning this fundamental lesson was a seminal experience for Nixon. He left Moscow 'depressed', admitting that he had achieved 'no success whatever in getting through to Khrushchev and the Soviet leaders'.[65] However, his apparent failure as a vice-presidential communicator had the long-term effect of making him a successful presidential negotiator. With hindsight it is clear that Nixon's formidable achievements in the field of US–Soviet relations as the architect of 'hard headed détente'; as the signatory of the first Strategic Arms Limitation Treaty and as an influential advocate throughout the 1980s of 'peace through strength' all stemmed from what he learned on his 1959 visit. From that time on, Nixon was no longer interested in soft options. He rejected most of the fashionable diplomatic nostrums of his time, such as the emphasis on establishing goodwill at the head of state level; the need to convince the Soviets of the merits of the US system; and the importance of persuading the Russian leaders that the US was 'sincere' in its desire for peace. Instead, he realised that the US should demonstrate in its national relations with the Soviet Union the same resolve he had shown in his personal dealings with Khrushchev. Only when the Soviets knew that the US was prepared to match them blow for blow in competition, would they recognise that their true interests lay in conciliation. Nixon thus became the ultimate real-ist in his handling of relations with the Soviet Union because Khrushchev had taught him that the language of strength and self-interest was the only language to which the Kremlin would respond.

VI. NOMINATION FOR PRESIDENT

In the final year of his Vice Presidency, Nixon devoted most of his energies to the upcoming election. He had some problems with his preparations for the coming battle inside the Government. The Eisenhower Cabinet was not interested in the electoral effects of its decisions. 'Time and again I would see Nixon get up from the table after Cabinet meetings so tense that beads of sweat were standing out on his brow', recalled Elliot Richardson* who often attended the Cabinet in 1959, deputising as acting Secretary of Health, Education and Welfare. 'The cause of his tension was that he had to keep his mouth shut while decisions were taken that he knew would erode his political base for 1960.'[66]

One occasion when Nixon did not keep his mouth shut at a Cabinet meeting in 1959 elicited the admiration and gratitude of Richardson, who was on the verge of resignation over the Administration's refusal to accept a bill which would provide certain federal guarantees and subsidies for bonds funding the expansion of higher education. The bill was brought back to the Cabinet for one last discussion. The HEW Secretary, Arthur Fleming, made his pitch and Eisenhower asked for views. 'Just about everyone was against it at first,' recalled Richardson. 'Ezra Taft Benson, the Agriculture Secretary, said it was an unwelcome intrusion of government. Bob Anderson, the Secretary of the Treasury, said it required an excessive commitment of federal funding. Our allies deserted us one by one. The bill looked completely lost, until the Vice President spoke up. In a series of well-timed interventions Nixon got Anderson to admit that the bill would have very little impact on the budget in the first year or two. Then he had everyone agreeing that there was no objection to the bill in principle since the Government was already giving all sorts of subsidies to higher education. Finally he gave his own interpretation of the HEW data of the needs for higher educational institutions, ending up by asking, 'Can there be any doubt Mr. President, that this bill meets an important national priority?' There was a tiny spluttering around the table but

---

* Elliot Richardson was Assistant Secretary for Legislation in the Department of Health, Education and Welfare 1957–60. After serving as Lieutenant Governor (1964–6) and Attorney General of Massachusetts (1966–8), he joined the Nixon administration in 1969 as Under-Secretary of State. He was promoted to the Cabinet in 1970 as Secretary of Health, Education and Welfare. He was Secretary of Defense January–May 1973 and Attorney General May-October 1973, until resigning in protest over 'The Saturday Night Massacre'. In the Ford administration, Richardson served as Ambassador to Britain (1974–5) and Secretary of Commerce (1975–6). He was sometimes called 'The Man for All Positions'.

no one opposed it any more, so Ike looking rather grim nodded and said, 'All right—send it up'. It was a quite extraordinarily skillful performance by Nixon. He had won the bill almost single-handed, and I was extremely grateful to him since I was saved from the need to resign. Quite an irony, when you consider what happened to me in 1973.[67]

This glimpse of Nixon performing successfully in Cabinet was matched by some good vice-presidential performances before the wider public. He played a prominent role during Khrushchev's tour of the United States in the fall of 1959, which reminded people through the television repeats of the Moscow kitchen debate how well he had stood up to the Soviet leader. Nixon's popularity in the Gallup Polls climbed high. 'He looked totally secure as the heir apparent', recalled Charles McWhorter, a thirty-five-year-old Republican lawyer, who had joined Nixon as a full-time political aide. 'There were several people around him who wanted to get his campaign bandwagon rolling. I was given the job of stopping this happening. Nixon was sensitive about the propriety of his relationship with Eisenhower. He was very careful not to look as though he was trying on the crown.'[68] Nixon's restraint was attributable to his reading of the mood of the Republican Party. The man who had been dubbed by his opponents as a chronic campaigner also had a finely tuned sense of when not to campaign. In the winter of 1959–60 he could afford to bide his time, for there was little doubt that he would be the nominee. Almost the only GOP leader who felt otherwise was Governor Nelson Rockefeller of New York. 'I hate the thought of Dick Nixon being President of the United States,'[69] Rockefeller told his intimate friends. A more accurate explanation of his motives might have been that he was in love with the thought of becoming President himself.

It was once said of the nineteenth-century British Prime Minister Lord Rosebery that 'he is one of those who like the palm without the dust'.[70] The same description can be applied to the twentieth-century ambitions of Nelson Rockefeller. In 1960 his method of campaigning for the nomination was more monarchical than political. Disdaining to enter any of the primaries, he preferred to hold court on his imperial estate at Pocantico Hills, surrounded by a retinue of expensive advisers, among them a still unknown foreign affairs specialist called Henry Kissinger.

Millions of Rockefeller dollars were spent on staff, offices, and private Gallup Polls. These purported to show that the Governor of New York would be a far more popular national candidate than the Vice President of the United States. However, the results were disregarded by the GOP activists to whom they were circulated—ironically, because Rockefeller had paid for them himself.

Disappointed by the lack of response to his private polls, Rockefeller sent emissaries across the country to hunt for convention delegates and made personal visitations to eleven states. He was cheered in the streets by the people but snubbed in the smoke-filled rooms by the party regulars. When the GOP power brokers cut their deals to control delegates, no one wanted to know the Johnny-come-lately from New York, even if he was a Governor and a billionaire. In the face of the Rockefeller charm offensive, the party regulars turned their backs. They stayed resolutely loyal to their foul weather friend Dick Nixon—a just and reciprocal reward for his loyalty to them in so many less promising campaigns over the previous decade.

To make matters worse for Rockefeller, Nixon was well supported by big business, and was streets ahead in his arrangements for the primaries. However, he did not feel as secure as he looked. 'Nixon spent a lot of time worrying about Rockefeller's challenge in the fall of 1959', recalled Bob Finch, who was soon to be appointed the Vice President's campaign manager, 'and he got us to focus early on New Hampshire. By the time the Rockefeller people started thinking about that primary we had the delegates, we had a statewide organization headed by the Governor, we had the halls booked, we practically had the votes counted. When Rockefeller saw that he backed off.'[71]

On Christmas Eve 1959 Rockefeller issued a dignified withdrawal statement, telling the world he intended to concentrate on his duties as Governor of New York. It ended: 'I am not, and shall not be, a candidate for the nomination for the Presidency. This decision is definite and final.'[72]

This decision, which turned out to be neither definite nor final, did not fill Nixon with much joy. He had looked forward to the primaries as sparring rounds in which he would decisively defeat his Republican rivals and take valuable television time away from his Democratic opponents. Moreover, he did not believe that Rockefeller was out of the running. These instincts proved right. Throughout the spring and early summer of 1960 Rockefeller continued his vain wooing of delegates, sending them unsolicited mailings and self-serving poll findings rather in the manner of a spurned lover despatching flowers and photographs to the already betrothed. On 11 June 1960 Rockefeller even tried to woo Eisenhower, calling him in the White House to ask 'whether or not he should be an avowed candidate'. According to the notes taken by a secretary, 'The President said he was afraid Nelson would be called "off again, on again, gone again, Finnegan"', and urged the Governor to 'support whoever was nominated'.[73] It was a position that Rockefeller was emotionally incapable of taking.

While he continued to keep a close eye on Rockefeller's pre-convention manoeuvres, Nixon's main focus was on the Democrats. Kennedy was the opponent he feared. The British Foreign Secretary, Selwyn Lloyd, called on the Vice President in April and learned this in a long talk about the election. 'Nixon seemed to think that if there was no recession he should beat everyone except Kennedy— about him he seemed doubtful', Lloyd reported.[74]

Observing the Democratic primaries, Nixon started to become psyched by the Kennedy style, the Kennedy family, the Kennedy money and the Kennedy ruthlessness. On the family he was much given to repeating a *bon mot* of Mrs. Alice Roosevelt Longworth's about the different characters of the Kennedy brothers: 'Teddy's a gregarious Irish barman. Bobby's a ruthless, humorless eighteenth-century Jesuit priest. But Jack's a debonair man of the world with all the looks and sex appeal of a Hollywood movie star.'[75]

Even with such talents on the campaign trail, Nixon did not believe that Kennedy would beat Senator Humphrey in certain key primaries. This view turned out to be wrong, first in West Virginia, where the population was 95 per cent Protestant, pro-New Deal, and with a high incidence of poverty. Nixon thought this was ideal Humphrey territory, and was astonished by the Kennedy victory, although his amazement turned to anxiety when he learned that the Kennedy people 'had spent enough money in West Virginia to pay every voter $50 ... poor old Hubert was just utterly outspent'.[76]

Most of all, the Kennedy ruthlessness worried Nixon: 'I know you can't just buy the voters in any state. But what really concerned me was what happened to Hubert in Minnesota and Wisconsin', he recalled. 'Hubert was from Minnesota, and it was particularly important for him to win the Wisconsin primary because after all Wisconsin's in his back yard. The polls predicted he would win it. But what happened was that just a few days before the election the Catholic precincts in Milwaukee and other areas of Wisconsin were flooded with vicious anti-Catholic literature postmarked from Minnesota. Everybody thought Hubert did it and the Kennedy people did nothing to dissuade them. There was a backlash and Hubert lost. Afterwards I learned that an aide to Bobby Kennedy did that mailing.'[77]

Despite his fears about such factors, Nixon's personal relations with the Kennedys remained good. During the early part of 1960 he had several cordial conversations with JFK in the Senate about the progress of the primaries, and other topics. After one such meeting Kennedy sent him a book, *To Light a Candle*, inscribed by its author, Father Keller. A month before the Democratic convention

Nixon had a chance encounter with the patriarch of the family, Ambassador Joseph P. Kennedy Snr. outside the Colony Restaurant in New York City. 'Poppa Joe' was standing on the pavement with his youngest son Teddy Kennedy when Nixon came walking along the street. They shook hands and Joe Kennedy said warmly: 'I just want you to know how much I admire you for what you've done in the Hiss case and in all the Communist activity of yours. If Jack doesn't get it I'll be for you.' Teddy nodded, but said nothing.[78]

That was Nixon's first meeting with Joe Kennedy. His second came a few days later in the first-class compartment of a United Airlines flight from Washington to Los Angeles. The seventy-two-year-old former ambassador was accompanied by a girl in her twenties, 'a real raving beauty' according to Nixon. Kennedy introduced his companion as 'my niece', accompanying his words with a broad wink which Nixon was too embarrassed to return.[79]

On 16 July John F. Kennedy was nominated as the Democratic Party's candidate for President. Nixon watched the acceptance speech at his office in Washington and liked what he saw. The Harvard accent, the staccato delivery, the high-falutin literary language; and the gaunt tiredness in his face made Kennedy look vulnerable to the predatory eye of his rival. Nixon told his companions that his performance had been poor. Remembering the proposals from the Democrats for a first-ever televised debate between the presidential candidates, Nixon felt inclined to accept. The Kennedy he had just seen could be beaten on television.

Later that month the Republicans assembled in Chicago for what promised to be more of a coronation than a convention. There was no rival in sight who could stop Nixon winning the nomination. However, Rockefeller was a loose cannon who might yet spoil the party. The common perception of these two GOP leaders was that Nixon was the conservative and Rockefeller the liberal. This was wrong. For all the fuzzy liberalism of his high-sounding speeches extolling 'The Brotherhood of Man and the Fatherhood of God' (known to journalists as 'the BOMFOG message'), Rockefeller was a right-winger on many specific issues. As Governor he had introduced mandatory life sentences for drug offenders in New York; he criticised Eisenhower for neglecting the nation's defences, and he favoured a major US military commitment to South Vietnam. Nixon, by contrast, was a centrist, attacked by a *Wall Street Journal* editorial in January 1960 for being 'far too liberal on such matters as foreign aid, international development and welfare legislation'.[80] Nevertheless, non-candidate Rockefeller was perceived as progressive, and non-conservative Nixon was viewed as a hardliner. With Rockefeller's liberal supporters airing policy differences as the Republican high command gathered in Chicago to draft their election platform, Nixon knew he had to accommodate his rival in order to unify the party.

This quest for party unity led Nixon to strike a deal with Rockefeller which was labelled by conservatives as 'Surrender on Fifth Avenue'[81] and 'The Munich of the Republican Party'.[82] When the epithets subsided the agreement could be seen as a simple matter of good politics. What happened was that the Platform Committee in Chicago drafted a manifesto which took as its guide the achievements of the past Administration rather than the aims of a future one. Rockefeller's representatives threatened to repudiate the text, which would have meant a damaging public split. To avoid this, Nixon flew to New York on the evening of Friday 22 July and dined alone with the Governor in his twenty-three room triplex apartment on 5th Avenue. Early in the meal the vice-presidential nomination was offered and refused. Then followed the real business of the evening, which was drawing up an agreed list of fourteen points for the consideration of the Platform Committee. These included a more imaginative foreign policy; increased expenditures for defence; a more positive domestic economic policy; and a firmer stand on civil rights.

'There was no question in my mind that reaching this compromise with Rockefeller was essential', recalled Nixon. 'To me it was just a fact of political life as without the wing of the party Rockefeller represented I might just as well have forgotten about the election. It was expedient but it was also realistic. Both Rockefeller and I knew what was happening. I had sewn up the nomination but I needed his backing and he made the most of it in what to him was a losing situation. The conservatives gave me unshirted hell for "surrendering", but in fact there was no surrender. I was glad to broaden the platform, but I also did not hesitate to turn down some of the portions of Rockefeller's draft statement which I could not accept either as a candidate or in my role as Eisenhower's Vice President.'[83]

The first blast of unshirted hell against the Compact of Fifth Avenue came from the President. Vacationing in Newport, Rhode Island, Eisenhower blazed with fury about the 'personal treachery' of Rockefeller, blaming him for the Compact's paragraphs on national defence which, in Ike's view, amounted to a near repudiation of his personal competence as Commander-in-Chief. 'If our rockets only had the same thrust that the President developed on Saturday morning we would not have to worry about Khrushchev', was Lucius Clay's description of Eisenhower's temper that weekend.[84] Meanwhile, in Chicago, the reaction was just as rough. 'No words of pain, outrage and fury can describe the reaction of the Republican Platform Committee', reported Theodore H. White. 'A single night's meeting of two men in a millionaire's triplex apartment in Babylon-by-the-Hudson, 830 miles away, was about to overrule them; they were exposed as clowns for all the world to see. It was too much.'[85]

Nixon had to work hard to repair the damage. After mollifying Eisenhower in a series of phone calls, he flew to Chicago and gave a press conference repudiating every allegation of surrender. He soothed the ruffled feathers of the Platform Committee and had one-on-one meetings with the Party's leading conservatives, bluntly reminding them that in order to win the presidential election 'a Republican candidate needed 90 per cent of his own party's vote, 50 per cent of the independent vote and 20 per cent of the Democratic vote. That argument finally quietened their concerns'.[86]

Nixon's toughest task was selling to the conservatives the liberal civil rights policy he had agreed with Rockefeller. The Platform Committee's draft proposal on this issue had been a moderate one but it avoided an outright declaration of support for Negro sit-in strikes at 'whites only' lunch counters in the South and made no promise of federal intervention to secure full job equality for Black workers. A discreet silence on these two issues, which had been the subject of strong interventionist pledges at the Democratic convention, would almost certainly have carried the Southern states for the GOP, and in retrospect would have won the election.

Nixon understood the political temptations of such a strategy, but rejected it. To his great credit he held out for the most liberal platform on civil rights ever to be accepted by the Republican Party. His decision, much praised by Theodore White and other commentators of the day, was a personal victory of principle over expediency. It was also a reminder that 'Tricky Dick', the ambitious political chameleon of the caricatures, was perhaps not so important in the Nixon persona as 'Young Richard', the boy whose Quaker heritage had instilled in him an unshakeable moral conscience on civil rights and racial equality.

After the struggle to win a moderate platform, the rest of the convention was an easy ride. On the evening of Wednesday 27 July Nixon was nominated on the first ballot as candidate for President by a vote of 1321 to 10. The following day he chose UN Ambassador Henry Cabot Lodge as his running mate. It was an odd choice, for the patrician Lodge was no vote-getter, having lost his Massachusetts Senate seat to John F. Kennedy in 1952. Nixon's main reason for preferring Lodge over the immediate alternatives of Congressman Walter Judd of Minnesota and RNC Chairman Thruston Morton of Kentucky was that experience in foreign policy would be a vital issue in the election. Many conservative delegates, however, were appalled by the choice of Lodge, Senator Barry Goldwater calling it 'a disastrous blunder'.[87]

Having achieved a platform of his liking, and a running mate of his choice, Nixon set about putting heart into his party with an acceptance speech which was the most remarkable feature of the convention, and which he described some thirty years later as 'the single most effective political address I ever made'.[88]

After three nights spent almost without sleep because of the wranglings over the platform, Nixon had not prepared his address as well as he had the other turning point speeches of his career. Even so it had many good lines:

> The Democrats 'promised everything to everybody with one exception: they didn't promise to pay the bill.'
>
> '...A record is not something to stand on, but something to build on.'
>
> '...Our next President must tell the people not what they want to hear, but what they need to hear. Why, for example, it may be just as essential to the national interest to build a dam in India as in California.'
>
> 'When Mr. Khrushchev says our grandchildren will live under Communism, let us say his grandchildren will live in freedom.'[89]

The final passages of the speech, which portrayed the making of a new world of peaceful coexistence and freedom under American leadership, caught the imagination of the delegates and of at least one international observer, the British Ambassador Sir Harold Caccia. He reported to London that Nixon had delivered

> a real *tour de force* which set the tone for the Republican campaign both in spirit and substance. The speech, which unlike Senator Kennedy's sounded better than it reads, struck all the right notes...personal humility, dedication to the Republican cause, awareness of the serious challenge of the 60s, a certain kindly condescension to his less experienced political opponents and a call to every last effort in a fight which he predicted would be one of the closest in American history. During both the acceptance speech and the whole convention ran this theme: 'Who is better qualified to run against the wily and bellicose Mr. Khrushchev?' It is plain that Mr. Nixon will run against Mr. Khrushchev as much as against Senator Kennedy...Mr. Nixon

intends to wage his own campaign with little thought for the past. While taking care not to criticise the President directly nor alienate the President's millions of admirers he will present himself as a young but experienced man with his face to the future.[90]

Nixon's decision to present himself as the candidate of experience was fully justified. In the past eight years he had prepared himself for the Presidency as no Vice President before him had ever been able to do. His participation at NSC, Cabinet and congressional leaders' meetings had given him a solid grounding in all matters of government from national security to national campaigning. As presiding officer of the Senate he had come to understand the ways of that powerful body better than any other living legislator apart from Lyndon Baines Johnson. In foreign affairs he had honed his intellectual and diplomatic skills to the point where he was respected all over the world as a coming international statesman. He had competently deputised for Eisenhower during two long periods of presidential illness. More than enhancing his own political prospects, however, he had transformed the office he held. Never before had a Vice President been so visible and influential on both the domestic and international stages. In part this was due to the accident of circumstance. Nixon was fortunate to have been given a significant role to play by a President who needed an active deputy. He was a politician in a Cabinet lacking politicians and so was drawn deeper into political battles than his predecessors had been. He represented the United States at a moment when its national prestige was at a peak, and when jet travel had for the first time made it possible for a Vice President to exert an influence around the globe. However, in larger part the increase in the power of the Vice Presidency was due to Nixon's own efforts. It was his character, industry and persistence that had allowed him to seize the opportunity to make his presence felt and his opinions heard.

Not all who listened liked what they heard. Domestic perceptions of him were still tarnished by considerable hostility, principally among opponents and the press. But any objective view of his performance and his qualifications would admit that he had raised the office of the Vice President to a new level, and that he was ready to ascend higher himself—to the White House. All he had to do was win the election.

FOURTEEN

A TALE OF TWO
DEFEATS

I. KENNEDY IN THE ASCENDANT

The 1960 presidential contest was the most exciting democratic election of the twentieth century. Mythology has always surrounded it. In that pre-Vietnam era of American supremacy the fight for the leadership of the free world's superpower was easily portrayed as a battle between supermen. Young, talented, and charismatic in their different ways, Kennedy and Nixon both lived up to this image. They would have been outstanding candidates at any time, and in the new age of television they were magnified to the status of heroic gladiators.

The events of the campaign, superbly recounted in Theodore H. White's seminal if partisan account, *The Making of the President 1960*, also contained the stuff of which legends are made. Some of the legends were true. The excitement inspired a higher percentage of the US electorate to go to the polls than at any time, before or since, in the history of the Republic. The televised debates became the political heavyweight championship of the world. Across the globe, a new generation of young people were turned on to politics by the vigour and passion of American democracy. The result, widely predicted as being too close to call, turned out to be almost too close to count. After an election night of heartstopping photofinishes in state after state, Kennedy was officially declared the winner by a margin of less than one tenth of one per cent. The agreed verdict of both myth and history is that no other presidential battle has come near to 1960 for glamour, drama, and suspense.

From Nixon's point of view, the legends looked rather different. The old saying that victory has a hundred fathers but defeat is an orphan was reversed in the Republican postmortems. At least a hundred excuses and 'if onlys' could be attached to Nixon's defeat, while Kennedy's victory had the one big question mark of electoral fraud hanging over it. Although these obsessions soon became academic, it is still relevant to try to answer two fundamental questions: Why did Nixon lose the 1960 election? Did he really lose it?

The vital statistics of the results give their own reasons why the answers to those questions are so problematical. 68.8 million ballots were cast for President, of which 34.2 million were for Kennedy (49.7 per cent) and 34.1 million were for Nixon (49.6 per cent), with minority parties accounting for the remaining 0.7 per cent. The margin between the two main candidates was 112,881 votes—less than one tenth of one per cent of all the votes cast. Kennedy won the election because his victories were concentrated in the more populous states which carried the greater number of electoral college votes. He was therefore declared to have been elected President by 303 electoral votes to Nixon's 219. However, when the results in individual states were studied, the question of who won what became more and more hair-raising.

Illinois was the most dramatic example of this uncertainty. Kennedy carried the state by a margin of 8,000 out of 4.7 million ballots cast. A switch of 4,000 would therefore have given the state's twenty-seven electoral college votes to Nixon. If Illinois had voted for a Republican President (and given the evidence of electoral fraud by Mayor Richard Daley's Democratic machine in Chicago, it may well have done), then Nixon would have needed only one other state to capture the White House. It could easily have been Missouri or South Carolina, where the margins were less than 13,000 votes each; or Texas—the principal state after Illinois in which there were serious allegations of fraud and ballot rigging. Without delving into the murky mysteries that clouded several such individual results, it can safely be asserted that Nixon would have won the Presidency of the United States in 1960 if only 12,000 voters out of 68,800,000* had switched their ballots to him in the one or two states which carry a high number of electoral college votes.

With a result that close, no definitive judgements are possible, and it seems reasonable to accept the mordant comment of Tom Wicker in the *New York Times*:

---

* This margin of defeat is the mathematical equivalent to the author losing his British Parliamentary seat by only nine votes, or to Speaker Tom Foley losing the 5th District of Washington State by only twenty-six votes.

'Nobody knows to this day whom the American people really elected President in 1960. Under the prevailing system John F. Kennedy was inaugurated but it is not at all clear if this was really the will of the people, or, if so, by what means and margin that will was expressed.'[1]

The will of the people, although impossible to measure by votes in the end result, was clearly affected by a clutch of pivotal episodes, six of which were significant enough to be described as 'swing factors', meaning that any one of them could have shifted enough votes to influence the outcome of the election. These swing factors were: the health of the candidates; the television debates; the Catholic vote; the Black vote; the choice of Vice President; and the Eisenhower factor. Nixon lost out on all of them; sometimes he was unlucky, sometimes he made wrong decisions, and sometimes he put decency before politics.

In the business of electioneering, good health is of paramount importance. A candidate communicates by transmitting energy. There are few better highs in public life than electrifying an audience with a personal supercharge of mental and physical vigour. There are not many worse lows than struggling through a period of campaigning while suffering from an illness. Nixon, who had never missed a speaking engagement in his entire career through bad health, had the supreme misfortune to be either sick or well below par for much of the 1960 campaign.

Nixon's health problems began on 17 August when he banged his knee against the edge of a car door in Greensboro, North Carolina. This seemingly minor injury became agonisingly painful as the joint swelled up with a severe infection which did not respond to hot compresses. The assistant White House physician, Dr. Walter Tkach, took a fluid tap and was so alarmed by the result that he ordered the Vice President to bed, with the warning, 'You'd better get out to the hospital or you will soon be campaigning on one leg.'[2] On 29 August Nixon was admitted to the Walter Reed Hospital where he underwent a two-week course of under-the-kneecap antibiotic injections to treat what had been diagnosed as a serious case of *hemolytic staphylococcus aureus*. Nixon was a fretful patient, saying afterwards that the pain 'was bad enough...but the mental suffering was infinitely worse'.[3] He was tortured by the TV news bulletins showing Kennedy drawing large crowds at Labor Day and other rallies throughout the early part of September.

With the polls showing that Kennedy had slipped into the lead by 51-49 per cent, Nixon left hospital prematurely. Instead of lightening his schedule, he intensified it, taking on a 9,000-mile speaking tour of fourteen states during the first week he was back on his feet. It was too much for him. A crack-up came on 12

September in St Louis, Missouri, where he woke at 3.30 a.m. shaking with a 103° temperature. His travelling physician, Dr. John Lungren, worked through the night to bring down the fever with massive doses of aspirin and antibiotics. These enabled Nixon to fulfil an 'essential' breakfast speaking engagement at 8.15 a.m. the same morning. He admitted afterwards that he had never felt weaker in his life as he walked to the podium.

This debilitating pattern repeated itself during the next two weeks. Nixon was plagued by night temperatures, chills and fevers. By sheer willpower he defied the laws of medicine and fought to maintain his schedule. Although he kept going, he lost ten pounds in weight and started to look like a sick man. Kennedy, meanwhile, looked and sounded in the peak of condition.

The contrast was paradoxical, for at the outset of the primaries Kennedy was thought to be the one contender for the Presidency who might have serious health problems. For all his outward appearance of youthful vitality he was a long-time sufferer from Addison's disease; he needed regular traction for his excruciating back pain; and he required daily cortisone injections. Nixon was aware of his rival's medical history. As Vice President he had visited Kennedy in hospital in November 1954, when the young Senator was feared to be dying from adrenal failure following a perilous spinal fusion operation. During the primaries, reports had reached Nixon about how Kennedy's hands had been seen shaking uncontrollably below the podium while he was making a speech— apparently a side effect of cortisone. Although urged by some of his supporters to make political capital out of his opponent's health troubles, particularly as the Kennedy team had not hesitated to exploit Lyndon Johnson's past problems of heart disease during the Democratic primaries, Nixon refused. He brushed aside suggestions of calling for the publication of Kennedy's medical records, saying that FDR had been an outstanding President in spite of polio, and that in any case, 'Anybody who can go through a presidential campaign is healthy enough to be President.'[4] It was ironic that Nixon came close to failing his own test in the early weeks of the election.

Health was to play a vital role in the first televised debate, which took place in Chicago on Monday 26 September. After a hard week of barnstorming through eleven states, a tired Nixon arrived just before midnight at O'Hare Airport, where he was greeted by a crowd of 5,000 supporters. Instead of going straight to bed with the fever that was still troubling him, he went on a tour of street rallies in each of the city's five wards, finally reaching his hotel at 1 a.m. On the Monday morning he delivered a major speech to the United Brotherhood of Carpenters and Joiners. This was a hostile union audience which gave him such a rough reception that it sapped his vitality and unnerved him.

As if to restore his confidence, Nixon went into purdah for the afternoon. For six hours he worked alone in his hotel suite, cramming his mind with facts and figures. The first debate was assigned to domestic policy issues, so he concentrated on making himself statistic-perfect on a wide range of economic and labour topics which he thought Kennedy was likely to raise. This solitary study session took longer than expected. Like an anxious law school examinee with case names swimming in his head, Nixon continued to sweat over his notes until it was time to go down to the studio. He even cancelled his afternoon appointment with his media consultants. The only briefing he received on the setting, make-up, lighting and other technical aspects of the debate came from an amateur television adviser, Ted Rogers, during the ten-minute car ride from the hotel to the TV station. Whatever Rogers said was obliterated by a small but agonising accident. As Nixon climbed out of his car he once again cracked his knee on the edge of the door. A reporter noticed that his face, already gaunt from a 100° temperature and loss of weight, went 'all white and pasty'.[5]

Kennedy's preparations were something completely different. Arriving in Chicago a day and a half before the debate, he had set up a relaxed Monday schedule. It included a suntan on the hotel rooftop; a carefree lunch with friends; a nap, and a couple of question-and-answer sessions with three of his closest advisers. These were conducted with Kennedy lying on his bed in a white, open-necked T-shirt and army suntan pants, gaily spinning fact cards to the floor once he felt he had mastered the brief on each subject.[6]

The final act of preparation was even more unconventional, according to Kennedy aide, Langdon Marvin.

> The night before the debate, Jack said to me, 'Any girls lined up for tomorrow?' So I made arrangements to have a girl waiting for him in a room at the Palmer House. I took him down there about ninety minutes before airtime, rode up in the elevator with him, introduced him to the girl (she'd been prepaid for her services), then stood guard in the corridor outside the hotel room. Jack evidently enjoyed himself, because he emerged fifteen minutes later with an ear-to-ear grin on his face.
>
> During the debate he looked the picture of self-assurance and good health. Nixon, meanwhile, looked like an escaped convict—

pallid, perspiring, beady-eyed. Jack was so pleased by the results he
insisted we line up a girl for him before each of the debates.[7]

Nixon, who had enjoyed no such horizontal diversions, did indeed look
macabre on camera. His shirt collar hung limply around his neck as a result of
his ten-pound weight loss. His face was pale and wan. He wore no make-up apart
from a light coating of powder, which accentuated the heaviness of his jowls. As
Theodore White saw him, Nixon was 'tense, almost frightened, at turns glower-
ing and occasionally haggard looking to the point of sickness...no picture in
American politics tells a better story of crisis and episode than that famous shot
of the camera on the Vice President as he half slouched, his Lazy Shave powder
faintly streaked with sweat, his eyes exaggerated hollows of blackness, his jaw,
jowls and face drooping with the strain'.[8]

From a more neutral diplomatic corner, the British embassy reported to
London:

> Neither candidate came through as a human being...Senator Ken-
> nedy, visibly keyed up, opened with a prepared speech which he
> rattled off like machine-gun fire in a harsh, almost croaking voice.
> Though much of what he said was an appeal to emotion, he might
> for all his expression or persuasiveness of style have been presenting
> a statistical analysis to a group of economists...Mr. Nixon was not
> dissimilar. But what struck me most about him was his appearance.
> He seems in the last few weeks to have aged and shrivelled and the
> way in which his tongue kept darting in and out of his lips was posi-
> tively reptilian. Although both candidates are trying to stress their
> ripe age and maturity, Mr. Nixon seemed to have gone too far. He
> looked small and old.[9]

Some of these appearance problems were exacerbated by the hardball tactics
of Kennedy's television advisers. Some years after the debates, Nixon's staff learned
from a reliable Democratic source that the Kennedy people had asked for the
principals to stand up throughout the debate in the belief that this would cause
discomfort to Nixon's weak knee; that they had demanded an unusually warm
temperature in the studio because they knew Nixon tended to perspire easily; and
that during the live transmission they had put pressure on the studio director in
the control room to make him show candid close-ups of Nixon mopping his brow.[10]

Whether these alleged activities by the Democrats had much effect on the perception of Nixon by the viewing audience of 73 million is open to doubt. The subsequent polls tended to confirm the judgement of the British embassy's report to London which concluded that most of the electorate were not moved in any direction by the first debate. However, the telegram also shrewdly noted that while 'Kennedy's detractors were reluctantly impressed... Nixon's supporters were dismayed by his performance'.[11]

The last part of that statement was entirely accurate. Many Republicans had been anticipating that the experienced Vice President would wipe the floor with his junior opponent. When this did not happen, their instant reactions of dismay ranged from Hannah Nixon in Whittier calling up to ask whether her son was ill, to Henry Cabot Lodge in Texas swearing to his aides 'that son of a bitch has just lost us the election'.[12]

Although the visual impression of Nixon was unfortunate, his actual performance on the substantive issues was good. The majority of the 12 million strong radio audience thought the Vice President had been the clear winner of the first debate, while among newspaper editorial writers, the general consensus was that the contest had been a draw. Nevertheless, the polls taken among the 73 million television viewers gave Kennedy the edge. That victory of the images came as a short-term boost for the Democrats, but it was not sustained. In the three subsequent debates, Nixon looked and performed much better. With the help of a new make-up artist, a fattening-up regime of four rich milk shakes a day with his meals; and some improvement in his general health, he regained most of his form. However, he did not recover what should have been his trump card of greater authority over Kennedy. Before the debates, the junior senator from Massachusetts was thought to be an unequal match for the two-term Vice President of the United States. After they were over, it was clear that the younger politician had held his ground. The debates were thus an equaliser for Kennedy, not a destroyer of Nixon. Even so, their effects on the polls were negligible. Before the first screen confrontation on 26 September, Gallup had shown Kennedy leading by 51 per cent to 49 per cent. After the final foreign policy debate on 21 October, the same poll showed Kennedy at 50.5 per cent and Nixon at 49.5 per cent. So at the end of three weeks of media hype and hullabaloo, public opinion put the candidates back where they had started—neck and neck. Subjectively, the laurels seemed to go to Kennedy, who was widely perceived to have won the debates, if only because he looked better and did not emerge as the loser. Objectively, the evidence suggests that voter loyalties were unaffected.

Voter loyalties did move in mysterious ways among two important minorities, the Catholics and the Negroes. Kennedy's Catholicism was initially seen as an electoral disadvantage. It might well have turned out that way if Nixon had not handled the religious issue with a sensitivity that was wholly honourable.

America had never elected a Catholic President. The previous Catholic candidate, Governor Al Smith in 1928, was thought to have lost many votes because of his religious affiliation. Thirty-two years later, there were still millions of voters in the Protestant majority whose prejudice affected their politics. Coming from a religious minority group himself, Nixon deplored such bigotry. He went out of his way to stamp on all manifestations of the Protestant backlash. Two days after leaving hospital, he appeared on 'Meet the Press' on 11 September, where he was questioned about Kennedy's possible conflict of loyalties between Pope and country. 'I have no doubt whatever about Senator Kennedy's loyalty or about his ability to put the Constitution of the United States above any consideration', replied Nixon. He said he intended to keep religion completely out of the campaign and that he had ordered his supporters 'not to discuss religion, not to raise it, not to allow anybody to participate in the campaign who does so'.[13]

Nixon maintained this position even when it became apparent that the religious issue was unexpectedly hurting him rather than Kennedy. In the closing days of the campaign, Republican Catholics were being urged by the Democrats to vote for JFK, while Republican Protestants were being asked to do likewise—in order to prove that they were not prejudiced! Democratic TV commercials also played the religious card blatantly, using the theme that no one had asked Kennedy about his Catholicism when he had fought for his country in the Pacific. Such tactics came close to an attempt to turn the election into a referendum between tolerance and intolerance.

As private polls began to indicate that the traditional Republican Catholic vote was avalanching to Kennedy, Nixon's staff unanimously advised him to make a speech criticising his opponent's use of 'reverse bigotry'. Among the most vocal advocates of this recommendation were the Catholic members of the Vice President's team. One of these was Peter Flanigan, a twenty-seven-year old New York investment banker who had been a contemporary of Bobby Kennedy's at the Benedictine school of Portsmouth Abbey, Rhode Island.

'I was appalled that we were doing nothing to deter the flight of the Catholic voters so I went to RN with some suggestions for advertisements that might stem the tide', recalled Flanigan. 'He chewed me out. "Don't you play the religious card under any circumstances whatever", he told me. "I absolutely forbid you to do anything which suggests that my campaign has a religious bias to it."'[14]

This abhorrence of making political capital out of religion was Nixon's strong moral conviction. It stemmed directly from his heritage of Quaker tolerance and touched something deep within him. He could not have been more sincere or more effective when it came to keeping religion off the Republican Party's campaigning agenda. He was deeply shocked when he realised that certain Democrats, particularly Robert Kennedy, were exploiting the issue with such ruthless cunning.

The contrast between the Republican and Democratic handling of the religious question cost Nixon vital support in key areas of the country. Post-election polls showed that he received less of the Catholic vote, 22 per cent, than any Republican candidate in the twentieth century. By contrast, Eisenhower in 1956 had received 60 per cent of the Catholic vote. In the northern industrial states, where the margins were agonisingly close, Kennedy's extraordinarily high Catholic support appeared to have made the difference. The Democrats captured seven of the ten states where the 1960 consensus statistics showed the Catholic population to be the highest. In Illinois, which was won by a plurality of 8,000 votes out of 4.7 million, the strong Catholic vote in Chicago was more than enough to give the Democratic ticket the edge it needed.

All this was distressing to Nixon, but he had no regrets about his handling of the Catholic question. The day after his defeat, on the flight back from Los Angeles to Washington, he told Flanigan, 'Pete, here's one thing we can be satisfied about. This campaign has laid to rest for ever the issue of a candidate's religion in presidential politics. Bad for me perhaps, but good for America.'[15]

Peter Flanigan was stunned by this conversation, later describing it as 'true nobility in defeat'.[16] Even when seen in more prosaic terms, the fact remains that Nixon, widely perceived as among the most unscrupulous of politicians, behaved so scrupulously about religion in politics that he allowed himself to be damaged by the politics of religion. It was a cruel and unlucky factor in his defeat.

Nixon also received a disappointingly low percentage of the Negro vote, again for unlucky reasons. At the start of the campaign he had expected to run well in Black districts. His record on civil rights was respected by many Negro leaders, especially by the influential King family. The Reverend Martin Luther King Junior had been generous in his praise of the Vice President from the time when they joined forces to support the 1957 Civil Rights Act, and Martin Luther King Senior had publicly endorsed Nixon early in the primaries. All this changed after 19 October, when Martin Luther King Junior was arrested during a sit-in at an Atlanta department store. The judge trying the case on 26 October sentenced him to four months' imprisonment on the grounds that King had broken the parole imposed on him some weeks earlier for driving without a valid licence.

With emotions running high in the South, the Kennedys were quick to appreciate the huge political potential of a sympathetic public response to King's misfortune. John Kennedy called Mrs. Coretta King to assure her that he would do everything he could to help her husband. Bobby Kennedy made an even more decisive call to the judge in the case, urging him to release the Black preacher because of fears that he could be lynched in prison. Nixon, who also believed that King had been treated shamefully, considered making similar calls but decided against them on the grounds that they would be 'grandstanding'.[17]

Nixon took the view that contacting the judge would be an improper act contrary to the American Bar Association's rules of professional conduct. Instead, he talked to Attorney General William Rogers, making the suggestion that the Justice Department should intervene to protect King's constitutional rights. Rogers agreed and sought White House approval for an intervention, but Eisenhower was reluctant to move. As these private discussions were going on within the Government, Nixon's Press Secretary, Herb Klein, put out a statement that the Vice President had 'no comment' on the incident. 'This was a fatal communication gap', Nixon said later. 'I had meant Herb to say that I had no comment *at this time*?[18] Meanwhile, the judge made a decision to release Martin Luther King. In Negro newspaper reports of the episode (the white media ignored the story completely), Nixon was condemned for his silence, while Kennedy was lauded as a saviour. Martin Luther King Senior reversed his earlier endorsement of the Vice President, declaring, 'I've got a suitcase of votes and I'm going to take them to Mr. Kennedy and dump them in his lap.'[19]

In Black churches all over the country, the faithful were advised from pulpits and in pamphlets that votes should be switched from 'No Comment Nixon' to 'The Candidate with a heart—Senator Kennedy'.[20] This message was fuelled by Kennedy money. In those days it was common practice for political parties to subsidise certain Black churches in order to sway the votes of their congregations. 'I wasn't up to speed on that. We didn't ever do it in California', recalled Nixon. 'But Len Hall knew all about it. The party had been doing it for years. So he made an attempt to give contributions and so forth to some of the black preachers in orders to get their support. He had a pretty good fund to do that. But he came back to me and said, "My God, I've never seen anything like it. I've paid these fellows more than they ever got before and Joe Kennedy's come in there and raised me every time. We didn't get one of 'em."'[21]

Outspent and outmanoeuvred, Nixon's loss of Negro support hurt him badly. The Republicans had held 40 per cent of the Black vote in 1956. Nixon was expecting to do at least as well in 1960, but he won only 20–25 per cent of it. In several individual states, this trend sounded the death knell to his chances of winning the Presidency. In Illinois Nixon lost by 8,000 with 250,000 Blacks voting for Kennedy. In South Carolina Nixon lost by 10,000, with 40,000 Blacks in Kennedy's column. In Missouri Nixon's margin of defeat was 35,000, with a Black vote for Kennedy of 100,000. It is hard to resist the conclusion that for the want of a telephone call, an election was lost.

II. TOO CLOSE TO CALL

Nixon was unlucky with individuals as well as with political groups in the 1960 campaign. His vice-presidential running mate, Henry Cabot Lodge, proved to be a drag on the ticket. Selected by Nixon for his foreign policy credentials and for his qualifications to step into the Presidency, Lodge emerged as the least industrious campaigner on either ticket and was prone to embarrassing gaffes. On 12 September, speaking in Harlem, he announced that 'there should be a Negro in the Cabinet...it is part of our program and it is offered as a pledge'.[22] Lodge had not cleared the statement with Nixon, who was justifiably furious and had to issue a correction saying that the Cabinet would contain 'the best men possible' and that 'a man's race or religion would not be a factor either for or against him'.[23] The crude attempt on the part of Henry Cabot Lodge to buy votes and his subsequent vacillations on the matter offended voters of all areas and races, particularly in the South.

By contrast, Kennedy's running mate, Lyndon Johnson, barnstormed brilliantly throughout the Southern states, presenting himself in various alternative roles as the grandson of a Confederate soldier; a homely Texas rancher; the Negroes' friend; the defender of traditional Dixieland values; and the 'good ole boy' turned 'pol' who would deliver for his friends in Washington. It was difficult for anyone to compete with LBJ going all the way, and particularly for Lodge. He was an aloof Boston Brahmin with a lackadaisical approach to campaigning. Following the Negro in the Cabinet shambles, a loyal Nixon secretary, Margery Petersen, was seconded to Lodge to act as a discreet minder and coordinator of statements. She was appalled by the attitude of her new boss: 'I got the feeling that Mr. Lodge thought campaigning was almost beneath him', she recalled. 'He would go off for weekends. He liked to take afternoon naps. He kept on making mistakes in his speeches, and he was surrounded by Boston people who were just so defeatist. I remember when we were close to winning in the final stages, Mr. Lodge and his team spent time preparing an election night statement. When I saw it, I just couldn't believe my eyes. It was a concession statement! I refused to type it.'[24]

In spite of the loyalists' strong feelings about Lodge, it should be remembered that one of the oldest axioms of presidential elections is that whatever the vice-presidential candidates do or say, they never affect the end result. Was 1960 the exception to this rule? Probably yes. By his bravura performance on the stump, Lyndon Johnson unexpectedly won Texas and other Southern states for Kennedy, whereas Lodge clearly cost the Republicans some votes. Although he never said so publicly, Nixon in later life admitted that he made a mistake in the selection of his running mate.[25] He wished he had picked Senator Thruston Morton of Kentucky, a gifted and energetic campaigner who would have been a worthy match for LBJ in the battle for the South.

The other eminent Republican who, on balance, had a negative effect on Nixon's chances was Eisenhower. The relationship between President and Vice President had always been a complex one and in the election year the complications were greater than usual. Ike certainly wanted Nixon to win. He was appalled by the Kennedy–Johnson ticket, holding a low opinion of JFK, whom he described as 'an upstart who knows nothing about military matters'[26] and taking an even poorer view of LBJ, whom he saw as 'the most tricky and unreliable politician in Congress'.[27]

In spite of his strong anti-Democrat attitudes, Eisenhower was not entirely helpful to the Republican cause. He had pressed for Lodge's selection as the running mate, which turned out to be a bad political judgement. He was defensive about the record of his administration, and became prickly whenever Nixon needed to take a more distinctive line of his own. The dispute over the handling of the economy was case in point. Towards the end of 1959, Nixon had correctly foreseen that a recession was on its way. Fearing the electoral consequences, he urged a policy of reflation. Ike, who predicted in January that America would have 'the most prosperous year in our history',[28] did not see any need to change course. When the unemployment figures started to rise during the summer, Nixon's advice was finally heeded. The Federal Reserve Board loosened credit in June, but it was a case of too little too late. By the time of the election in November, the numbers of newly unemployed workers in Illinois, New Jersey, Michigan, Minnesota, Missouri and South Carolina were greater than the numbers of voters by which Nixon lost those states. Nixon ran worst in the cities with the highest proportion of unemployed. A few months after the election, certain Republican financial experts came to believe that Eisenhower's reluctance to expand the economy was the single most important factor in the loss of the election. A belated convert to that point of view was Eisenhower's Treasury Secretary, George Humphrey, who told Nixon in 1962, 'I think we kept the reins too tight too long. If we had loosened up on the money supply just a bit in the spring, we would not have had that downturn and the election results might well have been different.'[29]

Eisenhower's refusal to reflate was at least an understandable error of judgement. No such qualification can be applied to the wounding public insult Ike delivered on the subject of the Vice President's role in the Administration. This bizarre episode occurred at a White House press conference on 27 August. Reporters were pressing for details about Nixon's record as a decision maker in government. Eisenhower gave vague replies. Charles Mohr of *Time* magazine persisted. Could the President give an example of one idea of Nixon's that he had adopted? Thoroughly irritated, Eisenhower snapped back, 'If you give me a week, I might think of one. I don't remember.'[30]

Those fourteen words could hardly have been more damaging to Nixon, whose principal campaign theme was his record of experience as Vice President. The Democrats, who were vulnerable to the claim that Kennedy was too immature, seized on Eisenhower's maladroit comment and exploited it mercilessly. The quotation was used against Nixon to greatest effect in the first television debate. He could only reply defensively: 'I would suggest that if you know the President, that was probably a facetious remark.'[31]

The explanation for Eisenhower's outburst lay in bad temper rather than good humour. Immediately after the 27 August press conference, the President called Nixon to apologise, putting forward several rather lame excuses. These were that he had been caught unawares; that he had been joking; and that his 'give me a week' remark had been intended to mean he would answer the question at his next press conference. None of these explanations sounded convincing. Nixon put a different interpretation on the gaffe, after hearing from his secretary Rose Mary Woods about her conversation on the subject with Eisenhower's secretary Ann Whitman. According to Whitman, the President had been in a spectacularly black mood throughout the whole week leading up to the press conference. The cause for this ill humour was that Eisenhower had suddenly begun to realise his term was ending. Disturbed by how the nation's attention was turning towards Nixon and Kennedy, he grew increasingly short-tempered with his staff, visitors and Cabinet officers. Eventually his frustrations boiled over in front of the journalists at the press conference. Nixon, who was sensitive to Ike's withdrawal symptoms, accepted this explanation and showed forbearance over the incident. Even in private, he did not criticise the President, saying, 'It was just one of those unfortunate slips',[32] but he was under no illusions about the political damage that had been done.

Eisenhower planned to make amends for any such damage by taking on a heavy schedule of electioneering. It was agreed that the most effective strategy would be for him to remain above the battle until late October and then to come out fighting. 'We felt that his appearances in the last two weeks of the campaign might tip the balance to me in some close areas in key states', explained Nixon,[33] who by that time was trailing three or four points behind his opponent in the polls.

At first the strategy worked superbly. When the moment came for him to enter the fray, Eisenhower was like a geyser ready to explode. He had been bottling up his anger over Kennedy's attacks on the Administration's defence policy, and was especially incensed by the bogus allegation of a 'missile gap' in the nation's security arrangements.

Ike with his dander up was an exhilarating campaigner. Those who travelled with him on his swings through Pittsburgh, Cleveland and New York thought he had never made sharper or more passionate speeches—even in his own presidential elections. 'Crisp, fresh and dramatic... I assume, as do most other observers, that the force of Eisenhower in the last ten days of the campaign was one of the great support bursts in the Nixon surge', wrote Theodore White.[34] One observer who agreed with this assumption was Nixon himself. Excited as he watched the gap in the polls narrowing fast, he arranged a lunch with Eisenhower on 3 October to make plans for enlarging the presidential campaigning schedule so that it included the crucial states of Michigan, Missouri and Illinois in the days running up to the poll.

This meeting was an embarrassment. According to White, Nixon 'was at the point of utter exhaustion, so beat that he couldn't think either clearly or quickly... the conversation at the table was completely irrelevant'.[35] This was all an act. By the time he reached the lunch table at the White House, Nixon had been put in the difficult position of having to tell the President that his services in the key states were no longer required. This was doubly painful because Ike was raring to go, and Nixon needed him badly.

The cause of the volte-face was Mamie Eisenhower. The night before the lunch she had made a highly emotional phone call to Pat Nixon. According to the distraught First Lady, her husband's heart was once again in bad shape. She was terrified that he might not survive the high-pressure schedule of electioneering. She begged Pat to get Dick to stop the plan, adding the rider, 'but Ike must never know I called you'.[36] Nixon received further corroboration about the state of the President's heart from the White House physician, Major General Howard Snyder. He told the Vice President that the strain of intense campaigning might be too much for Eisenhower's limited cardiac reserves. 'Please either talk him out of it or just don't let him do it for the sake of his health', urged Snyder.[37]

After these appeals, Nixon felt he had no option but to stand the President down. However, he was too inhibited to give Eisenhower a direct explanation. Nixon has recalled that his lame excuses made the President, 'confused, to put it mildly...at first he was hurt and then he was angry...he finally acquiesced. His pride prevented him from saying anything but I knew he was puzzled and frustrated by my conduct'.[38]

Who knows whether Eisenhower's magic would have made the vital difference in the razor-edge states like Illinois and Missouri? The question remains just one more of the tantalising 'if onlys' of the campaign. In his somewhat inept way, Nixon had again done the decent thing, but this pattern of decency was costing him dear. His reactions to the religious issue; to the suggestion that he should call the judge in the Martin Luther King case; and to the Mamie Eisenhower request, were all honourable responses. A really ruthless politician might have acted more self-servingly in all three episodes. Nixon in 1960 was beginning to bear a resemblance to the nineteenth-century British statesman Sir Austen Chamberlain, of whom it was written: 'He always played the game, and he always lost it.'[39]

Two weeks before polling day, Nixon looked like a loser. Gallup showed him five points behind Kennedy—and slipping. His staff were pessimistic. All sorts of small issues were going wrong. One of these, which received disproportionate attention at the time, was the story of the Hughes loan. This minor mystery featured Nixon's younger brother Donald, a small-time entrepreneur based in Whittier who had expanded the original family grocery store and gas station to include a coffee shop and a couple of drive-in restaurants serving 'Nixonburgers'. To develop his enterprises, Don needed to raise money and was granted a loan from a local bank of approximately $100,000. However, before anything was signed with the bank, representatives of the reclusive aviation tycoon Howard Hughes arrived at Don Nixon's office and offered him a loan from the Hughes Tool Company of $205,000.

'The strange thing was that Don never asked for that loan', recalled Clara Jane Nixon, Donald's widow. 'He never had any contact with Howard Hughes. He was as surprised as anyone when Frank Waters and Vic Johnson, who he thought of as friends, came and offered him the money. They told him, "The man says you are to have this", and Don, who was one of those people who float along with the tide, just accepted it. Dick never knew the first thing about it.[40]

This simple account, given by Clara Jane Nixon in 1990, is far more believable than the sensational tales of intrigue and corruption that rolled off the typewriters of certain journalists in 1960. Drew Pearson and other investigative reporters surmised that Hughes companies had received 'tens of millions of dollars'[41] worth of favours from the US Government in tax rulings and airline route authorisations in return for the loan to Don Nixon. Such theories were pure fantasy. They required a belief that the Vice President of the United States could exercise power over government agencies like the Justice Department, the Federal Aviation Agency and the Internal Revenue Service (Nixon certainly did not); that the Nixon brothers were in close financial cahoots (they never were); and that the various government rulings given on the Hughes company transactions involved bias by Cabinet officers of the stature of Attorney General Herbert Brownell and Treasury Secretary George Humphrey. Such scenarios were inconceivable.

The far more likely explanation is that Don Nixon was so naïve that he gladly accepted a loan for his business on over-generous terms without suspecting that the lender might have ulterior political motives. Just what Howard Hughes's ulterior motives may have been is pure speculation. He was a weird billionaire who enjoyed buying a hold over politicians. Perhaps he hoped that a favour to Don Nixon would provide him with some indirect influence on the Vice President. If that was the strategy it failed abysmally on this occasion, since Don Nixon's companies went bust; Hughes lost his loan money; and the resulting embarrassment all round destroyed any prospects for influence peddling. No one ever produced a shred of conflict of interest evidence against Richard Nixon. Seen in retrospect, the story looks as though it was an unjustified media stunt, which in any case made no impact on the presidential election. The episode did, however, have some later repercussions on Nixon's attitude to the press.

The media kerfuffle over the Hughes loan was symptomatic of a deeper Nixon problem—his difficulty in getting fair coverage in the press. This was a perennial complaint among Republican loyalists, who usually failed to acknowledge that the flaws in the relationship were by no means one-sided.

At the time of the 1960 election, the Washington press corps consisted of about one hundred columnists and specialist reporters. The majority of them were liberal in their politics and antagonistic towards the Vice President personally. This last attitude was mutual. Journalists often brought out the insecurities in Nixon. The chemistry of his response to their presence made him appear aloof, suspicious, and brusque. Such a stance was hardly likely to win the hearts and minds of the press contingent accompanying him. It should also be recorded that many of Nixon's speeches on the stump were full of those hackneyed and corny Republican clichés which caused 'the folks' of Middle America to throw up their hands and cheer while the accompanying liberal reporters just wanted to throw up. 'He was just so icky, so yucky—humorless, self-righteous and smarmy', recalled Mary McGrory of the *Washington Post*,[42] while Harrison Salisbury, who covered Nixon for the *New York Times,* remembered 'a terrible sleazy quality that crept into many of his appearances'.[43] These harsh comments were not always unfair, for Nixon when exhausted, demoralised, and campaigning on politician's autopilot, could indeed turn in some terrible performances. However, the grava-men of the charge of bias should not be directed against the scepticism of the reporters travelling with Nixon but rather to the adulation of those who were covering Kennedy.

Kennedy had many attractions to the press. He had a charming, outgoing personality. He was something of a journalist *manqué*. He enjoyed the company of reporters, understood their trade, and knew how to praise or criticise their writings with an interest that was highly flattering. Yet there was more to his success than media manipulation. As the campaign approached its climax, his charisma and sense of mission swept many journalists away from their moorings of objectivity, and converted them to willing swimmers on the floodtide of Ken-nedymania. Theodore White caught the spirit of JFK's press corps in a telling paragraph of *The Making of the President 1960*:

> By the last weeks of the campaign those forty or fifty national cor-respondents who had followed Kennedy since the beginning of his electoral exertions into the November days had become more than a press corps—they had become his friends and some of them his most devoted admirers. When the bus or the plane rolled or flew through the night, they sang songs of their own composition about Mr. Nixon and the Republicans in chorus with the Kennedy staff, and felt that they too were marching like soldiers of The Lord to the New Frontier.[44]

If Nixon had lost the press, he had not yet lost the people. All observers agree that the final week of the election produced a last-minute surge for him and his party. In spite of all the negative forces recorded in the last few pages, somehow or other Nixon fought back from the position of certain loser to neck-and-neck equal. The polls said it. The campaign teams felt it. The candidates knew it. In response to the pressures of the coming photo finish, the two contenders hero-ically increased the pace of their schedules on the stump. Kennedy shrewdly concentrated on the big states of the northeast and midwest, drawing ecstatic crowds of up to 250,000 people. Nixon, in obstinate defiance of his campaign manager's advice, insisted on an irrelevant deviation to Alaska in order to fulfil his convention pledge that he would campaign in all fifty states. It was a promise he could well have ignored, using the excuse of his two weeks in hospital, for the eighteen-hour trip to Anchorage cost him precious time away from the key districts. This was an error of judgement, but it was offset by other good decisions and effective speeches. On TV and on the hustings, Nixon was hurting his opponent with jibes about 'Jumping Jack... the Pied Piper who says give me your money and I will solve all your problems... who promises vast new spending programs but no new taxes who urges "intervention" in Cuba but then says he means only moral intervention... he's like the old town medicine man who gets out of town just before the people catch up with his quack remedies'.[45]

Such rhetoric seemed to be narrowing the contest, but the pace was a killer. California, which had been showing a clear lead for Kennedy, started to put Nixon ahead by a nose after a blitz of TV appearances and whistlestops. The eventual recapturing of his home state was a near miracle, although it left the candidate not only dead tired, but even on one occasion giving the impression that he might be dead.

The incident occurred after a backbreaking day which ended well after midnight in a hotel at Stockton, California. Arriving in his suite, Nixon slumped into a chair and fell into a sleep so deep that he could not be woken up, even by shaking or by shouting. Bill Rogers, who discovered him in this condition, feared a coma and called in Nixon's most trusted personal aide Don Hughes with the words: 'I think we've got a big problem.' For a moment Hughes also feared the worst, but knowing that Nixon had not touched pills or alcohol he correctly diagnosed a case of total exhaustion. Hughes and Rogers gently carried the comatose Vice President to his bed. 'As we tucked him in, suddenly Nixon stirred for the first time and mumbled, "I think God is with us"', recalled Hughes. 'It came from somewhere very deep inside him. It was quite a moment.'[46]

Don Hughes shared one other deep moment with his boss on the afternoon of Election Day, Tuesday 7 November. It occurred in the chapel of the Virgin Mary at the Mission of San Juan Capistrano, sixty miles south of Los Angeles. Nixon was there incognito. Just after casting his vote in front of the world's cameras in Whittier, he made an impulsive decision and told his police driver to escape from the cavalcade of press men and political supporters. Having given them all the slip, he headed south on the San Diego freeway, accompanied only by Hughes and a secret service agent. Suddenly he drove off the main road, saying to his aide, 'You're one of my favourite Catholics, so I'll take you to one of my favourite Catholic places.' They turned inland to the Mission of San Juan Capistrano.

Initially avoiding the nuns and the handful of tourists, they walked straight to the exquisite little eighteenth-century chapel, with its Indian paintings and sixteenth-century Barcelona altar. For about fifteen minutes Nixon and his companion sat alone in the empty pews, profoundly silent in their thoughts and prayers.[47]

If there was any Divine intervention on election night, it was on the side of the Democrats. In thirteen gripping pages of his book *Six Crises,* Nixon has described the agonies and the ecstasies he went through as the tide of votes ebbed and flowed. In state after state, the results were cliffhangers. Eventually, by the tiniest of margins, the luck moved in Kennedy's favour and he edged within four electoral college votes of the absolute majority required. Shortly after midnight, Nixon, who was being accused by some TV commentators of being 'a poor sport'[48] for not conceding, decided he must make a statement. With his arm around a tearful Pat, he made an emotional but gracious speech to his supporters, finally telling them, 'While...there are still some results to come in, if the present trend continues Senator Kennedy will be the next President of the United States.'[49]

To the ears of some Republicans, this comment seemed dangerously premature. 'No, no, don't concede!' they shouted. There was a certain logic in these protests since California, Michigan, Minnesota and Illinois had yet to declare, and if three of them were to go to Nixon, he could yet become the next President. To this day there are old GOP professionals who insist that Nixon's quasi-concession was a mistake because it caused the Republican scrutineers to abandon their vigils of the Chicago ballots, with disastrous consequences for the Illinois result. The criticism is misplaced, but it serves as yet another illustration of the heartbreaking closeness of the final result.

Around four o'clock in the morning, Nixon dozed off into an unhappy sleep. He was woken by thirteen-year-old Julie, wanting to know the election outcome. 'I'm afraid we have lost', answered her father.

Julie burst into tears, asking in her anguish: 'What are we going to do? Where are we going to live? What kind of a job are you going to be able to get?'[50]

Nixon had no answers.

III. DIGNITY IN DEFEAT

In the immediate aftermath of the election, there were calls for a recount. The evidence of fraud was too convincing for these to be easily ignored. Attention focused on Illinois and Texas, whose Democratic machines had a long history of corrupt electoral practices. In the Lone Star State, investigative journalists and others found widespread evidence of stolen ballot papers, dead men's votes, phoney registers and plain vanilla frauds. Earl Mazo, writing in the *New York Herald Tribune,* made the calculation that in Texas 'a minimum of 100,000 votes for the Kennedy–Johnson ticket simply were non-existent',[51] backing the claim with specifics such as the polling station in which 6,138 votes were counted although only 4,895 voters were registered.[52] In a state which had given its twenty-four electoral college votes to Kennedy by a margin of 46,000 out of 2.3 million (or less than 1/50 of the votes counted) the 'stolen election' allegation began to look plausible. That charge was even more convincing in Illinois, where the margins were far closer. Nixon had comfortably won a huge majority in the state's non-metropolitan areas, but was eventually defeated by a surprisingly strong Democratic surge from Chicago. The city went to Kennedy by 450,000, making him the overall winner of Illinois' twenty-seven electoral college votes by the nail-biting majority of 8,000 out of 4.7 million ballots cast (or less than 1/550 of the votes counted).

There was plenty of evidence to suggest that this was a false result. Suspicion focused on the conduct of Mayor Richard Daley, who had long controlled the Democratic machine in the Windy City with legendary ruthlessness. On election night 'King Richard' held back Chicago's returns until all the results from the rural areas were in, thus establishing precisely how many votes were needed for a statewide plurality. Then he went to work, calling Kennedy in the small hours of the morning to say, 'Mr. President, with a little bit of luck and the help of a few close friends, you're going to carry Illinois.'[53] Most of those 'few close friends' seem to have been the familiar collection of dead, bribed, ghost and multiple voters. Again it was Earl Mazo of the *New York Herald Tribune* who published the specifics. They included evidence of individual voters who had cast up to six ballot papers; of precinct captains giving cash payments outside polling stations; and pre-primed voting machines, one of which was caught recording 121 ballots cast after only forty-three people had voted.[54] With increasing evidence of fraud flowing in, particularly from Cook County, the temperature rose sharply on the 'stolen election' issue in Chicago. Many leading Republicans, including President Eisenhower, urged Nixon to make a formal legal challenge to the result. Nixon's refusal to demand a recount in the 1960 election was one of the finest hours of his career. His reasons were a mixture of *realpolitik,* responsibility and reverence for the Presidency.

America had never held a recount in a presidential election. The machinery for one simply did not exist. On his own initiative, Bob Finch checked out the legal position in the half-dozen or so states where there had been a combination of close results and allegations of voter fraud. 'The position was impossible. Every state law was different,' he has recalled. 'In Arkansas, Missouri, and the Carolinas you couldn't get a recount until the legislature had been recalled. In Illinois, a recount would have taken a year and a half and even then I doubt whether you would ever have gotten the truth about what happened on the night in Cook County. In Texas there were no provisions for any sort of recount. The whole business would have been a constitutional nightmare.'[55]

In the early days of December, Nixon carefully thought through the implications of this scenario.

> I didn't really have any doubts in spite of what some of my supporters were saying. Mind you, there were good legal grounds for a challenge. We could have financed it. Eisenhower was willing to raise money from his friends to support me. A lot of people said that if the shoe had been on the other foot, Kennedy would have contested it. So I thought about it... My heart told me to do it, my head said no. It said no for two fundamental reasons. One, it would have meant that the United States would be without a President for almost a year before the challenges in Illinois and Texas could be taken. I felt that the country couldn't afford to have a vacuum in leadership for that period. Two, even if we were to win in the end, the cost in world opinion and the effect on democracy in the broadest sense would be detrimental. In my travels abroad I had been to countries in Latin America, Africa and the Far East that were just starting down the democratic path. To them, the United States was *the* example of the democratic system. So if in the United States an election was found to be fraudulent, it would mean that every pipsqueak in every one of those countries would be tempted, if he lost an election, to bring a fraud charge and have a coup.... [56]

With such thoughts in mind, Nixon switched off Eisenhower and other prominent Republicans like Senator Everett Dirksen and Ray Bliss, who were pressing him to make a challenge. The *New York Herald Tribune* was still in full cry, however, having run only four of the twelve articles planned for its series documenting the election frauds. Nixon asked the author, Earl Mazo,* to come and see him. Mazo was excited by the invitation. He knew from Rose Mary Woods that the Vice President's office had received a deluge of fresh evidence on voting

---

* Earl Mazo's biography, *Richard Nixon: A Political and Personal Portrait*, was published in 1959. He went on to write *Nixon: A Political Portrait* with Stephen Hess, published in 1968.

irregularities over and above what had already been published in the press. He thought it would be in character for Nixon to stoke up the flames of controversy by handing over this material to a friendly journalist.

For once in his life, Nixon had no intention of fighting back. His first words to his visitor were, 'Earl, those are interesting articles you are writing but no one steals the Presidency of the United States.' He gave Mazo a lecture on the international and domestic dangers of a vacuum in the Presidency, saying: 'Our country can't afford the agony of a constitutional crisis and I damn well will not be a party to creating one just to become President or anything else.' The conversation ended with Nixon successfully pleading for the series of articles to be discontinued in the interests of national unity.[57]

Meanwhile, the victorious Democrats were becoming unsettled by the rumours of an election challenge. On 14 December President-elect Kennedy took the unusual step of flying to Key Biscayne to talk to his defeated rival. The ostensible purpose of the meeting was reconciliation and the offer of an ambassadorship to Nixon. However, it was clear from Kennedy's opening words when the two men were alone ('Well, it's hard to tell who won the election at this point'[58]) that he was concerned about the fraud allegations. Nixon quickly indicated that demanding a recount was not on his agenda, and with that, the possibility of a constitutional crisis was over.

Nixon's handling of the electoral fraud issue in 1960 was both sensible and statesman-like. 'I wouldn't classify what I did as magnanimous or noble', he said later. 'Responsible would be my word for it. I simply did the right thing.'[59] It was the shrewd thing, too, in terms of Nixon's political future. He was still only forty-seven years old and had no intention of abandoning his ambition to become President. He venerated the office and had every prospect of making another try for it. Although devastated by his first experience of rejection from the American electorate, he could see glimmerings of hope in the closeness of the result. He had run well ahead of his party; he had fought cleanly and fairly; he had shown dignity in defeat. All this credit would have been thrown away if he had plunged the Presidency into a cesspit of recrimination by demanding a recount. Being a good loser was therefore good politics as well as good sense.

In his last days as Vice President, Nixon had two final duties to perform. Both reinforced his image as a good loser. As presiding officer of the Senate, he was required to make the formal declaration of the electoral college vote and to announce the winner of the presidential election to Congress. This was almost the equivalent of officiating at his own funeral, but he carried out the necessary ceremonies with grace and eloquence, winning a prolonged standing ovation as he told his colleagues:

> This is the first time in one hundred years that a candidate for the Presidency announced the result of an election in which he was defeated and announced the victory of his opponent. I do not think we could have a more striking example of the stability of our constitutional system and of the proud tradition of the American people of developing, respecting and honoring institutions of self government.
>
> In our campaigns, no matter how hard fought they may be, no matter how close the election may turn out to be, those who lose accept the verdict and support those who win...It is in that spirit that I now declare that John F. Kennedy has been elected President of the United States and Lyndon B. Johnson Vice President of the United States.[60]

Before closing down his office, Nixon had hundreds of thank-you letters to write and many personal farewells to say. Amidst all the upheavals, he found time to worry about the one member of his staff who faced financial difficulties as a result of the election defeat. This was his appointments secretary Dorothy Cox Donnelly, who in addition to losing her own job, knew that her husband would automatically be removed from his political appointment as a lobbyist on the staff of the Civil Aeronautics Board.

Nixon called Kennedy to ask, as a personal favour, if one or other of the Donnelly's could be found a job. 'Oh yes, sure, I remember Dorothy from your Senate office—the little one with the bun on the back of her head', responded JFK. To the amazement of the CAB, its Republican appointee was confirmed in his post a few days later on the orders of the White House. 'When I found out afterwards about this act of mercy involving the Vice President and the President-elect which allowed our fragile family finances to survive, I was astounded', recalled Dorothy Cox Donnelly. 'Mr. Nixon never said a word to me about it, yet this little story is so characteristic of his sensitivity and his willingness to reach out to someone in trouble with a kindness.'[61]

Nixon's final duty was to attend the inauguration of the new President. Listening to Kennedy's eloquent address, its words ringing with the plenitude of power ('Let every nation know, whether it wishes us well or ill, that we shall pay any price, bear any burden, meet any hardship, support any friend, oppose any foe to assure the survival and the success of liberty'[62]), the thoughts of the loser were generous.

> I really didn't feel at all bitter. Inaugurations are for me almost a religious experience...to see and hear the change that is occurring. It is a change of power occurring peacefully in the greatest democracy in the world, and so one feels, as I did, that you're just fortunate to be there, to see and participate in a moment of history. I must say that as I heard John Kennedy's speech I thought it was very effective and he delivered it, as I would have expected, very very well. It had a great impact on almost everyone, although not on Eisenhower. As I stood beside him, I could hear Ike's teeth grating, grating....[63]

Nixon's comparative serenity at the inauguration may have been due to a combination of fatalism and mysticism. He had lost with honour. He was young enough to live and fight another day. The election had produced no great divide of principles or policies. If there had been a winning theme it was Kennedy's exhortation to 'Get America moving again'—a call with which Nixon privately agreed but could not publicly articulate. Yet as the power to move the country was transferred to other hands, he had to recognise that the choice of leadership had been made on the basis of men not measures. He was about to become yesterday's man. The present belonged entirely to John F. Kennedy.

Late in the evening of inauguration day, Nixon had an almost mystical foresight into his personal future. The trappings of power had already passed from him. His office had closed. His secret service protection had been withdrawn at noon. His car and driver would leave him at midnight. After a quiet supper at home with Pat, Nixon was on the point of going to bed when he suddenly decided to make a last visit to Capitol Hill. The building was completely deserted, apart from a surprised security guard, who let Nixon in.

> I walked past the entrance to the Senate Chamber and down the long corridor to the Rotunda, the dome of the Capitol rising above it. The only sound was the echo of my heels on the bare stone floor.
>
> I opened a door and went onto the balcony that looks out across the west grounds of the Capitol. I had stood there many times before. It is one of the most magnificent vistas in the world, and it never seemed more beautiful than at this moment. The mall was covered

with fresh snow. The Washington Monument stood out stark and clear against the luminous gray sky, and in the distance I could see the Lincoln Memorial. I stood there looking at the scene for at least five minutes. I thought about the great experiences of the past fourteen years. Now all that was over, and I would be leaving Washington which had been my home since I arrived as a young Congressman in 1947.

As I turned to go inside, I suddenly stopped short, struck by the thought that this was not the end—that some day I would be back here.[64]

IV. RETURN TO CALIFORNIA

Nixon's return to life as a private citizen was not easy. He had no job; no pension; no staff except for Rose Mary Woods; no political prospects; and very little money. His net worth on leaving the Vice Presidency consisted of $47,000 in savings and a second-hand Oldsmobile worth $1,500. With those finances, his priority had to be earning a living. He went west to California, where he accepted a $60,000-a-year consultancy with the Los Angeles law firm of Adams, Duque and Hazeltine. On his first morning at work, he turned up at 7.30 a.m., only to discover that the organisation did not open its doors until 9 a.m. 'He walked round and round outside those offices for the next hour and a half getting tense', recalled Rose Mary Woods. 'It was typical of the problem he had in adjusting to the slower pace of California.'[65]

Familiarising himself with the mundane tasks of everyday living needed other adjustments. In his first months after arriving from Washington, Nixon stayed on his own in a small bachelor apartment on Wilshire Boulevard, while Pat stayed behind in Washington so that their daughters could complete their school terms. He had problems with the locks on the door and on his briefcase, which he managed to jam with bewildering frequency. His ineptitude with anything mechanical caused him continuing difficulties, particularly in the kitchen, where he eventually settled on defrosted TV dinners as his staple diet. There were problems on the road as well. After eight years' absence from the wheel of a car, he was required to take a test to regain his driver's licence. Even after overcoming this hurdle, his skills as a motorist were limited and he spent many frustrating hours getting lost on the freeway system.

His troubles went wider than the world of machinery. He was bothered by three successive Internal Revenue Service Audits of his tax returns and by a Justice Department investigation of his mother and his brother Don in connection with the Hughes loan. These inquiries, initiated on the orders of Bobby Kennedy, the new Attorney General, turned up nothing to discredit any of the Nixons and eventually fizzled out. 'I thought that kind of harassment very hard to forgive or forget,' recalled Nixon, 'particularly when it's aimed at your family...but on the other hand the Kennedys play hardball. They had me down. They knew I wasn't out, and they wanted to put a couple of nails in my coffin. They almost succeeded.'[66]

In the early months of 1961 Nixon wilted under these strains and gave serious thought to quitting politics altogether. 'I found it difficult to concentrate and almost impossible to work up enthusiasm for anything', he recalled. 'It took me some time to realize that I was only just beginning to react to having lost the election. Up till then the emotional impact had numbed me, and the constant activity in Washington acted as a buffer between me and the enormity of what had just happened. Now that I was alone without Pat and the girls, trying to find my own way in the world as a private citizen, I found myself becoming very unhappy and lonely. It was then I realized that I was experiencing the let-down of defeat.'[67]

This mood gradually passed. One development that helped to jolt him out of it was the Bay of Pigs crisis in April 1961. As Vice President, Nixon had been a strong supporter of the secret CIA plot to overthrow Castro with an American-supported invasion by Cuban exiles. When the Kennedy administration implemented the plan, it badly misfired, largely because the new President had cancelled the air strikes that the CIA was counting on to destroy Castro's air force. Without this vital air cover, the invasion force suffered heavy losses. In the midst of the drama, Nixon came home to find a message from Tricia: 'JFK called. I knew it! It wouldn't be long before he would get into trouble and have to call on you for help.'[68]

Nixon immediately responded to the summons and went round to the White House for a one-on-one meeting with the President. '*He said "shit" six times!*'[69] wrote Nixon at the top of his notes on the conversation. Kennedy was in an explosive mood, pacing up and down the Oval Office like a snarling panther as he cursed the CIA, the Chairman of the Joint Chiefs of Staff, and his own White House staff for giving him such appalling advice. Eventually the profanities subsided and he asked his visitor, 'What would you do now in Cuba?' Nixon replied:

> I would find a proper legal cover and I would go in. There are several justifications that could be used, like protecting American citizens living in Cuba and defending our base at Guantanamo. I believe that

the most important thing at this point is that we do what is necessary to get Castro and Communism out of Cuba.[70]

Kennedy brushed aside this advice, saying that Khrushchev was 'in a very cocky mood'[71] and that he might move on Berlin if the US invaded Cuba. Nixon argued that any such bluff from Khrushchev should be called, if necessary by American military action in both Cuba and Laos. Kennedy had no stomach for such adventures, pointing out that if US troops went into Laos, 'we might find ourselves fighting millions of Chinese troops in the jungle'.[72]

The irony of this conversation is that it was a complete reversal of the positions both men had publicly taken during the election campaign. Kennedy had made several bellicose speeches on the need for action to save Laos. During the last of the TV debates, on 21 October 1960, he had called for US intervention in support of the Cuban exiles. Nixon had been briefed about the CIA plan for the imminent Bay of Pigs operation, and knew that his opponent had received a similar briefing. He was horrified by Kennedy's statement on television, believing it to be a serious breach of security which could jeopardise the project. Nixon had instantly rubbished Kennedy's proposal as 'immoral and dangerous', explaining afterwards that he had put on an act to protect the lives of the forces whom he knew were training for the invasion. 'This was the most uncomfortable and ironic duty I have had to perform in any political campaign. I shocked and disappointed many of my own supporters and received support from all the wrong places for all the wrong reasons.'[73]

Six months after their public clash on television, the two ex-candidates were reversing their hawk and dove roles in the privacy of the Oval Office. This ironic foreign policy discussion ended with Nixon saying that he would support the President to the hilt if the decision was taken to go into Cuba or Laos, and that he would urge all other Republicans to do likewise.

Kennedy was pleased by this offer of bipartisan support. He walked Nixon to his car, thanking him as they strolled through the Rose Garden and asking as a farewell politeness: 'What are you doing with your time these days?' Nixon's answer was that he had almost no spare time at all after commuting between LA and Washington and trying to get established in a law office.

'I hope you'll take the time to write a book', said Kennedy. 'It's a really good idea even if it sells only a few copies. There's something about being an author which really builds the reputation of a political figure. Look what *The Conscience of a Conservative* has done for Barry [Goldwater]!'

'And *Profiles in Courage* for you!' retorted Nixon.[74]

This jovial exchange in the Rose Garden of the White House was the genesis of *Six Crises*, an intensely personal account of the peaks and valleys of Nixon's career up to 1960. The book, like the author's character, was complex. Students of psychology could find all sorts of revealing insights into the mystic, the paranoiac, the spiritual, and the self-analytical aspects of the former Vice President's character. Students of history could discover much fascinating new material in the narrative description of six major events (The Hiss case; The Fund; Eisenhower's heart attack; Caracas; The Kitchen Debate; and the presidential election) in which Nixon had been the central participant. Ordinary members of the public simply found *Six Crises* a good read. It sold over 300,000 copies, was serialised extensively in *Time* magazine and stood high on the best-seller lists for seven months. Nixon received $125,000 from *Time* for the serial rights; $60,000 as an advance from Doubleday; and another $50,000 or so in additional royalties.[75] He was also making a further $40,000 a year from writing a syndicated newspaper column. This success with his pen, together with his growing income from the law firm, which had grown to over $100,000 per annum, made Nixon comfortably off for the first time in his life. By the middle of 1962 he estimated his net worth at $382,000—an eightfold increase since leaving office.[76] He used most of his literary earnings to buy and furnish a showcase, Grecian-style house on the brand new Trousdale Estates development* adjacent to Bel Air. It had seven bathrooms, four bedrooms, three fireplaces, a library, a thirty-foot-long living room, a swimming pool—all this plus Harpo and Groucho Marx as next-door neighbours.

Nixon's new surroundings and financial prosperity did not satisfy him. *Six Crises* had been a great strain. He had written every word himself, but found the task, as he told Eisenhower, 'the hardest work I've ever done from the standpoint of concentration and discipline'.[78]

The physical and mental pressures of authorship took their toll:

> I was more tired at the end of *Six Crises* than I had been at the end of
> the 1960 campaign. I was almost ten pounds underweight from the
> strain and fatigue. I became short-tempered at home and at the office,
> but I continued to push myself on, determined that I could do every-
> thing if I just set my mind to it and worked hard enough. It was ironic
> that while I was writing a book about how to handle oneself during
> a crisis, I let myself get so snowed under and run-down that I wasn't

---

* The advertising slogan for this development was: 'If you can afford to live where you please you belong in Trousdale Estates – California's most exclusive community'.[77]

in good shape to make the decision about running for Governor, thereby creating a new crisis for myself and my family.[79]

Deciding to run for Governor of California was one of the worst mistakes Nixon made in his life. It cannot be explained away quite so easily, even though his run-down state may well have been a contributory factor to the error of judgement. From the moment he arrived in Los Angeles, Republicans from all over the state urged him to mount a challenge to the incumbent Democratic Governor, Pat Brown. Nixon's first instincts were to refuse. 'It would be a case of running for the wrong office at the wrong time',[80] he told his early supporters. As the polls began forecasting that he would beat Brown by a margin of 5 to 3, a combination of press speculation and the urgings of old friends like Eisenhower and Dewey pushed Nixon into considering the proposition more carefully. He sent a circular letter to his political allies around the country asking for their advice, but bluntly stating his own position: 'I still lean strongly against the idea, primarily because my entire experience is national and international affairs, and the idea of concentrating almost exclusively on state issues for four years simply has no appeal for me.'[81]

This judgement was correct. Nixon's eight years in office had made him one of the world's leading foreign policy strategists. He had no particular interest in dams, freeways, school building programmes and all the other minutiae of pork barrel politics that come across the desk of a state Governor. If he had been elected to serve in Sacramento, he would have been disobeying one of his own oft-repeated maxims: 'What separates the men from the boys in politics in that the boys seek office to *be* something and the men seek office to *do* something.'[82]

The governorship of California did, however, hold out the paradoxical prospect of saving Nixon from becoming one particular somebody—the unfortunate Republican candidate who would have to run against Kennedy in 1964. By the fall of 1961, JFK's national political popularity was soaring. Nixon could visualise a situation in which he would be trapped, as *de facto* leader of the opposition, into becoming his party's sacrificial lamb in a doomed battle for the White House. Seen in this perspective, the Governor's mansion at Sacramento took on a new appeal as a place of political sanctuary. Nixon could promise at the beginning of his gubernatorial campaign that he would serve a full four-year term. Such a pledge would give him the perfect alibi for not seeking the Presidency in 1964.

Amidst all this confusion of conflicting motives, tiredness, and pressure from eminent friends, Nixon still needed to convince his wife that running for Governor was a good idea. He failed. Pat had come home to California with the fervent hope that her spouse would settle down to a new career. 'If you ever run for office again I'll kill myself', a friend had overheard her shouting during a husband and wife quarrel in the summer of 1961.[83]

No wonder Nixon 'dreaded bringing up the subject' with Pat once he had made up his own mind to run. She reacted so badly when he broke the news to her that he immediately reversed his decision. As Nixon recalled: 'We had a family conference and I went over the pros and cons. Then she said, "Well, I just want to say one thing. If you decide to run you're going to run on your own. I'm not going to be there campaigning with you as I did when you ran for the House, for the Senate, for Vice President and for President." And so she left the room, and the girls were in tears.'

Shaken by this scene, Nixon retreated to his study, changed his mind and drafted out a new announcement for the press conference he was scheduled to give the following day. About half an hour later, Pat came into the room: 'I have thought about it some more,' she said in a voice trembling with disappointment, 'and I am more convinced than ever that if you run it will be a terrible mistake. But if you weigh everything and still decide to run, I will support your decision. I'll be there campaigning just as I always have.'

Nixon, in an equally emotional state, told her that he was now preparing the announcement that he would not be running.

'No, you must do whatever is right for you', said Pat. 'If you think this is right for you, then you must do it.'[84] The couple sat together in silence for some minutes, until Pat kissed her husband and withdrew. Two days later Nixon announced that he would not be a candidate for President of the United States in 1964 and that he would be a candidate for Governor of California in 1962.

V. GUBERNATORIAL CAMPAIGN

Nixon had several new experiences in his 1962 campaign to become Governor of California—all of them bad. They included a bruising primary fight; an acute shortage of money; vitriolic attacks from the far right; an incumbent who was hard to attack; and an international crisis which was impossible to exploit. The election ended in defeat, followed by a petulant outburst against the press which rebounded against him. From start to finish, the California episode was a nightmare.

Nixon had not expected a serious challenge in the Republican primary. His opponent was Joe Shell, a lightweight from the ultra-conservative wing of the GOP, whose highest public office had been the minority leadership of the state legislature. The Nixon–Shell battle should have been a walkover, but it did not work out that way. The Republican Party is often at its worst in primary campaigns because of the bitter ideological furies that can come to the surface. Shell unleashed these in his role as an early harbinger of the New Right movement, which was later to advance the career of Barry Goldwater. In 1962, this constituency was still an inchoate repository of contradictory discontents, whose supporters ranged from the unelectable to the unspeakable. In the latter category came the John Birch Society, the Ku Klux Klan and a like-minded brotherhood of kooks and nuts who, in their kindest moments, regarded Nixon as a dangerous liberal. The Birchers, whose leader Robert Welch had called Eisenhower 'a conscious agent of the Communist conspiracy',[85] were a sizeable force in California in the early 1960s. Nixon fought them head-on. At a March meeting of the California Republican assembly, he asked its 13,000 members to 'repudiate once and for all Robert Welch and those who accept his leadership and viewpoints'.[86] Nixon's motion was easily carried, but he paid a price for it. 'Many observers believe that Birch opposition was one of the major factors causing my defeat', he wrote in a post-campaign letter to the *New York Herald Tribune*.[87] That may have been an exaggeration, but Nixon's troubles on his conservative flank certainly did him some damage. Having been heckled up and down California in 1950 by the far left, it was a novel experience for him to receive the same treatment in 1962 from the far right.

The extent of the New Right's hostility was revealed when the primary results were declared. Shell received 37 per cent of the vote to Nixon's 63 per cent. This was a blow to Nixon's chances in the main election. Because California's registered Democrats outnumbered registered Republicans by 3:2, a GOP candidate in a statewide election needed to win at least 90 per cent of the Republican vote, 25 per cent of the Democratic vote and 50 per cent of the independent vote. 'I saw that I would have to win back almost all of Shell's 37 per cent Republican support or be foredoomed to defeat', recalled Nixon. 'The political omens were not good.'[88]

The financial omens were not good either. For the first time since the early days of his 1947 campaign, Nixon had a problem raising money. In the primary, some of the most effective right-wing fund raisers defected to Shell's camp. In the main election, the Republicans' prospects were sufficiently doubtful to deter many contributors from being over generous. The consequence was that Nixon had to campaign on a limited and at times a shoestring budget.

In his seven previous elections, Nixon had been most effective whenever he was on the offensive. Such tactics were difficult to deploy against Governor Brown, who came across to the voters as a bumbling but reasonably competent people's candidate who had made no major mistakes in his first term. As Caspar

Weinberger, the Chairman of California's Republican Party in 1962 put it: 'Nixon was viewed as trying to push out an incumbent Governor who hadn't done anything very wrong. And that's a very hard role to play.'[89] Governor Brown's own assessment was similar: 'The fact was that I'd been quite a good Governor, having pushed through a water program and an education masterplan which the voters liked', he recalled. 'But even so, I thought at the start of the campaign that Nixon was going to beat me. I had a bit of an inferiority complex about him. He was such an extraordinarily able guy, while I was a kind of a dummy who had only just managed to struggle my way through night law school. But as the election went on I came through as a nice guy, while he came through as a tough guy. He didn't have much charm as a politician, in fact he had whatever the opposite of charm is. I was really amazed by how well I was doing in the polls against him, and how easy it was to get him on the defensive.'[90]

Brown had considerable help from the press in his efforts to push Nixon into a defensive position. One of their weapons was the Hughes loan to Don Nixon, which played a much more important part in this campaign than it had in the 1960 presidential election. Nixon dealt with the continuous harassment of him on this issue impressively. Questioned about it during a TV debate with his opponent, he said:

> Six years ago my brother was in deep financial trouble. He borrowed $205,000 from the Hughes Tool Company. My mother put up as security for that loan practically everything she had—a piece of property which to her was fabulously wealthy and which now is producing an income of $10,000 a year to the creditor...I had no part or interest in my brother's business. I had no part whatever in the negotiation of this loan. I was never asked to do anything by the Hughes Tool Company and I never did anything for them. And yet...Mr. Brown, privately, in talking to some of the newsmen here in this audience and his hatchetmen have been constantly saying that I must have gotten some of the money—that I must have done something wrong. Now it is time to have this out. I was in government for fourteen years as Congressman, as a Senator, as Vice President. I went to Washington with a car and a house and a mortgage. I came back with a car and a house and a bigger mortgage. I have made mistakes but I am an honest man. And if the Governor of this state has any evidence pointing up that I did anything wrong in this case, that I did anything for the Hughes Tool Company, that I asked them for

this loan, then instead of doing it privately, doing it slyly the way he has—now he has a chance.

All the people of California are listening on television. The people of this audience are listening. Governor Brown has a chance to stand up as a man and charge me with misconduct. Do it sir![91]

In the face of this broadside, Brown turned tail and ran for cover. He mumbled his way through a half-hearted denial that he and his staff had been raising the Hughes loan issue. Later he cancelled all subsequent joint TV appearances and debates with Nixon. From this retreat one might have deduced that the Hughes loan would die as a campaign issue. Instead, Brown's surrogates in the press kept it alive with a steady cascade of innuendo and insinuation. Anecdotal evidence suggests that Nixon was politically damaged by these smears, which reminded the electorate of Helen Gahagan Douglas's 'Tricky Dick' label twelve years earlier.

It is easy to sympathise with Nixon over the Hughes loan charges. His hands were clean. Indeed his only role in the episode was to try to intervene some months after the loan had been granted at the first moment he heard about the transaction. 'I was shocked', he recalled. '"My God" I said. "Why did they do it?" I was no fool and I remember so well.' Nixon immediately called his brother and tried to make him return the loan. When this proved impossible, Nixon then insisted 'that he put up my mother's property—you know, the service station, the store and all the rest—as security'.[92] This was done and the presumably surprised Hughes Tool Company found itself holding a secured loan with significant property collateral instead of the unsecured paper loan they had offered. Improving the loan's status was a well-meaning but futile gesture which eventually made Hannah Nixon poorer without saving Richard Nixon one iota of political embarrassment. The incident amounted to a rather sad little sideshow, revealing naivete on the part of all the Nixons but nothing worse.

The pinpricks over Don's loan disconcerted Nixon to an undue extent, not because he himself was vulnerable, but because he was hypersensitive to criticism involving his family. Some reporters began to notice that the easiest way to upset Nixon was to needle him from a personal angle on subjects such as money, relatives, his daughter's education, his 'lavish' new house, or Pat's occasional absences from the campaign trail. Nixon's thin skin on such topics might seem to some an understandable human weakness, but under the merciless spotlight of a partisan media he could easily be made to look nervous, jumpy and, once again, 'tricky'.

Dirty tricks were a feature of the late stages of the campaign and Nixon was personally implicated in one of them. On the recommendation of a public relations firm headed by a GOP supporter, Mrs. Leone Baxter, the Republicans created a phony organisation which they called 'The Committee for the Preservation of the Democratic Party in California'. This fake 'Committee', financed from Nixon campaign funds, sent out over 500,000 circulars to known conservative Democrats linking Governor Brown to a liberal organisation known as the California Democratic Council (CDC), which had supported left-of-centre policies on certain issues. The circular contained a poll asking if the recipients approved of the alleged CDC–Brown links and policies. Before the results of this loaded poll could be published, a watchful Democrat spotted that the literature of the non-existent 'Committee for the Preservation of the Democratic Party in California' did not identify its printer, or the names of its sponsoring committee of Democrats as the law required for literature soliciting campaign contributions. Writs and injunctions flew. The circulars were stopped.

At the time, Nixon was not personally associated with what the Democrats claimed was a serious election fraud. However, both Leone Baxter and Nixon's campaign manager Bob Haldeman subsequently confirmed that Nixon had approved the operation and the text of the circular.[93] Although a minor episode in itself, it is interesting as the first proven example of Nixon's direct involvement in an election manoeuvre which was a possible violation of the law rather than just another controversial item of the political crossfire.

Nixon's descent to this level of warfare was excusable on the grounds that the Democrats were getting up to far dirtier tricks and leaflets. Their notorious prankster Dick Tuck was active throughout the campaign, masterminding a multitude of smears. One of these was the publication of a leaflet by the so-called 'Independent Voters of California', which alleged that when Nixon had bought a house in Washington in the 1950s he had signed a restrictive covenant promising not to sell the property to Jews or Negroes.

Such allegations highlighted Nixon's wider problem in the election. For better or worse, *he* was the main issue of the campaign. Brown kept the pressure up by continuously asserting that Nixon was merely intending to use the governorship as a personal stepping stone to the Presidency. Seen from afar it might be imagined that many Californians should have been glad to elect a Governor who could in time move up from State House to White House, but that was not the mood in 1962. With parochialism in the ascendant, Nixon the California-born, educated, and thrice-elected legislator, was portrayed as an unwanted intruder. This was such a misrepresentation that inevitably the tide began to turn. By the later stages of the campaign the muddy waters of smears and personalised trivia were beginning to recede, as Nixon did his best to put forward a serious platform of policies for the state. They included education reforms; higher salaries for teachers; an enlarged police force; more freeways; more water projects; the death penalty for drug pushers with three convictions, and a reduction in the Sacramento bureaucracy. Some of the electorate seemed to be listening, for by mid-October the polls showed that the gap between the candidates was closing.

Nixon had assembled a new staff around him of bright young men, among them John Ehrlichman (thirty-seven), Dwight Chapin (twenty-one), Nick Ruwe (twenty-nine), Sandy Quinn (twenty-seven), Jerry Reynolds (thirty-three) and Ron Ziegler (twenty-two). The only major survivors from the 1960 campaign were Bob Finch, Herb Klein and thirty-six-year-old Bob Haldeman, who by 1962 had moved up to campaign manager. This was in some ways a nominal position, as it had been for Finch in 1960, because Nixon insisted on making all the major decisions himself. Haldeman was afterwards sharply critical of his boss's reluctance to delegate: 'The old adage that the lawyer who represents himself in court has a fool for a client applies to political campaigning. Nixon made one elementary mistake after another in 1960 and 1962 because he thought he knew it all. The campaign manager who might have saved him was Murray Chotiner, but he was in disgrace over a financial scandal by that time so wasn't around. Nixon was only just beginning to take my advice seriously.'[94]

Harry Robbins Haldeman was destined to become the pivotal member of Nixon's inner circle, eventually holding the appointment of Chief of Staff in the White House 1969–74. Born in Los Angeles in 1926, he was the third-generation scion of an 'old California' dynasty, whose patriarch, Harry M. Haldeman, had been a prominent leader in the commercial and charitable hierarchy of his city. Harry M. Haldeman's activities included being a leader of the Salvation Army; an activist in the Better America Federation (an early anti-Communist society); a founder of the Hollywood Bowl; and a civic father voted 'Los Angeles's most useful citizen'.

Bob Haldeman inherited from his paternal grandfather brains, money and a strong sense of social and religious duty. Throughout his education he combined an enthusiasm for scholarship with a zeal for militaristic discipline. He graduated high in his class from the Harvard School (the top boys' school in LA), and from USC and UCLA. He also found time to become a senior officer in his high school ROTC; the President of Scabbard and Blade (a USC honorary military fraternity) and an officer in the Naval Reserve. In addition he was the leader of his university's Christian Science organisation.

The austere side of Bob Haldeman was tempered by a laconic sense of humour, bounding energy, and a flair for unexpected entrepreneurial initiatives in his chosen field of management and marketing. He took a keen interest in showbusiness and had an early ambition to become a management executive in a circus ('not so different from managing a political circus', he later observed[95]). Diverted from this high-wire career, he went into advertising, serving for two decades as a senior executive with the J. Walter Thompson agency.

Politically, Haldeman was a conservative who by his early twenties had become an ardent free marketeer and anti-Communist. He first noticed and began to admire Nixon for his tenacity in the Hiss case. This admiration deepened into strong respect. On the night of the Checkers broadcast during The Fund crisis of 1952, Haldeman stood in the crowd outside the El Capitan Theater in Hollywood to deliver a letter volunteering his services for the Nixon campaign. That initiative did not work out, but later, after arranging an introduction to the Vice President through Loie Gaunt, a trusted Nixon secretary who had been a fellow UCLA classmate, Haldeman worked as an advance man under Bob Finch in the campaigns of 1956, 1958 and 1960.

Nixon was attracted to Haldeman by his family credentials, his keen intelligence and his ruthless efficiency as a campaign scheduler. For his part, Haldeman admired Nixon's political philosophy of limited government at home and staunch anti-Communism abroad. 'I became fascinated by Nixon's mind, particularly his incredible intellect. He was to me that rare species, the uncommon man', recalls Haldeman. 'He was difficult to work for, but I had somehow developed a talent for handling difficult people. At JWT I was in charge of the terror clients such as Walt Disney. Nixon wasn't that bad! In any case I am a total subscriber to the Peter Drucker theory of management which is don't bother to solve problems, go out and seize the opportunities. I could see in Nixon a supreme talent combined with all kinds of flaws and negatives. I wanted to capitalize on his talent.'[96]

In 1962 it was the flaws and negatives in Nixon that were most visible. Originally, Haldeman had advised his boss against running for Governor. 'I felt this quite strongly as a Californian myself', he recalls. 'I knew that Nixon didn't really want to do the job. The only reason why he wanted the governorship was to maintain his political profile and I thought this was a bad reason. In fact it doomed the campaign to disaster from the beginning.'[97]

The final disaster to Nixon's campaign was the Cuban Missile crisis, which broke in the last week of October. 'I just lost the election', said Nixon to Rose Mary Woods as he watched the first news bulletins describing the US naval blockade.[98]

He was right. As the world hovered on the brink of nuclear war, the voters of California lost interest in their domestic election. Brown was helped by the national wave of support for President Kennedy. He also benefited from being summoned to Washington to chair an emergency Governors' conference on Civil Defense preparations. Kennedy was not too busy to miss the political trick of sending Brown home with a presidential letter praising him for his calm and decisive leadership.

Nixon was completely stymied by the crisis. He gave his strong support for Kennedy's quarantine of Cuba and calmed down the atmosphere of panic food-buying in the shops of California with a speech perceptively forecasting a successful outcome to the naval operation. Supporting the President in an hour of national peril was good statesmanship, but it put an end to any remaining chances of achieving a political upset in the gubernatorial contest.

On election day, Brown won the governorship by a majority of 297,000 votes out of 6 million ballots cast. Nixon, who was expecting to lose, sat up through most of the night watching the returns. When Finch, Haldeman and Klein saw him around 8 a.m. on the morning after, he was red-eyed with tiredness. 'He looked bad,' recalled Klein, 'but his spirits did not seem as low as I had anticipated.'[99] In fact, Nixon was in a philosophical mood, attributing his defeat to the Cuban Missile crisis and quickly accepting his adviser's recommendation that he should not appear at any press conference. He agreed that Herb Klein should be left to release the concession statement and the text of a congratulatory telegram to Pat Brown. When Klein went downstairs to deliver these messages to the press, Nixon came out of his suite to thank members of his staff for their help. An emotional scene developed as secretaries began crying, some of them embracing 'The Boss', who was visibly moved. Amidst these hugs and tears, Klein came back to say that he was being harassed by reporters insisting on a personal appearance from the candidate.

'The anger and frustration, the disappointment and fatigue struggling inside me burst out', recalled Nixon. 'I said, "Screw them. I'm not going to do it. I don't have to and I'm not going to. You read them my concession statement to Brown, Herb, and if they want to know where I am you can tell them I've gone home to be with my family".'[100]

That seemed to be his last word, but a few moments later he glanced at the television and heard reporters lambasting Klein, with shouts of 'Where's Nixon?' in an insulting tone. Nixon snapped. 'I'm going down there', he declared angrily, calming down a little during the elevator ride as he sighed to his companions, 'Oh hell. It was a pretty good fight. We fought hard. We fought clean...Losing

California after losing the Presidency—well, it's like being bitten by a mosquito after being bitten by a rattlesnake.'[101]

Entering the press conference, Nixon strode to the microphone and opened on a defiant note: 'Now that Mr. Klein has made a statement, now that all the members of the press are so delighted that I lost, I would just like to make a statement of my own', he began. Then he checked himself, turning the other cheek to his tormentors as he told them:

> I appreciate the press coverage of this campaign. I think each of you covered it the way you saw it. You had to write it in the way according to your belief on how it would go...I have no complaints about the press coverage. I think each of you was writing it as you believed it. I congratulate Governor Brown, as Herb Klein has already indicated, for his victory. He has, I think, the greatest honor and the greatest responsibility of any Governor in the United States...I wish him well. I wish him well not only from the personal standpoint because there never were on my part any personal considerations.

So far so good. Nixon had sounded conciliatory and almost dignified. However, his next words revealed that the bitterness he felt welling up inside him was starting to seep out.

> I believe Governor Brown has a heart, even though he believes I do not. I believe he is a good American, even though he feels I am not...I am proud of the fact that I defended my opponent's patriotism. You gentlemen didn't report it but I am proud that I did that. I am proud also that I defended the fact that he was a man of good motives, a man that I disagreed with very strongly, but a man of good motives. I want that—for once gentlemen—I would appreciate it if you would write what I say in that respect. I think it's very important that you write it. In the lead! In the lead!

By now Nixon's voice was rising and he was off on a public roller-coaster ride of emotional turmoil. Listening to the speech was for one reporter, Jules Witcover, 'like stumbling unannounced into a man's monologue to his analyst'. It was a cruel but accurate description. Nixon lurched from generous tributes to his staff to specific grievances about press bias; back to complimenting the one newsman who he felt had been consistently objective and on through three rambling perorations; each one beginning, 'One last thing…' Finally he was on to his fourth 'One last thing', his phrases see-sawing between bitterness and sadness as they climaxed in the announcement of his withdrawal from political life:

> One last thing. The last play. I leave you gentlemen now, and you will now write it. You will interpret it. That's your right. But as I leave you I want you to know—just think how much you're going to be missing. You won't have Nixon to kick around any more, because, gentlemen, this is my last press conference… Thank you gentlemen and good day.[102]

The oratory of the defeated at elections is occasionally noble, frequently sad, and sometimes humiliating. Nixon provided glimpses of all three conditions at his 'last press conference'. Looking at the television videotapes of the event nearly thirty years after it happened, the impression is that of a man tottering on the brink of an emotional abyss. However, tottering is the operative word, for he miraculously avoided a real disaster. He stumbled but never fell. He spoke more in sorrow than in anger. Although his inner turmoil may well have been cathartic, his outer dignity (narrowly) remained intact.

To their dismay, the media experts of the Democratic Party also came to share a similar view in retrospect. When Nixon was running for President in 1968, his opponents eagerly turned to the videotapes of 1962, confident that they would be able to pick out some damaging clips as propaganda for their election commercials. Not an inch of the footage was found to be useable. The 'last press conference' was simply not as bad as it had been painted.

The press corps of 1962 could hardly have told it worse. Most of them had come not just to bury Nixon but to dance on his grave. 'Exit snarling'[103] was the comment of Mary McGrory in the *Washington Star*, and it was characteristic of the journalistic pasting Nixon received over the next few days. The nadir of the media's funereal rejoicings were reached the following week, when ABC Television screened a half hour special, 'The Political Obituary of Richard Nixon'. Apparently compiled in the spirit of *De mortuis nil nisi malum*, the broadcast overreached itself in bias by featuring, among many Nixon adversaries, the convicted perjurer Alger Hiss. Although Hiss's appearance provoked more than 80,000 letters and telegrams of protest to ABC, it did not diminish the valedictory thrust of the programme, chillingly encapsulated in the final words of its host, Howard K. Smith: 'Mr. Nixon has been referred to in the past tense so much in this report that we may forget that this is a political obituary and not a biological one.'[104]

Although the media's style of mourning at Nixon's demise was not universally appreciated, no one disputed their conclusion that his political corpse was as dead as the proverbial Dodo. Friend and foe alike were convinced that his career in public life was over. As *Time* magazine put it: 'Barring a miracle, Richard Nixon can never hope to be elected to any political office again.'[105]

The only secret dissenter from this epitaph was Richard Nixon. He believed in miracles. He believed in fighting back. He was determined to try again.

FIFTEEN

THE WILDERNESS
YEARS 1963–1967

I. PUBLIC PARTNER

Nixon spent five years in the political wilderness. It was one of the most remarkable periods of his life, culminating in a triumph that astonished both his friends and foes. In the journalistic judgement of the time, his recovery from being 'finished' after the California debacle of 1962 to recapturing the Republican presidential nomination in 1968 amounted to nothing less than 'a miracle' of political resurrection. This was largely hokum. Miracle stories sell newspapers. They also appeal to the mystic side of Nixon's character, which may well be the reason why he has so often emphasised the part played by the hand of fate in his comeback. 'It was not by dint of my own calculation or efforts', was one of his more lofty disclaimers. 'No man, not if he combined the wisdom of Lincoln with the connivance of Machiavelli, could have maneuvered or manipulated his way back into the arena.'[1]

All political careers are affected by luck. Yet after making ample allowance for the role of fortune in Nixon's return to power, it is impossible to avoid the conclusion that his comeback happened because he fought for it. The key elements in that fight were achieving professional success in the legal world closest to politics; exercising astute judgement to position himself in the centre of the Republican hierarchy; and campaigning like a warrior in the cause of his party during the leanest of lean years. Throughout this time, he prepared himself for his comeback with the discipline of a former heavyweight champion returning to the ring. On a more personal level, Nixon recharged his intellectual batteries; achieved financial security; confirmed his religious faith; learned lessons from his past mistakes; and enjoyed some disinterested personal friendships. It was a period when he discovered new strengths within himself, both as an individual and as a politician, without which he could not have won the Presidency.

At the beginning of 1963, Nixon's prospects for a re-entry into presidential politics looked hopeless. He was seen, even by his friends, as a two-time loser whose hour had passed. Just about the only people in the world who disagreed with that assessment were Nixon himself and the man whom he and his family called 'Uncle Elmer'. This was Elmer H. Bobst, the wealthy seventy-eight-year-old Chairman of the Warner-Lambert Corporation. Born in China as the son of an American missionary, Bobst had made his fortune from pharmaceuticals, an industry in which he was known as 'The Vitamin King'.

The friendship between Bobst and Nixon was ten years old. They had met in 1953 at a businessman's fund-raising dinner in New Jersey, and had taken an instant liking to each other. Thereafter, the relationship deepened. Nixon, who had a tendency to admire self-made men, came to revere Bobst so much that he regarded him almost as a surrogate father. 'Uncle Elmer', a lonely widower, became the closest of family friends. He spent several Thanksgivings and Christmases with the Nixons; settled trust funds on Tricia and Julie; and was one of the young Vice President's most intimate confidants. It was entirely natural, in the aftermath of his California defeat, that Nixon should have turned to Bobst for help and advice.

At that time, Nixon may have been down but he was by no means out—at least in his own eyes. The character lessons he had learned from Coach Newman on the Whittier College football pitch thirty years earlier stood him in good stead. His political prospects may have looked bleak to others, but at the age of only forty-nine he was sanguine about his long-term chances of regaining a leading role in the counsels of the nation. Although realistic enough to put his presidential aspirations on ice for the foreseeable future, he talked optimistically to Bobst about his hopes of becoming Secretary of State. With such thoughts at the back of his mind, Nixon in early 1963 turned down several lucrative business offers. These included the chairmanships of Chrysler and Pepsi Cola International, as well as a proposition from Jack Dreyfus, worth around $400,000 a year in salary and stock options, to be the Chief Executive Officer of the Dreyfus Corporation, a mutual fund group. He also refused invitations to become President of a Midwestern university and national commissioner for baseball. Instead, on

Bobst's recommendation, he opted for the career he had missed out on during his days at Duke University—practising as a New York lawyer. Contrary to his public utterances on the subject, his motivation for this choice was highly political.

The vehicle for Nixon's entry into legal practice was the Wall Street law firm of Mudge, Stern, Baldwin and Todd. This was a long-established but somewhat moribund partnership whose billings had been declining for several years. Among its peers the firm was admired for its old-fashioned rectitude but mocked for its lack of dynamism. Some Wall Street wags called it 'Mudge, Sludge, Fudge and Won't Budge'.[2]

Through his various business interests, Elmer Bobst was Mudge Stern's largest client. Early in April 1963, he called the senior partners with the suggestion that they should invite Nixon to join them. 'You need new blood at the top,' he told them in his basso profundo voice, 'someone who can serve to bring the firm into the eyes of Wall Street and to the attention of industry throughout the country.'[3]

The concept that Bobst outlined, almost in the form of a royal command, was that Nixon should become Mudge Stern's 'public partner'. This is a familiar device among top law firms whereby a senior lawyer who has been successful in government places his surname first in the list which designates the partnership. Rogers and Wells (William Rogers); Dewey Ballantine (Thomas E. Dewey); Donovan Leisure (Bill Donovan); and Davis Polk (John W. Davis) are past and present examples of this style of nomenclature. Bobst was so keen on his plan that he arranged for the leading figures in Mudge Stern to meet Nixon over a game of golf in New Jersey the following Saturday. The preliminary conversations in the bar of Baltrustol Golf Club went well and were continued over a formal lunch at the firm's 20 Broad Street offices a few days later. Nixon has recalled his reaction to the approach:

> We lunched in the conference room. I particularly remembered they
> had candles, lighted candles, for lunch which to me was quite impres-
> sive. My God, candles in the middle of the day! So we had a good lunch
> and a very good talk and I remember the sell was not particularly hard.
> I remember how Bob Guthrie—this was his trademark through the
> years—said, 'You know we have a lot of fun, we have a ot of fun.' So
> we talked about it and I just had a good feeling about them.[4]

These good feelings were evidently reciprocated for Nixon was offered a deal which gave him a $220,000 a year base salary and made him one of the joint

'Heads of the Firm'—whose name would be changed to Nixon, Mudge, Rose, Guthrie and Alexander. The clinching factor had apparently been Nixon's answer to the question, 'Have you really given up politics?' His reply was: 'Anyone who knows anything about politics knows that when you give up your base, as I've done in California, then you're finished.'[5]

Anyone who knew anything about Richard Nixon should have been able to detect the ambiguity in that response. In their political innocence the partners missed it. In fact Nixon was coming to Wall Street because it was the most propitious environment in which to build a new political base. He knew that in the previous hundred years, three Presidents, seven presidential candidates, eight Secretaries of State and over fifty Cabinet officers had emerged from the top law firms operating in the twenty acre enclave around Wall Street.[6] Surrounded by the leaders of the US foreign policy establishment; in touch with the big deals and money of corporate America; and in regular contact with the most influential brains in the country, Nixon was delighted to be on what he liked to call 'the fast track'. He was, however, careful to disavow all suggestions that this track might one day take him back to Washington, for he told questioners that by joining the firm he was 'taking the veil politically'.[7]

In his life 'under the veil' as a Wall Street lawyer, Nixon was a considerable success. He gave the firm a higher profile, brought in new accounts and recruited new talent. As a business getter he worked closely with Bob Guthrie, the Harvard-educated senior partner from Texas whose bustling style was described by one colleague as being 'more like Lyndon Johnson than Lyndon Johnson'.[8]

Although in many ways the ebullient Guthrie and the reserved Nixon made an odd couple, their joint teamwork earned millions of dollars in new billings as they travelled around the world together creating deals, acquisitions and new market opportunities for clients of the firm. Their greatest success was winning the Pepsi Cola account. This was directly attributable to Nixon's relationship with Pepsi's Chairman Don Kendall, who had admired the former Vice President ever since their encounter in Moscow at the time of the 1959 'Kitchen Debate' with Khrushchev. Thanks to 'the public partner's' personal contacts with foreign government leaders such as Chiang Kai-shek and Ayub Khan, Nixon Mudge opened the doors for new Pepsi franchises in Taiwan, Pakistan and other Asian nations. A grateful Kendall subsequently directed almost all of Pepsi's extensive legal work to Nixon Mudge. The account was worth more than $3 million in annual billings.

Success on such a scale soon bred more success. Nixon Mudge took on much more litigation and acquisition work for clients such as Studebaker, Precision

Valve Inc., Warner-Lambert and Dreyfus Corporation, all of whose chairmen considered themselves close to Nixon. The firm expanded by merging with two smaller law partnerships. This growth of the business may have looked natural, and there were many contributors to it besides Nixon, yet it only happened because the 'public partner' was in place and working exceptionally hard to build up the firm. As Nixon himself described his activities in this period: 'Believe me, it's an excruciatingly difficult thing. You go to board meetings and you go to dinners and you talk to people that you would rather, frankly, not talk to. You work and work and work. Nothing is very direct, and then eventually almost by osmosis, it begins to go.'[9]

In addition to the hard grind of expanding the firm's legal business, Nixon also found himself enjoying 'a lot of fun' from his new career just as Bob Guthrie had predicted at their initial lunch. Much of this came from his contacts with younger lawyers. One of Nixon's assignments was to restore the firm's faded prestige on law school campuses. He took the job seriously, setting off on the first of several personal recruiting tours in late 1963 to Harvard, Yale, Columbia, Chicago and Michigan. Students at these law schools were flattered to find themselves being interviewed by a former Vice President of the United States. Some of them were subsequently invited to dinners and lunches at the Nixon apartment in New York, where they found a genial, if sometimes initially nervous host, drawing them out in conversation across a wide range of intellectual, legal and sometimes political topics. Nixon developed an eye for young brainpower in this period of his life. He enjoyed the challenge of the selection and evaluation process. His recruiting record, which at this time was not complicated by questions of political loyalty, resulted in many good appointments.

For all his outward appearance of geniality towards his partners, Nixon remained a difficult man to get to know. The only member of the firm who took the considerable trouble needed to build a real human relationship with him was Leonard Garment.

Len Garment was an unlikely figure to become a friend of Richard Nixon. A liberal Democrat; a talented jazz clarinettist; a one-time drop-out from Brooklyn College; a film and theatre buff; a debunker of the Establishment; a sharp Jewish wit with a strong line in puns; above all a hip and irreverent gadfly, Garment was at first glance the antithesis of the *homme sérieux* that Nixon embodied. Yet Garment was a brilliant professional as well as an amusing pluralist. After he had dropped back into his university course after taking a prolonged sabbatical to play the clarinet in Woody Herman's band, Garment's intellectual talent took him straight from Brooklyn Law School to Mudge Stern, where after eight years he became Chief of the Litigation Department. He was, at thirty-nine, the unusual but rising star of the firm when he was introduced to his new public partner, Richard Nixon. 'Intuitively we took to each other as fellow outsiders', recalled Garment. 'We came from such similar backgrounds on the wrong side of the tracks. The animating force of our lives was the work ethic. Our driving force was that we so much wanted to succeed. We both had ambivalent attitudes towards the Establishment, towards the world we had left and to the world we aspired to. Instinctively we knew that we could be instruments for each other's purposes. We had the synergy of two live wires.'[10]

Nixon was stimulated by Garment and reciprocated some of these intuitive feelings. Yet he was never completely comfortable with his self-appointed gadfly. Garment bombarded Nixon with a daily flood of memos on every imaginable subject, ranging from restaurant and theatre recommendations to appraisals of the war in Vietnam. He provided a private clippings service of interesting articles. He offered a continuous stream of advice on politics, the media, show business and the law. The vitality and irreverence of these memos kept Nixon in a constant state of surprise. 'I guess I had an almost manic abandon in proposing ideas to him, but at the end of the day 85 per cent of my suggestions were rejected', recalled Garment.[11]

Even if the rejection rate on his memos was high, Len Garment still managed to exercise a beneficial influence on Nixon's wilderness years. For a start he was the purveyor of more 'fun' than any other Nixon associate. Outside the office, he played a significant part in broadening Nixon's general outlook and life style. As a professional colleague he did much to enhance Nixon's career as a lawyer. Garment's importance as a new friend was that he helped to rebuild Nixon's motivation and self-esteem to the point where serious political campaigning came back on to his agenda.

Within two years of moving to New York, Nixon found himself to be enjoying success, financial security and a considerable degree of personal happiness. Although he had never previously been particularly interested in money, there was a side of him that had sometimes resented his lack of resources during the lean years of facing expensive commitments on the Vice President's annual salary of $30,000. From 1965 onwards he was comfortably well off, earning over $250,000 a year from the law partnership, plus additional income from book royalties on *Six Crises* and other writings. He had moved with his family into a twelve-room apartment on 5th Avenue overlooking Central Park. He had limitless opportunities for foreign travel. With the new self-confidence that financial success brought him, he relaxed and blossomed. His tastes broadened in food, wine, culture—and people. At impromptu musical evenings in Garment's Brooklyn home (Len on the clarinet, Dick at the piano) he met a range of liberals, left-wingers, dissenters and Democrats whom he had never encountered in his more rigid years as a Republican leader. Sometimes he liked his new acquaintances enough to do them big favours. The Hollywood producer Jerome Hellman (*Midnight Cowboy, Day of the Locust* etc.) tells of how Nixon saved one of his early movies from disaster in 1964.

Hellman at that time was an independent producer making *A Fine Madness* starring Sean Connery, when a ferocious row erupted with the film's financial backers and distributors, Warner Brothers. The cause of the trouble was that no one had told Jack Warner, Head of the Studio, that *A Fine Madness* featured Connery as a poet suffering from writer's block, not in one of his more typical Bond-style adventure roles. This misunderstanding produced a subplot worthy of the movie's title. When Warner saw the rushes he flew into one of his notorious black rages; ordered Hellman off the lot; sent him a cheque for the balance of fees owed to him; and told his agent that the guards on the gate had instructions to shoot if he tried to re-enter the studio.

Distraught at this turn of events, Jerome Hellman arrived via Len Garment to tell his tale of woe to Richard Nixon. On his many visits to Jack Warner's office, Hellman (politically a man of the left) had noted that a large and affectionately inscribed photograph of Nixon adorned the main wall. It was dedicated to 'Colonel Warner', a title by which the mogul was inordinately fond of being addressed.

Nixon heard Hellman out, and apparently much amused by this story of a day in the life of Hollywood, decided to play a cameo part in the melodrama. He immediately called Jack Warner and, after exchanging pleasantries, launched into an introduction worthy of an impresario: 'Jack I'm sitting here with a young man whose future is very important to me,' began Nixon, 'a young man of quite outstanding talent, a young man of creative genius.' Listening in on an extension, Hellman could hardly believe his ears as Nixon continued to spread a warm mantle of praise and protection over his unidentified protégé. 'I understand this young man is a friend of yours too Jack', said Nixon, pausing for effect. 'His name is Jerome Hellman.' Warner's gasp of astonishment was clearly audible across three thousand miles of telephone wire, for there was no way he could have dreamt of making a connection between his political hero and the current *enfant terrible* of his studio. After listening to a few more minutes of Nixon's persuasive advocacy, Warner gracefully gave way, blaming someone else for the misunderstanding. He declared that he had always liked Hellman, who would be warmly welcome to come back to the studio with full powers of creative control restored. Nixon's magic intervention as the fairy godfather had worked a miracle. *A Fine Madness*, produced by Jerome Hellman, distributed by Warner Brothers, was completed on schedule—and they all lived happily ever after.[12]

Although Nixon worked several such wonders for clients of his firm by judicious use of his powers as an eminent fixer, there remained some nagging doubts about his capacity as a lawyer. 'Does he really practice law?'[13] was a question frequently asked by sceptical outsiders. The affirmative answer became possible in early 1966 when Nixon appeared as an advocate before the Supreme Court in the case of *Time, Inc. v. Hill*.

Time, Inc. v. Hill was an important milestone in First Amendment litigation, highlighting the issue of where the line should be drawn between personal privacy and press freedom. Nixon appeared on behalf of his firm's longstanding clients, James and Elizabeth Hill. This middle-class family from Philadelphia had been portrayed by *Life* magazine as the prototype victims for a ghoulish Broadway thriller *The Desperate Hours*. According to *Life* the play was 'a re-enactment' of the Hill family's ordeal of having been held hostage by three escaping convicts some years earlier. *Life* published an article showing photographs of the Hill's family home, and, without any reference to fictionalisation, made the claim that the Broadway play (whose plot involved heavy scenes of violence and sexual abuse) was the 'true crime' story of the Hill family's experiences re-created on stage. This claim was almost entirely unfounded. The evidence showed that *The Desperate Hours* had been drawn in a general way from a large number of hostage cases of which the Hill incident was only one. The Hills had, in fact, been relatively well treated by their captors, and had not been subjected to violence. For these reasons, the Hill family asked *Life* to publish a retraction. *Life* refused, citing the First Amendment. Advised by Len Garment, the family sued. After a decade of forensic battles up to the highest Appeal Court in New York, the Hills won their case and were awarded heavy damages. *Life's* parent company Time, Inc. subsequently sought to have the judgement reversed by the United States Supreme Court, which was where Nixon entered the story.

Nixon, who was sensitive to the charge that he was merely his firm's top 'fixer' for corporate clients, had been searching for the right piece of litigation with which to make his public debut as a courtroom advocate. *Time, Inc. v. Hill* was not the ideal case for his purposes. He would be appearing against one of the most powerful publishing groups in the United States in a role which could make him appear to be continuing his old war against the press. On the other hand he was excited by the intellectual challenge of the argument and moved by personal sympathy for the Hill family. Eventually, after much deliberation, he took the case, realising that the stakes were high for his own reputation.

Nixon prepared for the Hill case with almost as much intensity as he had devoted to the Hiss case nineteen years earlier. He committed to memory the full trial record, the state court appeals, and copious quantities of additional background material such as law review articles, philosophical writings on privacy and many case law precedents. As the date for the hearing grew close he set up numerous 'skull sessions'—question-and-answer dialogues with his law firm colleagues simulating court argument. Len Garment, who bore the brunt of these endeavours, was awed by Nixon's thoroughness, recalling: 'His preparation was almost obsessive; he left nothing to chance. His behavior was not only a matter of professional pride, but a sign of his determination not to let his recent defeats drive him from the political arena.'[14]

Nixon's debut before the Supreme Court, on 27 April 1966, won favourable comment from Bench, Bar and press. The *Washington Post* reported that he had presented 'one of the better oral arguments of the year'.[15] He was interrupted thirty-one times by the justices with questions on points of law and produced scholarly responses to every one. According to Garment, Nixon 'sounded like a polished professional of the Bar—his footing confident, his language lawyer-like, his organization of material sure and clear. He had true "bottom" responding to dozens of tough questions and the Court clearly relished the performance'.[16] Even his old enemy Earl Warren, now Chief Justice, expressed surprise that Nixon had done so well.[17] Justice Abe Fortas, President Johnson's most recent appointee, said that Nixon made 'one of the best arguments that he had heard since he had been on the Court' and that he could develop into 'one of the great advocates of our times'.[18]

Nixon himself was far more self-critical. When he arrived home late at night after his arduous day of forensic jousting, he found the energy to dictate a five-page memorandum, candidly analysing the strengths and weaknesses of his oral argument. This document, typed by Rose Mary Woods at 7.30 a.m., arrived first thing next morning on the desk of an astonished Len Garment, who later described it as 'the most instructive example of Richard Nixon's tenacity and work habits that I've read in all the time I've known him, including the presidential and post-presidential years'.[19]

Although most observers of the Supreme Court hearing thought the Hill family had won the day, Nixon's caution was justified. The justices were so divided that they took the unusual step of setting the case down for a further day of re-argument. Nixon, by his own perfectionist standards, felt he did better at the second hearing, but the final outcome was a disappointment. By a vote of 5-4, with five Justices writing separate opinions, the Hill family lost their case. The decision went against them largely on the basis of the view, forcefully expressed in the opinions of Justices Black and Douglas, that the First Amendment was absolute, and that it gave constitutional protection even to knowing or reckless falsity on the part of the press. Nixon took the narrow defeat somewhat personally, sourly telling his colleagues 'I always knew I wouldn't be permitted to win a big appeal against the press.'[20] He could, however, take consolation from the strength of the dissenting judgements and from the accolades of his peers on the high quality of his advocacy.* What the Hill case had demonstrated was that Richard Nixon the courtroom advocate possessed the ability to compete with the very best and brightest members of his profession.

Nixon's appearance before the Supreme Court in the Hill case marked the zenith of his legal career. In his own mind he had now proved himself on the fast track of the New York Bar. This made him feel ready to return to the even faster track of national politics. An interesting clue to the reawakening of these ambitions was to be found in the nocturnal memorandum of self-criticism which he had dictated a few hours after presenting his initial argument to the Court. Having somewhat grudgingly conceded that his oral presentation to the justices may have been good 'from a strictly legal standpoint', Nixon continued: 'On the other hand, in a broader context it will not help us in terms of getting the publicity which we deserve which might bring us more clients in the future who have possible Appellate problems, and naturally it does not help us in terms of other considerations which are *broader than our purely commercial interest* [author's italics].'[21]

When this memo was circulated within the firm, some of Nixon's less worldly legal colleagues were puzzled by the last six words of this sentence. What on earth were these mysterious 'other considerations' that Nixon felt were broader than the firm's commercial interests, they asked each other? Len Garment alone knew for certain what Nixon meant.

In the weeks before the Hill case hearing, Nixon had used every available moment of his time to fit in extra 'skull sessions' on points of law. Sometimes this involved taking Garment with him on long-distance trips to fill in time by playing the combined roles of debate coach and intellectual valet. On one such trip, to Florida, the planned accommodation arrangements went wrong. Nixon decided to solve the problem by going unannounced to the home of his friend

---

* Nixon eventually had the satisfaction of seeing the Supreme Court acknowledge in the case of *Gertz v. Welch* (1974) that private individuals should be given certain protections against press intrusion.

Elmer Bobst near Miami, only to encounter the further problem that no one would answer the door (it was after midnight). By the time that the visitors' predicament was clear, their driver had gone away. 'Come on Garment, it's over the wall we go', said Nixon[22] in a rare mood of derring-do. The two law partners clambered over the wall, briefcases and all, and found their way to a pool house in Bobst's garden, where they dossed down on a pair of mattresses like teenagers at summer camp. In this unusual setting, Nixon began talking to his companion with no less unusual intimacy. Before he fell asleep, he told Garment about his dreams of again playing a role in foreign policy, saying he felt his life had to be dedicated to the great purposes he had in this field. As Garment recalled the conversation:

> This man, so fiercely determined to stay in the political arena—for which he was in many ways so ill suited—told me that he felt driven to do so not by the rivalries or ideological commitments of domestic politics but by his pacifist mother's idealism and the abstract intellectual attractions of foreign affairs. That was the night's theme. Nixon declared that he would give anything or make any sacrifice to be able to utilize his talents and his experience in foreign affairs. Making money, belonging to exclusive clubs, and playing golf were not his idea of a worthwhile life, he said. Up to then he had lived 'in the arena' and that was where he wanted to be even if it meant 'a much shorter life'.[23]

In the elusive quest for 'the real Nixon' there are few more revealing moments than his conversation on the mattresses of Elmer Bobst's pool house early in 1966. By the standards of most high achievers in life, Nixon at this time had everything: prestige, financial security, family contentment, celebrity and a past history of high political triumphs. Yet to him, these green pastures were not enough. He was determined to fight his way back into the arena, to honour his mother's pacifist ideals and to pursue his intellectual theories of geopolitical statecraft. Nixon had a dream. Events far beyond his control were now moving to help him fulfil it.

II. BACK INTO THE ARENA

The landscape of American politics altered dramatically in the three years after Nixon's defeat for the governorship of California. When Nixon first arrived in New York at the beginning of 1963 to earn his living as a Wall Street lawyer,

John F. Kennedy seemed set to serve two full terms in the White House; Nelson Rockefeller was the most probable inheritor of the 1964 GOP nomination; and there was no expectation of an American military commitment to Vietnam. Kennedy's assassination; Rockefeller's divorce; Goldwater's candidature; and the deployment of 300,000 troops to Saigon changed these scenarios. Nixon's plans changed with them.

Nixon heard the news of Kennedy's death in a New York taxicab on the morning of 22 November. He had spent the previous day at a Pepsi Cola board meeting in Dallas, ironically advising the newspaper readers of that city to 'give a courteous reception'[24] to the President and his wife, who were scheduled to arrive the next morning. Coming back into New York from the airport Nixon, like millions of others, can recall exactly how he heard the fateful news.

> My cab halted at a stoplight in Queens, just before the 59th Street bridge. A man ran over from the kerb and said to the driver, 'Do you have a radio in your car?' The driver said no. The man said, 'President Kennedy's just been shot.' Well, as we didn't have a radio I could only sit in the cab for the next twenty-five minutes agonizing about what could have happened...When I arrived at my apartment the doorman ran out with tears pouring down his cheeks as he said, 'Oh Mr. Nixon, have you heard, sir? They've killed President Kennedy. It's terrible'...A few minutes later I got J. Edgar Hoover on the line and I said, 'What happened? Who was it? One of those right-wing nuts?' Hoover responded, 'No, it was a Commonest.' He never said Communist, incidentally, always Commonest. That was how I got the story. Hoover called me later to tell me that Mrs. Oswald said under questioning that the day before she had locked her husband into the bathroom because he had taken out his gun and said he was going to get me—because of course I had been reported as being in Dallas the day before. If that story is true, and I have no reason to believe that Edgar Hoover made it up, it means that this man was completely off his rocker and was out to get anybody that he thought was against whatever he stood for.[25]

Even after learning of Marina Oswald's testimony, Nixon claimed never to have had any 'there but for the grace of God go I' reactions to the assassination. Like almost everyone else in the world his feelings were those of deep shock and sadness. On the night of the assassination, he sat up into the small hours of the morning lamenting his dead rival. He wrote to Jacqueline Kennedy:

> Richard M. Nixon
> 810 Fifth Avenue
> New York, NY 10021
> November 23rd
>
> Dear Jackie,
>   In this tragic hour Pat and I want you to know that our thoughts and prayers are with you.
>   While the hand of fate made Jack and me political opponents, I always cherished the fact that we were personal friends from the time we came to the Congress together in 1947. That friendship evidenced itself in many ways, including the invitation we received to attend your wedding.
>   Nothing I could say now could add to the splendid tributes which have come from throughout the world to him.
>   But I want you to know that the nation will also be forever grateful for your service as First Lady. You brought to the White House charm, beauty and elegance as the official hostess for America, and the mystique of the young in heart which was uniquely yours made an indelible impression on the American consciousness.
>   If in the days ahead we could be helpful in any way, we should be honored to be at your command.
>   Sincerely,
>   Dick Nixon[26]

This graciousness was not immediately reciprocated by the Kennedy staff who, in the confusion of the hour, failed to invite Nixon to the funeral. He had to ask for his invitation with the intermediate assistance of Congressman Pat Hillings.[27] Walking behind the cortège to Arlington cemetery amidst all his emotions of sorrow, Nixon must have found a moment to reflect on the strange tides of fortune. From his perspective, Kennedy had been born with a silver spoon in his mouth. Good looks, athletic ability, inherited wealth, media charisma and a natural Irish wit—these were the gifts that had helped JFK to reach the summit of political power. Nixon, whose luck had apparently left him stranded in the quicksands of failed presidential dreams, would have been less than human if he had not entertained some thoughts along these lines. Nor would he have been alone in such reflections. Jackie Kennedy wrote in response to Nixon's letter of condolence a remarkably sympathetic letter, which expressed similar sentiments.

> Dear Mr. Vice President,
>
> I do thank you for your most thoughtful letter. You two young men—colleagues in Congress, adversaries in 1960 and now look what has happened. Whoever thought such a hideous thing could happen in this country.
>
> I know how you must feel—so long on the path, so closely missing the greatest prize—and now for you, all the question comes up again—and you must commit you and your family's hopes and efforts again. Just one thing I would say to you—if it does not work out as you have hoped for so long—please be consoled by what you already have—life and your family.
>
> We never value life enough when we have it and I would not have had Jack live his life any other way—though I know his death could have been prevented, and I will never cease to torture myself with that.
>
> But if you do not win, please think of all that you have. With my appreciation and regards to your family. I hope your daughters love Chapin School as much as I did.
>
> Sincerely,
>
> Jacqueline Kennedy[28]

For all his twinges of jealousy, Nixon long before the assassination believed that there was significantly less to his arch rival than met the eye. He respected Kennedy as a smart political operator. He resented some of Kennedy's superficial skills, such as his almost uncanny ability to conjure favourable coverage from journalists. However, when it came to substantive achievement, Nixon always believed that he himself would one day do better.

This deep-seated sense of destiny had kept Nixon working away at the substance of politics even when his prospects of regaining power were at their nadir. Despite his humiliation by the voters of California in 1962, he continued to think of himself as an international statesman-in-waiting who should keep in touch with world leaders and events. Nixon's idea of a family holiday in the spring of

1963 was to plan what was virtually a diplomatic circuit of international capitals. On his six-week tour he saw Generalissimo Francisco Franco in Barcelona; the British Foreign Secretary Lord Home in London; the German Foreign Minister Willy Brandt in Bonn; Italy's Defence Minister Giulio Andreotti in Rome and Egypt's President Gamal Nasser in Cairo. He drew huge crowds in Budapest and gave a press conference at the Berlin Wall.

The highlight of his trip was a two-hour private luncheon as the guest of President Charles de Gaulle. The invitation came as a last-minute surprise to the Nixons while they were sightseeing in Paris, and turned out to be an intimate occasion, with only six people present—the de Gaulles; the Nixons; plus US Ambassador Chip Bohlen and his wife. Nixon, who was something of a Franco-phile as a result of the childhood lessons he had received from his mother in French history and literature, had impressed de Gaulle when Vice President by his grasp of European affairs. This good impression was strengthened over the al fresco lunch in the garden of the Elysée Palace. Nixon quoted Rousseau (the fruits of his four-year French course at Whittier College) and gave a perceptive *tour d'horizon* of the strengths and weaknesses of the Atlantic alliance.

The French President spoke about the importance of the United States nego-tiating with the Chinese as soon as possible while they needed American friend-ship, instead of waiting too long until America would be compelled to negotiate with them because of their strength. He also talked about the need for 'détente' in US-Soviet relations. It was the first time Nixon had heard the word used in that context and he sat with rapt attention as de Gaulle told him: 'Well, what are you Americans going to do? Are you going to break down the Berlin Wall? If you are not ready to make war, make peace, but make it on a very strong basis, from strength rather than weakness.'[29]

It was at this 1963 lunch on the patio of the Elysée Palace that the seeds of certain political ideas were sown which later germinated into President Nixon's foreign policies. At the time, the notion that there might ever be a President Nixon looked an electoral absurdity. However, de Gaulle evidently did not share this conventional Washington wisdom, as he showed in the toast he proposed towards the end of the meal. Raising his glass to Nixon he said, 'I realise that you have been checked in the pursuit of your goals. But I have a great sense that some time in the future, without doubt, you will serve your country again in an even higher capacity.'[30]

This was heady stuff from Europe's greatest living statesman, and all four Americans were astonished by the tribute. Ambassador Bohlen seemed totally bemused by it, saying several times in the car journey from the Elysée, 'That was a really remarkable statement', to which Nixon replied 'Sure was. It's the first time I've ever heard anybody say I might have that kind of a political future.'[31]

De Gaulle's compliments were not the passing flattery of a good host. He was one of several international leaders in the mid 1960s who perceived in Nixon a stature, perhaps a greatness, which was not being accorded to him by his fellow countrymen. De Gaulle felt an almost visionary empathy for Nixon, telling aides and visitors on several occasions over the next few years that this was the man destined to lead the United States. One light-hearted illustration of this prescience came in 1965 when de Gaulle was inspecting some recently renovated guest quarters for state visitors at the Trianon Palace in Versailles. As he toured the suite intended for use by heads of state, passing through the bathroom an aide remarked, 'This bath looks as though it might be a little too small for Johnson.' De Gaulle smiled and replied, 'Yes, but it looks about right for Nixon.'[32] Two years later, he made a more serious prediction: 'Mr. Nixon is still young and he will be President', he told General Vernon Walters in 1967. 'There are strange parallels in our lives. Both of us have had our crossings of the desert. And both of us will have been exiles in our own country.' The comment gave Walters 'real goosepimples', and showed him that even at that early stage the French President had 'a deep and special feeling for Nixon'.[33]

Returning from his tour of Europe to New York in May 1963, Nixon faced the more mundane task of earning a living, but he soon became adept at combining business with statecraft. Thanks to his frequent Far East travels on behalf of Pepsi Cola and other clients, he foresaw, well ahead of other US politicians, that Asia was likely to be the most politically sensitive region of the coming decade. He also privately predicted that Kennedy's commitment of 16,000 US 'military advisers' to Vietnam in November 1963, together with US complicity in the assassination of President Diem in the same month, were policy decisions which would turn sour. With these thoughts in mind, Nixon began to build up his knowledge and expertise on Vietnam. He made several private fact-finding missions to the area between 1963 and 1965. These self-imposed journeys were often lonely and tiring. 'I had to do virtually all this non-legal work without any outside assistance', he recalled. 'On several of my trips to Asia, for example, I traveled alone with no security and no aide. This was difficult but in retrospect I think the experience toughened me up.'[34]

Toughened him up for what? A glimpse of Nixon's strategy in this early period of the wilderness years can be seen from an account of his speech on 17 September 1965 to an organisation known as the Advanced Donors of the United Funds of Northern Westchester County. This philanthropic group included some significant opinion formers, among them the editors-in-chief of *Saturday Review*, *Look*, and the *Reader's Digest*, as well as business leaders such as the Chief Executives of Morgan Guaranty, Goldman Sachs, and Morgan Stanley. The invitation sent out to these 'Advanced Donors' said: 'Former Vice President Richard M. Nixon will speak on the importance of using voluntary initiative to solve pressing community problems.'

The aide who prepared the research material and draft speech for Nixon was a thirty-three-year-old recruit to the law firm, Tom Evans. He travelled up to Westchester County with his boss, answering questions about voluntary initiatives for community problems until they arrived at the Bedford Golf Club. As Evans has recalled:

> The speech was not particularly well delivered or for that matter well received. The audience seemed somewhat restless as Richard Nixon occasionally confused the statistics (I remember he said 'eight thousand' rather than 'eight million' at one point) and otherwise proceeded through a fairly lackluster rendition of what must have been a familiar topic to these 'Advanced Donors'. A smattering of applause followed the speech, but then Hobe Lewis of the *Reader's Digest* invited all present 'to remain if you want to hear Mr. Nixon's personal observations on his recent trip to Vietnam'. No one left. Richard Nixon then delivered what he had undoubtedly prepared as his principal remarks for the evening. He used no notes. He spoke of conversations with world leaders on a trip through Asia and of military leaders in Vietnam. He had also talked to frontline troops. The audience was transfixed. It was like being in the briefing room at the White House. I believe that each person in attendance felt that he was in on something very special. At the end of the remarks the audience stood, clapping for a prolonged period.[35]

Vietnam gradually became the issue which brought Richard Nixon back from public partner to public figure. His talk to the Advanced Donors of Westchester County was later turned into an important article in *Reader's Digest*. It was the first of many such writings and speeches. Nixon's authority and expertise on this issue raised his political profile. By the end of 1965 public opinion in the United States was starting to simmer with serious discontent about the war. A few months later, there were signs that the nation might be going to tear itself apart. A voice of proven foreign policy wisdom speaking out on Vietnam was what many Americans longed to hear, particularly in the Republican Party, which had already torn itself apart for other reasons.

After Kennedy's assassination, Nixon flirted with the idea of seeking the Republican nomination in 1964. He did not go after it overtly, but with somewhat transparent coyness he played a waiting game. The longer he waited, the less hopeful his prospects became. In the White House the new President, Lyndon B. Johnson, displayed a master's touch as he cloaked himself in Kennedy's legacy, uniting the Congress and the nation behind a massive programme of social legislation, which he labelled 'The Great Society'. Within months it became obvious that Americans liked the programme and wanted political continuity rather than three different Presidents within a year. Johnson began to look unbeatable.

Among the Republicans, the contest was between Nelson Rockefeller, the liberal Governor of New York, and Barry Goldwater, the right-wing Senator from Arizona. Nixon at one stage hoped that he might emerge as a compromise choice after these two polarised candidates had wounded each other in the course of the primaries. Contrary to such expectations, Goldwater showed surprising strength on the road to the nomination. He was an ideological hero to large numbers of New Right conservative activists in the GOP and their fervour for his cause proved decisive. By contrast, Rockefeller stumbled, largely as a result of adverse publicity over his divorce. By the time the Republicans reached the Cow Palace in San Francisco for their convention in mid-July, Goldwater was unstoppable in his momentum and unrestrainable in his conservatism.

Nixon bowed to the inevitable and was considered sufficiently supportive of the nominee to be given the crucial task of introducing Goldwater to the convention. In party-political terms, Nixon's carefully crafted speech was a masterpiece, binding up the wounds, recapturing the centre ground, and profiling the candidate with a breadth and sympathy that was worth millions of uncommitted votes. The theme of the presentation was unity, as Nixon's closing words emphasised: 'Now I present to you the man who earned and proudly carries the title of Mr. Conservative. He is the man who, by the action of this convention, is now Mr. Republican. And he is the man who, after the greatest campaign in history, will be Mr. President—Barry Goldwater.'[36]

The convention erupted with a fifteen-minute ovation that followed Nixon's address. If Goldwater had picked up the unity theme and built on it, he might well have mounted a serious challenge to Johnson in the election. Instead he took the opposite course. 'Those who don't care for our cause we don't expect to enter our ranks in any case', he thundered, thus turning his back on at least a third of his own party. Goldwater then moved on to even dizzier heights of self-destructive oratory with the memorable line, 'Extremism in the defense of liberty is no vice; moderation in the pursuit of justice is no virtue.' As the New Right conservatives bellowed and bayed their approbation for these words with the blood-curdling enthusiasm of hounds on a hot scent, Nixon sat frozen with horror in the convention hall. 'I felt almost physically sick', he recalled. 'As soon as I heard those words I knew the election had gone down the tube. With that one line, Goldwater had split the party and given Johnson and the Democrats the opportunity to tag him with the extremist label.'[37]

In spite of his gloomy forebodings, Nixon was too loyal a servant of his party to start scrapping in public with the nominee as other leading Republicans were doing. However, he immediately foresaw that Goldwater's folly could lead to the revival of his own political prospects. One sign that he had grasped which way the wind might be blowing was his sudden decision in the last hours of the 1964 convention to hold a reception for all the surviving delegates from 1960 who had voted for him to be the nominee in the race against Kennedy. 'That was a party with a purpose', recalled Pat Hillings. 'Nixon stood in that receiving line for hours, remembering names, establishing links and subtly reminding everyone that he could be the great unifier. There was no doubt in my mind that he was putting down a marker for the future.'[38]

Such futuristic thoughts encouraged Nixon to suppress his political distaste for the New Right. Taking five weeks' leave from the law partnership, he campaigned vigorously for the ticket, making over 150 speeches in thirty-six states. In a conversation with Bob Finch, he compared his effort to joining the doomed army of Napoleon on the retreat from Moscow.[39] He knew the Goldwater cause was hopeless. But remembering his unhappy experiences with Joe Shell's supporters in California, he calculated that it was vital not to sever all political links with the conservatives in the GOP. 'I thought it important for them not to feel that they were completely abandoned by all of those who happened to disagree with some of Goldwater's views.'[40]

Thus, while other GOP chieftains like Rockefeller and Scranton sulked in their tents, Nixon was the good soldier, loyally fighting for the Party and its chosen candidate. In retrospect, Nixon regarded his decision to campaign for Goldwater in 1964 as the single most important step that he took on his return to power during the wilderness years.[41]

The results of the 1964 election were a catastrophe for the Republicans. In the presidential contest, Lyndon Johnson won 61 per cent and 486 electoral votes to Goldwater's 39 per cent and 52 electoral votes. The GOP held on to only 17 of the 50 governorships. In the House they lost 38 seats and were left as an enfeebled rump facing a 295-140 Democratic majority. In the Senate they were reduced to 32 seats, while in state legislatures across the country, nearly 600 Republican incumbents were defeated. Fierce recriminations inevitably followed such a massacre, but Nixon, the loyal campaigner, was immune from the orgy of backstabbing and backbiting that took place. Indeed, many more observers with long-range vision began to see that the misfortune of Goldwater might become the good fortune of Nixon. The GOP desperately needed a political Phoenix who could rise from the ashes; heal the wounds between the Party's liberal and conservative wings; and start attacking the increasingly vulnerable jugular of Lyndon Johnson. Almost the only visible and acceptable candidate for this role of Phoenix was Richard Nixon.

Back at 20 Broad Street the bright young men of the law firm were also quick to see that their public partner might have a presidential future. After many in-house 'skull sessions', now dedicated to the unfamiliar subject of politics, they came up with a plan which became known as Congress 1966. This was based on the proposition that the political pendulum had swung too far. Large numbers of the congressional seats lost in the Goldwater débâcle of 1964 were natural Republican districts which would come back with the tide at the next mid-term elections of 1966. Nixon should therefore spearhead a campaign to recapture such seats. If his efforts were seen to be successful it would leave him well placed to fight for the GOP presidential nomination in 1968.

This was the plan. It worked because an inner group of young men so fervently believed in Richard Nixon. 'I was talked into this campaign by amateurs',[42] he said afterwards, referring principally to Len Garment (thirty-nine); Tom Evans (thirty-three); and a new recruit to the law firm, John Sears (twenty-seven). This trio was later buttressed by more experienced fund-raising hands such as Maurice Stans and Peter Flanigan, who collected approximately $100,000 to pay the expenses of the Congress '66 operation. $30,000 of this came in a single donation from Robert A. Abplanalp, the inventor of the aerosol valve. 'Let us spray', said one 20 Broad Street humorist when the cheque arrived.

The money was used mainly for air travel, and for paying the salary of Nixon's sole full-time political aide Patrick J. Buchanan, a twenty-seven-year old conservative journalist recruited from the *St. Louis Post Despatch*. Outside volunteers included William Safire (thirty-six), the New York public relations executive who had been captivated by Nixon ever since witnessing his performance in the Moscow 'Kitchen Debate' against Khrushchev; Nick Ruwe, a privately wealthy advance man who had helped in the 1960 campaign; and Charles

McWhorter, an ITT lawyer and GOP activist whose encyclopaedic knowledge of his party was a Republican legend.

With this slender band of close supporters, Nixon embarked on the campaign trail of 1966. He was the only prominent Republican to be out on the battlefield, targeting his efforts on sixty-six congressional seats in thirty-five states. His party loyalty was much admired but his performances on the stump were not always convincing, as John Sears, who often accompanied him on these early speaking tours, has recalled:

> We weren't getting good vibes from many of the audience. Nixon was too often stiff and transparently insincere. He didn't look like a man who would be President, and the polls didn't suggest that his Congress '66 operation was likely to be all that successful—at least not until the very end. Sometimes he could come across as a complete phony. I remember that on one occasion in New England even he seemed to be quite ashamed of some pretty awful lies he told to an audience on quite substantive issues because he said to me afterwards, 'John, I can say things that when other people say them, they are lies, but when I say them people don't believe them anyway!' From then on I realized I was dealing with a very complicated person.[43]

The complexity of the Nixon character fascinated his young aides. They knew he had a dark side in which mendacity, deviousness, and personal disloyalty could come to the fore. There were times when they were offended by the nakedness of his opportunism, as for example in April 1965, when he rashly challenged the principle of academic freedom by demanding the dismissal of Professor Eugene Genovese of Rutgers University for making controversial statements about the desirability of a North Vietnamese victory in the war. Yet for all his frailties, Nixon could shine on the campaign trail with courage, humour and even kindness to his critics. When he swung through the Deep South he fought tenaciously against the GOP conservatives' efforts to dilute civil rights. In Mississippi, where the local Republicans had endorsed a platform calling for 'segregation of the races as absolutely essential to harmonious racial relations', Nixon rejected it completely, telling his audience in Jackson, 'I am opposed to any segregationist plank in a Republican platform. I would fight it in the national Republican platform and speak against it in any state I appear in.'[44] He also warned, in a syndicated newspaper column, 'Southern Republicans must not climb aboard the sinking ship of racial injustice.'[45]

When it came to humour, Nixon could be amusing in private, but in public he relied on a repertoire of somewhat stilted jests, which apparently hit the target with his audiences. 'Any Republican who believes LBJ is a conservative would believe Richard Burton married Elizabeth Taylor for her money', was one.[46] 'When I look at all the Democrats' mistakes that need attacking, I feel like a mosquito in a nudist camp—I don't know where to begin', was another.[47] As for Nixon the compassionate campaigner, Charles McWhorter remembers him at a 1965 press conference in Hartford, Connecticut.

> It was Nixon's practice to let the opening question go to a senior local reporter, so up gets this guy from some little rag out in the boondocks and really lets fly at Nixon with a whole string of 'have you stopped beating your wife' questions which were just awful—untrue, full of prejudice, the pits. Unfortunately all this was live on local state television, and I could feel Nixon getting mad. So when the reporter finally got all his bullshit off his chest, I expected Nixon to tear him to pieces, but no, instead he gave the guy a long, patient, totally courteous response answering every point in detail with unbelievable politeness. Eventually, as we were leaving Hartford, I asked Nixon: 'Why the hell didn't you hit out at that son of a bitch?' The Boss's answer was amazing. He said, 'At first I wanted to, but then I thought to myself, that's probably the first and only time a guy like that will ever get to ask a question of a national political figure, and then I realized that if I went for him he would be humiliated on television in front of his own community, his colleagues on his paper and his family. So I said to myself. This guy's got a mother. She's probably watching. I'd better go softly with him.[48]

The one opponent with whom Nixon did not deal softly was Lyndon Johnson. Knowing how to sting the President was his forte. He delivered many wounding barbs at the Johnson domestic record in his campaign speeches. However, on Vietnam, Nixon pulled his punches for most of 1966 in what he claimed was a bipartisan spirit.

Eventually, two weeks before the November elections, he got a chance to throw down a challenge to the President. Johnson had been to a summit in Manila with the leaders of South Vietnam. The communiqué announced a formula for mutual withdrawal by which American troops would be brought home as and when North Vietnamese forces pulled back. Nixon rightly saw this as an illusory offer which had not the slightest chance of being accepted by Hanoi. He also seized on the communiqué's central flaw, which was that its proposals for withdrawal referred only to the North Vietnamese Army and not to the Vietcong, who would still be able to continue their war inside the South. 'Is this a quest for peace or a quest for votes?' Nixon asked scornfully, issuing a statement asking the President a number of pointed questions. 'Are we really ready to stand aside and let the Vietcong and ARVN [Army of the Republic of Vietnam] slug it out? Will we limit our military response to the fluctuating intensity of Communist aggression? Or will we escalate in order to shorten the war and reduce American casualties? How many more American troops will victory require? Does the Johnson administration intend to raise taxes to pay for this war?'[49]

Within two hours of the publication of Nixon's statement in the *New York Times* (which had only printed it after some skilful lobbying by Bill Safire because news was slack that day), Lyndon Johnson exploded at a televised White House press conference. Caustically and emotionally he attacked the statement point by point. Then he laid into his tormentor.

> I do not want to get into a debate on a foreign policy meeting in Manila with a chronic campaigner like Mr. Nixon. It is his problem to find fault with his country and with his government during a period of October every two years. If you will look back over his record you will find that to be true. You never did really recognize and realize he had an official position... You remember what President Eisenhower said, that if you would give him a week or so, he would figure out what he was doing.
>
> Since then he has made a temporary stand in California, and you saw what action the people took out there. Then he crossed the country to New York. Then he went back to San Francisco, hoping that he would be in the wings available if Goldwater stumbled. But Goldwater didn't stumble. Now he is out talking about a conference, but obviously he is not well prepared on, or informed about... Mr. Nixon doesn't serve his country well by trying to leave that kind of impression in the hope that he can pick up a precinct or two, or a ward or two.[50]

'He *hit* us. Jesus did he hit us. You'll never believe how he hit us!'[51] was how an electrified Pat Buchanan reported the President's press conference to his boss, who was off campaigning in New Hampshire. Nixon was hardly less excited than his aide, seeing LBJ's attack as manna from heaven. Overnight the President's outburst put Nixon back on centre stage as the Republican Party's spokesman on the nation's most pressing issue. During the weekend before the elections, Nixon was given maximum exposure on the front pages, the news bulletins and the talk shows. The Republican National Committee (which had not been overly helpful to Nixon in 1966 on the grounds they did not wish to favour any individual con- tender for the nomination in 1968) changed course and provided him with a half-hour of network television prime time to answer the President.

The veteran of the Checkers broadcast knew how to make the most of such an opportunity. 'I was subjected last week to one of the most savage personal assaults ever leveled by the President of the United States against one of his political opponents...I shall answer it not for myself but because of a great prin- ciple that is at stake. It is the principle of the right to disagree, the right to dissent', was how he opened, going on to present a litany of questions and criticisms on Johnson's war policies. Nixon ended by returning to the subject of LBJ's irascible outburst, putting an artful 'more in sorrow than in anger' stab of the stiletto into the final passage of his broadcast. Purporting to speak directly to the President he solemnly intoned, 'I respect you for the great energies you devote to your office and my respect has not changed because of the personal attack you made on me. You see, I think I can understand how a man can be very very tired and how his temper can then be very short.'[52]

Nixon said later that his crocodile tears about LBJ's tiredness had been designed 'to send Johnson right up the cotton-pickin' wall'.[53] They must have had just such an effect, for by the time the weekend of intense media attention was over, Nixon had been elevated from chronic campaigner to Leader of the Oppo- sition. When the election results came in two nights later, on Tuesday 9 Novem- ber, they made the new Leader of the Opposition look like the next Republican President. The GOP scored a resounding victory, capturing forty-seven congres- sional seats, three Senate seats, eight governorships and 540 seats in state legisla- tures. 'It's a sweep, it's a sweep', Nixon kept repeating as he joyfully checked the returns in New York. It was also a personal triumph, for Nixon had been spec- tacularly successful both in the districts where he had targeted his campaigning efforts (forty-four of the sixty-six House candidates for whom he had spoken were victorious) and in his national challenge to Johnson, which was thought to have been a big factor in enhancing the swing to the Republicans.

Just after midnight, when most of the returns were in, Nixon was in a back- slapping mood of exultation at his headquarters in the Drake Hotel. 'It's too great a night to go home—let's go out and celebrate', he laughed to his aide Nick Ruwe.

With another friend, John Davies, they headed off to a fashionable Manhattan nightclub, El Morocco. Ruwe recalled:

> I've never seen Nixon on a greater high. He was over the moon at the magnitude of his achievement. He knew he'd turned the political world upside down more or less single-handed…as we drank two or three bottles of good claret and munched our way through a mountain of spaghetti bolognaise, people kept coming up to our table to shake Nixon's hand—it was that sort of an after-the-football-game atmosphere…I can remember two interesting things about the conversation. The first was how scathing Nixon was about various journalists who'd written him off and the GOP off in their columns. He seemed to have a total recall for every damn-fool phrase the prophets of doom had written. The second was that he'd already calculated exactly what 1966 meant to the 1968 election…He wasn't saying he would be the nominee, although I guess his hopes were strong for it. What he was saying was that whoever got the nomination would now only have to run 2 per cent ahead of the party to knock Johnson out of the White House. He kept on emphasizing how in 1960 he'd had to run 5 per cent ahead of his party, and how that had been an impossible task. 'But it's within reach now', I recall him saying as he checked the arithmetic.[54]

Returning to his apartment from El Morocco at around 3 a.m., Nixon telephoned John Sears back at the Drake Hotel to get one last check on the late results. Sears remembers him chortling after listening to the final tally: 'We'll kick their toes off in '68.'[55]

Against the longest of odds, Nixon had fought his way back into the arena of presidential politics.

III. PREPARING FOR THE PRESIDENCY

After successfully positioning himself as a probable Republican presidential nominee for 1968, Nixon did the oddest thing. He took a voluntary sabbatical from politics. This move was made against the recommendation of every member of his fast-expanding group of advisers. They wanted him to capitalise on his mid-term election triumphs with a series of national speeches and TV appearances. Nixon would have none of it. Although he instructed his team to work intensively at the tasks of fund raising, organisation building and delegate hunting, he decided to operate on an entirely different level himself. After announcing to universal surprise on 'Meet the Press' that he was imposing a personal six-month moratorium on campaigning, Nixon withdrew from the battle to prepare himself for the Presidency. He said afterwards that he took this decision 'because I understood the great rhythm of politics—when to be on stage, when to be off stage, when to stand back, when to insist on time to think things through, and when to work hard at preparation'.[56]

Nixon's preparations took the form of extensive travel and writings. Seen with the wisdom of hindsight, these activities gave the clear signal that he intended to devote his Presidency to foreign affairs and that he was planning sensational new policy initiatives in this field. At the time, however, few people in America got this message and even fewer believed it. The conventional wisdom among election watchers was that Nixon had decided to go on tour hoping that his rivals for the nomination might suffer from over-exposure at home, while he himself earned favourable media coverage by grandstanding abroad. There was a smattering of truth in this interpretation, but such domestic purposes were a secondary objective. Nixon was absolutely serious about preparing a new geopolitical strategy for America—and for the world. 'I realized that I had to get ready for the top job, and that the best thing I could do was to get to know the world', he recalled. 'Those six months became one of the most creative periods of my entire life, because it was then that I began to see what had to be done, with the Soviets, with China, and with our allies.'[57]

It is sometimes difficult with Nixon to see where the cynical politician in him ends, and where the visionary side of his character begins. On his overseas tours of 1967, however, it was clearly Nixon the intellectual strategist who was in the ascendant. The aides who accompanied him on these gruelling schedules around four continents that year were quick to realise that 'The Boss' was deep into policy not politics. Robert Ellsworth, the former Congressman from Kansas, accompanied Nixon on the European section of his travels. Their appointment schedule read like a *Who's Who* of international diplomacy. In London, Harold Macmillan, Edward Heath, and Prime Minister Harold Wilson. In Bonn, Konrad Adenauer, Chancellor Kurt Kiesinger, Foreign Minister Willy Brandt, and Finance Minister Franz-Josef Strauss. In Rome, Pope Paul VI, President Saragat, Prime Minister Moro and Foreign Minister Fanfani. In Paris, de Gaulle, and Couve de Murville. In Brussels, Paul-Henri Spaak, Secretary General Manuel Brosio of NATO and Commander General Lyman Lemnitzer, Supreme Allied Commander, Europe. 'Accompanying Nixon to appointments like these, I began to realize that here was a quite extraordinary mind at work', recalled Ellsworth. 'He saw international politics as the highest stakes game in the world. He was an intense listener who said afterwards how much he had learned when I really thought he knew it all. He analyzed everything, even the anecdotal stuff, the visits to shops as well as the talks with statesmen. He was often thinking two or three moves, sometimes even a generation ahead. As we went along I could gradually see what was forming in his mind—the notion that the European order had become rigid, sterile, bipolar and that America should move to help change all that.'[58]

After touring Eastern Europe and the Soviet Union (where Leonid Brezhnev alone of world leaders refused his American visitor an appointment) Nixon returned to 20 Broad Street to touch base with his law partners, several of whom were now dedicating large parts of their working days to presidential politics. However, he only stayed in New York for a week, setting off again in March on a long swing through Asia, accompanied by his latest and most cerebral recruit to the political staff, Ray Price, a former editorial writer from the *Herald Tribune*. In April, Nixon made a five-nation tour of Latin America, where he was received by the President of each country. In June he went to Africa and in the immediate aftermath of the 1967 Arab-Israeli Six Day War, he toured the Middle East.

If the purpose of these peregrinations was to produce favourable press coverage in the United States, it was unsuccessful. 'Around the world in 80 clichés', was the headline of an unfriendly *Newsweek* article on his visits.[59] The most vitriolic attack on Nixon the global presidential candidate came from the *New York Times*. 'What is he trying to prove?' asked the paper's senior columnist, James Reston. 'He is trying to prove the new theories of American politics, (a) that motion is progress, (b) that the road to the White House runs through all the other capitals of the world, and (c) that distance lends enchantment. He is proving that he knows not only all the Republican county chairmen of the United States, but all the Prime Ministers of the world as well.' Reston's judgement was that the Nixon travel schedule was an exercise in pointlessness. 'There is absolutely no evidence that travel has given him any new or deeper visions of America's problems in the world...He gives us straight Cold War dialogue...Few candidates have ever seen so many new things or had so little new to say about them.'[60]

This column was an illustration of the gulf that was starting to open up between the perception of Nixon by the East-coast media establishment and the perception of Nixon by well-informed international observers. All over the world in the late 1960s, members of that élite club of geopolitical statesmen and thinkers were coming to regard the former Vice President as one of the most enlightened minds in their own peer group. Konrad Adenauer; Charles de Gaulle; Lee

Kwan-yew; Lester Pearson of Canada; Eisaku Sato of Japan (a country to which Nixon made ten visits between 1963 and 1967); Ayub Khan of Pakistan; and Robert Menzies of Australia were among the world figures with whom Nixon talked and corresponded on a regular basis. In Britain, the foreign policy establishment regarded him as a worthy heir to John Foster Dulles. This author, working in 1967 as an aide to the former British Foreign Secretary Selwyn Lloyd (at that time a House of Commons Opposition front-bencher on whom Nixon occasionally called), retains a memory of Lloyd reading the Reston column, stamping his foot angrily, saying, 'Twaddle, absolute twaddle!...Nixon's a brilliant strategist, not a Cold War hack', later adding somewhat sadly (and wrongly), 'If even Scotty Reston has now got his knife into Nixon, there's not much hope for his chances of becoming President.'[61]

Reston's column did turn out to be 'twaddle' in one respect, for that very summer Nixon was writing a seminal article outlining his new foreign policy strategy. It was published in the October 1967 issue of *Foreign Affairs* under the title 'Asia After Viet Nam'. It was Nixon at his most original and prophetic, foreseeing the rise of Far East economic miracle in countries like South Korea, Hong Kong, Singapore, Malaysia and Taiwan; calling for an increased Japanese defence contribution; and raising the curtain on his future policy to China. 'There was no single moment when I suddenly said to myself like Saul on the road to Damascus, we've got to have an opening to China', recalled Nixon. 'The idea had been germinating with me for some months, particularly on those 1967 tours. But if I had to pick a time when my thinking crystallized I would say that it was when I was working with Ray Price on the *Foreign Affairs* article. The discipline of discussing the issue in depth with someone of Ray's intellect and of having to get my ideas down on paper helped me to see ahead to the China policy as it later came to be.'[62]

The vital sentences that Nixon published in *Foreign Affairs* on China were these: 'Any American policy towards Asia must come urgently to grips with the reality of China...This does not mean rushing to grant recognition to Peking...but we simply cannot afford to have China forever outside the family of nations, there to nurture its fantasies, cherish its hates, and threaten its neighbors.'[63]

He amplified this theme in an important private speech later in the summer at the Bohemian Grove in California. This establishment summer camp, well attended by the barons of corporate and Republican America, had in 1967 a considerable political importance for Nixon. He was still well ahead in the race for the Republican presidential nomination, but he feared that the charismatic Governor of California, Ronald Reagan, was coming up fast on the rails as the favourite with the conservative wing of the Party. Reagan's weakness lay in his inexperience, while Nixon's vulnerability lay in the fear that he might be unelectable. Both men were Lakeside speakers (star billing at the camp's auditorium overlooking a lake) at the Bohemian Grove.

Nixon, knowing that the stakes were high, prepared for battle. 'I took a week off before that appearance, rented a room in a motel, and with John Davies who was my volunteer aide bringing me in Kentucky Fried Chicken for dinner every night, made an extensive outline and delivered the speech without notes', he recalled.[64] The address was an inside summary of observations and conclusions from Nixon's recent travels through four continents. It was, according to its author, 'the best speech I made during my years out of office'[65] and it set the audience alight. The roaring standing ovation made it an event reminiscent of Nixon's *tour de force* before Tom Dewey's New York Republican State Dinner in 1952 which had opened up the road to the vice Presidency. By contrast, Governor Reagan was glitzy but lightweight. The many influential GOP power brokers present, including southern conservatives like Senator John Tower of Texas, and Governor Claude Kirk from Florida, shared the consensus that there had been no contest between the two speakers. Nixon alone had sounded ready to win the White House and to lead the free world. From the Bohemian Grove speeches onwards, Reagan's presidential prospects for 1968 began to ebb.

Another rival for the Republican nomination, Governor George Romney of Michigan, also started slipping as a result of Nixon's primacy in foreign affairs. Throughout 1967 the Vietnam issue was top of the political agenda. Nixon had a clear stance on it, which was that he believed in a level of military security that would bring about a credible settlement. Romney slithered from hawkish to dovish statements, his ultimate goof coming in September, when he returned from a visit to US troops in Saigon to tell a press conference: 'I just had the greatest brainwashing that anyone can get when you go over to Vietnam, not only by the generals but also by the diplomatic corps over there, and they do a very thorough job.'[66] The derision heaped on Romney's use of the word 'brainwashing' was the beginning of the end of his presidential prospects. The contrast with Nixon's firm expertise on the issue could hardly have been starker.

1967 was Richard Nixon's year of resurrection. His progress towards the Presidency was beginning to take on an air of inevitability as his GOP competitors fell away and Lyndon Johnson's unpopularity plummeted to irretrievable depths. Nixon's satisfaction at this growing public success was matched by the contentment of his private life. Pat, happy in the anonymity of New York, had accepted with good grace that there would be one more campaign and went back to her work in her old role as the volunteer secretary 'Miss Ryan', who came in to help Rose Woods with the rising tide of political mail at 20 Broad Street. Tricia and Julie had grown up to be vivacious daughters of whom any father would be proud. They were dating the young men Ed Cox and David Eisenhower, who later became their husbands. In November Julie broke the news of her impending engagement to her father. He was inwardly delighted but too overcome with emotion to say so with the warmth the occasion required. Julie was understandably upset by what she thought was paternal coolness. The episode says volumes for Richard Nixon's limitations as a human communicator. However, after a word from Pat, he put matters right, slipping this note under Julie's bedroom door:

> Dear Julie,
>
> I suppose no father believes any boy is good enough for his daughter. But I believe both David and you are lucky to have found each other. Fina* often says 'Miss Julie always brings life into the home.' In the many years ahead you will have your ups and downs but I know you will always 'bring life into your home' wherever it is.
>
> Love,
>
> Daddy[67]

There was plenty of life in the office too. 20 Broad Street was beginning to hum with political excitement. Nixon's full-time staff was small but superb, consisting of Pat Buchanan, Ray Price, Rose Mary Woods, and Dwight Chapin. By contrast, Governor Nelson Rockefeller, still a presidential hopeful, had a full-time staff of over 150. Buchanan and Price were the intellectual wordsmiths for speeches and statements; Woods as always was the workaholic private secretary; and Chapin looked after all the scheduling arrangements for speeches, appointments and travels. This last role was more important for Nixon than for most politicians. He had functioned badly in the past when the mechanical disciplines of his life were not working according to plan. Disruptions and interruptions bothered him to the point of fury. He needed to have his time protected and his schedule tightly regimented. Bob Haldeman, whose experience as California campaign manager in 1962 had given him a full understanding of Nixon's vulnerabilities, believed that 'a zero defect system' had to be put in place to safeguard the technical and administrative side of the candidate's body politic. Dwight Chapin, a twenty-five-year-old USC graduate whose fascination with politics had taken him to the 1960 convention as a teenager, was chosen by Haldeman to be

---

* Fina Sanchez and her husband Manolo were the Nixon family's beloved housekeeper and cook.

the keeper of this system. Its defects were not always zero, at least in Nixon's view. He could explode at unnecessary interruptions and on one occasion was so enraged by some scheduling transgression that he threw Chapin against a wall, bruising his arm—an uncharacteristic blow for which Nixon swiftly apologised. Such outbursts aside, the Chapin-Haldeman custodianship of Nixon's time worked well in the wilderness and early White House years, not least because it provided him with the hours of solitude in which he did some of his most creative thinking.

Although much of Nixon's 'thinking time' was devoted to the international scene, he had an intellectual appetite for new ideas which covered the whole spectrum of politics. Some of his administration's most successful domestic policies had their genesis in his dialogues with academic advisers during the 1967–8 period. For example, the radical proposal to abolish the draft and create all-volunteer armed forces first surfaced in a memorandum to him from Professor Martin Anderson of Columbia University. Anderson also introduced Nixon to the welfare reform writings of Daniel Patrick Moynihan of Harvard. These triggered Moynihan's subsequent appointment to the White House staff and paved the way for some highly original policies aimed at restructuring the nation's welfare system.

In addition to the flow of ideas from external advisers, the in-house brains trust of Price, Buchanan and Garment were prolific with policy suggestions. Among the older Nixon associates, Bob Finch came up with his thoughts on medical initiatives which later emerged as 'The War on Cancer' of the 1970s, while Maurice Stans advised on new economic strategies.

With so much think-tank activity taking place, there were times in 1967 and early 1968 when the atmosphere at 20 Broad Street seemed to be getting rather too academic. Theoretical ideas on how to govern appeared to be taking precedence over the practical plans for getting elected. Nixon in certain moods reflected this ambivalence. In his mind the high ideals of government and the low practices of politics were divided into separate compartments. One political associate who diagnosed this mild schizophrenia in the candidate-in-waiting was Charles E. Colson, a thirty-six-year-old lawyer and GOP activist from Boston. He presented some unusual ideas on how the Republican Party could broaden its base of support by wooing certain ethnic and occupational groups of voters. Nixon was impressed but hesitant. 'After our meeting he gave me a lift home,' recalled Colson, 'and he began talking almost as if I wasn't in the car with him. "Should I really run?" he was saying. "All that traveling. All that hard work. All those tired old pedestrian faces... The only reason that I could go through with it is that I know what has to be done...to counter the long-range ambitions of the Soviets...to build up NATO...to hold our own so that our democratic ideals will have time to take root.'"

Colson was captivated by this monologue. 'I thought to myself: "This man has got to be President. He is a true idealist."' Colson promptly signed up for the campaign. He was to become one of Nixon's most ardent disciples.[68]

As the countdown towards the early 1968 primaries began, what Nixon's team lacked was a manager. It was full of talent, but there was too much competitiveness among both the full-time and the part-time advisers. An older figure whose authority would be obeyed by the young turks was needed. After one or two false starts and wrong appointments, the finger of selection for this role started to point to John Mitchell. Mitchell had arrived at 20 Broad Street in January 1967 as a result of the merger between his law firm and Nixon Mudge. He was a man of considerable achievements and attributes, several of which were tailor-made to appeal to Nixon. In youth, Mitchell had been a sports star, carrying off national trophies in golf, athletics, and professional ice hockey. In education, he had won but turned down a place at Harvard, choosing to study at New York's unglamorous Fordham Law School because his father disliked Boston élitism. In war he had been decorated with the Silver Star and two purple hearts for gallantry in combat, and had commanded the South Pacific squadron of Navy Patrol Torpedo boats made famous for including among its skippers Lieutenant John F. Kennedy. In love he was a starry-eyed romantic, touchingly devoted to his erratic but glamorous Southern Belle wife, Martha. In law he had reached the top of his profession by becoming Dean of the Municipal Bond Bar. He earned over $400,000 a year from his practice, which gave him an encyclopaedic knowledge of the personalities and finances in state and local governments across the country. This expertise fascinated Nixon, who soon saw ways of harnessing his new partner's abilities to his own presidential ambitions.

Even more intriguing to Nixon was Mitchell's personality, for here was a man who outwardly radiated such strength. 'Mitchell exuded competence, calmness and toughness', recalls Tom Evans. 'He sat there at conferences in our office with his hands clasped around his pipe, hardly ever moving a muscle, usually saying very little. When he did speak he came across as the voice of authority.'[69] In fact, Evans and some of the other young men in the law firm soon saw that there were weaknesses in Mitchell's façade. They noticed that Mitchell had a shaky hand muscle, and that it was his determination to conceal this small infirmity that led to his elbows-on-the-table posture of pipe-clenching immobility. They also observed that Mitchell could be a bully to people he considered unimportant; that he was prone to small lies, often pretending to know much more than he really did; and that he zealously maintained the fiction of a long-standing friendship with Nixon going back over many years, whereas in fact the two men had met for the first time in 1966. These small chinks in Mitchell's armour were not perceived by Nixon. 'The Boss virtually fell in love with John,' said one insider, 'and it was a love that was blind'.[70]

One of the factors which brought about this 'love' for Mitchell was Nixon's need for a contemporary on his political team. All the other members of his entourage were ten or fifteen years younger than himself. They called him 'The Boss', 'The Man', even 'The Old Man'. Mitchell, at fifty-four, was Nixon's equal in age and seniority at the law firm. He was also seen as 'a heavyweight', in achievement if not in political experience.

This latter weakness did not bother Nixon, who had a strong instinct that his new law partner would make a good political partner. Within three months of Mitchell's arrival at 20 Broad Street, the Dean of the Bond Bar was having his first trial runs as a delegate hunter. Soon he was given important assignments, such as the setting up of the Nixon-for-President organisation in Wisconsin and other Midwestern states. After these missions were executed with impressive efficiency, Mitchell was sounded out on his availability for the job of campaign manager. He purported to be reluctant to accept any such role, but this was largely a pretence. At the start of the year he had taken a 60 per cent salary cut in order to fit in with the remuneration structure at Nixon Mudge. This, and his willingness to take on political chores, were among the many indicators of his eagerness to gain proximity to a future President. Nevertheless, Mitchell's posture during his early months at the law partnership was that of playing hard to get. Nixon needed him, he implied; he didn't need Nixon. It was a stance which had its own cleverly calculated appeal to the man who mattered.

The rise of John Mitchell to becoming the number one figure in Nixon's political life was due to more intriguing factors than executive efficiency or personal magnetism. The true explanation may be found in the psyche of the junior partner in the relationship. Even as he approached the threshold of the presidency, Nixon remained an insecure man who often suffered from endearingly humble doubts about himself and his electoral prospects. He was awed by Mitchell's strength of character and aura of competence. All that granite toughness and certitude overimpressed him. The cynicism of mind, brevity of tongue, and ruthlessness in executing decisions that were Mitchell's trademarks became artificially stamped on the President-in-waiting. Nixon had a strong intellect of his own, but his personality had a chameleon-like dimension to it. In the presence of forceful men he could shed the more sensitive and thoughtful side of his character in his urge, still largely unfulfilled since his college days, to be 'one of the boys'.

With the establishing of the Nixon–Mitchell relationship came the first seeds of the later troubles of Watergate. It was not that Mitchell was a bad man, it was that by encouraging the macho side of Nixon he created an atmosphere in which bad judgements were too easily made. Nixon the hater; Nixon the profane; Nixon the furious; Nixon the unscrupulous player of hardball were demons in his nature which had surfaced comparatively rarely during the first fifty-four years of his life. By contrast, there was Nixon the idealistic, the thoughtful, the sensitive, the kind-hearted and the thoroughly decent son of Hannah. These had been the stronger and more consistent characterisations of his multi-faceted personality up to 1967. It was the arrival of John Mitchell as the strong peer relationship in his life that began shifting the balance of these conflicting forces.

However, before casting too much blame in Mitchell's direction, certain caveats should be entered; for there were two important external catalysts also encouraging changes in Nixon's character. One was the temper of the times. By 1967 the twin poisons of Vietnam and racial discontent had firmly entered America's political system. Their feverish symptoms appeared everywhere. That summer saw race riots in Detroit and fifty other cities. The anti-war civil disobedience movement erupted on a thousand campuses. From Harvard to Haight-Ashbury, from Black power to flower power, there were signs that a revolution of alienated youth was on the march. Publicly Nixon kept his cool on these developments. Privately he was starting to share the outrage felt by his constituency of Middle America. One side of him responded to these pressures by searching for solutions, another side simply said 'hang tough'. While Mitchell's voice was in the forefront of those advocating the latter strategy, his simplistic law and order prescription would never have received much attention from Nixon had not the situation itself been crying out for stronger action. When, in the coming months on the campaign trail, Nixon began sounding angrier and tougher, his change of mood was reflecting the troubled spirit of America in the 1960s.

Second, Nixon's inclination to 'play hardball' was linked to the deteriorating standards of the Presidency. Life in the White House had moved a long way from the 'clean as a hound's tooth' morality of the Eisenhower years. Observing Kennedy and Johnson in power brought out the chameleon in Nixon and led to the development of a new ruthlessness in him. Bill Rogers, one of the few 'fast track' friends in New York whose connection with Nixon went back to the 1940s perceived this metamorphosis and was quietly troubled by it.

The Dick Nixon I knew was one of the most kind-hearted, straight-forward and ethical individuals you could ever hope to meet. In business and money matters he was always that way. Yet I think that around this time he began to make a difference between personal ethics and political ethics. He was affected by watching what went on in the White House, first with the Kennedys who stopped at noth-ing—womanizing, abusing the IRS and the Justice Department and so on—and then with Lyndon Johnson who was just totally unscru-pulous. I believe Nixon saw what happened with those Presidents and said to himself, 'That's the way the game's gotta be played.'[71]

John Mitchell encouraged Richard Nixon to play his game with the tough amorality that had been displayed by his immediate presidential predecessors. To that extent Mitchell was a bad influence, the Mephistopheles to Nixon's Faust. Yet his reach was limited. Mitchell was no intellectual. He did not participate in the geopolitical strategising or philosophical musings that were an important aspect of Nixon's nature. Their friendship involved considerable mutual trust but it never deepened into great mutual intimacy. As subsequent chapters will show, Mitchell had a great deal to do with building Nixon up and bringing Nixon down, but he did not have a lasting impact on those more personal characteristics that constituted 'the real Nixon'.

IV. READING, RELIGION AND RELAXATION

Nixon's preparations for the Presidency were personal as well as political. Although his wilderness years were busy ones, he remained a loner who relished his solitude. The child of Yorba Linda was still the father of the man approaching the White House. He did his best work, and had his greatest enjoyment, in his mind. A portrait of Nixon *circa* 1967 would picture him working on his own in the oak-panelled study of his Fifth Avenue apartment. Sitting in his armchair, with his feet up on a stool, he would be scribbling on a yellow pad. Perhaps he might be taking notes from some historical biography or magazine article. More likely he would be gazing out of the window towards Central Park, occasionally smiling while jotting down his thoughts and game plans. He might be phrase-making for a speech or world-changing by sketching out some new theory of foreign policy. He could be dreaming of what he would do in the Oval Office or scheming on how to capture an uncommitted slate of convention delegates. His ideas would range from local politics to global philosophy, from petty details to abstract concepts. If interrupted during these mental processes, Nixon could get unreasonably angry. Left alone, he could lock himself into creative concentration for several hours. This is a difficult side of the man to capture. Yet the attempt should be made, for no account of Nixon the public politician is complete without an understanding of Nixon the private intellectual, and no perception of the private Nixon is possible without some glimpses of the personal changes that came about in him during his wilderness period.

There was a part of Richard Nixon which went back to school between 1963 and 1967. On the political side of his life he showed an eagerness to learn from past mistakes and to listen to new tutors. This eventually led to an almost complete reversal of his 1960 and 1962 electioneering tactics when he entered his 1968 presidential campaign. On the personal front, his three Rs could be described as reading, religion and relaxation.

Nixon read widely and deeply during his wilderness years. Whenever possible he would put in three or four hours with a book before retiring for the night. His tastes were a mixture of the populist, the philosophical and the historical. On the first level he subscribed to a Book of the Month Club and made occasional selections from the *New York Times* non-fiction best-seller lists. But this was light froth in comparison to the staple diet of his reading. Somewhere inside him Nixon had a hunger for heavy intellectual study. He took pains to conceal it from his less intellectual cronies in the law and politics, but his private notes and memoranda of the period clearly illustrate the deeper nature of his literary tastes.

Ever since his university days Nixon had been something of a philosophy buff. He returned to this interest between 1963 and 1968 by spending long hours with the works of Plato, Aristotle, St. Thomas Aquinas, Kant, Pascal, Hegel, Rousseau, Hobbes, Locke, and Montesquieu. Among twentieth-century political philosophers he immersed himself in the writings of Karl Marx, and as an antidote to them, he took to the conservative authors Russell Kirk and Robert Nisbet.

Although fiction was generally not to his taste, he went back to his Tolstoyan roots, re-reading *Anna Karenina* and *War and Peace*. He turned to Dostoevsky, reading *Crime and Punishment* for the first time. He collected anthologies of famous speeches, copiously underlining eloquent passages from them, particularly in his four-volume edition of Edmund Burke's Parliamentary addresses. In his favourite fields of history and biography, among the books he enjoyed and annotated were: Barbara Tuchman's *The Guns of August*; Bruce Catton's *Centennial History of the Civil War*; A.J.P. Taylor's *Bismarck*; Elizabeth Longford's *Queen Victoria*; Boswell's *Life of Johnson*; H.G. Wells's *History of the World*; Clausewitz's *On War*; and Robert Conquest's *The Great Terror*. He had a particular penchant for mega-histories such as Will Durrant's ten-volume *A Story of Civilisation*;

Edward Gibbon's *Decline and Fall of the Roman Empire*; Arnold Toynbee's ten-volume *Study of History* and Carl Sandburg's six-volume biography of *Lincoln*.

By the standards of the late twentieth century this scale of reading is exceptional for a busy politician. But there was a side to Nixon in his hours of solitude that bore a closer resemblance to a nineteenth-century scholar-statesman eschewing newspapers and television for philosophy and history. Precise connections between his literary enthusiasms and his political activities are difficult to establish, as he himself has acknowledged: 'I can't say that any of this reading provided specific guidance for the foreign and domestic policies I developed during this period,' he wrote to this author, 'but I have always believed that anyone in the political arena is better prepared to address controversial current issues if he immerses himself in history, biography and philosophy and thereby gains perspective.'[72]

The only clear link between Nixon's reading and politics came from the books by and about the four statesmen he most admired. These were Woodrow Wilson, Theodore Roosevelt, Charles de Gaulle and Winston Churchill. He regarded Wilson as his hero among political intellectuals, and worshipped Teddy Roosevelt as the presidential 'man of action' who best embodied 'the mystique of leadership'.[73]

The mystique of de Gaulle fascinated Nixon. No book in his library was more heavily annotated than de Gaulle's 1960 autobiography, *The Edge of the Sword*. Some of the passages he underlined may have caught his interest as a result of self-identification. For example:

> Powerful personalities...capable of standing up to the tests of great events frequently lack that surface charm which wins popularity in ordinary life. Strong characters are, as a rule, rough, disagreeable and aggressive.[74]
>
> There is nothing harder for the human spirit to bear than being cold shouldered.[75]
>
> Great men of action have always been of the meditative type. They have without exception possessed to a very high degree the faculty of withdrawing into themselves.[76]

As for that great man of thought and action, Winston Churchill, Nixon had venerated him ever since officially welcoming him to Washington while Vice President in 1954. Now he saw a parallel in their common experience of a prolonged exile in the political wilderness. The precedent encouraged Nixon to devote a high percentage of his reading time to studying every one of Churchill's thirty-four published volumes, from *The Story of the Malakand Field Force* (1898) to *The History of the English Speaking Peoples* (1958). His favourites were *The Eastern Front* (1931), the final volume of Churchill's account of the First World War, and *Great Contemporaries* (1937). This collection of profiles, mainly of early twentieth-century politicians, is a gem of biography in miniature. Nixon annotated his copy heavily in the margins. An example of how his mind was working as he read it may be given by citing one particular passage from the chapter on Viscount Curzon, Britain's Foreign Secretary and former Viceroy of India, who failed to become Prime Minister in the 1920s, contrary to his own and most other people's expectations.

According to Churchill: 'Here was a being gifted far beyond the average level; equipped and comparisoned with glittering treasures of mind and fortune; driven forward by will, courage, and tireless industry; not specially crossed by ill luck; not denied a considerable span and yet who failed to achieve the central purpose of his life. Why did he fail and how did he fail?' On page 273 of his copy, Nixon underlined this passage and scribbled alongside it 'Taft? Dewey?'[77] He might even have stretched a point or two and added 'Nixon?', had it not been for his growing feeling that he was destined to achieve the central purpose in his own life.

This view was linked to his religious beliefs. 'Intensely personal, intensely private'[78] is how he has described them, taking great pains to screen this side of his character away from public attention. However, there are four pieces of evidence from the wilderness years which suggest that his religion remained important to him, and that he had not lost the faith which burned so brightly when he wrote the 'What Can I Believe?' essays in his college days.

First, Nixon was a regular reader of the Bible. 'I did not read it every day which was my custom in my earlier years, but I probably read it more often than many of those who wear their religion on their sleeves', he wrote to this author, adding a comment which illustrates his conservatism in religious matters: 'Incidentally, I always read the King James version. I am really turned off by all of these modern translations.'[79]

Second, he was a dutiful churchgoer in New York, attending Sunday morning services at the Marble Collegiate Church on West 29th Street. The Minister was the Reverend Dr. Norman Vincent Peale, a legendary preacher of the Gospel. 'From seeing him at those services and from one or two things he said I am darned sure that Nixon was stirred up by some of those sermons. Peale really got to him', observed Tom Evans.[80] Nixon has more or less confirmed that view, acknowledging that Peale became his closest spiritual adviser ('From a religious viewpoint he had more influence on me during this period than Billy Graham'[81]) and that he was uplifted by Peak's 'robust and inspirational' preaching.[82] The relationship deepened over the years. Peale conducted the marriage service of Julie to David Eisenhower; counselled Nixon after his resignation; and led the prayers at the Nixon Library and Birthplace dedication ceremonies at Yorba Linda in 1990.

Nixon's frequent attendance at the Marble Collegiate Church was remarkable because he had developed a considerable distaste for worshipping in public. These feelings led to the third indication of Nixon's strong interest in religious matters when, in or around 1967, he formed the idea that if elected he would like to hold Sunday services in the White House. No other President, let alone a presidential candidate, had ever considered such a religious innovation. He brought in this interdenominational practice during 1970, much to the appreciation of many members of his staff. It says something about Nixon's involvement in matters spiritual that he should have been planning an experiment of this kind as part of his agenda of preparation for the Presidency, even to the extent of drawing up lists of his favourite preachers, several of whom were later invited to give sermons in the White House.

The fact that the motivation for these services had a great deal to do with the President's overdeveloped desire for religious privacy was a throwback to his mother. During Nixon's childhood, Hannah had preferred to shut herself away in a broom cupboard when saying her prayers so that she could never be seen on her knees, even by her own family. It is not surprising that religion is still today the most private aspect of Nixon's life.

Even though Hannah Nixon had been bedridden from a stroke since 1963, she continued to exert a strong influence over her son. This fourth indication of Nixon's religious values surfaced from time to time in his private conversations about his mother. For example in the course of his revealing dialogue with Len Garment in Elmer Bobst's pool house in 1966, Nixon obliquely referred to his own spiritual dimension when he defined his political goals in terms of his mother's idealism. The link here is that Hannah Nixon, 'the Quaker saint', took all her ideals from Christ's teachings. As she lay dying in her Whittier nursing home she would have been proud that her son, who rarely in his life did anything by half measures, was still taking inspiration from the faith she had instilled into him during his childhood years.

Hannah Nixon died on 30 September 1967. Her death was not unexpected, but the event came as a deep, if delayed, emotional shock to her eldest surviving son. Richard Nixon owed everything to his mother. She had inspired his excellent education; shaped his strange emotions; and guided him to his strong spiritual beliefs. As long as Hannah was alive, the dark side of Nixon was rarely in the ascendant. She was the sheet anchor of his morality and the visionary spirit behind his highest political ideals.

It was not until the funeral that the full impact of bereavement hit Nixon. He had not been able to weep for his mother in New York or on the plane trip to California. This changed when he reached the small Friends Church in East Whittier, where Frank and Harold's funerals had taken place and where Hannah had worshipped for most of her life. Shown to the pew in which he had so often sat with his mother, his trapped emotions poured forth.

There had been a dispute within the family as to whether or not to leave the coffin open during the service. Unknown to Nixon, the open-coffin view had prevailed. At the sight of Hannah's frail body he cracked up. 'My mother was not pretty but she was beautiful, and she looked as beautiful in death as she had in life', he wrote in his memoirs.[83] His other thoughts on the day were less serene. On the journey from New York he had been racked by guilt feelings about whether he had neglected his mother in her declining years. Arriving at the church, he was incensed by the intrusive presence of reporters, some of whom were crass enough to ask him how he was feeling. The press filled the back and side aisles in such numbers that many local people were unable to get into the church. The sight of his mother's friends and neighbours being forced to stand outside increased Nixon's resentment to boiling point. There are some family intimates who believe that the time when he began to see journalists as enemies rather than adversaries can be pinpointed at Hannah's funeral.

The service was conducted by the Reverend Billy Graham, who had known Hannah as a devoted attender at one of his early California crusades before her son became famous. He preached a magnificent eulogy, after which the family filed past the open coffin for the last time. It was all too much for Nixon. When he reached the church door the floodgates of his heart burst open and he collapsed in tears on the shoulder of Billy Graham, who hugged him saying, 'Let it all out.' Nixon later observed that this was only the second time in his life that he had wept in public, the first being his breakdown on the shoulder of Senator William Knowland in 1952, just after the shadow of The Fund crisis had finally been lifted by Eisenhower.[84]

Hannah was buried in the family grave in Rose Hills Memorial Park along-side her husband Frank, her sons Arthur and Harold and her sister Elizabeth, Nixon's favourite 'Aunt Beth', who had died in her thirties of cancer. The last three were the lost loves of Nixon's youth, whose memories he could hardly bear to talk about in adult life. It must have been a searing afternoon of mourning and memories for him. Unable to sleep on the long 'redeye' flight back East that night, the recollection that both haunted and uplifted him the most was of his last visit to Hannah in her nursing home some weeks earlier. She had just undergone a major operation and was weak from acute pain. Nixon knew she had little hope of recovery. All he could think of to say to her was, 'Mother, don't give up.' At this the eighty-two-year-old patient sat upright in bed and with sudden strength in her voice said: 'Richard, don't *you* give up. Don't let anybody tell you you are through.'[85]

Touching though this maternal advice was, Nixon hardly needed it. His problem was not giving up, but knowing how and when to let up. He has often been portrayed as a man who could never relax. It has also been said of him that he had no real friends. Both assertions were true for certain periods in his early career. His shyness, his insecurities, and the private caution of the public office-seeker all made him a buttoned-up character. He often gave the impression of trying to be someone he was not. His unease with himself made others uneasy about him. The higher he rose, the more uptight he became.

These apparent flaws in the outer Nixon diminished considerably during his wilderness years. It was as though his defeats had unblocked a warmer side of his nature which had hitherto been repressed in the cause of ambition. Gradually this warmth spread outwards to a small circle of friends.

The young men who had become the praetorian guard of Nixon's political and legal colleagues in 20 Broad Street were among the beneficiaries of this more temperate climate in his human relationships. However, they were always 'staff', no matter how close they came to 'The Boss' on their assignments. A similar qualification applied to Nixon's business friends. He liked some of his backers enormously, but he maintained a barrier of reserve with them, perhaps because of a lingering hang-up from the days of The Fund crisis.

Where Nixon found his greatest intimacy was with two non-political, non-intellectual and in many ways highly unlikely characters to be his best friends—Robert A. Abplanalp and Charles G. 'Bebe' Rebozo.

Bob Abplanalp had, like Nixon, come up the hard way through life on the way to high achievement in his chosen profession of engineering. Born in 1922, he was the son of a Brooklyn auto mechanic. In his teenage years, Abplanalp had washed dishes in a restaurant four or five nights a week as his contribution to the family budget—a parallel with Nixon's teenage duties in the grocery store. 'Our similar backgrounds made it easy for us to feel comfortable together', he told this author.[86]

Abplanalp, who became a multimillionaire as a result of inventing the aerosol valve, first met Nixon in April 1961. Their appointment, for which Nixon was uncharacteristically late by forty minutes, fell on the morning when Nixon had been summoned to the White House by John F. Kennedy to give advice on the Bay of Pigs crisis.

Nixon returned to his home without noticing that a visitor was sitting quietly in a corner of the living room. Unaware that there was any need for civility, Nixon proceeded to blow up about the crisis to an aide, Cliff Folger, describing his meeting with Kennedy in profane terms. 'I just sat there amazed', recalled Abplanalp. 'Here was this guy I had always thought was so cold and wooden letting fly in sailor's language about Castro, Cuba, and how Kennedy had screwed up in his first test against the Communists. What I saw at once was that Nixon was burning with the anger of patriotism. He really cared about what this meant to the United States. "This is my kind of guy", I said to myself. When he saw me he cooled off. Then he sat down and gave a brilliant résumé of what the Bay of Pigs would mean to the Soviets and how it would result in far more trouble from Cuba—all of which came true later. I was really impressed...I gave him a little bit of legal business from our factory in California—I think we were the first new client he had landed for his law firm in Los Angeles. After that I began seeing a lot of him, and Rebozo too.'[87]

The chemistry of friendship that developed between Nixon, Abplanalp and Rebozo had several unexpected ingredients. They included laughter, practical jokes, teasing, story-telling, beer drinking, sports talk, beach life, three-hour swims, suntanning, midnight boating adventures and an idyllic atmosphere which combined carefree recreation with complete mutual trust. This does not sound in the least like Richard Nixon—but it was. Within the privacy of the triumvirate, the buttoned-up man unbuttoned himself and learned how to relax.

Nixon had done precious little in the way of relaxation since those happy vacations in Georgia and Hawaii with Pat in the early 1950s. Now, with middle age upon him, he realised that he must pace himself in preparation for the gruelling challenge of his last race for the Presidency. From his experiences in the 1960 campaign, he knew what a mistake he had made by ignoring his health and wellbeing. He was vulnerable to tiredness and low energy levels. To become less vulnerable he decided he should master the art of physical self-renewal, much in the the same way that he was mastering so many other subjects as he reached towards the pinnacle of power. This calculation that he must work hard at relaxing was soon sent cheerfully astray by the uncalculating warmth of the two men he had instinctively turned to in his search for companionship. The common thread between Abplanalp and Rebozo was that they were totally discreet men who wanted nothing from Nixon. They liked him as an individual and were not interested in what he might do for them as a politician. Uncomplicated characters too contented with their successful roles in life to be overwhelmed by the companionship of a potential President, they became his truest friends. In the wilderness and in the White House years they were the protectors of his privacy; the providers of his escapism and the nurturers of his health.

Bebe Rebozo had partially filled these roles on many occasions ever since 1951 when, at the instigation of Senator George Smathers, he had taken Nixon on boat trips off the Florida coast at a time when the thirty-eight-year-old junior Senator from California was on the verge of a physical breakdown. The environment of sun, sea and silence which the self-effacing Rebozo was glad to offer at the time of that first encounter proved wonderfully therapeutic. Nixon, whose California childhood had left him with a yearning for sunlight, subsequently returned to Rebozo's home on Key Biscayne for several visits. The relationship puzzled some of Nixon's Washington associates, who found it difficult to understand what rapport could possibly exist between the intense Vice President at the centre of the Republican political establishment and the laid-back Florida real estate fixer of Cuban parentage. Others were more perceptive.

'Bebe is a strong, silent, and suspicious kind of a guy who doesn't trust anyone. He's also warm hearted, generous and kind. Nixon's practically the same', observed Senator George Smathers. 'Once they discovered each other's qualities, they were bound to get along, particularly as they are both so comfortable with long silences. I've often been out with the two of them on the *Coco Lobo* [Rebozo's boat], and for three or four hours at a stretch they'd sit together without either of them saying a word. Nixon would scribble away on his yellow pad. Then he'd put his head back and look at the sky—meditating; contemplating; enjoying space and silence. Rebozo was just part of the landscape, but always attentive and helpful if required... I think Bebe brings out the mystic in Nixon. It's a profound relationship. Two men who separately trust nobody yet when together they trust each other absolutely.'[88]

Another dimension to the friendship was Rebozo's geniality and laid-back attitude to life. He provided his eminent guest with an emotional and conversational safety valve. As an aide, Stephen Hess, saw it: 'Bebe has an old shoe quality that helps Nixon relax.'[89]

Bob Abplanalp was a natural fit as the other half of the pair of 'old shoes' needed for Nixon's off-duty life. Unpretentious, unassuming and utterly discreet, he had an offbeat sense of humour which made Nixon laugh (normally a rare occurrence) as well as the resources to pamper his favourite guest in a cocoon of luxurious privacy. Abplanalp collected beaches and islands the way other men collect postage stamps. The jewels of his empire were in the Bahamas, where he owned Horseshoe Beach, Mermaid Beach, Walker's Cay, Little Grand Key Island and other tracts of unspoilt beauty which were secluded from public access. Nixon loved to meander deep in thought among the white sands and palm trees of the Abplanalp estate. He swam on his own for hours, read, reflected, then rejoined the human race for meals, drinks, and jokey conversation with the two other members of the triumvirate.

'It was good to watch him unwind and then start to have fun', said Abplanalp as he recalled the details of a Nixon visit on 10 January 1967.

That was a great but in its way fairly typical day on Little Grand Key. Nixon spent two or three hours in the sea until his skin was almost as wrinkled as a prune. Then we had a barbecue lunch at which Rebozo was teased a lot because of a practical joke we'd played on him, putting his jeans in a trouser press to improve his dress code, only unfortunately we set the temperature too high so the knees got burned. It sounds a little foolish now, but it's the kinda thing we laughed a lot about on a beach. Usually one of us was the butt of the other two's humor. That day it was Bebe's turn to be kidded. After lunch we sat around fishing and telling stories. Nixon himself almost never told stories, but he sure enjoyed them, and he had his favorites which he'd get us to repeat...in the evening we had a good dinner and towards the end of it I offered Nixon a cigar only to find that we'd run out of them in the house. Now we were on our own on Little Grand Key, so the only way to get new cigars was to go over by boat to the next island and buy some from a bar. This was a pretty wild idea as it was ten o'clock at night, but my Bahamian cook Woodfield said his sister had a bar on Grand Key and that he was willing to take the boat and go over there. When he heard this Nixon said, 'That's a great idea. I'd like to come.' By this time Rebozo had passed out on the sofa so he was in no mood for late night boating adventures, but Nixon was raring to go so we went down to the rickety old dock and set off—Nixon, me and Woodfield in a fifteen-foot Boston whaler. Nixon kept saying, 'This is fun', as Woodfield steered us around the rocks in pitch darkness until we reached Grand Key. Then we found his sister's bar, which had half the village in it because that happened to be the election night when Lyndon Pindling got elected. The Bahamians were absolutely amazed to see Nixon, but then they figured

he'd come to help them celebrate the election of the first ever Black
government in the Bahamas, so they gave him a big cheer. Nixon
really entered into the spirit of the evening. He sat down at this little
bar and had drinks with the local populace for the best part of two
hours…I had a helluva time getting him out of there but eventually
we navigated our way back across the water, where we found Rebozo,
who'd woken up. He was so mad with me, saying again and again,
'Do you realize you've risked the life of the next President of the
United States?' but Nixon just laughed and laughed.[90]

This anecdote well illustrates the point that Nixon could let himself go in the
right environment. Does it also raise the question of whether or not he had a
drinking problem? The issue needs to be raised if only because so much journalistic speculation has surrounded it.

The starting point of any such discussion has to be that Nixon was normally
a man of iron discipline in his personal and political habits. When campaigning,
speech-making or performing any sort of public duty, he lived like a Spartan,
preferring not to eat and almost invariably refusing alcohol. However, when the
pressure was off, he had his occasional lapses. Pat Hillings, who frequently accompanied him as an aide during the 1950s, recalled a private dinner *en famille* with
the Eisenhowers in Denver just before the 1952 campaign got under way. 'Nixon
had a glass or two more than he should have done. It didn't really show until he
came down in the elevator, but then he startled everyone by giving the wall a
smack and saying at the top of his voice, "I really like that Mamie. She doesn't give
a shit for anybody—not a shit!"'[91]

Significantly perhaps, there are no recorded examples of any similar loose-
tongued incidents during Nixon's eight years as Vice President. In the wilderness
years, however, there were occasional rumours of his being the worse for wear for
drink. One senior aide who concerned himself about this problem was John
Ehrlichman. At the 1964 Republican National Convention, Nixon gave a party
in his hotel suite after his well-received speech of reconciliation following Goldwater's nomination. According to Ehrlichman, Nixon got 'pie-eyed'[92] and gave
offence by his behaviour, making some clumsy passes at an embarrassed young
woman in the group. Ehrlichman, himself a teetotal Christian Scientist, took the
view that such behaviour could cost Nixon his chances of returning to public life.
So when Ehrlichman was invited by his friend Bob Haldeman to join the Nixon
For President campaign team in 1968, he initially declined. Haldeman then urged
Ehrlichman to come to New York and talk to Nixon about the problem. This led

to an interview which showed moral courage on the part of both participants. Ehrlichman levelled with Nixon, bluntly telling him that he was troubled by his drinking habits and continuing: 'I have a feeling that you are highly susceptible to alcohol. I'm not interested in coming away from my practice and my family and going out and beating my brains out if this is going to be a problem.'[93]

Instead of ducking the subject as Ehrlichman had anticipated, Nixon faced up to it immediately. 'He got very serious with me; he said he thought I was right', was Ehrlichman's version of the conversation. 'He made me a very solemn pledge that it would not be a problem. He asked me to come and help him and I was persuaded...He kept that promise all through the campaign. He was very fit; drinking was not a problem.'[94]

Thereafter Ehrlichman believed that Nixon had no difficulties with alcohol while on duty, either on the campaign trail or during his White House years. However, Ehrlichman later told Tom Wicker that he had been uneasy about Nixon's off-duty periods, particularly those 'weekends at Key Biscayne where little real work was done and the ever-present Bebe Rebozo acted not only as untiring listener but as bartender'.[95] Ehrlichman also told Wicker: 'Physiologically this fellow [Nixon] has a disability...One drink can knock him galley west if he is tired. Even if he is not tired, about two and a half drinks will do it. So he is much more susceptible than a lot of people I've met...He simply has to watch it.'[96]

Largely on the basis of these and other similar comments from Ehrlichman, a journalistic legend grew up that Nixon had a drinking problem. It was given wider circulation and credence by the portrayal of Nixon as an inebriated President in *The Final Days* by Bob Woodward and Carl Bernstein. History should reject it as a canard. Nixon was no more than an occasional drinker and when he did consume alcohol it was in moderation. Comments on this subject given to this author during interviews with over a hundred Nixon staffers, friends, Secret Service men, critics and even enemies confirm this general picture. If he had some lapses into alcoholic excess, as most people do in the course of a lifetime, they were extremely rare. Moreover, even these lapses as perceived by Ehrlichman and others may not have been due to alcohol on its own.

A little known fact about Nixon is that, during the wilderness years, he began taking a stress-reducing drug known as Dilantin. He was introduced to it by its enthusiastic promoter Jack Dreyfus, who had come across this 'wonder drug' in the course of his charitable work for his Dreyfus Medical Research Foundation. He advised Nixon early in 1964 that he should try Dilantin, telling him that one pill each day would have the effect of 'calming down your tension without slowing down your performance'.[97]

Nixon, who all his life had suffered from periods of over-stress and tension gave Dilantin a try. 'He called me several times to say how well it was working for him', recalled Dreyfus. 'He made a big fuss of me for putting him on to it, calling me "his guru" and sending me notes saying I was his, "favorite genius"—all that sort of thing…he said he was working better, sleeping better, performing more evenly. None of this was in the least surprising as Dilantin users all know…then in the run-up to the election he called me and said, "Can I take two a day?" So I said that was fine in periods of high pressure and gave him a large supply of tablets…He continued using them for several years into his presidency and then stopped some time before Watergate. I wish he'd stuck with it—he could have been helped a lot.'[98]

There is nothing strange or improper about Nixon having used a pharmaceutically respectable drug such as Dilantin. However, it did have side-effects, as Jack Dreyfus has acknowledged. 'Dilantin can have some mild side-effects, particularly in the evening just after it's been taken, when you're up too high anyway and you use both alcohol and Dilantin to bring you down. The consequences can be that your speech gets slightly slurred and you sound a bit woozy, although in fact your brain is clicking away just as well as ever. It doesn't last long, and you're right on the button all the time yourself, but you don't sound too good to someone who doesn't know you.'[99]

Could Nixon's use of Dilantin be the cause of the rumours that he had difficulty in holding his liquor? It is a rather more credible theory than the crude suggestion that he was something of a drunkard. One voice which has given unwitting confirmation to the former explanation came from Ray Price, a loyal aide who knew nothing about Nixon's use of Dilantin. Questioned in an interview by Tom Wicker on the alcohol issue, Price 'strenuously objected' to the idea of Nixon as a 'problem drinker'; he conceded, however, that 'when Nixon was tired, particularly if he'd had a sleeping pill—one drink or even a beer could make him appear drunk'.[100]

The sum total of the allegations about Nixon's drinking habits in the end comes down to an appropriately blurred mish-mash of isolated incidents, subjective impressions, unconfirmed rumours and contradictory accounts. Against such flotsam and jetsam of unfriendly journalism stands the rock of hard fact. No man of Nixon's work habits, application, and achievements could possibly have had an alcoholic tendency. He may have occasionally given a poor impression of himself because of drinking when under stress. Indeed, he obliquely admitted as much in the chapter on 'Temperance' in his 1990 book of reminiscences when he wrote, 'Based on my experience…a drink on vacation or with family and friends may have little effect. A drink when you are tired or tense can have an explosive effect.'[101] There were many explosions of various kinds in Nixon's life, but the pattern of them cannot be credibly linked to alcoholic excess. It was never a serious problem for him. The rumours of Nixon's excessive drinking were often linked to his friendship with Bebe Rebozo. In Kissinger's memoirs,[102] and other accounts of the period, Rebozo tends be caricatured as some sort of hyperactive Latin barman who led the President astray. This is unfair. The relationship between two men of their background and generation would have been almost abnormal if it had not included enjoying an occasional drink, but the ties that bound these two strange characters together into a lifelong friendship were tele-pathic—not alcoholic. Nixon has described Rebozo as 'a very very unusual friend…he knew that I was something of a loner, so he left me alone and did not ask questions. He was not one that wanted to sit down and have me confide in him. Often I knew what he was thinking and he knew what I was thinking without having to ask my opinion. That's why he was such a good friend.'[103]

One good illustration of the Rebozo–Nixon intimacy occurred during three days of silences and spiritual guidance at Key Biscayne from 28 to 31 December 1967. Although Nixon had long been preparing for his second attempt at the Presidency, he claimed not to have made up his mind until the New Year's Eve of election year. He surrounded this final moment of decision in an atmosphere of theatrical suspense. After getting the blessing of his family, he took himself down to Florida and spent many hours walking on the beach, sometimes alone, some-times with Rebozo. Although the purpose of these ruminations supposedly was to decide whether or not to become a candidate in 1968, Nixon never once asked his greatest friend for his views, saying afterwards, 'I knew Bebe's opinion without asking him.'[104] Instead, Nixon invited the Reverend Billy Graham to join the conclave.

Graham was one of the few men in America who had done more travelling in 1967 than his host. He had also become a close spiritual adviser to Nixon in the aftermath of Hannah's death the previous September. Graham spent his first evening talking theology, praying for guidance, and reading aloud to Nixon the first two chapters of St. Paul's Epistle to the Romans. The following day the three men set out for a walk to the old Spanish lighthouse on the tip of Key Biscayne. Graham was suffering from a lung infection, coughing so badly that he could not finish the walk. So they sat down on the beach and Nixon asked the crucial ques-tion, 'Billy, do you think I should run?' Graham replied, 'I have just come back from a trip around the world, and in every country the United States is in trouble. In every area of the world it is essential that the US should provide better leadership than is currently being provided. If you don't run and provide that leadership, I think the world is going to be in deep trouble.'[105] Nixon said later that these words made a deep impact on him, and the time when he finally decided to run again for the Presidency was this 'Billy Graham moment' on Key Biscayne beach.

Cynics will pour scorn on such a claim. Nixon had been dreaming of the White House for more than twenty years. His progress towards his chosen goal had required enormous qualities of hard work and fighting spirit. For the last few months he and his staff had been engaged in the most exhaustive of plans, preparations and fund raising activities. As 1968 dawned he looked a near certainty to be the nominee of his party and a strong probability to be the victor in the election. Against this background, it is surely absurd to suggest that a New Year's Eve walk on the beach with the silent Bebe Rebozo and the coughing Billy Graham could somehow have become the critical moment of decision in Nixon's presidential candidature.

The comments in the previous paragraph are entirely logical, but they miss the point that Nixon's personal ambition, powerful though it was, needed to be fired by the spark of emotional idealism. His odd references during the wilderness years to his mother's Quaker ideals as the foundation for his political dreams had nothing phony about them. Those ideals were an important dimension in this multidimensional man. In Nixon's mind there was a symmetry between Billy Graham's role as the preacher at Hannah's funeral some twelve weeks earlier, and his appearance on Key Biscayne beach as the oracle of truth on the question of whether to run for President. 'I don't mean I was asking Billy to be the judge on high to decide it,' recalled Nixon, 'but when he talked about the people around the world and the leadership that I might provide, he was reminding me that I would be running not just for personal purposes but for a cause.'[106]

This sense of purpose was vital to the temporal politician who was still striving to honour his dead mother's spiritual values. Most of Nixon's hard work in the wilderness years had been devoted to the greasy mechanics of presidential politics, to activities such as fund raising, delegate hunting and organisation building. He needed this practical machinery, but within himself he needed a sense of vision more. With the help of Billy Graham's words and Hannah Nixon's legacy, as the New Year dawned he could see his great cause—the creation of a new international framework for peace. The fact that he believed in this cause and felt confident of both his inner and outer fortifications was important, for 1968 was to be a year of political turbulence on a scale unequalled since the time of Abraham Lincoln.

SIXTEEN

1968

I. PROTEST, REBELLION AND ASSASSINATION

1968 was the year when the sixties exploded. The passions and poisons that had been fermenting inside American society for most of the decade suddenly boiled over with a fury that traumatised the nation. It was a melodrama in four acts. Act One consisted of anti-war protests, youth rebellions, political upheavals, scarifying riots and tragic assassinations. Act Two was the counterrevolution, the fearful and sometimes hateful reactions of the older America that was deeply disturbed by the country's lurch towards anarchy. Act Three was the story of how democracy responded to these conflicting pressures and elected a new President. Act Four, the least understood but perhaps the most historically enduring element in the saga, was the legacy of '68 that Richard Nixon inherited as President.

Merely to record the calendar of events in the early part of the year is enough to set the pulse racing. In January came the Tet offensive in Vietnam. This dramatic escalation of the war by the North Vietnamese army sent shock waves through the electorate, especially when the battle reached the grounds of the US Embassy in Saigon. People, particularly young people, were appalled because the ferocity of the hostilities so clearly made liars of the government spokesmen who had repeatedly claimed that the war was being won.

In February, the effect of Tet caused an upheaval in the New Hampshire Democratic primary. A determined cadre of anti-Vietnam Liberals persuaded Senator Eugene McCarthy of Wisconsin to run against Lyndon Johnson on a stop-the-war ticket. By all the known bench marks of American political experience, McCarthy's 'kids' crusade' should have been an exercise in futility, for a maverick candidate normally has no hope when challenging an incumbent President from the same party. This received wisdom evaporated in the snows of New Hampshire. When the result was declared on 12 March, McCarthy received the astonishing total of 18,000 votes to Johnson's 22,000. From that near-triumph, McCarthy moved on to the Wisconsin primary with his raggle-taggle army of student volunteers, where he was well on the way to inflicting even greater shocks on the Democratic Party when two sensational events forestalled him.

The first came on the Ides of March, when Robert F. Kennedy finally decided that he would mount his own challenge for the Democratic presidential nomination. Kennedy had been brooding on this decision for months. The manner and timing of his announcement on 15 March had the effect of throwing petrol on an already raging fire. Bitterness towards him erupted throughout the anti-war movement, many of whose supporters denounced his action as an opportunist act of treachery towards their new hero McCarthy. However, the split on the campuses was dwarfed by the emotional response that Kennedy's campaigning style evoked in the country. He had a huge constituency of his own—the Blacks, the poor, the underclass of society—who loved him with a fervour that was frightening. Bobby Kennedy reached out to the crowds who flocked to hear him not as a politician after votes, but as a saviour who could stir their souls. There was something messianic in his appeal as he rekindled the memory of his martyred brother and sounded his clarion call for an end to racial discrimination, to economic deprivation, and especially to the war in Vietnam. McCarthy was outshone, but by no means eclipsed by Kennedy's oratory. The radical cause now had two champions in the field, fighting against each other as well as against the President.

Watching these developments from the White House, Lyndon Johnson was plunged into despair. For the last year, his stewardship of the war had made him not merely unpopular but so hated that he was a virtual prisoner in Washington. Every time he ventured out to make a speech in the country, the event was ruined by the viciousness of the anti-war demonstrations.

Hey, Hey LBJ
How many kids did you kill today?
Ho, Ho, Ho Chi Minh
The Viet Cong are going to win
One, Two, Three, Four
We don't want your fucking war
Two, Four, Six, Eight
Organize and Smash the State

were the chants that filled the air on all LBJ's excursions as protestors hurled themselves in front of the White House limousines; threw excrement at the Secret Service; and used every imaginable dirty trick to weaken the Presidency with the politics of disruption. The increasing size and savagery of these demonstrations would have shaken any leader. However, until New Hampshire, Johnson was able to assert that the anti-war movement was a small minority of agitators. When the results and the polls gave a different message, his confidence crumbled. To make matters worse, sharp divisions among LBJ's inner circle of advisers on the war were beginning to emerge. From his battle headquarters in Saigon, General William C. Westmoreland was promising victory but requesting the deployment of another 206,000 troops, in addition to the 500,000 already in Vietnam, to achieve it.

From the Pentagon, the recently appointed Defense Secretary Clark Clifford advised the President that the war could not be won within the foreseeable future. LBJ's White House aides were in similar disarray. On top of all this discord from within and without, Kennedy's entry into the presidential power struggle came as the final straw. In Johnson's words to his confidante Doris Kearns: 'The thing I feared from the first day of my Presidency was actually coming true. Robert Kennedy had openly announced his intention to reclaim the throne in memory of his brother... The whole situation was unbearable to me.'[1]

On the evening of 31 March, Johnson broadcast to the nation. Ostensibly his message was about new moves for peace in Vietnam, but his final peroration, kept secret from all except a handful of intimates, came as a thunderbolt:

With America's sons in the fields far away, with America's future under challenge right here at home, with our hopes and the world's hopes for peace in the balance everyday, I do not believe that I should devote an hour or a day of my time to any personal, partisan causes or to any duties other than the awesome duties of this office—the Presidency of your country.

Accordingly, I shall not seek, and will not accept, the nomination of my party for another term as your President.[2]

Like everyone else listening to the broadcasts, the Republican front-runner, Richard Nixon, was astounded by the President's withdrawal. He listened to it on a radio in Bob Abplanalp's private jet as they were approaching La Guardia airport. He immediately made the astute remark, 'I'd be very surprised if President Johnson let Bobby Kennedy have it on a platter.'[3]

The atmosphere of civil war among the Democrats intensified rather than abated in the aftermath of the President's speech. Vice President Hubert Horatio Humphrey now entered the race with the backing of Johnson and that large part of the Democratic machine which felt threatened by the destabilising radicalism of Kennedy. Humphrey was, on paper, a strong candidate, but his ever-optimistic garrulity was a handicap in the sombre atmosphere of the times. Lyndon Johnson once memorably described his Vice President as 'a man who prepares for a good solid thought provoking speech by taking a deep breath'.[4] Humphrey lived up to this description on the morning when he launched his presidential campaign, merrily telling his supporters: 'Here we are, just as we ought to be, the very way politics ought to be in America, the politics of happiness, the politics of purpose, and the politics of joy. That's the way it's going to be, all the way from here on in.'[5]

The politics of joy and happiness were a long way from the agenda of most voters in 1968, as events soon confirmed. On 4 April, the Reverend Martin Luther King was assassinated by a white gunman in Memphis, Tennessee. Immediately, a wave of rioting struck 125 cities in 29 states. The toll from these disturbances was 46 killed, 2,600 injured, 21,000 arrested, and damage to property estimated at over $50 million. The street fighting was at its worst in Washington DC, where bullets and bombs exploded two blocks from the White House. As the double horrors of racial violence and anti-war hysteria tore America apart, columnists ran out of adjectives to describe the prevailing atmosphere of fear and loathing. Many of them fell back on two quotations, so often repeated in 1968 that they became journalistic clichés. 'The centre cannot hold; mere anarchy is loosed upon the world' (Yeats) and 'Events are in the saddle and they ride mankind' (Emerson).

One more tragedy was yet to darken the first half of 1968. After the political moratorium that followed King's murder, the California primary came to be regarded as the next trial of strength in the race for the Democratic nomination. For Kennedy it was a make or break contest. After an extremely effective campaign, he won it decisively, defeating McCarthy by a margin of 46 to 41 per cent. Among Kennedy supporters on the election night of 5 June, jubilation was followed by horror. Seconds after making his victory statement, Robert F. Kennedy lay groaning in a pool of his own blood felled by the bullets of a lone gunman.* He died in hospital a few hours later. So ended the first act of the 1968 melodrama.

II. COUNTER-REVOLUTION

While these seismic shocks were causing agony to the Democratic Party, Nixon stayed steadily on course for winning the Republican nomination. His priority was to shed the image of a loser. This he proceeded to do with a remarkable show of strength in the early primaries. His well-financed campaign took on the momentum of a steamroller as he crushed the already fading Romney in New Hampshire by capturing 79 per cent of the poll, going on to win Wisconsin with 80 per cent and Nebraska with 69 per cent. The primary that mattered most was Oregon, where Governor Ronald Reagan of California and Governor Nelson Rockefeller of New York were on the ballot for the first time. Nixon thrashed them both, winning 73 per cent of the vote compared to Reagan's 23 per cent and Rockefeller's 4 per cent.

In spite of these victories, Nixon still feared that he could get squeezed out at the convention by a Rockefeller—Reagan pincer movement in which a cabal of Southern conservative delegates might ally themselves with California and New York in a 'Stop Nixon' movement that would hand the prize to Reagan. To prevent such a nightmare, Nixon began working on a Southern strategy of his own. On 31 May he travelled to a meeting in Atlanta with his supporters from all over the South. To his delight he found that the majority of the delegates had already been delivered to him, largely as a result of pro-Nixon leadership from that icon of Southern conservatism, Strom Thurmond. The legendary South Carolina Senator was one of the GOP's king-makers. His staunch support for Nixon was due to what Thurmond thought was their shared belief in a strong military and foreign policy.

After the meeting, Nixon rode out to the airport with his benefactor, accompanied by Bob Ellsworth. As the drive was ending, Nixon made a little speech of appreciation, concluding with the rather nervous question, 'Senator, is there anything you want from me?' Nixon was fearful that Thurmond might be going to spring unacceptable demands on him, such as requesting his support for the 'Freedom of Choice' (all-white schools) movement in education. Thurmond, for

---

* Kennedy had been shot by Sirhan Sirhan, a Palestinian, who was violently opposed to Kennedy on account of his support for Israel.

all his anti-civil rights views, had even higher priorities: 'Why Dick, when you're President, all I want is that you never, never let up against them Communists', said Thurmond. 'Senator, you know I never will', responded Nixon. 'I sure know you won't', answered Thurmond, pumping the candidate's hand, evidently in the belief that a solemn bond had been sealed, for he sorrowfully reminded Nixon of these words during his Presidency at the time of the antiballistic missile (ABM) treaty and the China initiative.[6]

To those with a keener eye for the nuances of foreign policy than Strom Thurmond, it was noticeable that by mid-1968 Nixon was steadily moving away from his hardline anti-Communist position of the past. For many months he had been refining his stance on Vietnam, and had quietly dropped his earlier talk of escalation for military victory. In an important speech on 5 March in Hampton, New Hampshire, he introduced his concept of linkage, declaring that in the search for 'honorable peace' (an important semantic change from his familiar phrase 'victorious peace') he believed that the United States should use its diplomatic, economic and political leverage with the Soviet Union as the key to a possible settlement. In a revealing conclusion he made a pledge that his leadership would 'end the war and win *the peace in the Pacific* [author's italics].'[7]

It says much about the perception of American journalism of the time that the significance of Nixon's carefully crafted words at Hampton were entirely missed. He was speaking as a geopolitician, but the reporters were only interested in listening to him as a politician. Instead of following up the intriguing new route to peace that Nixon had signposted, the press set off on a false trail of their own invention. Far from being praised, or at least questioned for his new thinking, Nixon was accused of concealment and political gimmickry. The main charge against him was that he had spoken of 'a secret plan' for peace in Vietnam without giving any further specific details. In fact Nixon had never used the phrase 'a secret plan'. That adjective came from a questioner in the audience. It was mistakenly attributed to Nixon and put on the wires by a UPI staffer editing the incoming copy at the agency's Boston office. The mistake was eventually acknowledged, but not until long after Nixon's critics had enjoyed a field day. Nelson Rockefeller, in particular, used the error to pour scorn on his rival, sarcastically wondering how Nixon could keep his peace plan to himself 'while hundreds of Americans die each week in Vietnam'.[8]

The row over 'the secret plan' with the press in New Hampshire was one of the factors that moved Nixon towards a new style of political campaigning. Another, more minor irritation had been the activities of the Democratic Party's expert on dirty tricks, Dick Tuck. Posing as an accredited journalist, Tuck's standard prank in New Hampshire was to bribe the band at each rally to play the tune 'Mack the Knife' just as the candidate came on stage. As a result, when the smiling, waving Nixon entered the room he was greeted with the strains of 'and the shark has pearly teeth'. Nixon himself was only mildly disturbed by this somewhat juvenile jape, but Nick Ruwe, the chief advance man in New Hampshire, remembered how angry John Mitchell became with Tuck, saying ominously, 'We'll get even. We'll get even.'[9]

Nixon had already received detailed advice on changing to a more aloof style of campaigning. The recommendation was first made in a memorandum sent to him by H.R. Haldeman at the end of 1967. Its thesis was that the modern presidential candidate should restrict his activities on the stump in order to concentrate on television to the maximum. ('The reach of the individual campaigner,' wrote Haldeman, 'doesn't add up to diddly-squat in votes.'[10]) The potential flaw in Haldeman's strategy was the fear that Nixon would be no good on television. This anxiety was based on the belief that Nixon had lost the 1960 election because of his poor showing in the debates against John F. Kennedy. However, it ignored Nixon's early triumph with the 'Checkers' broadcast of 1952 and also his more recent record of successful TV appearances during the wilderness years.

One of the first aides to spot that there was a new television Nixon had been Len Garment. He sent in a memorandum on the subject as early as mid-1966. 'Television: Jerry Hellman, Tom Evans and I ran tapes of a number of your major appearances in a screening room last week. All agreed that your recent work is extremely effective and by far the best you have ever done. "Meet the Press" (1965) gets the highest marks for thoughtful, balanced tone, grasp of subject matter, and pertinence of response. The Vanderbilt U press conference (1966) is also top drawer for lightness and physical mobility, a "hip" quality which we all agreed was enormously attractive.'[11]

Reproducing to order Nixon's 'hip' and attractive qualities on television was at first glance a difficult task, since he had a tendency to freeze into distinctly un-hip and unattractive postures when under pressure from critical journalists. However, towards the end of the New Hampshire primary, Nixon's staff tried him out with an experimental TV format. At Hillsboro Town Hall, he faced a panel of representative citizens who interrogated him for over two hours. Initially 'grouchy' at these arrangements, Nixon gradually relaxed and, according to Theodore White, became 'crisp, direct, real and convincing'.[12]

The key to the Hillsboro experiment was that only local voters were allowed to participate. The absence of reporters out to get him (as he usually imagined they were) noticeably contributed to Nixon's confident performance, which was also boosted by the knowledge that editorial control of the mastertape remained in the hands of his own media experts. They cut it into segments, packaged but genuine, and screened them to good effect in New Hampshire and across the nation. Seeing the end product, Nixon and his advisers were ecstatic. They had found a TV formula that really worked.

The Hillsboro format was from then on used extensively throughout the campaign. It pleased the public almost as much as it infuriated the press corps. Some of the reporters, whose opportunity for a regular, rough-and-tumble press conference with the candidate became extremely limited, worked themselves into a frenzy of indignation about the new arrangements. A hilariously bitchy attack on this aspect of the Nixon campaign by Joe McGinnis, *The Selling of the President 1968*, captures the venom felt by some of the media representatives. Their general line was that Nixon was not discussing the issues but falsely packaging himself for sale as a bogus product. It is not an argument that stands up to serious examination, unless one believes that journalists are infallibly superior to voters when it comes to questioning candidates on election issues.

Nixon's campaigning methods in 1968 were full of tactical and technical innovations. Most of them were suggested by Bob Haldeman, who in the words of one colleague 'virtually lived and breathed for making the Boss President'.[13] With the arrival of Mitchell, Haldeman became guardian-in-chief of the Nixon body corporate, while Mitchell assumed overall command of the campaign. 'We had a good relationship,' Haldeman recalled later, 'a relationship born in heaven. Mitchell was not at all prepared to deal with the problems of managing the candidate and I was not at all prepared to deal with the problems of managing the campaign. We both welcomed the fact that the other was there and divided the task. It worked extremely well.'[14] Haldeman controlled all access to the candidate, organised his schedule and maintained an iron grip on the smallest personal details of Nixon's on- and off-duty programme. 'He doesn't want to organize, he wants to *be* organized',[15] was Haldeman's justification for the tightness of his regime. In the election of 1968 it was a wholly justified policy. Nixon thought and spoke best when all the physical movements of campaigning were operating on autopilot. Haldeman understood this perfectly and his 'zero defect system' was largely devoted to eliminating the mistakes that had cost victory in 1960.

The contrast between Nixon's 1960 and 1968 campaigns is a study in tactical reversal. In 1960 Nixon brought himself to the brink of exhaustion as a result of impossibly hectic scheduling and the neglect of his personal health. In 1968 he had a leisurely programme of early nights, weekends off and regular trips to Key

Biscayne to refresh his suntan. In 1960 he insisted on campaigning in all fifty states; in 1968 he confined himself to twenty-seven. In 1960 he lost much of the Black vote by his unintentional 'no comment' snub towards the imprisoned Martin Luther King. In 1968 he flew to Atlanta to attend King's funeral. In 1960 he allowed himself to be upstaged by Kennedy in the televised debates and disturbed by adversarial journalists at press conferences. In 1968 there were no televised debates and few clashes with reporters. Nixon reached out to the voters by commercials; by televised, citizen panel shows modelled on the Hillsboro format; and by a series of thirty-minute radio addresses on major issues. All this elaborate packaging cost money. In 1960 Nixon had been heavily outspent by the Kennedys. In 1968 he outspent all his rivals. His fund raisers provided him with a budget of $9 million to win the nomination and another $24 million to fight the main election. At the time, it was the most expensive campaign for the Presidency in history.

Nixon's progress towards the nomination became so serene in its closing stages that it resembled a stately Spanish galleon coasting home under full sail from a fair wind. After his good showing in the primaries, he came to the convention rested, confident and looking like a winner. So confident, indeed, that he initially stayed away to work in seclusion on his acceptance speech at Montauk Point, Long Island. When he arrived in Miami halfway through the proceedings, he asked Mitchell, 'John, what's the count?' Mitchell chuckled and replied, 'I told you you didn't need to worry, Dick. We've got everything under control.'[16] So it turned out. Disproving the widespread press reports about last-minute defections to other camps, the first ballot for the Republican presidential nomination for 1968 gave decisive victory to Richard Nixon with 692 votes to 277 for Nelson Rockefeller and 182 for Ronald Reagan. Resurrection had been accomplished. The only complaint (mainly among journalists) was that the final stages of the comeback were so calm and predictable that the actual proceedings of the convention became utterly boring. One Nixon advance man said that the atmosphere of tedium had been deliberately created. 'The country was on the edge of a nervous breakdown. Our mission was to calm everyone down.'[17]

Almost the only excitement in Miami arose over the selection of the vice-presidential nominee. Nixon's first choice was Robert Finch, the forty-two-year-old Lieutenant Governor of California, who had been his most trusted aide and liberal conscience since the 1940s. The bonds between them were deep, so much so that some observers saw their relationship as that of an elder and younger brother. Although Finch was not a national political figure, Nixon was sure he had presidential qualities in him, so he pressed his old friend to accept the role of running mate on two or three occasions in the weeks before the convention. Finch would not be persuaded: 'I thought that becoming Vice President would be so destructive of family life', he has recalled. 'I could see police cars escorting my kids to school, and an end to all privacy. That was the major element in my decision...I was also concerned about how my selection would appear. It smacked of nepotism, and I thought it could rebound on Nixon.'[18]

With Finch taking himself out of the running, Nixon began leaning towards the choice of Governor Spiro T. Agnew of Maryland. The two men had met for the first time at 20 Broad Street at the beginning of the year, when Agnew had still been one of Nelson Rockefeller's supporters. Nixon was impressed by his visitor's outward appearance and 'inner strength'.[19] This favourable assessment was championed by John Mitchell, who saw outer strength in Agnew's rise from a humble Greek immigrant background to becoming a successful trial lawyer, a World War II company commander, the Chief Executive of Baltimore County, and the top elected politician in his state. Agnew's projection of toughness was much enhanced in Mitchell's eyes by the Governor's performance during the riots in Baltimore that broke out in the aftermath of Martin Luther King's assassination. Agnew summoned the Black leaders of the city to a conference, but instead of delivering the expected conciliatory speech he blasted his listeners for their alleged complicity in the disturbances. He called his audience of Black preachers and politicians 'circuit-riding, Hanoi-visiting, caterwauling, riot inciting, burn-America-down type of leaders', and accused them to their faces (or rather to their backs since most of them walked out of the conference) of 'breaking and running' to stop the riots.[20] Such a tough stance on the law and order issue played well in the South, where Nixon had to be watchful about the emerging third party candidacy of Governor George Wallace of Alabama.

Agnew's strength was that he was a good political fit for the ticket. As a border state governor, he was acceptable to all regions. He had a respectable record on civil rights which would appeal to the ethnic and urban voters in the big city states, while his angry adjectives about civil disorders would reassure Strom Thurmond and other Southern conservatives that there would be no liberal sellout. Agnew's weakness was that so little was known about him, but Nixon preferred picking a nonentity to a charismatic figure such as Ronald Reagan. Interestingly, in view of subsequent events, enough was known about Agnew at the time of the convention for Nixon to have given some thought to the notion that the Maryland Governor might have been a regular recipient of kick-backs. As Nixon recalled his reasons for selecting Agnew:

First, I wanted someone who would be a bridge between North and South. I didn't have a qualified Southerner. If I'd had a qualified one, I'd have put him there because it was time for the South to be on the ticket, but Agnew coming from a border state met that.

Second, Agnew had very good credentials as a 'moderate' Republican. He had defeated a racist Democrat. He had been highly praised in the *New York Times* editorially for having done so after he was elected Governor of Maryland.

Third, in terms of Agnew himself, he was an able man. He was intelligent. He was a well-trained lawyer. He was a fighter for what he believed in.

Now let's look at the negatives there, and let's put it in context since we're speaking historically. Agnew, unfortunately, had been Governor of Maryland. Maryland realistically for as long as anybody can remember had been a state in which contractors doing business in the state were asked to, and gladly complied with, provisions to kick back part of amounts they got for their contracts into funds to be used for the Governor for his political purposes, and was to an extent, since the Governor wasn't paid all that much, even to take care of some of his personal expenses. Now that wasn't limited to Maryland. That's happened in many other states. Adlai Stevenson, according to John Bartlow Martin his biographer, had a fund of $60,000 which was taken from contractors doing business with the state of Illinois. It was used to pay for some of his charitable contributions, for parties that he gave for his staff, for a dance that he gave for his children and so forth and so on. It was considered perfectly proper in his case. Agnew did the same. He accepted contributions...I didn't anticipate a problem because I did not dream that he would go on accepting the contributions after he became Vice President.[21]

These comments, made by Nixon in 1978 but presumably an accurate reflection of his thinking in 1968, illustrate the validity of the remark by Bill Rogers quoted in the previous chapter: 'Around this time he began to make a difference between personal ethics and political ethics.'

Nixon himself would never have accepted kick-backs in cash from contractors at any stage of his career. Yet he was not unduly bothered that the sleazy, backhander-taking culture of Illinois or Maryland was part of his running mate's profile. To Nixon that was 'just politics'.[22] It was a weakness of judgement in him which was to reappear with disastrous consequences during his White House years.

Agnew's selection received neither a good press nor a friendly response from the convention. Boos and cries of 'Spiro *who?*' greeted Nixon as he made the announcement.

On the floor, a liberal splinter group staged a disruptive protest by putting forward Governor Romney as an alternative vice-presidential nominee. This rebellion, even though it got nowhere, infuriated Nixon, but he had to face the fact that his choice had not gone down well even with the faithful. The cheekiest word on Agnew came from Theodore Roosevelt's seventy-seven-year-old daughter Mrs. Alice Longworth. In a reference to the Eisenhower administration's rule that the President and Vice President must never travel together on the same aircraft, Mrs. Longworth said to Nixon, 'Promise me, Dick, that if you're elected, you'll *always* make Governor Agnew travel with you on your plane.'[23]

Although the disappointed reactions to the running mate selection ruffled a good many feathers, these were soon smoothed over in the general euphoria that customarily attends the final stages of conventions. Nixon's acceptance speech was not one of his finest performances, but it contained many good lines and a clear definition of the constituency to which he was reaching out. Although he did not use the phrase on that occasion, his appeal was directed to 'the silent majority'.

> As we look at America, we see cities enveloped in smoke and flame. We hear sirens in the night. We see Americans dying on distant battlefields abroad. We see Americans hating each other; killing each other at home.
>
> And as we see and hear these things, millions of Americans cry out in anguish: Did we come all this way for this? Did American boys die in Normandy and Korea and in Valley Forge for this?
>
> Listen to the answer to these questions.
>
> It is another voice, it is a quiet voice in the tumult of the shouting. It is the voice of the great majority of Americans, the forgotten Americans, the non-shouters, the non-demonstrators. They're good people. They're decent people. They work and they save and they pay taxes and they care. They work in American factories, they run American businesses, they serve in government. They provide most of the soldiers who die to keep it free. They give drive to the spirit of America. They give lift to the American dream...[24]

The speech was full of dreams, most of them introduced as the antithesis of the current nightmares afflicting America. Instead of the flag being burned; the crime wave increasing; the pollution getting worse; the traffic choking up; the welfare spending being wasted; the President unable to travel round the country; and the nation's prestige plummeting abroad, Nixon had a series of optimistic visions, usually introduced by the phrase (which he used eight times), 'I see a day when…'

The best of these dreams was the most personal. In his closing remarks, Nixon returned to the philosophy of his father. Frank Nixon had always told his sons that anyone born in the United States could achieve anything. Richard Nixon was the living embodiment of this faith. He was the ideal spokesman to proclaim the view that, in the land of opportunity, the American child need not end up on welfare or in despair. After commiserating with any such unfortunate children, he concluded with a moving passage which went back to his own roots:

> I see another child tonight. He hears a train go by at night and he dreams of faraway places where he'd like to go. It seems like an impossible dream, but he is helped in his journey through life.
>
> A father who has to go to work before he finished the sixth grade, sacrificed everything he had so that his sons could go to college.
>
> A gentle Quaker mother, with a passionate concern for peace, quietly wept when he went to war, but she understood why he had to go.
>
> A great teacher, a remarkable football coach, an inspirational minister encouraged him on his way.
>
> A courageous wife and loyal children stood by him in victory and also in defeat. And in his chosen profession of politics, first there were scores, then hundreds, then thousands, and finally millions who worked for his success. And tonight he stands before you—nominated for President of the United States of America.[25]

The words of the acceptance speech may not resonate in cold print today, but at the time their symbolism struck home with millions of voters. By invoking the American dream, Nixon was signalling that he was 'one of us'—an accredited member of the silent and decent majority. Against the background of 1968's alien turmoil, he looked the part. He had come up the hard way. He had worked for his success. He was reassuringly square. His history of resilience proclaimed both his determination and his talent. He was smart, tough, and maybe even a little tricky. But at least he understood the new anxieties and wanted to lead America back towards the old values. In an election where every other candidate was beginning to look unhinged, Nixon represented stability, continuity and firmness of purpose. To Middle America, he was the man for the hour. It was no surprise that the first Gallup Poll taken after the convention showed Nixon comfortably ahead in the race for the Presidency, leading Humphrey by sixteen percentage points.

III. ELECTED PRESIDENT

Nixon's image as a rock of stability in a world where his rivals were going mad was enhanced by the off-stage drama of the Democratic National Convention in Chicago. On the floor, Hubert Humphrey comfortably secured the nomination but on the streets mayhem erupted. In a year already shamefully stained by bloodshed and violence, no event made a nastier impact than the clash between the Chicago police and the anti-war demonstrators on the night of 28 August.

Chicago's political passion play that unravelled in so much sickening brutality is incidental to this biography. Suffice it to say that its Cecil B. de Mille-sized cast included 11,900 over-tired city policemen; 7,500 soldiers of the Illinois National Guard; some 20,000 demonstrators provocatively commanded by the confrontation-seeking National Mobilization Committee to End the War in Vietnam; several hundred Yippies (or crazies), whose main purpose was to nominate a pink effigy called Pigasus J. Pig for President; the Poor People's March, complete with wagons and mule-trains demanding 'Jobs and Food for All', and a leadership of semi-professional agitators (among them Tom Hayden and Bobby Seale of the Black Panthers), determined to cause maximum disruption. Cram this gallimaufry of troublemakers into a few streets close to the convention hall; start a cacophony of chants such as '*SiegHeil!*' 'Fuck you LBJ' and 'Kill the Pigs'; urge the crowd to advance on the police barricades and you have a recipe for certain disaster. Although many of the demonstrators behaved appallingly, their demeanour was almost genteel in comparison to the conduct of Chicago's police who, quite literally, went berserk. At about 8 p.m. on the night of Humphrey's nomination, all control snapped as flying phalanxes of officers suddenly went on the rampage, flailing their billyclubs, squirting Mace into the eyes of their tormentors, beating viciously at heads, limbs or genitals; and generally savaging the mob in what one British journalist called 'a sadistic romp'.[26]

The media coverage of the pitched battles outside the convention hall was both magnified and distorted by the coincidence of a telephone technicians' strike.

This meant that the street violence could not be transmitted live during the forty minutes or so when it was happening. Instead, the raw cameramen's film was rushed to the control rooms of the networks inside the hall, where it was edited into emotive segments and intercut with the Democrats' proceedings. Its juxta-position of the speeches with repeated clips of horror film showing the carnage of the earlier fighting left the impression that Hubert Humphrey was being nominated in a sea of blood.

'Like millions of other Americans watching television that night, I did not want to believe my eyes', wrote Nixon in his memoirs. 'It seemed as if the Demo-crats' convention was confirming every indictment of their leadership that I had made in my campaign speeches.'[27] Theodore H. White, on the spot in Chicago, drew an even blunter conclusion from the scenes he was witnessing. 'The Demo-crats are finished',[28] he scrawled in his reporter's notebook.

In the aftermath of the convention, law and order became the number-one issue of the presidential campaign. Nixon exploited it, but in responsible language. He promised his audiences he would bring in a new attorney general (hardly an innovation, since new Presidents invariably pick a new Cabinet) who would crusade against all forms of law breaking with unprecedented vigour. 'The wave of crime is not going to be the wave of the future'[29] was one of his most frequent applause lines.

The candidate who was making the eagles scream with a special brand of applause lines on law and order was George Corley Wallace. The Alabama Gov-ernor, racist and demagogue though he was, propelled himself on the wings of humour and hysteria into becoming the most dangerous third-party challenger for the Presidency since 1912.* He had taken his circus act from the Deep South to the big cities of the North, where he was pulling in huge crowds and rising steadily in the polls. It is difficult now to understand the flavour of Wallace's appeal. In his philosophy he was little better than a pied piper of negativism. Yet he had a certain tawdry charisma ('aggressive and darkly venturous, he has the dingy, attractive air of a B-movie idol, the kind who plays a handsome garage attendant', according to the description of journalist, Gary Wills[30]) and his rhetoric could be hilarious. In the early months of the year he put out the message that he was the candidate with a difference.

---

* In 1912, Theodore Roosevelt had led the famous 'Bull Moose' Progressive Party revolt against the incumbent President, William Howard Taft. This Republican in-fighting allowed Woodrow Wilson to win the election, but not before Roosevelt had displayed characteristic bravado when, having been shot in the chest minutes before he was due to make a speech, he refused medical assistance, declaring, 'I will make this speech or die. It is one thing or the other.'

Now you take a big sack and you put LBJ in there, and you put Hubert
Humphrey in there, and you put Bobby Kennedy as the blood-giver
in there, and you shake 'em all up. Then you put this Richard Milhous
Nixon, who with Eisenhower put bayonets into the backs of the
people of Little Rock and in your backs, and you put in Earl Warren,
who doesn't have enough legal brains in his head to try a chicken feed
in my home county, and you shake 'em all up. And then you put in
that Socialist Nelson Rockefeller from the most liberal state in the
country, and that left-winger George Romney, who was out in the
streets with the demonstrators, and that Clifford Case of New Jersey,
and that wild Bill Scranton of Pennsylvania, and that radical Jacob
Javits of New York, and you shake 'em all up.

Then you turn that sack over and the first one that falls out, you
pick him up by the nape of the neck and drop him right back in again,
because there's not a dime's worth of difference in any of 'em, National
Democrats or National Republicans.[31]

Having pulverised all his opponents, their advisers ('pointy headed liberals')
and the East-coast press into one identical tribe ('feedin' and breedin' together
like one big family of Mississippi rabbits when they settle down in them there
comfortable burrows in Washington DC'), Wallace told his audiences how he
would sort out the nation's number one problem.

Instead of being soft on crime, he would turn the country over to the police
for a couple of years so that 'a good crease in the skull' could be given to rioters
and protesters could be 'drug through the courts by the hair of their heads and
thrown into a big strong jail'. The crescendo of his invective was always the same:
'Ah hadn't meant to say this tonight, but yew-know, if one of them hippies lays
down in front of mah car when Ah become President, that'll be the last car he lays
down in front of.'[32]

Instead of turning their backs on this rhetorical claptrap, a sizeable minority
of the American electorate pledged their support for Wallace. By September 1968
the polls showed him holding steady with 18 or 19 per cent of the vote. This would
have been enough to deny either major party candidate an overall majority of
electoral college votes, thus raising the spectre of a constitutional crisis with the
Presidency having to be decided by the votes at the House of Representatives. That
such a scenario had to be taken seriously was yet another indication of the madness of 1968.

The Republicans were the party who stood to lose most from the Alabama challenge. Polls showed that Wallace was taking away two votes from Nixon to every one he drew from Humphrey. Wallace was therefore an opponent to be fought and not a collaborator to be accommodated. Although there were journalists who accused Nixon of competing for the racist vote, such a charge is baseless. Nixon's rhetoric was always respectable on the law and order issue, and he attacked Wallace's negativism, deftly turning the Governor's favourite punch line: 'We need politics at home that will go beyond simply saying that, "Well, if somebody lies down in front of my Presidential limousine it will be the last one he lies down in front of",' Nixon told an Atlanta television audience. 'No President of the United States is going to do that and anybody who says that shouldn't be President of the United States.'[33]

Later in the campaign Nixon put his own spin on the time-honoured argument used by major parties against minor parties: 'Do you want to make a point or do you want to make a change?' he asked his audiences. 'Do you want to get something off your chest or do you want to get something done? Do you want to get a moment's satisfaction by your vote of protest or do you want to get four years of action?'[34]

Under pressure of this kind, the Wallace bandwagon started to slow down, slewing to a halt on 3 October when he introduced retired Air Force General Curtis LeMay as his running mate. LeMay stunned even the wildest rednecks at his first press conference by advocating the use of nuclear bombing as part of his ticket's foreign policy: 'I think there are many times when it would be most efficient to use nuclear weapons...I don't believe the world would end...If I found it necessary, I would use anything we could dream up—including nuclear weapons if it was necessary.'[35] After these surrealistic statements, which included LeMay's opinion that nuclear explosions did no permanent ecological damage except perhaps to land crabs, Wallace's support crumbled and he was no longer a serious force in the election.

In the final months of the campaign, Nixon launched 'Operation Extra Effort', which was a surge of media spending using the campaign's $24 million war chest. TV time was purchased across the nation on a mammoth scale, but the most impressive part of the blitz was a series of radio talks from the candidate. Subjects covered in these broadcasts included the reform of the draft; the future of NATO; the state of American youth; and one particularly interesting one, 'A New Alignment for American Unity', calling for a coalition of interest groups ranging from Blacks wanting jobs to enlightened Southerners, new liberals and traditional Republicans. These measured and thoughtful addresses (reprinted in booklet form) were a good reflection of Nixon the serious political leader. They contrasted well with Humphrey's frenetic burblings about 'the politics of joy'.

By mid-October Nixon looked so assured of victory that he was even pre-pared to describe his future presidential plans for foreign affairs. He had a private and historically significant conversation on this subject on 18 October with Har-rison Salisbury, the Assistant Managing Editor of the *New York Times*, a news-paper man whom Nixon respected for his expertise on Soviet matters. 'Nixon outlined the foreign policy he would put in place', recalled Salisbury. 'He said his initial move would be to go to Western Europe. He felt our allies there had been neglected. He wanted to strengthen the Atlantic alliance before anything else could be done.

'His next move, he said, would be to end the Vietnam war. "We can't have a foreign policy with Vietnam hanging around our necks. I will deal with it within six months", were his words...He also told me he planned to make an opening to China. He said it was not possible to conceive of a secure world without China's co-operation and that it would only be possible to deal with the Russians after he had struck up an accord with the Chinese. "I don't want to bargain with Brezhnev until I'm holding all the chips", he said. "We want to have the Chinese with us when we sit down and negotiate with the Russians."'[36]

Harrison Salisbury's record of his discussion with Nixon in October 1968 is important. The conversation took place some six weeks before Nixon met Henry Kissinger, thus conclusively answering the question as to who was the real archi-tect of the Nixon-Kissinger foreign policy. It also demonstrates how much care and thought had gone into Nixon's preparations for the course he would later follow as President.

In spite of all his outer confidence about the election result, Nixon was inwardly scared of secret developments on the one issue that transcended all others in importance, the Vietnam war. His strength on this issue was his general air of foreign policy authority, but the vagueness of his proposals for ending the hostilities still left many voters confused. By contrast, President Lyndon Johnson, beleaguered and sidelined in the White House throughout the campaign, was working on a specific peace plan of his own. If successful, LBJ's plan might yet secure his place in history and win the election for the Democrats. It was the ace up the President's sleeve. Astonishingly it had been deliberately put there by Moscow.

The story of how the White House and the Kremlin collaborated to 'Stop Nixon' has been chronicled by Johnson's former Defense Secretary Clark Clifford in his memoirs *Counsel to the President*. According to Clifford, Moscow sent a secret message to Johnson three weeks before election day. It proposed that 'If the US stopped the bombing of North Vietnam, Hanoi would agree to the participation of the Saigon Government in the negotiations that would follow immediately.'[37]

President Johnson was at first suspicious of this sudden reversal of Communist policy until Clifford reminded him of Averell Harriman's prediction 'that Moscow would try to prevent a victory by Nixon, whom they still regarded as an unreconstructed Cold War warrior'.[38]

Having thus been alerted to the Soviet interest in stopping Nixon, Johnson was nevertheless prepared to work with them. He agreed to Moscow's bombing halt, even making it a condition 'that negotiations begin within twenty-four hours after the cessation of the bombing'.[39] This was to ensure that the negotiations would have maximum impact on the presidential election.

Nixon got word of these byzantine manoeuvres from Henry Kissinger, still at that time a Harvard professor and foreign policy adviser to Governor Nelson Rockefeller. Kissinger also had a role as a 'trusted consultant'[40] to the Johnson administration. The trust was evidently not all that mutual, since it was from Kissinger that the Nixon headquarters received their first warning of the imminent bombing halt and peace talks agreement. Describing Kissinger as 'a very good source we had in this period...who talked regularly to Mitchell but who never talked to me', Nixon was appreciative of the professor's willingness to leak this top-secret information, although later adding the comment: 'Henry's role here may not have been too admirable because he seems to have had a foot in both camps.'[41]

All political camps were electrified when, on 31 October, five days before the election, President Johnson went on national television to announce a breakthrough on Vietnam. He said that North Vietnam had agreed to participate in peace talks with all parties, to respect the neutrality of the Demilitarized Zone, and to stop attacking South Vietnamese cities in return for an end to the bombing north of the DMZ. 'I have now ordered that all air, naval, and artillery bombardment of North Vietnam cease as of 8 a.m. Washington time, Friday morning', declared the retiring President. 'I have reached this decision...in the belief that this action can lead to progress towards a peaceful settlement of the Vietnamese war...What we now expect...are prompt, productive, serious and intensive negotiations in an atmosphere that is conducive to progress.'[42]

At first hearing, Johnson's announcement sounded wonderful. The American public's reaction may be measured by the polls, which approved the bombing halt by an enormous margin and put Hubert Humphrey into the lead in the presidential race. According to the Lou Harris Poll of 2 November, Humphrey had 43 per cent, Nixon 40 per cent, Wallace 13 per cent and 4 per cent undecided. On the face of things, Nixon's worst fears had come true. The President was hailed as a hero, and the Vice President looked like winning the election in a last minute surge of peace euphoria.

However, all was not what it seemed, for behind LBJ's statement lay a political saga of labyrinthine complexity, which had more twists and turns to come.

Although the US Government negotiators had been struggling in Paris and Saigon to come up with a deal that would bring all parties to the conference table, they had been unable to get agreement from President Thieu of South Vietnam. Without such agreement from the Government of Vietnam (GVN) the peace talks would be pointless—a diplomatic version of *Hamlet* without the Prince. Thieu was therefore under heavy pressure from the US to agree to Johnson's deal and at one stage had allegedly accepted the proposals. Nixon and the other presidential candidates had been briefed to this effect in a call from President Johnson on 16 October. However, between 16 and 31 October, the GVN became evasive about whether or not it would attend the peace talks. A more cautious President would have signed up the South Vietnamese before proceeding further, but with only five days to go before the polls in America, patience was at a premium, so in a gambler's throw, Johnson had gone ahead and made his announcement (without Thieu's agreement) that South Vietnam was 'free' to participate in the negotiations.

Nixon was watching these events. Ever since Kissinger's leak, he had been anticipating both the bombing halt, and its probable effect on his election prospects. He made speeches preparing the public for such an initiative, and reacted cautiously to the President's announcement when it came. Nixon strongly suspected that the South Vietnamese would not agree to come to the peace table, and that the whole of LBJ's strategy would therefore crumble. This judgement was correct. On Saturday 2 November, President Thieu issued the shattering statement: 'The Government of South Vietnam deeply regrets not to be able to participate in the present exploratory talks.'[43] With that announcement and the headlines that accompanied it around the world, all bets were off—both for peace in Vietnam and for the outcome of the Presidential election.

Nixon's reputation suffered some damage from these events many months later when his critics began accusing him of having deliberately sabotaged Johnson's peace initiative. The basis for this charge lies in the interpretation placed on the contacts that took place between Nixon's senior staff (principally John Mitchell) and Mrs. Anna Chennault.

Mrs. Chennault was a wealthy and well-connected figure on the Washington social scene, with business interests in many parts of Asia. Skilled in the art of self-promotion, she cut a dashing figure as a hostess and influence broker in the diplomatic milieu then known as the China lobby. The Chinese widow of the World War II hero General Claire Chennault, she had become a US citizen in 1950, and was active as a Republican supporter. In 1968, Mrs. Chennault had become Co-chairwoman (with Mamie Eisenhower) of Republican Women for Nixon and had helped this organisation to raise $250,000 for the election campaign. She claimed to be a close friend of Nixon's (untrue) and also to be close to several political leaders in the Far East, among them Chiang Kai-shek and President Thieu.

In Mrs. Chennault's twilight world of international influence-broking, it was difficult to know where to draw the line between fact and fiction. During the month of October she became aware, as did millions of Americans, that a peace deal on Vietnam might be in the offing. Mrs. Chennault was opposed to any such development and made several telephone calls to her friends in Saigon, urging them to resist. In the course of these conversations (which were monitored by US Intelligence agencies), Mrs. Chennault gave the impression that stalling by Thieu on the peace talks would be welcomed by Nixon.

She was overheard telling an official of the South Vietnamese embassy that no peace terms should be accepted before the election. When the official asked whether Nixon knew what she was doing, Mrs. Chennault replied, 'No, but our friend in New Mexico does.'[44] After much head-scratching among the eavesdroppers, they surmised that this might be a reference to Governor Spiro Agnew, who happened to be spending that day campaigning in Albuquerque, New Mexico.

President Johnson immediately put a personal wiretap order on Agnew, but it revealed nothing. He also had Mitchell's telephone tapped and ordered the FBI to place bugs on Nixon's campaign plane.[45] None of these eavesdropping activities produced any evidence of collusion. Johnson nevertheless remained convinced that the Nixon camp was doing its best to undermine his peace efforts through Mrs. Chennault. The President's paranoia, and the leaks that flowed from it, were the basis for the subsequent sabotage allegations against Nixon.

Seen in retrospect, the Chennault affair has the feeling of two and two being added together to make seven. There is, however, evidence to confirm that John Mitchell had at least one telephone conversation in October with Mrs. Chennault about the peace talks, in which he made the obvious point that they would collapse and rebound on the Democrats if Thieu refused to come. Mitchell later said that he was aware that Mrs. Chennault's telephone was being tapped and, as a result, was careful and guarded in his remarks. It would perhaps have been wiser if no such conversation had ever taken place. Yet even if Nixon, through Mitchell, was something more than an innocent bystander in the contact with Mrs. Chennault, he was certainly not a guilty party to the breakdown of the peace talks.

Nixon was far too experienced a practitioner in national security affairs to involve himself in a conspiracy to derail a bombing halt for domestic political purposes. Advance knowledge of such activity would have appalled Nixon as a patriot and alarmed him as a politician. He would have been the first to realise that his electoral prospects could be severely damaged if any connection between his staff and Mrs. Chennault's manoeuvres had been exposed.[46]

Moreover, there is evidence that Nixon had long steered clear of Mrs. Chennault, mistrusting her as a self-promoting chatterbox. She had given offence during a 1967 visit by Nixon to Chiang Kai-shek, showing up in the same Taiwan hotel with persistent suggestions for meetings and dinner invitations.

Nixon had responded to these unwelcome overtures from Mrs. Chennault by instructing his aide, Pat Hillings: 'Keep her away from me, Hillings, she's bad news.'[47] It seems unlikely that this attitude would have changed in the tensest moments of the election a year later.

In any case, President Thieu had compelling reasons of his own for refusing to co-operate with LBJ's peace moves, regardless of suggestions from Washington lobbyists. His cabinet, his rebellious Vice President Nguyen Cao-ky, and the majority of members in his national assembly, were vehemently opposed to negotiations with the North. They saw South Vietnam's domestic position both militarily and economically as a strong one. In their eyes it was the cities of the North which were crying out for a relief from the bombing. The South, shored up by the presence of half a million US troops, was in no danger of losing further territory. Its economy was booming, particularly around Saigon, and many members of the Government were happily becoming rich through corruption. Time therefore was on South Vietnam's side. Delaying tactics were the Government's preferred option. Moreover, President Thieu realised that if he yielded to Johnson's pressure he might face serious trouble at home (there were rumours of an impending coup) in addition to the even more serious risk of humiliation by Hanoi at the negotiating table.

Above all, Thieu did not need to be told by Mrs. Chennault that his interests would be better served by having Nixon rather than Humphrey in the White

House. He already knew that Nixon was a hardliner, deeply sceptical of North Vietnamese intentions, and far more supportive of South Vietnam than the dovish Vice President was ever likely to be. These were the real reasons why South Vietnam refused to go along with Johnson's last-minute ploy to have peace talks on the eve of the election. Mrs. Chennault's shadowy activities could not, at the most, have been anything other than marginal to the making of President Thieu's decision.

Insignificant in Saigon, the role of Mrs. Chennault might have been explosive in the final days of the US elections. Some Democrats actually believed that Nixon was responsible for sabotaging the peace talks. They urged Humphrey to make the charge public. As Theodore H. White wrote: 'I know of no more essentially decent story in American politics than Humphrey's refusal to do so; his instinct was that Richard Nixon, personally, had no knowledge of Mrs. Chennault's activities; had no knowledge of Mrs. Chennault's activities; had no hand in them; and would have forbidden them had he known. Humphrey would not air the story.'[48] Prudence as well as decency must have entered Humphrey's calculations. The telephone intercepts had, after all, specifically recorded Mrs. Chennault telling the South Vietnamese embassy that Nixon did not know what she was up to. She may well have taken Nixon's name in vain during her conversations with her friends in Saigon, but as Theodore White and other leading reporters of the time concluded, that was all there ever really was to this episode. As White put it himself: For the sake of the record, this reporter's judgement was that Humphrey's decision was morally, if not tactically, correct.'[49]

Because of the confusion over the Vietnamese peace talks, the presidential election of 1968 ended as a cliffhanger. Nixon, comfortably ahead a few weeks before election day, had to endure the agony of seeing Humphrey narrowly overtake him in some of the polls taken on Saturday 2 November, two days after Johnson announced his bombing halt. If the belief that peace was at hand had consolidated, Humbert Humphrey might well have become the next President of the United States. Saigon's repudiation of the peace talks, headline news in the Sunday papers of 3 November, halted the Democrats' momentum. By Monday 4th the election was too close to call. The final act of drama took place in Los Angeles, where both parties staged mammoth telethons. Calls poured in from the public at the rate of 130,000 per hour. Humphrey and his running mate, Senator Edmund Muskie, had the edge in endorsements from Hollywood stars, Kennedy nostalgia and vice-presidential credibility. They made much of the fact that Nixon appeared alone, an embarrassing but wise decision in the light of Agnew's numerous gaffes on the campaigning trail. Nixon, live on national television for four hours, was generally thought to have pulled ahead by the quality of his substantive answers to questions. One of the most telling points he made was on the latest escalation of the war by the North Vietnamese. After lamenting the fact that the peace negotiations had fallen apart at the seams, Nixon claimed to have heard 'a very disturbing report' that 'the North Vietnamese are moving thousands of tons of supplies down the Ho Chi Minh trail and our bombers are not able to stop them'.[50]

This report, which according to Nixon came to him 'from a very reliable and secure intelligence source',[51] was immediately disputed by the Democrats and by journalists, some of whom claimed it was an invention. But subsequent events showed that Nixon and his source were right, for aerial reconnaissance photographs did indeed confirm that the North Vietnamese had been moving supplies south in this period. Even without the photographic evidence, Nixon's warning was thought by some observers to be the nail in the coffin of the peace talks factor in the election. For if the enemy were on the march down the Ho Chi Minh trail, there was not much sense in voting for the notion that peace would come imminently under the Democrats.

The election night of 5 November 1968 was initially almost as agonising for Nixon as its unhappy predecessor in 1960 had been. There was much bad news for him in the early returns from Ohio and Illinois and the networks were full of speculative comments about a possible Humphrey upset. The popular vote tally was on a nerve-racking see-saw.

> At 9.30 p.m. Nixon had 41 per cent to Humphrey's 39 per cent
> At 10 p.m. they were on a dead heat.
> At 10.30 p.m. the results were still dead even.
> At 11 p.m. Humphrey had a slight lead.
> At 11.30 p.m. Humphrey's momentum was building.
> At midnight Humphrey was leading in the popular vote by 43.5 per
>   cent to 42.6 per cent—a majority of 600,000.

The popular vote figures were, however, misleading. By midnight Nixon had won 231 of the electoral college votes out of the 270 he needed to win the White House. With California and its forty electoral votes a near certainty, by 12.30 a.m. he was looking like the next President of the United States. As favourable returns from Ohio, Illinois, and California flowed in during the early hours of the morning, his victory seemed assured. At 3 a.m. Nixon emerged from the seclusion of his bedroom clutching the yellow legal pad on which he had been making his calculations. With Mitchell, Haldeman, Finch and Chotiner, he doublechecked all the results, trends, projections and likely final figures. He was sure of it. 'Any objections?' he asked. There were no objections. Richard Nixon had won the Presidency.

The first formal acknowledgement came a few seconds later from John Mitchell. Overcome with emotion, the great strongman had dissolved into tears. Nixon put his arm round his campaign manager. 'Thank you Mr. President-elect', said Mitchell as he recovered his composure. 'It was like a gong going off', said Dwight Chapin, an eyewitness of the scene. 'From that moment on everything started to get different.'[52]

IV. VICTORY

'Nothing except a battle lost can be half as melancholy as a battle won', wrote Wellington in his despatch from the field of Waterloo on 18 June 1815, the day after he had defeated Napoleon.

Nixon was in a similarly pensive mood as he surveyed the political battlefield in the aftermath of his 1968 victory. Jubilation was scarcely on his agenda. Even on the morning of his triumph he made just one concession to the ecstatic mood of his supporters. 'Having lost a close one eight years ago and having won a close one this year, I can say this—winning's a lot more fun',[53] were his first public words as President-elect. Then he stilled his praetorian guard of cheering loyalists by taking up a more sombre theme based on the 'in victory—magnanimity' philosophy of his hero, Winston Churchill. 'I saw many signs in this campaign. Some of them were not friendly and some were very friendly', said Nixon. 'But the one that touched me the most was the one that I saw in Deshler, Ohio, at the end of a long day of whistle-stopping, a little town, I suppose five times the population was there in the dusk, almost impossible to see—but a teenager held up a sign, "Bring Us Together". And that will be the great objective of this Administration at the outset, to bring the American people together. This will be an open Administration, open to new ideas, open to men and women of both parties, open to the critics as well as those who support us. We want to bridge the generation gap. We want to bridge the gap between the races. We want to bring America together.'[54]

Bringing America together was an activity that became more honoured in the breach than the observance in Nixon's White House years. This failure has usually been attributed to the President's own attitudes. These were frequently flawed, and in the end they were partly responsible for the eventual disaster of Watergate—but only partly. Watergate was a tragedy with many authors and sources. It could only have been staged against an historical backdrop of looming disaster. As a drama it had a prologue, not unlike the opening scene of Shake-speare's *Macbeth*, when witches dance round a cauldron of sinister potions and foretell a black future.

The prologue of Watergate was the legacy of 1968. By the end of that year, the American body politic had become poisoned with political violence, racial hatred, youth rebellion and Vietnam. As they simmered together, these ingredients formed a noxious concoction which sapped the nation's strength and threatened its stability.

The unpopularity of the war in Vietnam was the principal catalyst for the changes that were sweeping across the country. On a private level, millions of families were torn apart as silly slogans ('Make love not war'; 'Don't trust anyone over forty'; 'Turn on, tune in, drop out') started to take effect. The generation gap became a behavioural revolution as the children of the 1960s rejected their parents' values, often swinging away into promiscuity, long hair, soft drugs, hard rock, hippie life styles and many other weird and wonderful indulgences dressed up as protests against society.

This atmosphere of disequilibrium, although led by youthful anti-war activists, was by no means confined to them. 'There was a quiet, sour fear at the centre of American life in 1968', wrote Gary Wills in *Nixon Agonistes*, a strange and sometimes brilliantly insightful book of campaign reportage. 'What is hard and essential to convey is the interaction of resentments. The bitterness moved in crossing tides, an acid weave of right and left, old and young.'[55]

This 'interaction of resentments' and its 'acid weave' corroded institutions as well as families. Two great power centres of American life were particularly affected by the convulsions of 1968—the media and the Congress. On their respective quests for viewers and voters they both made concessions to the temper of the times. The TV networks, with their hunger for colourful pictures, exaggerated the importance of essentially trivial symbols of the youth rebellion at home. They also introduced a new dimension to modern warfare abroad by giving so much prominence in their nightly news bulletins to the unpleasantness of the fighting in Vietnam. These changes were not mere shifts of emphasis or editorial judgement. At some point in the late 1960s a new spirit of adversarial reporting became part of the news industry's culture. Long before Nixon entered the White House, too much of the media's coverage of Vietnam had slipped from objectivity to opposition. Many young recruits to the ranks of the fourth estate went a stage further and became self-proclaimed opponents not just of the war but of the political system that had created it. This meant that the Presidency itself was no longer an institution to be revered but a target to be attacked. Leading this movement was the *Washington Post.* 'You could certainly say that from the mid-60s onwards we became a far more anti-establishment paper than we ever had been', recalled Ben Bradlee, its editor. 'As far as the Presidency was concerned there was an awe for the office under Wiggins, my predecessor. I guess I changed all that. By the time Nixon got in we were already anti-White House, and we sure stayed that way.'[56]

Ben Bradlee and his staff had plenty of imitators in the Vietnam era. For journalists of their persuasion, the fall of Lyndon Johnson was the first taste of blood. From that time on they were no longer scribes but carnivores. As long as the war continued their teeth would remain sharp in anticipation of a further onslaught against the sacred cow of the Presidency.

These thought-forms of 1968 journalism pervaded the Washington press corps. The feeling that the White House and its incumbent were adversaries who needed to be cut down to size was also gaining ground among politicians and their advisers in the groves of academe. Arthur Schlesinger's influential book *The Imperial Presidency* (an attack on the over-mighty nature of the office) had its genesis in much earlier academic concerns about the unconstitutional nature of the 1964 Tonkin Gulf Resolution and the apparently unlimited scope of the President's powers to wage war. Another highly praised book on this theme was *The Twilight of the Presidency*, in which the author, LBJ's former Press Secretary George Reedy, deplored the evolution of the White House into a royal court whose King, the President, now needed to be constrained by countervailing new pressures. It was not long before similar concerns were being voiced in and around the Congress. Indeed, the first opinion on Capitol Hill that Nixon would have to be impeached was recorded in 1969, a few days *before* his inauguration. This startling view was expressed by Robert Smith, the chief counsel of a key Senate committee on Government Operations to James Humes, a young Philadelphia lawyer and Nixon supporter who later became a White House aide. Humes was taking his friend to lunch, and the conversation turned to Nixon's prospects. Chief Counsel Smith voiced the (then extraordinary) opinion that the Nixon Presidency would end in impeachment. He argued that Congress was a political body; that impeaching a President was a political act; and that impeachment was 'not such a difficult thing to do', recalled Humes. 'Robert Smith then showed me the list of votes that had recently been cast on the Senate Judiciary Committee motion to impeach Supreme Court Justice Abe Fortas,' recalled Humes, 'although that vote had been defeated by the Democrats, who were in the majority. Smith said they would one day be turned right around to carry a motion for the impeachment of Richard Nixon. He added that LBJ would have been impeached for his handling of Vietnam if he had been a Republican. Now that there was a decisive anti-Republican majority in both the Senate and the House, Smith argued it was only a matter of time before the legislature used its powers of subpoena and impeachment to break an unpopular President.'[57]

James Humes thought the conversation was getting ridiculous and ended it by accepting a 50–1 bet against Nixon's Presidency collapsing before the end of his first term. Because of the time limitation, Humes won his wager financially and collected the magnificent sum of one dollar. Politically his victory was pyrrhic.

It would be wrong to imply that such pre-inauguration stirrings towards a Nixon impeachment were widespread. Nevertheless, the Humes conversation, together with the attitudes of many journalists, legislators and political observers of the period were indications of a prevailing trend in liberal thinking. The Presidency was too powerful; Nixon was awful; both the man and the institution needed to have their wings clipped.

Two other factors were part of the legacy of 1968, both of them related to Nixon personally. One was that Nixon was the first President to be a victim of class prejudice. This assertion may shock those who believe in the American dream of a classless society, but it was a dream that had not yet penetrated the Washington of the 1960s. In those days the nation's capital was still an élitist village in which the movers and shakers of journalism, government and society tended to belong to an identifiable establishment that was predominantly liberal in its attitudes, Democrat in its politics, wealthy in its finances, and Georgetown in its geography. The luminaries of this Washington establishment had spent the last quarter of a century despising Nixon for his rough edges, his uncomfortable political abrasiveness, and his social insecurities. They did not stop their sneering just because he was President—if anything they intensified it. Nixon had long been aware of these class attitudes and deep down was upset by them. He was not the only one to feel that way. The incoming British Ambassador to Washington, John Freeman, was shocked by the anti-Nixon snobbery he encountered on taking up his appointment in February 1969.

'Nixon was treated abominably by Georgetown society', recalled Freeman. 'It was not just a question of political disagreements. Really beastly attitudes were on display towards him, largely to do with social class...I remember one not uncharacteristic example of this at Mrs. Alice Longworth's house one evening. Over drinks before dinner, she asked me what I thought of the new President. I gave some sort of respectful reply. Alice then hushed the whole company, saying in her wickedest voice 'How extraordinary! Listen. The Ambassador thinks well of Mr. Nixon! Such a common little man!' and her guests all roared with laughter.'[58]

Although he had a chip on his shoulder about the attitudes of the Georgetown set towards him, there was nothing common about the way Nixon treated Hubert Humphrey on inauguration day. Remembering his own Cinderella-like exit from the Vice Presidency in 1960, when all facilities, including his car, were withdrawn at the stroke of midnight, Nixon showed a touching sensitivity towards the feelings of his defeated rival.

In addition to the warm public and private tributes he paid to his election opponent, Nixon personally supervised all the arrangements for Humphrey's last hours in Washington. These included putting an Air Force jet at the ex-Vice President's disposal, choosing a bouquet of Muriel Humphrey's favourite flowers to be handed to her as she got on to the aircraft, and attaching to them a handwritten note of presidential thanks for the couple's twenty-five years of public service. The son of Hannah Nixon had not forgotten the importance of small acts of kindness.[59]

Other aspects of inauguration day brought out the angry side of Richard Nixon. His address was both eloquent and conciliatory. After some fine words on the theme of peacemaking abroad, he urged the nation at home 'to lower our voices' and added, 'We cannot learn from one another until we stop shouting at one another.'[60]

A few minutes later the inaugural parade was ruined by shouters. It was a national disgrace, the first time in the 180 years of the Presidency that any such disruption had occurred. 'Four more years of death', chanted the demonstrators along with their familiar obscenities against the war and in favour of Ho Chi Minh. All the way along Pennsylvania Avenue flags were burned, smoke bombs were ignited and debris was hurled at the presidential limousine. Inside it, Nixon was understandably furious. When the parade had passed the worst of the demonstrators, he threw open the sun roof and stood up alongside Pat making defiant V for Victory signs to the cheering crowd.

The gesture symbolised Nixon's determination to fight back against his adversaries. It was the second most important personal ingredient he added to the combustible legacy of 1968. Perhaps if he had been blessed with a more emollient personality he might just have been able to dampen the fire storms of those tormented times, particularly if he had followed his own inaugural's advice 'to lower our voices'. This was the right strategy but Nixon was the wrong man to make it work. He simply did not have the temperament to turn the other cheek, especially when he found himself on the receiving end of the slings and arrows of outrageous opposition. Like his father, he was a man who bore grudges. He wanted to take on all comers, even when the odds against beating them looked insurmountable. Such a fighting spirit had been the quintessence of his struggle to become President. He could not abandon it now that he was the President.

Thus, from the first day he took office, Richard Nixon was destined to be a combative leader. In a less turbulent period of America's history, that combativeness might have been channelled into high achievement. Indeed, to a remarkable extent there were such results, but they were accompanied by bitterness and divisiveness on an unprecedented scale.

It has been fashionable among American writers to place all or at least most of the blame for the tragic developments that tarnished and ultimately destroyed the Nixon Presidency on the shoulders of Nixon personally. He must certainly bear his full share of responsibility as later chapters will show. Yet there should also be a wider perspective which is perhaps more easily perceived by non-Americans schooled in the great clashes of European history, such as the seventeenth-century warfare between the English King and his Parliament or the earlier confrontations across the Holy Roman Empire between the medieval church and state. In those epic battles of centuries past, the roots of the power struggles went far deeper than the follies of the personalities who eventually provoked them. So it was with Watergate. Before Nixon arrived in the White House, the historical stage was set for a whole tournament of jousting—between President and Congress; President and media; presidential authority and youthful rebellion. These clashes were always likely to be exciting and passionate, and to have important results. But in the absence of the three witches from *Macbeth*, almost no one could foresee either the ferocity of the jousting or that it would unfold into the greatest trauma of twentieth-century American politics.

SEVENTEEN

THE PEAKS AND VALLEYS OF THE PRESIDENCY

I. THE COURT OF KING RICHARD

'The first opinion of a ruler is based on the quality of the men he has around him' wrote Machiavelli in *The Prince*[1] and on that basis Nixon measured up well at the start of his first term. The White House in 1969 contained a galaxy of managerial and intellectual talent. The principal stars each reflected an aspect of the President's personality and power drive, having been chosen by him, sometimes instinctively, because they fitted into his long-conceived masterplan for the Presidency.

The managerial leader of the team was H.R. 'Bob' Haldeman, who effectively created the modern office of White House Chief of Staff. Previous Presidents had their principal aides, their senior assistants or their court favourites, but it was Haldeman who institutionalised the post of Chief of Staff and created for it an executive system which has endured. Nixon himself was a poor administrator. He had never managed an organisation larger than a small platoon of servicemen in the South Pacific. In his wilderness years he had even found it difficult to manage his personal and business routines without staff assistance. A thinker who yearned to be a doer, he recognised that as President he would be a conceptual leader who had to rely heavily on others to make his concepts work. Haldeman understood Nixon's needs well. He built a machine for the White House staff, designed to ensure that the ideas coming out of the Oval Office were followed through with an elaborate system of action memos, job numbers, and 'ticklers' (sharp reminders), ultimately getting translated into policies and results.

The Haldeman system worked far better than has generally been acknowledged. However, it had its weaknesses too. The Presidency is about people as well as paperwork, and Haldeman could be too hard on the people in the middle and junior echelons of the White House. No one liked to argue with the Chief of Staff, let alone say 'no' or 'it shouldn't be done' to his orders. 'The staff were scared of Bob's ruthless approach', recalled Charles Lichenstein, who worked in the White House as a Special Assistant to the President in 1970. 'They lived in terror that he might catch them relaxing. They didn't dare go home until the light in the Haldeman office went out. And they swallowed all his nonsense about how the President must have a zero-defect system.'[2]

Such retrospective grumbles have some validity but they obscure the total dedication that the Chief of Staff and most other senior White House personnel gave when driving towards the goal of making the President's will be done. Haldeman was a believer as well as a manager. He subsumed his own creative intelligence (he was a top scoring member of MENSA) and critical faculties under his devotional faith in Richard Nixon. 'If Bob had a failing it was that he accepted the President's views too easily', said Haldeman's friend, UCLA classmate and fellow Christian Scientist John Ehrlichman, who had joined the White House staff as Counsel to the President. 'We often argued about this or that idea that had come down from Nixon but time and again Bob would end the discussion by saying, "But he's right", and go out and get some staffer to do it. That happened much too easily.'[3]

Although Haldeman's control over the White House staff was formidable, it was by no means total. For all its Republican antecedents, the office of President of the United States has, in the twentieth century, become increasingly comparable to the role of an elected King, who passes power not through a system of management and organisational charts, but by far more personal nods and winks to the barons and court favourites closest to his throne. Nixon had several such favoured courtiers around him, often seeking to handle them by a philosophy of divide and rule.

On the domestic front, the President put two top aides simultaneously in charge, thus sowing the seeds of a creative tension that eventually delivered, after some early disappointments and changes, a remarkable record of results. The two aides in question were Arthur Burns and Daniel Patrick Moynihan. Burns was an intellectual giant but slow and methodical in his policy planning, using a series of task forces staffed by distinguished experts. Moynihan was an intellectual firecracker, who had never met the new President until his appointment, although his writings on welfare reform had been an important influence on Nixon's thinking.

Effervescent in wit, erudite in scholarship and skilful in flattery, Moynihan threw his Irish leprechaun's spell of charm over Nixon at their first meeting and continued to captivate him for the next two years. Despite his opposition to the Vietnam war, his Harvard background, and his history of service to the Kennedy White House, Moynihan found himself being sounded out on the President's plan to establish an Urban Affairs Council as the domestic policy equivalent to the National Security Council in foreign affairs. 'That's a capital idea!' he enthused.[4] Nixon immediately appointed him to be its first head, a role in which Moynihan excelled. 'I came to the White House as the absolute outsider', he recalled.

> I had no idea what to expect but almost immediately I found myself in an entirely congenial, entirely workable environment. The President was enthusiastically receptive to new ideas, easy to see, easy to convince. It was amazing what he would say yes to. I remember putting up an early paper advocating Home Rule for the District of Columbia. In those days that was quite a step. Elected Black Mayors running the nation's capital—dangerous radicalism in the eyes of some Republicans! But Nixon was all for it. 'I've always been for Home Rule', he said, somewhat to Haldeman's and Ehrlichman's consternation. So we went ahead and did it, just as we did a lot of good things for which we weren't given much credit... On the domestic side, the Administration was full of clever, energetic people. What did we all achieve? Well, for a start we changed the atmosphere. There was an expectation when we came in that every city in the country was going to have a race riot. The cliché was, 'It'll be a long hot summer.' But there wasn't any long hot summer and there weren't any more race riots under Nixon, partly because local communities could see that his administration was moving on jobs, schools, decentralization of power and welfare reform. By August 1969, just seven months after taking office, the President approved and sent to Congress a message proposing a guaranteed cash income scheme for poor families which we called the Family Assistance Plan (FAP); a revenue-sharing program shifting money and responsibilities to the states

and local communities; and a reworking of manpower programs. Nothing quite like it had ever happened! We may well have been the most progressive administration on domestic issues that had ever been formed.[5]

Moynihan's euphoric reminiscences have a touch of the 'Bliss was it in that dawn to be alive'[6] spirit of the French Revolution. He was one of very few White House aides who found Nixon 'easy to see, easy to convince'. Nevertheless, he does recapture a flavour of the idealism and the zest for reform which characterised the early months of the Nixon Presidency. Where was Nixon himself amongst all that zest and idealism? Notorious for his cynicism about individuals, he had a touch of the romantic when he encountered attractive new ideas, and could surprise everyone by the strength of his commitment to a policy concept he had carefully thought through and approved. One such idea was Moynihan's proposal for welfare reform, the FAP. Welfare reform was a political minefield for a Republican President, as it could expose him to criticism from conservative members of his party, as Nixon was to find out. Moynihan was nonetheless able to convince Nixon to embrace reform by playing on his sense of history. Comparing Nixon to Disraeli, the great British Prime Minister who owed to his conservatism his ability to carry out reforms that were more daring than his liberal opponents could dream of achieving, Moynihan persuaded Nixon that a role as a reformer was entirely compatible with his Republicanism.*

Convinced also that Moynihan's FAP reforms would strengthen family life and help the working poor to rise out of poverty, Nixon became more enthusiastic than the enthusiasts, urging his staff to accelerate their schedule and sending up the appropriate legislative messages to Congress. 'A year was simply too long,' he has recalled, 'so I pushed the Cabinet and staff to develop a program of creative and innovative social legislation as soon as possible.'[8]

The Moynihan reform programme, after an initially favourable welcome, came under heavy shelling from the very people who might have been expected

---

* Nixon was first introduced to Disraeli when Moynihan sent him a memorandum dated 4 December 1970 responding to a request for his list of 'the ten best political biographies'. Moynihan's recommendations were:

John Adams, *Autobiography* (published 1802); Lord Charnwood, *Abraham Lincoln* (1917); Henry Adams, *The Education of Henry Adams* (1918); Duff Cooper, *Talleyrand* (1932); Lord David Cecil, *Melbourne* (1939); Alan Bullock, *Hitler, A Study in Tyranny* (1952); John Morton Blum, *The Republican Roosevelt* (1961); Robert Blake, *Disraeli* (1966); John Womack Jr., *Zapata and the Mexican Revolution* (1969). Five weeks later Nixon told an astonished Moynihan: 'I've read them all. Now about Disraeli . . .'[7]

to be its strongest supporters—liberals in Congress and the media. Gradually the Family Assistance Plan and the Revenue Sharing Programs began to founder, losing support inside and outside the Administration and eventually sinking in the Senate. Many years later, Moynihan described the onslaught against his programmes in a letter to Anthony Lewis of the *New York Times*: 'Liberals commenced to denounce the proposals as reactionary, racist, Lord knows what. From the outside this might not have seemed much harassment or rejection. From the inside it seemed a continuous, relentless barrage. I watched the high spirits of the reformers gradually subside. It was no use. They would never be accepted as reformers. And so? And so, why bother?'[9]

Nixon was among those who stopped bothering. Just as the initial support for the reforms waned, so Nixon's enthusiasm disappeared. The war in Vietnam was proving to be far more intractable than he had hoped and he was forced to devote more and more of his attention to the effort to end it. Had it not been for Vietnam, Nixon might well have stuck by his domestic reforms and his early aspirations might not have been disappointed. As it was, his disappointment over the fate of FAP and Revenue Sharing took two forms—a reversion to cynicism and a demand for better public relations. He believed that his old liberal enemies had shafted the programmes because they could not bear to see a conservative Republican President achieve what liberal Democrat Presidents had failed to achieve. On a Moynihan memorandum giving an assessment of 'final thoughts' on the demise of the programmes, Nixon scribbled, 'I agree completely—an utter PR failure on our part.'[10]

Nixon had an obsession with public relations. Even as President, journalists brought out some of his worst insecurities. He was convinced that he could never get favourable or even objective coverage from the White House press corps. 'The Press is the enemy' was a phrase he used to his aides on numerous occasions.[11] Although the generalisation was too sweeping, it was not entirely wide of the mark for a visceral opposition to the President personally sometimes showed among the reporters covering the White House.

Instead of rising above that personalised antagonism, Nixon reciprocated it. He got into the habit of sending angry notes to his staff denouncing this or that story and ordering that the offending writer and his publication should in future be cut off from all White House sources. The older hands in the Administration tended to ignore these instructions, knowing from experience that Nixon himself did not really mean these 'off with his head' edicts, which in any case were almost unenforceable. But within the White House there were few experienced figures with the political sophistication to filter, or at least finesse, the President's *obiter dicta*.

One group which did have political sophistication were the speech-writers, who included Pat Buchanan, Ray Price, David Gergen, Bill Safire, Ken Khachigian and Lee Huebner. This was probably the most gifted team of professional word-smiths to have served any President, for all of them enjoyed previous or subse-quent careers as journalistic commentators of high distinction. Nixon worked well with them, enjoying the intellectual stimulation of such first class minds, yet for obscure reasons the speech-writers were secondary in White House PR activities to Haldeman's 'beaver patrol'.

This eager collection of aides in their twenties were political greenhorns. They knew little about the art of running a government and even less about their multifaceted President and his ways of working. When they received a memo ending 'Do it', or 'Get it done' (characteristic Haldeman sign-offs), they reacted in the spirit of 'theirs not to reason why', for they knew they would be judged mainly on how fast they jumped. Haldeman has recalled that he chose this type of enthusiastic but inexperienced aide 'because it was not necessary for them to know about running a government. They were administrative functionaries.'[12] Such functionaries, who were all too anxious to please, were incapable of mod-erating the orders they received, and Nixon's expressions of anger were too often translated into ill-considered action.

Nixon's instincts to fight the press were combined with attempts to practise the doubtful art of news management using both carrots and sticks. Every day in the White House there was a ten o'clock and a five o'clock meeting at which aides competed with one another to provide responses for the President's insis-tent demands for better PR. Well understanding that the Achilles heel of many journalists is their indolence, the President's PR men were adroit in feeding the media. The means used included giving the heaviest possible bias to television coverage at the expense of print journalism; favouring friendly news organisa-tions with exclusive facilities; and putting 'spin' on news releases by attaching explanatory summaries glorifying the President. There were also attempts to withhold sources from those journalists who were perceived as adversaries. The Federal Communications Commission was used to threaten unfriendly media companies' television licences, and on one occasion the FBI carried out 'checks' on hostile television studios and their reporters. On other occasions, presidential addresses were met with an overwhelmingly favourable response, expressed in telegrams and telephone calls which had been previously organised by the White House. In addition, Vice President Agnew was unleashed as the Administration's Rottweiler to bark menacingly against the liberal media in a series of extrava-gantly worded speeches.

None of this did much good. 'We thought these PR techniques were bizarre in their lack of subtlety', recalled Ben Bradlee, the Editor of the *Washington Post*. 'It was like they were running some sort of sleazy hotel in the Caribbean. "Give 'em a free trip, and fill 'em up with booze if they're for us. Buy 'em off if they're neutral. Knee 'em in the groin if they step out of line." It was just so darn unsophisticated.'[13]

It was not quite as bad as that. The Administration had its successes as well as its failures in news presentation. Nixon himself frequently contradicted his 'the press is the enemy' line, giving interviews and 'backgrounders' to a wide range of reporters. In the early weeks of his Presidency he even made a series of Saturday morning calls to Ben Bradlee. The first one got off on the wrong foot because Bradlee thought the deep-voiced caller was Art Buchwald playing a joke. Even after this had been ironed out, Nixon's efforts to build bridges with the *Post* proved counterproductive. Bradlee felt the President's Saturday calls 'had no purpose, no intellectual foundation…I used to say to myself after each of these conversations, "What the hell was all that about?"'[14]

The fact that the President of the United States and the Editor of the *Washington Post* could only engage in a dialogue of the deaf was an ill omen for the Administration's drive for better public relations. Inside the White House, Nixon communicated to his over-zealous aides his inherent dislike of journalists and his requirement that strong action should be taken to counterbalance any of their critical comments. This led to a downward spiral towards negative PR. Was there a conspiracy on the part of the Administration to discredit and malign the press? Did Nixon himself encourage, direct, and urge on the anti-media campaign? Did the us-against-them mentality boomerang against Nixon in his second term? 'The answer to all those questions is, sadly, yes', wrote the President's friend and speech writer, William Safire.[15]

What the PR difficulties could not distort was that the President was active and successful in his handling of foreign affairs. From the day he took the oath of office, Nixon the foreign policy strategist was in his element, his feelings similar to those of his hero Winston Churchill on entering 10 Downing Street in 1940: 'I felt as if I were walking with destiny, and that all my past life had been but a preparation for this hour and for this trial.'[16] To help him in his rendezvous with destiny, Nixon chose as his National Security Adviser Henry A. Kissinger, who quickly became the closest of his courtiers. Nixon's initial attraction to Kissinger was intellectual. He had only met Kissinger once before he invited him to his transition headquarters at the Pierre Hotel in New York. He had, however, read one of Kissinger's books and was familiar with his thinking on foreign policy, recognising it to be similar to his own. The two men shared a common conception of America's role in the world that was radically different from their predecessors' views. Previous Presidents and their advisers had tended to follow narrow approaches to foreign policy that were based single-mindedly on either ideology or pragmatism. Nixon and Kissinger, by contrast, were conceptualists who believed in a wider, geopolitical approach. They were advocates of the Balance of Power, a concept long applied within the continent of Europe, and now for the first time tried out on a global basis by an American President.

When the two men had their first substantive discussion at the Pierre, Vietnam was dominating most experts' thinking on US foreign policy. The President-elect did not see it that way. He told Kissinger that he was determined to avoid the trap of devoting all his time and energy to Vietnam because 'it was really a short-term problem'.[17] Instead, Nixon was determined to address those longer-term problems that he felt posed a real threat to the security of the United States. In an outline of his foreign policy that was similar to the one he had given to Harrison Salisbury during the election campaign five weeks earlier, he stressed the importance of the Atlantic Alliance, and the primacy of the United States' relationships with the Soviet Union and China. In advocating such a geopolitical philosophy to Kissinger, he was preaching to the converted.

The conversation then turned to structural matters. Nixon told Kissinger how much he distrusted the State Department, whose personnel, he felt, had no loyalty to him, having disdained him as Vice President and ignored him during his wilderness years. He also told Kissinger how he thought it 'imperative to exclude the CIA from the formulation of policy' because 'it was staffed by Ivy League liberals who...had always opposed him politically'.[18] This apparent determination on the part of the President-elect to exclude the bureaucracy and concentrate all power in foreign policy-making within the White House also won Kissinger's enthusiastic approval.

The conversation brought about a meeting of more than minds. Nixon wrote in his memoirs, 'I had a strong intuition about Henry Kissinger, and I decided on the spot that he should be my National Security Adviser.'[19] Intuition often played a strong part in the decisions of Richard Nixon, and few instinctive judgements can have been better than his selection of Kissinger for such a pivotal role in his administration. For Nixon's intuition was able to tell him what no one could have predicted from such a short meeting: the grocer's son from Whittier and the refugee from Hitler's Germany had minds and characters that were uncannily complementary. The two men shared a childlike enthusiasm for springing surprises; a conspirator's love of secrecy; a guerrilla's contempt for the regular forces of the bureaucracy; and a manipulator's enjoyment of power politics. These traits gave them the guile and cunning they needed to carry out the tortuous diplomatic manoeuvres of their negotiations with Vietnam, the Soviet Union and China.

Although their relationship soon became a strong one, it also had its shadows. Both men had a tyrannical streak, which Nixon displayed towards his enemies and Kissinger towards his staff. They were each capable of towering rages and of deep reflection; of high elation and of black depression. The same willingness to engage in duplicity, and at times mendacity, that served the national interest so well abroad, proved disastrous when used to defend the President's interest at home. Their dark moods rarely coincided, but when they did, as at the time of the Pentagon Papers, the results could be catastrophic. To their credit, they both had unexpected virtues. Nixon was the humbler and kinder member of the partnership; Kissinger had the better sense of humour. Kissinger had a horse trader's skill in bargaining; Nixon had a horse breeder's gift for conceiving geopolitical winners. Dedicated patriots, inspired by the highest ambition for their country, they were both deeply insecure men within themselves. They understood each other's faults and complemented each other's talents. Rarely before in the field of international relations had two such strange individuals welded themselves together in so effective a partnership.

The first fruits of the Nixon–Kissinger collaboration in foreign policy came during the President's trip to Europe just five weeks after his inauguration. The itinerary was Brussels, London, Paris, Bonn, Berlin and Rome. The objectives were to demonstrate the US commitment to NATO; to revitalise the Atlantic Alliance by detailed consultations; to show the world that the American President was not completely obsessed with Vietnam; and to seek President de Gaulle's co-operation for the US opening to China. Nixon was received with positive enthusiasm by the European crowds and by the European leaders, most of whom knew him well from his travels in the past five years. On this first presidential journey, Kissinger was not much more than an efficient codifier of briefing papers but his first impressions of Nixon on an overseas tour are worth recording despite their condescending tone: 'He [Nixon] was exuberant; he adored the vestigial ceremonies and was new enough to it to be thrilled at the succession of events. To land with *Air Force One* on foreign soil, to be greeted by a King and then a Prime Minister, to review honor guards to visit Chequers—all this was the culmination of his youthful dreams, the conception of high office, seemingly unattainable for a poor, and somewhat resentful young man from a little town in California. It all produced one of the few occasions of nearly spontaneous joy I witnessed in my acquaintance with this withdrawn and elusive man.'[20]

Although these words were written by Kissinger about Nixon, there are close colleagues of both men who think that the author may have been subliminally transposing his own reaction. 'Henry was the one who was orgiastic about it all—Nixon had been through many similar ceremonies of state as Vice President', observed Bob Haldeman.[21] Nixon certainly gave every appearance of being an experienced practitioner in the art of presidential dignity, as he showed in the episode involving John Freeman, the Editor of the left-wing weekly the *New Statesman*, and a personal friend of Senator Hubert Humphrey.

Freeman, at the beginning of 1969, was the British Ambassador-designate to Washington. He had been appointed to the post by Prime Minister Harold Wilson some months earlier in unwise anticipation of the safe arrival in the White House of President Humphrey. Soon after Nixon won the election he suggested through intermediaries that the Ambassador-designate's appointment might be reconsidered, coming to this view after his attention had been drawn to a 1962 *New Statesman* article in which Freeman had described him as 'a man of no principle whatsoever except a willingness to sacrifice everything in the cause of Dick Nixon', adding that Nixon's defeat for the Governorship of California was 'a victory for decency in public life'.[22]

In spite of the President's umbrage at this article, Harold Wilson refused to consider changing the Freeman appointment. This offended Nixon and even affronted Eisenhower who, from his hospital bedside, expressed the opinion that a Freeman ambassadorship would be an insult not only to Nixon personally but to the Presidency as an institution. Fired up by this counsel from his old chief, Nixon made one or two macho remarks during the planning sessions for his trip to the effect that he might refuse to meet Freeman in London. For the first, but by no means the last time in his Presidency, Nixon's private grumblings were listened to by his courtiers in much the same way as King Henry II's knights heard the grumble, 'Who will rid me of this turbulent priest?' An over-zealous aide* translated the comment into a message that the President would boycott the Prime Minister's dinner in his honour unless Freeman was removed from the guest list. A diplomatic tizzy ensued, causing much heartache to the US Ambassador at the Court of St. James, David Bruce, who was unable to persuade either the White House to change the President's mind or No. 10 Downing Street to change its invitations.[24] Just as the tizzy was on the verge of developing into a diplomatic incident, the problem was solved by a young advance man for the presidential

---

* The identity of the over-zealous aide is a mystery. In his memoirs, Henry Kissinger fingers John Ehrlichman, but Ehrlichman resolutely denies the charge, saying, 'It was Henry—typical of him to try and shift the blame.'[23]

party, Ron Walker. 'The whole trip was going to blow apart over this according to David Bruce,' recalled Walker, 'so I took an initiative and went backchannel to Secretary of State Rogers who was at a State Dinner with the President when I got him on the phone. He saw the point at once, spoke to the President, and gave me immediate instructions to stop all the fuss about Freeman.'[25]

Despite this last-minute climb-down, the stage seemed set for a chilly encounter between President and Ambassador at No. 10 Downing Street. But Nixon loved to surprise. In his toast after dinner he poured charm over Freeman, saying that American journalists had written far worse things about him than the *New Statesman*. 'Some say there's a new Nixon', he went on. 'And they wonder if there's a new Freeman. I would like to think that that's all behind us. After all, he's the new diplomat and I'm the new statesman.'[26] As the men thumped the table and called 'Hear Hear', Wilson wrote Nixon a note on the back of his menu. 'That was one of the kindest and most generous acts I have known in a quarter of a century of politics. Just proves my point. You can't guarantee being born a lord. It is possible—you've shown it—to be born a gentleman."*[27]

The European trip was a success and all its objectives were achieved. Its most substantive part was Nixon's meeting with de Gaulle. The French President, who five years earlier had been a lone voice in predicting that his guest would one day reach the White House, was warm in his welcome and sagacious with his advice. The two leaders discussed China and Vietnam, opening the way for Washington's subsequent French channels to Hanoi and Peking. Nixon's success in establishing a Franco-American relationship of trust was to prove vital for his subsequent triumphs in superpower diplomacy.

During these European travels, there came the first overt signs that the traditional role of the Secretary of State would be downgraded in the Nixon administration. The eclipse of Bill Rogers and the rise of Henry Kissinger has usually been ascribed to Nixon's not-so-reluctant connivance with Kissinger's determination to eliminate a rival influence. This is an oversimplification.

Although Nixon was no admirer of the State Department, he retained considerable respect for his old friend Bill Rogers and originally saw him as a counterweight to Kissinger as a foreign policy adviser. The concept of maintaining a

---

* John Freeman was to become an effective Ambassador and a considerable admirer of Nixon. At his farewell audience with the President in 1971, Freeman said he thought the time had come to apologise for his 1962 article. Nixon brushed him aside, but Freeman persisted, saying, 'I'm apologising not for my manners but for my judgement. I got you so wrong.' Nixon responded cheerily, although not entirely in the language of a gentleman: 'Ah, I understand. Well, you couldn't have said that before without browning your nose.'[28]

balance of power in his administration as well as in the world was never far from Nixon's mind, even though he always intended to be his own Secretary of State. However, it was Rogers who spoilt this strategy of man management by opting out of the philosophical discourses on geopolitical theory in which Nixon loved to engage. No one understood this better than Rogers's chosen deputy, Elliot Richardson, the Under-Secretary of State. 'There was something in Bill Rogers which caused him to look down on Nixon and his musings on geopolitics', recalled Richardson. 'Bill was good when it came to advising on a specific problem, such as how the US should respond to the shooting down of one of our Navy aircraft by the North Koreans.* But he suffered from that failing of lawyers who tend to look on situations as though they were cases. He did not seem to understand that every foreign policy decision is an intervention into a flow. He spoke slightingly of "all that geopolitical thinking" and turned most of the interaction discussions at the NSC over to me. The impression he gave was that he was opting out. He stopped competing for Nixon's attention. Kissinger has been blamed too much for maneuvering himself into the key position. The truth was that Kissinger owed his rise to a default on the part of Rogers.'[29]

Bill Rogers was steadily shifted to one side as a foreign policy adviser from the time of the European tour onwards. The same fate befell many former Nixon intimates. High on the casualty list was Rose Mary Woods, his faithful personal secretary for over twenty years. She had every right to expect that her role and influence in the White House would be the same as those exercised under previous Presidents by such formidable confidantes as Kennedy's Evelyn Lincoln; Eisenhower's Ann Whitman; and Franklin Roosevelt's 'Missy' Lehand.

Instead, 'RMW', as she had appeared in lower case type on innumerable Nixon letters over the decades, found that her access to the President was severely restricted by Haldeman, although not without a fight. On one memorable occasion in the early weeks, a Secret Service man tried to stop Rose Woods from slipping through to see her old boss in the Oval Office. The unfortunate agent proved no match for RMW, who, after a heated exchange which included the challenge 'go ahead and shoot but I'm going in there',[30] sailed in unshot to the presidential presence. Rose Woods won that particular battle, but, although she remained Nixon's personal secretary, she lost the war of regular access, which was a pity because with her fell the access of the several old Nixon friends who might

---

* On 14 April 1969 an unarmed Navy EC-121 reconnaissance plane was shot down over Korea. Kissinger called for an airstrike against a North Korean airfield. Rogers was successful in persuading Nixon not to retaliate militarily.

occasionally have spoken to the President with greater candour and wiser advice than was offered by his new inner circle of staff.

The exclusion zone around Nixon was ruthlessly controlled. Even senior Cabinet members found it difficult, and sometimes impossible, to get appointments with the President. This led to stories appearing in the newspapers about 'The Berlin Wall', blaming the Teutonic trio of Haldeman, Ehrlichman and Kissinger. Although there was some truth in the criticism—Kissinger in particular exploited Nixon's shyness about meeting strangers in order to tighten his personal monopoly on foreign affairs advice—the so-called wall was largely erected by the President himself. Haldeman was the ultimate personal loyalist who would just as obligingly have operated a revolving door policy, if Nixon had so instructed. But the fact was that the President disliked the glad-handing, stroking and socialising side of his job. He was awkward in encounters with new faces or even old faces with whom he did not feel wholly comfortable. His preference was for a schedule which provided him with long periods of solitary 'thinking time' and equally long hours of 'staff time', which usually consisted of carefully compartmentalised one-on-one sessions with a court favourite. John Ehrlichman has colourfully recalled the atmosphere of these dialogues, or near monologues. 'Richard Nixon was like a cow...He would chew his cud over and over on a subject and turn it over and chew it some more, and turn it over and chew it some more...Probably you'd grunt at the right times or make some comment or other.'[31]

In 1979, Ehrlichman had a conversation about Nixon's penchant for monologues with Henry Kissinger, who also at times resented what he called his 'excruciatingly long conversations' with the President in which the same subject was endlessly regurgitated. The two former White House aides were worried about how they might be viewed by historians listening to the White House tape recordings of their private sessions with Nixon. 'We are going to look like perfect fools when those tapes come out', said Kissinger.[32] Ehrlichman agreed that they both had problems. 'At times we will be heard responding to Richard Nixon's truly outrageous statements with silence or even acquiescence, when an outsider might have yelled or pounded the desk in outrage.'[33]

These comments highlight the difficulties in relying on the famous tapes (of which more later) as a source of historical truth. For just as Kissinger and Ehrlichman can justifiably argue that their silences or words of acquiescence should not be taken at face value, so Nixon can enter the same plea about a good many of his 'truly outrageous statements'. These sessions of intimate conversation were Nixon's way of thinking aloud. His technique was to review a situation or an item of information from every conceivable angle. He would consider all the options from the hair-raising to the statesman-like. As his mind roamed back and forth, the most extraordinary and contradictory ideas floated in and out. Sometimes it seemed as if he was exorcising the dark side of his thinking. Sometimes it was a way of letting off steam. More often it was a device for separating the practical from the impractical. One of his favourite manoeuvres was to say something elliptical or even outrageous in order to test the reaction of his fellow conversationalist. Henry Kissinger caught this aspect of his boss with a perceptive sentence in the first chapter of his memoirs, *White House Years*: 'I learned that to Nixon words were like billiard balls; what mattered was not the initial impact but the carom.'[34]

What gradually emerged from these games of verbal billiards and Nixon's other methods of dealing with his inner circle was that no single adviser enjoyed the President's complete confidence. After the first few months, the White House became a mistrustful and secretive place in which to work, reflecting both the President's introvert personality and the external pressures of the Vietnam war. But if there was a Number Two man in the Administration, whose relationship with the President was more trusting and whose influence stretched across more of the compartments and barriers that separated one aide's territory from another's, that man was the Attorney General of the United States, John Mitchell.

Mitchell was consulted by Nixon on anything and everything. It is far from clear why the President relied on him so much, since the record shows that Mitchell had a record of misjudgements ranging from his recommendation of Supreme Court Justices to the ITT fiasco and on to Watergate. But he was a strong man who filled Nixon's curious need, even as President, for a peer relationship. Moreover, his strong advice was particularly welcome in one area because it reinforced Nixon's instinct to tough it out with the anti-war protesters and to take the long view on Vietnam—the problem that was deteriorating into a quagmire.

The intractability of the war cast the first shadow over the golden morning of the Nixon Presidency. As peace hopes were deferred and disappointments grew, all the other problems such as bad PR, presidential remoteness, and anger with opponents began to magnify.

Bob Haldeman, from his vantage point as Chief of Staff, came to understand the impact of Vietnam as well as anyone: 'No matter what facet of the Nixon Presidency you're considering, don't ever lose sight of Vietnam as the overriding factor in the first Nixon term', is his advice to historians. 'It overshadowed everything else all the time, in every discussion, in every decision, in every opportunity, in every problem.'[35]

II. THE SILENT MAJORITY

Vietnam was the curse of the Nixon Presidency. Like a growing tumour it corroded the norms of democracy, debilitated the nation and raised the still unanswered question of whether American public opinion could stomach a long war with heavy casualties in the age of television.

Vietnam was not Nixon's war, but he knew that he had been elected to end it. He relished this challenge of peacemaking, initially in a mood of excessive optimism. He was too confident that the peace with honour he had promised in his campaign speeches could be delivered within a relatively short timescale. Reluctant to accept that the war bitterness among young liberals and opinion-formers might be the barometer signal of a changing national mood, Nixon believed that he would be given sufficient time by his countrymen and sufficient concessions by the North Vietnamese to move the peace process forward. What he did not foresee was that the road to an acceptable settlement was going to be far rougher and longer than anything he had anticipated.

During his early months in the White House, Nixon made all the right pre-liminary moves on Vietnam. He reviewed America's options in depth with the NSC and consulted several foreign leaders, of whom the most influential was de Gaulle. The French President advised him to establish a timetable for troop with-drawals; to enter into direct negotiations with the North Vietnamese on political and military issues simultaneously; and to be both strong and patient until a settlement was reached. De Gaulle added, 'I do not believe that you should depart with undue haste.'[36]

This advice was in tune with Nixon's private thinking. During his wilderness years he had often described the United States' position in Vietnam as that of 'a cork in a bottle'.[37] Pulling the cork out too quickly could, he believed, have disas-trous consequences for the non-Communist people of South Vietnam. He there-fore would not contemplate a defeat, a scuttle, or even 'an elegant bug-out'. He told aides that he did not intend to be 'the first American President to lose a war', adding that such a defeat would mean a US 'retreat from the world', which would 'destroy the confidence of the American people in themselves'.[38]

These attitudes were wholly honourable and did not detract from Nixon's deep personal desire to be the architect for peace in Vietnam. If anything, his peacemaking instincts led him into some uncharacteristic naïveté about the timetable for ending the fighting. He genuinely believed that he would be seeing 'light at the end of the tunnel' within a year and that a peace settlement would be reached in time for the congressional elections in 1970.[39]

The North Vietnamese were not operating on any such schedule. Indeed, it is doubtful whether they were interested in anything other than total US capitulation. Nixon approached them through foreign intermediaries with several clandestine messages. They were ignored. In February 1969, the North Vietnamese Army (the NVA) opened a new offensive. Nixon believed that they were testing his resolve and was determined to take strong action in response. He decided to bomb the NVA sanctuaries in Cambodia. In his mind this would be neither an extension of the war nor an unwarranted invasion of another country's neutrality: the NVA had already violated that neutrality and was using the sanctuaries for bases and supply lines for its military operations against South Vietnam.

While the bombing could be justified both militarily and morally, politically it would be much more problematic, as Nixon soon found out when his Secretaries of State and Defense objected to it. Nixon also knew that the reaction among the anti-war protesters to such an 'extension' of the war and 'violation' of a neutral country would be violent, and he wanted to avoid such opposition so early in his administration. He therefore instinctively followed a course that would become second nature to his administration when faced with situations that were likely to cause public outcry: he kept the bombing secret. An elaborate system was instituted within the Air Force's reporting procedures to ensure that the bombing of Cambodia was not even mentioned in the military's own records.

The secret bombing was the punitive side of Nixon's policy. The positive side was that he withdrew 25,000 combat troops and put forward, via the Soviets, his first peace proposals. These included phased withdrawals of US, Allied and North Vietnamese forces from South Vietnam; internationally supervised elections; and a cessation of hostilities. Disappointed by Hanoi's lack of response, Nixon sent an emollient letter to Ho Chi Minh which was followed up by a secret meeting in Paris between Henry Kissinger and Mai Van Bo on 4 August. These discussions were almost worthless, since the North Vietnamese maintained the absurd fiction that there were no NVA troops in South Vietnam at all. They stuck to their hard-line position that the entire US military presence must be withdrawn immediately and that President Thieu must be overthrown before negotiations could commence. This stance was reiterated in a letter from Ho Chi Minh which Nixon described as 'a cold rebuff'. It was hardly surprising that Nixon's early optimism began to fade. 'I had never thought that peace in Vietnam would come easily; for the first time I had to consider the possibility that it might not come at all', he wrote of that period.[40]

It became clear that the North Vietnamese intransigence was partly based on a belief that American anti-war protests would force Nixon to pull US troops out unilaterally. Premier Pham Van Dong went so far as to broadcast a public message to this effect, calling on 'US Progressive People' to join the struggle against US aggression, ending with the words, 'May your fall offensive succeed splendidly.'[41]

This extraordinary appeal from Radio Hanoi referred to an impending series of mass demonstrations, known as the Vietnam Moratorium, which were planned for 15 October in several US cities. The build-up to this day of protest was enormous. The ferocity of the advance wave of rallies, 'teach-ins', and other anti-war activities disturbed several thoughtful commentators: on 7 October David Broder wrote in the *Washington Post*: 'It is becoming more obvious with every passing day that the men and the movement that broke Lyndon Johnson's authority in 1968 are out to break Richard Nixon in 1969. The likelihood is great that they will succeed again.'[42]

A week later, on the eve of the Moratorium, syndicated columnist James Kilpatrick was even more alarmist: 'From one end of the country to the other drums are rolling for the head of Richard Nixon and for the surrender to Hanoi', he wrote, saying of the demonstration leaders: 'They are insatiable. Nothing that Nixon might do short of absolute and precipitate withdrawal would cool their fevers...They want his head.'[43]

These prophetic comments were given further credibility by the sheer size of the Vietnam Moratorium. Several million people took part in the demonstrations. The biggest crowds were in Washington (250,000), Boston (100,000) and San Francisco (100,000).

A significant new factor was the high percentage of middle-aged, middle-class and middle-of-the-road participants. Their protests were peaceful and far removed from those of the Chicago crazies a year earlier. To many it seemed as though the President's own constituency had joined the chorus of dissent. Some White House staffers, including Kissinger, were shaken by the scale of the Moratorium and by the announcement that a second day of even bigger protest known as New Mobe was to take place a month later. Nixon was himself thrown on to the defensive. On the night of 15 October, with the demonstrators still besieging the streets and the White House, he settled down to compose the first draft of a national television speech on Vietnam planned for delivery on 3 November. At the top of the page he wrote, 'Don't get rattled— don't waver—don't react.'[44]

Nixon did not stay on the defensive for long. One of the strongest influences on his change of mood was a visit to the White House two days after the Moratorium by Sir Robert Thompson. Thompson was a British military expert on

Vietnam who had the reputation of being one of Asia's most successful counter-insurgency specialists.* He had been head of the newly created British Advisory Mission in Saigon, which was where he first met Nixon in 1967. Thompson's briefings and writings soon became well known to the *cognoscenti* among Vietnam observers. Both Nixon and Kissinger were admirers of his book *No Exit from Vietnam*, and were intrigued by his thesis that the North Vietnamese could be defeated by a long-haul low-cost strategy. It therefore came as no great surprise to Thompson when, in mid-October 1969, he was contacted by the CIA at his home in Somerset and asked if he would travel to Washington under conditions of elaborate secrecy for a meeting with the President. His influence on Nixon's strategy was to be considerable.

When Thompson came into the Oval Office on 17 October, he found the President in an undecided, almost volatile, mood. They ran through the options. 'What do you think of the option to the right?' Nixon asked him. 'What would you think if we decided to escalate?'[45] Thompson was opposed to escalation on the grounds that the South Vietnamese army (ARVN) was not yet ready to defend itself against the new wave of Communist offensives which escalation would produce. However, he believed that a determined policy of Vietnamisation would succeed in strengthening ARVN and that the North Vietnamese could be contained and steadily pushed back. Thompson thought that these results would be achieved over a two-year period provided Nixon made it clear that there would be no US pull-out and that American troops would stay for the duration.

The discussion then turned to the strategic importance of Vietnam. As Thompson recalls it, 'Although Nixon did not have a particularly good grasp of the tactical situation on the ground, he had a tremendous strategic grasp of the wider picture. He understood perfectly the role of the big outside influences in Vietnam, Russia and China. He saw that the whole attitude and future policy of those two superpowers towards the United States would be decided by their perception of the American resolve on Vietnam.'[46]

According to Nixon, his visitor took an equally broad view. In response to the President's question whether it was important for the United States to see it through in Vietnam, Thompson replied: 'Absolutely. In my opinion the future of Western civilisation is at stake in the way you handle yourselves in Vietnam.'[47]

---

* The son of an English country parson, Thompson had been on active duty in Asia throughout the Second World War, serving from 1942 onwards as one of General Orde Wingate's guerilla warfare commanders in Burma, for which he was awarded the Military Cross and the Distinguished Service Order. He was later appointed Secretary of Defence by the Malaysian Government and was one of the masterminds in the defeat of the Communist Emergency.

Thompson left Washington the next day with an appointment as a White House consultant and a mission to travel out to Vietnam and produce an 'Eyes Only' report for Nixon. 'I think my contribution was that I convinced the President that by going for the long haul he could come out of Vietnam if not smelling like a rose at least leaving behind a non-Communist South which could defend itself,' recalled Thompson. His expertise did not, however, extend to being able to forecast the influence of the domestic anti-war movement. On that issue, Thompson's advice was robust but simplistic. 'Bugger your critics! Just make sure you've got your own supporters behind you', he told the President.[48]

Fortified by Thompson's counsel, Nixon returned to the preparation of his 3 November speech. He was determined that it would mark a watershed in US policy towards Vietnam. Suggestions on what he should say flowed in from both hawks and doves. Kissinger, who had been present at the meeting with Thompson, was the principal hardliner, advising that the Communists would feel they could control US foreign policy through domestic public opinion if the speech gave a message of impending retreat. Softliners included Secretary of State Bill Rogers; Defense Secretary Melvin Laird; and Senate Majority Leader Mike Mansfield, who went further than anyone else by submitting a memorandum which advocated an immediate unilateral withdrawal. The media was one big dovecote whose only disagreements revolved around such questions as how many troops would be withdrawn, and what sort of a ceasefire agreement would be proposed.

Nixon encouraged these flutterings of feverish suspense. Ever since the 'Checkers' speech he had fully appreciated the advantages of allowing speculation to build up in advance of a major broadcast. He kept his cards close to his chest and withdrew to the seclusion of Camp David. There he worked alone on the speech for up to fourteen hours a day. At least twelve drafts of the text survive in his own handwriting. Their existence makes the point that Nixon has been the only President in the modern age of speech writers who had the ability and application to sit down and compose an important nationwide address entirely on his own.

Delivered to a television audience of 70 million on the evening of 3 November, the speech was a stunning surprise. Far from getting out of Vietnam precipitately, Nixon's message was that the United States would stay there and fight until the South Vietnamese were able to defend themselves, or until the North Vietnamese negotiated an honourable peace settlement. After giving a résumé of the origins and progress of the war under three Presidents, he gave this stern internationalist warning:

For the future of peace, precipitate withdrawal would be a disaster of immense magnitude. A nation cannot remain great if it destroys its allies and lets down its friends. Our defeat and humiliation in South Vietnam without question would promote recklessness in the councils of those great powers who have not yet abandoned their goals of world conquest. This would spark violence wherever our commitments help maintain the peace—in the Middle East, in Berlin, eventually even in the Western Hemisphere.

Nixon then took his audience through his record of hitherto secret peace initiatives, making the point that the obstructions to a settlement were coming exclusively from Hanoi: 'The obstacle is the other side's absolute refusal to show the least willingness to join us in seeking a just peace. And it will not do so while it is convinced that all it has to do is to wait for our next concession, and our next concession after that one, until it gets everything it wants.'

Having surprised everyone by his determination to hang tough and continue the fighting, Nixon qualified his apparently hawkish stand by promising US troop withdrawals linked to the progress of Vietnamisation, which he defined as the taking over by ARVN of combat responsibilities. This policy, he said, had already produced results. Infiltration numbers, bombing operations and US casualties were all down. If these trends continued, so would American withdrawal, coupled with the diplomatic search for a negotiated settlement. The speed at which the troops could be brought home would depend on the progress of these policies in Vietnam and would not be affected by demonstrations in the streets.

Nixon had explained his plan, which he said was 'not the easy way but the right way'. After summarising the principles on which he would seek to build a structure for peace in Vietnam and the whole Pacific area, Nixon moved to the peroration whose opening line gave the speech its name:

And so tonight—to you the great silent majority of my fellow Americans—I ask for your support.

I pledged in my campaign for the Presidency to end the war in a way that we could win the peace. I have initiated a plan of action which will enable me to keep that pledge.

The more support I can have from the American people, the sooner that the pledge can be redeemed; for the more divided we are at home the less likely the enemy is to negotiate at Paris.

Let us be united for peace. Let us also be united against defeat.
Because, let us understand: North Vietnam cannot defeat or humil-
iate the United States. Only Americans can do that.[49]

Given the polarised state of American society in 1969, it was inevitable that
reactions to these remarks would differ sharply. Nixon's biographer, Stephen
Ambrose, himself an anti-war campaigner in the 1960s, has described the ending
as 'sweeping and silly'.[50]

This was more or less the reaction of the network TV reporters on the night.
To a man they abandoned all pretence of making impartial summaries of the
address (the usual practice following nationwide presidential broadcasts) and
instead launched their own adversarial attacks on it. This was a misjudgement,
at least in terms of their viewers' response. Within forty-eight hours of the broadcast it became evident that Nixon had struck a deep chord within the silent
majority itself, so much so that it briefly became the vocal majority. A Gallup
television poll taken immediately after the speech showed a 77 per cent approval
rating. Letters and telegrams of support poured into Congress and the White
House at unprecedented levels. Nixon's presidential approval rating in the polls
soared to 68 per cent.

Congressional opinion swung sharply. Within a week of the broadcast, 300
members of the House of Representatives (119 Democrats and 181 Republicans)
responded to the views of their constituents by co-sponsoring a resolution backing the policies described in the speech. Fifty-eight Senators (twenty-one Democrats and thirty-seven Republicans) signed letters expressing similar support. All
the evidence suggested that against overwhelming odds the President had rallied
the country behind him and had sidelined the anti-war movement to the status
of a noisy but impotent minority.

Nixon was elated by this triumph, not least because it was such a slap in the
face to his media opponents. 'The White House Press Corps is dying because of
the effect of that television speech', he said on 5 November. 'I'm not saying all the
press is bad—some are responsible—but when you get on television you can get
across your point without having what you say strained through the press. And
that drives the press right up the wall.'[51] Nixon's pleasure at discomfiting the
journalists of the day was matched by his confidence in the favourable judgement
the speech would receive from the historians of the future. 'Very few speeches
actually influence the course of history. The November 3 speech was one of them',
he opined in his memoirs.[52]

This is a doubtful claim. Seen in perspective, the brilliant feat of leadership which Nixon performed was to prove transitory in its effects. The paradox of the 'Silent Majority' speech was that it made history yet had little impact on the course of history. In terms of Nixon's ability to use his Presidency as 'a bully pulpit' (Theodore Roosevelt's phrase) and to reach out to the people of America over the heads of the liberal media, the speech was a political masterpiece. However, it did not mark any great turning point in the Vietnam war. Far greater disappointments lay ahead in that vale of tears, but they were not yet visible from the Oval Office. At the time, the international response to the Silent Majority speech was distinctly encouraging, not least in Vietnam. From Saigon, Sir Robert Thompson's assessment was that the speech had put new heart into the South Vietnamese. His report concluded:

> A winning position in the sense of obtaining a just peace (whether negotiated or not) and of maintaining an independent non-Communist South Vietnam has been achieved but we are not yet through. We are in a psychological period where the greatest need is confidence. A steady application of the 'do it yourself' concept with continuing US support in the background will increase the confidence already shown by many GVN leaders. The year 1970 could then end decisively in our favour...[53]

As 1969 came towards its end, Nixon remained buoyed up by the success of his 3 November broadcast. He believed it had bought him enough time to move both Vietnamisation and the Vietnam peace process significantly forward. It was undoubtedly one of the peaks of Nixon's White House years. He had proved himself to be a President who could lead. Whether Vietnam would allow him to become a President who could deliver was still an open question.

III. THE SUPREME COURT AND THE SOUTH

The support given to Nixon on Capitol Hill in the immediate aftermath of his 'Silent Majority' speech was not characteristic of his relations with Congress. He was the first President for more than a century to begin his term with both the Senate and the House of Representatives controlled by the Opposition party. This situation, impossible under most other Western nations' constitutions, made his task of governing extremely difficult. In his first year Nixon sent forty domestic proposals to Congress, only to have thirty-eight of them rejected. Even in foreign affairs and national security issues, where the President traditionally gets bipartisan support, Nixon had a perilous passage. His plan to reform US foreign aid was voted down and his request for an antiballistic missile defence system (ABM) was carried only on the casting vote of the Vice President in the Senate. It was not surprising that he was soon complaining of being frustrated in his policy making agenda.

These frustrations came to a head on the issue of nominations to the Supreme Court. During his 1968 election campaign, Nixon had consistently expressed the view that the Court had gone too far in the direction of freewheeling judicial activism. He had promised that he would use his power of appointment to bring the majority of justices back towards the traditional and more conservative pattern of 'strict construction' of the Constitution. This much-needed correction of the Court's tendency towards overt political liberalism began with Nixon's appointment of Warren Burger as Chief Justice. In the summer of 1969 the unexpected resignation of Justice Abe Fortas gave Nixon the opportunity to fill a second seat on the Supreme Court. On the advice of John Mitchell, he nominated Clement F. Haynsworth, a distinguished Fourth Circuit Appeals Judge from South Carolina and a strict constructionist. Nixon particularly wanted a Southerner. He felt that the South had been discriminated against for too long in the matter of top political and judicial appointments.

This thinking was in tune with his overall Southern Strategy, but its origins went right back to his days at Duke Law School, where he had first formed the view that it was high time to forget the legacy of the Civil war and to treat the South as a fully fledged part of the Union.

Haynsworth's judicial credentials were good, but within days of his appointment a variety of liberal bandwagons rolled out to oppose him. The first group of critics were from the Jewish lobby. They fought the appointment because it was taking away 'the Jewish seat' on the Court, which had been held in turn by Abe Fortas, Arthur Goldberg, Felix Frankfurter and Louis Brandeis. Nixon found this claim offensive. 'There is not a Jewish seat or a Catholic seat or a Negro seat on the Court', was his retort.[54] Even more offensive were the claims from civil rights and union groups that Haynsworth was 'a racist' and 'anti-labor'. The weakness of these charges did not prevent an unpleasant campaign of character assassination against the nominee.

A witch hunt was led on the Judiciary Committee by Democratic Senator Birch Bayh of Indiana, who produced some slender evidence that Haynsworth had failed to discharge himself from sitting on a case in which he had a small pecuniary interest through his portfolio of stocks and shares. By the accepted standards of judicial guidelines, no impropriety had occurred, but Bayh and his allies in the press built this up as the 'appearance of impropriety' issue. Although Haynsworth's record showed merely minor peccadilloes, they were enough to sink him. Nixon was advised to withdraw the nomination, but he took this sort of political combat far too personally to contemplate such a surrender: 'If we cave in on this one, they will think if you kick Nixon you can get somewhere',[55] he said furiously, instructing his White House aides to twist every available arm in the Senate. It was to no avail. Haynsworth's nomination was defeated on 21 November 1969 by fifty-five votes to forty-five. The real reason for his rejection was his political background not his judicial qualifications. He fell for the very reasons that Nixon had selected him—he was a Southerner and a conservative.

Nixon took the defeat badly. According to John Ehrlichman, it 'rankled and itched. It was inevitable that the President would try to scratch the itch. If they were going to get one of ours, Nixon decided, perhaps we should be going after one of theirs.'[56] Accordingly, the White House tried to start a campaign for the impeachment of William O. Douglas, a liberal Supreme Court Justice who was far more vulnerable than Haynsworth to charges of impropriety. This petered out but Nixon's anger did not. Declaring that he would 'show them',[57] he instructed his aides 'to find a good federal judge further south and further to the right'.[58] The Justice Department came up with the name of G. Harrold Carswell of Florida, who had recently been appointed to the Fifth Circuit Court of Appeals. It was a poor choice. Carswell was on the record as a supporter of white supremacy in his early political career. None of his judicial decisions appeared to have moved him from that position. Indeed, his career on the Bench had been notable only for its being second-rate.

Objections to his 'mediocrity' poured in from all sections of the legal profession. Although one congressional supporter put forward the original argument that the mediocre people in the country were entitled to a representative on the Court, most senators remained unconvinced. 'They think [Carswell's] a boob, a dummy', White House congressional aide Bryce Harlow told the President. 'And what counter is there to that? He is.'[59]

In his post-resignation years, Nixon privately admitted that he had erred in the selection of Carswell. At the time he fought like a tiger for his indefensible choice. Part of the reason for his tenacity was a misplaced loyalty to John Mitchell. If the Attorney General had done his homework properly, Carswell should not have been recommended for an Appeals Judgeship, let alone for the Supreme Court. Mitchell was also vulnerable to criticism for not having checked Haynsworth out with the thoroughness that the nature of the appointment required. These were fundamental errors, but Nixon was protective towards his Attorney

General out of political loyalty and because of the personal sympathy he felt over the increasing problems Mitchell was having to endure from his alcoholic and unstable wife, Martha.

So Nixon went in to bat to help both Mitchell and Carswell, but again to no avail. On 8 April 1970 the Senate rejected the nomination by fifty-one to forty-five. It was the first time since 1894 that two consecutive Supreme Court appointments had been rejected in this way.

Nixon was undaunted. Within days of the Senate's rejection of Carswell, he nominated Harry Blackmun of Minnesota, and later, in 1971 (following the retirements of Hugo Black and John Harlan), Lewis Powell and William Rehnquist. All three were quickly approved by the Senate, which had no stomach for further in-fighting. All were conservatives and strict constructionists, and Powell was a Southerner from Virginia. With these nominations, Nixon had succeeded in his aim to redress the balance of the Court and to put an end to the era of liberal judicial activism. In so doing, he showed his fighting qualities of determination and resilience. But his success came at a price. The Haynsworth–Carswell débâcle was a humiliation for him and it had a deleterious effect on his future relations with Congress.

In the meantime, Nixon had moved fast to turn the rejection of Carswell to his political advantage. The day after the Senate vote, Nixon made a statement for the TV cameras:

> I have reluctantly concluded that I cannot successfully nominate to the Supreme Court any Federal Appellate Judge from the South who believes as I do in the strict construction of the Constitution. Judges Carswell and Haynsworth have endured with admirable dignity vicious assaults on their intelligence, their honesty, and their character. They have been falsely charged with being racist. But when all the hypocrisy is stripped away, the real issue was their philosophy of strict construction of the Constitution—a philosophy that I share—and the fact that they had the misfortune of being born in the South.[60]

Every Southerner watching the news that night could see that Nixon was speaking from the heart. His press release went even further than his televised statement, for it contained the sentence, 'I understand the bitter feelings of millions of Americans who live in the South about the act of regional discrimination that took place in the Senate yesterday.'[61]

These were fierce words from a northern President and they were to have far-reaching Southern consequences. The short-term result was that Nixon's political stock soared throughout the Old Confederacy. The long-term result was that Nixon quietly used his newly perceived empathy with the South to accomplish one of the most important achievements of his Presidency—the desegregation of Southern schools.

When Nixon became President, school segregation in the South was but a small step ahead of apartheid, despite having been declared unconstitutional by the Supreme Court ruling in *Brown v. Board of Education* some fifteen years earlier. In 1969 only 5.2 per cent of Black children were in unsegregated schools. By 1972 that figure had increased to 90 per cent.

The story of how this turnaround was accomplished is too long to relate in detail in this biography, but suffice it to say that presidential leadership was the crucial ingredient in making it happen. Moynihan, Ehrlichman and others who worked closely with Nixon on this issue were impressed by the sincerity of his commitment. It seems to have been triggered by a 'white paper' written by Ray Price on school desegregation policy which was published by the White House in the middle of the Haynsworth–Carswell furore. The acceptability of its recommendations grew because Nixon was seen as a President who was for the South as well as for enforcing the law and the Constitution. He treated the ending of educational segregation not as a stick with which to beat Southern schools, but as a balm with which to heal the wounds in divided local communities all over the country. He encouraged reform among gerrymandered school districts in both North and South alike, sugaring the pill with generous financial assistance, and making the issue one of education not race. All this involved more than a little sleight of hand, but according to those closest to him the President's firmness of purpose was never in doubt. As John Ehrlichman has recalled: 'Nixon was realistic about the intent of the courts that the law required desegregation. He took his role seriously as the executor of that law. At the same time he saw the political peril in his determination to get it done, so through the White House staff he reached down into the entrails of the bureaucracy, enforcing the strategy his way, because he knew that only by moving sensitively could the political and legal irreconcilables be reconciled.'[62]

Moving sensitively often meant dissembling and doing the good deed by stealth. 'We don't poke our fingers in their eyes. We don't rub their noses in it. We don't get our name in the newspapers—but we do it', he told his staff.[63] Whatever retrospective criticism may be made of his methods, the end result was that Nixon solved a huge and intractable national problem on which his three presidential predecessors had failed to make progress. A decade and a half after being declared unconstitutional, the dual school system of the South was virtually intact in 1969 as a hated symbol of racial subjugation. By 1972 it was dismantled for ever.

This was one of the most remarkable and least remarked of Nixon's achievements. It was almost the domestic equivalent of the opening to China, for only Nixon with his strong credentials in the South and his feel for the clandestine methods required could have accomplished it. One of the few liberal writers to give Nixon his due for this success story was Tom Wicker, who wrote in his 1991 biographical study *One of Us*:

> The indisputable fact is that he got the job done—the dismantling of dual schools—when no one else had been able to do it. Nixon's reliance on persuasion rather than coercion, his willingness to work with Southern whites instead of denouncing them, his insistence that segregation was a national, not just a Southern problem, the careful distance he maintained between himself and the 'liberal establishment', the huge political credit he earned in the South with his Supreme Court nominations and his other gestures to the Southern sensibility—particularly local leadership—all resulted in a formula that worked.[64]

There were some who later argued that Nixon's Southern strategy was a masterpiece of Machiavellian cunning from start to finish, and that he had even nominated Haynsworth and Carswell as sacrificial lambs to make himself popular. This is nonsense. Ever since those days of youthful rapport with his roommate Bill Perdue and other Southern classmates at Duke, Nixon had understood and sympathised with the region. He had a much better feel for it than most national politicians. His respect for the South was real, and his legacy to it has proved enduring. Peaceful desegregation led to a diminution in the Black violence that had been the scourge of 1967–8. Nixon's schools policy had been the harbinger of a steadily improving climate in America's race relations. It also changed the presidential electoral prospects for Southern politicians. In 1968 senators and governors from the Deep South were thought to be almost unelectable to national office, but by 1976 President-elect Jimmy Carter of Georgia was on his way to the White House. Although Nixon might not have wished for this particular consequence, he succeeded in bringing the South, its schools and its leaders back into the mainstream of American life.

IV. THE DOMESTIC PRESIDENT

Nixon was an active President in domestic affairs. His choice of the innova-tive Patrick Moynihan to be the head of the first Urban Affairs Council signalled that intention and he proceeded to record several enduring achievements in this field. His successes included the ending of the draft; the setting up of the Envi-ronmental Protection Agency; the quadrupling of federal support for the arts; the War Against Cancer medical programme; and the expansion of the National Parks. His interesting experiments, thwarted by Congress at the time but revived in later Presidencies, included the New Federalism (a plan to share tax revenues between Washington and the states on a fairer basis) and the Family Assistance Plan (a radical reform of the welfare system). Nixon was also much more of a hands-on manager of the economy than has been generally realised, sometimes with unorthodox methods but with the political skill to engineer a favourable economic climate for his re-election in 1972.

This brief list in itself undermines the contemporary journalistic view that Nixon was 'not interested' in domestic policies. His record in this area was initially obscured by the drama of his foreign policy initiatives and later eclipsed com-pletely by Watergate. However, looked at with hindsight, he appears as an original and progressive domestic President. Nixon never intended to be his own domes-tic affairs supremo in the same way that he wished to be his own Secretary of State. He therefore delegated much more to his appointees in the domestic policy arena. Yet he had his usual feel for the programmes that would have voter appeal. He was successful in choosing good people to run those programmes and in pushing them to get the job done. Above all, he had a clear philosophy which governed his administration's domestic policy.

Nixon believed that federal government spending programmes should gen-erally be reorientated so that decisions on spending were shifted into the hands of locally elected representatives even when the funding was coming from Wash-ington. However, this was no simplistic 'power to the people' attitude, for Nixon also believed that only the federal government could direct certain resources from Washington and could take certain crucial decisions on domestic policy issues of national importance. His New Federalism and Revenue Sharing proposals (now back in fashion, having been stalled by Congress in the 1970s) were the first serious attempt to devolve decision-making powers to the states and local com-munities. This was a trend Nixon wanted to develop much further, but the biggest domestic decisions of his Presidency on the draft, the environment, and the economy were taken by him at national level.

The plan to end the draft had started its journey as an academic paper put forward to Nixon during his wilderness years by Professor Martin Anderson of Columbia University. Although a popular proposal with the younger generation, it seemed politically unworkable owing to entrenched opposition in Congress and the Pentagon. However, Nixon remained captivated by the concept of an all-volunteer army. After carefully studying Anderson's paper and soliciting reactions to it from thoughtful military experts, he came to believe that America's security would be increased rather than diminished by such a reform. Realising that an early bill to end the draft would be doomed to strangulation in Congress, Nixon put forward no such legislative proposal at the beginning of his term.

Instead, he shrewdly turned the issue over to a Presidential Commission. Even more shrewdly, he did not pack its fifteen-man membership with supporters of his own position, recognising that on a national security issue of such importance, the Washington power structure would react negatively towards recommendations from a stacked body. For Chairman Nixon approached Thomas Gates, a pillar of the military establishment who had been Eisenhower's Secretary of Defense. 'But Mr. President, I'm opposed to the whole idea of a volunteer force. You don't want me as the Chairman', said Gates. 'Yes I do, Tom', replied Nixon. 'That's exactly why I want you. You have experience and integrity. If you change your mind and think we should end the draft, then I'll know it's a good idea.'[65]

Gates somewhat dubiously agreed to serve and went on to chair a remarkable Presidential Commission. Its report, published in February 1970, unanimously recommended that the United States should switch to an all-volunteer defence force system.

The original differences of view among Commission members had been subsumed by the weight of the evidence. However, even with such a strong Commission report on his side, Nixon still had a political battle on his hands and it took much presidential arm twisting of recalcitrant Senators before the Bill passed into law in September 1971.

The ending of the draft was a reform of the highest strategic importance, for which Nixon deserves full credit. His vision was not fully vindicated until twenty years later, when the all-volunteer armed forces of the United States were able to show in the Gulf War of 1991 how infinitely superior they had become in morale, training, and expertise to the conscripted US forces of the pre-Nixon 1960s.

On environmental issues, Nixon responded effectively to the pressures of the age. Although a late and at times reluctant convert to the causes of the conservation movement, he nevertheless delivered more results to it than any other president before or since. Throughout the 1960s, concern for the environment was still a minority interest led by authors and academics which barely registered on the nation's political agenda. In the 1968 campaign, neither Humphrey nor Nixon did much more than pay passing lip service to the issue for the good reason that they were hardly ever questioned about it, either by voters or by journalists. A private White House poll taken in the spring of 1969 confirmed this apparent apathy by revealing that only one per cent of respondents considered the environment the most important issue facing the new President.

One of the first manifestations that conservation was moving to centre stage as a subject with mass political appeal came in April 1970 with Earth Day. This was a national programme of teach-ins, clean-ups, 'ecofairs', vigils, marches, and other environmental events. Its success astonished everyone, for at least three million enthusiasts across the country participated in Earth Day activities. This was the birth of America's Green movement, although no one was yet calling it by that name.

Nixon recognised the arrival of a new political constituency and reacted to it with speed and thoroughness. Two months after Earth Day he announced the setting-up of the Environmental Protection Agency (EPA). This was a formidable new regulatory organisation which centralised the hitherto uncoordinated environmental functions of the US Government under one roof and assumed sweeping new powers to control pollution. Nixon's 1970 State of the Union message contained the most far-reaching environmental agenda ever set by a President. 'Clean air, clean water, open spaces—these should once again be the birthright of every American', he told Congress,[66] putting forward a slate of thirty-six proposals to improve the quality of life. When passed into law during the next two years, these changes were radical in their effect. They included the National Environmental Policy Act, whose impact study requirements opened the floodgates to pollution control litigation and regulation; the Clean Air Act, which imposed exhaust emission restrictions on cars; the Oil Spill Act; the Noise Control Act; the Clean Water Act; the Ocean Dumping Act; the Coastal Zone Management Act and many lesser anti-pollution regulations in such fields as pesticide and chemical control. Virtually all of this was ground-breaking legislation, which, with one exception, had strong and consistent support from the Nixon administration.

The exception was the Clean Water Act of 1972, which Nixon initially vetoed on cost grounds in the knowledge that his power would be overridden by a subsequent vote of Congress—as it was. This veto had been seized upon by his critics to make the claim that Nixon was insincere in his commitment to the environment and that his role in the anti-pollution revolution of 1970–2 was that of an opportunist but secretly hostile bystander. Such a charge is unfair. As an intelligent and hands-on President, Nixon fully understood the implications of his 1970 environmental message to Congress. His establishment of the EPA was the real breakthrough, for it opened the doors of government to much stronger executive and legislative initiatives than were possible so long as the stewardship of the environment was fragmented among several weak bureaucracies in different departments. However, Nixon did develop a critical ambivalence towards those environmentalists, whose enthusiasm caused them to disregard the economic implications of their proposals. He was ahead of his time by insisting on a cost-benefit analysis of environmental legislation. This is now standard practice, but in those first heady months of kneejerk congressional enthusiasm for each and every item of environmental legislation, Nixon the cost-conscious centrist was severely criticised for seeking to strike a balance. He vetoed the Water Bill 'purely for dollars,' said his White House aide John Whittaker. 'He knew he was going to be wiped out but he also knew he was dealing with a credit card Congress spending $18 billion they didn't have.'[67]

Whittaker had no doubt that Nixon's participation in the environmental movement of the 1970s was sincere, even if he did sometimes attempt to curb the big spending excesses of the most ardent conservationists by bringing in the Office of Management and Budget (OMB) to exercise some degree of financial control over their proposals. Nixon's critics have complained that OMB represented a Trojan horse whose mission was to halt the environmental bandwagon, but this is an absurd claim. Nixon's political achievements on the environment may have been motivated by electoral self-interest and tempered by economic realism, but they also had his personal commitment, a point well illustrated by his policy on National Parks. 'He felt very strongly about parks, particularly because he'd been brought up in a reasonably poor environment and he realized that the folks in his area couldn't afford a trip to Yellowstone or the great pristine parks, so somehow we had to bring the parks to the people', recalled Whittaker, citing Nixon's instructions on how to deal with excess federal land released by the Property Review Board: 'When in doubt, make a park out of it'.[68] It was an order which resulted in the creation of 642 new parks during his Presidency.

Nixon became an environmental reformer because he was in power at the right moment. He saw the tide of history and swam with the stream. He had to put up with attacks from both sides of the argument on his policies. The great economic interest of the nation thought he was going too fast (a view shared by several members of his Cabinet) while the environmental crusaders thought he was moving too slowly. Characteristically, he steered a middle course, recognising as he always did that politics is the art of the possible. He understood, for example, that he could only achieve automobile emission restrictions by recommending legislation that was almost equally unpopular with the Detroit manufacturers and the clean air activists. In such matters, Nixon's centrism was the source of his effectiveness. During his serpentine negotiations between businessmen, legislators and lobbyists, he delivered more by taking credit for less. This meant that his environmental record was underrated at the time of his Presidency, but it can now be seen as one of his most enduring achievements. Signing all the basic legislation, setting up the EPA, and giving formidable new powers to his appointees, Nixon laid the foundation for America's quality of life revolution of the 1970s. With the possible exception of Theodore Roosevelt, no President has yet done more for the causes of conservation and the environment.

As a manager of the economy, Nixon achieved mixed results. In particular he was vilified by conservative economists for his unorthodox decision to introduce temporary wage and price controls in 1971. He paid the penalty for that initiative when the distortions flowing from it, together with the oil price rises in 1973, caused considerable economic problems soon after the election.

Although not even Nixon's greatest admirers would call him an economist, it is interesting to realise the extent to which he became involved in economic decision-making during his first term. 'Of the time he devoted to domestic issues, I would say that 35 to 40 per cent was spent on the economy', recalled John Ehrlichman, who, by November 1969, had been promoted to become the Special Assistant to the President for Domestic Affairs. 'Once he had moved Arthur Burns to be Chairman of the Federal Reserve, John Connally to be Treasury Secretary, and George Schultz to be Director of OMB, he saw those people very frequently. They educated him and he translated their education into policy. Soon he was so much on top of it all that not a sparrow fell without him getting involved.'[69]

Nixon's involvement took the form of hands-on intervention to help areas of high unemployment. He directed government contracts to problem districts such as the San Francisco Bay area, and the Northeast. He ordered Peter Flanigan to accelerate all government assistance or contracts in the pipeline that might assist pockets of deprivation around the country. He sent John Ehrlichman off on a 'Hey Fellas, you've got to help the President get the price of meat down' exercise to the Cattlemen's Association in Texas—one of many jawboning exercises which did slow some price rises for a few months.[70]

Such initiatives had their roots in Nixon's youthful experiences of the Great Depression. He knew what it meant for a community to be suffering from the twin scourges of unemployment and inflation. Unfortunately, his small interventions achieved only small results. With political pressure mounting, Nixon moved towards a dramatic reversal of orthodox, free market economic policies, which finally took place in August 1971. Worried by the upward economic spiral in labour costs, inflation and unemployment, the President gathered his advisers for a weekend at Camp David. After much agonising discussion he took the electrifying decisions to impose controls on wages and prices; to allow the dollar to float; and to suspend the convertibility of the dollar into gold. This was pure political expediency and it worked—at least in the short term. Inflation temporarily halved and there were satisfactory falls in unemployment and labour costs. The polls showed that the public liked Nixonomics and they certainly helped his re-election campaign in 1972, even if the price had to be paid later.

Nixon had no illusions about what he was doing. 'Politically necessary and immensely popular in the short run. But in the long run I believe that it was wrong', was how he described it in his memoirs.[71] Acutely conscious of how his narrow election defeat in 1960 could probably have been avoided by a small dose of political management in the economy, he was not going to let the same mistake happen twice. So he broke the free market rules but won the election. Only an economist would blame a politician for doing that.

Nixonomics were a political and public relations success story. That was more than could be said for the rest of the President's domestic programme, admirable though it looks in retrospect. The problem was that the substantive achievements of the Administration kept on being outweighed by insubstantial negatives. John Ehrlichman, who was doing more than almost anyone else in the government to further the President's domestic programme, felt frustrated. He wrote a perceptive memo to Bob Haldeman about his fears on 15 April 1970:

> In terms of social programs, e.g. manpower training, anti-poverty, environment, health and education, we are doing as much or more than Johnson or Kennedy.
>
> In terms of sound legislation on the domestic side, experts agree that we have made more good proposals for significant reform (draft, post office, manpower, occupational health and safety etc.) than any for ten years.

We have loaded aboard a lot of bright, young, able people who can present the President and his programs in an excellent light.

Nevertheless, among young business executives, among municipal officials, and on the campuses, we are epitomized by the Vice President, the Attorney General, and Judge Carswell.

We are presenting a picture of illiberality, repression, closedmindedness and lack of concern for the less fortunate...

The widespread negative impression on campuses and in urban areas can directly result in urban and campus unrest and I think that's where we are, coming into the spring.[72]

The last sentence was prophetic. All the good work being achieved on the domestic front was obscured and almost obliterated by the wave of anger that broke over the nation in May 1970 when Nixon took the decision to widen the Vietnam war by invading Cambodia.

V. CAMBODIA AND LINCOLN

Nixon's desire to find a swift and honourable ending for the war in Vietnam was running into trouble by the spring of 1970. Tension was rising on three separate fronts. In Paris, Hanoi's negotiators were stalling the peace talks by deliberate procrastination. In Southeast Asia the North Vietnamese army was engaged in a massive build-up of troops and equipment in its Cambodian sanctuaries. At home, the breathing space won by the 'Silent Majority' speech was about to be dissipated by a new wave of anti-war demonstrations.

The violence on the campuses was far worse than expected. In April a rash of arson attacks struck Yale, Stanford, Berkeley, Santa Barbara, Kansas and Ohio State. Some of these were firebombings against Reserve Officer Training Corps buildings, administration offices and banks. Others involved the torching of libraries and academic institutes. One of the most serious outrages was the burning down of the Center for Behavioral Studies at Stanford, which destroyed much unique research material, including the lifetime's work of the celebrated Indian anthropologist, Professor M.N. Srinivas.

These horrors affected Nixon personally. He wrote a consoling letter to Srinivas and made an emotional call to his old Whittier history professor, Dr. Paul Smith, asking for guidance on the root causes of the student uprising in California. The most direct blow came when Nixon was forced to cancel his visit to Julie's graduation ceremony after being advised by the Secret Service that over 100,000 demonstrators planned to besiege him at the Smith campus. Mortified as a father at having to miss his daughter's big day, he was alarmed as a President at finding himself coralled in the White House in a manner that was painfully reminiscent of the last days of Lyndon Johnson.

In spite of the worsening military situation in Cambodia, Nixon saw some hopeful signs in the progress of Vietnamisation and decided to take a risk. Believing that 'the time had come to drop a bombshell on the gathering spring storm of anti-war protest'[73] he announced on 20 April, that he was withdrawing 150,000 troops from Vietnam. This broadcast surprised his critics but dismayed his military advisers. They believed that the North Vietnamese divisions building up in the sanctuaries, and the supplies they were receiving from Russian and Chinese ships arriving daily at the Cambodian port of Sihanoukville constituted a serious threat to Saigon. Nixon was specifically warned by Admiral John D. McCain Jr., the Commander-in-Chief of the United States Forces in the Pacific, that there would soon be a North Vietnamese offensive against Saigon's western flank. The only effective way to pre-empt such an offensive, said McCain, would be to attack the NVA sanctuaries in the Parrot's Beak district just thirty-three miles from the South Vietnamese capital.

Additional military support for neutralising the Cambodian sanctuaries came from General Creighton Abrams, the Commander of US Forces in Vietnam. He wanted to send his troops in to attack the Fishook district, which he claimed contained COSVN (the Central Office of South Vietnam), the Communists' strategic command post and central supply depot. A third point of pressure on Nixon was the political situation in Cambodia, where, according to the CIA, the pro-Western government of Lon Nol looked likely to fall as 40,000 Communist troops closed in on the capital Phnom Penh.

In the last week of April, Nixon considered his options in the light of the conflicting advice he was receiving. His senior Cabinet Secretaries, Rogers and Laird, were opposed to direct US military involvement in such a high-risk operation. 'It will cost us great casualties with very little gain. And I just don't believe it will be a crippling blow to the enemy,' said Rogers.[74] Kissinger, whose NSC staff was bitterly divided, wanted an attack on the sanctuaries but conducted only by ARVN forces. The Joint Chiefs favoured an all-out deployment of US troops inside Cambodia. Against such recommendations Nixon had to balance the anticipated domestic backlash: 'I never had any illusions about the shattering effect a decision to go into Cambodia would have on public opinion at home', was how he summarised it.[75]

After a weekend of contemplation, much of it spent alone with Bebe Rebozo at Camp David, Nixon reached his decision. It was to authorise a joint US–ARVN incursion into the Fishook and to support an ARVN attack on the Parrot's Beak sanctuaries. The news of the operation broke on the morning of 29 April. Nixon went on television the next night to explain his policy.

Inevitably perhaps, in view of the tale it told, Nixon's speech polarised the nation, causing deep divisions of opinion even within his own circle of aides and appointees. The doves were contemptuous of the President's claim that he was not widening the war into neutral Cambodia but striving to make a peace settlement more attainable by weakening the enemy. The hawks were exhilarated by the toughness of his tone and language, as well as by his emphasis on the wider consequences, as when he declared: 'If, when the chips are down, the world's most powerful nation, the United States of America, acts like a pitiful helpless giant, the forces of totalitarianism and anarchy will threaten free nations and free institutions throughout the world.'[76]

There were also sharply divided reactions to Nixon's claim that he had risen above all domestic political considerations in reaching his decision:

> Whether I may be a one-term President is insignificant compared to whether by our failure to act in this crisis the United States proves itself to be unworthy to lead the forces of freedom in this critical period in world history. I would rather be a one-term President and do what I believe is right rather than to be a two-term President at the cost of seeing America become a second-rate power and to see this Nation accept the first defeat in its proud 190 year history.[77]

The gauntlet of a one-term Nixon Presidency was eagerly taken up in the liberal media and on the seething campuses. Over the next few days, a hurricane of hostility hit the White House. It was intensified by an off-the-cuff remark Nixon made on the morning after his speech. He was walking through the crowded lobby of the Pentagon just after receiving an upbeat military briefing. Accosted by an emotional but supportive wife of a US soldier serving in Vietnam, Nixon became equally misty-eyed, telling the woman how much he admired men like her husband:

> I have seen them. They're the greatest. You see these bums, you know, blowing up the campuses. Listen, the boys that are on the college campuses today are the luckiest people in the world, going to the greatest universities, and here they are burning up the books, storming around about this issue ... Then out there, we have kids who are

just doing their duty. And I have seen them. They stand tall, and they are proud.[78]

The media interpretation of this 'bums' remark was so far over the top in umbrage and outrage that it might easily have been thought that the comment outranked the fighting in Cambodia for its importance. The public were given the impression that Nixon had condemned all students as bums, whereas in fact his criticism had been aimed at the firebombers and arsonists. Reaction on many campuses became violent. The most tragic of these disturbances came at Kent State University on 4 May. After rioters had burned down the campus ROTC building, the Governor of Ohio called out the National Guard to maintain order.

Some of the young guardsmen on duty panicked during a rock-throwing incident and fired a volley into the crowd. Four students were killed and eleven wounded. Two of the dead were girls, uninvolved in the demonstration, who had been on their way to classes.

This shocking event caused mayhem and madness across the country. As horror turned to rage and rage escalated into violence, the groves of academe became battlefields. One campus demonstration after another lurched out of control, often exploding into mindless fighting and destruction. From Harvard (where rioting students threatened to burn down the home of Daniel Patrick Moynihan) to the University of New Mexico (where blood flowed in the street from a series of stabbings at a protest march) the atmosphere was one of vicious retaliation against authority. Over 200 incidents involving the burning, ransacking or wrecking of university property were recorded. Confronted by so much destructive savagery, most police forces recognised their own helplessness and became notable for the hastiness of their retreats or the conspicuousness of their absence.

The National Guard had to be called out to twenty-one campuses in sixteen states, but they, too, remained impotent, perhaps wisely, in the face of such profound disorder. Within days of the Kent State shootings, 450 colleges were closed down by this hysterical wave of student or faculty protest strikes. It was the worst turmoil America's educational institutions had ever seen, their darkest hour of revolutionary upheaval and collective insanity.

The tides of political emotion were not, however, running in the same direction. In New York on 7 May, a crowd of construction workers stormed City Hall and beat up student demonstrators. The cause of the violence was Mayor John Lindsay's decision to hold a ceremonial lowering of the Stars and Stripes to half mast. This was too moderate an act of symbolism for the students, who preferred to burn their own flag in the streets as an improvement on the Mayor's protest. It was too much for the watching 'hard hats' on a nearby building site. About 300 of them spontaneously downed tools, rescued Old Glory from the flames, thumped a few students and hauled City Hall's flag back to full mast.

The confrontation was repeated the following day with much larger marches and counter-marches. The political irony of these clashes was extraordinary. The students were mainly drawn from élitist backgrounds, coming from schools such as Harvard, Columbia, Dartmouth, New York University and the Massachusetts Institute of Technology. The hard hats were almost to a man proletarian, Irish-Americans, Italian-Americans and Kennedy Democrats. Yet Cambodia had apparently turned the natural blue-collar Democrats into Nixon supporters and the natural young Republicans into Nixon haters. By the end of the second day of street confrontation, the construction workers' leaders had been invited (by White House aide Charles Colson) to have coffee with the President in the Oval Office. Not to be outdone, the New York student leaders announced that they were also travelling to Washington—but to sleep and march in the streets as participants in a national weekend of anti-war protest. America was indeed turning itself upside down at this time of torment.

Inside the White House, the national reactions to Cambodia and Kent State caused much soulsearching. From the President downwards, everyone felt the pressure and some cracked under it.

Four members of the NSC staff, including Nixon's future biographer Roger Morris, resigned in protest. The Cabinet split publicly, with those opposed to the Cambodian strategy (Hickel, Rogers, Laird, Finch) leaking their priorities to the press with varying degrees of indiscretion. Kissinger was unsteady, wobbling between anger with his dissident staffers; distress over the hostile letters he received from his old friends at Harvard; and self-reproach at having misjudged the domestic backlash. He became moody and disconsolate. Nixon pulled him out of one of his blackest troughs with a pep talk ending with the words: 'Henry, remember Lot's wife. Never turn back. Don't waste time rehashing things we can't do anything about.'[79]

For all his bravado and Bible references, Nixon suffered great personal anguish during the Cambodian crisis. Ray Price remembers him one evening in a dejected and lachrymose state, downing scotches with the reproachful refrain, 'Everyone misunderstands me.'[80] This was a manifestation of some bad bouts of insomnia and depressed feelings which Nixon took sufficiently seriously to send for his former mentor and psychosomatic medicine practitioner, Dr. Arnold Hutschnecker of New York. Their unlogged secret meeting in the White House on 6 May was a failure. Nixon wanted a consultation but had not made this clear through Rose Mary Woods. Hutschnecker, who had become an ardent dove, thought he had been summoned to offer political advice. 'Mr. President, I think you should rename the Department of Defense the Department of Peace', was his prescription. Nixon listened patiently for a few minutes then excused himself. 'Our old intimacy was not there', concluded Hutschnecker.[81]

What was there was Nixon's determination to keep up a brave face in public, although this sometimes left him looking cold and unfeeling. Unwisely, he followed John Mitchell's advice to hang tough. This led to him approving an insensitive White House statement issued on the day of the Kent State killings, which failed to express a single word of sympathy for the dead students and their families. The killings, the statement read, 'should remind us all once again that when dissent turns to violence it invites tragedy. It is my hope this tragic and unfortunate incident will strengthen the determination of all the nation's campuses... to stand firmly for the right which exists in this country of peaceful dissent and just as strongly against the resort to violence as a means of such expression.'[82] Such sentiments were not the true feelings of the private Nixon, as he later recorded:

> In the newspaper the next day I saw the pictures of the four young people who had been killed. Two had been bystanders; the other two had been protesting a decision they felt was wrong. Now all four were dead, and a call was going out for nationwide demonstrations and student strikes. Would this tragedy become the cause of scores of others? I could not get the photographs out of my mind. I could not help thinking about the families, suddenly receiving the news that their children were dead because they had been shot in a campus demonstration. I wrote personal letters to each of the parents, even though I knew that my words could not help.
>
> Those few days after Kent State were among the darkest of my Presidency. I felt utterly dejected when I read that the father of one of the dead girls had told a reporter, 'My child was not a bum.'[83]

Throughout his life, Nixon always found it difficult to say sorry, particularly when under fire from criticism, so these sympathetic and almost apologetic musings were not disclosed at the time of the crisis.

However, at his White House press conference on the evening of 8 May, he did succeed in lowering the temperature, promising to pull all American troops out of Cambodia by the end of June and taking a conciliatory line towards the demonstrators.

His calm demeanour in front of the television cameras was a reassuring performance, but did not give the full picture of the gentler sensitivity Nixon felt towards America's angry young people. This emerged during the strange and sleepless night of 8–9 May, one of the most revealing episodes of his Presidency.

After his press conference was over, Nixon behaved as he often did after public addresses. Too keyed up to go to bed and energised by a mood which he described as 'agitated and uneasy',[84] he sat up into the small hours of the morning telephoning around the country to friends and staffers, among them Billy Graham, Norman Vincent Peale, Tom Dewey, Bebe Rebozo, John Mitchell, Bob Haldeman (seven times) and Henry Kissinger (eight times). The White House switchboard recorded fifty-one such calls between 10.35 p.m. and 3.50 a.m.

Just before 4 a.m., Nixon went to his favourite room in the White House, the Lincoln sitting room, where he put on a Philadelphia Orchestra recording of Rachmaninov's Second Piano Concerto. Listening to the music, he looked out of the window towards the Washington Monument where he could see groups of young people gathering on the Ellipse in preparation for the coming day of protest. His valet, Manolo Sanchez, appeared offering tea or coffee. Still gazing out of the window, Nixon said he considered the Lincoln Memorial at night the most beautiful sight in Washington. Sanchez replied that he had never seen it. 'Let's go and look at it now', was Nixon's impulsive reaction. A few minutes later, the President and his valet were on their way. The time was 4.30 in the morning and the accompanying Secret Service men were, according to Nixon, 'petrified with apprehension'[85] as their code-named 'Searchlight' headed through the dawn twilight and the gathering demonstrators to the Lincoln Memorial.

What was Nixon up to? The answer lies not so much in his nocturnal restlessness as in the roots of his upbringing and education. His grandmother, Almira Milhous, had caught his childhood imagination with her near-religious adulation of Lincoln as 'The Friend of Slaves'. The young Richard had been further inspired in Paul Smith's classes at Whittier by the full historical drama of Lincoln the President. By the end of his student years, Nixon was something of an expert on the Great Emancipator, knowing by heart not only the classic Lincoln speeches but also long passages from his ten-volume biography by Nicolay and Hay.

The bond that linked America's 16th and 37th Presidents was that they had both come to power at a time of extraordinary turmoil. Nixon inevitably saw a parallel between the Civil War of the 1860s and the civil strife of the 1970s. There was, he believed, a common thread between the two misunderstood leaders who, in their different eras, had to battle against ferocious and irrational opposition in order to achieve their higher purposes for the good of the nation.

Within the White House, Nixon's feelings for his great predecessor bordered on the mystical. Not only was his favourite retreat the Lincoln sitting room, but adjacent to it was the Lincoln bedroom, where, as he recalled long after his resignation from the Presidency, 'On special occasions, for example before we went to China, before we went to Russia, before I had a major speech or a major press conference I would stop…and have a moment of silent prayer because I sort of gathered strength just from being in this room where Lincoln had been.'[86] Now, at 4.30 in the morning of 9 May 1970, he was going even further in his quest to gather strength from Lincoln. As the first rays of sunlight shed a rose-pink glow on the white marble of Henry Bacon's soaring monument, Nixon was climbing its steps towards his hero, searching for guidance and inspiration at one of the bitterest turning points of his own Presidency.

Arriving at the foot of the statue, Nixon read out to Manolo Sanchez his favourite phrases from the carved inscriptions, particularly relishing the line, 'In this temple, as in the hearts of the people for whom he saved the Union, the memory of Abraham Lincoln is enshrined forever.' As this presidential teach-in progressed, some eight or nine amazed but respectful male students drew near to listen. They were joined by Egil 'Bud' Krogh, a thirty-year-old aide on John Ehrlichman's staff who was the night duty officer responsible for White House security. He described Nixon at the Lincoln Memorial as 'a surrealistic scene. Here were these kids who had come from all over the country to demonstrate, many of them in combat fatigues with long hair, peace badges, hairbands, and so on, looking pretty dishevelled. And there was the President in the middle of them, talking quietly and earnestly. It was a moving feeling being there, and I know the kids felt it, as I did.'[87]

Nixon was doing his best to get onto the students' wavelength. He shook hands with them, asked them where they were from, and what they were studying. He accepted that most of them disagreed with his policy for ending the Vietnam conflict, but said he hoped that they would not let their hatred of the war turn into a hatred for their own country. Getting little response, he tried to capture their support with an historical analogy:

> I know that probably most of you think I'm an SOB but I want you
> to know that I understand just how you feel. I recall that when I was
> just a little older than you, right out of law school and ready to get
> married, how excited I was when Chamberlain came home from

Munich and made his famous statement about peace in our time. I had heard it on the radio. I had so little in those days that the prospect of going into the service was almost unbearable and I felt that the United States staying out of any kind of a conflict was worth paying any price whatever. As a result I thought at that time that Chamberlain was the greatest man alive and when I read Churchill's all-out criticism of Chamberlain I thought Churchill was a madman.

In retrospect, I now realize I was wrong. I think now that Chamberlain was a good man but that Churchill was a wiser man and that we in the world are better off than we would be because Churchill had not only the wisdom but the courage to carry out the policies he believed were right even though there was a time when both in England and all over the world he was extremely unpopular because of his 'anti-peace' stand.[88]

After thirty minutes or so of Vietnam discussion, Nixon began talking about the importance of travel as a mind-broadening experience. He hoped his listeners would one day be able to go to China, to the Soviet Union, and to the cities of Eastern Europe such as Prague.

A student interrupted him. 'We are not interested in what Prague looks like. We are interested in what kind of a life we build in the United States.'[89] Nixon responded with a discourse on racial desegregation ('You must find a way to communicate with Blacks in your universities'[90]) and on the environment, soaring away on to a spiritual theme, which included an oblique reference to his 'What Can I Believe?' college essays of 1930.

Cleaning up the air and the water and the streets is not going to solve the deepest problems that concern us all. Those are material problems. They must be solved. They are terribly important... But you must remember that something that is completely clean can also be completely sterile and without spirit.

What we must all think about is why we are here. What are those elements of the spirit which really matter... Forty years ago I was searching, as some of you may be searching now for an answer to this problem. But I want to be sure all of you realize that ending the war, and cleaning up the streets and the air and the water is not going to solve spiritual hunger that all of us have and which of course has been the great mystery of life from the beginning of time.[91]

After this revealing homily inside the Lincoln Memorial, Nixon looked at his watch, saw it was five to six, and decided to move on. Before getting into his car he made some characteristically awkward efforts at smalltalk to a larger crowd of students at the foot of the steps, asking one group from Syracuse University about their football team and another Californian group about surfing. He posed for a final photograph with a red-bearded student from Detroit. 'I know you came a long way for this event. I know you are terribly frustrated and angry about our policy and opposed to it. But I just hope your opposition doesn't turn into a blind hatred of the country. Remember, this is a great country with all of its faults', Nixon told him, getting a warm smile and a friendly handshake in return.[92]

By now, Krogh and the Secret Service detail were getting increasingly nervous. Their concern was understandable since Washington that morning resembled an armed camp of troops and policemen, surrounding the principal buildings and institutions of the government whose President was now so unexpectedly on the loose amidst the potential trouble makers. Nixon, however, was not finished yet. 'Have you ever visited the Capitol?' he asked Manolo Sanchez. He had not. So off they went, first to the Senate Chamber (still locked at that early hour) and then to the House Chamber, which they managed to get a surprised custodian to unlock after a five-minute hunt for the keys. After showing Sanchez the seat in which he had sat as a young Congressman in the 1940s, the President was approached by three Black cleaning ladies. One of them, Mrs. Carrie Moore, asked him to sign her Bible. Nixon said he was glad to see that she carried her Bible with her, adding as he signed it, 'The trouble is that most of us these days don't read it enough.' 'Mr. President, I read it all the time', replied Mrs. Moore, a solemn and dignified lady.

Nixon took her hand, evidently moved by some deep thoughts about Hannah. 'You know my mother was a saint. She died two years ago. She was a saint.' There was a long pause as he struggled with his emotions. 'You be a saint too', he told Mrs. Moore, squeezing her hand. 'I'll try, Mr. President', she replied.[93]

Moving on, Nixon told the Secret Service he would like to have breakfast at one of the restaurants along Connecticut Avenue. It was now 6.40 a.m. Outside the Capitol the party was joined by Bob Haldeman, Dwight Chapin, and Press Secretary Ron Ziegler. They urged the President to return to the White House but he was determined to include a downtown breakfast in his outing, so the group took their custom to the Rib Room of the Mayflower Hotel. Nixon, visiting his first Washington restaurant since he became President, ordered corned beef hash with an egg on top. After this hearty repast he announced his intention of walking back to the White House. He set off on foot down Connecticut Avenue, much to the further consternation of the Secret Service, who realised that his route would take him through a large crowd of demonstrators in Lafayette Park. After walking a block or two, Bud Krogh took Nixon by the arm and tried to manoeuvre him into the presidential limousine, saying, 'We can't walk back. We've got to ride back.'[94] With some reluctance, Nixon abandoned his role as a pedestrian and was driven through the long line of police buses and barricades, arriving back in the White House via the E Street entrance at 7.30 a.m. almost exactly three hours after he had set off for the Lincoln Memorial.

The sunrise expedition was a public relations disaster. The White House press corps, none of whose members had been eyewitnesses to the story, seemed affronted that the President should have embarked on his sortie without making arrangements for their attendance. Their resentment showed in the eventual coverage. Nixon was pilloried for pulling a stunt; being on the verge of a nervous breakdown; and talking to the students with condescension and insensitivity. The last charge was based largely on the comments of a Syracuse University sopho-more who had not heard Nixon talking to the group inside the Lincoln Memorial. She had joined the discussion just before 6 a.m., and had therefore missed more than an hour of the dialogue. She was entitled to her view that the President's small talk about the Syracuse University football team sounded patronising, but this was hardly a rounded view of the conversation.[95]

A different perspective of the episode came from Bud Krogh, whose opinion of his boss took on a new and almost messianic dimension after being in atten-dance for all three hours' worth of the morning's exchanges. On the basis of what he had heard, Krogh now saw Nixon as 'a compassionate and profoundly misun-derstood man', full of faith in his country and sympathy for its young people. 'I am sure that what he was doing at the Lincoln Memorial was seeking and giving spiritual refreshment', was Krogh's view.[96] This was not an opinion which found its way into any newspaper or television broadcast.

Like its junior offshoot, Nixon's sunrise expedition, the Cambodian incur-sion was also a public relations disaster. So fierce were the continuing protests, and so scathing the journalistic indictments which it continued to provoke, that the episode came to be regarded as the first sounding of the death knell for the Nixon administration. This assessment has been given added credence by Bob Haldeman, who wrote in his memoirs that the events of May 1970 'marked a turning point for Nixon; a beginning of his downhill slide toward Watergate'.[97]

How and where the slide to Watergate started is a subject which will be examined later. But what may be said with some certainty is that during the tumultuous summer of 1970 Nixon did not feel himself to be on any sort of slide.

He believed that the decisions he had taken on Cambodia, however unpopular at home, were correct in the context of bringing an honourable peace settlement to Vietnam. This view was justified.

Although no liberal historian has been able to accept it, the Cambodian incursion brought about many of its intended tactical and strategic results. By the end of May it was clear that most of the sanctuaries had been either destroyed or severely damaged. The one omission, hurtful in public relations terms, was the failure to uncover COSVN, but the absence of this elusive totem pole was more than compensated for by the taking of other military scalps.

The US and ARVN attackers between them captured enough enemy weapons and munitions to equip seventy-four full-strength NVA battalions; enough enemy food supplies to sustain the entire Communist forces in Vietnam for four months; and enough heavy military equipment and vehicles to make the anticipated offensive against Saigon an impossibility.

The ARVN had fought with sufficient confidence and courage to show that Vietnamisation was working and that US troop withdrawals could proceed with safety. Most important of all, Lon Nol's anti-Communist government survived because the military pressure against it was relieved. This meant that Sihanoukville, the leading port of entry for Soviet and Chinese ships delivering heavy weapons to the North Vietnamese, was permanently closed down as the receiving point for Communist military supplies to the area. It was two years before the North Vietnamese would launch a major offensive against the South.

One international expert who fully appreciated the strategic gains from the Cambodian incursion was Sir Robert Thompson. He made an extensive tour of Vietnam five months after the attack on the Parrot's Beak and Fishook sanctuaries. He reported that the Communist forces on the ground had been so badly affected by the loss of weapons and equipment that it would be two years before they could rebuild their stocks to previous levels. This breathing space was already allowing the South Vietnamese government (GVN) to make huge gains in their pacification of the countryside and the strengthening of ARVN. According to the secret report Thompson sent to Nixon on 12 October 1970:

> In military capability, manpower and territorial security, the GVN is immeasurably stronger and the enemy very much weaker. The main reason for this, apart from the success of the [Vietnamisation and Pacification] programs themselves has been the destruction of the enemy's bases and stocks in Cambodia and the loss of Sihanoukville as a port of supply.[98]

Thompson's optimism was confirmed by the fall in the US casualty figures. They had been running at an average of ninety-three per week before May 1970. By October they were down to fifty-one per week, and falling. Far more important than the numbers game was the fact that the breathing space was giving both non-Communist Cambodia a chance to resist the Hanoi-organised Khmer Rouge and non-Communist South Vietnam a chance to survive against the North. That these hopes were ultimately dashed was not the fault of Nixon. He had acted with courage to achieve some important tactical military successes in Cambodia. He had also sent a clear signal to the enemy that there was no lack of presidential resolve to stand firm until the Paris peace talks produced an honourable settlement.

In the race between the strengthening of the South Vietnamese army, and the ability of the North Vietnamese army to thwart that improvement by launching offensives, some useful ground had been gained for America's allies. Unless one subscribes to the view that the best policy was the immediate capitulation to the Communists, Nixon's strategy looked a sound one. The majority of the American public seemed to be backing him, for a *Newsweek* Gallup Poll taken at the end of May showed that 65 per cent of the voters approved of his handling of the Presidency and that 50 per cent approved of his decision to send troops into Cambodia. If that level of domestic support had been maintained, the eventual outcome of the drama in Southeast Asia might have been very different. Unfortunately for Nixon, his level of support in the two vital power centres of the Congress and the media was much lower.

VI. WIRETAPS, THE HUSTON PLAN AND CHUCK COLSON

Throughout his Presidency, Nixon fought a running battle with the press. He viewed most of its representatives not as objective reporters but as political opponents. This judgement, though at times distorted in individual cases, was by no means wrong. During the 1960s the Vietnam war had created its own adversarial ethos in the Eastcoast media establishment. As a result, Nixon's arrival in the White House coincided with an era of anti-government hostility in the big news gathering organisations of the United States. Although occasional voices of editorial conservatism made themselves heard, these were the exceptions that proved the rule. America's national journalism, in harmony with the opinions of its younger readers and viewers, had by 1970 taken on a mind set of antagonistic liberalism.

Any President would have had difficulty with his press relations in such a climate. Nixon himself was temperamentally unsuited to engage in the sort of tactical subtleties that might have been able to change the journalistic weather. Yet in the beginning, he did try much harder than has been recognised to build bridges to the media. Haldeman has recalled that 'his attempts were often heavy handed and rarely successful but he did try to conciliate [the press] fairly often'. There were several White House dinners for correspondents; small press briefings were held in the Oval Office in the style of FDR; and after-hours cocktail sessions took place in Nixon's hideaway office in the Executive Office Building where the President would himself 'cook up' the Martinis.

All these efforts met with failure. 'He would say it had not worked because he would be shafted by one of the press people present, and then he would say, "See? It was no use. You can mess around all you want. It won't make a difference…To hell with them!"'[99]

These aggressive instincts became sharpened by the Administration's early problems with leaks. In the first five months of Nixon's Presidency, twenty-one major leaks from classified NSC files appeared as stories in the *New York Times* or *Washington Post*. Later that year, the CIA sent to the White House a list of forty-five newspaper articles which were regarded as serious violations of national security. It would have been difficult for any government to ignore such a haemorrhage of secret information and it was hardly surprising (especially with a war on) that the Administration took measures to try and detect the culprits.

On 9 May 1969, a story appeared in the *New York Times* revealing the secret bombing of Cambodia. Nixon met soon afterwards with Kissinger, Mitchell, Haldeman, and FBI Director J. Edgar Hoover to discuss how to stop such leaks. Kissinger and Hoover both recommended the use of wiretaps and Nixon issued a general authorisation which led to intercepts being placed on the telephones of thirteen government officials and four journalists. Great indignation was expressed in the media when this eavesdropping activity eventually came to light in 1973, not least because of uncertainty about whether the proper legal procedures had been followed.*

---

* The legality of such wiretapping was somewhat obscure at the time. Nixon was advised that he was empowered to authorise wiretaps without obtaining a warrant under the 1968 Omnibus Crime Control Act, Title III, which gives the President such power to defend the nation against foreign attack and spying, or to protect the government from overthrow by unconstitutional means. On 19 June 1972, however, the Supreme Court found that such presidential use of wiretaps, while justifiable in the interests of maintaining domestic security, must be in conformity with the Fourth Amendment's requirement that searches and seizures be judicially approved.[100]

Much of the criticism was directed at Kissinger, whose advice on whom to tap looks curious in retrospect. Several of his own closest aides and journalistic friends were bugged, among them Henry Brandon of the London *Sunday Times*, a particularly bizarre suspect since his stories owed much to the close relationship he enjoyed with his frequent weekend guest, the National Security Adviser. Nixon was not given the names of all those whose phones were tapped. As President he saw the issue as a broadbrush matter of protecting national security, leaving the details to the FBI, Kissinger, and Kissinger's senior staff assistant Colonel Alexander Haig, who according to Haldeman 'was much more the manager of the project than Henry'.[101] The whole exercise was a failure anyway. Nixon's view of it emerged in a discussion three years later about the intercepts placed on two of Kissinger's NSC staffers, Morton Halperin and W. Anthony Lake. Nixon said: 'I know that he [Kissinger] asked that it be done. And I assumed it was. Lake and Halperin. They're both bad. But the taps were too. They never helped us. Just gobs and gobs of material: gossip and bullshitting—the tapping was a very, very unproductive thing.'[102]

The failure of the wiretaps to prove a single definite link between any government official and a specific leak of national security was frustrating. According to Haldeman, by May 1970 'Nixon had given up on the intelligence and investigatory agencies such as the FBI to help in his battle to quell the national uproar...As far as he was concerned, the FBI was a failure; it hadn't found the leakers of military secrets; it hadn't found Communist backing for the antiwar organizations which he was sure was there.'[103]

The President's concern about the adequacy of the FBI was understandable. In a bewildering outgrowth of political extremism, the sinister forces of terrorism were starting to spread their tentacles across the United States. Between January 1969 and May 1970 there were 40,000 bomb threats, 3,000 bombings, $21 million worth of damage to property, and forty-three deaths attributable to political violence. J. Edgar Hoover's investigators were getting nowhere in finding the culprits. Caught in their own time warp of Soviet anti-Communism techniques, the FBI's intelligence division could detect few leads on the perpetrators of the new subversion. Statistics given to the President showed that 64 per cent of all the bombing incidents had no suspects, let alone arrests, although rumours abounded about mysterious terrorist organisations such as the Weathermen or the Black Panthers.

Against a background of rising fear across the nation, Nixon summoned the chiefs of the American intelligence community to the White House on 5 June 1970. Among those present were J. Edgar Hoover of the FBI, Richard Helms of the CIA, General Donald Bennett of the Defense Intelligence Agency and Admiral Noel Gayler of the National Security Agency. Haldeman, Ehrlichman, Bob Finch, and a twenty-nine-year-old White House aide Tom Huston were also present.

The President delivered a blistering dressing down to his intelligence barons, accusing them of being over-staffed, overfunded, bedevilled by rivalry, lacking in co-ordination, and failing in their duty. He told them to form a committee and to produce a report recommending a programme of action to fight the terrorist challenge. Hoover would chair this committee; Huston would be the White House staff representative.

The President's sharp criticism resulted in 'The Special Report Interagency Committee on Intelligence (Ad Hoc)'—more usually and memorably called 'The Huston Plan'—which called for an expanded range of covert activities against suspected terrorists, including mail opening; 'black bag jobs' (surreptitious break-ins); wiretapping; increased infiltration of left-wing groups; recruitment of informants on campuses and greater use of electronic surveillance. All these activities were to be co-ordinated by a new committee of intelligence agency leaders on which Huston would sit as the President's personal representative.

In short, here was a blueprint for counter-terrorist action. Yet neither the President nor four of the Principals who had approved it—Helms, Bennett, Gayler, Huston—appeared to be concerned by the difficult questions it raised about the legal basis for such methods. The times were too turbulent and the perceived dangers too great. The United States constitution has an inherent contradiction between the President's oath of office to 'insure domestic tranquility' and to 'provide for the common defense' when those objectives conflict with the civil liberties of individual citizens under the Bill of Rights. Nixon decided that his duty lay on the side of strengthening the common defence. He therefore gave his approval to the Huston Plan on 23 July.

Opposition to his decision came from an unaccustomed source of libertarian protest, J. Edgar Hoover. He argued that the dangers of the unconstitutional methods recommended by the plan, and their risk of public exposure far outweighed the intelligence-gathering gains. A secondary and unspoken reason for his objections may have been that the new co-ordinating committee would have taken power away from the FBI. Hoover won the support of his immediate boss, Attorney General John Mitchell, and Mitchell convinced the President that the unconstitutional methods were not worth the risk. Five days later, Nixon withdrew his approval and the Huston Plan was dead. The bombings and the violence continued. Ironically, it was discovered five years later, in 1975, that the FBI had been using the investigative methods in the plan long before and long after Nixon rescinded his approval of it.[104]

Although the Huston Plan was killed off, the thinking behind it lived on and became part of the culture in one corner of the White House. Nixon's most senior men knew their boss well enough to protect him from his own worst ideas. The Berlin Wall of Haldeman, Ehrlichman, and Kissinger around the Oval Office was not only a fortification to stop people getting in. It also protected some of the President's darker impulses from getting out. Nixon was appreciative of this service in the early months of his Presidency. As he said in a memo to Haldeman on 16 June 1969, 'I have an uneasy feeling that many of the items that I send out for action are disregarded when any staff member just reaches the conclusion that it is unreasonable or unattainable... I respect this kind of judgement.'[105]

This unusual White House filtration system worked well for the first phase of Nixon's Presidency. But a combination of frustration about the anti-war opposition and fears over the upcoming election gradually caused him to reach out beyond the Berlin Wall. Gresham's law of economics ('Bad money drives out good') applied to the White House staff. Zealots, sycophants, and climbers started to replace or at least circumvent the old loyalists. John Ehrlichman saw and understood what was happening:

> Nixon had an energetic, constantly churning mind which was forever throwing out a flow of ideas, some good, some awful. I think he considered it one of the luxuries of the office that he could vent his spleen and not affect the outside world. It was our job to direct that part of the flow which could be full of disgust and divisiveness. Bob [Haldeman] in particular did a good job there. But in time, it became apparent that Nixon had found a way of getting around us. If I turned one of his bad ideas down, that would not be the end of it. He would rummage around in his bag of personnel until he found the guy who would do this or that dastardly deed. Someone who would salute him and say, 'Yes sir, Mr. President' and go out and get it done.[106]

The principal purveyor of what Ehrlichman and others saw as 'dastardly deeds' was Charles E. Colson, a thirty-eight-year-old political zealot whose originality of thought and ruthlessness of action soon made him a new court favourite who captivated the President. 'Chuck's got the balls of a brass monkey', was Nixon's early assessment of his most unusual aide,[107] although it was another part of Colson's anatomy, his head for political strategy, that first brought him into the White House in November 1969.

Colson was a practitioner of 'bloc politics'. He had grown up on the wrong side of the tracks in Boston as a member of an ethnic group known as 'Swamp Yankees'—the poorer white Protestants who had been left behind by the upwardly mobile denizens of the Harvard and Brahmin establishments to jostle 'in the swamp' of the old city alongside the Italians, the Irish Catholics, the Jews, the Slavs, and other newcomers.

From this background, and from his own struggle to become a scholarship boy and successful lawyer, Colson instinctively understood what Nixon was trying to achieve when he talked about putting together a new Republican majority. This strategy consisted of shaking loose from their traditional Democratic allegiances any organised voting blocs that might be tempted to switch their support to a Republican President who more sympathetically represented their values and aspirations than anti-war Democrats like Senators George McGovern or Edmund Muskie.

Described by Theodore H. White as 'the shrewdest political mind, after Richard Nixon's, in the White House',[108] Colson made it his business to build the new majority by reaching out to the labour unions, the Catholic blue-collar voters, the European ethnic blocs and other such groups. He did so with positive presentational skills that were brilliant but also with negative tactics that were unscrupulous. Discrediting a political opponent was meat and drink to Chuck Colson, and he cared little about the ethical proprieties of the methods he used to serve the President's interests. It was not as though the President cared much about those ethical proprieties either. Sitting together in the White House late at night talking tactics over a scotch, Nixon and Colson could hot one another up to the most feverish bouts of plotting and scheming. 'Those who say that I fed the President's darker instincts are only 50 per cent correct,' recalled Colson, 'because 50 per cent of the time he was feeding my darker instincts.'[109] Misinformation and gathering political intelligence that could be used against opponents were priority items on their mutual agendas. One evening, when they were both watching TV news reports of the Democratic presidential front runner, Senator Edmund Muskie, campaigning in New Hampshire, Nixon remarked, 'Wouldn't it be kinda interesting if there was a Committee of Democrats supporting Muskie *and* Bussing. Couldn't you arrange that Chuck?'[110]

Arranging that one should have been Mission Impossible. The compulsory bussing of schoolchildren (a policy aimed at desegregating schools by transporting children from racially and culturally unmixed areas to racially and culturally mixed schools) was anathema to the Catholic and ethnic groups that made up Muskie's strongest base of support among registered Democrats. But Colson was a 'can-do' political operator, who never shrank from 'breaking the china' when it came to carrying out the President's wishes. So by pushing and shoving, paying and pressurising, he somehow unearthed enough oddball voters to form such a committee. 'Democrats for Muskie and Bussing' duly published 100,000 leaflets with funds provided by Colson. The false propaganda coup delighted Nixon, and threw the Muskie Democrats into some disarray.[111]

On the intelligence-gathering front, a typical Colson coup involved a rumour that Senator Edward Kennedy had been dating a starlet named Maria Pia in Paris. After much long-distance telephoning and manoeuvring, the resourceful Chuck managed to get Kennedy and the young lady photographed together in a Champs Elysee nightclub. 'Nixon was really wowed that I was able to bring him that picture', recalled Colson with some amusement.[112]

Such escapades of hardball playing were the froth on the top of the Nixon–Colson relationship. The real substance was their work in building the New Republican Majority, an achievement which not only won the 1972 election with a landslide; it also changed the landscape of American political loyalties for at least two decades. Yet Colson was seen by his contemporaries in the White House not as a big gun but as a loose cannon. Haldeman, Ehrlichman, and Mitchell were continually worrying that his activities might be going to misfire or implode.

But other more impressionable junior aides saw Colson as a role model, pointing the way on how to rise in the President's esteem. It was in the wake of Colson that an underground began to form in the White House, whose most important and fateful members were John Dean and the Plumbers.

VII. DEAN, THE UNDERGROUND AND THE PLUMBERS

John Dean, destined to become the President's accuser and betrayer, was a figure of no importance when he arrived at the White House in July 1970.

How he came to get his job and how he used it to advance himself is a cautionary tale of how not to select and supervise presidential appointees. Nixon was not to blame for it, but nor was he entirely blameless.

As his relationship with Chuck Colson was beginning to show, there were dark corners in the world of Nixon the politician that seemed incompatible with the shining image of Nixon the President. One of those corners existed in the office of Counsel to the President long before John Dean was appointed to it.

Nixon's first Counsel was John Ehrlichman, a political heavyweight who did many good deeds for the Administration in the field of domestic policy. However, before being promoted to the post of Special Assistant to the President for Domestic Affairs, Ehrlichman was in charge of what he called 'a rag bag' of duties at the Counsel's office.[113] Some of these were routine legal chores, some were policy matters, some were investigations. This last function required investigators. Ehrlichman had two of them at his disposal, both former undercover detectives from the New York Police Department's Bureau of Special Services and Investigations (BOSSI). The senior investigator was Jack Caulfield, who had been assigned by BOSSI to act as protection officer for ex-Vice President Nixon on his public appearances in the city during his wilderness years, 1963–7. In this role Caulfield established enough of a personal relationship to ask Nixon for a job in Washington after the 1968 election. The request was granted and Caulfield gravitated via the Department of Justice to Ehrlichman's office at the White House.

'Nixon was often asking for odd jobs that required investigation', recalled Ehrlichman. 'Sometimes these were research tasks. I remember him saying, "History is going to want to know where I lived. Check out all the addresses Pat and I had". So we checked them out. Sometimes they were more personal investigations. Julie had been attacked in print by someone and Nixon wanted the guy investigated to see why his motivations were so hostile. There were other family jobs, such as checking out one of Don Nixon's business deals which could have been embarrassing. Or most often he wanted political investigations done on opponents like Ted Kennedy. As the pattern developed I became concerned that this sort of work could not legitimately be funded by the taxpayer—who was paying Caulfield's salary, so on Caulfield's recommendation I hired Ulascewicz, another NYPD man, to work for us privately. His salary was paid by a Nixon trust fund left over from previous campaigns. This was an effort to keep the show legitimate and clean, which I think is what I did.'[114]

For all Ehrlichman's disclaimers there is something surprising, and perhaps faintly seamy, about a President of the United States needing the services of a couple of gumshoes to carry out political and personal investigations on opponents. Yet in defence of these curious arrangements, it should be remembered that presidential politics is a rough game and that incumbents of the White House seeking re-election need both a defensive and an offensive capability to deal with the slings and arrows of outrageous opposition. Nixon may have had a somewhat unhealthy bias towards investigators, going back to his days with the Hiss case, but the Ehrlichman–Caulfield–Ulascewicz set-up seems to have been a fairly benign and insignificant operation which might well have petered out completely had it not been for John Dean.

When Ehrlichman was promoted he took many of the Counsel's functions with him to his new post, leaving behind the minor legal chores. What was needed to carry them out was a minor legal functionary. Having downgraded the job, although not its title or salary, the White House set about finding a suitable apparatchik to fill it and came up with the name of thirty-one-year-old John Dean.

Dean was a transparently flashy chancer whose track record was as full of ill-smelling holes as a slice of Emmenthal cheese. After graduating from Georgetown Law School, Dean's first job had been with a Washington law partnership. He was ignominiously fired from his junior associateship there because of an ethical conflict of interest row which erupted when he was discovered to be secretly working on a TV station licence application for a competitor of one of his firm's clients.[115] Narrowly escaping disbarment, Dean moved to Capitol Hill, where he used his family connections (he was briefly married to the daughter of a Missouri senator) to become a minority counsel to the House Judiciary Committee. In that job he also had ethical problems, for at least one of his colleagues denounced him as 'an idea thief' after he had been observed lifting other people's research work and claiming credit for it.[116]

In 1969, following Nixon's election victory, Dean was one of several Republican lawyers who secured political appointments in the Department of Justice under Attorney General John Mitchell. After a year at Justice, Dean pushed himself, through his acquaintanceship with White House aide Bud Krogh, on to the shortlist for the job of Counsel to the President. Because he was erroneously assumed to be 'Mitchell's man', Dean became the favourite for the post. After only perfunctory checks on his record, he was flown to San Clemente for an interview with Haldeman. 'I thought he was ambitious and bright and he came highly recommended', Haldeman has recalled. '[Egil] Krogh recommended him and another lawyer thought highly of him. I acted on that recommendation.'[117] Dean was appointed Counsel to the President at a salary of $42,500 a year. This was nearly six times greater than the $7,500 salary he had been earning from his unhappy associateship with the law firm three years earlier. He was rising fast.

Nixon had no interest or involvement in Dean's appointment beyond a ritual introductory handshake. He had only three meetings with his Counsel during the first two years of Dean's employment, on subjects of peripheral importance. However, despite this lack of presidential interest, Dean's stock began to rise in the White House, for he was presentable, pliable and ambitious. Nicknamed 'the golden boy' on account of his long blond hair, Gucci shoes, Porsche sports car and swinging bachelor life style, Dean carved out a useful niche for himself, first as an in-house legal adviser to White House staffers and later, far more ominously, as an intelligence-gatherer. He had listened to the gossip about Colson's activities and concluded that the best way to ingratiate himself with the high command of the White House was either by bringing in political intelligence (digging up the dirt on the President's opponents) or by negative PR work (spreading that dirt). There were several young aides running around with similar thoughts in their heads, among them Jeb Magruder and Gordon Strachan. However, Dean had a headstart on them because he had inherited as members of his staff Ehrlichman's two undercover investigators Jack Caulfield and Tony Ulascewicz.

Although Nixon and Ehrlichman appeared to have forgotten all about the investigative unit attached to the President's Counsel's office, Dean found plenty of work for it to do. Some of its operations were straightforward, for example gathering intelligence on forthcoming anti-war demonstrations. Others were more dubious, such as investigations into the personal affairs and backgrounds of Congressmen. Dean even directed the unit into territory worthy of Damon Runyon's stories. In the summer of 1971 he made Ulascewicz investigate the 'Happy Hooker' callgirl ring operated by Xaviera Hollander in New York to see if any prominent Democrats were on her list of clients. As the basis of a 'pols and dols' scandal, this unusual White House initiative had to be abandoned when it was discovered that the number of well-known Democrats on the Happy Hooker's list was equalled by the number of well-known Republicans.

Dean also sought to ingratiate himself by making some original suggestions in the area of negative political action. He composed a memorandum, dated 16 August 1971, entitled 'Dealing with our Political Enemies', in which he addressed the question, 'How can we use the available federal machinery to screw our political enemies?' His suggestion was that a list should be compiled of Administration opponents to whom 'we should be giving a hard time' and that various government agencies such as the IRS should be encouraged 'to screw them'.[118] Mysteriously, this Dean memorandum had no addressee. Nixon, Haldeman, and Ehrlichman all subsequently denied ever having seen it and no action was taken to implement its recommendations. However, it was to make a major impact as 'The White House Enemies List' when Dean produced it as part of his evidence to the Senate Watergate Committee nearly two years later.

In the great strategic master plans of the Nixon Presidency—on China; Russia; Vietnam; the desegregation of schools, the environment, and the New Majority—the activities of John Dean and his peer group were insignificant pimples on the body politic. But nobody discouraged them, for the word among insiders was that the President was amused by their seedy little initiatives. Thus the Dean–Magruder–Strachan–Caulfield–Ulascewicz methods of operation developed a certain momentum. Indeed, 'the underground' as it was later to be labelled, received some visible signs of encouragement from on high. 'It was like a culture taking root in a corporation', recalled Chuck Colson. 'Haldeman, no doubt with the President's blessing, ran a sort of system by which a nod, a smile, a word of approval or an invitation to a White House function was bestowed on those who brought in the dirt on our opponents. You could always get rewarded if you showed up in the White House with a bit of negative intelligence, so the puppies kept coming in with their bones.'[119]

The underground might well have continued at the level of puppies and pimples with no discernible impact on the Presidency if it had not been for the episode of the Pentagon Papers. This burst upon the world on 13 June 1971 when the *New York Times* ran a front page story headlined, 'VIETNAM ARCHIVE: PENTAGON STUDY TRACES THREE DECADES OF GROWING US INVOLVEMENT'.

The text described a 7,000-page survey of American involvement in Southeast Asia from the end of World War II until 1968. The project had been commissioned by Robert McNamara, Defense Secretary under Kennedy and Johnson, with the title 'The History of US Decision Making in Vietnam'. It was based on an archive of documents drawn from the Defense Department, the State Department, the CIA, the White House, and the Joint Chiefs of Staff. Many of these materials were classified top secret. In defiance of that classification, the *New York Times* announced that it thought it fit to print not only extensive extracts from the study but many of the original secret documents as well.

Despite the journalistic excitement that accompanied their publication, 'The Pentagon Papers', as they soon became known, were yesterday's news. Their disclosures were embarrassing to the Kennedy and Johnson administrations but covered nothing that had happened since Nixon's inauguration. Perhaps for that reason, the President's initial reaction was calm. His mood at the time was mellow.

As President, he believed his clandestine overtures to China were about to result in a spectacular breakthrough. As a peacemaker, he was hopeful that the North Vietnamese negotiators in Paris would respond favourably to the radical new proposals he had just sent to them. As a father, he had just enjoyed great family happiness with the marriage of Tricia to Ed Cox, a Princeton graduate in his second year at Harvard Law School. The ceremony was held in the Rose Garden, at Tricia's request, and was followed by a reception in the East Room. Nixon clearly enjoyed himself, dancing first with Tricia, then Pat, Julie and even Lynda

Bird Johnson (LBJ's daughter). It was the first time he had danced at the White House. This was one of very few days Nixon devoted to his family during his Presidency, and it was one of his happiest. 'It was a day that all of us will always remember,' Nixon wrote in his memoirs, 'because all of us were beautifully, and simply, happy.'[120] His happiness, however, was marred when the reports of the White House wedding shared the front page of the *New York Times* with the disclosure of the Pentagon Papers.

The last thing Nixon needed in the summer of 1971 was a bitter fight with the nation's most powerful newspaper. His first inclination was to regard the leak as a nine-day journalistic wonder, troublesome only to the Democrats.

This cool approach by the President was shattered by a white-hot rage on the part of Henry Kissinger. 'He went completely into orbit...It was a case of wild over-reaction...He talked passionate nonsense about how we were in a revolutionary situation...how the security of the United States was at risk...how we must have a British type Official Secrets Act to protect ourselves...and how the *New York Times* must be stopped whatever it took. It was Henry in his worst tantrum ever...absolutely beyond belief, was Bob Haldeman's recollection of the scene in the Oval Office on 17 June when he, Ehrlichman and Kissinger first met with the President to discuss the problem.[121]

Kissinger certainly knew how to wind up his boss. The main thrust of his warning was that the release of the Pentagon Papers imperiled other world leaders' perception of Nixon. 'It shows you're a weakling, Mr. President', declared Kissinger. 'The fact that some idiot can publish all of the diplomatic secrets of this country on his own is damaging to your image, as far as the Soviets are concerned, and it could destroy our ability to conduct foreign policy. If the other powers feel that we can't control internal leaks, they will never agree to secret negotiations.'[122]

Although there was no evidence that the Soviets or any other nation were reacting to the Pentagon Papers in this way, Kissinger's punchline, 'It shows you're a weakling, Mr. President', galvanised Nixon into action. John Mitchell was immediately ordered to launch an all-out battle in the courts against the *New York Times*. When the Government's case failed, for predictable First Amendment reasons, the White House turned its fire on the perpetrator of the leak, one Daniel Ellsberg, a forty-year-old Rand Corporation employee who had been a member of the team of researchers working on the study Robert McNamara had commissioned.

Kissinger was sensitive about Ellsberg, with whom he had an academic connection going back to the 1960s when they had both been lecturers on a Harvard course of Defense Policy seminars. As Haldeman and others saw it, Kissinger felt vulnerable because yet another of his protégés had been unmasked as a leaker of secrets. If this was his concern, Kissinger certainly over-compensated for it by portraying Ellsberg to Nixon as a psychotic weirdo.

According to the National Security Adviser, Ellsberg was a genius, a drug abuser, a sexual pervert, and a hawk turned peacenik who, in his militaristic period, had enjoyed taking pot shots at Vietnamese peasants from helicopters.[123] Kissinger's political diagnosis was that Ellsberg 'must be stopped at all costs' because he was 'the most dangerous man in America today'.[124]

Wound up still higher by such descriptions, and by the media's subsequent lionisation of Ellsberg, Nixon came to regard him as an unstable and subversive traitor. John Mitchell fanned these flames by reporting from his Justice Department sources that the leak had been part of an international conspiracy; that the Soviet Embassy had received a set of the Pentagon Papers before their publication in the *New York Times*; and that the FBI was pulling its punches in its investigation of the case because its Director J. Edgar Hoover was a personal friend of Ellsberg's father-in-law. Enraged by these reports and by further rumours that Ellsberg was in possession of an even greater cache of other secret documents, Nixon started to cast around for alternative ideas on how to handle the problem. 'If we can't get anyone in this damn government to do something about the problem that may be the most serious one we have, then, by God, we'll do it ourselves', he told John Ehrlichman. 'I want you to set up a little group right here in the White House. Have them get off their tails and find out what's going on and figure out how to stop it.'[125] Ehrlichman responded by summoning one of his most trusted aides, Egil 'Bud' Krogh, to San Clemente on 17 July. Sitting on the sun-drenched patio of the President's office at the Western White House, the thirty-one-year-old Krogh was given two alarming briefings, first by Nixon and then by Ehrlichman. 'I don't think any young person in government could have been more frightened than I was by what I was told', recalled Krogh. 'I came away knowing that I was being asked to deal with a national security crisis of the utmost importance. My mission was simply to find out why these documents had been stolen and what lay behind the theft.'[126]

The President did not give any instructions on the methods needed to carry out this mission. However, such was the intensity of the briefings that Krogh felt he had been given the highest authority to do whatever was necessary. That feeling was shared by David Young, who was seconded from his NSC post as Kissinger's administrative assistant to join the new anti-leak unit. Young, however, remained on the National Security Advisers' payroll for the duration of his partnership with Krogh and reported regularly to Kissinger on what he and his new colleagues were doing.[127]

In the early stages of their research on Ellsberg, Young and Krogh came across enough material to persuade them that desperate measures were necessary to establish the facts about the leak. The Soviet angle was the one that troubled them most, particularly when it was discovered that the source notes of the Pentagon Papers, if analysed by an expert KGB specialist, could jeopardise a whole range of CIA codes and operations. One of the most sensitive of these was the CIA's facility for recording the car-telephone conversations of members of the Politburo. Such revelations at one stage convinced Young and Krogh that Ellsberg was a Soviet spy. They thought he might have been recruited in the 1950s by the notorious Cambridge espionage ring of Philby–Blunt–Burgess–Maclean and others. At the request of the FBI, Britain's security services followed up this lead and made a massive effort to check every aspect of Ellsberg's student days at Cambridge. The result of MI5's investigations were inconclusive.[128]

Desperate in their quest for facts on Ellsberg, Krogh and Young sought assistance from harder men. They recruited G. Gordon Liddy, a former FBI agent working for the Justice Department. Liddy was not the sort of hard man to do things by halves. Within days of joining the team he was recommending that LSD should be put into Ellsberg's soup at a dinner in order to destabilise him. When that idea was turned down Liddy recommended that a 'black bag job' (a surreptitious entry) should be carried out at the office of Ellsberg's psychiatrist, Dr. Lewis Fielding. This recommendation was strongly supported by another new member of the unit, E. Howard Hunt, a former CIA counterintelligence specialist who had been recruited on the recommendation of his friend Charles Colson.

'The Plumbers" as the quartet of Krogh, Young, Hunt and Liddy jokingly called themselves, sent a memo to John Ehrlichman on 11 August requesting approval for their recommendation that 'a covert operation be undertaken to examine all the medical files still held by Ellsberg's psychoanalyst'.[129] Ehrlichman then returned the memorandum to Krogh with the annotation, 'Approved with your assurance that it is not traceable'.[130] He did not consult the President or anyone else before giving this approval.

---

* The name of 'The Plumbers' originated from David Young's grandmother, a lady with a droll sense of humour. On learning that her grandson had been assigned to a White House unit in charge of stopping leaks, she wrote to say that her late husband, who had been a New York plumber, would be proud that David was returning to the family trade. Young was much amused by the letter and replaced the names on his office door with the word 'Plumbers'.

Hunt and Liddy recruited a team of Cuban burglars and broke into Fielding's offices a few days later. They found no files on Ellsberg. To cover their traces they smashed up the office in order to make it look as though they had been thieves after money. They took photographs of their handiwork which they brought back to the Plumbers' headquarters in the Executive Office Building of the White House. Young and Krogh were horrified by the wanton destruction of Fielding's property. They had expected the 'covert operation' to take the form of some mild deception such as posing as the janitor.[131]

'There are some things that happen when your stomach turns over and you know that your whole life is going to change', recalled Bud Krogh. 'When I saw those photographs that was one of those moments for me. I realized that somewhere along the line we had lost touch with reality.'[132] Krogh showed the photographs to Ehrlichman, who said angrily: 'This is far beyond anything I ever authorized.' 'In a way it's far beyond anything I ever authorized either', was his aide's ashamed reply.[133]

Surprisingly, nobody expressed shame or anger to Hunt and Liddy. Young later regretted this. He came to believe that the violent damage to Fielding's office and the photographic record of it was Hunt's way of getting something on the White House for future blackmail purposes.[134] In the light of Hunt's subsequent behaviour, that theory appears credible.

From Nixon's point of view, the episode of the Plumbers marked an unseen turning point in his Presidency. He had not known about the specifics of the Fielding break-in but afterwards he recognised that he had contributed to making it happen. It was another recurrence of the Thomas à Becket and King Henry II syndrome—'Who will rid me of this turbulent priest?' Nixon more or less admitted.this in his memoirs when he wrote:

> I do not believe I was told about the break-in at the time, but it is clear
> that it was at least in part an outgrowth of my sense of urgency about
> discrediting what Ellsberg had done and finding out what he might
> do next. Given the temper of those tense and bitter times and the peril
> I perceived, I cannot say that had I been informed of it beforehand, I
> would have automatically considered it unprecedented, unwarranted,
> or unthinkable.[135]

The trouble was that what the President negatively considered 'not unthinkable' became the positive thinking of Hunt and Liddy. The Fielding break-in by the Plumbers was thus the crossing of the Rubicon. By condoning what the hard men had done, the White House was signalling to them that burglary under the cover of national security was acceptable. From there it was but a small step for Hunt and Liddy to conclude that if the President's men were willing to condone such activity for national security purposes in 1971, it would not be much of a stretch to condone it again in 1972 for political purposes.

Thus the slide towards Watergate began with the misconceived reaction to the Pentagon Papers, whose ripple effects were felt far beyond the actual Fielding break-in. The first such ripple was the change in the White House underground. Before the Plumbers, it had consisted of a group of weak young puppies, like Dean and Huston, running around in circles. After the Plumbers, it was augmented by the two rough, tough pit bull terriers, Hunt and Liddy. It was hardly surprising when the pit bulls and the puppies began working together on the Committee to re-elect the President that the pack got out of control.

Another important ripple effect of the Pentagon Papers drama was its effect on the *Washington Post*, which had followed the *New York Times* in publishing huge extracts from Ellsberg's stolen documents. Nixon had been enraged by both papers but for some reason the brunt of his anger appeared to fall hardest on the *Post*. In addition to fighting a full-scale legal battle against the Administration in the courts, the *Post's* television licences in various parts of the country began to be opposed at Federal Communication Commission hearings in the fall of 1971 by groups of businessmen known to have close links to the President. The move first alarmed and then angered the paper's editor, Ben Bradlee:

> All of us here were scarred by Nixon's reactions to the Pentagon Papers because his actions were so damn mean and hostile. For the first time in the history of the Republic the Government tried to silence the press, not only using the civil doctrine of prior restraint but even the Statute of Treason for God's sake! And when they lost that battle in the courts, they became even meaner and more hostile... At that time the law said that if you owned a TV station you had to have your licence renewed every three years by the FCC. This was usually an automatic procedure but in the fall of 1971 several of our licence renewals were challenged by friends of Nixon, groups organized by Bebe Rebozo and so on. Our stock price nosedived as the word got around that the *Post* was going to lose its TV station income. It was a scary time, and it had an absolutely critical impact

on us internally. From that time on we knew that Nixon hated us and
we reciprocated. Without that, the *Post* would never have behaved so
confidently in its reporting of Watergate.[136]

It is clear from Bradlee's description that both the *Post* and the President were
caught up in the vortex of what Nixon called 'those tense and bitter times'.[137] The
reality was that the importance of Ellsberg's theft of the Pentagon Papers was
wildly exaggerated. Both the press and the White House were at fault here. For
his part, Nixon was unbelievably badly advised about the national security implications of Ellsberg's grave misconduct. On the basis of that advice he overreacted
and his responses had the unforeseeable knock-on effects of transforming the
underground of the White House from a juvenile sideshow to a sinister force; and
of converting the *Washington Post* from an adversary to an enemy. The Plumbers
had sowed the wind. Eighteen months later Nixon would reap the whirlwind.

EIGHTEEN

PEACEMAKING AND ELECTION WINNING

I. THE OPENING TO CHINA

He went to China. These simple words describe the most enduring achievement of Richard Nixon's Presidency and America's most outstanding foreign policy initiative in the postwar period. In one, week-long visit Nixon shifted the global balance of power in the West's favour. It took his internationalist conviction, his uncompromising courage and the strange forces that shaped his character to pull it off. No other President had both the high strategic vision to conceive of such a policy, and the low political cunning to implement it. The United States was fortunate that, when opportunity called, Nixon was in the White House to answer it.

Nixon had been dreaming of making a presidential visit to China for at least five years before he set off on his historic mission to Peking in 1972. He had given his first clear indication that he favoured a US–China rapprochement in his 1967 *Foreign Affairs* article. Soon after becoming President he instructed Kissinger to prepare a study of how to implement such a policy. 'Henry was very surprised at the priority I was giving to China', recalled Nixon,[1] who initially encountered considerable foot-dragging by his National Security Adviser. 'This crazy guy really does want to normalize our relations with China',[2] Kissinger despairingly told his deputy, Colonel Alexander Haig, in the spring of 1971. But the 'crazy'

President kept the pressure up, and slowly made some progress although there were some obstacles, not the least of which were the difficulties in making contact with the Chinese.

Some weeks after Nixon's initiative had begun, the White House became alarmed by intelligence reports suggesting that an attack by Soviet bombers on China's military installations at Lanchow might be imminent. An American message of warning and support to Peking was considered. To Kissinger's chagrin he discovered that there was no way of delivering such a message. There were no backchannels; no reliable third party channels; and of course no official channels because there had been no diplomatic relations between the US and China since 1949. Mercifully, this particular intelligence scare faded, but there could hardly have been a starker example of the dangers in continuing the antagonism between the world's most powerful and most populous nations.[3]

In order to get the message to the Chinese that Washington wanted a new relationship with them, Nixon embarked upon a diplomatic minuet. Its choreography was complicated, involving at least four foreign governments (France, Pakistan, Romania and Norway); two US Ambassadors in Warsaw and Paris conducting secret talks with their Chinese opposite numbers; and other private intermediaries. Nixon orchestrated all the early manoeuvres himself, minimising the role of Kissinger in the preliminary moves, and excluding the State Department from all serious knowledge of what was going on.

One of the reasons why Nixon kept such tight control of the diplomacy was that it involved partners such as de Gaulle, Ceauşescu of Romania, and Yahya Khan of Pakistan, whom he alone could approach. It also required some particularly delicate footwork whenever Taiwan was mentioned, as Chinese pride and philosophy made it almost impossible for them to talk to an American President who had not conceded that there was only one China. On the other hand, the pressures of American domestic politics, expecially those personified by Nixon's own brand of Republicanism, made it almost impossible for any President to abandon the two-China policy and the commitment to Taiwan. This great divide seemed insuperable, but if there was any chance of bridging it, Nixon was the one twentieth-century President sufficiently bold, devious, and right wing to have the chance of pulling it off. As he said in an unguarded moment in his retirement years, 'We could never have brought off the opening to China if we hadn't lied a little; could we?'[4] It was dissimulation in a great cause.

During the geographical and intellectual travels of his wilderness years, Nixon had foreseen his opportunity to break up the old bipolar confrontation between East and West. He regarded the Sino–Soviet split as the most important international development of the postwar era.

In response, he invented 'triangular diplomacy', an ingenious concept balancing the national interest priorities of the three great powers involved.

The Chinese priority was to end their vulnerability to a Soviet attack. They regarded this as a realistic threat after the 1968 Soviet invasion of Czechoslovakia and the subsequent announcement of the Brezhnev Doctrine, which claimed the Kremlin had the right to correct deviationism in other Communist governments by military intervention. With one million Soviet troops on its borders; a large number of Soviet missiles targeted at its cities; and deviationism rampant inside its government, there were good grounds for China's fears. There could not have been a more propitious moment for Peking to consider ending its anti-American isolationism.

The Soviets had their own worries. Their economy was overstretched by the combination of low-level productivity and high-level military commitments. These were on the verge of leaping upwards in cost if the arms race moved on to a new and more expensive generation of nuclear weapons. It was therefore a Kremlin priority to reach agreement with Washington in the Strategic Arms Limitation Talks (SALT), and to persuade the US to lower its trade barriers, thus gaining access to American food and technology exports.

For Nixon to move between the two Communist giants, offering arms reductions and trade to the Soviets and friendship to the Chinese, was a masterstroke of creative foreign policy. In return, he hoped to persuade both countries to cease supplying the North Vietnamese with armaments and to assist him in his efforts to make peace. Yet for all his conceptual thinking about triangular diplomacy, Nixon regarded China on its own as his real priority. 'Even if there had been no Soviet Union, and no Vietnam War, I would still have taken the initiative on China. It just had to be done',[5] he recalled.

The view that it had to be done was not uncommon at that time in some US academic circles, but actually doing it was an operation fraught with political peril. The secret overtures to China made Nixon vulnerable to over-reaction by the Soviets; to alienation from his conservative base of support at home; and to serious trouble from a Congress which contained many staunch supporters of the US–Taiwan alliance.

As far as the Soviets were concerned, Nixon lulled them into a false sense of complacency. He told Ambassador Dobrynin that whatever the United States was doing in China (he did not specify what it was), the Soviets should not be alarmed that he was concerned solely with China and Chinese affairs, and not in having an influence through China on the Soviet Union.[6] This was a case of being economical with the truth, but at the time Moscow appeared to be convinced that nothing of great import would happen.

As for the Republican right wing, Nixon kept them, like everyone else, completely in the dark. When the news broke he maintained that the opening to China did not mean a lessening of US commitment to Taiwan. Nixon was again being economical with the truth, but he knew that his conservative supporters had nowhere else to go. He believed that most of them would eventually accept that he had acted in the best interests of US national security.

Congress was kept in the dark too. This was quintessential Nixon who loved the big play, the big secret and the big surprise. Yet by sending Kissinger on such a momentous undercover mission to Peking, Nixon was implicitly challenging the authority of the legislature to have a say in the formulation of foreign policy. It was a huge risk as Kissinger well realised, writing in his memoirs: 'Having made the decisions without executive or congressional consultation, Nixon had left himself quite naked should anything go wrong; in such lonely decisions he was extremely courageous.'[7]

The chances of Nixon's China policy going wrong in its early stages were far higher than has generally been acknowledged. For most of the period when America's secret diplomacy was at its most active, China's leaders were convulsed in a life and death power struggle. This was the knock-on effect of Mao's Cultural Revolution, when senior political figures were being arrested, imprisoned or killed in large numbers.

It took considerable nerve for Nixon to discount such serious instability within the People's Republic of China, and to press on so determinedly with his initiative.

One other potential problem was the fear of a backlash from Chiang Kai-shek and his US supporters in the China Lobby. Nixon had considerable personal regard for the aging generalissimo, who had been politically gracious to him as Vice President, and commercially generous to him as a lawyer at Nixon Mudge seeking the lucrative Pepsi Cola franchise. A sudden pang about Chiang Kai-shek's sensitivities seems to have struck Nixon when the China initiative was on the verge of becoming public knowledge. During the first week of July 1971 he asked his old friend Don Kendall, the Chairman of Pepsi Cola, to visit Taiwan and to deliver an oral message to the generalissimo: 'Whatever the future may hold, I'll never forget my old friend.'[8] Kendall duly recited these cryptic words to Chiang Kai-shek, who nodded gravely but said nothing. Kendall had no idea of their significance, until a week later, when it was announced that the President of the United States would be visiting Peking.

The story of how Nixon communicated with the Chinese leaders and despatched Henry Kissinger to the Middle Kingdom in conditions of high subterfuge and secrecy is a gripping tale. The fullest version of it is to be found in Kissinger's memoirs *White House Years*, an account which not uncharacteristically gives fullest credit to the author. However, even while Kissinger was en route for his secret destination, Nixon was calling the shots with last-minute signals of his own to the Chinese.

Kissinger had left Washington on 1 July with an itinerary that took him to Saigon, Bangkok and New Delhi before reaching Islamabad, where he would feign a stomach upset and purport to spend two days in bed. During this 'illness' period of 9–11 July he would be flown to Peking. Before departure he had received the most detailed presidential negotiating instructions, ranging from the cards he should play in the game of triangular diplomacy, to the blocking moves he should insist upon to prevent Democratic presidential hopefuls, such as Senators Kennedy and Muskie, from being issued with visas for China during the run-up to the election. However, after Kissinger was airborne, Nixon became convinced that the Chinese leaders might need certain further reassurances of US intentions.

Accordingly at a presidential media briefing in Kansas on 6 July, scheduled to be devoted to the subject of domestic policy, Nixon unexpectedly began making unscripted comments about China. He told the assembled journalists:

> The goal of US policy must be in the long term ending the isolation of Mainland China and a normalization of our relations with Mainland China...Mainland China outside the world community completely isolated with its leaders not in communication with world leaders, would be a danger to the whole world that would be unacceptable. So consequently this step must be taken now.[9]

Amazingly the entire White House press corps missed the significance of these comments. The same mistake was not made in Peking, which received a transcript of them through an approved channel. On 10 July Premier Chou En-lai embarrassed Kissinger by asking detailed questions about this presidential speech which the National Security Adviser had not read.

Chou En-lai was particularly interested in the Kansas City transcript because it contained Nixon's futuristic prophecy of a multipolar economic world in which China would have a seat at the top table as one of 'five great economic superpowers'.[10]

This well-timed shift in emphasis by Nixon from military to economic strategy in Sino–American relations showed that he had a vision fully in accord with the latest Chinese thinking. In subsequent meetings with the Americans, Chou En-lai deprecated any references to China as a military superpower, well understanding that for the foreseeable future his country had no hope of catching up with US or Soviet military technology. However, China as an economic giant was a more likely prospect, especially if helped towards that goal by American trade and investment as the President was now hinting. In accomplishing the final stage of the US diplomatic breakthrough to China, Nixon's public intervention from Kansas City was just as important as Kissinger's secret discussions in Peking.

Apart from the gap in his knowledge about the Kansas City press briefing, Kissinger's negotiations with Chou En-lai were highly successful. They allowed Nixon to stun the world with a 15 July television broadcast lasting for just three minutes and twenty seconds in which he announced that he had accepted the Chinese leader's invitation to visit Peking 'to seek the normalization of relations between the two countries and also to exchange views on questions of concern between the two sides'.[11]

Response to the announcement in a war-weary America was amazed but awestruck. 'The politics of surprise leads through the Gates of Astonishment into the Kingdom of Hope', wrote columnist Max Lerner.[12] In the diplomatic capitals of the world, with the exception of outraged Taipei and affronted Tokyo, there was an immediate realisation that the news presaged a positive change in the global power structure. In London, the former British Prime Minister Harold Macmillan recalled the historic comment of the nineteenth-century statesman George Canning: 'I have brought the new world into existence to redress the balance of the old', and added, 'Nixon has reversed Canning. He's brought the oldest civilisation in the world back into the game to redress the new Russian empire.'[13]

The preparations for the President's trip to China were a mixture of global statesmanship and domestic electioneering. Nixon immersed himself in briefing papers and books, annotating and memorising with an intensity equalled only in the preparations for his first Soviet visit in 1959.

He also saw a succession of China experts of whom the most impressive was the great French writer and philosopher André Malraux. He captivated Nixon with a brilliant discourse on Chairman Mao. 'You will be dealing with a colossus, but a colossus facing death', he told Nixon. 'You will meet a man who has had a fantastic destiny and who believes that he is acting out the last act of his lifetime. You may think he is talking to you, but in truth he will be addressing Death.' Malraux also told Nixon that he was setting out on a journey into the unknown:

'I think of the sixteenth-century explorers, who set out for a specific objective but often arrived at an entirely different discovery. What you are going to do, Mr. President, might well have a totally different outcome from whatever is anticipated.'[14] Nixon was riveted by Malraux's insights, which were on his mind as Air Force One rolled down the runway, bound for Peking, on 17 February 1972. He wrote later, 'As the plane gathered speed and then took to the air, I thought of Malraux's words. We were embarking upon a voyage of philosophical discovery as uncertain, and in some respects as perilous, as the voyages of geographical discovery of a much earlier time.'[15]

Running in parallel with these noble thoughts were Nixon's more cynical calculations that the voyage might also provide a unique public relations and election-winning opportunity. At his direction, an overwhelming amount of White House effort had been devoted to the media coverage of the visit. This familiar obsession with presentation for once succeeded brilliantly. Peking, thirteen hours behind New York, was perfectly located for maximum, primetime live reporting on the evening and breakfast TV news programmes. Although the Chinese must initially have been bemused by the strange scheduling and locationing requests from Haldeman's legions of advance men, they gave their co-operation to the full and the results were stunning. From the first moment when Nixon came out alone from his aircraft for a deeply symbolic handshake with Chou En-lai, with the Red Army band playing the Star Spangled Banner, and a 350-man guard of honour saluting, it was clear that this was going to be the television political spectacular to beat all others. So, indeed, it proved. With presidential talks, toasts and tourism set against backdrops like the Great Wall, the Ming Tombs, the Forbidden City, Hangchow, and the Great Hall of the People, the viewers at home were mesmerised.

In one sense, the medium truly was the message. With the Chinese and American leaders appearing continuously together on the world's television screens, warmly toasting one another at banquet after banquet while the Red Army musicians played 'Home on the Range' or 'America the Beautiful', it became clear to every viewer that a vital new international relationship was in the process of being formed.

Nixon instinctively understood the importance of this symbolism, not just for the American electorate but for the audiences in the Kremlin and in China itself. What really mattered at this stage was that a quarter of a century of alienation between the United States and the People's Republic of China was seen to be ending. The two symbols that counted most were the handshake with Chou En-lai and the meeting with Chairman Mao Tse-tung.

One of the best-kept secrets of Nixon's China initiative was that he took off from Washington without any promise of an appointment with Mao. The absence of such a commitment from his hosts baffled and disturbed him. For the President not to meet the Chairman would be interpreted as a massive snub on both sides of the bamboo curtain. The impact of the visit would have been diminished and perhaps seriously damaged. Nevertheless, Nixon decided to take the gamble.

It has since become known that the reason for Chinese evasiveness on the Mao–Nixon meeting was the Chairman's health. Throughout the spring of 1972 Mao was critically ill with a respiratory infection and complications from his stroke. He was still bedridden, surrounded by nurses, oxygen canisters and ventilation equipment on the morning of 17 February when Nixon's plane touched down in Peking. But fired up by the excitement of the occasion, Mao found the will to struggle out of bed; to order the removal of the medical equipment from his home and to issue the command: 'Bring Nixon here now.'[16]

In their respective memoirs, Nixon and Kissinger have waxed lyrical about the wit and wisdom of the Chinese leader at this first meeting. It is difficult to see why from the printed exchanges, which consisted largely of jests and generalities. Mao indulged in much heavy-handed humour about Chiang Kai-shek's bandits and Kissinger's girlfriends. Continuing in this jocular vein, he told Nixon that he liked 'rightists' and added, 'I voted for you during your last election.' 'I think the most important thing to note is that in America, at least this time, those on the right can do what those on the left can only talk about', was Nixon's pointed response.[17]

For all his alertness and banter, Mao was not well enough to maintain a substantive conversation, tiring after some fifty minutes had passed. This was just enough for Nixon to set the agenda by referring to the Soviet threat and by making it clear that their shared perception of it was more important than their ideological differences. 'What brings us together,' Nixon told Mao, 'is a recognition of a new situation in the world and a recognition on our part that what is important is not a nation's internal political philosophy. What is important is its policy toward the rest of the world and toward us.'[18]

Mao did not make a particularly significant reply to these preliminary overtures. However, by the warmth of his response (elicited mainly by Nixon judiciously quoting from the Chairman's sayings and writings), he stamped his leader's seal of approval on the visit and the new *entente*. From then on, all the Chinese officials, from Chou En-lai downwards, seemed to redouble their efforts to accommodate the extraordinary public relations and political requirements of their American guests. The result was pageantry on an epic scale in public, and in private the first stirrings of the international realignment that was to follow.

Nixon's long negotiating sessions with Chou En-lai were more in the form of two disparate monologues than a dialogue. On most regional issues, such as North and South Korea, the Philippines, the security pact with Japan, the two leaders could only agree to disagree. This was the formula used in the Shanghai communiqué, a most original diplomatic document which avoided the usual bland newspeak of international summitry and instead spelled out both sides' profound disagreements on the issues that divided them.

There were, however, two crucial areas of understanding. The first, and most delicate one from the US viewpoint, was on Taiwan. Here Nixon and Kissinger performed a verbal conjuring trick of consummate skill, which can best be appreciated by quoting the full words of the relevant paragraph in the US communiqué.

> The United States acknowledges that all Chinese on either side of the Taiwan Strait maintain there is but one China, and that Taiwan is a part of China. The United States Government does not challenge that position. It reaffirms its interest in a peaceful settlement of the Taiwan question by the Chinese themselves. With this prospect in mind it affirms the ultimate objective of the withdrawal of all US forces and military installations from Taiwan. In the meantime, it will progressively reduce its forces and military installations on Taiwan as the tension in the area diminishes.

Decoded, what the paragraph meant for the Chinese was that, if they reduced their support for the North Vietnamese, the US would not think it necessary to maintain as large a force in Taiwan. The final phrase 'as the tension in the area diminishes' was the key to the code. Many latched onto this section of the communiqué, claiming that it amounted to a sell-out on Taiwan, but Nixon's strategy was more subtle than this criticism suggests. In fact, the opening to China had enhanced Taiwan's security by complicating China's options. Now, if the Chinese attacked Taiwan, they would lose their new and valuable relationship with the US. It was Nixon's belief—and history would seem to have confirmed it—that the Chinese had invested so much in this relationship that they would never think it worth their while to take offensive action against Taiwan.

The second understanding concerned the Soviet Union, whose leaders must have been watching the week's developments in Peking with rising apprehension.

The basis of the Chinese–American rapprochement was that old axiom, 'The enemy of my enemy is my friend.'

In that spirit, Nixon had assured Chou En-lai in their private talks that he was ready to 'turn like a cobra on the Russians'[19] if they attempted the military domination of Asia. This pledge was affirmed in diplomatic language by the sentence in the communiqué that stated that neither America nor China 'should seek hegemony in the Asia-Pacific region and each is opposed to efforts by any other country or group of countries to establish such hegemony'. Behind the opaque phraseology lay a magnificent achievement of statesmanship. A peaceful new alliance had been created. Its purpose was to deter Soviet expansionism with a realigned balance of power, and to bring permanent peace to the Asia-Pacific region.

As the principal architect of this new Chinese–American relationship, Nixon had every right to feel euphoric as he signed the Shanghai communiqué. 'This was the week that changed the world', he declared as he raised his glass to honour his hosts on the final night of his visit. The words were not an exaggeration. China was where Nixon's peacemaking ideals and political skills had combined to the greatest effect. It was his finest hour.

II. DÉTENTE WITH THE SOVIET UNION

Nixon came to power more feared by the Kremlin than any previous President of the United States. With his track record of unmasking Hiss as a Soviet spy; worsting Khrushchev in the 1959 Moscow 'Kitchen Debate'; and championing the anti-Communist cause in twelve election campaigns since 1946, Nixon was the American leader the Russians least wanted to see in the White House. However, once he got there, he surprised them. The more the Soviets dealt with Nixon during his Presidency, the more they grew to respect him. They found him, to borrow Margaret Thatcher's phrase on Gorbachev, a man they could do business with. The business accomplished included a major breakthrough in arms control treaties; a wide range of mutual cooperation agreements; and a generally improved atmosphere of détente. Although there were several rough passages in the relationship between Moscow and Washington before these goals were reached, it is interesting to note how positive the official Soviet Government view of the Nixon Presidency became in retrospect.

'We rate highly that period in Soviet–American relations as the most fruitful and productive in the postwar years', the Soviet Ambassador to Washington stated in a paper presented to the Hofstra University Conference in 1987. 'We cannot fail to pay tribute to Nixon's far-sightedness in matters of foreign policy strategy.

In spite of all the existing constraints at the time, in spite of the conservatism and anti-Communist bias of President Nixon himself, the agreements and treaties concluded between the US and USSR between 1970 and 1974 signify a substantial progress on the road of strengthening international security and mutual trust.'[20]

This Soviet verdict is now widely accepted by all except a handful of ultra-conservative critics. Nixon came to earn it because in matters of superpower diplomacy he was both a clever conceptualist and a ruthless realist. In his wilderness years he had devoted much intellectual effort to various theories of how to deal with the Soviets, and had come up with three concepts: strategic sufficiency; linkage; and triangular diplomacy.

At his first presidential press conference on 27 January 1969, Nixon stated that, under his leadership, the United States would seek 'sufficiency not superiority' in nuclear weapons. The phrase marked a historic change from the defence policy of postwar administrations for it had been an article of faith with every President from Truman to Johnson that American nuclear supremacy over the Soviets must be maintained. A few lone voices had criticised the pointlessness of seeking such an ascendancy in the age of nuclear parity, notably Senator William Fulbright, who made a celebrated speech attacking America's 'arrogance of power'. Nixon was the first President to put forward a practical alternative. This did not mean he was about to give something away for nothing. Knowing that the Soviets were worried by the cost to their economy of escalating the arms race, Nixon merely signalled his willingness to enter into arms limitation negotiations. However, he qualified this at his first press conference by saying that any such negotiations would be more productive if they were conducted 'in a way and at a time that will promote, if possible, progress on outstanding political problems at the same time'.[21]

At his first meeting with Soviet Ambassador Anatoly Dobrynin, on 17 February 1969, Nixon made the same point more explicitly, saying 'History makes it clear that wars result not so much from arms, or even from arms races, as they do from underlying political differences and political problems. So I think it is incumbent on us, when we begin strategic arms talks, to do what we can in a parallel way to defuse critical political situations like the Middle East and Vietnam and Berlin, where there is a danger that arms might be put to use.'[22]

Having thus propounded the doctrine of linkage, Nixon waited in vain for a Soviet response. In Berlin, in the Middle East, and above all in Vietnam, the White House could discern nothing but the usual unhelpful intransigence from Moscow. This situation led to one of the toughest Soviet–American diplomatic exchanges on record, when Nixon saw Ambassador Dobrynin on 20 October and told him how disappointed he was with the lack of progress in US–Soviet relations. 'As of today I have been in this office for nine months. The babies should have been born by now. Instead there have been several miscarriages', began Nixon, listing the Soviets' sins of commission and omission, particularly in Vietnam where he believed they were obstructing the search for peace. 'Mr. Ambassador, I want you to understand that the Soviet Union is going to be stuck with me for the next three years and three months, and during all that time I will keep in mind what is being done right now, today. The whole world wants us to get together. I, too, want nothing so much as to have my administration remembered as a watershed in American and Soviet relations. But let me repeat that we will not hold still for being diddled to death in Vietnam.' On that note Nixon terminated the discussion and asked Kissinger to show Dobrynin out. When he returned, Kissinger said, 'I wager that no one has ever talked to him that way in his entire career. It was extraordinary! No President has ever laid it on the line to them like that.'[23]

Nixon followed up his chewing out of Dobrynin by temporarily escalating the arms race. He asked Congress to vote for an antiballistic missile system (ABM), arguing that it was essential for America's present defence to counterbalance the existing Soviet missile threat, and that for America's future diplomacy ABM might be a vital bargaining chip in arms-control negotiations.

To a Democratic Congress heavily infected by anti-war sentiment, these arguments were not entirely persuasive. Nixon, on the other hand, saw the ABM vote as a litmus test of America's moral resolve and strategic credibility. He fought for congressional support like the proverbial tiger, nuzzling, snarling, and even occasionally roaring. 'Make sure that all our guys are there all the time. Don't let anyone get sick. Don't let anyone go to the bathroom until it's all over', he shouted to his congressional aide Bryce Harlow on the eve of the vote.[24]

Such dramatic measures were justified. After a cliffhanging debate, the ABM proposal was approved in the Senate by one vote—that of the Vice President. Nixon had secured his first big bargaining chip. His victory, as he had foreseen, greatly discomfited the Soviet leaders as they now had to direct substantial resources to increase their own ABM construction programmes.

Once the Kremlin realised they were dealing with a resolute President ready to fight for America's national interests with the same tenacity that characterised their own approach to Soviet interests, Moscow's attitude changed. The Dobrynin–Kissinger channel gradually became the conduit for a flow of give-and-take negotiations of singular creativity. Because of Nixon's distrust of the State Department, and Kissinger's antipathy towards its leading arms-control negotiator, Gerard Smith, the White House circumvented the official Strategic Arms Limitation Talks (SALT). Conventional diplomacy was replaced by cloak-and-dagger deal-making. Kissinger was the star of these clandestine bargaining sessions. He enjoyed comparing himself to the peripatetic nineteenth-century Austrian Foreign Minister Metternich, but Nixon, in more down-to-earth language, likened his National Security adviser to 'a rag merchant, who starts by haggling at 50 per cent in order to get to 25 per cent. That's why he's so good with the Russians.'[25]

In May 1971, after months of haggling and a personal message from Nixon to General Secretary Leonid Brezhnev, the Soviets made a major concession. They agreed that the arms control negotiations should cover both offensive and defensive weapons, and not merely mutual ABM limitations as Moscow had previously insisted. This breakthrough led to a flurry of diplomatic activity, and the decks were cleared for a Moscow summit in September. The Soviets then proceeded to become obstructive and to indulge in delaying tactics, eventually requesting a postponement. By agreeable coincidence this request arrived when Kissinger was on his way to Peking. He recorded his reaction in his memoirs: 'The Soviets had unwittingly done us an enormous favor; they had outfoxed themselves. The Kremlin's reply freed us from the complexity of managing two parallel summits. Moscow could not blame us for opening first to Peking. We could now complete our design with a minimum of friction.'[26]

Nixon's grand design of triangular diplomacy, when revealed to the world with his 15 July announcement of the opening to China, produced a marked improvement in most aspects of US–Soviet relations.

By 19 July Dobrynin was back in Kissinger's office meekly asking whether the summit the Kremlin had just postponed could now be brought forward, ahead of the President's meeting with the Chinese leaders. It could not. Nixon insisted that his visits to the Communist capitals would take place in the order in which they had been announced. He went to Peking in February and to Moscow in May.

Apart from the fact (and the television coverage) of the Peking visit, Nixon played the China card by not playing it. He assured the Soviets that the new Chinese–American relationship was not hostile to them. As Kissinger has described this tactic, 'This is the conventional pacifier of diplomacy by which the target of a maneuver is given a formal reassurance intended to unnerve as much as to calm, and which would defeat its purpose if it were actually believed.'[27] Having in this way raised the Soviets' anxiety threshold, Nixon said nothing to exploit it. The atmosphere this created produced great progress in the negotiations. In September 1971, an agreement was finally reached on one of the most dangerous flashpoints of the Cold War: Berlin. The Soviet Union guaranteed unhindered access to West Berlin and agreed to allow West Germany to represent the West Berliners. There were also breakthroughs on SALT and on other bilateral negotiations in areas such as the environment, direct communications links and weapons on the seabed.

In the period between the two summits, the North Vietnamese Army invaded South Vietnam. On 30 March, 120,000 NVA troops, equipped with Soviet tanks and artillery, surged across the internationally recognised limits of the Demilitarised Zone (DMZ).

As the invasion forces carried out terrible atrocities and destruction deep in the South Vietnamese heartlands, Nixon was impaled on the horns of a dilemma. If he did not support the South Vietnamese with heavy bombing of the NVA's troops and supplies, a US ally might well be defeated. But if he did escalate the war by a new surge of bombing, he would face the probable cancellation of the Moscow summit by the Soviets and a consequent backlash of increased anti-war protests on the domestic front.

In a deliberate move to increase the pressure on Washington for a soft response to the NVA invasion, Brezhnev sent Nixon a letter on 1 May warning him against taking any actions in Vietnam that might hurt the chance of a successful summit. On the same day, pressure of a different kind came from Saigon in a report by General Abrams. He advised the President that the South Vietnamese were crumbling in the face of the NVA onslaught. Quang Tri province had fallen to the Communists; the battle for Hué was about to begin; and there were now serious doubts whether the increasingly well-supplied invasion could be repulsed at all.

1–8 May 1972 was one of the darkest periods of Nixon's Presidency. It could easily have become another 'week that changed the world', but this time to America's detriment. If Nixon had gone along with the soft response option suggested by Brezhnev's letter, South Vietnam would have been defeated; US foreign policy would have lost all credibility; and the Moscow summit would have been an exercise in Soviet triumphalism. Nixon alone saw this scenario of impending doom with clarity, and realised that he was caught between a rock and a hard place: 'It was hard to see how I could go to the summit and be clinking glasses with Brezhnev while Soviet tanks were rumbling through Hué or Quang Tri. That would show callousness, or weakness, or both. For us to cancel the summit, however, would inevitably be criticized as an impulsive action that dashed the hopes for progress toward a more peaceful world.'[28]

Against this sombre background, Nixon evaluated his political and military options. Eventually he took one of the boldest and most effective decisions of his Presidency. He resolved to take dramatic military action in support of South Vietnam and to gamble that the Soviets would not respond to it by cancelling the summit.

Nixon's plan was to cripple the North Vietnamese invasion by destroying the supply lines at the ports and railroads by which Soviet military equipment was being delivered in huge quantities to the NVA for a further surge into South Vietnam. To achieve this, he ordered the blockade by mining of Haiphong and other North Vietnamese ports. He also approved plans for bombing Hanoi's supply depots and the railway lines leading to them. This would be a huge escalation in American military involvement in Vietnam. The advice from the defence experts was that it would succeed in halting the NVA invasion by cutting off its supplies. The advice from just about everyone else (the CIA; the State Department; the NSC; Henry Kissinger; and most of the Cabinet with the exceptions of Vice President Agnew and Treasury Secretary John Connally) was that the repercussions would cause the Soviets to cancel the summit. Nixon nevertheless remained adamant that not losing the war was the vital priority. As he told his divided Cabinet:

> The real question is whether the Americans give a damn any-more…If you follow *Time*, the *Washington Post*, the *New York Times* and the three networks, you could say that the US has done enough. 'Let's get out; let's make a deal with the Russians and pull in our horns.' The US would cease to be a military and diplomatic power. If that happened, then the US would look inward towards itself and remove itself from the world. Every non-Communist nation in the world would live in terror. If the US is strong enough and willing to use its strength, then the world will remain half Communist rather than becoming entirely Communist.[29]

At 9 p.m. on the evening of 8 May, Nixon made a nationwide TV broadcast to the nation. It was one of his most subtly crafted addresses, showing the iron fist to the North Vietnamese and the velvet glove to the Soviets.

'There is only one way to stop the killing', he said. 'That is to keep the weapons of war out of the hands of the international outlaws of North Vietnam.' He announced the mining of all entrances to North Vietnamese ports and the bombing of railway lines and military targets. To the Soviets his tone was conciliatory.

'We respect the Soviet Union as a great power. We recognize the right of the Soviet Union to defend its interests when they are threatened. The Soviet Union in turn must recognize our right to defend our interests.'

After making the point that much had been achieved in recent US–Soviet negotiations, he appealed for new progress: 'Let us not slide back toward the dark shadows of a previous age. We do not ask you to sacrifice your principles, or your friends, but neither should you permit Hanoi's intransigence to blot out the prospects we together have so patiently prepared. We, the United States and the Soviet Union, are on the threshold of a new relationship that can serve not only the interests of our two countries, but the cause of world peace. We are prepared to continue to build up this relationship. The responsibility is yours if we fail to do so.'[30]

In spite of these sentences, Washington opinion was virtually unanimous in its view that the Kremlin would cancel the 20 May summit. Inside the Government and the Congress, every Soviet expert, real or self-appointed, agreed with this assessment. In the media the reaction was close to apoplexy. Nixon was condemned by all the TV networks and the East-coast newspapers. The pack was led by the *New York Times*, which urged Congress to cut off all funds for the war to 'save the President from himself and the nation from disaster'[31] and by NBC, whose Moscow correspondent reported that Nixon's decision to mine Haiphong would 'practically kill prospects of a summit'.[32]

Fortunately, the Soviet leaders were more restrained than the American journalists. Nixon had judged the mood in Moscow with exquisite precision. After a brief hesitation and an argument in the Politburo, the Kremlin's plans to receive the American President stood firm. The Politburo member who had pushed for the summit to be cancelled, Pyotr Shelest, was demoted from his post as Ukrainian Party Chief. A day or two later, when attending a birthday party in honour of the Army Chief of Staff, Marshall Matvey Zakharov, Brezhnev was heard to deride Shelest saying: 'After Nixon went to Peking we had no choice. Now that we have a situation when the Americans are moving closer to China, how can we shut the door in front of their noses?'[33]

Brezhnev's remark illustrated the Soviets' greatest anxiety. Now that Nixon had invented triangular diplomacy, it would be alarming for them to be left out of the triangle. A Washington–Peking relationship not balanced by a Moscow–Washington relationship would be a nightmare for the Kremlin leaders. Moreover, if they turned their back not only on triangular diplomacy, but also on Nixon's two other concepts of sufficiency and linkage, the cost to the Soviet economy could be horrendous. Moscow needed a strategic arms limitation agreement for financial as well as for military reasons. It needed the trade, technology, and communications deals that would be linked to the signing of the SALT treaty. There were a range of lesser bilateral treaties, scheduled for signing at the summit, which would also be lost if cancellation occurred. For all these reasons it is easy to see with hindsight why the Politburo underreacted to the escalation of the Vietnam war by the US in response to the NVA invasion. Nixon alone understood their reasons and foresaw the outcome of their internal argument. In so doing he had paved the way for a second triumph in superpower diplomacy. On 20 May he became the first President of the United States to go to Moscow,* an achievement which greatly appealed to his enthusiasm for 'firsts' that made history.

He was installed in splendour on an entire floor of the Grand Palace inside the Kremlin. Within an hour of his arrival he was alone with Brezhnev and an interpreter. The bear-like toughness and sharp intelligence of the Soviet leader impressed Nixon, who wrote in this diary, 'Like an American labor leader, he has what it takes, and we can make no greater mistake than to rate him either as a fool or simply an unintelligent brute.'[34]

The diary comment underlines an important element in Nixon's dealings with Communist leaders. He usually respected them, never underestimated them, and always treated them as his political equals.

'One of the key ingredients in Nixon's success as a negotiator with the Soviets was that he never gave them any sense that Americans felt superior', says Dimitri Simes, who in 1972 was a Soviet policy adviser at Moscow's Institute of World Economy. 'He handled the top men in the Politburo in the smartest possible way. He was tough but never polemical. He didn't bother them with moralizing or by preaching at them like President Carter did. He spoke to them in the language they understood, of national self interest and realism—and always with respect.'[35]

The Peking summit had been all about the mood and atmospherics of the new relationship. In Moscow the summit was one of greater substance with SALT and other significant agreements on the agenda. Finalising and signing these agreements, was comparatively easy because the basic work had already been done so thoroughly by the negotiators. From Nixon's point of view he had to be watchful that the Soviets did not try to pull any last-minute tricks to change the basic principles that were in place. He also had to create a working relationship with Brezhnev that would further enlarge the areas of mutual trust and détente between the two governments. In both objectives he was successful.

---

* He was the second President to go to the Soviet Union, the first being Franklin D. Roosevelt, who went to Yalta in 1945.

True to form, the Soviet leaders did put Nixon to one or two sharp tests during the summit. At one point during the first session of negotiations, Brezhnev casually cut 300 kilometres from the agreed limits on how far the new Soviet ABM systems would be situated from Moscow. Nixon immediately pounced on that one, and without further argument Brezhnev reverted to the original figure as if no trick had been attempted.

The next Soviet manoeuvre was on Vietnam. At the end of a day of good-humoured visits and discussions, Brezhnev suggested a short, private meeting just before dinner in his dacha, almost as if he was offering an aperitif. Instead it turned out to be a stagey confrontation on Vietnam. 'I momentarily thought of Dr. Jekyll and Mr. Hyde when Brezhnev, who had just been laughing and slapping me on the back, started shouting angrily',[36] Nixon recalled. The row consisted of three hours of emotional tirades from Brezhnev, Kosygin and Podgorny on the evils of US involvement in Vietnam, delivered by yelling, table-thumping, angry stalking around the room, and with insults thrown in such as 'Barbaric!' or 'Just like the Nazis!'[37] Dinner had to wait.

Nixon, a man who could sometimes lose his temper under small provocations, maintained an impassive demeanour, remaining almost completely silent apart from the occasional icy interjection. 'Are you threatening, here?'[38] he asked after one particularly savage blast from Brezhnev, which brought a temporary halt to the invective.

Eventually the President of the United States was allowed to speak. With the calm precision of an experienced debater, Nixon firmly rebutted all the Soviet's noisy arguments point by point. His central theme was that, since becoming President, he had withdrawn about 500,000 troops from Vietnam; he had shown great restraint and flexibility in his peace-seeking efforts; it was only the North Vietnamese invasion which had compelled him to meet force with strong action. It was a cool and effective performance, much admired by Kissinger, who praised his chief in his memoirs for behaving 'with remarkable dignity throughout'.[39]

This extraordinary session may well have been a charade for the purposes of sending a record to Hanoi. For when the Soviet leaders had exhausted their stock of indignant theatricals, the mood suddenly changed from fury to joviality as if a magic wand had been waved, and at 11 p.m. the party sat down to a splendid dinner amidst jokes, toasts, and the cheeriest of atmospheres.

The night was, however, still young. At 12.30 a.m. Kissinger and Foreign Minister Gromyko met in the Kremlin to resolve the critical questions still standing in the way of the proposed SALT agreement. This negotiating session went so badly that at 2.15 a.m. Kissinger returned to Nixon's quarters in the Grand Palace with the news that the Soviets would not make any concessions on limiting the size of their missile silos (which meant they would be able to place far larger ballistic missiles in the existing SS-9 sites) or on the expansion of their nuclear submarine building programme. Nixon received these tidings when he was having a back massage from his osteopath. He also heard that there was trouble among congressional conservatives back at home after leaks from the Pentagon about the SALT details. His reaction was to hang tough on both fronts. He would stick to the proposed agreement now under fire from critics at home; he would make no further concessions on missile silos or submarines. Those who witnessed the scene of this decision making process have given accounts of it verging on hyperbole:

'He took one of the most fateful decisions of his Presidency, and of the postwar generation, there on the massage table', wrote William Safire, quoting Nixon as saying, 'Go to your negotiations, Henry. Do the best you can. But we don't have to settle this week.'[40] Kissinger's version is similar: 'Lying naked on the rubbing table, Nixon made one of the more courageous decisions of his Presidency... He would not be swayed by politics at home; and he would not be pushed by the Soviets beyond what I had suggested. Nixon took a heroic position from a decidedly unheroic posture.'[41]

The message from the massage table succeeded. At a meeting of the Politburo two days later, the Soviet government agreed to accept the American final terms. The way was now clear for signing the first arms control agreement of the thermonuclear age.

Although Nixon was subsequently criticised for not fully understanding the technical details of the armaments concessions he was making; and for failing to drive a harder bargain, such comments were irrelevant nit-picking when seen alongside the magnitude of his accomplishment. The ABM treaty he signed in Moscow was the first step towards an ending of the nuclear arms race. The two superpowers had agreed to set limits on their power of mutual destruction. This principle, and the verification and reduction procedures which accompanied it, changed the climate in the age of nuclear terror.

It is interesting to speculate on what might have happened if there had been no such breakthrough. The Soviet Ambassador to Washington in his 1987 speech to the Hofstra Conference offered a chilling scenario in response to a question on this point when he said, 'Had there been no ABM treaty it would be difficult even to say at what level of the nuclear arms race the Soviet Union and the United States would find themselves now, or whether you and we would exist at all.'[42]

Crucially important though it was, the ABM treaty should be seen as the first step in a much wider process of détente. At the Moscow summit, and in subsequent months, a range of ground-breaking accords and agreements were signed. The most important of these was the Interim Agreement on Strategic Missiles (known as SALT 1), which froze the levels of strategic missiles to those actually existing or under construction. It was accompanied by an agreement on 'basic principles of mutual relations between the US and USSR', the first legal framework for co-operation between the two superpowers. From this flowed a wide range of subsidiary agreements on matters such as the exploration and peaceful use of outer space (which culminated in the 1975 Apollo-Soyuz docking); the prevention of incidents on the high seas; the prohibition of weapons on the sea bed; the exploration of oceans; co-operation on environmental protection; joint-initiatives in science, technology and health care; the establishment of new trade and communication links; and the peaceful use of atomic energy.

These agreements set a completely new tone, not only in US–Soviet relations, but in international relationships. The world was becoming a safer place as the threat of nuclear war was replaced by greater co-operation, openness and mutual understanding. Nixon, ever the realist, was not particularly starry-eyed about his achievements in the Soviet Union, seeing them only as a useful beginning. In retrospect, they look much more important than that. By implementing his concepts of sufficiency, linkage and triangular diplomacy, Nixon had done more than any other statesman to bring the Soviet Union in from the cold. He had laid the foundations for the era of peace between the superpowers which still endures today.

III. THE 1972 ELECTION

By the end of May 1972, Nixon was assured of re-election. His superpower summitry in Peking and Moscow had won him great popularity at home. His stewardship of the economy, although marked by some uncharacteristic zigzags into wage and price controls during 1971, had come good. Inflation was down to 2.7 per cent; GNP was growing at the rate of 6.3 per cent; real incomes were rising at 4 per cent; Federal taxes were down by 20 per cent since 1969 for an average family; and the stock market was rising steadily to the 1,000 point all-time high it reached by election day. This combination of peace and prosperity was virtually unbeatable. If Nixon had any re-election worries they focused on two unpredictable factors: events in Vietnam and the third-party candidacy of George Wallace.

The course of the war in Vietnam could easily have shattered the morale of the American people and the electoral prospects of the President. Unlike some of his closest advisers, Nixon was quick to appreciate that the NVA's spring invasion raised the nightmare possibility of both a military and a political débâcle. As the South Vietnamese forces crumbled in the face of Hanoi's offensive, he wrote in his diary of 30 March:

> Both Haldeman and Henry seem to have an idea—which I think is mistaken—that even if we fail in Vietnam we can still survive politically. I have no illusions whatever on that score, however. The US will not have a credible foreign policy if we fail, and I will have to assume the responsibility for that development.[43]

This blunt realism, so characteristic of Richard Nixon, was responsible for the biggest gamble of his career. He had staked the Moscow summit, the security of South Vietnam, the future of his Presidency and the credibility of the United States on his judgement that by mining North Vietnam ports and bombing its supply lines, he could halt the NVA invasion. The gamble succeeded, not only in Vietnam and Moscow, but with the American voters. Despite the vehement denunciations of his liberal critics, Nixon had the public behind him. A Harris poll taken three months after the blockade had begun found that 55 per cent supported continued heavy bombing of North Vietnam; 64 per cent supported the mining of Haiphong Harbour; and 74 per cent thought it was important that South Vietnam should not fall into the hands of the Communists. War-weary though they were, it appeared that the American people preferred Nixon's policy of fighting on for peace with honour rather than the liberals' alternative of peace through surrender. Once that trend of public support was clear, it denied the President's opponents their only strong card for the election.

The wild card was Governor George Wallace. All the polls confirmed that his potential third-party candidacy consistently attracted between 9 and 13 per cent of the vote, no matter what successes Nixon enjoyed in economic or foreign policy. The early primaries suggested that Wallace could deny the President victory over the Democrats in a number of crucial Northeastern states, thus making it difficult for him to achieve the 270 electoral college votes he needed for certain re-election. This spectre of a hung result haunted the White House until Wallace's bandwagon was violently halted when a madman shot the Alabama Governor while he was addressing a rally at Laurel, Maryland on 15 May. Wallace was paralysed from the waist downwards and had to retire from the campaign. Nixon's security of tenure in the White House was assured.

The one political group Nixon had no need to worry about were the Democrats. They were busy committing political suicide. Their convention, which nominated Senator George McGovern, had the atmosphere of a mad hatter's tea party. Its new rules, introduced in the aftermath of Hubert Hum-prey's defeat in 1968, downgraded the traditional power blocs such as congressional support groups and organised labour unions on the grounds that these represented the 'old politics'. Instead, the rules transferred power to the 'new politics' and its twin sister 'open politics'. In practice, this meant that the places in every state delegation were allocated on a quota basis by age, sex, ethnic groupings, and minority interests. As a result of this bizarre method of delegate selection, the Democratic convention was a shambles. The colourful representatives of the 'new politics' exploited the television coverage of the convention by coming to the podium not to support their party but to advocate the causes dearest to their hearts. This turned the platform debate into an undisciplined filibuster, heavily biased towards the radical and the ridiculous. There was a preponderance of speeches favouring instant and unconditional withdrawal from Vietnam; women's liberation; homosexual equality; amnesties for draft dodgers and illegal immigrants; special rights for Mexican farm workers; better welfare for single parent families; improved compensation for dispossessed Indian tribes; the lowering of the age of sexual consent—and many other issues far removed from mainstream politics in 1972. Nothing like it had ever been seen at the national convention of a major political party. With millions of other Americans, Nixon recalled sitting in front of his television screen unable to believe his eyes. 'The scene had the air of a college skit that had gotten carried away with itself and didn't know how to stop'.[44]

After a three-hour debate on the vice-presidential nomination in which candidates like Mao Tse-tung and Martha Mitchell were proposed, finally, at 2.48 a.m. in Miami ('prime time in Guam' remarked some acerbic commentator), George McGovern was at last allowed to make his acceptance speech. Using the theme 'Come home, America', he pledged a total withdrawal of all US forces from Vietnam within ninety days; swingeing cuts in the defence budget; an amnesty for draft dodgers and a programme of job creation to be paid for by higher taxation.

Watching this performance in San Clemente, Nixon saw in his opponent an unelectable Goldwater of the left. He also decided that McGovern must be pilloried as an extremist—exactly the tactics that the Democrats had used against Goldwater in 1964. 'Attack McGovern on his wildest, most radical position', Nixon instructed John Ehrlichman a few days later. 'This is the line—McGovern is left wing; ADA [Americans for Democratic Action] left wing. He is a dedicated radical, pacifist left winger.'[45]

The line succeeded brilliantly so far as fund raising was concerned. Under the direction of Maurice Stans, who had raised $36 million for the Nixon campaign in 1968, an all time record of $60 million was raised in 1972. A significant percentage of this arrived in cash. Owing to a technical gap in electoral legislation, campaign contributions could be made without the amounts or the names of the donors being publicly disclosed as long as they were made before 7 April 1972, when Congress's new Federal Election Campaign Act came into force. This secrecy appealed to many big-money contributors, some of whom were lifelong Democrats running so scared of McGovern that they gladly put their money where their mouths were not. Such donors often preferred the anonymity of cash contributions. After 7 April, the law required each party to record publicly all its sources of funds over $10 and report to the General Accounting Office details of any contribution over $100.

Before and after the reporting deadline, Nixon's election coffers were awash with funds. 'Money is the mother's milk of politics'[46] runs an old campaigning axiom, but Stans was so good at financial lactation that he found himself presiding over a financial dairy. The safes in his office were like over-full milk churns bursting and dripping with banknotes. From mid-April onwards the campaign had an overfunding problem, which some zealots were later to solve by ingenious and unscrupulous methods.

The recipient of the fund-raising largesse was CRP (unofficially dubbed CREEP), the Committee to Re-elect the President. CRP was headed by John Mitchell, who resigned in January 1972 as Attorney General for this purpose. Jeb Stuart Magruder, previously an aide of Haldeman's, acted as Mitchell's deputy. Also to be found on CRP's personnel list were Gordon Liddy and Howard Hunt, who had been reassigned there after the Plumbers had been disbanded in 1971. When CRP was first set up in the spring of 1971, Nixon was standing so low in the polls that his re-nomination, let alone his re-election, was open to doubt. Haldeman recalled that Nixon's original intent was to have an effective and independent campaign. 'He was determined that the campaign be separate from the White House and not be with the [Republican] National Committee. This was because…he wanted to run the campaign himself and thought that the National Committee was not efficient enough.'[47] Later, after two Republican challengers (Congressman John Ashbrook of Ohio and Congressman Peter McCloskey of California) threw their hats into the ring, CRP became a legal necessity. 'Nixon couldn't use the Republican National Committee before the Republican Convention', recalled Rob Odle, an aide to John Mitchell who was seconded from the Justice Department to become the committee's director of administration. 'If we'd claimed to be the Republican Party, we'd have had lawsuits so fast it would make your head swim.'[48]

Swimming in cash and all-party support was infinitely preferable. Democrats for Nixon, headed up by John Connally, were so successful that the President was delighted to sail on without the Republican banner. Even more importantly, McGovern's rejection of the traditional Democratic power blocs made it possible to fulfil an ambition he had cherished for the past seven years—creating a New Republican Majority as the leading electoral force in American politics. With this dream in mind he courted all the old strongholds of the Kennedy–Johnson era, including the Catholic vote, the Jewish vote, small farmers, blue-collar workers, ethnic groups, and the bosses of organised labour. The wooing of these interests, much of it handled from the White House by Charles Colson, was highly successful. Several unions, led by the Teamsters, took the unprecedented step of endorsing a Republican President, and prominent individual defectors from the Democratic party abounded. These seismic shifts in political loyalties, which may be said to have started with the 'Silent Majority' speech of November 1969, are Nixon's enduring legacy to the GOP. The Republicans have won six out of the last seven presidential elections, a record of successes which owes much to the break-up in the traditional Democratic voting patterns which Nixon initiated.

With so much going his way, neither Nixon nor his election high command at CRP needed to exert themselves unduly to fight the Democrats. By early June the election result was a foregone conclusion. Perhaps that was why the start of the Watergate drama made such a relatively small impact when it occurred. The public's first knowledge of the affair came on the morning of 18 June 1972, when some newspapers reported the arrest of five men attempting to bug and burgle the offices of the Democratic National Committee. These offices were located on the sixth floor of the Watergate building—a fashionable hotel, office and apartment complex in downtown Washington overlooking the Potomac.

The published details of the break-in made it sound more like a spoof on a spy movie than a serious crime. At around 2.30 a.m. on the morning of 17 June, an alert security guard noticed that the doorlatch to one of the stairways in the Watergate building had been tampered with. The guard called the police who checked the entrances to the office suites leading off the stairway and discovered that the locks on the Democratic National Committee's headquarters had been broken with a jemmy. The police burst in with guns drawn. From behind a partition close to the office of a DNC secretary named Maxie Wells came the cry 'Don't shoot!' Five men put up their hands and surrendered. They were all wearing surgical gloves. Three of the five were Cubans; the fourth was a Miami businessman with a weird history of adventurous escapades; the fifth was a former CIA security specialist. They were found to have in their possession a bag of burglar tools; two 35mm cameras; forty rolls of unexposed film; three tear gas canisters; a walkie-talkie radio; assorted electrical equipment including bugging devices; a wig; and $5,300 in new, consecutively numbered $100 bills. Caught red-handed, the five intruders were marched off in handcuffs to police headquarters where an investigation began. Such were the facts first reported in the press.

The notion that this episode might be the start of the American Presidency's most cataclysmic political drama of the twentieth century is unlikely to have occurred to anyone reading their newspaper on 18 June. Such a thought certainly did not cross the mind of Richard Nixon, who was weekending in Key Biscayne. He first learned of the Watergate break-in from the *Miami Herald*, which covered the item as a small story low down on its front page under the headline: 'Miamians Held in DC Try to Bug Demo Headquarters'.[49] Nixon's first reaction was: 'It sounded preposterous: Cubans in surgical gloves bugging the DNC! I dismissed it as some sort of a prank.'[50]

Nixon's role as the central figure in Watergate and the subsequent cover-up will be examined in detail in Chapter 19. Only two points should be made at this stage in the narrative of the 1972 election: First, that Nixon has always denied all prior knowledge of the break-in; Second, that he claims to have given Watergate a low priority in terms of his time and attention in the days following the arrest of the burglars. The justification for these claims will be analysed later, but few would quarrel with at least one part of Nixon's Watergate story as stated in his memoirs: 'I have sometimes wondered whether, if we had only spent more time on the problem at the outset, we might have handled it less stupidly.'[51]

At least there was nothing stupid about the way Nixon was handling the 1972 election campaign. Presidential authority and an Eisenhower-like posture above the battle were his tactics. He had a triumphant convention, then left the fray to political surrogates, making only occasional appearances as his PR men unleashed a tidal wave of commercials blanketing the networks with the finest footage from the Moscow and Peking summits. Meanwhile the Democrats continued to flounder in the quicksands of their own mistakes. One of George McGovern's earliest errors was the fiasco over his running mate, Senator Thomas Eagleton of Missouri. Six weeks after the Democratic convention, a campaign of press rumours forced Eagleton to disclose that he had been in hospital three times between 1960 and 1966, suffering from mental depression. His treatment had included electro-shock therapy. When this news broke, McGovern issued an immediate statement saying Eagleton was 'fully qualified in mind, body and spirit to be the Vice President of the United States and if necessary to take over the Presidency at a moment's notice.'[52] The following day, McGovern spoke out even more strongly, stating that he was '1000 per cent' behind Eagleton and had no intention of drop-ping him. A week later, in circumstances which made the nominee look incom-petent and inconsistent, the '1000 per cent' endorsement was reversed and Eagleton was kicked off the ticket. Nixon made no public comment on the epi-sode, but privately he felt moved to make one of his unusual but not untypical gestures of personal kindness. Remembering how the Missouri Senator had brought his teenage son to the Oval Office some weeks earlier, the President found time to send a two-page handwritten letter to thirteen-year-old Terry Eagleton with the closing line: 'I hope you do not allow this incident to discourage or depress you. Years later you will look back and say, "I am proud of the way my dad handled himself in the greatest trial of his life"—Sincerely, Richard Nixon.'[53]

The Eagleton affair made McGovern look like a fool but Watergate was not yet tarnishing Nixon as a knave. If a cover-up was going on, it was succeeding. In spite of frantic Democratic efforts to stir up outrage over the mysterious burglary of their headquarters, the voters yawned and looked the other way. Watergate was seen as a 'Washington story'. One survey suggested that 52 per cent of the elector-ate had never heard about the episode. Another showed that by a 70 to 13 margin, those polled regarded the break-in as an acceptable case of espionage. By a 57 to 25 margin they believed political spying to be a common occurrence, particularly during the heat of a campaign. Media coverage reflected these attitudes. With the exception of the *Washington Post* (which had Watergate stories on its front page during the election seventy-nine times), the hot breath of investigative reporters chasing leads on the break-in felt distinctly tepid. Less than 15 of the 430 journal-ists based in Washington for different newspapers and television stations were working on Watergate. To all but the keenest of editorial noses, the scent of a big story was fading.

---

* Terry Eagleton wrote back to Nixon: 'I guess very few thirteen-year-olds get handwritten letters from the President. Although I am a Democrat, I think you must be a wonderful man to take the time to write to some unimportant person like me. Do you know what Dad said when he read your letter? He said, 'It's going to make it all the tougher to talk against Nixon.' I think both Dad and you are excellent politicians. Even though you and Dad don't always agree, I think the country is lucky to have both of you...Thank you, Mr. President, very, very much. With appre-ciation, Terry Eagleton.'[54]

In its lonely and dogged pursuit of the Watergate trail, the *Washington Post* made some startling revelations. On 10 October the paper ran a front-page story which began: 'FBI agents have established that the Watergate bugging incident stemmed from a massive campaign of political spying and sabotage conducted on behalf of President Nixon's re-election and directed by officials of the White House and the Committee for the Re-election of the President.'[55] There followed an account of the activities of one Donald Segretti, a college friend of Nixon's appointment secretary Dwight Chapin. Segretti had apparently been hired by Chapin as a dirty tricks expert, with a brief to be 'A Republican Dick Tuck'.[56]

There was nothing new in dirty tricks during a presidential election campaign. Although Segretti's repertoire seemed excessive, in that it combined the puerile with the poisonous (sending unwanted pizzas to a Democrat rally, or smearing Senator Ed Muskie with sexual and racist rumours), the real danger in the *Post's* story was that it alleged a Watergate–White House–dirty tricks connection. This was the first indication that the threads of Watergate might unravel to ensnare the President's closest aides. However, at the time, the indignation of the *Washington Post* was balanced by the insouciance of the Democratic Party's nominee: 'I always thought that these dirty tricks were exaggerated by the press', recalled Senator George McGovern. 'Everything Nixon's wild men got up to, including the break-in to our own National Committee's headquarters, was low level, superficial, and utterly peripheral to the mainstream of campaigning. I don't think all those dirty tricks put together changed more than 10,000 votes in either the battle for the nomination or the election itself.'[57]

Nixon's opinion of the matter was close to McGovern's. He thought the *Post* was guilty of exaggeration and double standards. He regarded the story as 'the last burp of the Eastern establishment'.[58]

By this time the liberal establishment was bleeding as well as burping. Despite a strong endorsement of McGovern by the *New York Times*, the Democrats' presidential campaign was proving a disaster. Throughout October the polls put Nixon in the lead by margins of between 28 and 34 per cent. This should have kept him in a mood of euphoria, but as he said himself 'instead it was one of the most frustrating and least satisfying of all my campaigns'.[59]

Private worries about the gathering storm clouds over the Watergate affair may have been one part of that frustration, particularly as threats of various congressional investigations into aspects of the mystery were looming. On a more public level, Nixon was enraged by the viciousness of his opponents' personalised attacks. He was compared to Adolf Hitler in three of McGovern's speeches, and accused of leading a party worse than the Ku Klux Klan. This was inexcusable rhetoric, far more unpleasant than Nixon's own worst oratorical excesses twenty years earlier, yet McGovern escaped lightly in terms of media criticism.

The answer to McGovern and the President's other tormentors seemed overwhelming when the ballots were counted on the night of 7 November. Nixon achieved a stunning triumph. He won 47 million votes or 60.7 per cent of the total, compared to McGovern's 29 million or 37.5 per cent. It was a national as well as a numerical landslide,* changing the contours of America's political geography. Nixon carried every state in the Union except Massachusetts. He was the first Republican ever to win a majority among blue-collar workers, Catholics, members of labour union families and voters with only grade school educations. His support in most of the major ethnic communities had doubled. The New Majority of Nixon's dreams had been turned into a glorious reality.

And yet…in the hour of his greatest electoral triumph Nixon was weighed down with feelings of divine discontent, once again bringing to his mind the quotation from Wellington after Waterloo: 'Nothing except a battle lost can be half as melancholy as a battle won.'

Explanations for this strange mood of melancholia, which was temporarily aggravated by a broken tooth, were not hard to find. Although Nixon had won the Presidency, his party had again lost the Congress. The Democrats were in a majority in the Senate by 57 to 43 (a gain of two seats) and in the House by 243 to 192 (a loss of twelve). This made the President a political leader without a secure base. A combination of premonition and intuition told him that he would face some hard pounding from the 93rd Congress, particularly over appointments, Watergate, and the determination of foreign policy. He also felt frustrated by his inability to control the federal bureaucracy, and was fuming against his real and imaginary enemies in the media.

In his reflective moments Nixon must have felt apprehensive about some of the shadows that so incongruously persisted in the sunrise of his election victory. Always ready to evaluate his options, he should have considered dispelling this apprehension by implementing the 'bring us together' theme of his first inaugural. Using a formula of conciliation towards the Congress; magnanimity towards the media; and (hardest of all) a public apology for the errors of his aides over Watergate, Nixon could have disarmed his adversaries and enjoyed a full second term as President just as rich in historical achievement as his first four years of power. Alas, it was not to be. Conciliation, magnanimity and apology did not

---

* Nixon's victory was the greatest numerical landslide in history and the second-highest percentage result. Only Lyndon Johnson, running against Goldwater in 1964, had scored fractionally better with 61.1 per cent.

come easily to Nixon at this stage in his Presidency. Encouraged by sycophants, he followed his worst instincts. Instead of turning the other cheek he unsheathed his sword. Rather than reaping in joy, he seemed determined to sow in tears.

This aggressive mood had been simmering within the President's mind for several weeks. On 15 September he had a conversation with his Chief of Staff in which he expressed many complaints against the federal bureaucracy, coupled with regrets that he had not reorganised the executive branch at the start of his administration. 'We're going to have a house cleaning', he declared. 'It's time for a new team. Period.' He told Haldeman to act quickly after the election: 'You've gotta do it fast because then they'll take off for Christmas you know, then after the first of the year it's too late.' As the conversation continued, Nixon's anger blazed as he suggested to Haldeman what he might say to the departing bureaucrats: 'You've got one week to plan your holidays now. You're out, you're out, you're finished, you're done, done, finished.' He gave one final succinct order: 'Knock the hell out of there.'[60]

This hell-knocking strategy surfaced on the morning after polling day, when at 11 a.m. on 8 November the triumphantly re-elected President addressed the White House staff in the Roosevelt Room. His thanks were perfunctory; his demeanour appeared chilling and remote. There was hardly any acknowledgement of the fact that he was surrounded by loyal associates who had worked their hearts out to make his first term so monumental in accomplishment. There was no expression of elation over the election results. After five minutes' worth of mundane remarks delivered with all the warmth and humanity of a telephone answering machine, Nixon stalked out, turning the meeting over to Haldeman, and leaving him to perform the role of Lord High Executioner.

Wielding his axe with brutal equality, Haldeman announced that every member of the staff was required to submit his resignation immediately. Mimeographed forms for this purpose were promptly distributed. Haldeman also asked everyone to submit a full list of documents in their possession and said that further personnel announcements could be expected within a month. The same ruthless performance was repeated to the Cabinet an hour later. Both audiences were stunned.

In fact, the purpose of Haldeman's announcement had been misunderstood. While he and Nixon had intended to reorganise the White House staff and the Cabinet, they had also wanted, as Haldeman later explained, 'to give individuals the chance to say whether they wanted to leave government and go into the private sector, or to stay in government but change their post, or stay right where they were'.[61] Unfortunately, they failed to make this intention clear, and their attempt

to give the staff a say in their own futures seemed, instead, to be ingratitude for
their past services.

This extraordinary display of how to lose friends and influence with people
who support you was the opening shot in Nixon's campaign to reorganise the
government. For at least two years he had been dissatisfied with several of Washington's great bureaucracies. High on his list of targets for reform were the CIA;
the State Department; the Pentagon; and Health, Education and Welfare. Moreover, he was determined to break the links between these departments and their
often overprotective congressional sub-committees. 'The relationship between
the executive branch and the congressional staffs had long struck Nixon as being
an unhealthy one', recalled Haldeman. 'These people had been able to manipulate
both the legislature and the executive for far too long.'[62]

Nixon was not far wrong in his diagnosis. The federal bureaucracy had grown
bloated in size and sclerotic in its ability to perform many of the functions of
government. The relationships between the departments and the staffs of the
congressional committees had become incestuous. But what Nixon and his advisers failed to appreciate was that curing these maladies required dexterous wielding of the scapel. Instead, what the White House was proposing appeared to be
an operation by blunderbuss—at least in the eyes of those likely to be reorganised.
As the plans for the restructuring of government became known, a self-protective
fear (and in some cases loathing) began to spread among Washington's top
bureaucrats. These individual responses may have been a considerable factor in
the events that were later to unfold during the drama of Watergate, for a frightened
government servant can be a dangerous and disloyal animal. 'In retrospect we
made a strategic error', Haldeman has admitted. 'It backfired on us.'[63] But at the
time there were no such second thoughts. Nixon withdrew to Camp David with
only a handful of his closest aides and continued to fulminate against his real and
imagined enemies. Charles Colson recorded a chilling encapsulation of the
President's mood at this time. He, together with Kissinger, Haldeman and Ehrlichman, were discussing the problem of the anti-war liberals in Congress: 'One
day we will get them—we'll get them on the ground where we want them', growled
Nixon. 'And we'll stick our heels in, step on them hard and twist—right, Chuck,
right?' Colson agreed. 'Henry knows what I mean', Nixon went on. 'Get them on
the floor and step on them, crush them, show them no mercy.' 'You're right, sir,
we'll get them', said Colson, as Kissinger also nodded.[64]

But who was going to get whom? In politics, as in life, enmity begets enmity.
As Nixon's first term drew to its close what should have been a happy ending was
already being overtaken by an angry beginning. The hostilities soon became

mutual. With snipers from the fourth estate conducting increasingly effective guerilla warfare on Watergate; with the executive branch in a mood of insecurity and truculence; and with the Democratic majorities in the legislature spoiling for a fight, Nixon was in no position to start 'getting people'. Instead of behaving so aggressively, he needed to start doing a little peacemaking at home. He was still a past master at doing it abroad—as his latest moves in Vietnam were once again demonstrating.

IV. PEACE IN VIETNAM

In the middle of the 1972 election campaign, Nixon's long-planned strategy for peace with honour in Vietnam suddenly started to bear fruit. The breakthrough occurred because the North Vietnamese leaders were feeling the heat from several different pressure points, all of which had been brought into play by Nixon's successes.

First and foremost, the triumph of triangular diplomacy meant that Hanoi could no longer rely on Peking and Moscow for unqualified support. By September, both Communist patrons were limiting assistance for their militant ally to food supplies only. This development crippled North Vietnam's long-term capacity to wage war against the South.

Second, the success of the American bombing and blockading of the ports meant that the NVA spring offensive had been halted in its tracks. Hué had not fallen, and the Communist occupiers of Quang Tri were expelled on 15 September by an ARVN counterattack. Although many problems remained, South Vietnam's military security now seemed assured for the foreseeable future. Nixon's 8 May decision to escalate the bombing had been the turning point.

Thirdly, the success of Nixon's election campaign was troubling the North Vietnamese, who could read the opinion polls as well as anyone. Early in October, French diplomatic sources in Hanoi reported a conversation with Premier Pham Van Dong in which he expressed regret at having paid too much attention to American anti-war leaders; recognised that Nixon would have a freer hand after the election; and made optimistic noises about the chances of a peace settlement. Nixon meanwhile sent a signal to Hanoi through the Soviet Foreign Minister, Andrei Gromyko, warning that if the next US peace offer was rejected when the American and North Vietnamese met in Paris on 8 October, then he would turn to 'other methods' after the election.[65]

On the night of 8 October, Kissinger reported from Paris in terse and cryptic terms: 'Tell the President that there has been some definite progress at today's first session and that he can harbor some confidence that the outcome will be positive.'

The following day, Kissinger's personal cable to the President was even more delphic. 'The negotiations during this round have been so complex and sensitive that we have been unable to report their content in detail due to the danger of compromise. We know exactly what we are doing, and just as we have not let you down in the past, we will not do so now. Pending our return and my direct report to you it is imperative that nothing be said in reply to McGovern* or in any other context bearing on the current talks.'[66]

Nixon found this one paragraph message 'more tantalizing than enlightening'[67] but went along with it. His tacit acceptance elicited the admiration of Kissinger, who wrote in his memoirs:

> Few Presidents would have acquiesced in such a procedure. But maddening as Nixon's conduct could be in calm times, it verged on the heroic when really critical issues were at stake. He must have been tense; he could not avoid being uneasy...It took unusual fortitude not to try to affect a negotiation that might decide the election and that would certainly determine whether or not his second term would be tranquil or ridden by crisis. Such was Nixon's self-control that he refrained even from indulging natural human curiosity by a phone call.[68]

The news that Kissinger brought back to the President from Paris on the evening of 12 October was startling. On the second day of the talks, North Vietnam's chief negotiator Le Duc Tho had unveiled a new peace plan. Its essential ingredients were a complete ceasefire; the withdrawal of US forces; the return of all prisoners of war by both sides; and no further infiltration of the South by the NVA and Vietcong. Hanoi had dropped its demands for President Thieu's resignation and for Communist power-sharing in a coalition government. Instead, they had separated the military and political issues, just as Nixon had proposed early in 1969. The political structure of South Vietnam would be left to the Vietnamese people to settle. The only political concession requested was a face-saving formula for a National Council of Reconciliation and Concord, in which the Vietcong would have the right to participate but would not have the power to out-vote Thieu.

When Kissinger first listened to Le Duc Tho's droning voice setting out these peace proposals, he regarded it as 'my most thrilling moment in public service'.[69] Nixon, hearing the full account of the offer for the first time in his Executive

---

* McGovern was due to make a nationwide broadcast on Vietnam the following day.

Office Building hideaway three days later, was almost as ecstatic. He saw the deal as 'a complete capitulation by the enemy: they were accepting a settlement on our terms'.[70] He ordered a celebration dinner of steaks and a bottle of Château Lafite-Rothschild to be brought into the office. With a beaming smile Kissinger told him: 'Well, Mr. President, it looks like we've got three out of three'—a reference to Nixon's original trio of policy objectives: the opening to China, détente with the Soviet Union, and peace in Vietnam.[71]

The mood of euphoria was heady, but it did not last. As Kissinger had empha-sised to Le Duc Tho, the United States could not make peace unilaterally. The agreement also had to be accepted by the Government of South Vietnam (GVN). Persuading President Thieu to sign up to the deal proved an extremely difficult task. He was slow, maddeningly obstructive, and full of genuine doubts about the prospects for his country's survival. Nixon did his utmost to convince the GVN leader that the peace terms were workable and enforceable. 'I believe we have no reasonable alternative but to accept this agreement', he wrote to Thieu in a letter hand-delivered by Kissinger on 19 October. 'I am personally convinced that it is the best we will be able to get and that it meets my *absolute* condition—that the GVN must survive as a free country.'[72]

Thieu, however, remained unconvinced. He stalled and objected, not without good reason, for ever since the deal appeared imminent the North Vietnamese had been moving up their forces around Saigon in an attempt to seize the maxi-mum territory in advance of the ceasefire. In this context it is important to remember that a total withdrawal of all NVA forces from the South had long been regarded as a practical impossibility unless the US resorted to all-out war against Hanoi. Thieu had accepted this reality at least three years earlier when he endorsed the 1970 ceasefire plan, but now he balked at it. Nixon sympathised, and urged Kissinger not to push Thieu too fast. 'As you continue discussions with Thieu, I wish to re-emphasize again that nothing that is done should be influenced by the US election deadline', the President cabled to his National Security Adviser in Saigon on 20 October. 'I have concluded that a settlement which takes place before the election which is, at best, a washout, has a high risk of severely damaging the US domestic scene, if the settlement were to open us up to the charge that we made a poorer settlement now than what we might have achieved had we waited until after the election... We must have Thieu as a willing partner in making any agree-ment. It cannot be a shotgun marriage.'[73]

Nixon's reluctance to bless a shotgun marriage was bad for his image as a domestic politician but good for his historical reputation as an international statesman. The temptation to override the GVN protests and to sign the ceasefire before the election was considerable. Such a course of action was urged on him, for different reasons, by Kissinger from Saigon, by Brezhnev from Moscow, and by Premier Pham Van Dong from Hanoi. As the timetable for signing slipped in the face of further obstructionism from Thieu, the North Vietnamese increased the pressure by going public with the story of the peace agreement and its delayed implementation. Kissinger immediately held a press conference to ensure that Hanoi's version of events was superseded by the American account. As a short-term public relations exercise it was successful, but it brought long-term trouble because Kissinger exceeded his brief. In his opening remarks to the White House press corps on 26 October he told reporters, 'We believe that peace is at hand. We believe that an agreement is within sight.' Later in the press conference he added 'We believe, incidentally, what remains to be done can be settled in one more negotiating session with the North Vietnamese negotiators, lasting, I would think, no more than three or four days, so we are not talking of a delay of a very long period of time.'[74]

These were reckless words and the President was greatly displeased by them. As the phrase 'peace is at hand' made headlines around the world, Nixon's familiarity with the Winston Churchill story caused him to see an ominous parallel with Neville Chamberlain's claim of 'Peace in our time' in 1939. Enraged by the thought that Kissinger had been grandstanding in order to claim the credit for the imminent election victory, Nixon was fearful that his National Security Adviser's boastful forecast might weaken the US bargaining position with the North Vietnamese and lessen the chances of getting President Thieu's co-operation. These fears were justified. Within a week, Thieu publicly rejected parts of the announced terms and made it clear that South Vietnam would not honour any peace agreement it had not signed. The North Vietnamese said they would not meet Kissinger again for negotiations on what he had called 'minor details' of the deal. Nixon extricated himself from this growing chaos by making a nationwide TV broadcast on 2 November in which he captured the high ground of principle by rhetoric. 'We are not going to allow an election deadline or any other kind of deadline to force us into an agreement which would be only a temporary truce and not a lasting peace', he told the viewers. 'We are going to sign the agreement when the agreement is right, not one day before. And when the agreement is right, we are going to sign, without one day's delay.'[75] This phraseology was sufficiently opaque to satisfy all those who were beginning to wonder what 'peace is at hand' had meant. Four days later Nixon won the election.

Winning a landslide victory from the voters proved an easier achievement than making peace between the Vietnamese. In the weeks of stalemate after polling day, Kissinger compared his role to that of an animal trainer cracking the whip at two tigers, one North Vietnamese, one South Vietnamese, who refused to move in disciplined unison on their stools. 'When one is in place, the other jumps off.'[76] By late November it was apparent that most of the jumping off was being done by Hanoi. Nixon delegated the handling of Thieu to General Alexander Haig, the Deputy National Security Adviser. Their good relationship strengthened the fragile confidence between Saigon and Washington. Haig believed that Thieu would sign the agreement in the end, particularly after receiving a personal letter from the President guaranteeing US military action in the event of ceasefire violations by the North Vietnamese. 'You have my absolute assurance that if Hanoi fails to abide by the terms of this agreement it is my intention to take swift and severe retaliatory action', wrote Nixon.[77]

Meanwhile, the North Vietnamese were playing games with Kissinger in Paris. They reneged on some parts of the 8 October agreement; refused to accept even the most minor textual changes; and embarked on labyrinthine manoeuvres of bluffing, delaying and double-crossing. Kissinger became angry and frustrated. He was sure that in spite of their long-term need for a settlement, the North Vietnamese were preparing to break off the talks and to go another military round in the war. He believed that Hanoi was gambling on a collapse of US will, thinking that Nixon would be forced by pressures from the new Congress to sell out on Thieu and accept peace on North Vietnam's terms.

Not for the first time, Hanoi underestimated Nixon. He realised that he was back at the same cruel crossroads he had faced in May. However, now that domestic expectations had been raised by the 'peace is at hand' headlines, he did not feel he could rally the American public to accept another extension of the war along the lines of his 8 May broadcast. Instead he thought his only option would be to escalate the bombing of North Vietnam without explanation at home in the hope that this last demonstration of strength would bring Hanoi back to the negotiating table with a more constructive attitude. Accordingly, Nixon made contingency plans with his military advisers for a new bombing campaign. At the same time he gave Kissinger further and more flexible negotiating instructions to enable him to reach an agreement on outstanding points of difficulty with Le Duc Tho in Paris at their meeting scheduled for 11–13 December.

At these meetings, Le Duc Tho stalled and side-stepped in such a cynical manner that the only conclusion to be reached was that he was negotiating in bad faith, with no intention of reaching an agreement. Kissinger conveyed the atmosphere of these non-talks in vivid language. Gritting his teeth and banging his fists on the table, he told Nixon the North Vietnamese were 'just a bunch of shits.

Tawdry, filthy shits. They make the Russians look good, compared to the way the Russians make the Chinese look good when it comes to negotiating in a responsible and decent way.'[78]

It did not take much to convince Nixon of Hanoi's perfidy. He had followed every move of the negotiations and saw clearly that the North Vietnamese were trying to regain by delaying tactics at the peace table what they had lost through their military failures on the battlefield. He therefore had to face up to what he called 'the most difficult decision I made during the entire war'[79]—whether or not to order a bombing campaign of military targets in North Vietnam the week before Christmas. He was influenced by some late-night reading of Winston Churchill's World War I memoirs, particularly the passage in which Churchill observes: 'One can have a policy of audacity or one can follow a policy of caution, but it is disastrous to try to follow a policy of audacity and caution at the same time.'[80]

No one could criticise Nixon's eventual orders for what became known as 'the Christmas bombing' for lacking in audacity. For the first time in the war he sent large numbers of B–52s over the northern part of North Vietnam on a sustained basis. During the period 18–30 December (with the exception of Christmas Day) he authorised up to 120 B–52 strikes a day against military targets in the Hanoi–Haiphong areas. Shipyards, docks, radio transmitters, power stations, armaments factories, military bases, communications units, and command centres were blitzkrieged. Haiphong harbour was once again blockaded by the reseeding of mines. Nixon was tough on his own military commanders, telling Admiral Moorer, Chairman of the Joint Chiefs of Staff, 'I don't want any more of this crap about the fact that we couldn't hit this target or that one. This is your chance to use military power effectively to win this war, and if you don't, I'll consider you responsible.'[81]

As soon as the Christmas bombing campaign became known in the US, Nixon had to suffer the moral equivalent of B-52 raids pounding down on him from his critics in Congress and the media. 'War by Tantrum' (James Reston), 'Shame on Earth' (Tom Wicker), 'Acting like a maddened tyrant' (Anthony Lewis), 'Beyond all reason' (the *Los Angeles Times*) were some of the more vituperative headlines. From Capitol Hill, Senator Saxbe suggested that the President had 'taken leave of his senses'; Senator Kennedy said the action 'should outrage the conscience of all Americans', while Senate Majority Leader Mike Mansfield described it as 'a Stone Age tactic' and announced that the Democrats would introduce legislation setting a terminal date for the war. The prevailing sentiment in Congress left no doubt that funds for the continuation of hostilities would soon be cut off.*

Apart from the aspersions on the President's sanity, the gravamen of the charge against him was that he had ordered the B-52 raids as a terror tactic aimed at civilians. Indiscriminate carpet bombing of heavily populated areas'[82] was a frequent accusation, and comparisons with the bombing of Dresden, or even Hiroshima, abounded.

When the facts replaced the hysteria, the picture looked rather different. The evidence confirmed that the B-52 crews had implemented their commander-in-chief's orders to attack only selected military targets with considerable accuracy. The total estimate of fatalities from the North Vietnamese was between 1300 and 1600, many of them killed by falling debris from their own SAM missiles, of which they fired over 1,000. No massacre of civilians had taken place and terror bombing had no part in Nixon's strategy. Several authoritative reports later confirmed this.†

The Christmas bombing, far from destroying the peace negotiations, accelerated them. Hanoi's previous intransigence ebbed in inverse proportion to the rising tide of outrage from American liberal opinion. Following an exchange of conciliatory messages, the North Vietnamese Politburo sent its negotiating team back to the Paris peace talks with instructions to settle. There was no more stalling or obstructionism. On 9 January Le Duc Tho accepted the proposals that had been put forward in November. Kissinger cabled this news to the President with cautious optimism: 'We celebrated the President's birthday today by making a major breakthrough in the negotiations. In sum, we settled all the outstanding questions in the text of the agreement... The Vietnamese have broken our heart several times before, and we just cannot assume success until everything is pinned

---

* On 2 January, the House Democratic Caucus voted by 154 to 75 to cut off all funds for Indo-China military operations. On 4 January, Senator Kennedy proposed a similar resolution to the Senate Democratic Caucus, where it passed by 36 to 12. Although these votes, cast before Congress officially reconvened, had no legislative significance, they clearly showed which way the wind was blowing.

† 'Hanoi has certainly been damaged but evidence on the ground disproves charges of indiscriminate bombing', wrote Peter Ward of the *Baltimore Sun* on 25 March 1973, after a visit to North Vietnam. 'Several bomb loads obviously went astray into civilian residential areas but damage there is minor compared to the total destruction of selected targets.' *The Economist* in London on 13 January 1973 took a similar line, pointing out that: 'The Hanoi death toll is smaller than the number of civilians killed by the North Vietnamese in their artillery bombardment of An Loc in April or the toll of refugees ambushed when trying to escape from Quang Tri at the beginning of May. That is what makes the denunciation of Mr. Nixon as another Hitler sound so unreal.'

down, but the mood and businesslike approach was as close to October as we have seen since October',[83] to which Nixon replied: 'I greatly appreciated your birthday greetings and your report... You should continue a tough posture and, above all, not let the other side filibuster. If the other side stays on this track and doesn't go downhill tomorrow, what you have done today is the best birthday present I have had in sixty years.'[84]

The North Vietnamese side of the peace equation did not go downhill this time, but Nixon still had an uphill struggle on his hands in order to get President Thieu's agreement. 'Brutality is nothing. You have never seen it if this son-of-a-bitch doesn't go along, believe me',[85] the President told his aides as he despatched Haig to Saigon with a menacing letter to the South Vietnamese leader on 14 January. Its crucial paragraph read:

I have therefore irrevocably decided to proceed to initial the Agreement on January 23, 1973 and to sign it on January 27, 1973 in Paris. I will do so, if necessary, alone. In that case I shall have to explain publicly that your Government obstructs peace. The result will be an inevitable and immediate termination of US economic and military assistance which cannot be forstalled by a change of personnel in your government. I hope, however, that after all our two countries have shared and suffered together in conflict, we will stay together to preserve peace and reap its benefits. To this end I want to repeat to you the assurances that I have already conveyed. At the time of signing the agreement I will make emphatically clear that the United States recognizes your government as the only legal government of South Vietnam; that we do not recognize the right of any foreign troops to be present on South Vietnamese territory; and that we will react strongly in the event the agreement is violated. Finally, I want to emphasize my continued commitment to the freedom and progress of the Republic of Vietnam. It is my firm intention to continue full economic and military aid.[86]

Although Thieu continued to quibble right down to the wire, he could not resist this sort of pressure and on 21 January he gave way. His brinkmanship denied Nixon the opportunity to announce the coming of peace in his second inaugural address on 20 January, but this was only a minor irritation. On 23 January, the South Vietnamese Foreign Minister Tram Van Lam was authorised to sign the agreement at a meeting in Paris alongside Le Duc Tho and Henry

Kissinger. That night Nixon broadcast to the nation. He announced that the peace settlement had been reached in Paris and that the ceasefire would begin on 27 January.

At long last, America's agony in Vietnam was over. More than two million US military personnel had seen active service in that faraway country during the last ten years. Forty-five thousand of them had laid down their lives there. The cost in personal suffering and public bitterness had been horrendous.

Yet in early 1973, the claim that all had not been in vain looked soundly based. The peace agreement secured the cessation of hostilities between North and South Vietnam, and offered tranquillity to the neighbouring countries of Laos, Thailand and Cambodia. Much would depend on whether the Communists would ever dare to violate the terms of the agreement, and if so what action a future American President would take to defend the deal that had been made. With four more years of Nixon in power, it seemed extremely unlikely that the North Vietnamese leadership, chastened by the Christmas bombing, would have any illusions about the cost of breaking their word. Peace with honour had been achieved. Peace in perpetuity had been given a chance.

V. NIXON, KISSINGER AND THE VERDICT OF HISTORY

Nixon's reputation as an international statesman rests principally on his foreign policy towards 'The Big Three'—China, the Soviet Union, and Vietnam. At the time of his Presidency and for some years afterwards his peacemaking achievements among these nations were seen through a glass darkly. Ephemeral passions such as the hostility of the anti-war movement; the emotions of betrayal from the conservative right; and the furore over Watergate, diminished much of the credit that was due to him. The journalistic canonisation of Henry Kissinger, which has also proved somewhat ephemeral, was an additional factor in this process of diminution. Yet on the stock exchange of history, Nixon shares are now rising. There is a growing school of thought that recognises him as the most innovative and successful foreign policy President of the twentieth century. How far can such claims be justified? How large a share in Nixon's foreign policy achievements belongs to Henry Kissinger?

The starting point for any discussion of Nixon's role as a foreign policy President should be a recognition of the fact that the world was a dangerous place when he took the oath of office in January 1969. At that time, Vietnam was the cockpit of a savage and deteriorating ideological power struggle involving Chinese, Soviet and American interests. The chances of ending that struggle by peaceful means looked slim. Chinese–American relations did not exist except in a mutual exchange of insults across the air waves. Soviet–American relations were frozen in the hostile attitudes of the Cold War. Soviet–Chinese relations had become so antagonistic that the two Communist giants were on the brink of major hostilities.

In the wider world, many countries were disappointed in their relations with the United States because Washington had become obsessed with Indo-China to the exclusion of all other considerations. Even the European allies were growing restless, and in some cases disaffected, because of this phenomenon. In the midst of so much uncertainty, many of the world's leading military nations had embarked upon an extension of the arms race. It was a time of nuclear parity, political volatility, and diplomatic stalemate.

The prospects for changing this climate by means of Western leadership appeared poor. There was a widespread perception that America's economic power was waning and that Washington's will to exert international influence was waning with it. The US failure in Vietnam and the domestic turmoil that accompanied it seemed almost a mortal sickness. Most international observers understood that America would have to get out of Vietnam, but how to achieve this with honour; how to retreat without surrender; and how to conduct a credible foreign policy while engaged in the process of withdrawal were questions that had gone unanswered in the 1968 election campaign.

Fortunately for the United States and for the international community, the man who became America's 37th President turned out to be one of the most determined and original foreign policy strategists his country has ever produced. After an eight-year apprenticeship in statecraft as Vice President, Nixon had travelled extensively and thought creatively during his wilderness years. He had developed his own blueprint for a new geopolitical architecture. Long before the election result, and before he had met Henry Kissinger, Nixon outlined his foreign policy agenda to his confidants. Its main objectives were: to revitalise the Atlantic Alliance; to find an acceptable peace settlement in Vietnam; to create an opening to China; and then to negotiate a formula for peaceful coexistence with the Soviet Union. In 1968 such plans sounded like fantasies, but by January 1973 Nixon had achieved them all.

His greatest frustrations came in Vietnam. The peace agreement that he had hoped to reach in six months took more than four years. Every week of that delay deepened the bitterness that tortured America's body politic like a suppurating wound. Even though Nixon steadily reduced both the US military numbers in Vietnam (from 550,000 troops in 1969 to 60,000 in May 1972) and the level of casualties they were suffering (down from 300 killed per week in December 1968 to under 10 killed a week in early 1972), his liberal critics gave him scant credit. Instead, they attacked him with two principal accusations: that he needlessly prolonged the war, and that at certain stages he escalated it to unjustifiable levels of horror. These charges deserve examination.

Nixon came to power knowing that he had been elected to end the war and overconfident that he could do it quickly. In the first few days of his administration he sent a message to Hanoi proposing a ceasefire, a mutual withdrawal of forces, and an agreement that the political future of Vietnam should be decided by the Vietnamese people alone. This offer was brutally rejected. Three weeks after receiving it, the North Vietnamese launched an offensive which was to kill more than 1,000 Americans each month for most of the first year of Nixon's Presidency. It became clear that Hanoi was not interested in any sort of peace compromise but only in outright victory. What the North Vietnamese leadership demanded was an unconditional American withdrawal, coupled with the overthrow of President Thieu and his government. They offered no other terms until 1972.

Faced with this impasse, Nixon had to consider the consequences of acceding to Hanoi's ultimatum. It would have meant abandoning the South Vietnamese people to the tender mercies of their Northern Communist enemies, in violation of the assurances given by three previous US Administrations. Nixon was not prepared to reverse America's commitment in this way. Unpopular though it made him with the anti-war activists, he decided to hold out for peace with honour. He believed that to withdraw on Hanoi's terms would be humiliating in its global political implications and tragic in its regional humanitarian consequences—as the later travails of the boat people subsequently demonstrated.

In standing firm for peace with honour, Nixon held the support of what he called 'the silent majority' of his fellow countrymen, but he alienated an extremely vocal minority. The enmity of the latter was often virulent. Nixon had the wrong temperament for defusing such an atmosphere. He grew defensive and angry. He had to rely on actions rather than words to win the argument.

Unfortunately, the progress towards peace with honour was slow. This was not the fault of the United States government. The peace terms which were finally signed in January 1973 were first proposed by Nixon in a secret message to Hanoi in May 1971, and reiterated publicly in January 1972. Although attacked by both the North Vietnamese and the anti-war lobby as totally unacceptable, these were the terms which were ultimately accepted. Most of the blame for delay rests with Hanoi for its extraordinarily stubborn intransigence.

Against the background of the factual record, it is unjust to accuse Nixon of prolonging the war or to suggest that he could have secured peace in 1969 on the same terms that he settled for in 1973. These criticisms are still fashionable in some circles of American liberal opinion but they are unjustified. Nixon's policy of peace with honour was certainly agonising, but his critics' policy of peace by surrender would have led to far deeper dimensions of tragedy.

As for the charge that Nixon unjustifiably escalated the war at certain stages, this is principally based on three episodes: the incursion into Cambodia of May 1970; the mining of Haiphong and other ports in May 1972; and the Christmas bombing of December 1972. Each one needs to be examined on its merits in terms of strategic objectives and results. To anti-war liberals, all three were morally objectionable in principle. To Nixon admirers all three were successful in practice. To a more neutral observer it might seem that the Cambodian incursion was militarily somewhere between a half-success and a half-failure, but that the political price at home was too costly; that the mining of Haiphong was a bold gamble which paid off handsomely; and that the Christmas bombing was a cruel necessity without which the war would have dragged on for many more months.

What all these episodes revealed in Nixon was his willingness to use American power to its limits and to face up to the toughest of decisions with one paramount consideration—the long-term interests of the United States. Unpopularity at home troubled him much more than he liked to admit, yet he always discounted it as a factor in his decision making. Reactions from abroad concerned him more, but in this field he was a brilliant judge of his adversaries' responses to a difficult call. Most of his advisers told him that the mining of Haiphong would cause the cancellation of the Moscow summit. It did not. The same pessimists warned against the campaign of Christmas bombing, believing that it would drive Hanoi into even greater intransigence. It did not. In both situations, the President was almost alone in his judgement that the reactions from the Soviet and North Vietnamese leaderships would be the reverse of what had been predicted by the establishment of Washington. Under Nixon's carefully calculated formula of sticks and carrots, the Communist powers became more, not less, accommodating to the interests of the United States.

This ability to read the minds of Communist leaders was one of Nixon's greatest strengths. He understood his ideological adversaries better than any previous President, partly because he had studied them for so long and partly because he was capable of thinking in their terms. In his bilateral dealings with Moscow and Peking he was realistic in identifying their national interests and ruthless in advancing the interests of the United States. This was a philosophy of deal making that the Communists understood.

When it came to the practicalities of deal making, Nixon was effective for three reasons. First he treated his fellow superpower leaders with complete equality. The lecturing, sermonising, and rhetorical berating that has characterised several US Presidents' dealings with Communist leaderships had no part in Nixon's arsenal of diplomacy. Not for him the posturings of moral superiority or the pretence that personal charm works wonders in international negotiations. He was the ultimate realist who got to the bottom line quickly in order to do business at the lowest common denominator level of mutual respect, or even mutual cynicism.

Second, Nixon abroad had a personal style that was far more assured, confident and dignified than the image he portrayed at home. At close quarters with his fellow Americans he could be socially inept and visibly insecure. Yet when travelling overseas, as if by wave of a magic wand, he discarded his domestic complexes and resentments. From the moment of arrival on foreign soil he exuded strength and often warmth. A small part of this transformation may have been due to the realisation that he was usually being welcomed by people who admired him for his humble origins; who neither knew nor cared whether Whittier was an Ivy League university; and whose respect for his abilities went back a long time to the days when he had first begun to acquire his detailed knowledge about the affairs of their own country. However, the rapport between Nixon and foreign leaders went far deeper than these superficialities. In terms of international expertise he was admired by his peers as a professional's professional. If he had a job of diplomacy to do, both he and his hosts knew that it would be done well. If he had to propose a toast, Nixon could be relied upon to deliver remarks which would combine subtlety and statesmanship. He was known to be a deep thinker and a hard bargainer. Above all Nixon carried with him not only the aura of leader of the free world but also the reputation of a tough and clever President who was determined to exert international leadership in the arena of geopolitics.

The ability to conceive and conduct a geopolitical strategy was the third ingredient in Nixon's effectiveness. This was an idea whose time had come, but which no American President had ever tried to implement. In the United States there had been an ideological tradition in foreign policy making (Dulles) and a pragmatic tradition (Kennedy and Johnson) but the concepts of geopolitics and linkage were Nixonian innovations. The story of how he reached out to China, and then went on to make an accord with the Soviet Union, is an epic of creative statesmanship. In his insistence on absolute secrecy and in his disregard for

Congress, it might be said by his detractors that Nixon's approach to superpower summitry had more than a whiff of totalitarianism. However, this high-handed 'L'etat c'est moi' approach may be pardoned because the ends clearly justified the means. Triangular diplomacy was Nixon's invention, and it made the world a safer and more peaceful place. To have brought China back into the family of nations and to have made the first breakthrough in détente and arms reductions agreements with the Soviet Union were historic achievements by a giant of peacemaking.

Nixon was fortunate to have had Henry Kissinger as his assistant in these grand designs of geopolitics. In its earliest and most creative period their relationship was like that of Talleyrand and a clever Louis XVIII. However, there was no doubt as to who was the dominant figure in the relationship. Kissinger was an intellectual valet of prodigious industry; an in-house encyclopaedia of diplomatic history and a courtier skilled in the arts of flattery and manipulation. He had considerable charm, and a sense of humour which eased many internal and external frictions. He was a shrewd diplomatic bargainer, an indefatigable traveller and an effective collator of briefing papers and options. These qualities made him an excellent presidential assistant, but he was a follower, not a leader; a brilliant draftsman, not an innovator of conceptual thinking. Throughout his Presidency, Nixon was the architect and the originator of US foreign policy.

The chemistry between the President and his National Security Adviser worked well for good and bad reasons. On the plus side, both men were the staunchest of patriots with a clear vision of where America's long-term strategic interests lay. They both had outstanding and complementary intellects. They shared an enthusiasm for philosophical and dialectical chess games of geopolitical theorising. They had prodigious energies and strong determinations to make their policies succeed. They were fascinated by history and the future record of their own roles in its evolving tapestry.

On the minus side, they were both overly fond of complex intrigues; too insistent on unnecessary secrecy; and excessively contemptuous of associates. They were rudely dismissive of all institutions of government outside the White House, reserving particular venom for the State Department and the Congress.

On the personal front, Kissinger knew how to exploit Nixon's darker nature because he had one of his own. Having gained his stronghold on the President's confidence, he maintained it by dubious methods. These included cutting out all other foreign policy advisers with a jealous brutality and pandering to Nixon's worst instincts with cunning sycophancy. When it came to wiretapping journalists, bad-mouthing colleagues, encouraging attacks on opponents, or blitzkrieging enemies, Kissinger could be a force for revenge rather than for restraint. 'Henry plays the game hard, all right', said Nixon in tones of some admiration early in 1971.[87] From such an expert source, that was a double-edged compliment.

In the aftermath of the opening to China, Kissinger's vanity underwent a quantum leap of growth. His high voltage egotism had often caused difficulties, now it became a serious problem. In his own mind, and in the perception of the media whom he so assiduously cultivated, he had been promoted to the rank of superstar. He became more of a prima donna; more vindictive in his long-running feud with the Secretary of State Bill Rogers; more prone to temperamental outbursts and threats of resignation. Nixon was troubled by these mood swings, and at one stage considered whether this National Security Adviser should seek psychiatric care.[88] There was also public evidence that Kissinger needed to calm down. In November 1972, he gave an extraordinary interview to the Italian journalist, Oriana Fallaci. She asked him to explain his popularity. 'The main point stems from the fact that I've always acted alone. Americans admire that enormously. Americans admire the cowboy leading the caravan alone astride his horse, entering the village or city alone', he told Fallaci. 'This romantic, surprising character suits me precisely because to be alone has always been part of my style, or if you like my technique.'[89]

This vainglorious nonsense drove Nixon up the wall, largely because it confirmed a disturbing new development in Kissinger's approach to his duties, namely that he *had* begun to show signs of acting alone, behaving as a principal and not just as an adviser. The first symptoms of this tendency had shown up in the preparations of the Moscow summit, when Nixon suspected his National Security Adviser of being so keen to strike a bargain with the Soviets that he was exceeding presidential instructions. A more blatant case of Kissinger's Lone Ranger arrogance occurred when he exceeded his brief at the press conference about the Vietnam negotiations on 26 October by announcing, 'Peace is at hand', when it manifestly was not. This was a turning point in the Nixon–Kissinger relationship, which deteriorated further as Kissinger started to behave erratically during the difficulties in the final stages of the Vietnam peace talks. A flavour of this is captured in John Ehrlichman's memoirs, describing a conversation with Bob Haldeman at Camp David 6 December 1972.

> Haldeman showed me Henry's cables of December 4 and 5. They were pessimistic and predicted the failure of the current talks. 'I don't know if you realize it, but Henry was very "down" when he left for Paris', Haldeman said. *'He's been under care. And he's been doing*

some strange things. When he was in Saigon twice he cabled the
North Vietnamese in the President's name to accept their October
proposal. Henry did that over Al Haig's strong objection and beyond
any presidential authority.'[90]

A presidential assistant who does not observe presidential authority is at best
a worry, at worst a liability. Nixon grew more and more restless with his junior
partner. Further strains occurred when *Time* magazine made Nixon and Kissinger joint Men of the Year, a sharing of credits which did not gladden the President's New Year celebrations. The rift widened further when several columnists,
headed by Joseph Kraft, reported in early January that Kissinger had been opposed
to the Christmas bombing campaign all along. Nixon was disturbed by repeated
rumours that these stories had been planted by Kissinger himself. He told Charles
Colson to have the calls on the National Security Adviser's direct telephone line
monitored by the secret service. On the evening of 5 January Colson telephoned
the President with some damning evidence of Kissinger's duplicity. The conversation, as recorded on the White House tapes, gives a graphic picture of the
mistrust that had soured the relationship.

> Colson: Mr. President, after we started keeping the log on Henry's
> calls—this is in total confidence because Henry should never
> know that we could find out—after we started keeping the log
> we found out real evidence that Joe Kraft and Jerry Schecter and
> those kind of people...
> Nixon: Was Joe Kraft on the list?
> Colson: Oh yes, on January 2nd.
> Nixon: You saw Kraft, January 2nd?
> Colson: Oh yeah.
> Nixon: You saw his column today?
> Colson: Yeah, and how. So you know where that comes from...the
> hypocrisy of it is that he was saying to me on Sunday how we
> mustn't talk to anybody and then he picks up the phone and calls
> Joe Kraft.

After a short gap on the tape (the segment has been withheld by the Archives
on the grounds that it would constitute an invasion of personal privacy), Nixon
started to demand further confirmation of Kissinger's behaviour.

Nixon: Now I think Henry ought to be taken out on calling. Just say, 'Henry, did you talk to—have you talked to Kraft?'

Colson: Yeah, I can hit Henry on that.

Nixon: No, I want you to ask him...Henry, uh, uh,—Gee this is a terrible article—and if he lies on that, I want to know. Will you do it?

Colson: Yes, sir. I can check it.

Nixon: It is very important that I know that.

Colson: I probably won't be able to get him tonight. I'll probably get him in the morning.

Nixon: No, Oh God, no. I don't mean now, some time tomorrow say—and you know, I don't want him to be too irritated before he goes to Paris. But say, 'What the hell? Did—did anybody in your shop, or you, talk to Kraft?' He called him? Or did Kraft call Henry?

Colson: No, he called—it's an outgoing call. He called Kraft.

Nixon: I'll be Goddamned!

Colson: You see, the incoming—we couldn't monitor all those.

Nixon: He—called—Kraft...I'll be a son-of-a-bitch!

Colson: We only know the outgoing, 'cos the incoming you can't always check.

Nixon: That is unbelievable![91]

Unfortunately it was all too believable. Colson brought in yet more evidence of Kissinger's self-serving leaks to journalists over the next few days. At one point in these revelations Nixon said firmly, 'Henry will be leaving in six or eight months.'[92] Kissinger soon recognised the new atmosphere of disenchantment, and began to talk about resigning. In anticipation of his departure, he began making plans to resign in the fall of 1973. He was to be preserved by Watergate.

Having been united in so much accomplishment, it was sad that these two remarkable statesmen became divided by the pressures of temperament, jealousy, and Vietnam. When the final settlement in that last saga was made, Kissinger had no confidence that it would last, whereas Nixon was utterly determined to make it endure. Their respective attitudes illuminated a profound difference between their characters. Kissinger was a supple pragmatist, who regarded foreign policy as the art of the possible. Nixon was a granite realist who believed that by determined exercise of American power the impossible could be done. 'If they're lucky they (the South Vietnamese) can hold out for a year and a half', Kissinger told Ehrlichman on 23 January 1973, the day of the peace announcement. Nixon had a far tougher attitude: 'The North Vietnamese would never have dared to break the terms of the peace agreement, because they knew that I would have upheld those terms with every damn option I'd got—political, diplomatic, and military. And if it hadn't been for Watergate, by God that's what I'd have done.'[93]

'If it hadn't been for Watergate...' What an ocean of sorrows and disappointments lie behind those six words. For Nixon was planning a series of global and domestic initiatives which would have made his second term even richer in achievement than his first four years.

On the foreign policy front, he was intending to consolidate his breakthrough with the superpowers and then to turn his peacemaking efforts to the Middle East. On China he planned 'to encourage economic and political reform through massive increases in person-to-person exchanges and in trade...I strongly believed that while we had been brought together by a common concern about the threat of Soviet aggression, we could only stay together if we developed a common interest in increasing our economic, cultural, and political relationships.'[94]

On the Soviet Union, the President's credo was an observation by Winston Churchill: 'The Russians fear our friendship more than they fear our enmity.' With that Churchillian dictum in mind, Nixon intended 'to push for massively increased trade and cultural exchange programs. In addition on the diplomatic front my first priority was to negotiate an offensive weapons agreement which would move eventually towards reduction of nuclear arms as well as limitations.'[95]

As for the rest of the world, the President had a disagreement with his National Security Adviser on what America's priorities should be. Kissinger wanted to make 1973 the 'Year of Europe' and to concentrate on developing closer relations with the European Community. Nixon thought 'we should concentrate primarily on what I believed was the explosive situation in the Mideast...it was my belief then and it is my belief now that the only time it is possible to make progress on Middle East issues is in non-election years. In election years the hardline supporters of Israel in the Congress will always have a veto power over any even-handed approach to Arab–Israeli problems. Unfortunately we did not seize the moment and the inevitable conflict occurred in the Yom Kippur War.'[96]

Other Nixon international schemes included a Western Hemisphere Free Trade Zone; a series of visits to improve US relations with Latin America; and a new focus on Eastern Europe, where he believed that 'peaceful change was inevitable. I intended to do everything possible in my second term to increase contacts, exchange trade etc. in order to encourage that change.'[97] It was also a *sine qua non* of Nixon's second term plans that he would uphold the Vietnam peace agreement both by economic carrots and if necessary by military stick.

Many of these thoughts were first sketched out in a handwritten sheet of notes headed 'Goals for 2nd Term' on 11 January 1973. Were they the impossible hopes of a pipe-dreaming President or the realistic and realisable plans of the strong and overwhelmingly re-elected leader of the free world? Alas, we shall never know. But on the basis of his track record, it seems fair to assume that an unweakened Nixon would have achieved some and perhaps most of his targets. If that is a correct conclusion, then those lost international achievements were heartbreaking. For if he had succeeded in widening and deepening the American opening to China, there might have been no Tienanmen Square and a far more positive atmosphere in Chinese–Western relations today. If he had accelerated the process of détente and disarmament with the Soviet Union, the world might have avoided the punitively expensive return to Cold War atmospherics and rearmament programmes of the 1980s which pushed the American economy into debt and the Soviet economy into collapse. If he had achieved serious progress on the road to peace in the Middle East, the tragedies and losses that might have been avoided in that troubled region are almost incalculable. If the United States had extended the hand of friendship to Eastern Europe in the 1970s instead of the 1990s, several of those countries might have achieved both their freedom and their prosperity much sooner and with far less suffering.

The 'if onlys' can be made to resonate on and on like the tolling of a church bell. On the domestic scene, Nixon had bold plans to check the drug problem, to revive his welfare reforms, and to revitalise the education programmes in America's schools. In politics he intended to create a 'New Establishment' based on his New Majority of labour groups, Hispanics, European ethnic groups and middle-class Blacks. He set himself personal goals as well. The last section of his scribbled page of notes of 11 January 1973 poignantly reads:

> Restore respect for office
> New idealism, respect for flag—country
> Compassion—understanding[98]

Sadly, Nixon had no understanding that his blueprint of second-term dreams and schemes was doomed to go unfulfilled. It was a tragedy for the world, for the United States, and for himself that none of his far-sighted plans ever came to fruition. The cause of the doom and tragedy was to be summed up in one word— Watergate.

NINETEEN

WATERGATE AND RESIGNATION

I. A REVISED VERSION OF THE BREAK-IN

Watergate was a Shakespearean tragedy for Richard Nixon. According to most Washington reviewers, he was the actor who played all the most villainous parts: motivator of the break-in; architect of the cover-up; betrayer of the constitution; tape-wiper extraordinary; venal tax dodger; obscenitor most foul; and criminal-in-chief. Such characterisations brought comfort to America's liberal establishment and joy to its journalists. Their righteous certainty that Nixon got what he deserved has, until recently, been the authorised version of history.

Challenging this version is an uphill struggle, for the President's role in this self-inflicted crisis was undoubtedly an ignoble one. Even the most generous explanations for his conduct do not bring him exculpation. In his frenzied efforts to fight his way out of the quicksand of Watergate, Nixon made himself guilty of many 'crimes'—among them deceit, negligence, bad judgement, mendacity, amorality, concealment, and a disastrous reluctance to face up to uncomfortable personal confrontations with the individuals who were creating the worst problems. But were these 'crimes' simply personal and political acts of folly or did they become real criminal actions so serious in nature that Nixon deserved to be ejected in disgrace from the Presidency of the United States? Did the punishment fit the 'crime'? Did Congress handle the crisis in the best interests of the United

States? Was the media's judgement on Watergate a fair one? So strong has been the tide of anti-Nixon sentiment that such questions have rarely been asked, let alone answered. Yet as the twentieth anniversary of Watergate passes there are increasingly strong reasons for asserting that some revisionism is justified. The important new research presented by the authors Len Colodny and Robert Gettlin in *Silent Coup* (1990) is one of those reasons. Others can be found in some of the interviews and conclusions which appear later in this book. All that can be said with certainty is that the judgement of history on Watergate is a long way from being final.

Watergate began with the burglary at the Democratic National Committee headquarters in the early hours of the morning on 17 June 1972. Although this was neither the original starting point nor the most pivotal episode in the drama, nevertheless the important unanswered question remains: 'Who ordered the break-in?'

The one fact that is now well established is that the order did not come from Nixon. After the most exhaustive investigations by the FBI, the Congress, and the office of the Special Prosecutor, not one single piece of evidence has emerged to suggest that the President gave any direct or indirect instructions for the break-in. There is nothing to confirm that he knew about it in advance or that he received any information from the bugging operation that preceded it. This exoneration does not depend, as Nixon's principal biographer Stephen Ambrose has uncharitably suggested, on the investigators' failure to uncover a memo that said, 'Break into the Watergate and bug Larry O'Brien—Richard Nixon'.[1] Instead it relies on two propositions, both well supported by evidence. The first is that Nixon's immediate reactions to the break-in were consistent with ignorance of what had happened. The second is that there were other figures, in or extremely close to the White House, who had their own personal motives for ordering the break-in, and operated accordingly.

Nixon's first responses to the news of the burglary were those of surprise and cynicism, followed by a reflex action designed to ensure political damage limitation. The two men who were with him at Key Biscayne, Florida when he first heard about Watergate were his closest friends Bob Abplanalp and Bebe Rebozo. Both have given accounts of the President taking the call which came in from Bob Haldeman on the morning of Sunday 18 June, reporting on the break-in. 'Hell, I was with him in the room', recalled Abplanalp. 'I heard him say, "They did WHAAT?" to Haldeman. He was so astonished he was practically shouting. He came off the phone shaking his head.'[2] Rebozo has confirmed this atmosphere of mystification. 'First he was amazed. Then he sat down and laughed about it. He said two or three times, "What in God's name were we doing there?"[3] It seems improbable that Nixon would put on such an act for the benefit of his two best friends, or indeed for Haldeman, who was equally convinced at his end of the call that the President's surprise was genuine.

Nixon's next move was to telephone Charles Colson. 'I was suspect number one with the President', recalled Colson. 'At that time in my life I would have gladly organized the bugging of a political opponent, but the plain fact was I had nothing whatever to do with it. I think I got this through to the President, but my strongest memory of that call was his anger. He kept saying it was stupid. Over and over again he asked "Why? Why?"[4]

The initial presumption on which Nixon (and later everyone else) worked was that the break-in to the Democratic National Committee Headquarters must have been a bugging operation directed at the Democratic Party Chairman Lawrence F. O'Brien. Nixon was certainly interested in O'Brien's activities, particularly after Bebe Rebozo had passed on some evidence that O'Brien was receiving a large personal retainer from Howard Hughes. A financial connection with Hughes could be an albatross around the neck of any politician, as Nixon had learned to his cost in 1962 when the Democrats had raised hell over the Hughes loan to his brother Donald. So with the thought in the back of his mind of playing the Hughes card back against the Democrats, Nixon sent a memo to Haldeman asking for the story to be checked out.

> January 14th 1971
> ABOARD AIR FORCE ONE
> To: H.R.Haldeman
> From: The President
>
> It would seem that the time is approaching when Larry O'Brien is held accountable for his retainer with Hughes. Bebe has some information on this although it is, of course, not solid but there is no question that one of Hughes's people did have O'Brien on a very heavy retainer for 'services rendered' in the past. Perhaps Colson should make a check on this.[5]

Haldeman scribbled 'Let's try Dean' on the bottom of this memo and passed the assignment to the Counsel's office.

It is part of the mythology of Watergate that this presidential memo in January 1971 was the motivation for the break-in to the DNC offices eighteen months later. This is untrue. Dean and his team did try to investigate Rebozo's report, but got nowhere. However, six months later, an Internal Revenue Service contact of John Ehrlichman's came up with the information that O'Brien was receiving a consultancy fee of $160,000 a year from the Hughes Tool Corporation. Thus, by the middle of 1971, the request in Nixon's 14 January memo had been answered, although not through the Haldeman–Dean channel, whose efforts to find the information had fizzled out.

In fact, John Dean had an interest of his own in the DNC offices: in November 1971 he gave his two investigators, Jack Caulfield and Tony Ulasewicz, an intriguing order.

'Dean wants you to check the offices of the Democratic National Committee', Caulfield instructed Ulasewicz.[6] The ex-policeman obeyed his instructions. Ulasewicz went over to the Watergate building and entered the DNC's headquarters. No break-in was necessary. Full access was achieved by the simple subterfuge of masquerading as a visitor. Ulasewicz walked all around the DNC's floor, noting the location of the various offices. 'It was a similar business office to what the Republicans would have, a place for records of donors, sending out brochures, making arrangements for dinners and fund-raising programs, hiring people out in the field, contacts with newspapers and all the routine matters', he reported to Caulfield, adding: 'I don't know what you think is in this office. My street smarts told me when Dean's asking me this kind of thing, there's something that they are after. Something hot. I told him "It's not there".'[7]

In the familiar accounts of Watergate, little or no attention has been paid to this strange episode of Ulasewicz 'casing the joint' at the DNC headquarters. His walk through, ordered by Dean, took place seven months before the 17 June 1972 break-in. At that time no other White House source or CRP official had the faintest notion that the DNC headquarters was being targeted in this way. Nixon was oblivious of such an activity. Equally ignorant were John Mitchell, Jeb Magruder, Gordon Liddy and Howard Hunt. So if all the principal *dramatis personae* of the later break-in drama were unaware of this reconnaissance mission, what on earth was John Dean up to when he sent his investigators into the Watergate building in November 1971?

The answer to this question is stranger than fiction. Only a brief summary can be given here, although serious students of the preliminaries to Watergate are strongly recommended to immerse themselves in *Silent Coup* as required reading on this phase of the story. According to the authors of *Silent Coup*, Dean's interest in the DNC was based on prostitution rather than politics. He was desperately anxious to acquire hard information on leading Democrats sleeping with call girls. As we have seen, he had made an abortive effort to deal in this type of dirt earlier in 1971, when he acquired the 'Happy Hooker's' list of clients through an Ulasewicz operation. In the winter of 1971/2 he started to plan a similar dirt-digging project. The essence of his plan was to bug the telephones of certain junior employees of the Democratic National Committee whom Dean believed to be in the business of putting visiting politicians in touch with a Washington call-girl ring. The target, therefore, was not O'Brien's office, but offices on the other side of the building.

Bugging these particular telephones required two break-ins. The two veterans of the Plumbers break-in, Howard Hunt and Gordon Liddy, became the masterminds of the operation. Liddy had by this time been appointed as Counsel to the Committee to Re-elect the President (CRP). In that role, at Dean's urging, Liddy had prepared a $1 million security and intelligence gathering plan called Operation Gemstone. He first unveiled it at a meeting in January 1972 attended by Dean, John Mitchell (who was about to become Chairman of CRP) and Jeb Magruder, who was to be Mitchell's deputy at CRP. Mitchell at first vetoed Gemstone, but Dean encouraged Liddy to resurrect it and to re-present it in a modified form at a further meeting on 30 March with Mitchell and Magruder.

Magruder's testimony as to what was said at this crucial meeting has been erratic. In the account he gave to the Senate Watergate Committee in 1973, Magruder claimed that Mitchell approved a scaled-down Gemstone operation and specifically authorised the burglary of the DNC offices in the Watergate building. But in his interview with the authors of *Silent Coup*, Magruder said Mitchell did not approve the DNC as a break-in target. 'The first plan we got had been initiated by Dean. Mitchell didn't do anything. All Mitchell did is just what I did, was acquiesce to the pressure from the White House...The target never came from Mitchell.'[8]

Magruder was undoubtedly in a tight spot at the time of the 30 March meeting. He was being relentlessly bullied by Liddy, whose charm offensive had recently taken the form of threats to tear his arm off. He was being pressed for a favourable decision on Gemstone by Dean, who claimed to have the White House behind him. As a character, Magruder was congenitally weak and anxious to please. Like a feather pillow, he gave way to the person who last sat on him. It was entirely in character for him to take the line of least resistance. As the authors *of Silent Coup* summarised his situation: 'Magruder was trapped between the pressure from Dean at the White House and Mitchell's repeated annoyed refusals to approve Gemstone on behalf of the CRP. So trapped, we believe, that Magruder gave the CRP's go-ahead to fund the scaled-down Gemstone without Mitchell's approval, using the funds that were already under Magruder's own control.'[9]

The extension of Gemstone's electronic surveillance plans into the Watergate bugging operation again had Dean's fingerprints all over it. His principal motivation seems to have been his desire to gather intelligence on the link between the call-girl ring and the Democrats. A secondary motivation may have been his alleged wish to gain access to a call-girl address book and some compromising photographs in the desk of one particular DNC official.

The notion that the break-in that led to the President of the United States' downfall was all to do with John Dean seeking salacious gossip about call girls and Democrats seems, at first glance, impossibly far-fetched. Impressive though *Silent Coup*'s research has been in establishing the theory, this author would have hesitated in accepting it had it not been for Gordon Liddy.

'Without doubt the man who commanded and conceived the Watergate operation was John Dean', said Liddy. 'Mitchell and Nixon had nothing whatever to do with it. I didn't realize that at the time. Like most other people I was fooled by Dean's facile lies. "Oh you don't understand Mitchell's ways", he told me when I was assuming from everything Mitchell said to me that he wanted Gemstone aborted. It was Dean who got the show on the road again. His meal ticket at the White House was to pass up the line the sort of who-sleeps-with-who-material that J. Edgar Hoover used to feed the various Presidents. That was Dean's level of sleaze. But he was a nasty, cunning little ferret so he didn't tell anyone except Howard Hunt that what he was really after was the call-girl address book and a bug on the phones that were used to book the call girls. He duped Magruder on that one and he duped me. I remember Magruder saying to me, "what we want is what they've got right here", pointing at the middle draw of his own desk. Now he didn't mean Larry O'Brien's desk. When the Cubans went in they didn't go near O'Brien's office in the DNC. Hunt gave them their orders and on the second break-in they went straight to the office and the desk of a secretary called Maxie Wells.* Our look-out post from the hotel over the road was angled to that office not to O'Brien's... The whole damn Watergate break-in was Dean's show. All the evidence confirms it. I thought I was involved in an operation that was politically

---

* According to *Silent Coup*, the FBI was able to establish that Wells's desk was the burglars' target, because when the burglars were being arrested, one had tried to conceal a key that fitted Wells's desk. For some mysterious reason, this fact was ignored throughout the investigation of the break-in.[10]

important to the President. I now know it was an operation that was personally important to John Dean. Period"[11]

If Gordon Liddy, in theory the physical commander of the Watergate break-in, was deceived in this way, how much greater must have been the deception of the President. As already recounted, Nixon was completely baffled when the first news of the break-in reached him in Key Biscayne on the morning of 18 June.

While his first reactions were those of ignorance, his secondary responses were those of anger towards some of his senior aides. That was sound, if misplaced, thinking. For the one member of his staff he never suspected of having anything to do with the burglary was John Dean. Yet it was to Dean, the true author of the Watergate break-in, that the President and his Chief of Staff turned for advice on the damage-limitation exercise that became the cover-up. That was a fatal error.

II. THE COVER-UP BEGINS

It was the cover-up of Watergate that ruined Richard Nixon. Why he started it; how he allowed it to get out of control; and how it became the many-headed monster that destroyed his Presidency were separate phases in his downward spiral towards political catastrophe.

In all the early stages of the cover-up, Nixon's Achilles heel was his reliance on John Dean. If there had been a different Counsel to the President there would have been no presidential resignation. Yet for all Dean's astounding acrobatics of double-crossing and deceit, his role in the cover-up was only that of best supporting actor. In Shakespearean terms, he played Iago to Nixon's Othello. His self-serving manipulation of the President and other senior White House figures was abhorrent, but distaste for the serpentine manoeuvrings of Dean does not diminish the fundamental responsibility of Nixon. His participation in the cover-up was profound, having its origins in the longstanding conflicts of his character.

Throughout his career, Nixon had a tendency to rise to the big challenges and diminish himself in the face of petty controversies. By 1972 he had won the laurels of a peacemaker without losing the instincts of a street fighter. Having shown great vision in his approach to international statecraft, he could be myopic in lesser matters, retaining a mean streak which he could display in inverse proportion to the size of the problem that was needling him. When he first learned the details of Watergate, it seemed to him to be no more than a minor political irritant. In his characteristic street-fighter style, one of his earliest thoughts was to see if it could be turned to the disadvantage of his lifelong enemies, the Democrats.

Nixon's first substantive meetings on Watergate took place at the White House on 20 June. His primary purpose was to find out what had happened. He did not get very far or try particularly hard. Haldeman was the President's principal source of information but he could not shed much light on the origins of the break-in since *his* principal source was Dean, who had maintained a judicious silence on the subject at a staff meeting earlier that morning. In the absence of hard information, Nixon chewed away at the Watergate bone in two meetings* and telephone conversations with Haldeman; a meeting with Colson; and a phone call to Mitchell. From these conversations he got nothing except a general impression that his senior aides were as much in the dark as he was. Colson said he was clean. Mitchell sounded embarrassed but innocent, merely expressing regret that he had not policed the people at CRP more effectively. In any case, Nixon's main concern was not internal discipline but external worry that the Democrats and the media might turn Watergate into an election issue. He suggested sarcastically that there should be a call for the Watergate burglars to be awarded a Pulitzer Prize as a match for the one the *New York Times* had been given for publishing the stolen Pentagon Papers. Later he became more combative, telling Haldeman that the way to handle the story was to play up the Cubans' involvement with the anti-Castro community in Miami. He thought Bebe Rebozo might get these Cubans 'to start a public bail fund for their arrested countrymen and make a big media issue out of it. If they used it to revive the Democrats' inept handling of the Bay of Pigs and to attack McGovern's foreign policy ideas, we might even make Watergate work in our favor.'[12]

This comment shows that Nixon's gut instinct from the outset was to go on to the attack over Watergate as the best form of defence. What he wanted to defend himself from was the Democrats' instantly announced intention of setting up a congressional investigation into the break-in, which he feared would turn into a political fishing expedition for other embarrassing activities such as Colson's dirty tricks. To Nixon, all this was routine hardball in the rough-house atmosphere of an election year. Having been at the sharp end of the campaigning ethics of John F. Kennedy and Lyndon B. Johnson, he needed no conversion course on presidential amorality. That was the way he thought the game had to be played. He therefore never even considered rooting out the culprits of Watergate and dismissing them from his administration. He simply wanted to solve what he thought was a small political problem in the most expedient way. As Bob Haldeman later put it, 'The President was involved in the cover-up from Day One.'[13]

---

* The first of these 20 June meetings was subsequently the object of great suspicion because of the mysterious eighteen and a half-minute gap on the tape.

The cover-up formally began three days later, on 23 June when the President and his Chief of Staff had a conversation reviewing the latest developments. By this time Haldeman had established that Liddy had been the operational leader of the break-in; that his funding had come from CRP; and that the FBI under its new Acting Director, L. Patrick Gray, was close to tracing the original sources of that funding. Haldeman explained this to the President, adding that he had been informed by Dean that Dean and Mitchell had conferred and recommended that the CIA be called in to obstruct the FBI. The crucial exchanges went as follows:

> Haldeman: Now on the investigation, you know, the Democratic break-in thing we're back to the—in the, the problem area because the FBI is not under control, because Gray doesn't exactly know how to control them, and they have, their investigation is now leading into some productive areas, because they've been able to trace the money, not through the money itself but through the bank, you know, sources—the banker himself. And it goes in some directions we don't want it to go...Mitchell came up with yesterday and John Dean analyzed very carefully last night and concludes, concurs now with Mitchell's recommendation that the only way to solve this, and we're set up beautifully to do it, uh, in that and that...the only network that paid any attention to it last night was NBC...they did a massive story on the Cuban
>
> President: That's right.
>
> Haldeman:—thing.
>
> President: Right.
>
> Haldeman: That the way to handle this for now is for us to have [Deputy CIA Director General Vernon] Walters call Pat Gray and say, 'Stay the hell out of this...this is, ah, business here we don't want you to go any further on it'. That's not an unusual development...Ah, he [Pat Gray] will call [Assistant Director of the FBI] Felt in and say: 'We've got the signal from across the river to put the hold on this'. And that will fit rather well because the FBI agents who are working this case, at this point, feel that's what it is. This is CIA.

Haldeman then told Nixon that the FBI examination of the cheques found on one of the burglars would lead to Kenneth Dahlberg, a CRP fundraiser. Nixon was astonished, for he had no idea who Dahlberg was. Indeed, one of the most striking features of the 23 June tape is that it is full of Nixon's exclamations of astonishment at the news Haldeman was giving him about the history of the break-in. This presidential amazement is a further indication that Nixon had no prior knowledge of Watergate. However, despite his innocence of the break-in, he apparently had no qualms about the cover-up, instantly endorsing what he thought was Mitchell's plan to block the FBI's investigation.

> Haldeman: And you seem to think the thing to do is to get them [the FBI] to stop.
> President: Right, fine.
> Haldeman: They say the only way to do that is from White House instructions. And it's got to be [CIA Director] Helms to ah...Walters...And the proposal would be that Ehrlichman and I call them in and say...
> President: All right, fine...well we protected Helms from one hell of a lot of things.

Further on in the conversation, Nixon asked about the role of John Mitchell.

> President: Well, what the hell, did Mitchell know about this thing to any much of a degree?
> Haldeman: I think so. I don't think he knew the details but I think he knew.

A few moments afterwards, Haldeman explained the role of Liddy, saying that he had been under pressure to get more information.

> President: Pressure from Mitchell?
> Haldeman: Apparently.
> President: All right, fine, I understand it all. We won't second guess Mitchell and the rest. Thank God it wasn't Colson.

These exchanges became notorious in the final days of the Nixon Presidency as 'the smoking gun'—the direct evidence on tape of criminal guilt. Yet in the atmosphere of the conversation as recorded, two features stand out. The first was that the President did not appear to have the faintest understanding that he might be sliding across the line into illegality. The criminal statutes of obstruction of justice clearly never entered his consciousness. On tape, Nixon and Haldeman sound like two business managers briskly solving a discrepancy in the firm's accounts department. They make calling in the CIA like asking for assistance from an outside firms of auditors. The entire conversation took less than five minutes of their attention in a ninety-minute agenda on the affairs of the Presidency. They made their decisions quickly because they thought they were taking the most effective route towards getting rid of a troublesome but minor political difficulty in accordance with the anarchic rules of the game. As Nixon himself said towards the end of the discussion, 'Play it tough. That's the way they play it and that's the way we are going to play it.'[14]

The second remarkable feature of the 'smoking gun' conversation was that the gun itself had been loaded, primed and pointed in the wrong direction by John Dean. This was, of course, unknown to Nixon and Haldeman at the time. It has only recently been discovered by the authors of *Silent Coup*, but their evidence appears conclusive.

In *Silent Coup*, Dean is portrayed as the self-appointed secret controller of the cover-up. He receives and transmits all the inside information on Watergate. For different reasons the key players trust him. Liddy regards him as the damage control officer of the break-in. Haldeman and Ehrlichman give him the assignment of conducting an internal White House inquiry into what happened. Acting FBI Director Gray allows Dean to sit in on all FBI meetings and interviews on Watergate after being told by him that as President's Counsel he will report what he learns directly to the President. This was pure fiction, but it provided Dean with a most advantageous listening post on the progress of the FBI's investigation. Thus it was from Gray that Dean learned that the FBI were confused about the motives for the break-in and had formed a theory that it might have been a CIA operation. Gray also gave Dean a remarkable new idea for getting everyone off the hook. 'I remember telling Mr. Dean in one of those early telephone calls or meetings,' Gray later testified to the Senate Select Committee, 'that the FBI was going to pursue all leads aggressively unless we were told by the CIA that there was a CIA interest or involvement in this case.'[15]

This indication that the FBI could be halted in its search for the truth by the right word from the CIA came as manna from heaven to John Dean. As one of the most ardent instigators of the break-in, he was in an extremely vulnerable position. Disgrace and imprisonment faced him if the FBI uncovered the truth about his involvement. That was why he worked so frantically and duplicitously in the days after the break-in. He secretly offered hush money to the burglars and to Liddy. He assumed the key role in Ehrlichman's White House inquiry while concealing most of his information from his bosses. He inserted himself into the FBI investigation on a false premise. In short, a great deal of power and knowledge was in Dean's hands, and he used it to perform the conjuring trick which dragged Nixon into the cover-up.

At 8.15 on the morning of 23 June (later to become the day of Nixon's 'smoking gun' conversation), Dean telephoned Haldeman. He began by delivering the unwelcome information that the FBI was hot on the money trail and had traced a link between a cheque found on one of the burglars and a Mexican bank account used by CRP. 'Great news', responded Haldeman sarcastically. 'What else has the FBI found?'[16] Dean heightened the panic threshold by saying that the money trail from the Mexican bank could lead to the FBI uncovering the names of many CRP contributors. Although this was irrelevant to Watergate it unsettled Haldeman, who knew that many of the big contributors to CRP had insisted on anonymity (to which they were then legally entitled) and that the revelation of their identities could be politically explosive.[17]

Having dropped his bombshell, Dean now offered a way of damping down the flames.

'Gray has been looking for a way out of this mess', he told Haldeman. 'I spoke to Mitchell, and he and I agree the thing to do is for you to tell Walters that we don't know where that Mexican investigation is going to lead. Have him talk to Gray—and maybe the CIA can turn off the FBI down there in Mexico.'[18]

The Chief of Staff was impressed by both the logic and the source of authority of this suggestion. If John Mitchell was recommending such a course of action to halt the FBI in its tracks, Nixon needed to know about it. So, less than two hours later, at 10.05 a.m. on 23 June Haldeman went into the Oval Office, faithfully relayed Dean's message and started the conversation which eventually destroyed the Nixon Presidency.

It is one of the strangest ironies of Watergate, that what Nixon so fatally endorsed on the 'smoking gun' tape was nothing more than a Dean falsehood. For John Mitchell had never at any time made the suggestion that the CIA should be asked to obstruct the FBI. Dean simply invented that ploy to save his own skin, attaching Mitchell's name as author in order to give the scheme more credibility with Haldeman and Nixon—which it certainly did.

There is a temptation at this point in the narrative to sympathise with Nixon, for at first glance the President seems to have been a most unlucky victim of the curse of Dean.

A spider's web of deceit had led Nixon to believe that Mitchell had instigated the break-in; that Mitchell wanted his mistake covered up; and that Mitchell was responsible for the ingenious suggestion that the White House should get the CIA to block the FBI's investigation. In fact, Mitchell had done none of these things. So when Nixon finally said on the 'smoking gun' tape, 'All right, fine, I understand it all. We won't second guess Mitchell and the rest', he was talking nonsense. He still did not understand Watergate at all. What he had done was to fall hook, line and sinker for his Counsel's conjuring trick.

Sympathy for Nixon's gullibility does not, however, equate to an acquittal for his involvement in the conspiracy. Nixon was a victim, but by no means an innocent victim. He showed himself perfectly willing to give his blessing to a cover-up, although admittedly a cover-up for Mitchell. This brings the focus back to Nixon's character. The 'dark' side of his nature was already pulling him towards fighting back against the Democrats with any weapon he could lay his hands on. If low blows, dirty tricks, and illegal acts had to be part of the weaponry that was all part of the game.

Yet Nixon might have backed off from such a strategy, from fear or caution, if the 'good' side of his nature had not also weighed in on the side of covering up for personal reasons. These centred on the fact that John Mitchell was his truest political comrade. From 1967 onwards, the relationship between the two men had, for all its complexities, been as near as either of them ever got to a close friendship. Nixon felt he owed a lot to Mitchell; and he confided in him more than anyone else, effectively regarding him as the number two man in his administration. To complicate the picture still further, Mitchell was at a low point in his personal life—depressed, drinking too much, troubled by ill health, and plagued by the instability of his wife Martha.

A more ruthless leader might have seen these difficulties as an additional reason for dispensing with Mitchell's services. Not Nixon. He could be almost as headstrong in his compassion for a friend as he was in his combativeness towards an enemy. The instincts of his parents, Hannah and Frank, were still strong forces within him, and they both seemed to point in the same direction. Cover up for John Mitchell for reasons of kindness and loyalty (Hannah). Cover up against the coming attack by the Democrats because toughing it out and fighting back is t^ way to win in politics (Frank).

There was one other factor which encouraged Nixon's participatio cover-up. His reluctance to face up to personal confrontations. As he hi admitted, this was a fear that went back to his childhood,[19] but if ev a moment in his adult life when he needed to vanquish it, it was the diately following the Watergate break-in. For once Nixon kne knew, that Mitchell was heavily implicated, the obvious and move for the President to make was to call in his old friend for a one-on-one confrontation. Had this happened, it is extremely unlikely that Watergate would ever have exploded into a political crisis. For Mitchell did not need to be protected by a cover-up. His hands, though not completely clean, were far from being tainted by criminal guilt. Although he had flirted unwisely and perhaps dangerously with the Gemstone plan, he had vetoed it three times. He had never authorised the break-in. He had never suggested blocking the FBI with the CIA.

If only Nixon had heard all this from Mitchell's lips, how different history might have been.

The confrontation that never was allowed the cover-up that need not have happened. Within hours of the 'smoking gun' conversation, Haldeman and Ehrlichman were playing Dean's music at a meeting with Richard Helms, Director of the CIA and his Deputy, General Vernon Walters. Nixon had added a few notes of his own to the score, by telling Haldeman to mention that the Watergate break-in would be 'likely to blow the whole Bay of Pigs thing' if it went any further.[20] This mysterious reference to the CIA's past incompetence over the 1961 Bay of Pigs fiasco initially seemed to have the desired effect when dropped into the conversation. 'Turmoil in the room', was how Haldeman later described the scene. 'Helms gripping the arms of his chair and shouting "The Bay of Pigs had nothing to do with this. I have no concern about the Bay of Pigs."'[21] But when the shouting stopped, the meeting ended with the impression that the CIA was going to be constructive.

Later that same day, General Walters met with Gray. He told him that the FBI investigation was about to uncover CIA operations in Mexico and reminded him of the agreement between the FBI and CIA not to expose each other's sources. Walters soon changed his tune, however, when he returned to CIA headquarters that evening and discovered that no CIA operations were threatened by the FBI investigation. From then on, determined to keep the CIA out of any cover-up, Walters refused to comply with Dean's efforts to involve it. Three he was summoned to see Dean (on 26, 27 and 28 June) who asked for the lp in containing the Watergate investigation and even in paying for the ail. Walters denied him thrice. His explanation for rejecting these prophetic. 'Involving the Agency would transform what was now d conventional explosive into a multi-megaton explosion and orth the risk for all concerned',[22] he told Dean, whose strategy d now failed.

onwards, the cover-up spiralled slowly but steadily out of arge of it and he used bribery, perjury, and the manipulation of both prosecutors and witnesses to keep the scandal from unravelling before the election. In the short term his methods were successful, but expensive. In fulfilment of his promise to Liddy that the burglars would get their legal and support costs paid, Dean organised a cash-raising and distribution operation which at times resembled a gold-plated farce. Throughout the summer, Dean's gumshoe Tony Ulasewicz was kept in almost perpetual motion, picking up large bundles of dollars from CRP and delivering them to the defendants' representatives by spy-movie methods such as brown paper bag handovers, left luggage locker drops and nocturnal assignations in strange places. Hunt was by far the most financially demanding of the burglars, requiring separate cash payments of $40,000, $43,000, $18,000 and $53,000 to be handed over to his wife. Hunt later admitted that he had extorted these tranches of money as 'a quid pro quo for silence'.[23]

It was a silence that Dean was particularly anxious to buy, for Hunt was the Watergate operative who knew most about Dean's involvement in the planning of the DNC break-in. The details of that involvement and the whole chronology of Gemstone had been recorded in two Hermès notebooks lying in Hunt's White House safe. While he had them in his custody, Dean destroyed them.

In addition to paying hush money and destroying evidence, Dean also gave coaching lessons in perjury. His pupil was Magruder, who was in the prosecutor's frame for possible indictment as a co-conspirator of the burglars. The object of the lessons was to give Magruder a story to tell to the Grand Jury which would result in the indictments stopping short of the Hunt—Liddy level. Thus, after many rehearsals, Magruder dutifully explained on oath that the legitimate intelligence gathering operation he had commanded at CRP had escalated into the illegal Watergate break-in without any knowledge on his part. He assured the Grand Jury that the burglary of the DNC was solely due to excessive zeal on the part of Hunt and Liddy, acting on their own without higher authority. Dean's talents as a perjury tutor must have been considerable, for the Grand Jury believed Magruder. When the indictments were handed down on 15 September they went no further than Hunt, Liddy, McCord and the rest of the Watergate burglars. The second conjuring trick of the cover-up had worked.

How much did Nixon know about Dean's illegal activities in the June–September period? The answer is virtually nothing. He had no direct contact with Dean, and the reports he received from Haldeman gave few details beyond the fact that the young Counsel was doing his best to stop the indictments reaching higher than the break-in team.

On the day the indictments were announced, the President and Haldeman had a meeting with John Dean to thank him for his good work. The tone of the conversation was upbeat and mutually confiding. It opened on a congratulatory note:

> President: Hi, how are you? You had quite a day today, didn't you?
>   You got Watergate on the way, didn't you?
> Dean: We tried.
> Haldeman: How did it all end up?
> Dean: Ah, I think we can say 'well' at this point. The press is playing
>   it just as we expect...

The stroking session lasted for almost an hour and left Dean basking in the warm glow of his boss's approval. As a middle-level White House official, he had rarely met the President before, and had never been involved at such a level of intimacy. All three men seemed to be confident that the indictments would end the affair. At one point Dean reported, 'Three months ago I would have had trouble predicting there would be a day when this would be forgotten but I think I can say that fifty-four days from now [the date of the presidential election] nothing is going to come crashing down to our surprise.'[24] Nixon sounded appropriately grateful, praising his young aide for his 'skillful' job. Dean took the opportunity to indicate that he had other skills that could be useful in future. He said he had been keeping notes on those who had behaved 'as less than our friends'. 'Great!' exclaimed Nixon as Dean warmed to his theme with a homily on the importance of being earnest about enemies. It was a message guaranteed to wind up Nixon. 'I want the most comprehensive notes on all of those who have tried to do us in', he instructed Haldeman in tones of mounting enthusiasm. 'They are asking for it and they are going to get it... We have not used the power in this first four years, as you know. We have never used it. We haven't used the Bureau and we haven't used the Justice Department, but things are going to change now.' 'What an exciting prospect', was Dean's ecstatic reply.[25]

Haldeman, who had often heard Nixon in these excitable moods before, did not take any of this too seriously. But Dean went away exhilarated, believing that he had received the President's blessing for his past actions and some 'exciting' marching orders for the future. Dean and Nixon did not talk again until more than five months later, on 28 February 1973. By that time Watergate was threatening to close in on the White House, because what both the President and the President's Counsel had seriously underestimated was the power of Congress, aided and abetted by the power of Judge John Sirica.

III. CONGRESS UNSHEATHES ITS SWORD

Long before Watergate, Congress was spoiling for a fight with Nixon. The roots of this conflict went deep and have been traced in a previous chapter. But the 93rd Congress that assembled in January 1973 was in a particularly pugnacious mood for several reasons. First there was the battle cry 'No more Vietnams', which the Democrats converted into their proposal for a War Powers Act. This was a device to impose a sixty-day limit on any presidential commitment of troops to hostilities abroad, unless congressional approval was granted. They also planned, in separate legislative proposals, to refuse funding for continuing military aid to Saigon and to reject the administration's package of reconstruction aid to Hanoi. These were profound challenges to the President's right to control foreign policy, a right which had not been seriously questioned since the disputes over the Neutrality Acts in 1935.

A second rallying cry was 'The Imperial Presidency'. This was the title of a best-selling book by the liberal historian Arthur Schlesinger Jr., and its central theme, that the President's powers had increased, were increasing and ought to be diminished, won much support on the campuses and in the op-ed columns of some newspapers. Nixon regarded the 'Imperial Presidency' thesis as an outrageous exercise in political hypocrisy. He pointed out to his aides that Schlesinger and his liberal camp followers had been all in favour of a strong presidency so long as the Democrats occupied the White House. He also emphasised that the Truman, Kennedy and Johnson administrations had been far more overbearing than his own when it came to numbers of wiretaps; extensions of executive privilege; and other accusations of presidential excess made in the book against himself. Nixon was justified in complaining about these double standards. However, his complaints fell on deaf ears among the Democrats, who did not wish to see the argument about the President's power reduced to an embarrassing squabble about which recent occupant of the Oval Office had behaved worst. Instead, they hoped to elevate the dispute to a constitutional epic on the level of an historic struggle between King and Parliament in seventeenth-century Britain. These signs and portents were ominous because the Democrats were exceptionally powerful on Capitol Hill in 1973, and Nixon was exceptionally vulnerable. Democrats controlled both the House and the Senate, whereas Nixon was the first President since Zachary Taylor in 1849 to start his term without a majority for his own party in either body. So if there was to be a power struggle, Nixon would face it at a severe political disadvantage.

The Democrats' third cry was 'We were robbed'. Considering the size of the Nixon landslide that had defeated their candidate, this sounded a ludicrous attempt to make bricks out of straw. The only straws they had were the stories published in the *Washington Post* about Republican dirty tricks by a prankster named Donald Segretti and the Watergate break-in. However, since both examples of foul play were reported to have links with the White House, there was a feeling that the 1972 presidential election excesses by the Republicans might prove to be far more serious than the dirty tricks both sides had played on each other in the past. One powerful Democrat was the majority leader in the Senate, Senator Mike Mansfield. He was bitter about the underhand attacks and smears that had been perpetrated on his old friend Senator Ed Muskie. He sensed that there was much more to Watergate than had yet come out. Mansfield thus became the prime mover in turning the machinery of Congress's investigational power towards Watergate.

The first congressional inquiry into Watergate-related matters was instigated by the House Banking and Currency Committee of the 92nd Congress under the chairmanship of Wright Patman. He was a formidable opponent. His staff concentrated on the money trail and by October 1972 they had unearthed enough evidence of strange financial goings-on at CRP for Congressman Patman to announce that the campaign contributions might have been used to finance 'the greatest political espionage case in American history', which reached 'right into the White House'.[26] The White House did all it could to block the Patman Committee's inquiry, preventing Dean, Mitchell, Stans and others from testifying. This led to Patman staging a theatrical 'hearing' with empty chairs symbolising the missing witnesses. Although his inquiry ran out of time and steam, it caused a great deal of defensive footwork within the White House, particularly by Dean, who realised how vulnerable he was to further congressional investigations. 'We really need to turn Patman off', he told Haldeman.[27] Nixon shared that view. According to the Speaker of the House Carl Albert, the President lived 'in constant torture' from the time when the Patman Committee began its inquiry, making Nixon's life 'a living hell from then on. He knew that this thing had been done, he knew that... there had been a cover-up and he had not stopped it. He was afraid all the time that they might find that out. So he must have had a life of real misery.'[28]

If that view was correct, Nixon's misery must have been multiplied by the news that the gauntlet thrown down by Patman was going to be seized by a far more menacing congressional body. This was the Senate Select Committee on Presidential Campaign Activities, which was established on Mansfield's initiative under the chairmanship of Senator Sam Ervin. Its terms of reference were to 'conduct an investigation and study of the extent, if any, to which illegal, improper or unethical activities were engaged in by any persons…in the presidential election of 1972'.

The Democrats used their majority to block all Republican amendments to restrict this investigation to specific areas of concern, or to widen it to topics which might embarrass previous Democratic presidential candidates. It was all highly political. In the end, the Republican minority gave up and acquiesced to the original wording of the terms of reference. So the Committee, which soon became known as the Watergate Committee, received full Senate approval by 77–0 on 7 February.

The Chairman of the Watergate Committee was Senator Sam Ervin, an old-style Southerner from North Carolina who had the manner of a country lawyer and the voting record of a reactionary. Ervin's two great loves were the English language and the United States Constitution. His repertoire of Biblical, Shakespearean, and country-boy allusions combined with his mystic reverence for the constitutional rights of the citizen made him sound like America's favourite grandfather on television. Nixon saw him differently, regarding Ervin, for all his homespun stylism, as 'a sharp, resourceful, and intensely partisan political animal'. In the President's view, Ervin's selection for the Watergate Committee chairmanship meant that 'the Democrats actually are starting four years early for their run for the White House'.[29]

The Vice Chairman of the Committee was the Republican Senator from Tennessee, Howard Baker. An able lawyer, who later in his career was destined to become Senate Majority leader and White House Chief of Staff, Baker was consistently outfoxed by Ervin. He has recalled that he accepted the minority leadership of the Committee with considerable scepticism: 'I approached this job with the mind set that this was just a partisan caper by the Democrats. I didn't think it would get anywhere.'[30] He did his best to reassure Nixon, telling him at a private meeting before the hearings began: 'Mr. President, I am your friend and a loyal Republican. I want you to know that I want you to get a fair shake.'[31]

Nixon was far from reassured. He thought it outrageous that the investigation should be limited to the 1972 election and urged that the presidential campaigns of 1964 and 1968 should be included in the Committee's remit since this would result in the exposure of LBJ's buggings; the dirty tricks of the Democrats' favourite prankster, Dick Tuck, and many other skulduggeries. Howard Baker suggested this wider approach but was thwarted by Ervin, who used one of his many bucolic metaphors to declare that it would be 'as foolish as the man who went bear hunting and stopped to chase rabbits'.[32] It was the first of several preliminary skirmishes lost by the Republican minority. The most important of these concerned the selection and funding of the Committee's staff. The Majority Counsel was Samuel Dash, an experienced Philadelphia prosecutor and criminal law professor who towered over the Minority Counsel, Fred Thompson, in experience and in his ability to recruit a large and often highly partisan staff. 'We were completely outgunned in staff terms from day one', recalled Thompson's deputy, the Committee's Assistant Minority Counsel, Howard Liebengood. 'The majority staff just trampled all over us. They outnumbered the minority staff by a factor of 5–1. We had about 12 guys and they had 60. Some of the most active members of Dash's team were total Nixon haters, just out to get him, and they ran amok. Scott Armstrong, for example, was extremely close to Bob Woodward of the *Washington Post*, and he wasn't just a source of leaks to journalists, he was more like an open pipeline pumping all the Committee's confidential material directly to Woodward on a daily basis.'[33]

This incestuous relationship between the press and the Ervin Committee staff, combined with the network's later decision to televise the hearings, meant that the White House was completely outflanked in the public relations battle. In any event, the President's men soon had much greater worries than public relations on their hands. The Senate Judiciary Committee's confirmation hearings in February on the nomination of Patrick Gray for Director of the FBI were a disaster for the White House. Gray admitted under questioning that he had regularly submitted the FBI investigative reports on Watergate to Dean. He also testified that Dean had taken a week to turn over the contents of Howard Hunt's White House safe to the FBI. This drew the President's Counsel into the spotlight of congressional and public attention for the first time. There were immediate demands for him to come before the Committee and testify. This prompted Nixon into meeting with Dean on 28 February to discuss the Gray hearings, and another looming problem—the sentences that were about to be passed on the Watergate burglars by Judge John Sirica.

It is clear from the transcript of this conversation that Nixon was getting shaken by all the bad Watergate news that was flooding in on him. He began, as he so often did in this phase of the crisis, with a ramble of reminiscences about the Hiss case. Then he turned to the sentencing of the burglars, expressing incredulity at the rumours that Judge Sirica was intending to give them exemplary sentences in order to force them to talk.

'You know when they talk about thirty-five-year sentences,' said Nixon, 'here is something to think about. There were no weapons! Right? There were no injuries! Right? There was no success! It is just ridiculous.' Dean agreed. 'What the hell do they expect though?' continued Nixon. 'Do they expect clemency in a reasonable time? What would you advise on that?' Dean, who had already promised clemency to some of the burglars without asking anyone's permission, kept quiet on that one, merely supporting the President's view that clemency could not be offered for the foreseeable future and that nothing should be said about any of the burglars while their cases were being appealed.

'Maybe we will have to change our policy', said Nixon. 'But the President should not become involved in any part of the case. Do you agree with that?'

'I agree totally, sir. Absolutely', responded Dean.

Nixon returned to the theme of his own ignorance of, and isolation from, the break-in. 'Of course, I am not dumb and I will never forget when I heard about this [expletive deleted] forced entry and bugging. I thought, what in the hell is this? What is the matter with these people? Are they crazy? I thought they were nuts! A prank! But it wasn't. It wasn't very funny. I think that our Democratic friends know that too. They know what the hell it was. They don't think...I'd be involved in such stuff. They think I have people capable of it—and they are correct in that Colson would do anything.'[34]

Dean agreed with that too. After their meeting, Nixon dictated his impressions for his diary. 'I am very impressed by him [Dean]. He has shown enormous strength, great intelligence, and great subtlety...I am glad that I am talking to Dean now rather than going through Haldeman or Ehrlichman. I think I have made a mistake in going through others, when there is a man with the capability of Dean I can talk to directly.'[35]

That was probably the biggest error of judgement Nixon made in his life. For the next few weeks he put his trust in Dean, with whom he confided on over twenty occasions during the month of March. The subject of their confidences was always Watergate. The President seemed to be caught in a maze of confusion, often repeating his questions and sounding stunned by some of the answers. Who knew what and when? Who should testify? Who would be good witnesses? What would Sirica do? Who were the Ervin Committee gunning for? Did they have someone 'higher up' in their sights? Roaming around in this undergrowth of speculation, Nixon observed to Dean on 13 March that Haldeman was the Committee's main target because one of his key aides, Dwight Chapin, was linked to Segretti's dirty tricks operation which the press persisted in presenting (erroneously) as part of Watergate. Dean reassured the President that Chapin had not known anything about the break-in. Almost as an afterthought, Nixon asked if Gordon Strachan, Haldeman's other key aide, had advance knowledge of Watergate. On receiving an affirmative answer, he exploded in angry astonishment.

President: Haldeman's problem is Chapin, isn't it?

Dean: Bob's problem is circumstantial.

President: Why is that? Let's look at the circumstantial...Bob didn't know any of those people like the Hunts and all that bunch. Colson did, but Bob didn't, OK?

Dean: That's right.

President: Now where the hell, or how much Chapin knew I will be [expletive deleted] if I know.

Dean: Chapin didn't know anything about the Watergate.

President: Don't you think so?

Dean: Absolutely not.

President: Strachan?

Dean: Yes.

President: He knew?

Dean: Yes.

President: About the Watergate?

Dean: Yes.

President: Well, then, he probably told Bob.

Dean: Yes.

President: I will be damned! Well, that is the problem in Bob's case. Not Chapin, then, but Strachan. Strachan worked for him, didn't he?

Dean: Yes. They would have one hell of a time proving that Strachan had knowledge of it, though.

President: Who knew better—Magruder?

Dean: Magruder and Liddy.

President: Oh, I see. The other weak link for Bob is Magruder. He hired him, et cetera.

The significance of this dialogue is that this is the first time Nixon has been told that any White House aide had advance knowledge of the break-in. Until this moment, Dean had been assuring the President for nine months that there was 'no White House involvement' in the burglary. Now Nixon learned that one of Haldeman's aides (and therefore by implication Haldeman himself) had been involved from the beginning.

Nixon's attitude to this bombshell was extraordinary. His most obvious course of action would have been to call in Haldeman and to ask whether Dean had got his facts right.* Was Strachan implicated? Did Haldeman have advance knowledge of the break-in? But the President never put these vital questions to the Chief of Staff, whom he saw alone every day for long periods. Why not? The answer again lies in Nixon's aversion to personal confrontation. At the second critical crossroads in the unfolding story of Watergate, Nixon was faced with a devastating revelation about a close personal colleague.

But just as he had avoided asking John Mitchell for the full facts about his involvement in the break-in on 20 June 1972, Nixon again avoided discussing Dean's allegations with Haldeman on 13 March 1973. The omission was a disaster. For if the confrontation had taken place, Nixon would have discovered that Haldeman (like Mitchell) did not have the advance knowledge of the break-in imputed to him by Dean. If only the President had established those facts, it would have been much easier for him to face up to the truth.

Even though he now believed that both Mitchell and Haldeman were at risk from Watergate, Nixon began to contemplate full disclosure. As if it had finally dawned on him that he was facing a new dimension of undefined vulnerabilities from the Senate inquisition that was coming, Nixon suddenly asked Dean a vital question. 'Is it too late to go the hang-out route?' This would have meant hanging out all the dirty linen in public; admitting precisely what had happened; firing those responsible; and allowing the American people to decide how significant or insignificant a matter Watergate really was. At long last, Nixon was on the right track, but Dean swiftly deflected him. It is easy to see why. For Dean, the hang-out route would have been the route to his own hanging. A strategy of full disclosure would have meant that Dean's pivotal role in the break-in, the cover-up, and the hush-money payments, would all have been exposed. Responding to the President's question, Dean sounded rattled and almost incoherent: 'There is a certain domino situation here', he said. 'If some things start going, a lot of other things are going to start going, and there can be a lot of problems if every-thing starts falling. So there are dangers, Mr. President. I would be less than candid if I didn't tell you there are. There's a reason for us...no—not everyone going up and testifying.'[36]

---

* The facts were frequently fluid in John Dean's hands. Having told the President in categorical terms on 13 March that he knew Strachan was involved in the planning of the break-in, Dean reversed this in a further conversation with Nixon on 17 March. In his testimony to the Senate Watergate Committee, Dean again denied all knowledge of Strachan's involvement. Yet in his memoirs, *Blind Ambition*, he admitted that he had known of Strachan's role from the beginning.

Nixon backed away from the idea of mass testimony, but returned to another version of the hang-out route after a difficult press conference on 15 March at which he was shocked by the intensity of the media's inquisition on Watergate. As he later wrote in his memoirs: 'The questioning kept returning to Watergate with a relentlessness, almost a passion, that I had seen before only in the most emotional days of the Vietnam war. It was during this conference that for the first time I began to realize the dimensions of the problem we were facing with the media and with Congress regarding Watergate. *Vietnam had found its successor.*'[37]

In the aftermath of the press conference, Nixon decided to press Dean for a written statement setting down all the oral assurances he had given since June 1972 about the non-involvement of senior White House aides. He met Dean on 16 March and suggested that he should go away for a few days to Camp David to prepare such a report which could be used as the basis for a full presidential statement. But Dean was now changing his tune. He pointed out that several White House aides could be vulnerable, including himself, and he introduced a new unexploded bomb, telling the President about John Ehrlichman's role in the Hunt–Liddy break-in at the office of Ellsberg's psychiatrist.

Nixon professed to be staggered by this information, although according to Ehrlichman he had been briefed on it at San Clemente several months earlier. To Dean, the President sounded suitably appalled. 'What in the world—What in the name of God was Ehrlichman having something in the Ellsberg…This is the first I ever heard of this! I can't see that getting into, into this hearing.'

But Dean by now could see the prospect of almost everything getting into the hearings. The whole cover-up was unravelling in his hands. Senator Ervin's Watergate committee was on the scent of several White House and CRP horror stories. Hunt was making extortionate demands for more money. Judge Sirica was expected to try to break the burglars' silence by handing out savagely punitive sentences in a few days' time. Some senior White House aides, notably Ehrlichman, were supporting the hang-out or full disclosure route. The President was unsteady and undecided. John Dean was a frightened man. In response to a lighthearted question from his White House colleague, Bud Krogh, on 19 March, 'How are things?' Dean replied, 'Bud I'm scared, really scared. I'm so scared I can't even make love to my wife.'[38]

IV. DEAN TURNS ACCUSER

Dean soon conveyed his fear to the President, although in less colourful language than he had used to Krogh. Sounding 'slightly agitated'[39] he spoke to Nixon on the telephone on 20 March and requested an audience 'just to paint the whole picture for you, the soft spots, the potential problem areas'.[40] At this one-on-one meeting, which consisted of what was later to be known as the 'Cancer on the Presidency' conversation, Dean began by stating baldly that the White House defences had crumbled and that the 'plan' had failed. He continued:

> Dean: I think there's no doubt about the seriousness of the problem we've got. We have a cancer—within—close to the Presidency that is growing. It's growing daily. It's compounding, growing geometrically now because it compounds itself. That will be clear as I explain, you know, of why it is and basically it is because (1) we're being blackmailed (2) people are going to start perjuring themselves very quickly that have not had to perjure themselves to protect other people in the line. And there is no assurance—
> President: That it won't bust.
> Dean: That it won't bust.

After this apocalyptic opening, Dean began reciting his version of the Watergate story. Most of his account was familiar territory but he made some startlingly new disclosures. 'The most troublesome post thing,' said Dean referring to the cover-up following the break-in, 'is that Bob [Haldeman] is involved in that; John [Ehrlichman] is involved in that; I am involved in that; Mitchell is involved in that. And that is an obstruction of justice.' Nixon reeled with astonishment at this suggestion that his senior aides might be involved in a criminal conspiracy. 'How was Bob involved?'[41] he asked, believing that Dean must be 'over dramatizing'.[42] Dean explained that Haldeman had let him use a $350,000 cash fund in his safe to make payments to the defendants. He said that he, Haldeman and Ehrlichman had decided that 'there was no price too high to pay to let this thing blow up in front of the election'.

Dean then came to his primary concern, which was how to handle the burglars' demands for money. Hunt wanted 'by the close of business yesterday' a payment of $122,000 in cash, otherwise he would tell all about the Ellsberg break-in and other 'seamy things' he had done for the White House. With Judge Sirica's exemplary sentences expected in two days' time, this was an alarming threat. Dean added, 'This is going to be a continual blackmail operation by Hunt and Liddy and the Cubans.' 'How much money do you need?' the President asked a few moments later. 'I would say these people are going to cost a million dollars over the next two years', replied Dean. 'We could get that', said the President. 'If you need the money, I mean, uh, you could get the money...You could get a million dollars. And you could get it in cash. I know where it could be gotten...I mean it's not easy but it could be done.'

This exchange, at first reading, seems devastating to Nixon for it appears to confirm his willingness to pay a million dollars in hush money to the burglars. However, later on in the conversation, there is some evidence that he was speaking hypothetically, making the remark a few seconds afterwards, 'I'm just thinking out loud here, for a moment'.

The interpretation that the President was merely flying a hypothetical kite in this dialogue is further supported by the fact that he took no further action to find such mega-funding or to pay continuous hush money to the defendants. On the other hand, later in the conversation Nixon seemed to get rattled by the urgency of the threat from Hunt. The 'immediate thing,' he declared, 'is you've got no choice with Hunt but the hundred and twenty or whatever it is. Right?' Dean agreed. 'You better damn well get that done, but fast', ordered the President. Done it was.

Nixon was by now lurching into a deep and possibly criminal involvement in the cover-up. He was willing to pay Danegeld to Hunt to stave off a crisis, but not to any more Danes in future. This was equivalent to becoming a little bit pregnant and then stopping. Perhaps a more generous interpretation is that Nixon temporarily yielded to the temptation to pay Hunt's eve of sentencing blackmail demand for reasons of expediency, but thereafter decided as a matter of principle that it would be wrong to get into any further blackmail payments. He took a rather firmer line on the next problem Dean raised, which was Hunt's expectation of clemency. Dean said the other defendants would also be seeking a commutation of sentence, and added, 'I'm not sure that you will ever be able to deliver on the clemency. It may just be too hot.' 'You can't do it till after the '74 elections that's for sure', responded Nixon. 'But even then your point is that even then you couldn't do it.' 'That's right', said Dean. 'It may further involve you in a way you shouldn't be involved in this.' 'No, it's wrong, that's for sure', was the President's last word on clemency.[43]

The helplessness of his position was dawning on Nixon. After some wobbling he had decided to go no further in paying blackmail. He had rejected clemency. These decisions meant that sooner or later the storm would burst. The only way to pre-empt it was for the President to make his own full disclosure statement. Yet, after one or two feints in this direction during the dialogue with Dean and in subsequent conversations over the next two days with Dean, Haldeman and Ehrlichman, Nixon faltered and decided that honesty was not yet the best policy. 'There was just something in the makeup of the man that made it impossible for him to bare his breast to the nation', was Ehrlichman's interpretation of the President's refusal to accept the hangout route.[44]

The 21–22 March meetings ended in amoral stalemate. The only conclusion was that Dean should go to Camp David and write a report. 'See what you can come up with', said Nixon optimistically. The prospective revisionist historian immediately expressed his discomfort. 'I was everywhere—everywhere they look they are going to find Dean', he muttered, as he prepared to depart for the Catocins.[45]

Dean's sojourn at Camp David from 23 to 28 March was a major turning point in the Watergate story. While he composed his thoughts on the mountain top, events were moving fast in Washington. On the morning of 23 March Judge John Sirica announced his provisional sentences on the Watergate burglars. He gave thirty-five years to Hunt, forty years apiece to the Cubans, and twenty years to Liddy.* However, James McCord was freed on bond because he had sent a letter to the Judge offering co-operation for leniency. These sentences went far beyond Sirica living up to his nickname 'Maximum John'. For unarmed first offenders who had not stolen anything, the prison terms were sheer judicial terrorism. Sirica was quite blatant about his motives, saying the sentencing was harsh in order to make the defendants talk.

By the evening of 23 March, McCord was talking to the Ervin Committee's Chief Counsel Sam Dash, who announced that the secret testimony was 'full and honest'.[46] It was promptly leaked to the *Washington Post*, who ran a story on 25 March saying that McCord had told the Committee's investigators that Dean and Magruder had prior knowledge of the break-in. All this put the heat on Dean. Seeing that 'the dam was cracking',[47] he decided not to write a report for the President but to change sides in order to save his own skin. So he hired a lawyer and began to bargain with the prosecutors for leniency or immunity. He had changed his role from the President's Counsel to the President's Judas.

In the month of April, blow after blow rained on Nixon. Once it was clear that Dean had turned state's evidence, the top men in the White House fell apart. The President had serious worries of his own over his remarks in the 21 March 'Cancer in the Presidency' conversation about the payment of hush money, but the more immediate victims of Dean's treachery were Haldeman and Ehrlichman. On 15 April the Attorney General Richard Kleindienst and Henry Petersen, the Chief Assistant US Attorney, came to tell the President what Dean had been

---

* Liddy's sentence was announced later, in November 1973, because he had been cited for contempt by refusing to testify on his own behalf or against his colleagues and superiors. President Carter later commuted his sentence and he was released from prison in September 1977.

saying to the prosecutors. Haldeman was accused of knowingly allowing his $350,000 fund to be used for the payment of hush money to the Watergate defendants; Ehrlichman of ordering Dean to get Hunt out of the country and to 'deep six' the material in Hunt's safe.

Petersen advised the President to dismiss his two top aides. Nixon balked at this on the grounds that Dean's accusations were not sufficient evidence for such a step.* 'I can't fire men simply because of the appearance of guilt. I have to have proof of their guilt', he said. 'What you have just said, Mr. President speaks very well of you as a man', responded Petersen. 'It does not speak well of you as a President.'[48]

There followed two weeks of agony for Nixon as he wrestled with advice from all quarters, his conscience, and his loyalty to his two senior aides. Even after being taken through the obstruction of justice statutes by Attorney General Kleindienst, he seemed unable to grasp the criminal implications of what had been alleged. As he later explained his feelings, 'I was faced with having to fire my friends for things that I myself was a part of, things that I could not accept as morally or legally wrong, no matter how much that opened me to charges of cynicism and amorality. There had been no thievery or venality. We had all simply wandered into a situation unthinkingly, trying to protect ourselves from what we saw as a political problem.'[49]

The political problem, meanwhile, was getting worse as Dean's allegations leaked into the newspapers, making Haldeman and Ehrlichman's positions increasingly untenable. Eventually Nixon steeled himself to ask for their resignation. He tried to avoid even this confrontation by getting his old friend Bill Rogers to do the job for him. Rogers refused, so Nixon had to be his own butcher, a role he dreaded. In a tearful farewell to Haldeman he said, 'You know, Bob, there's something I've never told anybody before, not even you. Every night since I've been President, every single night before I've gone to bed, I've knelt down on my knees beside my bed and prayed to God for guidance and help in this job. Last night before I went to bed I knelt down and this time I prayed that I wouldn't wake up in the morning. I just couldn't face going on.'[50]

Haldeman was much moved by the President's anguish, as was Ehrlichman, whom he saw separately. In that farewell interview, Nixon wept uncontrollably. 'It's like cutting off my arms, you and Bob', he sobbed as Ehrlichman tried to comfort him.[51]

---

* Nixon's initial reaction was right in Ehrlichman's case. Dean had invented those allegations about Ehrlichman and Hunt. But Ehrlichman was still vulnerable for his role in the Ellsberg break-in.

The resignations were announced by Nixon in a national television broadcast on 30 April. Considering the depressed state of his feelings ('It's all over',[52] he had told Ziegler the previous day) his performance was a resilient one, although unconvincing to his critics. He had evidently decided to tough it out on Watergate by throwing up a smokescreen of half truths and excuses. He made a gracious reference to Haldeman and Ehrlichman ('two of the finest public servants it has been my privilege to know') and did not blame them for anything. He was also careful not to admit any culpability himself, although as 'the man at the top' he accepted responsibility.[53] Since he did not say what he was responsible for, this abstraction was nothing more than an evasive fudge. The speech sounded good on the night but when the text was analysed by the media, it weakened Nixon's position still further. He was now a crippled President.

The summer of 1973 was a season of hate and hysteria in Washington DC, bringing to mind an American version of Macaulay's dictum, 'We know no spectacle so ridiculous as the British public in one of its periodical fits of morality.'[54] The dismissal of Haldeman and Ehrlichman released a whirlwind of rumours, allegations, and accusations about what had been going on around the President. Some were true, many were untrue, most fell into the doubtful category of half lie or half truth. All got an airing in one way or another. Among the wilder falsehoods appearing in print were that Senators had been wiretapped; that FBI 'suicide squads' had conducted undercover campaigns against opponents of the Administration; and that there had been an 'elaborate, continuous campaign of illegal and quasi-legal undercover operations conducted by the Nixon administration since 1969'.[55]

As the temperature of the anti-Nixon fever rose, some observers publicly compared Washington's witch-hunt atmosphere to the McCarthy era, among them Democratic Senator William Proxmire and Bernard Levin, leading columnist of *The Times* of London. Yet for all the smoke in the media, the place where the fire was genuinely burning was in the Senate Caucus Room, where the Watergate Committee hearings commenced on 17 May.

'The Greatest Show on Earth', was Theodore H. White's billing for those hearings.[56] Whether they would amount to anything more than a political show depended on the proceedings. Congressional investigations had a history of being long on sound and fury but short on significant results. The line-up of witnesses looked dramatic enough. Burglars, bankers, policemen and payoff men in the first two weeks; then the minor players such as Strachan and Magruder; finally the superstars of this how-are-the-mighty-fallen pageant—Mitchell, Ehrlichman, Haldeman—and topping the bill John Dean, the President's accuser.

Dean's testimony was sensational but uncorroborated. He began by reading a 245-page statement lasting over seven hours. Its essential message was summarised in the *New York Times* headline the following day: 'DEAN TELLS INQUIRY THAT NIXON TOOK PART IN COVER-UP FOR EIGHT MONTHS'.[57] Unlike all the previous witnesses, who had simply confessed to their own complicity in a variety of nefarious activities at a low or medium level, sometimes implicating others, Dean launched an all-out assault on the integrity of the President.

On the cover-up he implicated Nixon with full knowledge dating back to 15 September 1972. He re-created his conversations with the President with a fair degree of accuracy, although using some selectivity and mendacity to magnify the impression that Nixon had been a willing partner in the crime of conspiracy to obstruct justice.

Nixon did not watch Dean's testimony on television, unlike well over 100 million of his fellow citizens. But the reports of it made him angry and frustrated. He accused Dean of 're-creating history' by 'an artful blend of truth and untruth'. He claimed he was able to identify many lies and deliberate omissions. He worked hard with his aides to draw up a list of these distortions and had them fed to friendly Republican Senators on the Committee. Under the cross-examination based on these materials, Dean's credibility weakened to some extent. Senator Howard Baker's private characterisation of him was 'a sleazy lying little sonofabitch'.[58]

This anger of the Republican Vice-Chairman of the Committee was reflected among its Republican staffers. 'Dean was the Democrats' ace, and they played him in a highly partisan way', recalled Assistant Minority Counsel Howard Liebengood. 'Sam Dash kept him completely away from the minority staff and didn't give us a chance to ask him any questions in advance of his appearance as we did with all other witnesses. So we were left in the dark and could make no preparations. The result was that Dean was treated with kid gloves. He wasn't asked questions about his role in the break-in. His testimony was deliberately skewed to a "Get the President attack". The partisan swords were well and truly drawn over Dean, and the result was that he got away with a lot.'[59]

Yet however angry the professionals on the Republican side of the Committee might be getting, in the eyes of the wider audience, much of the mud thrown by Dean was sticking to the President. Nixon failed to recognise this point at the time, belatedly acknowledging his mistake when he wrote his memoirs four years later:

> I worried about the wrong problem...the real issue had already changed. It no longer made any difference that not all of Dean's testimony was accurate. It only mattered if *any* of his testimony was accurate...I did not see it then, but in the end it would make less difference that I was not as involved as Dean had alleged than that I was not as uninvolved as I had claimed.[60]

That was an afterthought. At the time, Nixon dissipated his energy getting angry with his accuser rather than shoring up his own defences. These were further weakened by an extra thunderbolt from Dean which had nothing to do with the break-in or the cover-up. For in order to set the scene for his self-portrait of ambition led astray by corruption, Dean portrayed the atmosphere of the Nixon White House as some sort of satanic cavern dedicated to devilish machinations against opponents and devoid of all honourable ideals or achievements. To bolster this image, he dredged up several unsavoury items from the cache of negative evidence he had been hoarding for leniency bargaining purposes. The items included a copy of the Huston Plan; the story of the Plumbers; the intelligence-gathering activities; and most spectacularly of all, the White House 'Enemies List'. As Dean had himself created and largely prepared this list on his own initiative it deserved to boomerang against its author rather than to besmirch the President.

But in all the indignation following the disclosure, the media did not mention that there was no direct connection between the enemies list and Nixon—who had never seen Dean's original memo. Nor was it reported that nobody on the list had been audited by the Internal Revenue Service (IRS) let alone harassed in the way that the Nixon family had been harassed by the Kennedy-directed IRS in 1961. The truth was that inside the White House the enemies list had been a non-event, but when revealed to the outside world it became one of the biggest news stories of Watergate. The prominence of the coverage was not unconnected with the appearance of many leading journalists' names among 'the enemies'.

The furore over the enemies list was just one more indication of the damage the hearings were doing to Nixon's standing in the country. His support continued to haemorrhage as the testimony of other witnesses was heard. Yet he was bloodied but unbowed. His approval rating in the opinion polls in July was standing at 40 per cent. Many Presidents before and since have recovered from lower ratings than that. He had enjoyed some presidential successes while the Watergate story had been raging, including a productive summit with the Soviet leader Leonid Brezhnev and the safe return of America's prisoners of war from Vietnam, a happy and emotional event which moved Nixon more deeply than any other single episode in his Presidency up till that date.

Moreover, a measure of stability had returned to the White House with the appointment of General Alexander Haig as Chief of Staff. Chosen by Nixon on the recommendation of the departing Bob Haldeman, Haig showed a sure touch in his early weeks. He persuaded the President to fill many of the ninety vacancies in the Administration caused by resignations and attrition. He quietened the near-anarchy in the Justice Department. He brought the Pentagon's talented General Counsel Fred Buzhardt over to the White House to give new legal advice on the President's Watergate problems. He strengthened morale and discipline at all levels on the White House staff.

Almost the only bad reaction to Haig's appointment came from Henry Kissinger. He took umbrage at the prospect of having to report to a Chief of Staff who had once been mere Colonel Haig, his NSC assistant. Flying into a tantrum on hearing of the announcement, Kissinger insisted he would resign the following day. Although he had often made such threats in the past, this one looked real. Kissinger started clearing out his office and made an appointment for 9 a.m. the next morning to break the news of his departure to the President. Brent Scowcroft, the new deputy to Kissinger, thought the crisis was so serious that he visited Rose Mary Woods, who had been restored as the President's confidante after Haldeman's resignation, in her apartment at 11.30 p.m. to warn her of the situation. 'Make sure I see Henry before he goes in to talk to the boss', Woods told Scowcroft.

At five minutes to nine, Kissinger arrived in Woods's room, next to the Oval Office. 'Are you really going to resign?' she asked. Kissinger said he was, because the situation 'had become intolerable'.

Woods possessed a legendary Irish temper and she lost it with a vengeance. She reminded Kissinger of his previous status in life as an obscure academic and Rockefeller employee. She referred to the transformation in that status which the President's patronage had conferred on the once humble adviser. She listed the many kindnesses that Nixon had shown when Kissinger's fortunes had been low, and asked why such favours could not be returned now the President was in trouble. The polemic ended with the memorable line: 'For once in your life Henry, just behave like a man.'[61]

The visibly shaken Kissinger went into the Oval Office.

He did not mention resignation to the President.

The resignation of the President was not getting much serious attention either, bad though the Watergate Committee hearings had been. Dean's accusations had severely wounded Nixon's credibility, but as the dust on his testimony began to settle it was clear that those wounds were not mortal. For this was a case of one man's word against another's. Dean had taken no notes of his conversations with the President and vice versa. The evidence on both sides was therefore entirely oral with no corroboration available. Whether it was thought to be a clash between a perjurer and a maligned President; or the case of an honest witness accurately pointing the finger at a crooked President; or a plague on both their houses, was a matter of opinion. It was incapable of proof.

So where did the accusations go from here? And how much further could the Watergate Committee take the whole mess once the superstars had all testified? The show could not stay on the road for ever. Despite the embarrassingly unanswered question from Senator Howard Baker, 'What did the President know and when did he know it?' and despite much constitutional huffing and puffing about access to presidential files from Senator Sam Ervin, by mid-July 1973 the Watergate Committee was beginning to run out of steam. No doubt it would, in due course, have produced a censorious report, but Nixon could easily have survived that. He would have been resilient enough to pass off the worst findings of the Committee as a politically motivated extravaganza and to have served out the remainder of his presidential term until 1977. He might have been diminished in terms of domestic perception, but he would certainly not have been destroyed as a foreign policy President exercising leadership on the international stage.

So Nixon was going to survive. That was the likely outcome of Watergate until, on Monday 16 July, the existence of the White House taping system burst upon the world and changed everything.

V. TO BURN OR NOT TO BURN THE TAPES

'Why didn't he burn the tapes?' is one of the most frequently asked questions in the saga of Watergate. The answer is almost as complex as Nixon himself. The full story began with Lyndon Johnson and has many strange ingredients, including a snub from General Vernon Walters; a security leak to the British government; conspiracy theories involving the CIA; blood stains on the President's pillow; quarrels between White House advisers; resignation threats from a lawyer nicknamed 'the nuclear overreactor'; fear of accusations from Haldeman and Ehrlichman; incendiary advice from Vice President Agnew; a possible leak by Deep Throat; and the ghost of Benjamin Disraeli. It is a tangled tale which takes some explaining.

Nixon had a love-hate relationship with the very idea of a taping system. It started in December 1968 when, as President-elect, he toured the White House at the invitation of Lyndon Johnson. In the course of his tour, Nixon was told about the existence of LBJ's secret recording system which consisted of a concealed network of manually operated microphones. They bugged conversations in the Cabinet room; in the visitors' waiting room; and in the President's office as well as tapping all the key telephone lines.

The full details of how the LBJ tapes worked were given by Johnson's aide Joe Califano in a briefing to Bob Finch. Finch reported to the President-elect. 'Nixon's reaction was instant', recalled Finch. 'He said "Get them out of here." It was the gut response of a decent guy shocked to find himself surrounded by all that privacy-invading stuff.'[62]

Nixon's orders were carried out, and the White House had no taping system from his inauguration day until twenty-five months later, in February 1971. During this period Nixon's aides wrestled with the problem of how to keep accurate records of meetings in the Oval Office. 'We would get people going out saying, "The President says such and such", when he had said no such thing', Haldeman has recalled. Several solutions were tried. For a time, a note-taker attended every meeting, but this irked Nixon and tended to inhibit his visitors. Then someone was assigned to debrief the President and his visitor after each meeting, but this proved to be both inefficient and inaccurate. Haldeman recounted the last and most imaginative attempt, which was made in June 1970:

> We came up with the idea of having General [Vernon] Walters in. At that point Walters's claim to fame was as an interpreter and speaker of languages. He also had an incredible memory. So to keep track of what had been discussed, we thought we would get Walters to sit in on all presidential meetings and from memory write a practically verbatim account. Nixon bought the idea so we brought Walters back from Europe. I remember his reaction when I put the idea to him. He drew himself up to his full height and said, 'A general commands troops. He is not a secretary.'[63]

In the end, a decision to reintroduce recording devices to the White House was taken, partly because it was the last available option, and partly because Nixon succumbed to a bout of historian's insecurity which started from the unlikely source of the LBJ ranch.

After the 1968 election, the Johnson–Nixon relationship became surprisingly good. Even when they had been active political opponents, they stalked each other with the mutual wariness of big beasts in the political jungle. Once they were members of that special group of Presidents who have carried the burden of supreme power in time of war, their feelings for each other warmed towards mutual admiration. In his declining years Johnson described Nixon to various visitors as a good President, a great President, and even to his close friend Bobby Baker as 'probably the best President in history'.[64]

For his part, Nixon was punctilious in his courtesies to his predecessor. He kept LBJ well briefed on national security issues and ensured that the full privileges and perquisites of a former President were extended to him. In January 1971 a hiccup in these arrangements occurred when some over-zealous official in the General Services Administration decided it was his duty to make detailed enquiries about the spending of $30,000 at the LBJ ranch on the installation of a high-tech shredding machine. Johnson flew into a rage over the GSA's impertinence, and broke off diplomatic relations with the Administration. As soon as he was aware of the contretemps, Nixon despatched his old friend Don Kendall to Texas on a pacification mission.

Johnson was soothed within five minutes and then switched tack from the problems of shredding machines to the problems of presidential memoir writing. He told Kendall he had some important advice for Nixon. 'You should tell your friend that I'm having a helluva lot of trouble writing my history', Kendall recalls LBJ saying. 'Tell him to watch his back. Cabinet officers lose their notes and then rewrite them. Secretaries lose their files. You can't rely on anyone. I've been having one helluva time. But now I'm on to the period when I started taping, and suddenly it's becoming real easy. You tell your friend from me that when he comes to write his memoirs he'll find it a darn sight easier if he's kept good tape recordings of everything. I only wish I'd used my taping switch more often.'[65]

This advice fell on fertile ground. Nixon was already feeling frustrated by what he regarded as a lack of fair treatment from the press. He was dismayed at the prospect of today's journalism becoming the primary source for tomorrow's historians. He also knew that other Presidents, including Eisenhower, Kennedy, Johnson, and Franklin Roosevelt had recorded some of their conversations. With his own memoirs in mind, he accepted LBJ's counsel and on 9 February 1971 ordered the installation of a new White House taping system. 'Bug P's office', was Haldeman's note of the instruction.[66]

This move might have been just as inconsequential for Nixon as it was for his predecessors had it not been for the President's clumsiness problem. Notoriously inept in his handling of all things mechanical, Nixon could not be relied on to press the simplest button correctly. So, at least, thought Bob Haldeman, who looked for a fail-safe method of helping his boss to switch on. The search ended in the installation of a voice-activated system which could not be switched off.

Haldeman's zero-defect philosophy of management had efficiently circumvented Nixon's clumsiness but at the price of creating an electronic monster which was eventually to destroy the Nixon Presidency.

The taping system was installed in February 1971 with the utmost secrecy. According to Haldeman the only people who knew about it beyond Nixon and himself were his two personal aides, Alexander Butterfield and Larry Higby, plus the Secret Service technicians. Elaborate security precautions were taken to ensure that no military or intelligence community personnel became aware of it. Within the White House, even such trusted members of the inner circle as Kissinger, Ehrlichman and Rose Woods were kept in the dark.

The first breach in this wall of secrecy occurred in September 1971, when the British government became aware of the tapes as a result of an amateur but shrewd piece of detective work on the part of its Foreign Secretary, Sir Alec Douglas-Home.

In the course of a detailed Oval Office discussion on 30 September about Laos, Douglas-Home observed that neither Nixon nor Kissinger were taking notes even of his substantive points. 'I immediately drew the obvious conclusion, which was that every single word was being taped', recalled Douglas-Home. 'I was not particularly put out, but as they had decided not to tell us I thought it was perfectly in order that we should take our own steps to check it. I remember talking to Roly Cromer* about it the next day. He rather pooh-poohed my theory at first, but then he got one of his people to talk to our friends in the CIA, who owned up. Apparently they were absolutely flabbergasted that we knew about it and kept wanting to know how we'd found out. Had I been carrying a bug in my pocket—all that sort of nonsense...I can't say it affected our relationship at all. It certainly didn't worry me, although I think perhaps Ted [Heath] did clam up a bit with Nixon.'[67]

The Douglas-Home disclosures are intriguing, not only from the British diplomatic viewpoint, but also because they appear to confirm that the CIA had knowledge of Nixon's White House recording system from its inception. After his resignation, Haldeman alleged that his aide Alexander Butterfield might have been a CIA agent planted on him to 'spy' for the agency on the White House.[68] This British anecdote gives credence to that theory, for Haldeman insists that only Butterfield and Higby were privy to the precautions taken to ensure that no agency of the US government—especially the CIA—could possibly be aware of the tapes.

At the time, however, the exchanges between the British embassy and the CIA remained unknown, so the White House tapes rolled on in deepest secrecy for twenty-nine months. Nixon had little or no anxiety that their existence would

---

* The Earl of Cromer, British Ambassador to Washington 1971–4.

leak. In the first place he had been reassured by Haldeman that the system was known only to a tiny circle of trusted aides and Secret Service men. Secondly he was confident that if any member of this circle was to be questioned by Watergate investigators about the possibility of recording devices in the White House, such questioning would be deflected by claiming executive privilege. Both these beliefs turned out to be wrong.

The story of the tapes disclosure began on Friday 13 July 1973 when Alexander Butterfield came to the Senate office building for a routine interview in private session by two staff members of the Watergate Committee. The former Haldeman aide, who by this time had moved from the White House to become Director of the Federal Aviation Administration, was not expected to have much in the way of Watergate-related information to impart to the Committee. Yet under direct, but by no means intensive, questioning about the President's possible use of recording equipment in the White House, Butterfield opened up and revealed the full details of the voice-activated equipment. This was a sensational breakthrough for the investigators, who sprinted away to their superiors to report the news. Immediate action, including the serving of a subpoena, was taken to put Butterfield on the witness stand at the next public hearing of the Committee on Monday 16 July.

Why Butterfield was being interviewed by the Committee's staff at all and why he disclosed, with noticeably little resistance, the President's vital secret, are questions that have provided fertile ground for conspiracy theorists. One early area of speculation related to Haldeman's claim that Butterfield might have been a CIA agent planted at the White House to spy on the President. In this theory, agent Butterfield was primed by his spymasters at Langley to inflict maximum damage on Nixon at a critical moment.*

A second theory, proclaimed by the authors of *Silent Coup* and others, is that the ubiquitous Bob Woodward of the *Washington Post* received a tip-off from his subversive source 'Deep Throat' that Butterfield had been the former administrator of the White House tapes. In order to get the story confirmed, Woodward allegedly shared the information with his friend Scott Armstrong of the Committee staff. The rest, as they say, is journalism.

Although many such exciting rumours are still in circulation, the truth is more prosaic. Butterfield was interviewed as part of a methodical trawl through dozens of Nixon aides and contacts. By this time the Watergate Committee staff had grown to ninety-six and was extending its lines of inquiry into every nook

---

* This theory has long been ridiculed by the CIA. Its former director, Richard Helms, when asked about it by this author, replied 'Haldeman is full of shit.'[69]

and cranny of the President's circle. One of the purposes of this huge fishing expedition was to try to substantiate the rumours about bugging devices in the Oval Office. 'We strongly suspected that the President had been operating a recording system,' recalled the Committee's Chief Counsel Sam Dash, 'because Dean had told us he believed Nixon used one. Once he said that, we systematically started asking questions to every White House staff member who might know about such a set-up. It wasn't Providence that took us to Butterfield. He was on our list because he was one of Haldeman's satellites.'[70]

As for Butterfield, he was under no great pressure from the White House to maintain a Trappist-like vow of silence about the tapes. The reverse was nearer the truth. Nixon's old law partner Len Garment, who had become the President's Counsel since the departure of Dean and who was in charge of briefing witnesses before they testified to the Committee, took an almost fatalistic attitude to the potential disclosure. 'If anything, I thought the taping system would come out earlier', he said. 'A good many people knew about it by that time. I told our witnesses, "Don't volunteer it, but don't dance around it, and be careful you don't go to jail over it."'[71]

This insipid legal advice was unknown to the President. He had been taken to Bethesda Naval Hospital on the night of 12 July suffering from viral pneumonia. 'I had the hell of a time getting him to go into the hospital', recalled the President's Chief of Staff, Alexander Haig. 'Although he had a high fever he kept on with his schedule, holding meetings with the German Foreign Minister and so on. We had to bring X-ray equipment into the White House to prove to him that he'd got pneumonia, and even then it wasn't until I saw blood all over his pillow that I could convince him to go. He was real sick.'[72]

While Nixon was in hospital, his senior aides in the White House received word on the afternoon of Sunday 15 July from an aide of Senator Baker that Butterfield would reveal the existence of the tapes to the Committee the following morning. 'My immediate thought,' recalled Haig, 'was that executive privilege must apply to such conversations and that the President's "devil's advocate" way of talking issues through could cause problems. So I called in [White House legal adviser] Fred Buzhardt and said, "Jesus, Fred, I just don't think these tapes can be made public. If they are, from now on they're going to be the focus of everything." "Amen, brother," responded Buzhardt.'[73]

Haig and Buzhardt spent hours discussing the new situation. Buzhardt's view as a lawyer was that, until the tapes were put under subpoena, the President could do what he liked with them. Destroying them was the right course of action. His recommendation was challenged by Len Garment, who had been out of Washington for the weekend. Arriving back at National Airport he was rushed to the White House and told the news. His advice was dramatic. He declared that the President must not destroy the tapes; and that if he did, then he [Garment] would resign and attack the decision. Angry words flew at this announcement. Garment was at one point accused of being 'a nuclear over-reactor', but he stood firm.[74] Haig was furious, but realising that an impasse had been reached, he cut short the discussion.

The next morning, Haig called Nixon in hospital and told him that Butterfield would be testifying in public that day and was going to reveal the existence of the taping system.[*] Nixon was thunderstruck. 'As impossible as it must seem now,' he wrote in his memoirs, 'I had believed that the existence of the White House taping system would never be revealed. I thought that at least executive privilege would have been raised by any staff member before verifying its existence.'[75] Forced to confront the unimaginable, Nixon spent several hours with Haig discussing the problem and considering whether to destroy the tapes. Reaching no decision, they put off further discussion for the next day in order to consult with the White House lawyers.

On Tuesday 17 July, Haig, Garment and Buzhardt gathered around the President's bedside and offered their contradictory advice. 'My recollection is that Haig was fairly silent, and that Buzhardt made out the case for destruction in a low key way', is how Garment remembered the meeting. 'I felt strongly that destroying the tapes would be an obstruction of justice and a felony. A subpoena did not have to be served. If it was clear that the evidence was going to be required and that a subpoena would be served, then destroying that evidence could still technically qualify as an obstruction of justice. I could see the destruction of the tapes being Count Number One on an impeachment petition, and that was what I told the President.'[76]

The discussion took one or two surrealistic turns. Haig asked whether the tapes would be hurtful or helpful to the accusations made by Dean. Nixon said they would be helpful, citing Haldeman's reports to this effect. In a rhetorical flourish of his opposition to the conflagration option, Garment asked: 'Who will fire the torch—Bebe?'[77] There were no volunteers for the arsonist's role within the hospital room. Later in the conversation, Nixon said he wanted the tapes stored under his bed in the White House. The order was never carried out, not least because it would have required raising the roof of the bedroom by at least twenty

---

[*] Why Haig waited until the Monday morning to tell Nixon about this is one of the many mysteries of Watergate.

feet, so vast was the stockpile of tapes. With the President sick and fretful, the meeting drifted into irresolution.

Later the same day, Haig returned to the hospital with Spiro Agnew, who was blunt and to the point. 'You've got to have a bonfire and right now', the Vice President advised.[78] Nixon, however, continued to vacillate. Haig reported that Kissinger was strongly in favour of destruction, but that the lawyers were still at loggerheads. Haldeman was contacted, and repeated his odd (in retrospect) advice that the tapes should not be burnt because they would be so useful to the defence against Dean. Haig supported Agnew's recommendation of a bonfire but felt obliged to add that this would create an impression of guilt in the eyes of the public.

Alone with Haig, Nixon said something extraordinary: 'Al, I don't know what Haldeman and Ehrlichman are going to accuse me of. I know what I did and didn't do. I don't think I knowingly committed any crime. But I need those tapes to protect me.'[79]

There is a strong echo of this in Nixon's memoirs, published five years later. Explaining why he did not destroy the tapes, he wrote: 'I was prepared to believe that others, even people close to me, would turn against me just as Dean had done, and in that case the tapes would give me at least some protection.'[80]

This urge for protection from the men who, three months earlier, had been his two most trusted aides reflects a growing paranoia in the mind of the President. It is particularly hard to fathom in Haldeman's case, since the former Chief of Staff was, at face value, still a trusted confidant and loyalist. Ehrlichman, by contrast, was making increasingly bitter noises, although these were hardly a serious threat in comparison to other problems.

On the other hand, it is easy to understand why Nixon should by this stage in Watergate have been exceptionally susceptible to feelings of mistrust. For more than a year he had been suffering at the sharp end of Murphy's Law—'If something can go wrong, it will'. Battered by political disasters; beleaguered by opponents; betrayed by incompetent and sometimes disloyal aides, he was crumbling both mentally and physically. Nixon at the peak of condition would surely have resolved to burn the tapes with the ruthless celerity advised by his Vice President. But in the face of conflicting advice and confusion around his hospital bed, decisive action was postponed. Discussions meandered on until the moment of opportunity had passed.

Although burning the tapes has often been presented as a close call, such an impression is superficial. Deep down Nixon was always leaning against this course of action, for his own reasons of political and historical judgement. 'I never thought he came near to having a bonfire,' recalled Haig, 'because it was clear to me that he genuinely believed that those tapes would be exculpatory and protective.'[81] That was the political judgement, and wrong though it turned out to be, it represented Nixon's state of mind at the time.

The historical judgement was and still remains more complicated. From the time when Nixon installed the taping system it was clear that his real objective was to establish a unique record of his Presidency. The contemporary influence urging him to do this was the voice of Lyndon Johnson, but the unseen influence from the past was the ghost of Benjamin Disraeli. Ever since Daniel Patrick Moynihan had introduced the President to the notion that Robert Blake's biography of the nineteenth-century British Prime Minister demonstrated many parallels between their two careers, Nixon was fascinated by the comparison. Several other thoughtful readers could see some historical validity in it, among them Elliot Richardson, who said to Nixon in early 1971, 'The similarities are great Mr. President, but what a pity that Blake could not quote Disraeli's conversation.'[82] Richardson believes that this conversation had a considerable impact on Nixon at the time.[83]

Be that as it may, Nixon developed a deep sense of the importance of the tapes as a source for posterity. Believing that many of his motives and actions had been misrepresented by journalists, he hoped that his Presidency would be seen in a fairer perspective by historians. Who can say that he was wrong? So far only sixty hours out of four thousand hours of the White House tapes have been made public. Those now in the public domain show the worst of Nixon, for they consist exclusively of recordings required by the Special Prosecutor for the purpose of Watergate indictments. Snippets of conversation from these segments are often misleading and always unrepresentative, for they portray only one dimension of Nixon in a single and thoroughly miserable episode of his Presidency. When the full sweep of the Nixon White House years can be seen through the entire collection of tapes, the judgement of history will certainly be different, and probably more favourable.

All that can be said about such matters in July 1973 is that a subliminal desire to preserve the tapes as a historical record was probably one of the unspoken factors that played a part in Nixon's decision not to burn them. But the whole process was so blurred and fleeting that it was more of an indecision than anything else, in which thoughts about Disraeli, Garment, Agnew, Ehrlichman, Buzhardt, Haldeman and Haig and the Watergate Committee all jumbled together in a sick

President's mind, resulting in no immediate action. Nixon has long regretted that he missed his chance. 'I should have destroyed them. Stupid. They should have been burned', is his retrospective judgement.[84]

By the afternoon of 16 July Butterfield had testified, the media had erupted in shock horror headlines, 'NIXON BUGS HIMSELF'; the Committee had issued a subpoena; and the political world was a different place. Burning the tapes was no longer an option. The slide towards resignation had begun. As Nixon later saw it: 'From the time of the disclosure of the existence of the tapes and my decision not to destroy them, my Presidency had little chance of surviving to the end of its term.'[85]

VI. COX, AGNEW, ISRAEL AND THE SATURDAY NIGHT MASSACRE

Butterfield's revelations undermined the morale of the White House staff and reinvigorated Nixon's adversaries. Like hounds scenting a fresh fox, they now had an exciting new quarry to pursue in the form of the tapes. The Senate Watergate Committee duly set off in full cry only to find themselves outgunned by a formidable new group of hunters in the Watergate jungle—the Special Prosecutor's Office.

The concept of a Special Prosecutor had been introduced by Senate Resolution in the days following the firing of Haldeman and Ehrlichman. The timing had coincided with the confirmation hearings on the new Attorney General, Elliot Richardson. Nixon publicly promised in his 30 April broadcast that Richardson would have 'absolute authority to make all decisions bearing upon the Watergate case and related matters'.[86] The President's pledge was used by the Democrats as a reason for withholding the confirmation of Richardson until he selected an acceptable Special Prosecutor. Richardson yielded to this pressure and announced the appointment of Professor Archibald Cox. It was a choice that might have been calculated to bring euphoria to Nixon's enemies and paranoia to the White House. For Cox was the apotheosis of the demons the President loved to hate. Aloof, patrician, and ardently liberal, he was a pillar of the East Coast establishment; a Harvard professor; a former Solicitor-General in the Kennedy administration; and a McGovern voter. At his swearing-in ceremony, Cox seemed to be flaunting a partisan approach to his Special Prosecutor's duties by inviting as his principal guests Senator Edward Kennedy and Mrs. Ethel Kennedy, Robert Kennedy's widow. The impression that Cox was crusading as a Kennedy Resurrectionist was further strengthened by his pattern of staff recruitment. Seven out of his eleven most senior appointees had previously worked for

John, Bobby, or Teddy Kennedy. Other aides were drawn from McGovern's campaign team. Of the total of thirty-seven lawyers (average age thirty-one) recruited for the Special Prosecutor's Office, only three were Republicans and all but four had attended Ivy League universities. As Cox's young men swung into action, Nixon saw them as 'partisan zealots abusing the power I had given them in order to destroy me unfairly' and was infuriated by the way 'the media presented them...as the keepers of the sacred flame of American justice against a wicked President and his corrupt administration'.[87]

While Cox's staff and the Ervin Committee's staff (often in acrimonious competition with each other) began the early moves in the coming legal battle for control of the tapes, the White House seemed almost paralysed. This was partly a matter of numbers. Nixon had a team of twelve working on Watergate. Ranged against them were an official opposition of over 200 professional employees or consultants from the Cox and Ervin empires, supplemented by the unofficial battalions of opponents in the media and on Capitol Hill. However, the deeper cause of the White House paralysis at this time lay in the Administration's latest and most secret unexploded bomb—the impending criminal indictment of Vice President Agnew.

The Justice Department had been investigating allegations of bribery, extortion and tax fraud against Agnew since April. On 6 August, Attorney General Elliot Richardson came to see the President to discuss the prosecution's findings. Nixon already knew from his White House lawyers Buzhardt and Garment that the case against the Vice President was a strong one. While Governor of Maryland, Agnew had regularly accepted kick-backs from contractors. Delayed payment of some of those kick-backs had been handed over in envelopes containing $1,000 or more in cash to Agnew at his office in the White House. There were over forty counts in the potential indictment against the Vice President, all of them supported by solid evidence.

When the Attorney General explained the details of the case in the Oval Office, he was startled by Nixon's cynicism. 'He wasn't in the slightest bit shocked', recalled Richardson. 'His first reaction was to say, "That sounds just like a Maryland politician. They're all like that." Then he wanted me to get Henry Peterson to make a fresh assessment of the case, which I agreed to. After I explained how cut and dried the evidence was in terms of documentary proof as well as sworn testimony, he told me I would have to confront Agnew directly with everything we had.'[88]

Nixon's reactions to the prospect of losing his Vice President were more complex than mere cynicism. Self-interest must have played a part in his thinking, for Agnew was a good insurance policy. An echo of King Charles II of England's celebrated remark to his heir apparent brother, 'They'll never kill me, James, to make you King', might well have run through Nixon's mind at this time. Another consideration was that Agnew, who had been strongly supportive throughout the Watergate crisis, was needed to shore up support among conservative Republicans, where his popularity was high. But more basic than any such political calculations was the President's gut instinct that Agnew was being pilloried for venal sins much in the same way that a young vice-presidential candidate named Richard Nixon had been pilloried (for noncriminal and infinitely less serious matters) in 1952.

'There was nothing to indicate that Agnew ever did anything as Vice President for which he took money,' recalled Nixon, 'but because some of the money that was supposed to be contributed by contractors was delivered to him after he became Vice President, he was forced to resign. Was it a double standard? Yes. Why was it worse in Agnew's case? Because he had the temerity to take on the press. There was no one, even more than me, than Agnew as a target, because he'd been effective against the press and understandably once they caught him out in what they thought was a politically vulnerable activity they hung him out to dry...I still think it was a double standard. I think he deserved certainly some condemnation, but I do not believe that he deserved the almost hysteria that went on in the US Attorney's Office and everywhere else that he had committed the crime of the century. It had happened before to Governors in Illinois and I'm sure it happened in a lot of other states...But with the problems I had at that particular time there was nothing I could do for him. I only wish I'd been stronger. If I had been I would have stopped him from going.'[89]

Nixon did make at least one effort to prevent Agnew's departure. He consulted Eisenhower's Attorney General, Herbert Brownell, and asked him to help on the case, but Brownell refused, telling Nixon that the Vice President 'hadn't a hope of surviving' and that it was 'all wrong' to try and defend him.[90] Apart from taking such private soundings, Nixon was a model of fairness and propriety throughout the vice-presidential crisis. This was more than could be said for the Vice President, who vacillated between noisy bellicosity and abject surrender. Since Agnew was fully capable of fighting the charges all the way to a Senate trial and impeachment (or so he said), the White House regarded him as a dangerously unguided missile during this period. In the end, with the press baying for his blood; the evidence against him incontrovertible ; and the Justice Department offering him favourable terms for a *nolo contendere* plea to one count of tax evasion, Agnew bowed to the inevitable. On 9 October, after an emotional leave-taking from Nixon, he resigned.

The greatest sigh of relief over Agnew's departure came from Alexander Haig, the White House Chief of Staff, who was quietly becoming a surrogate President. 'Forty indictable offences against Agnew did not just mean you had a Vice President in trouble', he recalled. 'Because of the President's increasing vulnerability over Watergate, what we were facing was a converging double impeachment of both the President and the Vice President. I was looking at a constitutional crisis of an unbelievable magnitude, whose end result would mean the Presidency passing to the third in line of succession, Speaker Carl Albert, who was an alcoholic under care. That was my nightmare! No wonder we had to ignore Watergate until Agnew had gone.'[91]

There were other more important reasons for ignoring Watergate. On 6 October war broke out in the Middle East as Syria and Egypt attacked the territories occupied by Israel since 1967 with air strikes, missiles, tanks and infantry. The hostilities took almost everyone by surprise, including the CIA and the Mossad. After four days of heavy fighting, the unprepared Israelis had suffered heavy losses, including one fifth of their 500-plane air force and a third of their 650 tanks. Without resupply they were doomed. Nixon had 'absolutely no doubt or hesitation about what we must do'. He told Kissinger (who had been appointed Secretary of State a few weeks earlier) to 'let the Israelis know that we would replace all their losses'[92] and instructed him to work out the logistics for doing so.

The logistical problems proved complicated. Chartered private planes could not get insurance. Access to the international air space around Israel was difficult. Even the British government became obstructive towards US requests for overflying, refuelling and landing rights controlled by their Royal Air Force base in Cyprus. The Defense Secretary, James Schlesinger, anxious not to offend the Egyptians, would not permit El Al cargo aircraft to use US military airports. The Pentagon, led by the Chairman of the Joint Chiefs of Staff, Admiral Thomas Moorer, who was notoriously antagonistic towards Israel, came up with a proposal to deploy only three of its C-5A transport aircraft on resupply missions. The Joint Chiefs justified this minimal response on the grounds that a larger number of American planes would alienate the Arabs and the Soviets.

Nixon became angry and imposed his will on the military obstructionists. On 13 October he called Schlesinger and told him to stop worrying about the Soviet and Arab reactions. The airlift was a presidential decision. 'We are going to get blamed just as much for three planes as for three hundred', declared Nixon, saying that he would take full personal responsibility if the Arabs retaliated by cutting oil supplies.[93] He told his Defense Secretary to make unlimited use of USAF transport aircraft if private charters were a problem. 'Whichever way we have to do it, get them in the air *now!*' was his order. A few hours later, on learning that there were disagreements in the Pentagon about which kind of plane should be used in the airlift, Nixon exploded to Kissinger, 'Goddamn it, use every one we have. Tell them to send everything that can fly.'[94]

The military finally obeyed their Commander-in-Chief. Later that day, the first thirty USAF C-130s were airborne for the 6,400-mile flight to Lod airport, near Tel Aviv. The news had an electrifying effect on Israeli morale and on the combat situation. Within seventy-two hours the airlift was operating at its peak rate, making daily deliveries of over 1,000 tons of military equipment and ammunition. So it continued for 566 USAF missions over the next thirty-two days, handsomely outstripping the Soviet resupply airlift to the Arabs, which averaged barely 500 tons of *matériel* per day. Nixon's decisiveness saved Israel. It was his last major international achievement.

While the Middle East hovered on the brink of an apocalypse, Washington was preoccupied by two more parochial subjects, the choice of a new Vice President and the challenge of Cox. Nixon wanted to appoint John Connally as Vice President. There was no man he admired more than 'Big Jawn' on the political scene. He had long nurtured the hope that the former Governor of Texas would succeed him in the White House after the 1976 election. But in the climate of congressional hostility that prevailed in October 1973, Connally, for all his qualities of leadership, had no hope of getting through the confirmation hearings. A larger than life visionary whose business and political record was not without blemishes, he had a plethora of powerful enemies on Capitol Hill. The same disqualification applied to other candidates whom Nixon considered presidential timber, notably Governors Nelson Rockefeller and Ronald Reagan. Compelled to take the low road of congressional acceptability rather than the high road of presidential suitability, Nixon chose Congressman Gerald R. Ford. The decisive factor in this selection was the advice from several sources that Ford was the only Republican who could be certain of confirmation by the Democratic majority. Secondary considerations were that Ford was a loyal team player, a supporter of the President's foreign policy and a long-time political associate whose links with Nixon went back to 1948, when as freshman Congressmen they were inaugural members of the Chowder and Marching Society.

In his post-resignation years, Nixon expressed the view that his own political demise may well have been hastened by Ford's unthreatening personality and his easy acceptability to Congress. He came to believe that 'the coalescence of forces' against him eventually included a significant number of Republicans in the House and Senate who thought 'they could get along better with Ford than with me'.[95]

This retrospective view may well be right, but at the time quite different calculations prevailed. Ford was perceived both by Nixon and by many of his fellow Congressmen as decent but dumb. He would be loyal, useful in coralling Republican votes against an impeachment resolution, but his peers did not regard him as a potential President. He was another 'insurance policy', or so Nixon told Chuck Colson.[96]

Unfortunately for the President, there was no insurance policy that would take care of the Special Prosecutor. Nixon saw Cox as a 'partisan viper we had planted in our bosom'.[97] On 12 October he discovered that the viper's sting could be deadly. That was the day when the Court of Appeals handed down a 5–2 judgement that the President must obey Cox's subpoena to hand over nine of the White House tapes related to Watergate. The decision presented Nixon with another dilemma. If he released the tapes he would be breaching the important principle that a President's private conversations must be protected by executive privilege. Yet disobedience of the court order was unthinkable, for it would make the President a lawbreaker. The only escape routes from the dilemma were either to seek a compromise, or to dismiss Cox.

The story of the plan that became known as 'The Stennis Compromise' will forever baffle historians because the conflicts of evidence about who agreed to what; who misinformed whom; and who broke their word are so confusing and contradictory. The essence of the plan was that the President would preserve the constitutional principle of executive privilege by providing summaries of the nine tapes required under Cox's subpoena. Once the nine summaries had been delivered, there would be no further attempts by the Special Prosecutor to obtain additional tapes of presidential conversations. The summaries would be verified for accuracy by Senator John Stennis of Mississippi. As the Chairman of the Senate Select Committee on Standards and Conduct, a former judge, and a senior Democrat, Stennis was respected in all political quarters for his integrity and impartiality. His imprimatur of authenticity should make each summary an acceptable substitute for the tape itself—or so the White House hoped.

The week in which the Stennis compromise was floated coincided with the fiercest days of fighting in the Middle East war. It was one of the most momentous dramas in Nixon's career as an international statesman, and he rose to the occasion magnificently. Not only did he save Israel from annihilation, he also put forward, in a far-sighted letter to Brezhnev, the concept of the two superpowers co-operating to impose a joint US–Soviet peace settlement on the Middle East. Had Nixon been strong enough at home to see this initiative through to a successful conclusion, it might well have been his crowning glory as a peacemaker.

With the pressure of great events occupying his time on the international stage, the President had to leave peacemaking on the tapes issue to Haig and the White House lawyers. At first they did well, at least according to Haig's account. Their job was to sell the Stennis plan as a genuine compromise between the Special Prosecutor's right to evidence and the President's right to claim executive privilege over the tapes. Cox was always unlikely to buy any such compromise. As a result of the abrasive methods he was using to conduct his investigation, he was perceived by the Administration as an incorrigible Nixon-hater, brazenly out to get the President by any means at his command. But there were other key players in the Watergate saga who, in Haig's version of events, did agree to support the Stennis formula. They included Senator Sam Ervin, Senator Howard Baker, and most important of all the Attorney General, Elliot Richardson.

Richardson's position was pivotal. As Cox's old law pupil, friend and boss, he had more influence over the Special Prosecutor than anyone else. It was just possible that he might be able to persuade Cox to accept the Stennis compromise. But if Richardson accepted Stennis and Cox refused to do so, then Richardson would have the right and duty to fire Cox. That was an outcome that would have delighted both Haig and Nixon.

What happened in the negotiations between Haig and Richardson is murky, and both men are sharply divided on the subject to this day. 'There was no doubt in my mind that Richardson agreed to it, and that he accepted that he would have to fire Cox if Cox refused to go along with the Stennis plan', recalled Haig. 'In fact when we worked out the details of the compromise we took every step at Richardson's behest. He was on board.'[98] This version is contradicted by Richardson. 'I regard the events leading up to the Saturday night massacre as one of my greatest failures', he said. 'We all have the defects of our qualities, in my case diffidence and objectivity, so perhaps it was my fault that I didn't get it across to Haig in sufficient time that I would not tolerate any restriction on Cox's right to the tapes. On the latter part of Friday [19 October] I don't know whether I wasn't making myself clear enough to Haig or whether Haig wasn't making my position clear enough to the President. But the end result was a disaster.'[99]

The ingredients in the disaster were not of Nixon's making. He believed that he had the agreement of Ervin, Baker, and Richardson to the Stennis compromise. So, in a presidential statement, he announced it on the evening of Friday 19 October. The immediate congressional and public reactions were favourable. In the *Washington Post* the following morning David Broder wrote a column praising Stennis as the logical man for the job.

Cox, however, thought differently. At 1 p.m. on Saturday 20 October, he called a press conference at the National Press Club. 'I am certainly not out to get the President of the United States. I am even worried, to put it in colloquial terms, that I am getting too big for my britches', he began disarmingly, but his message was one of outright defiance. He rejected the Stennis compromise, said that he must have the full tapes, and declared that the President's statement violated the guidelines of the Special Prosecutor's Office.

Nixon watched the press conference on television and was outraged. 'I thought that Cox had deliberately exceeded his authority; I felt that he was trying to get me personally, and I wanted him out', was his reaction.[100]

On Nixon's instructions, Haig telephoned Richardson and formally told him that the President was ordering the Attorney General to dismiss the Special Prosecutor. Richardson said he would resign, a threat he had made for the first time late the previous evening, when Haig had tracked him in a telephone call to Cox's home. An appointment was made for the Attorney General to see the President at 4.30 p.m. on Saturday 20 October.

Nixon was calm and collected at this meeting. He was fully aware that Richardson's resignation would have a seriously adverse impact both on domestic public opinion and on the fragile international negotiations towards a Middle East ceasefire which Kissinger was conducting in Moscow. On the other hand, he felt that his authority as President would be irreparably undermined if Cox's defiance was not halted by the dismissal Richardson had been commanded to carry out. 'If I can't get an order carried out by my Attorney General, how can I get arms to Israel?' he lamented to Len Garment as he wrestled with the problem.[101]

There was one last attempt at a compromise, or at least a postponement. Haig, although inwardly furious with Richardson for breaking what he regarded as a clearly understood agreement on the Stennis formula, outwardly took pains to butter up the Attorney General before he went into the Oval Office. 'By hint and implication Haig offered me the vice-presidential slot on the 1976 Republican ticket', recalled Richardson, who remained unmoved by such blandishments.[102] More surprisingly, he also remained unmoved by the President's request that he should delay his resignation for a few days because of the delicate state of the Middle East ceasefire negotiations. Nixon emphasised that Brezhnev would never understand such upheavals inside the US Administration and would only interpret them as signs of weakness to be exploited. This cut no ice with the Attorney General. Nixon said coldly, 'I'm sorry that you insist on putting your personal commitments ahead of the public interest.' 'Mr. President, I can only say that my resignation *is* in the public interest',[103] replied Richardson, formally resigning a few moments later.

This made William Ruckelshaus, Richardson's deputy, the Acting Attorney General. Haig telephoned him at the Department of Justice and said that the President was ordering him to fire Cox. Ruckelshaus refused. 'Well,' said Haig, 'you know what it means when an order comes down from the commander in chief, and a member of the team can't execute it?'[104] Shortly afterwards, on the President's authority, Haig dismissed Ruckelshaus. The third-ranking member of the hierarchy at the Department of Justice was the Solicitor General, Robert Bork. A renowned constitutional scholar, he agreed that the President had the legal right to dismiss any employee of the executive branch, including Cox. Bork therefore accepted the role of Acting Attorney General and duly performed the duty of dismissing the Special Prosecutor.

At 8.22 p.m. on Saturday 20 October, White House Press Secretary, Ron Ziegler, announced that Cox was being fired; that Richardson and Ruckelshaus had resigned; that the office of the Watergate Special Prosecutor was being abolished; and that its functions were being transferred back to the Department of Justice. The news broke like an exploding firestorm. The TV networks interrupted their regular programmes with apocalyptic bulletins and special reports. NBC's anchorman John Chancellor reflected the mood of the media as he opened his newscast with the words, 'The country tonight is in the midst of what may be the most serious constitutional crisis in its history...nothing even remotely like it has happened in all of our history'.[105]

This author was in New York at a dinner party given by CBS Chairman William S. Paley and retains a vivid memory of how a pleasant social evening suddenly erupted into a maelstrom of hysteria. Amidst a flurry of incoming telephone calls, the meal was abandoned for the television set. One of the most dramatic images was the CBS footage of FBI agents arriving at the Department of Justice to seal off the Special Prosecutor's office, forbidding access to Cox's staff. Excitable phrases like '*coup d'etat*'; 'What's next? Gas ovens?'; 'Reichstag fire'; 'thump of jackboots'; 'White House madman'; and 'Nixon's insane' filled the air. Around midnight, Bill Paley made the prophetic forecast, 'It's the last straw. He's bound to be impeached now.'[106]

The press labelled the event 'The Saturday Night Massacre' and Congress stoked the flames still higher. Public comments from eminent Senators over the next few days were almost as inflammatory as the heat-of-the-moment remarks at the Paley dinner party. Senator Robert Byrd accused the President of a 'Brown-shirt operation' using 'Gestapo tactics'; Senator Edmund Muskie said the Cox firing 'smacks of dictatorship'. Senator Edward Kennedy described the event as 'a reckless act of desperation by a President...who has no respect for law and no regard for men of conscience.'[107]

Nixon was rocked by the ferocity of the reaction. He had severely misjudged the mood of the nation which seemed to be a strange mixture of fear, frenzy and fury. As far as the legal progress of the Watergate investigations was concerned, Cox's dismissal turned out to be a far less important event than it appeared to be on the night. For the Acting Attorney General Robert Bork did not impede the work of the Special Prosecutor's staff, from which there were no significant res-ignations. If anything, the prosecutors intensified their efforts under the aegis of the Justice Department. Cox's plans to increase the number of subpoenas and to extend the life of the Watergate Grand Jury for six months were quietly imple-mented by Bork. On 1 November the appointment of a new Special Prosecutor, Leon Jaworski, was announced. The law was still taking its course.

Although the firing of Cox turned out to be relatively unimportant in legal terms, its impact on the political landscape was like an earthquake. Nixon's Gal-lup Poll approval ratings plummeted to an all-time low of 17 per cent. All across the country, newspaper columnists and TV commentators called for his impeach-ment. On 12 November *Time* magazine published the first editorial in its history calling on the President to resign. Many other newspapers and magazines of all political persuasions followed suit. Perhaps the most telling indicators that the Saturday Night Massacre had been cataclysmic in its effect were the huge mailings of anti-Nixon letters that flooded into the Washington offices of Senators and Congressmen. Middle America was finally turning against its President.

The politicians were not slow to respond to such pressures. By the end of the month, over twenty impeachment or impeachment enquiry resolutions had been tabled in the House of Representatives. The countdown to resignation had begun.

VII. THE ROAD TO RESIGNATION

The last nine months of Nixon's Presidency consisted of an inexorable slide towards resignation. There was little he could do to avoid this outcome. Although he made several attempts to stem the congressional pressure for impeachment, such efforts were doomed to failure. Every time there was a lull in the storm, it was soon followed by new hurricanes of bad news with catchy labels like 'the missing tapes'; 'the 18½ minute gap'; 'I am not a crook'; and 'expletives deleted'.

Journalistically exciting at the time, these episodes were historically almost irrelevant, for the President's fate was already sealed. However, the episodes themselves deserve some closer examination, since Nixon's personal reputation was so severely damaged by them.

The two tape stories about the 18½-minute gap and the 'missing' recordings were sideshows in which Nixon was a demonstrably innocent bystander. The 'missing tapes' rumpus was the first to hit the headlines. It began on 31 October 1973, when Judge Sirica was informed by the President's Counsel Fred Buzhardt that two of the subpoenaed tapes Nixon had promised to hand over to the court did not exist. They were nonexistent for the simple reason that no recordings had ever been made of the conversations concerned. The first subpoena related to a phone call between John Mitchell and the President on 20 June 1972. This happened to have been made from a telephone in the residential quarters of the White House, which was not connected to the taping system, hence the absence of a recording. The second subpoena was for a Dean–Nixon meeting in the Oval Office on 15 April 1973. There was no recording of that one either, because the machine had run out of tape earlier in the day.

These explanations were genuine, as the Secret Service technicians later confirmed. Ironically both tapes might have helped the President. The 20 June conversation would have been yet another item to confirm that Nixon had no foreknowledge of the break-in. The 15 April tape would have shown him backing away (albeit with somewhat unconvincing references to his previous 'joking') from earlier indications that he might be willing to let blackmail money be paid to the Watergate defendants. In the event, the newspaper headlines about 'two missing tapes' strengthened the public's perception that suppression of evidence was the name of the game at the White House, and Nixon was unfairly castigated. In the wake of the furore, the *New York Times* published an editorial calling for the President's resignation, and Senator Edward Brooke of Massachusetts became the first Republican in Congress to endorse this demand. Angry and frustrated, Nixon scribbled on the top of a briefing paper on 1 November:

> There were no missing tapes.
> There never were any.
> The conversations in question were not taped.
> Why couldn't we get that across to people?[108]

He was right on all counts, but no one was listening.

The next disaster with the tapes was the 18½-minute gap. At the end of Sep-tember, Nixon had given Rose Woods the task of transcribing the tapes. On 1 October, she ran into Nixon's office distraught because she had found a gap in a tape of Nixon's conversation with Haldeman on 20 June 1972, which she thought she might have caused. She had been listening to the tape when the telephone rang. She turned the tape recorder off, answered the phone and returned to the tape only to find that it had been interrupted by a mysterious buzz for four to five minutes.

At first, Nixon and his aides were unconcerned, because they thought that the conversation with Haldeman was not subject to the subpoena. But on 15 November Haig had two pieces of bad news for Nixon. The tape had, in fact, been subpoenaed, and the gap had somehow grown to 18½ minutes. Nixon could scarcely believe his ears. 'It was a nightmare', he remembered later.[109]

By this time, there had already been hints in the news that something untow-ard had happened to the tapes. Before the facts had been properly investigated inside the White House, the *Washington Post* of 8 November printed a story on its front page, suggesting that the tapes might have been 'doctored' and that the problems 'were of a suspicious nature'.[110] This speculation was based on a tip-off to Bob Woodward of the *Post* from his mysterious source 'Deep Throat', who claimed the tape contained 'deliberate erasures'.[111] The story triggered a fusillade of rumours, most of which cast the President's personal secretary Rose Mary Woods as the villainess of the piece. She had been transcribing tapes for some weeks and some members of the White House staff believed that she had con-sciously destroyed a portion of the 20 June tape because it was incriminating to her beloved boss.

'There's no question but that Rose did it. She's in bad trouble', was how Alex-ander Haig greeted Woods's lawyer Charles S. Rhyne as he arrived at the White House for his first consultation with his client. 'How do you know, did you see her do it?' was Rhyne's response. 'No of course not', snapped Haig. 'But the CIA, the FBI, and the Secret Service have all confirmed that she did it.' 'Take me to these confirmers', demanded Rhyne. Somewhat non-plussed, Haig took him instead to Len Garment. The two lawyers had a vigorous argument, which ended with Rhyne walking out saying, 'I'm going to ask the President to fire you.'[112] His next stop was Rose Woods's office ('Welcome to the snake pit' was her tearful greeting), where attorney and client talked until Nixon came in to join them, solicitously asking, 'Well, what are we going to do for Rose?' *'We're* not going to do anything', retorted Rhyne, whose days as Nixon's fellow classmate at Duke Law School had left him with a robust familiarity towards the President. 'My priority is not to let her be tried as Richard Nixon', he went on. 'When I walk out of the court house with her free then I'll talk to you. Until then—get out of the room.' Nixon complied.[113]

Charles Rhyne, who was a former President of the American Bar Association, took great delight in demolishing the case against Rose Woods. After many hours of testimony before the Grand Jury, it was clear that the electronic evidence was incomprehensible; that criminal intention was unprovable; and that even the acrobatic demonstration (which became known as the Rose Mary Woods stretch) as to how she might have erased the tape accidentally while reaching for the telephone, was ludicrous. After an intense investigation by the Special Prosecutor's office, Jaworski took Rhyne out to lunch and offered not to press any charges in return for a promise of silence. The deal was struck. Conceding Woods's innocence with a cover-up of the prosecutor's incompetence was a distinctly odd way to proceed, particularly as it left open the question of who was responsible for the 18½-minute gap. Accusing Nixon of it made no sense. As Haldeman's notes of the 2 June conversation showed, the dialogue between them had been innocuous, with no instructions or moves towards a cover-up at that stage. Moreover, if Nixon was trying to make deliberate erasures of the tapes (improbable in view of his notorious mechanical ineptitude), it seemed unbelievable that he should wipe out a section of a recording that was *prima facie* benign, while leaving intact so many incriminating tapes.

To this day, the 18½-minute gap remains one of the great unsolved mysteries of Watergate. But the key to it lies in the probability that the erasure was done not to protect the President from a harmful tape, but rather to use a harmless tape in order to damage his reputation still more grievously. This opens up an area of fascinating speculation about the identity of Deep Throat. When Deep Throat leaked the information about 'deliberate erasures' to Woodward in the first week of November 1973, only six people in the White House, or for that matter in the world, knew about the problem of the gap in the tape. They were: Richard Nixon; Rose Mary Woods; Alexander Haig; Fred Buzhardt; Butterfield's replacement, Steve Bull; and Haig's deputy, Major General John C. Bennett. There must therefore be the strongest of presumptions that Deep Throat was one of the six, or rather four, since neither Nixon nor Woods could conceivably be guilty of leaking stories about themselves to the *Washington Post*. Moreover, since none of the remaining four should have had any knowledge, at the time of the Deep Throat–Woodward conversation, that the gap had been caused by deliberate erasures, it seems likely that Deep Throat (DT) and Deliberate Eraser (DE) were one and the same person.

Four suspects remain. Which of them is the elusive Deep Throat? A combination of the laws of libel and an unwillingness to name Woodward's source this side of absolute certainty has caused this author to draw a veil at this stage in the DT/DE detective game. In any case, the name of DT/DE is less important than the devastating conclusion that should be drawn from the episode of the 18½-minute gap from Nixon's point of view. For what it really pointed to was that somewhere in the highest echelons of the White House there was, by November 1973, an individual who was willing to take secret hostile action against the President. The purpose of such action, it must be presumed, was to accelerate Nixon's departure from office. Someone close to him was greasing the skids.

By early 1974 there was a bunker mentality inside the White House. Many aides accepted that Nixon's days were numbered once they took stock of the congressional machinery for impeachment. This was in the hands of the House Judiciary Committee which consisted of twenty-one Democrats and seventeen Republicans. Although its Chairman, Congressman Peter Rodino, made strenuous efforts to lead the Committee towards an objective approach, the plain fact of the matter was that impeachment is and always has been a political rather than a judicial process. For all the theoretical eighteenth-century language in the Constitution about the proof of 'Treason, Bribery or other High Crimes and Misdemeanors' being a pre-condition of impeachment, the practical examples of history show that the exercise consists of politicians sitting in judgement on their fellow politicians. Political justice is not the same as natural or ordinary justice. For this reason Nixon from the outset regarded the House Judiciary Committee as 'a stacked deck'. Before the proceedings opened, he noted that eighteen of the twenty-one Democrats on the Committee were certain to vote for his impeachment because they were 'hard-core partisans' from the liberal wing of their party. He thought he had some hope of retaining the votes of three Southern conservative Democrats, but he was less sanguine about holding the support of all seventeen Republicans, of whom six were thought to be personally or politically disaffected. 'My only hope of averting a recommendation for impeachment from the Committee,' he observed 'would be either to hold every Republican and pick up two of the Southern Democrats, or to hold sixteen Republicans and win all three of the Southerners. Either of these outcomes was possible, but extremely remote.'[114]

The prospects of avoiding an impeachment vote were made still more remote by two additional knocks that hit Nixon in early 1974. One involved allegations of venality and tax evasion. The other was the 'expletives deleted' uproar.

In the view of Nixon's inner circle, the most unfair of all the charges levelled against him during Watergate were those which alleged that he had feathered his own nest at the expense of the public purse. In the opinion of his closest friends, such conduct would be completely out of character. Throughout his pre-presidential career Nixon had been scupulously correct in his stewardship of public money and punctilious in handling his own private resources. Even in his brief period as a high-earning Wall Street lawyer he had displayed a disinterest, almost a distaste, for the accumulation of wealth. He had never lived high on the corporate hog or aspired to a lavish life style. Yet, in the last months of Watergate, he acquired the reputation of a greedy, grasping, tax-dodging President. Was this myth or reality?

The main charge of venality was launched in almost identical headlines in the *Washington Post* and *New York Times* on 2 August 1973, '$10 MILLION SPENT ON NIXON HOMES'.[115] Both newspapers were referring to figures provided by the General Services Administration which, on closer analysis, showed that $8.9 million of the headlined total had been spent on administrative and security installations which were close to, but totally divorced from, Nixon's personal property. Of the remaining $1.1 million that had been spent on his houses at Key Biscayne and San Clemente, all but $13,400 was specifically requested by the Secret Service and related to items such as bullet-proof glass, security lighting, and alarm systems. Seen in retrospect, the Secret Service expenditure on protecting two sizeable houses owned by a Head of State does not look excessive. Yet from the howls of rage on this subject in the media 1973–4, it might have been thought that Nixon had personally decorated his houses with gold bars stolen from Fort Knox.

The President was more vulnerable to charges of tax evasion. An IRS audit of his returns, which leaked to the press, showed that in 1969 (on his previous year's income as a private citizen) he had paid $72,700 in taxes on an income of $328,000. In 1970 he made $263,000 and paid taxes of $793. In 1971 he made $262,000 and paid $878. In 1972 he made $269,000 and paid $4,300. These figures shocked Middle America. Yet there was a justification for the low tax payments. In shorthand terms it was that Nixon, after receiving professional and legal advice, had donated his private papers for his vice-presidential years to the National Archives in return for a tax deduction worth over $300,000. This should have been an entirely proper transaction. Nixon delivered the 600,000 documents covered by the arrangement on 27 March 1969. They were valued and accepted by the National Archives. So far as he knew, the deal was legally consummated for tax purposes when delivery and acceptance took place.

Unfortunately for Nixon, the member of his staff who was in charge of the paperwork did not process the documentation for another five months. This was significant because Congress subsequently passed (and Nixon as President signed) a law which disallowed deductions for such gifts after 29 July 1969. Without disclosing his subsequent action, the staffer signed the deed of gift for the papers on Nixon's behalf but back-dated it prior to the date on which the new law took effect. To this day, legal opinions differ as to whether the staffer concerned was wrong to do this, for it can be argued that the date of delivery, not the date of deed, was what governed whether the gift qualified under the deadline for tax deductions. In any case, Nixon had no knowledge of the back-dating by his adviser. He said he was shocked and frustrated by the discovery and that he would abide by a ruling on whether the deduction was right or wrong from the congressional committee investigating the matter. Because the explanation for this transaction was tortuous, Nixon sounded unconvincing. He had made matters worse for himself when, under pressure from questioners on financial matters, he said: 'I welcome this kind of examination, because people have got to know whether or not their President is a crook. Well, I am not a crook.'[116]

The quote; the subsequent ridicule; and the later ruling by a congressional committee that the President had underpaid his taxes by some $400,000 caused a further haemorrhage in his support. But worse was to come. In April 1974, Nixon had to respond to a subpoena for forty-two tapes from the House Judiciary Committee's Impeachment Inquiry. After much agonising, he decided to supply full transcripts of the conversations required.

Soon afterwards, the *New York Times* published the transcripts. It was only then that, for the first time, a majority of Americans polled expressed the opinion that Nixon should resign or face impeachment. In large part, this reaction was caused by what they found in the transcripts, but the greater sensation was caused by what had been left out. For the 1,300-page *'Blue Book'* delivered to the Committee did not consist of totally verbatim transcripts. Nixon decided to expurgate from them a considerable amount of dialogue he considered irrelevant or offensive, such as 'material unrelated to presidential action'; personal remarks about individuals; and profanity. This was a reasonable enough arrangement in principle, but in practice it turned out to be a disaster, causing a moralistic cyclone of opprobrium to engulf the President. The reasons for all the outrage look exaggerated in hindsight.

It was the missing swear words which caused the fuss. Nixon had directed that every time he or anyone else was recorded swearing, the offending epithet should be replaced by the words 'expletive deleted'. The effect was to make hundreds of pages in the *Blue Book* heavily spotted by this resonant phrase. The public's imagination ran riot. It was universally assumed that the deletions covered up the worst of obscenities. Nixon was denounced from pundit to pulpit. For many God-fearing Americans, the President's bad language was the last straw of Watergate. Such reactions were based on ignorance. Nixon was condemned for curses he had not uttered. Even the *New York Times* reflected the national mood of inaccurate sanctimoniousness when it stated in the foreword to its paperback on the tapes, 'Shit was the mildest of the deleted expletives.'[117] That was untrue. Those who have actually listened to the unexpurgated tapes know that Nixon went in for Sunday-school swearing and precious little else. His deleted expletives overwhelmingly consisted of 'Goddamn'; 'Hell'; 'Damn'; 'Christ'; 'For Chrissake'; 'What in the name of Christ'; 'Oh God'; and so on. The dirtiest words in the President's vernacular were 'crap'; 'shit'; and 'asshole'. Pornographic swearing by Nixon was recorded nowhere on the tapes. The familiar locker-room expressions for sexual intercourse were not used by him, nor were any of the commonplace four- and six-letter word obscenities. This analysis is supported by Nixon's principal American biographer, Stephen Ambrose, who wrote, 'Never—at least in the sixty hours of tapes available for listening in the National Archives—does he refer to a woman's anatomy in an obscene way. In fact, he was rather circumspect in his word choice, old-fashioned, generally avoiding rough language; when he used words like "Hell" and "damn" he did so in a low-key, almost embarrassed sort of way.'[118]

If Nixon's expletives were so mild, why on earth did he remove them from the transcripts? Undeleted they might have caused a negative reaction in the Bible belt but that would have been a flea bite in comparison to the mauling he received. The explanation is that the tapes were censored with Hannah Nixon in mind. The President himself admitted as much to Fred Buzhardt's assistant Geoff Shepard, who had argued that all those 'Gods' and 'Damns' were innocuous and should be left in. 'If my mother ever heard me use words like that she would turn over in her grave', replied Nixon.[119]

All through 1974, the President's political grave was steadily being dug by the House Judiciary Committee. Yet by June, there were some glimmerings of hope that the pendulum might be starting to swing away from the certainty of impeachment. When the Committee published its 7,000 pages of evidence, there were some optimists, like Congressman Joe Waggoner of Louisiana, who remained unconvinced. He told Nixon on 22 June that he thought there were seventy Southern Democrats, like himself, who would balk at impeachment in the full House vote. If that total was correct, only 150 Republicans would be needed to create an anti-impeachment majority in the House. However, that possible majority would depend on two factors: first, on holding the Southern

Democrats together; second, on there being no further surprises such as Nixon refusing to comply with or being in contempt of the Supreme Court—which was due to give its ruling on the tapes in a month's time.

In his own mind, Nixon became deeply pessimistic about the congressional arithmetic despite the encouraging signals he was receiving from Waggoner and others. The truth was that he had lost the moral high ground that sanctifies the American Presidency. The lies; the suppression of evidence; the dismissals; the financial irregularities and the expletives deleted had gradually eroded the bed-rock of his presidential respect from the country. Unfair though some of those allegations had been, their cumulative effect was a killer. Nixon had become an unlucky general and now that the final assault was on its way he could not per-suade enough of his natural supporters to fight for him. He was shrewd enough to recognise this before others came to the same conclusion. He thought that his real problem lay not with the antagonism of the liberal Democrats but rather with the fears of the Republicans running for re-election in the mid-term November polls. He thought that many of them wanted to distance themselves from the President, because they viewed him as 'an albatross around their necks'.[120]

This was a prophetic forecast. The first crack in Nixon's defence strategy came on 23 June when Congressman Lawrence Hogan, one of the Judiciary Committee's conservative Republicans, called a press conference to announce that he would be voting for the resolution to impeach. Later that day the three Southern Democrats let it be known that they, too, had defected from their expected positions of support for the President. Nixon was shattered. He made a last, desperate effort to claw back the Southern Democrats by calling Governor George Wallace. The purpose of the call was to get Wallace to lean on his fellow Alabamian on the Committee, Congressman Walter Flowers. The conversation lasted just six minutes. Wallace said he was praying for the President; that he felt sorry for the President; but that he could not help the President. He felt it would be improper for him to call Rowers, who would resent such pressure. He would call back only if he changed his mind. Nixon got the message. As he hung up, he turned to Haig and said, 'Well, Al, there goes the Presidency.'[121] That night, 24 July, Nixon wrote in his diary, 'Lowest point in the Presidency and Supreme Court still to come.'[122]

It was all over. Three days later, after a long and dignified debate, the House Judiciary Committee voted to recommend impeachment to the full House by twenty-seven votes to eleven. All twenty-one Democrats and six of the seventeen Republicans voted in favour of the resolution. The political consensus for impeachment was established.

After that vote, there was never any doubt that the full House of Representatives would follow the Committee's lead. But had such doubt existed, it would have been dispelled by the consequences of the Supreme Court's verdict in the case of *United States v. Nixon*. The Court ruled that the remaining subpoenaed tapes must be handed over to Judge Sirica. 'The generalized assertion of privilege must yield to the demonstrated specific need for the evidence in a pending criminal trial', said Chief Justice Warren Burger, as he delivered the unanimous opinion. Nixon had no option but to comply. His compliance led to the revelation of the famous 'smoking gun' tape of 23 June, which all this time had lain concealed and unknown to everyone except the original participants, Nixon and Haldeman. The passage where the President supports the suggestion that the FBI should be diverted from its investigation of the Watergate break-in by the CIA was what really shocked the insiders in the high command of the White House, who now listened to the 23 June tape for the first time. During the next few days a transcript of the 'smoking gun' conversation was secretly shown to some of the President's few remaining loyalists on Capitol Hill, such as Congressman Charles Wiggins and Senator Robert Griffin. They were equally stunned. All the professionals agreed that the President's position was now untenable. Nixon's natural instincts told him the opposite. 'End career as a fighter'[123] he scribbled on a handwritten pros and cons memo that he composed in the early hours of the morning during his sleepless night of 30–31 July. But twenty-four hours later, the realities of common sense, politics, and daylight gave him a different message. He had no support left in Congress; his own staff, headed by Haig, were telling him that he could not possibly survive; and he knew he could not defend the indefensible in such a political climate. On Thursday 1 August 1974 he decided to resign.

VII. THE FINAL DAYS

Nixon's final days as President of the United States were often emotional, sometimes theatrical and occasionally mystical. He had accepted the inevitability of resignation from 23 July onwards, but during his last week he made several zig-zags over the timing and choreography of his departure. According to Haig, 'He went up and down the mountain at least three times.'[124] However, there was no wavering on the question of whether he was going. He had made up his mind to do, as he often put it, 'what was best for the country',[125] and that meant resigning in a matter of days rather than weeks.

One of his problems in this phase was handling the pressure from his family, who were passionately urging him not to quit. Haig had recommended a resignation date of Friday 2 August, prior to the publication of the tapes. Nixon at first inclined towards this, but then changed his mind, saying it would be 'skulking away'.[126] Instead, he spent 3–4 August at Camp David with Pat, Julie, Tricia and his sons-in-law David Eisenhower and Ed Cox. 'An eerie weekend' was how he subsequently described it, consisting of walks in the woods, movies, swims and saunas with surprisingly little talk about what Tricia called 'subject'—her euphemism for resignation. However, there was one family discussion of 'subject' after dinner on Saturday night. At the end of it, Nixon slipped into rhyme as he told them that he would accept their recommendation to delay his decision until after the 23 June tape had been released on Monday 5 August. 'It's fight or flight by Monday night', he said.[127]

Reactions to the 'smoking gun' tape were so cataclysmic that flight soon looked like the only option. The transcript itself was bad enough but Nixon made it worse by issuing an accompanying statement in which he confessed to having withheld facts from his lawyers (who insisted he made this clear) and to misleading the public. The evening news bulletins on Monday 5 August were incandescent in their denunciations of the President's deceit. On Capitol Hill, Nixon's few remaining defenders were deserting him. The eleven Republicans on the Judiciary Committee who had voted against impeachment all reversed their positions in angry television interviews. From the Senate, it was reported that the President could not count on more than a dozen sure votes. This collapse of political support was brought about by an instant revulsion over the President's lies, not by a measured judgement on his deeds. Watergate, even at one minute to midnight, was again being fuelled by emotion rather than logic.

The emotional avalanche continued for the next forty-eight hours. However, the Cabinet remained calm. With one notable exception, none of its members rocked the boat. At their meeting on Tuesday 6 August, they even managed to have a surrealistic business-as-usual discussion on economic policies for the coming six months. Nixon deliberately gave the impression that his options were open and that he might be staying on for some time. 'I respected the Cabinet, but I wasn't about to allow them to push me into resigning', he said afterwards. 'I knew I was going in two days time, but if I said that it would have leaked. There are times when you have to keep your own counsel and this was one of those.'[128] The Cabinet tacitly understood this so played along with the charade of a discussion on inflation. There were one or two grumbles and *sotto voce* comments, such as Budget Director Caspar Weinberger whispering to Defense Secretary James Schlesinger, 'All that talent—all those flaws.'[129] However, most of those present made no direct or indirect references to 'subject'. The principal exception was George Bush, in attendance as Chairman of the Republican National Committee.

'As the President talked economics, Bush kept raising his hand', recalled Haig. 'Finally when he was recognized he said straight out, "Mr. President, you *have* to resign." That hit like a ton of bricks. In an atmosphere where everyone was trying to be so careful, it was an unbelievably insensitive contribution.'[130]

Soon after the Cabinet meeting, Nixon called in Haig and Ziegler and told them, 'Well, things are moving very fast now. I think we should do it on Thursday.' He gave orders for work to begin on the resignation speech, and made suggestions for Haig to pass to Ray Price. Give it 'dignity and no rancor' he said. 'Your exit will be as worthy as your opponents are unworthy', responded Haig. There was a long pause. 'Well, Al, I really screwed it up, didn't I?' said Nixon sadly.

There was no reply.[131]

The tone was different in the family quarters. That same evening over dinner 'Pat was emphatically against resigning' recalled Nixon. 'She was a fighter to the last. She was the last to give up in the Fund thing, the last to give up in 1960, and she was the last to give up this time. Very hard for her.'[132] However, Nixon later discovered that his wife, for all her fighting talk, had already started the momentous operation of packing for exile. 'Very perceptive of her', he was to observe. 'With us sometimes, as it is between people who are very close, the unspoken things go deeper than the spoken. She knew what I was going to do.'[133]

Julie also resisted resignation. She wrote a note which melted her father's heart when he found it lying on his pillow at 2 a.m. on the night of 6–7 August.

August 6th

Dear Daddy,
    I love you. Whatever you do I will support. I am very proud of you.
    Please wait a week or even ten days before you make this decision. Go through the fire just a little bit longer. You are so strong! I love you.
    Julie
    Millions support you[134]

Nixon wrote afterwards: 'If anything could have changed my mind at this point, this would have done it. But my mind was made up past changing…I had made the decision that was best for the country.'[135]

The following day he decided it would also be best for the country not to have any sort of bargaining about leniency, clemency, or pardons. He rejected all suggestions along these lines, including a strong recommendation from Haig and an even stronger plea from Haldeman arguing that the best way to wipe the slate clean would be grant a blanket pardon to all Watergate defendants and to match it with an amnesty for all Vietnam draft dodgers. Nixon rejected the proposal as 'unthinkable'.[136] He told Haig that he was not interested in special deals for himself. 'I will take my chances', he said.[137]

Nixon's last two full days in office were largely devoted to seeing political leaders and working on his resignation speech. His most important appointment was with his Vice President Gerald Ford. For an hour they talked about the challenges a new President would face, particularly on the foreign policy front. Nixon emphasised that Henry Kissinger was indispensable as Secretary of State. Ford said he was intending to keep Kissinger for as long as he would be willing to stay. Nixon also recommended that Haig should be retained as Chief of Staff, at least for the next six months. As the conversation ended, with some desultory talk about the plans for the swearing-in ceremony, both men's eyes filled with tears. Shaking hands at the door of the Oval Office, Nixon told Ford he would be praying for him in the days and years ahead.

There was similar talk, and even action, on the subject of prayer in one of Nixon's last meetings with Henry Kissinger. For nearly two hours they sat alone together in the Lincoln sitting room on the night of 7 August, reminiscing about their foreign policy triumphs. 'History will treat you more kindly than your contemporaries have', remarked Kissinger at one point. 'That depends who writes the history', retorted Nixon. They sipped brandy from the same bottle of Courvoisier they had opened on the night in 1971 when the message came through that the President had been invited to China. No one else had drunk from it since. Nixon defiantly proposed a toast: 'To the past—and to the future'.[138] When the time came for Kissinger to go, Nixon started to escort him out, but as they passed the Lincoln bedroom he halted. 'Henry, just wait a minute here', said Nixon. 'On special occasions in times past before we went to China, before I had a major speech or a major press conference, I would stop in this room and have a moment of silent prayer because I sort of gathered strength just from being in this room where Lincoln had been.' Awkwardly the President asked his Secretary of State if he would join him in prayer. The two men knelt and prayed together in silence for less than a minute.

A few minutes after they had parted, Nixon called Kissinger. 'Henry, you know that prayer was a very private matter', he said. 'I hope it didn't embarrass you.' 'Not at all', replied Kissinger. 'This is not going to leak'.[139] A few days later, the story was leaked to *Washington Post* journalists. Asked afterwards by a friend if he had been hurt by Kissinger's disclosure, Nixon replied, 'Nope, I was beyond the point of being hurt by then.'[140] Nixon might have been more hurt had he known how another senior figure in his administration, the Defense Secretary James Schlesinger, was behaving in the final days. In what would surely win first prize in a competition for the wildest over-reaction of Watergate, Schlesinger somehow got the thought into his head that Nixon was planning a military coup to avert his own resignation. This weird notion caused Schlesinger to issue an order to the Joint Chiefs of Staff that no alert or major movement of US forces should take place without his countersignature as Defense Secretary. Somewhat to the embarrassment of the Joint Chiefs, the Schlesinger Protectorate, created by this order, lasted for three days. 'Incredible' was Nixon's reaction when he later learned about it.[141]

In fact the outgoing President was doing nothing more sinister than saying goodbye to old friends and working on his resignation speech. His most traumatic leave-taking was held on the evening of Thursday 8 August, less than an hour before he was due to make the resignation broadcast. Fifty-five Congressmen, Senators, and senior aides had crammed into the Cabinet Room, which normally seats a maximum of thirty. Nixon recalled:

> You could just feel the emotion rising and rising in that hot room. These were my oldest friends and supporters. I talked about what we had been through together and I thanked them for their help in my campaigns, in the tough days in Vietnam, over the China initiative, and on other difficult issues. I don't think they were paying much attention to what I said. They just felt the tension in the room. I looked across the table and directly across from me, Les Aarons the Whip on the Republican side, my friend for 25 years, started to cry. He put his head down on his arms and just sobbed. Now I just can't stand seeing somebody else cry. So I just sort of quit talking. And then I choked up. I said 'I just hope I haven't let you down.' Of course I knew I had. And then I broke into tears. Somebody pulled the chair back and I left the room.[142]

Exit sobbing. He was now only fifteen minutes away from air time. Haig was fearful that the President might not be capable of delivering the resignation broadcast. Those fears were shared by others. 'He was under such great emotional stress that it seemed unbelievable that he could pull himself together for the television speech', wrote Congressman Glen Davis, who was present in the

Cabinet Room. Even the make-up artist thought the President was a 'basket case' as he sat down in front of her mirror[143] 'I don't know how I got myself together but I did', recalled Nixon.[144] He entered the Oval Office at two minutes to nine and sat behind his desk. After a voice level check, the transmission light on the principal camera glowed red and at forty-five seconds past nine he was broadcasting live to a record American television audience of 110 million viewers. Another 40 million were listening on radio.

'This is the 37th time I've spoken to you from this office', he began in a composed voice. 'Throughout my public life,' he continued, 'I have always tried to do what was best for the nation.' He had thought it was his duty to complete the term of office for which he had been elected, but he now recognised that his lack of congressional support would paralyse the nation's business if he stayed on.

'In the past few days,' he continued, 'it has become evident to me that I no longer have a strong enough political base in the Congress to justify continuing that effort. As long as there was such a base, I felt strongly that it was necessary to see the constitutional process through to its conclusion, that to do otherwise would be unfaithful to the spirit of that deliberately difficult process, and a dangerously destabilizing precedent for the future.

'But with the disappearance of that base, I now believe that the constitutional purpose has been served, and there is no longer a need for the process to be prolonged.'[145]

He then came to the fateful words ('the most difficult sentence I shall ever have to speak'[146]), which he delivered with a steady voice and eye line.

'Therefore I shall resign the Presidency effective at noon tomorrow.'

He continued: 'By taking this action, I hope that I will have hastened the start of that process of healing which is so desperately needed in America.

'I regret deeply any injuries that I may have been done in the course of the events that led to this decision. I would say only that if some of my judgements were wrong—and some were wrong—they were made in what I believed at the time to be in the best interest of the nation.'[147]

The last part of the sixteen-minute broadcast consisted of Nixon putting down some markers for history. He ran through his achievements, reminding the American people that in his inaugural address he had promised to dedicate himself to the cause of peace.

'I have done my very best in all the days since to be true to that pledge. As a result of these efforts, I am confident that the world is a safer place today, not only for the people of America, but for the people of all nations, and that all of our children have a better chance than before of living in peace rather than dying in war.

'This, more than anything, is what I hoped to achieve when I sought the Presidency. This, more than anything, is what I hope will be my legacy to you, to our country, as I leave the Presidency.'[148]

With the final words, 'May God's grace be with you in the years ahead', he faded from the screen. A few minutes later, back with his loving family in the private quarters of the White House, he started to shake violently, either from a chill or as a release from the high tension of the broadcast. The spasms passed in a few moments and he was back to normal. He spent the rest of the evening making calls to supporters all around the country, saying time and time again, 'I hope I haven't let you down.'[149]

The next day, Friday 9 August, there was one last official duty to perform and one last farewell speech. The duty consisted of signing an eleven-word letter addressed to the senior member of the Cabinet, Secretary of State Henry Kissinger. It read: 'I hereby resign the Office of President of the United States.' Nixon said later about his final presidential signature, 'I was just numb, so I didn't have any special feeling about it. After all in my own mind I had resigned two weeks before, and from then on each step was like water dripping on a rock and wearing it away. The signature was just one more drop of water on the rock, so I had no reaction. Nothing gave me a reaction at that point.'[150]

In fact there was plenty of reaction in the speech he delivered half an hour later to some 300 members of his administration in the grand ballroom of the White House. This was Nixon with the bark off, brimming with emotion, giving a performance that was at times moving and at times mawkish but utterly riveting throughout.

'I spoke from the heart',[151] he said afterwards. Flanked by his family, with Pat in dark glasses to hide her tears, Nixon let it all hang out in an unscripted address which was one part appreciation, one part inspiration, and one part mysticism.

The appreciation was gracious, if at times awkward. He thanked his staff and Cabinet for their service to their country, saying he was proud of every one of them and proud also that no one in his administration 'ever profited at the public expense or the public till...Mistakes yes, but for personal gain never...I only wish that I were a wealthy man—at the present time I have got to find a way to pay my taxes, [laughter] and if I were I would like to recompense you for the sacrifices that all of you have made to serve in the government.'

He took up these themes of sacrifice and service. Young people, he said, should go out and take up careers with these ideals in mind. As he talked about careers, the image of his childhood home in Yorba Linda flashed into his mind

and suddenly, now on the unpinioned wing of his innermost thoughts, he began
to talk about his father and mother:

'I remember my old man. I think that they would have called him sort of a
little man, common man. He didn't consider himself that way. You know what
he was? He was a streetcar motorman first, and then he was a farmer, and then
he had a lemon ranch. It was the poorest lemon ranch in California, I can assure
you. He sold it before they found oil on it.

'And then he was a grocer. But he was a great man because he did his job, and
every job counts up to the hilt, regardless of what happens.

'Nobody will ever write a book, probably, about my mother. Well, I guess all
of you would say this about your mother: my mother was a saint. And I think of
her, two boys dying of tuberculosis, nursing four others in order that she could
take care of my older brother for three years in Arizona, and seeing each of them
die, and when they died, it was like one of her own.

'Yes, she will have no books written about her. But she was a saint.'[152]

To many in the viewing audience of millions (the speech was televised), these
tributes were bizarre. How on earth could such an unsaintly President claim to
have had a mother as a saint? Was he going crazy in his last hours of office? And
if this was the moment for family compliments, why was he ignoring Pat? Her
omission looked still more peculiar as Nixon read out a description from Theodore Roosevelt's diaries of *his* beautiful wife, Alice, who had died young.

In fact there was method in Nixon's apparent madness. His mother *had* been
the lodestar of his life. She *had* been called a saint long before her son rose to
prominence. 'Honour thy father and thy mother' was the commandment which
Richard Nixon had kept well all his life, and it was natural for him to speak these
strange words in praise of his parents in his hour of travail. As for the criticism
(widely made in the media during the next few days) about his failure to mention
Pat, there was a simple answer to it. Nixon feared that a public tribute might cause
her to have an emotional collapse. 'She had just been in tears', he later explained.
'I wasn't about to mention her or Tricia or Julie and have them break down in
front of all the people in the country. That would have destroyed her. She had too
much dignity, and she was always proud of that. That's why I didn't mention her.
She knew that I was mentioning her in my heart—that's what mattered.'[153]

For students of Nixon's psychology, the speech contained several intriguing
signposts to both his insecurities and his strengths. His feelings of inferiority
about his education showed up when he joked: 'As you know I kind of like to read
books. I am not educated but I do read books [laughter].' There were hints of

childhood resentment about his family's financial misfortunes ('the poorest lemon ranch in California...sold...before they found oil on it') and other people's attitudes towards his father ('I think they would have called him a sort of a little man, a common man'). On the positive side, his peroration revealed his indomitable willpower, that iron determination to keep fighting back.

'We think when someone dear to us dies, we think that when we lose an election, we think that when we suffer a defeat, that all is ended. We think, as TR said, that the light had left his life forever.

'Not true. It is only a beginning, always. The young must know it; the old must know it. It must always sustain us, because the greatness comes not when things go always good for you, but the greatness comes and you are really tested when you take some knocks, some disappointments, when sadness comes, because only if you have been in the deepest valley can you ever know how magnificent it is to be on the highest mountain...'

In that credo was the first hint of a future comeback. At the time it seemed absolutely inconceivable that any sort of return from the disgrace of resignation could be possible, so the message of his words was universally missed. A few moments later, he offered another good piece of advice, which the cynics were quick to note had been more honoured in the breach than in the observance during his own career. '...never be petty; always remember, others may hate you, but those who hate you don't win unless you hate them, and then you destroy yourself'.

He ended on a spiritual note. 'And so we leave you with high hopes, in good spirits, with deep humility and with very much gratefulness in our hearts...Not only will we always remember you, not only will we always be grateful to you, but always you will be in our hearts and you will be in our prayers.'[154]

The audience rose and applauded. Many were weeping as he and Pat walked to the waiting presidential helicopter *Marine One*. He shook hands with Gerald Ford and wished him good luck.

'Have a nice trip Dick', said Betty Ford.

Nixon then climbed the steps of the helicopter. He turned back to the White House for one last defiant wave and one last proud but painful smile. Seconds later, as *Marine One* lifted off to take them to Andrews Air Force Base and the flight home to California, Pat observed to no one in particular, 'It's so sad, it's so sad.'[155]

By contrast, Nixon's own thoughts on that short helicopter ride were more futuristic than sorrowful:

> I must say I didn't have any feelings of bitterness or rancor or self-pity.
> I found myself thinking of what I had seen in that room, and how

hard it had been for me to finish the speech without breaking into tears myself…I thought how much I owed to all those people and how much the country owed to them and how fortunate we were to have such marvelous people in our administration. And then I thought of Julie down there and Tricia and Ed and David and Mrs. Nixon and how no one could have had a more supportive, loving, kind family and how lucky I was there.

And then as the helicopter moved on to Andrews I found myself thinking not of the past but of the future. What could I do now? What? It seems presumptuous that I thought it then, but I did. That's the way it was. A little couplet kept coming into my head that I had received from Clare Booth Luce in the spring of 1973 when Watergate had just exploded all over the place. It was the Ballad of Sir Andrew Barton:

> I am hurt but I am not slain
> I'll lay me down and bleed awhile
> Then I'll rise and fight again.[156]

It was to be the theme of the next chapter in Richard Nixon's life.

IX. WATERGATE THOUGHTS FROM ABROAD

No foreigner has ever understood Watergate. The same may be said for a great many Americans, particularly those who are too young to remember the passionate and often poisonous atmosphere created by Vietnam.

Without the war, Watergate would never have happened. Only in a political climate that was already severely polluted by mutual bitterness could so minor a scandal have burgeoned into so momentous a catastrophe. To that extent Richard Nixon was the last casualty of Vietnam and Watergate was its final battlefield.

There was nothing in the early ingredients of the drama to suggest that it might bring about the downfall of a President. In the beginning, the break-in was a low-level problem: an irresponsible act carried out by over-zealous aides without Nixon's knowledge. It was deplorable but not particularly evil in its intentions, at least by the standards of presidential campaigns from 1960 onwards. What transformed an incident into a crisis was Nixon's endorsement of the cover-up which began clumsily and continued stupidly. This, too, was clearly deplorable, but was his behaviour sufficient for him to be impeached?

Nixon's single worst action was to have ordered the CIA to block the FBI's investigation. The dialogue of the 'smoking gun' tape is damning on this count.

However, the CIA did not in the end make any move to stop the FBI, so no obstruction of justice occurred as a result of that infamous conversation. His second most damning piece of dialogue took place on 21 March when he discussed the possibility of paying a million dollars in blackmail money to the burglars. It was appalling that he even countenanced such an idea, but the one million dollars were never paid and at the end of the conversation he ruled out any White House payment of money to the defendants, rejecting the option of clemency as 'wrong'. These and many other ambiguities make it far from certain that Nixon would have been found guilty had the law taken its full course in 1974 with an impeachment and trial before the Senate. 'I don't believe that in the final analysis the Senate would have convicted him', is the view of Senator Howard Baker, who had a ringside seat at Watergate as minority leader of the Senate select committee. 'I thought that the historic dimensions of impeachment would have mitigated the partisan fervour, and that my fellow Senators would have seen the evidence as sufficiently ambiguous either to acquit or at least not to have removed him from office.'[157]

Such sanguine views on Nixon's prospects at the bar of justice depend heavily on whether the Senate trial would have been conducted as a court of law; a court of morals; or a court of politics. These very different tribunals became merged and confused in the Washington atmosphere of 1973–4. In the court of morals, Nixon fared badly. From day one of Watergate, he clearly set out to cover up the affair for misguided reasons of loyalty to John Mitchell. He was, at best, less than helpful in assisting the course of justice. He was vulnerable for having created in the White House an atmosphere that encouraged illegality among his staff. He made matters worse with self-inflicted wounds. His verbal gyrations, recorded on tape as he explored the cover-up possibilities, revealed a tawdry cynicism which caused even his best friends to cringe with embarrassment. Whether his behaviour was legally criminal or not, his morals were certainly awry.

In the court of politics Nixon fared even worse. One of the outstanding features of Watergate is that it was the climax of a highly politicised power struggle which centred on a whole range of Vietnam-related issues. There can be little doubt that both the power struggle and the future of Nixon's Presidency would have been resolved in a completely different way if the Republicans had held a majority in either the House or the Senate. Without the supremacy of the Democrats on Capitol Hill there would have been no resignation. Nixon's opponents had the votes. The court of politics always contained a stacked jury.

Non-Americans, distanced by culture and geography from the battlefield of Watergate, were always uneasy about the courtrooms of morals and politics that sat in judgement on Richard Nixon. This is where the domestic and international opinions began to divide. Were the President's misdeeds really so terrible? Did they merit the punishment received? Was the damage the uproar did to America's prestige and strategic interests worth it? Foreign observers who asked such questions have remained perplexed as to why the Watergate misbehaviour of the thirty-seventh President of the United States was, and apparently still is, seen as so much more heinous than the misconduct of the thirty-fifth and thirty-sixth Presidents, bearing in mind such matters as LBJ's corrupt financial practices and JFK's criminal links with the Mafia. Some strange double standards seem to have been used to discriminate between recent occupants of the White House. The obvious explanation for these double standards is that Kennedy and Johnson never got caught, partly because the state of party politics during their Presidencies made them impregnable to hostile congressional investigations.

Although Watergate was full of partisan politics, the legislators could never have ousted the President unless the tides of public opinion had also been pulling strongly in the same direction. When assessing that opinion and the forces that moved it, such as the media and the Congress, once again the atmospherics of Vietnam were paramount. Not since the Civil War had the times been more tempestuous or the hatreds more divisive than they were between 1968 and 1974. Nixon's temperament compounded these problems. By instinct a fighter, he was unable to play the role of conciliator which the domestic pressures required. From the first day of his Presidency there was a significant section of the political community that regarded him as an illegitimate usurper whose policies must be opposed, often violently, at every turn. Confronted by so much hostility and unreason, there were moments when Nixon responded with hostile words and unreasonable deeds. Some of his actions during Watergate fell into this category. He was certainly guilty of making the tragedy even worse than it need have been.

From an international perspective, Watergate looked a tragedy of errors, not a catalogue of crimes. Those errors were compounded by Nixon's own follies, yet one is left with the impression that these were only one element in his destruction. Perhaps the strongest destructive force was the sheer momentum of blows, accusations, and amazing events which crashed down on the President in the twelve months leading up to his resignation. Most of these were totally unpredictable. Just when it looked as though Nixon might have weathered the storm of the break-in; the cover-up; and the Dean testimony, he was struck by lightning, not once but several times in succession. The Butterfield disclosure; the Cox appointment; the Agnew disgrace; the missing tapes accusation; the tax dodging allegations; the 18½-minute gap furore; and the 'expletives deleted' uproar were knife-thrusts into Nixon's weakened body politic, and in retrospect they each look, to a greater or lesser extent, unlucky and unfair. Moreover, in most of these episodes the case for the prosecution was proclaimed in the media, while the case for the defence was never put at all.

As the juggernaut for impeachment rolled forward, it was left to non-Americans to argue for restraint, or at least for a sense of proportion. From foreign shores there was unremitting astonishment that this peculiarly Washingtonian extravaganza might end in the fall of one of the outstanding international statesmen of the twentieth century. Compared to his achievements as a peacemaker and geopolitical strategist, Nixon's domestic sins looked venial. Suzanne Garment, in her much acclaimed book *Scandal*, noted this dichotomy:

> Political morality and moral fashions can vary enormously from one country or era to another. Even countries whose sense of right and wrong is more or less like ours can have jarringly different notions of what constitutes politically scandalous behaviour. Those who lived through Watergate need no further demonstration of this fact. As the event unfolded, commentators in Britain and France, our fellow heirs in the Judeo–Christian moral tradition of the West, repeatedly scratched their heads and concluded that our massive agitation over wiretaps and break-ins was just another fascinating tribal ritual in the primitive and endlessly strange politics of the New World.[158]

Many primitive tribal rituals end in bloodletting. So it was with Watergate. Yet in a more dispassionate age, the thirty-seventh President's political execution takes a great deal of explaining. It does not seem convincing to this author that what Nixon *did* deserved the supreme penalty of resignation. What he *said* at certain moments in the protected privacy (or so he thought) of his own resentments, rages and duplicities was much more deserving of rebuke or even punishment. But there are no sentencing guidelines for Presidents who break the rules. To be hanged by his own tapes seemed excessively severe. Perhaps the appropriate penalty would have been a motion of censure or condemnation by the Senate.

In the view of this author, the forcing of Nixon's resignation was a political overreaction, a human injustice, and a strategic mistake. That was the consensus of international opinion at the time, and one which has strengthened with the passing of the years. American opinion still leans the other way, but it would not be wise to bet on where the consensus of history will be in fifty or one hundred years' time.

TWENTY

EXILE AND
RENEWAL

I. DE PROFUNDIS

During the early months after his resignation Nixon was a soul in torment. Shut away behind the well-guarded walls of his oceanside home at San Clemente, California, he made a brave show of keeping up appearances while deteriorating both emotionally and physically to the point where he had close calls with a nervous breakdown and with death.

The atmosphere at San Clemente in August and September 1974 lurched between surrealism, fatalism, and despair. The surrealism came from Nixon's efforts to remain presidential without the Presidency. Each morning he arrived in his office at 7 a.m. prompt, immaculately dressed in coat and tie despite the 100° heat. He was guarded by a detail of eighteen Secret Service men; given medical attention by Navy corps men; provided with transport by the Marines and supplied with secure communications by the Army. He was attended upon by a retinue of some twenty assistants, aides, and secretaries who had volunteered to accompany him to California. This façade of a court in exile was made possible by a unique arrangement to create a 'presidential transition' period of six months. A grudging Congress eventually approved the funding of the federal employees' salaries for this purpose, plus an expenses grant of $200,000—sharply reduced from the original allocation of $850,000. It enabled the former Western White

House (as the prefabricated offices in the San Clemente compound were known) to create a Ruritanian illusion of business as usual, even though in reality Nixon had no business except for the unusual. Occasionally, he tried hard to pretend otherwise. One morning he called his senior staff together in the office that had served as the National Security Conference room. After scowling at one aide who had rushed to this unexpected meeting in Bermuda shorts, Nixon sat up in his chair as if he was presiding over a meeting of the Cabinet. 'I've called you here to discuss an important topic,' he announced, 'and that is, what are we going to do about the economy this year?'[1]

Those who observed such stiff upper lip aspects of the ex-President were getting only one side of the story. In private he was crumbling as a human being. The aide who bore the brunt of this personal agony was Ron Ziegler. He had become something of a surrogate son to his boss during the last months of Watergate. At San Clemente he combined the roles of constant companion and therapist. Every day, seven days a week, the former Press Secretary was closeted alone with the former President for up to six or eight hours at a stretch. Sometimes the two men sat in long, brooding silences; sometimes they drowned their sorrows in beer or scotch; but most of the time Nixon just let it all hang out in a sometimes incomprehensible monologue of ramblings and ravings about what had happened to him.

Part of the problem was that Nixon genuinely did not know what had happened in some of the pivotal episodes of Watergate. One of the first visitors he invited to San Clemente was Bud Krogh. He had just come out of prison after serving a sentence of four months and seventeen days for his part in the Plumbers' break-in to the offices of Dr. Lewis Fielding, Daniel Ellsberg's psychiatrist. 'Tell me about what prison is like', asked Nixon, visibly moved at meeting the first of his White House aides to have undergone the trauma of incarceration. 'You have to choose between making it a positive or negative experience', replied Krogh, explaining that with the help of his religious faith he had managed to find his work as a prison farmhand 'spiritually enriching'. Nixon showed great interest in Krogh's spiritual survival plan for coping with life in jail. Eventually, the conversation turned to the Ellsberg burglary. Nixon asked Krogh whether he (Nixon) had known about it. Krogh was astonished by the question. He categorically assured Nixon that he had neither ordered the break-in nor had any advance knowledge of it.

'I came to the conclusion that Nixon was so down, and feeling so bad about what had happened that he wanted to assume the guilt for it himself', recalled Krogh. But even after responsibility for the crimes of the Plumbers had been lifted from his shoulders, Nixon still seemed to be tortured. 'Do you think I should plead guilty?' he asked in a low voice. 'Do you feel guilty Mr. President?' responded Krogh. 'No I don't. I just don't.' 'Then you can't, you can't do that', was Krogh's advice.[2]

While Nixon was discussing a plea of guilty, his successor in the White House was wrestling with the question of a pardon. Opinion in the country was massively opposed to such an exercise of the presidential prerogative, while in official Washington the subject aroused almost a lynch-mob atmosphere. In the end, Gerald Ford took his decision on the basis of simple human decency. He ignored the congressional clamour to have Nixon punished; the legal pressure to make him stand trial in equality with his indicted aides; and the media baying for his blood. Instead, Ford's heart was ruled by compassion and his head by common sense. The new President saw clearly what any objective observer (of whom few were around him) should have known: that a Nixon trial would prolong and embitter still further the national nightmare of Watergate; that it would be almost impossible to find an impartial jury; and that it was doubtful whether the man in the dock would be capable of withstanding such an ordeal. As reports reached the White House from various San Clemente visitors and telephone callers about Nixon's physical and psychological decline, Ford made up his mind. He despatched Benton Becker of the White House legal staff to southern California with instructions to work out the details of a pardon linked to an agreement about access to Nixon's presidential papers.

This proved to be an exceptionally difficult assignment, since Nixon was almost irrational when asked to discuss the proposal. Amidst wild swings of mood and concentration he veered from bathos to bravado. At one point he told his lawyer Jack Miller, 'I'd just as soon go through the agony of a trial so we can scrape away at least all the false charges and fight it out on those where there may be a doubt.'[3] In another display of defiance he told a member of his staff that he thought he could adjust to a prison sentence. 'All I'd need would be a good supply of books and a hard table to write on. Some of the best literature in history has been written in jail—look at Gandhi and Lenin.'[4] When he saw Becker he could not bring himself to discuss the pardon at all. He was tearful; his attention wandered; and he was incapable of finishing his sentences. His only coherent conversation came when he talked about the prospects for the Washington Redskins and presented his visitor with a presidential tie pin, telling him, 'You're a fine young man. You've been a gentleman. We've had enough bullies.' If it was an act, it was a convincing one. When Becker returned to Washington he reported to President Ford that he doubted whether Nixon would still be alive by the end of the year.[5]

In spite of the difficulties of communicating directly with Nixon, Becker did manage to hammer out an agreement with Miller and Ziegler. They, in turn, persuaded their principal that the pardon was the only way of closing off the prospect of spending several years in emotional agony and financial penury—with no certainty of a fair trial at the end of it. After much heart-searching Nixon eventually agreed, commenting later:

> It was the most painful decision of my political career, and one in which I had no other choice. To accept a pardon is to, in effect, admit guilt of a crime. I would have preferred to have fought that issue out in the impeachment proceedings before the resignation or in a trial after the resignation. But as Miller made abundantly clear to me, I did not have the financial resources or the physical strength to go through not only one but several trials which would have undoubtedly resulted had there been no pardon.[6]

One last stumbling block was Ford's requirement for 'a statement of contrition'. Initially Nixon resisted issuing any such statement, other than the nine-word sentence: 'In accordance with the law I accept this pardon.' When told by Becker that if that was the best they could do, Ford would withhold the pardon, Ziegler consulted with his boss and produced a draft which summarised Nixon's true feelings about Watergate, then and now. Its last paragraphs read:

> No words can describe the depth of my regret and pain at the anguish my mistakes over Watergate have caused the nation and the Presidency—a nation I so deeply love and an institution I so greatly respect.
>
> I know that many fair-minded people believe that my motivations and actions in the Watergate affair were intentionally self-serving and illegal. I now understand how my own mistakes and misjudgements have contributed to that belief and seem to support it. This burden is the heaviest of all to bear. That the way I tried to deal with Watergate was the wrong way is a burden I shall bear for every day of the life that is left to me.[7]

Becker returned with this statement to Washington and twenty-four hours later, on the morning of Sunday 8 September, President Ford announced that he had granted 'a full, free and absolute pardon unto Richard Nixon for all offenses against the United States which he, Richard Nixon, has committed or may have committed or taken part in during the period January 20th 1969 through August 9th 1974'.[8] Simultaneously, Nixon's statement of contrition was released. Far from damping down the controversy, these announcements had the impact of a volcanic explosion.

The political firestorm that exploded after the pardon damaged the Ford Presidency—possibly fatally. On 9 September, Gallup recorded the sharpest single fall in presidential popularity in the history of polling as Ford's approval rating crashed overnight by twenty-two points. The accompanying media indignation was no less censorious. The *New York Times* led the pack of hostile newspaper editorials with its comment: 'In granting President Nixon an inappropriate and premature grant of clemency, President Ford has affronted the Constitution and the American system of justice. This blundering intervention is a body blow to the President's own credibility and to the public's reviving sense of confidence in the integrity of its government.'[9]

On Capitol Hill, the Democrats queued up to heap insults on the pardoned President. One group of liberal Congressmen sought to have Nixon's pension withdrawn. Another tried to have him voted 'a security risk' who should not be given access to classified government material.[10] The GOP reeled under the general onslaught, as the polls recorded the public's opposition to the pardon by a factor of 2 to 1. As Senator Howard Baker recalled the atmosphere: 'We Republicans paid a terrible price for the pardon politically, but it was the right decision both morally and intellectually. Ford was virtually offering up his body and I think he knew that. He deserves enormous credit for an act of statesmanship.'[11]

Nixon had expected some negative reactions to the announcement but he was shocked by the savagery of the backlash. In addition to the external onslaught from his enemies, he even had to face some internal criticism from his family. They had not been told of his decision in advance, and when Pat heard the news she was furious. 'Pardon for what?' she exploded.[12] Having been ambivalent about accepting the pardon in the first place, Nixon now felt a sense of revulsion, so much so that he even tried to give it back. The telephone call in which he made this quixotic gesture tested the new President's politeness to the limit. The conversation was terminated at Ford's end with uncharacteristic abruptness.

The mental strain that Nixon was so obviously suffering at this time became matched by severe physical problems. His left leg swelled up with phlebitis as a large and potentially life-threatening blood clot formed. After anticoagulant drugs failed to work, his doctors decided they must operate. To obtain his patient's consent, Dr. Wiley Barker, chief of the surgical section at the UCLA Medical Center showed Nixon the venogram of his leg.

'If you look at this clot cross-eyed,' said Barker 'it will kill you.'

'So it's surgery then?'

'If you want to go on living, it is.'

Nixon smiled. 'I can assure you about that. I've got too many things to do to go on being sick. Let's just get it out of the way.'[13]

At 5.40 a.m. on 30 October, Nixon underwent a seventy-minute operation at Long Beach Memorial Hospital. Seven hours after emerging from the theatre, his recovery seemed to be going well, but suddenly he had a relapse. His valet, Manolo Sanchez, was alone with him when his eyes closed and he whispered, 'Is that you Manolo? Manolo, I don't think I'm going to get out of here alive.'[14] Seconds later, Nixon slumped into unconsciousness. His eyes rolled back into his head; his blood pressure fell to sixty over zero; he was in a state of critical trauma. The cause of the emergency was an internal haemorrhage, for it later transpired that at least four pints of blood had seeped away into an abdominal cavity.

The medical team, headed by Dr. John Lundgren, launched a desperate fight to save their patient. It took three hours of continuous blood transfusions and countershock measures before his condition stabilised. Nixon's only memory of the crisis was of a nurse slapping his face and shouting, 'Richard, wake up! Richard!'—a name only ever used by his mother. Pat, Tricia, and Julie kept an all-night vigil by his bedside. When he eventually came round and focused on Pat, he told her in a faltering voice: 'I don't think I'm going to make it.' 'Don't talk that way', she said fiercely, gripping his hand. 'You have got to make it. You must not give up.'[15] Through the fog of pain Nixon remembered she had used almost the same words just before The Fund crisis broadcast in 1952. It helped him to rally slightly, but he knew he was still perilously close to death. He said he wanted to dictate some last memories. Pat was brought pencil and paper and took down his comments for over two hours. When she tired, Ron Ziegler took over as the note-taker until he became exhausted. His replacement at the bedside was Frank Gannon, a young Ziegler protégé from the White House press office. 'Nixon looked utterly helpless with tubes up his nose and drips going into his veins, but his voice was surprisingly strong', recalled Gannon. 'He said he knew he might not live through the night. His doctors had warned him that his embolism could move at any time and that it would be at least twelve hours before his anticoagulant drugs might start to dissolve it. So he wanted to use what could be his last hours to talk for posterity—

mainly about what he had achieved and what he'd hoped to do. It was a moving and rather terrifying experience.'[16]

This energetic burst of 'deathbed' dictating at least demonstrated that Nixon had some fighting spirit left in him. The following day he began taking liquids; his fever dropped; his blood pressure returned to normal and the clot began to break up. But he remained in intensive care, still desperately weak. On the third day following the relapse, he was woken by a frenzied hammering and hacksawing at the door of his hospital room. The catch had jammed. Outside in the corridor stood President Ford, who had broken off from a day's electioneering in California to pay an unexpected visit. When the emergency carpenter finally got the door open, Ford entered and, according to Ziegler, 'turned gray'[17] at the sight of the patient's spectral appearance. However, it was the ex-President who did most of the talking. Nixon asked several questions about the progress of the midterm election campaign and on hearing it was going badly, he advised his successor 'to hang in there with [Vice President] Rockefeller' because 'the situation was bound to improve'.[18] Ford, who addressed Nixon as 'Mr. President' throughout their eight-minute conversation, made sympathetic small talk. He ended by saying, 'I just want to thank you for all you did for me.'[19] Tears came into the new President's eyes as Nixon said his goodbyes, croaking through the tubes in his mouth, 'I'm not feeling too well, but I'm going to make it...your visit has meant a lot to me, Mr. President, I'm deeply grateful.'[20]

Not everyone was as kind as President Ford. Back in Washington there were many who were sceptical about the bulletins from the hospital, including Judge Sirica. He sent a team of three doctors to investigate the medical condition of the star witness under subpoena for the forthcoming Watergate trial of Mitchell, Haldeman and Ehrlichman. After a detailed examination, Sirica's doctors unanimously agreed that Nixon was unfit to travel or testify. When this announcement was made, the *Washington Post* published a cartoon which had Puck the Penguin saying: 'Somebody tell him he has the wrong foot up.'[21]

The charge of malingering, popular though it was at the time, does not begin to stand up. In addition to the weight of medical opinion, there is the hitherto unpublished (and to some extent unprintable) evidence of Nixon's private diaries for the months of November and December 1974. They are full of references to his humiliating physical difficulties with tubes, bedpans, and urinals. In one almost illegible entry of 10 November, he recorded his despair when 'I didn't recognize Pat when she brought a chair into the room'.[22]

He had trouble with his drugs, especially painkillers, recalling in one passage: 'I took codeine because of the pain. I would wake up at night and the room would be upside down...like I was standing straight up in bed with the bed at my back. And I have to get my bearings to get back so I knocked off the codeine.'[23]

This was the first reference in Nixon's post-resignation diaries to getting or coming back. It slowly developed into a recurrent theme, although frequently qualified by mentions of his depressed feelings:

> Since returning home I have been terribly weak but have been gaining a little bit of strength each day. I've had these long sleeps that mean I must be catching up on all that I have lost. And yet as it reaches a quarter of one this Monday the 18th [of November] I have a rather depressed feeling again. I have simply got to get over this because we just can't continue to exist with nothing but depression or bad news coming in.[24]

Two days later, Nixon's fighting spirit was flickering again:

> Pat doesn't want to go out at all at this time. I have the same feeling but I've got to move out just a little bit although I must say I have no stomach for it having in mind that I don't like for people to come up and say they are sorry and I also don't want to run into unpleasant situations where people come up and snarl around. So be it. We will see it through. We've had tough times before and we can take the tougher ones that we will have to go through now. That is perhaps what we were made for—to be able to take punishment beyond what anyone in this office has ever had before particularly after leaving office. This is a test of character and we must not fail the test.[25]

In Nixon's mind, this self-imposed test soon started to take the form of a theoretical comeback. 'Some way there must be a way to come back', he wrote on 2 December. 'To come back from this vale of tears through which we have passed. Not just a vale of tears, buckets of them have been shed. I think of all the little people who must have been scared when I think of the fact that I have been afraid of the unknown in all this...it really makes me heartsick.'[26]

Although the notion of a comeback would have seemed insane to almost anyone else in America four months after the resignation, Nixon was beginning to prepare himself for this next extraordinary step in his life.

On 7 December 1974, noting that it was Pearl Harbor Day, he gave himself the following pep talk in his diary:

I simply have to pull myself together and start the long journey back—live through the agony of the balance of the tapes whatever they are; fight over the papers, whatever comes at the trial, and do the only creative thing that perhaps I have left to do which is to write a book—maybe one, maybe more—and to follow it with speeches, television of course where possible, which will maybe put some of these things in perspective. I think that Ron [Ziegler] and Frank [Gannon], both in a kind way are trying to tell me that there is a hell of a lot of hatred out there and mistrust and that we cannot underestimate it...

I do not want to feel depressed today. I rather feel it however, and yet maybe such a day is the day to start coming back—maybe this afternoon—to make the first outline on the book and during the next week to try to continue along this process.[27]

In spite of these upbeat words the totality of the December diaries, together with the eyewitness accounts of close friends, reflect a constant see-sawing in Nixon's spirits. On the whole, he was much more down than up. As the year drew to its close his cup of misery was still full. His convalescence remained slow and painful. He had lost fifteen pounds and his appearance was visibly shrunken and more concave. His emotions seemed to have imploded into a depression, which deepened into black gloom when he received the news that Mitchell, Haldeman and Ehrlichman had each been sentenced to serve two and a half to eight years in prison.[28] Meanwhile in the outside world the hurricane of public hostility towards him showed no signs of abating. One way and another, the seasonal atmosphere at La Casa Pacifica could hardly have been less peaceful, nor the climate of opinion more lacking in goodwill. As his daughter Julie put it: 'Christmas 1974 was the lowest point in my father's life.'[29]

II. STIRRINGS TOWARDS RECOVERY 1975–78

As soon as he was well enough to think clearly, Nixon had to face up to his three most overwhelming problems—health, money, and disgrace. A less indomitable spirit could well have lost heart in the circumstances that confronted him at the end of his *annus miserabilissimus* of 1974. He was an invalid, a near-bankrupt and a pariah. Some of his difficulties were worsening, particularly on the legal front, where he faced a plethora of expensive civil lawsuits not covered by the pardon. Denuded of staff (when the transitional period of federal funding which paid their salaries came to an end) and distanced by most of his friends,

Nixon was deeply demoralised. However, unlike everyone else, he did not regard his plight as hopeless.

The extraordinary resilience of Richard Nixon has its roots in the combative aggression he inherited from his father; the spiritual beliefs he accepted from his mother; the 'never give up' philosophy he learned from his teenage football coach Chief Newman; and the mystic sense of destiny he acquired for himself. All these factors came into play on his 62nd birthday, 9 January 1975, when he sat alone in his study overlooking the Pacific Ocean and scribbled on a yellow legal pad the outlines of a strategy for personal recovery.

Health was his first priority. To regain it he devised a regime of walking, swimming, and golf. His sporting companion and mentor was his former military aide Jack Brennan, whose brusque Marine Colonel's exterior concealed a gentle and compassionate sensitivity. Brennan officially left the Nixon staff on 9 February when the transition period ended. He was under orders to attend the Naval War College, a career appointment that usually leads to the rank of General, but while waiting to take up this posting he was temporarily assigned to Camp Pendleton, a Marine base fifteen minutes' drive from the Nixon compound. Bored by his duties at Camp Pendleton, Brennan came to spend many of his off-duty hours in Nixon's company. A rapport developed between them because of their similar upbringings; their common expertise at different ends of the military spectrum in Vietnam; and their shared conversational tastes which ranged from macho 'man talk' to global stra-tegising. As their communication deepened, Brennan felt such a strong pull of loyalty towards his former Commander in Chief that he decided to resign his commission in the Marine Corps and to stay permanently at San Clemente as Nixon's administrative assistant.

Brennan was much more than an office administrator and golfing partner. He recognised that Nixon was a convalescent in emotional self-esteem as well as in physical health. 'Almost every day I said to myself, "Don't make mistakes; the guy is still fragile; don't let him get hurt." So on that basis my priority was to take him to places where he'd be sure to get a good welcome. I remember the first time we played golf how terrified he was that someone on the course would shout abuse at him. When the opposite happened and people kept coming over to him to shake his hand, he was boosted right up. That taught me something and set a pattern.'[30]

The pattern was that Brennan tried to heal Nixon's shattered self-confidence by gradually bringing him into contact with people and situations likely to strengthen his morale. To this end a carefully screened programme of outside visits and incoming visitors was arranged. The friends who came to cheer him up meant a lot to him and are listed like a rollcall of honour in his 1990 book of memoirs, *In the Arena*. Among those not listed was his former psychosomatic medicine practitioner Dr. Arnold Hutschnecker from New York. Hutschnecker told him, 'You are in a depression which could be suicidal if you allow it to deepen or which could linger on in your mind until you work it out of yourself.' He found Nixon 'grateful for a chance to talk, extremely humble, full of enormous sadness, but somehow determined not to be defeated'.[31] That determination first flickered into life on the golf course, where Nixon began to show considerable competitiveness, not only in his own game but in his selective arrangement of the partners and handicaps which often enabled him to end up on the winning side.

In addition to these therapeutic golf foursomes there were trips to baseball games and other sporting events where the spectators could be relied on to give him a cheer. There were occasional parties, such as the one organised by his barber Ken Allan at Corona Del Mar, at which John Wayne presented him with a Boehm sculpture of a horse: 'You know, Mr. President,' drawled the film star, 'it's kinda ironic giving this horse to you after the rough ride you've been having in Washington.' Nixon laughed and held up the horse to the guests: 'You never know, one day this horse may gallop again.'[32]

The horse that was galloping fastest was Nixon's book. Originally he had hoped to postpone writing his memoirs for several years but economic necessity compelled him to start working on them a few weeks after coming out of hospital. He set up a book office in the San Clemente compound headed by three principal researchers drawn from the former White House staff—Frank Gannon, Diane Sawyer, and Ken Khachigian.

The chief editorial assistant was Gannon, a twenty-nine-year-old graduate of Georgetown University's Foreign Service School; the London School of Economics; and Oxford. During his years in England, Gannon had been a member of the team working for Randolph Churchill on his filial biography of Sir Winston. This experience proved invaluable. 'We followed the "Randolph system" of chronological files for every significant day of the subject's life; of background papers on individual issues; even of outside "young gentlemen" hired by the hour as historical researchers to come in and write briefs on particular subjects', recalled Frank Gannon. 'But for all the depth of our preparations it was very much Nixon's own work. His application was amazing. He would get to his office between six or seven every morning and would stay there dictating, discussing and correcting the text until about five in the afternoon, when he would go for a swim with Mrs. Nixon or play some golf. That was his routine seven days a week, 365 days a year for three years.*

Every time Christmas Eve came round I remember him saying rather diffidently, "I know it's Christmas tomorrow, but—uh—I'll be in the office if you need me." That was the kind of dedication which made us give a 365 day a year commitment too. I only took one weekend off in all my time in San Clemente and even then he was on the phone to me talking about the files I had taken to read! He was a demanding taskmaster, but at the same time kind, considerate and always fascinating to work with.'[33]

The toughest part of the book (approximately 300 pages of it) was Watergate. The researcher who bore the brunt of this was Diane Sawyer, then twenty-eight years old. She had become the White House press office's expert on the saga during the year leading up to the resignation, and as a consequence had been hired to work on the memoirs. She spent her first six months in San Clemente creating a mammoth compendium of the legal documents, the public record, and the journalistic coverage—right down to the craziest of speculations. Her challenge was to lead her boss through these minefields in order to ensure that Nixon as an author did not repeat in print the mendacious follies that had destroyed him as a President. This was no small task, particularly as the answer to the old chestnut 'What did he know and when did he know it?' was far from clear, even in the calmer atmosphere of historical research.

Sawyer spent more time alone with Nixon than any other member of the research team. Her longest stretch was six and a half hours without even a bathroom break. Part tutorial, part confessional, part editorial, these sessions left her emotionally and physically exhausted. 'She would come back from them looking harrowed and sick,' recalled Gannon, 'but she always recognized that Nixon had to do it his way, which was to talk himself through each phase of Watergate before dictating. He hated having to think and write about it, not least because there really were a lot of things he simply didn't know about, but in the end he faced up and did it.'[34]

At the outset of the project, Nixon laid out the parameters of his memoir-writing philosophy to his staff: 'We won't grovel; we won't confess; we won't do a *mea culpa* act; but we will be one hundred per cent accurate', he said.[35] The final text fulfilled these requirements. No critic was able to identify any major mistakes or inaccuracies in its 1090 pages and several of the reviews were surprisingly complimentary. The public liked it too, buying 330,000 hardback copies in six

---

* In fact Nixon broke the routine only twice—when he prepared for the Frost interviews in March 1977 and when he visited China in 1976.

months, a figure which made *RN* the best-selling presidential autobiography of the twentieth century.

The memoirs were not only Nixon's testament for history, they were also his financial salvation. The Hollywood agent, Irving 'Swifty' Lazar, had secured a $2.5 million advance from the publishers, payable by instalments. These literary earnings, plus Nixon's congressional and presidential pensions worth around $80,000 a year, should have been enough to keep the wolf from the door, but they were not. So large were his liabilities and expenses that his budget was running at a serious deficit. Such assets as he had were in heavily mortgaged property, so the end result was a negative net worth. On paper at least, Nixon was insolvent.

The main problem, which seemed to have no end in sight, was litigation. Over sixty lawsuits were filed against him in the first four years after his resignation, many of them by individuals seeking redress by government actions which had never involved presidential decisions in the first place. Most of these were dismissed, but they all had to be defended, as did the more substantial proceedings involving matters such as access to Nixon's tapes and papers or depositions required by the Special Prosecutor's office. A few days before the resignation, Nixon's son-in-law Ed Cox, a New York lawyer, had warned him that the team of young attorneys at the Special Prosecutor's office might prove a heavy cross to bear in years to come: 'I know these people. They are smart and ruthless. They hate you', said Cox. 'They will harass you and hound you in civil and criminal actions across the country for the rest of your life.'[36]

There was some truth in this prediction. For several years Nixon was tangentially and unfairly enmeshed in a great deal of Watergate-related litigation and investigation. One of the most painful of these legal episodes came in June 1975, when he was questioned under oath for eleven hours as part of a federal investigation into Bebe Rebozo. The interrogation was an ordeal, but it took the Special Prosecutor's office no further forward. Rebozo was never indicted. No evidence could be found to sustain charges against him. Nixon to this day regards the hounding of his closest friend* as a disgraceful abuse of power by the US attorneys concerned. All this activity cost serious money. Nixon found himself facing legal bills of over $750,000. In addition, he had other liabilities such as the salaries for his staff after the transition period ended (more than $150,000 a year); back tax demands of over $200,000; property taxes on the San Clemente house

---

* In a touching diary reference to Rebozo's legal troubles, which centred on what he had or had not done with a $100,000 campaign contribution from the Hughes Tool Company, Nixon wrote: 'I must say Bebe is a strong man, the best friend anyone could possibly have and my heart just breaks when I think of what he has been through and what he is going through now.'[37]

($37,000 a year); and overdue mortgage loan repayments, which at one stage were running at $226,000 a year. Nixon simply did not have the resources to meet these commitments nor, in the early days, did he understand the depth of his financial plight. In one recklessly generous gesture on Christmas Day 1974 he gave $5,000 each to Tricia and Julie in anticipation of his book advance. At first Julie refused to take it, but Nixon insisted, saying that he wanted his daughters to have some fun now.[38] Such paternal kindness did not improve his bank balance. By mid-January, just after he had paid the $23,000 medical bills for his treatment at Long Beach Memorial Hospital, he was left with exactly $500 in his bank account.[39]

Drastic action was needed to remedy this situation. Most of the staff had to be laid off, including Ron Ziegler. The two beach houses at Key Biscayne were sold at generous prices to a trust owned by Bob Abplanalp and Bebe Rebozo. Cuts were made in household and garden expenditure at San Clemente. The weeds growing over La Casa Pacifica's unkempt miniature golf course, which had once been maintained by political volunteers, were a telling symbol of both the ex-President's financial difficulties and the eroding support among his friends.

Nixon, however, never lost heart, even when his economic position looked desperate, or when Congress struck him a low blow by reducing the anticipated $100,000 a year office expenses allowance for a former President to $60,000. 'He would sit there figuring away on his yellow pads, and even when the sums just couldn't be made to add up, he would end up by saying "Oh well, it will work out"', recalled Ken Khachigian.[40] This cheerfulness in the face of adversity was based on Nixon's steadfast belief in his own long-term earning power. How best to activate this was a problem. He could not go back to the law, because the New York Bar Association had humiliatingly disbarred him in a public court action. He could not earn honoraria from lecturing, partly because of the general hostility towards him but more because he had (and still has) a quaint but honourable belief that former Presidents should never accept paid speaking engagements. The book was potentially a big earner but the instalments on the advance were slow while the expenses of the research team stayed high.

Discreetly, through the resourceful Brennan, Nixon began to explore the possibilities for private business deals overseas. Operating as an adviser, a consultant or a provider of introductions, the services of a former President had considerable value. Discussions about these possibilities took place in San Clemente with a handful of international entrepreneurs such as Adnan Khashoggi of Saudi Arabia, Sir James Goldsmith of Britain, Ardeshir Zahedi of Iran, and Omar Zawawi of Oman. However, before any of these business deals could come to fruition, Nixon faced a cash flow crisis. It was precipitated by his lawyers, who threatened to resign if their bills remained unpaid. He solved it by signing a contract to record twenty-four hours of television interviews with David Frost, who, after some casting around, was the only bidder for such a series.

The Frost interviews were a strategic mistake but a financial necessity. Every cent of the $600,000 Nixon received (less 'Swifty' Lazar's ten per cent) went straight to his lawyers. It was a high-risk project on each side. Frost's own production company, David Paradine Productions, Inc., had invested heavily in it, and both Frost and Nixon had reason to worry about the eventual content of the interviews, as one verbal exchange during the negotiations emphasised:

'How do we know that you are not going to screw us on the editing?' demanded Jack Brennan.

'And how do we know that you are not going to screw us with the stonewalling?' retorted Frost.[41]

When the interviews took place in March 1977, the early rounds of the screwing contest went to Nixon. Stonewalling was not the problem. Nixon did his fair share of it, but his supremacy as an interviewee came from the fact that he was smarter, better prepared, and more in command of the subject matter than his British interviewer. This caused much despondency in the Frost camp as the cans filled with hours of film on Vietnam, Cambodia, the Soviet Union and the domestic side of the Presidency without Nixon losing the initiative. Even when he made the breathtaking claim, 'When the President does it, that means it is not illegal', during a discussion of the Pentagon Papers, Frost failed to follow up in cross-examination. 'You sound like two old chums sitting around a pork barrel talking about a bowling game', remonstrated his senior researcher Bob Zelnick.[42]

Because of the softness of the interviews, Frost eventually felt obliged to negotiate for extra time. His bluff was that without additional taping, he would not be able to cover China. In reality, the extension was needed to allow an in-depth interrogation on Watergate. Nixon fell for the ploy and agreed to record four more hours without extra charge.

In the Watergate sections of the interviews, Frost sharpened up his act considerably. Nixon was discomfited to no small extent, visibly sweating and stuttering as Frost wrong-footed him in various passages, most notably when he produced unpublished transcripts from the White House tapes which appeared to confirm the President's involvement in the cover-up.

Frost: So March 21st was the first time you really knew about the cover-up?

Nixon: March 21st was the date in which the full import, the full impact of the cover-up came to me...

Frost: But in that case... why did you say in such strong terms to Colson on February 14th—which is more than a month before... 'The cover-up is the main ingredient. That's where we gotta cut our losses; my losses are to be cut. The President's losses gotta be cut on the cover-up deal.'

Nixon looked stunned as the damaging quotes continued. 'It hasn't been published yet, you say?' he asked nervously, later falling back on the assertion that Frost had been reading 'out of context'.[43]

Nixon's unhappy body language, which became highly prominent in the editing, made admissions even more telling than his unhappy words. As the cameras rolled, he himself seemed to be overwhelmed by some sort of catharsis, saying emotionally: '...It was my fault. I'm not blaming anybody. I'm simply saying to you that, as far as I'm concerned, I not only regret it—I indicated my own beliefs in this matter when I resigned. People don't think it was enough to admit mistakes—fine. If they want me to get down and grovel on the floor, no, never, because I don't believe I should.' He continued with increasing passion: 'I brought myself down... I gave them a sword. And they stuck it in. And they twisted it with relish. And I guess if I had been in their position I'd have done the same thing.'

In the final moments of the interview, Nixon declared through moist, half-closed eyes:

I let down my friends. I let down the country. I let down our system of government and the dreams of all those young people that ought to get into government but think it's all too corrupt and the rest... I let the American people down. And I have to carry that burden with me for the rest of my life.[44]

Ironically the screening of the Frost interviews seemed to lift Nixon's burden a little. Public reaction to them was predictably mixed. A Gallup Poll taken among the estimated 55 million US viewers showed that 44 per cent came away from their TV sets feeling more sympathetic towards Nixon, although 72 per cent thought he was guilty of obstruction of justice and 69 per cent believed he had lied during the interview itself.[45] Nixon did not watch his own performance, once again citing the old testament advice to Lot's wife, 'Never look back.'[46] However, those around him thought that a boil had been lanced by the interviews, and that when he soon afterwards completed the memoirs section on Watergate, he felt within himself that he had expurgated a black corner of the past.

By early 1978, other clouds were lifting at San Clemente. The money problems were easing as one or two of Brennan's international business deals came off, with the result that sizeable commissions were paid into the 'silent partner's' bank account at the Bank of Key Biscayne. Nixon's physical health was improving also. Golf had become something of an obsession, and gradually his game improved to the point where he was breaking ninety and frequently doing holes in par. With his rounds of the course, long walks on the beach, and swims in the Pacific, he had made himself a fit man again. But fit for what? Almost his only activity for three years had been working on the memoirs. These came to an end with the correction of the proofs in March 1978. On the final night of this operation when all that remained to be done was to pack the pages into a carton for flying to the publishers in the morning, Nixon came into the book office with three glasses and a bottle of brandy on a tray. 'I guess this calls for a celebration', he declared to Frank Gannon and Diane Sawyer. Explaining that they were about to drink from a very special cognac, the one he and Kissinger had sipped in 1971 to mark the conclusion of the secret negotiations for the China trip, he raised his glass to propose a toast. After expressing his gratitude in emotional terms to his researchers, he finally concluded: 'To the book! And to the future !'[47]

Nixon's future in 1978, at the age of sixty-five did not look particularly bright. He was still continuously referred to in the press as 'the disgraced ex-President'. The Carter White House was treating him with a pronounced meanness of spirit, restricting his briefings and other courtesies normally extended to former Presidents, to the minimum. There were no indications in the polls that his low standing with the public was improving. Yet, on the wider horizons, Nixon knew he had both a domestic and an international constituency whose admiration for his achievements had not been unduly diminished by the shenanigans of Watergate. It was to these groups that he now turned in his quest for political acceptance.

China was his first port of call. In 1976, on the fourth anniversary of his historic visit to Peking, the Chinese government sent an aircraft to pick him up in Los Angeles. He was given an almost presidential tour of the country, complete with bands, state banquets and a meeting with the ailing Chairman Mao. He also had nine hours of politically important talks with Chou En-lai's successor, the newly appointed Premier Hua Guofeng, whom no American official had ever met. 'We Chinese do not forget our friends', Nixon was told many times during these meetings and receptions. Almost the opposite message was being given out by the White House, where President Ford, battling in the New Hampshire primary, was doing his best to forget the predecessor by whom he was being upstaged 8,000 miles away.

Whatever the irritations felt by the Ford administration over Nixon's ex-presidential diplomacy in Peking, the China trip sent his morale soaring. As soon as the memoirs were finished, he began planning another Asian journey, this time to the rim of the Pacific with stops in Australia, Singapore, Thailand and a nostalgic tour of the Solomon Island bases such as Green Island, where he had served as a naval officer in World War II. This expedition was blocked by the new Carter administration which, in an underhand way, persuaded the Australian government that it would be in the best interests of Canberra's relations with the White House if Nixon's feelers for an official invitation could be rebuffed. He was understandably angered by these manoeuvres, particularly when the Australian rejection was made public.[48] As a consequence, Nixon shelved all travel plans for some months, making one exception when an unexpected invitation came in from Hyden, Kentucky (population 500), which wanted to name its new swimming pool and gymnasium complex the Richard M. Nixon Recreation Center.

Hyden was the perfect setting for Nixon's first public speech since his emotional farewell address to the White House staff three years and eleven months earlier. It was a loyal Republican stronghold of small town, blue collar, Middle America, and it showed its appreciation by giving Nixon a welcome worthy of the second coming of the Messiah. Six thousand citizens of Hyden and the surrounding Leslie County turned out on 2 July to roar their applause as Nixon delivered a forty-two-minute oration full of tub-thumping rhetoric and familiar cheer lines. It was a memorable occasion, not so much for the speech but for the emotional warmth of the faithful towards their exiled hero. A few weeks later, Nixon repeated the experiment in front of a much larger crowd at Biloxi, Mississippi. Once again his speech appeared to unleash passionate feelings of restoration mania as the audience cheered themselves hoarse. On his way back to California, he stopped off at Shreveport, Louisiana, where Congressman Joe Waggoner, his most steadfast supporter in the House of Representatives, hosted a 500-guest barbecue party in his honour. As he was leaving the barbecue, a chant started up: 'Keep coming out, keep coming out.' Nixon strode back to the microphone and said with a beaming smile, 'Don't worry. I will. I guarantee you this is not the last of my public appearances. This is just one of many I plan in the future. Officially you can say that I'm out.'[49]

The Hyden, Biloxi, and Shreveport speeches were the culmination of the Brennan 'friendly faces only' strategy. However, much of the rest of the country was still unfriendly, or so a New York Times editorial, criticising the 'officially I'm out' remark, sharply suggested.[50] But Nixon was now in the mood to spread his wings. His next move towards recovery was in the international arena, with a European trip to engagements in Britain and France.

III. A JOURNEY TO BRITAIN—1978

In 1978, when Nixon made his visit to Britain (his first post-resignation trip to a Western country), the stakes were high. If successful, the trip could mark an important milestone on his road back to public acceptance. If it failed, his aspirations to regain the normal international status of an ex-President could be set back several years.

The first sign that a journey to Britain might be on Nixon's agenda came in a telephone call to the House of Commons from San Clemente on the afternoon of Friday 3 November. When the ex-President came on the line he was in an upbeat mood. 'I'm thinking of coming to your country towards the end of the month,' he told me.* 'I've had an interesting invitation to address the Oxford Union. Would you think it—uh—advisable for me to accept?' I was against it. The Union in those days was notorious for giving its visiting speakers a rough ride. However, my forecast of heavy heckling seemed to leave Nixon underwhelmed. 'Oh I'm quite used to all that…I've been to Oxford before, you know',[51] was his response. As the conversation continued, it became apparent that he was not seeking advice: he had already made up his mind to go to Oxford. What he was after was some assistance in lining up other appointments. He transferred the call to his aide, Colonel Jack Brennan, to run through a list of those whom he would like to see. They included: the Prime Minister; the Foreign Secretary; senior members of the Cabinet; The Queen—although he recognised there could be 'some problems' with Buckingham Palace; all the former Prime Ministers— Macmillan, Wilson, Home and Heath; 'distinguished intellectuals' such as Robert Blake and Paul Johnson; 'sympathetic columnists'—the only nomination was Peregrine Worsthorne; 'old friends' like Sir Christopher Soames and Sir Robert Thompson. He would also be glad to address Britain's Members of Parliament in session at Westminster.

By the time the call came to an end I was beginning to regret my conversation with Nixon in California some months earlier, when I had more or less volunteered my services for the task that now lay ahead. The problem was that the view from San Clemente of the level of welcome Britain might accord to the fallen President was out of tune with reality. There was no doubt that Nixon would be

---

* Because of the author's personal involvement in Nixon's visit to Britain, this is the only section of the book to be written in the first person singular.

courteously, if perhaps a little coolly, received as a private citizen coming to London for meetings with former associates or for delivering a lecture to an invited audience such as Chatham House.* But Brennan's request list sounded more in the nature of a royal tour. I was apprehensive and felt the need to take further soundings.

On a Friday afternoon, the House of Commons is usually quiet and soporific. When I went back into the chamber after the telephone call from San Clemente, it was almost empty save for three or four MPs debating hospital services in Worcestershire and the Speaker, the Rt. Hon. George Thomas, in the chair. Although I hardly knew him, on impulse I went over and asked if he could possibly see me for five minutes later that afternoon. The kindliest of men, George Thomas evidently sensed that he had a worried young backbencher on his hands. He immediately invited me to come up to his private quarters when the House rose at four o'clock.

Over tea in the Speaker's study, I outlined what I thought might be my problem. George Thomas did not seem to think it a problem at all. This devout Welsh Methodist preacher and former Labour Cabinet Minister was almost beside himself with excitement. His main concern was how best to roll out the red carpet for such a historic visitor. 'President Nixon, God bless him!' declared the Speaker. 'I have always thought him to be one of the world's greatest men. I shall never forget the inspiring speech he gave to Harold Wilson's cabinet.' He added that he now admired Nixon even more 'because he has suffered for his sins and has repented'. With mounting enthusiasm, George Thomas suggested some generous hospitality arrangements. He would personally welcome the ex-President to the Palace of Westminster; he would give a reception for him in the State Apartments of Speaker's House; he would invite the Cabinet, the Shadow Cabinet and at least 100 MPs. 'It will be a *pleasure* to do this for President Nixon', he enthused. 'It will make my heart sing.'

This euphoric mood was reflected in a 'Dear Mr. President' handwritten letter Speaker Thomas there and then composed. It outlined the arrangements we had been discussing, ending with the line, 'I do hope you will feel able to accept my invitation to Speaker's House, which is extended to you with a full heart. Yours sincerely, George Thomas.'[52]

The Speaker was soon in trouble for his good intentions. On returning to my home in London after a weekend in the constituency on Sunday evening, three telegrams were waiting. 'Please ring me urgently—219 3610—George Thomas';

---

* The Royal Institute of International Affairs, located at Chatham House, St. James's Square.

'Please ring me at Cardiff 613921—Very urgent—George Thomas'; 'Please come and see me first thing Monday morning—George Thomas'.

The Speaker was in a state of visible agitation when I arrived in his office. 'Have you posted that letter to Mr. Nixon I gave you on Friday?' was his first question. On receiving an affirmative answer he seemed utterly downcast.

'Oh dear, oh dear, now we are in a mess.'

'Why?'

'Because when I told the Foreign Office, they reacted extremely badly. They say President Nixon may be regarded as *persona non grata*, and that even if he is allowed to come in, the Government will boycott his visit. I gather the young squire himself is furious about it.'

This reference to the 'young squire' was to the recently appointed Foreign Secretary, Dr. David Owen, whose youth (forty) and high-handed ways had recently been attracting some adverse comment in the press. After more expressions of dismay at the turn of events, George Thomas came up with the solution of inviting Nixon to his home in Cardiff instead of to Westminster. 'He might enjoy a visit to Wales', he said optimistically. This vision of the former leader of the free world being led round Cardiff docks as a tourist had to be tactfully deflected. Eventually George Thomas said he thought he could perhaps give Nixon a cup of tea with his two Deputy Speakers 'completely privately' as a prelude to an all-party meeting of MPs which could be arranged separately in a committee room.

A few minutes after this discussion, I happened to encounter Margaret Thatcher in one of the corridors of the House. As the Leader of the Opposition she had been included on Brennan's list of requested appointments. I had sent her a note to this effect over the weekend, mentioning the Speaker's reception. 'Just got your letter', she said as she bustled past. 'I would be absolutely *delighted* to meet President Nixon. I shall come to George's reception for him.' It did not seem to be the moment to tell her that George's reception had just been cancelled. Instead, I retraced my steps back into the Speaker's office and reported the Leader of the Opposition's intentions. This news put great heart into George Thomas. 'What a woman! What courage!' he exclaimed. 'That puts a completely different complexion on matters. I think I shall give my reception after all...but a small one, just for a few friends. If Ministers don't want to come they needn't come, need they? I'm not going to have the Foreign Office telling me what I can or can't do in my own house.'

Similarly unpredictable swings of the pendulum continued during the rest of the preparations for the visit. Alec Douglas-Home was happy to come down from Scotland to meet Nixon. Harold Macmillan refused, saying 'I couldn't face it...I was too fond of Jack.' Ted Heath was 'otherwise engaged'. Harold Wilson booked a private room at the Dorchester Hotel in which to give the ex-President dinner. No senior Conservative MP could be found to take the chair at the proposed all-party meeting, but Dick Crawshaw, a respected Labour Privy Counsellor, volunteered for the task on hearing that there were difficulties. All Government Ministers, with one exception,* refused to meet the former President or to attend the meetings at which he spoke.

Nixon, who was unaware of these preliminary skirmishings, arrived at Heathrow airport on a scheduled flight on the morning of 29 November, where [as related in the Prologue] he was met somewhat ungraciously by the US Ambassador to the Court of St. James, Kingman Brewster. Nixon had four speaking engagements in Britain. All of them were successes, for he was adept at converting even his most sceptical listeners into at least grudging and sometimes enthusiastic admirers.

The Oxford Union was the noisiest of these events, although the hostility was confined to about 150 demonstrators outside the hall calling themselves CREEP—The Campaign to Resist the Efforts of the Ex-President. Hearing their predominantly American accents chanting 'Jail to the Chief' at him as the police pushed a way through the mêlée, Nixon muttered, 'Rhodes scholars from Ivy League schools, I'll bet', an unproven assertion that seemed to psyche him up for his speech. This was a vigorous *tour d'horizon* of foreign affairs which won him a fifty-second standing ovation. He then spent the next two hours answering the students' questions, some of which were hostile. He was asked if he regretted ordering the invasion of Cambodia in 1971. He replied that he only wished he had done it sooner and continued: 'Accusing the United States of invading the North Vietnamese occupation zones in Cambodia is the equivalent of accusing the Allies of invading German Occupied France in 1944.' Questioned about his personal future, he declared, 'My political life is over...but so long as I have a breath in my body I am going to talk about the great issues that affect the world. I am not going to keep my mouth shut. I am going to speak out for peace and freedom.'

On Watergate, he said: 'Some people say I didn't handle it properly and they're right. I screwed it up. And I paid the price. *Mea culpa.* But let's get on

---

* The exception was Dr. Dickson Mabon, Minister of State for Energy, who turned up at the Speaker's reception saying that he had admired Nixon ever since meeting him as Vice President and that he 'wasn't going to be buggered about by any damnfool orders from Number 10'.

to my achievements. You'll be here in the year 2000 and we'll see how I'm regarded then.'

Nixon left the Oxford Union to one more standing ovation and much cheering. He drove straight to the House of Commons. After drinks with the Speaker and an animated discussion with Mrs. Thatcher ('Wow, you can see how she became a leader, she's really got it', he remarked immediately after the encounter), he addressed approximately 180 MPs of all parties in a jam-packed committee room. 'I stand before you as the only American-born citizen who cannot seek election to the Presidency of the United States', was his opening line, which played well with a Westminster audience that had been somewhat overwhelmed by visits from two US presidential contenders in the previous ten days. After more of this endearingly self-deprecating humour, he dazzled the assembled parliamentarians with an ex-President's foreign policy seminar. After over an hour of questions the only note of mock dissent came from the Labour backbencher Andrew Faulds, who said: 'I deplore the outrageous sycophancy of this meeting,' (long pause for effect) 'but I have to admit, sir, that warts and all you were a bloody good leader of the Western world' (thunderous applause).

In fact, there was not much sycophancy at either Oxford or Westminster. What Nixon was encountering was the first manifestation of the swing in international opinion away from the obloquy that had been heaped on him at the time of Watergate. This swing continued during the last two days of his visit. He addressed a lunch for establishment figures hosted by Sir Charles Forte (who sent out 120 invitations and received 102 acceptances) and saw a steady flow of private visitors in his suite at Claridges.

One of Nixon's most testing engagements in intellectual terms was a talk he gave to the Conservative Philosophy Group, a gathering of academics, editors and politicians. There, in a private setting, he was challenged and closely questioned by journalists of the calibre of William Rees-Mogg (Editor of *The Times*); Simon Jenkins (Political Editor of *The Economist*); Peter Utley (*Daily Telegraph* columnist); Alastair Burnett (ITN anchor man); Peregrine Worsthorne. (*Sunday Telegraph*); Ronald Butt (*The Times*); and Alexander Chancellor (Editor of the *Spectator*); by academics such as Professors Hugh Thomas, Hugh Trevor-Roper, Robert Blake, Kenneth Minogue, and Shirley Letwin; and by an assortment of businessmen and politicians including Robin Leigh-Pemberton, Lord Sieff, Norman Lamont, Maurice Macmillan, Kenneth Baker and Julian Amery. Several of those present had come to bury Nixon, but by the time he had presented and defended his cerebral discourse on foreign policy, most of them were more than ready to praise him.

Nixon stayed long into the night to dine and talk with the Conservative Philosophers. One of his most memorable predictions, made just three weeks after the papal election of John Paul II, was: 'Watch out for the long-term impact of a Polish Pope with such qualities of spiritual leadership. He will change the map of Eastern Europe.'

On a more personal note, Nixon said afterwards that one of the highlights of the evening had been his conversation with Robert Blake, the Oxford historian and author of *Disraeli*. This much-acclaimed biography was widely reported to be Nixon's favourite reading during his White House years. At that time, some American commentators were puzzled by the President's self-identification with the nineteenth-century British Prime Minister. Blake's account of his talk with Nixon, given in a 1990 letter to the author, shed some interesting light on this historical association.

> I only met Nixon once and that was at your house in 1978 when I sat next to him at supper. He talked at length about Disraeli and was very flattering about my biography. He had obviously read it—one can always tell whether someone really has read one's book or merely been 'briefed' about it—and he referred more than once to Disraeli's handicaps and problems as someone of 'humble' (relatively) origins overcoming them and rising to the top of the Conservative rather than the Liberal Party which he thought would have provided a more natural or probable ladder to climb for someone of Disraeli's origins. Gladstone, he said, had all the advantages, Eton, Christ Church and money. I could not help wondering whether there was some parallel in his mind with himself and Jack Kennedy, but, if so, it was not made explicit.
>
> He referred to Disraeli's letter to Peel when seeking office in 1841 and actually quoted it: 'I have had to struggle against a storm of political hate and malice which few men ever experienced' (p. 164 of my book). Did I think this was true? As far as I can remember my reply was that Disraeli had incurred much hatred in his youth. So indeed did Winston Churchill. But people who are making their way over obstacles often do, and the fact that the obstacles are sometimes self-imposed does not help. He was silent for a moment and then said he remembered though not verbatim a shrewd remark by Lord Derby to Queen Victoria about people who are obliged to make their way in the world having to say and do things which were not necessary

for people who were already established*...I thought it was interesting that Richard Nixon remembered it.

We discussed the famous *mot* about climbing to the top of the greasy pole. He asked me if that was Disraeli's only object. I said no but it was an important one. He was very ambitious, but he had purposes; a strong Britain, belief in Empire, social reform. He would seize his chances as and when they came, but circumstances were always changing. He would take a striking initiative if there was a sudden opening—like the Suez Canal shares purchase—but he was not a man with a conscious detailed programme. He was there to govern and deal with events as they came along. Nixon said that this was really just about all that a politician could do. He said that Disraeli must have been a very tough character. I agreed, and Nixon said that he remembered, though again not verbatim, a good quotation in my book from Gladstone about Disraeli being a man who was never long defeated but would always make a comeback. He was evidently alluding to the quotation on p. 600 l.15 from bottom:

'Disraeli is a man who is *never beaten*. Every reverse, every defeat is to him only an admonition to wait and catch his opportunity of retrieving and more than retrieving his position.'

I think that Nixon does and did see a certain parallel between himself and Disraeli, though I do not know whether this was a cause or result of his reading my book. Obviously they are very dissimilar personalities. But it is true that both rose from relatively obscure origins to the top of the right-wing parties of their day. Neither had the advantages of wealth or high connections. Both were in a sense adventurers, slightly alien figures on their respective scenes. Both were involved in questionable episodes on their way up the ladder and both inspired a great deal of animosity in the process. Finally both had a remarkable capacity—as of india rubber—to bounce back after apparently permanent defeat.[53]

After many more good conversations on that evening (with Paul Johnson on philosophy; with Julian Amery on the Middle East; and with Robin Leigh-Pemberton on international economics, to name but three), Nixon might well

---

* Lord Derby's actual words in 1851 were, 'Madam, Mr. D. has had to make his position, and men who make their positions will say and do things which are not necessary to be said or done by those for whom positions are provided.'

have felt that he was bouncing back rather effectively so far as British opinion formers were concerned. The aide who accompanied him to the Conservative Philosophy Group, Ray Price, evidently thought so. 'I've never seen The Boss on better form', was his comment. 'He was stimulated intellectually and he really relaxed socially. He had fun.'

This feeling of having fun was epitomised by Nixon's dinner with Harold Wilson the following evening. The former Labour Prime Minister had spared no expense to entertain his guest. A private suite in the Dorchester; beautiful flowers; the finest food and wine (of which Nixon, apparently something of an expert on Bordeaux vintages, was highly appreciative) and the most jovial of greetings set the scene. Apart from the two principals, the only guests were Wilson's long-standing personal secretary Lady Falkender and myself. Falkender and I were almost completely silent throughout the meal as the elder statesmen roamed through recent political history with a glorious panoply of reminiscences. When the brandy came round Nixon observed, 'Well Harold, you and I are two surviving members of a small club. We have held real power, but now we're out.' 'Down but not out', interjected Wilson, who at this time was regarded as something of a political pariah by his own Labour Party. 'Right, right, we'll show 'em,' continued Nixon, 'but what I really want to know from my fellow club member is how do you fill your days? Do you read, do you write, are you preparing some great testament?' Wilson seemed to find this a difficult question. After much puffing on his pipe he eventually replied: 'As a matter of fact, Dick, I'm spending a lot of time on Gilbert and Sullivan.'

Nixon nodded seriously as if to convey the impression that he thought this an entirely suitable occupation for a world statesman. 'I'm quite a Gilbert and Sullivan buff myself', was his unexpected comment. 'In my college days I was one of the stage managers for a couple of productions—*Pinafore* and *The Pirates of Penzance*.'

Not to be outdone, Wilson countered: 'As a matter of fact I'm word perfect on both of them myself.' He explained that as a lifelong Gilbert and Sullivan enthusiast he was campaigning to save the D'Oyly Carte opera company which owned the copyrights. A few moments later, he decided to prove his musical expertise with a demonstration.

> When I was a lad I served a turn
> As office boy in an attorneys' firm
> piped up the former British Prime Minister.
> I cleaned the windows and I swept the floor

And I polished up the handle of the big front door

carolled the former President of the United States.

I polished up that handle so carefullee
That now I am the ruler of the Queen's Navee

the singing statesmen warbled together in passable unison, beating time on the table. They were off—for at least four verses of 'When I was a Lad'. As they reached the final refrain

Stick close to your desks and never go to sea
and you all may be rulers of the Queen's Navee

the enthralled audience of Falkender, Aitken, and a Dorchester waiter, gave rapturous applause for this unique Anglo-American duet. 'Harold sure knows how to make a party go', said Nixon as he left the Dorchester at 1.30 a.m.

Relaxed and enjoyable as the evening had been, it was not typical of Nixon's schedule. Indeed, to those who spent many hours of the visit in his company, one of the principal impressions was how unrelaxed he remained. He was obviously not on some retired politician's junket down memory lane. In spite of having pointed out to every audience that the US Constitution made it impossible for anyone twice elected to the Presidency to make a third attempt at it, he seemed to be winding himself up as if he was running for some new office. He prepared intensively for each speaking engagement, memorising passages of his remarks (which were always delivered without notes) and rehearsing potential answers to questions. When he had one-on-one meetings, they were not chats but substantive discussions, sometimes on matters of great detail. For example, when the former Foreign Office Minister and disarmament expert Lord Chalfont came to his suite in Claridges, Nixon grilled him for an hour on the interstices of the current East–West arms control negotiations, asking complex questions about matters such as the range limits of the latest Soviet ICBM's and SLCM's. When Christopher Soames dropped in, he was surprised by the depth of knowledge Nixon had, and wanted to acquire, on the developing Franco–German relationship.

Another interesting feature of these private meetings was the degree of Nixon's interest in Margaret Thatcher, who some domestic observers were writing off as a one-term Opposition Leader. After their brief talk on East–West relations at the Speaker's reception, Nixon by contrast seemed to have a strong intuition about her future, questioning everyone he saw from Alec Douglas-Home to the President of the Cambridge Union about Thatcher's policies, even using the term Thatcherism, which was not in common parlance in 1978.

On a more personal note, there were several attractive features in Nixon's character revealed during the trip. He took considerable pains to be agreeable to the young, spending a disproportionate amount of his time in dialogue with students, candidates for Parliament and junior MPs. He went out of his way to be kind to the 'little people' who were of service to him, talking with no hint of condescension to the maids in his hotel, waiters, drivers and policemen, about their homes and families. On his last morning, he said he wanted to show his appreciation to the two secretaries in my office who had carried a heavy load of typing on his behalf. So he came over to their room at Westminster to thank them in person, spending several minutes in conversation and posing for a photograph.

There were occasional glimpses of his vulnerabilities too. In the middle of a day of friendly responses, a passer-by unexpectedly goaded him in the street with rude gestures, and for a fleeting second his face crumpled in pain. A few moments after finishing a mutually warm meeting with Alec Douglas-Home, he suddenly had a pang of guilt about the prospects of his departing guest being badgered by journalists at the hotel entrance. 'Shall we tell Alec to find some other way out?' Nixon asked nervously. 'I wouldn't like to embarrass him about having had a meeting with the—uh—disgraced ex-President.'

More of these self doubts surfaced when he said goodbye to me. Had the visit really been a success? I assured him it had. Would the weekend press continue to be friendly? I thought (correctly) it would. He knew there had been 'a number of rather sensitive issues'—had they been too difficult, too much of a burden? Not at all. Why had the audience reactions been so favourable? 'Because you worked so hard to give them speeches that were as good as you would have given if you'd still been President', was my attempt at an answer.

This set Nixon off. He said he would like to offer some advice 'to a young politician from an old politician'. This was how I recorded his words in my diary:

> Preparations for a speech are important. So is delivery. So are all the political skills. But two things really sort out the men from the boys. Belief in a cause, and determination to fight for it. You have to be ready to fight through all life's ups and downs. There is really no such thing as a down because the only thing that finishes a politician is quitting. I've been down a few times so I know. Disappointment doesn't finish you. Being in what your enemies call disgrace doesn't

finish you. Only quit does that. You have to stay in the arena...Even when you're down and bleeding and being kicked in the nuts, you have to get up and fight back. You can always do it. And when you feel you can't go on, you must do it. If the cause is great enough, it's always worth fighting back...that's what makes a politician.

Nixon's eyes were misty as he spoke these words, which seemed to be coming from somewhere deep within him. Although he was ostensibly addressing me, on a more profound level he was talking to himself. I already knew that the reactions to his speeches and appearances in Britain had been good therapy for him. Now I realised that he would never rest until he regained his foothold of respect and influence as a former President.

IV. INFLUENCE 1978–1984

After his return from Britain, Nixon quietly stepped up his drive towards political rehabilitation in the United States. His relations with the Carter administration, which had been cold and distant, suddenly became much warmer after an 'Eyes Only' correspondence with the President on China in December 1978. These secret exchanges were a breakthrough for Nixon. They led to him being invited to his first visit back to the White House a few weeks later, and were the beginning of a steady flow of influential letters and memoranda to three Presidents over the next fourteen years.

The opening of the 'Nixon channel' to the White House began on 20 December 1978. The trigger was the Administration's decision to normalise diplomatic relations with the People's Republic of China. Nixon had been briefed in advance of the 15 December announcement and naturally supported it. However, he saw from the international and congressional backlash to the concomitant announcement of the break in diplomatic relations with Taiwan, that the issue was in danger of being mishandled. Accordingly, he sent President Carter a four-page letter of suggestions. The first of these was that certain additional reassurances must be given to the Taiwan lobby in Congress: 'Unless their opposition is mitigated...the fall-out on future foreign and defense policies will make the Panama Canal controversy look like a Sunday school picnic in comparison', he wrote, listing some specific moves that he thought would soothe congressional critics.

Nixon's second suggestion was that the President should reassure America's nervous allies, particularly South Korea, that the abrogation of the Taiwan treaty was a special case, and that no other treaties were going to be renounced. 'It would be most helpful to increase substantially the budget for military aid to Korea as a symbolic move to put North Korea and others on notice that the action on Taiwan should under no circumstances be interpreted as the beginning of a US withdrawal from other parts of Asia', he advised.

The third suggestion was a thinly veiled hint that Carter should temporarily suspend his moralisings about the human rights record in countries sensitive to the Taiwan decision. 'I believe it is important to publicly and privately give them [the Philippines, Indonesia, Iran and other countries with doubtful human rights records] our unqualified support. It would be ironical to qualify our support to any country which allows some human rights at a time when we have dramatically moved towards normalization with full co-operation with a nation which allows none—the PRC', wrote Nixon. 'I don't mean to criticize your eloquent commitment to this cause but I feel the greatest threat to human rights today is on the totalitarian left rather than on the authoritarian right.'[54]

Far from being offended by these implied criticisms of his policies, Carter responded by sending a handwritten note out to San Clemente on 22 December. 'I appreciate your excellent letter which is very helpful', he began, telling Nixon that 'with some difficulty' he had accepted his recommendations.[55] A few days later Carter wrote again, inviting his new adviser to attend a dinner on 29 January in honour of China's Vice Premier, Deng Xiaoping. The Chinese had themselves played some part in this invitation, specifically requesting Nixon's inclusion on the guest list, but however it came about, this was the first time the Carter White House treated him with the customary recognition normally accorded to a former President.

Nixon relished his return to 1600 Pennsylvania Avenue, despite being picketed by several dozen demonstrators carrying signs such as 'YOU BELONG IN PRISON NOT IN THE WHITE HOUSE'.[56] He sat at a table immediately behind Carter's, surrounded by senior administration figures such as National Security Adviser Zbigniew Brzezinski; US Ambassador to China Leonard Woodcock; Assistant Secretary of State for Asian Affairs Richard Holbrooke, and Chinese Deputy Premier Fang Yi. The following day he met privately for over two hours with Deng Xiaoping, who invited him back to China for a third visit. Despite some predictable media sniping, the dinner and the publicity it received were another milestone on Nixon's road to recovery.

The process of returning to the more public life style of an ex-President was quickened by the decision to come back East to live in New York. Pat was the prime mover in this. In 1978, the first of their grandchildren was born to Julie and in 1979 the second to Tricia. Both families were living on the East Coast and Pat was longing to be in closer contact with them. Meanwhile, the trip from La

Casa Pacifica to Los Angeles was a long two hours and her feelings of isolation in San Clemente were becoming unbearable. 'We're just dying here slowly',[57] she complained to Julie some months before La Casa Pacifica was sold for a price of $2.5 million. Nixon did not initially share these feelings. He was working on a new book; he enjoyed the sunshine and the golf; and he did some of his best thinking and reading in his secluded garden, spending long hours looking out over the cliffs in solitary communion with the Pacific. 'In the end the decision was made for him', recalled Jack Brennan. 'Pat absolutely insisted. She was just about ready to go off on her own without him.'[58]

After the Nixons' return to New York in February 1980, they soon found themselves enjoying life on 'the fastest track in the world' almost as much as they had during their wilderness years' sojourn in the city from 1963 to 1968. For $750,000 they bought a four-storey brownstone town house at 142 East 65th Street, five minutes' walk from the apartment of Tricia and Ed Cox, and their youngest grandson Christopher. Gradually they began to sample the traditional Manhattan pleasures of theatre-going, shopping, walking in Central Park and eating in good restaurants. With its veneration of celebrities, toleration of sinners, and admiration for fighters, the Big Apple was the ideal environment for the return of the exile. Fortified by cheerful greetings from strangers and warm welcomes from friends, Nixon soon swam with the New York stream and began to bask in the sunshine of increasing public acceptance.

The tide of politics was also beginning to turn in his favour. In the eyes of its critics, the Carter administration was turning out to be a disaster. The sanctimonious idealism of the President had led to a series of humiliating reverses in the field of foreign policy, most notably in Iran and in US-Soviet relations. Many voices began to be heard, hankering for the more ruthless but far more successful approach to international relations of the Nixon era. These voices multiplied after the publication of Nixon's new book, *The Real War* in the summer of 1980. It was a clarion call for a return to tough *realpolitik* in US diplomacy and an increase in America's military strength.

Learned in its historical references, and subtle in its twin-track approach to Soviet expansionism, *The Real War* argued that the two superpowers would continue to be in dangerous conflict until the United States showed that it had the will and the strength to contain aggression, coupled with the wish to cooperate in areas of mutual interest. A secondary theme was that the free world needed an American President with the character to convince the Kremlin that the US would be prepared to deploy its military power to halt further Soviet adventurism.

The Real War was a global and domestic best-seller. It bestowed a new status on its author as an influential advocate of strategic change in foreign policy, catching the mood of rising anxiety and reviving will in the Western Alliance. As a critique of Carter's foreign policy and a vindication of the Nixon approach to 'hard-headed détente', its shots went home, but the major impact of *The Real War* was that it became central to the thinking of the next US administration.

One of the book's most avid readers was Ronald Reagan, who was to become the Republican nominee in the presidential election of 1980. Nixon quietly moved close to the Reagan camp during the long campaign. He rarely talked directly to the nominee but was in close touch with Richard V. Allen, the chief foreign policy adviser; John Sears, the manager of the early phase of the campaign; Lyn Nofziger the press secretary and William Casey, one of Reagan's closest confidants. All these men had held posts in the Nixon administration and were admirers of their former chief's political and foreign policy expertise.

Nixon's dialogues with these members of the Reagan inner circle were carefully calculated to increase his influence. The extent of his growing confidence may be measured by the impact of the memorandum he sent to the President-elect on 18 November 1980. It concentrated mainly on appointments. Two of Nixon's strongest recommendations were for Bill Casey to head the CIA and for Alexander Haig to be appointed Secetary of State. Nixon's assessment of Haig's suitability for the appointment was this:

> He [Haig] would reassure the Europeans, give pause to the Russians, and in addition because of over five years as Henry's deputy in the White House and two years at NATO, he has acquired a great deal of experience in dealing with the Chinese, the Japanese, and the various factions in the Mideast, the Africans, and the Latin Americans. He is intelligent, strong, and generally shares your view on foreign policy. Those who oppose him because they think he is 'soft' are either ignorant or stupid. Others who raise the specter that he was somehow involved in Watergate simply don't know the facts. On the contrary, I can vouch from experience that he did an outstanding job helping to keep the wheels of government moving during the time we were under such enormous assault in the Watergate period. He would be personally loyal to you and would not backbite you on or off the record. He has one potential weakness. Because he is a career man he might be reluctant to clean house in the State Department to the extent the situation demands.[59]

Reagan was highly appreciative of this memorandum, which was a decisive factor in both Haig's and Casey's appointments, and also in William French Smith's appointment as Attorney General. However, the President-elect did not follow Nixon's other principal suggestions which were for John Connally to be Defense Secretary; Bill Simon to be Treasury Secretary; and John Swearingen to be Energy supremo. The memo concluded with a suggestion about the future relationship between the 37th and 40th President. 'As far as my own personal situation is concerned I do not, as you know, seek any official position', wrote Nixon. 'However, I would welcome the opportunity to provide advice in areas where I have special experience to you and to members of your Cabinet and White House staff where you deem it appropriate. President Eisenhower said to me when I visited him at Walter Reed Hospital after the election of 1968, "I am yours to command." I trust that that can be our relationship in the years ahead.'[60]

Reagan responded positively to this suggestion, and as a result 'the Nixon channel' stayed open as an unacknowledged but much appreciated source of advice for the next eight years. Most of the advice related to foreign policy issues and was given in telephone calls and secret briefing meetings with the National Security Adviser. The exchanges were busiest when William Clark (1982–3) and Robert C. McFarlane (1983–5) were in that post. Clark, who had formerly been a leading partner in the Los Angeles law firm of Gibson, Dunn and Crutcher developed a political friendship with his fellow Californian. He made a point of travelling once a month to Nixon's office in New York or to his new home in Saddle River, New Jersey (purchased for $950,000 in 1982) in order to give the former President classified briefings on current National Security issues. This exercise was much more than a courtesy. So up to date was Nixon's knowledge, particularly in relation to Chinese and Soviet affairs, that Clark readily admitted that he would begin the meetings as the briefer, yet end up as the briefee.[61] The talks were supplemented by calls to and from the White House five or six times a month. Sometimes Clark would start the conversation with Nixon and then pass the phone to Reagan. The President was highly appreciative of his predecessor's wisdom and used it to the full, even to the extent of authorising his National Security Adviser to show Nixon the super-secret handwritten correspondence with General Secretary Andropov of the Soviet Union. However, it was considered essential to keep the relationship between the Presidents both confidential and deniable. Clark particularly regretted this veil of concealment and wanted to make some public acknowledgement of the contribution made by 'The Sage of Saddle River', as NSC insiders dubbed him. The National Security Adviser twice recommended in 1983 that Nixon should be sent on special official missions for the Administration—one to Peking and one to Western Europe—but on both occasions the trips were vetoed by Haig's successor as Secretary of State, George Schultz. It was a pointed reminder that some ex-Presidents were more equal than others.

Clark's successor as National Security Adviser, Robert 'Bud' McFarlane, had a rapport with Nixon that was personal as well as professional. 'I often called him to talk about my frustrations,' recalled McFarlane, 'which could center on my relationships in the White House or most usually my difficulties in overcoming President Reagan's inability to understand foreign policy. Nixon was extraordinarily considerate and helpful. He would say, "Put it to him this way", or "Put it to him that way", and when I tried his suggested approach it often worked…Nixon was consistently a strong source of advice to me and to the President, particularly on Soviet affairs. He was way ahead of anyone else.'

Nixon's relationship with McFarlane had a touching footnote to it. Fourteen months after resigning as National Security Adviser, McFarlane attempted to take his own life, for reasons connected with the Iran–Contra arms sales controversy. The morning after he was coming round from his drug overdose in February 1987, his first visitor at Bethesda Naval Hospital was the 37th President of the United States. 'Nixon had flown down from New Jersey specially to see me and he was just unbelievably sympathetic', recalled McFarlane. 'He urged me to remember that Churchill and de Gaulle had suffered their 'black dogs' and said that even though I would be portrayed by the media as a weak figure, I could overcome the setback of my suicide attempt. We talked about prayer and Bible reading. I said I was doing a lot of that. He said, "That's good. You need an anchor. Your strong faith will take you through this." He asked a lot of questions which set me thinking about what I was going to do when I got out of hospital. I recall the warmth in his voice when he said, "From now on, don't look back. Get busy, go earn yourself some money. You've done the right things in the past, now look to your future. You can do it." Coming from him, I can't tell you what a tonic that encouragement was.'[62]

Good though his relationships with McFarlane and Clark were, Nixon did not rely exclusively on oral messages to the National Security Advisers for getting his recommendations to the President. There were many occasions when he wrote directly to Reagan. Over two hundred pages of these 'Eyes Only' letters and memoranda survive in his files. Some extracts from them are worth quoting as illustrations of the advice Nixon was offering.

On early White House personnel difficulties involving Richard V. Allen, National Security Adviser, and David Stockman, the Director of OMB:

Putting it bluntly the problem that all conservative administrators face is that those who are loyal are not bright and those who are bright are not loyal. The Stockman–Allen incidents illustrate this point. Allen is loyal but unfortunately not bright enough. Stockman is bright, but as anyone who reads the entire *Atlantic Monthly* interview article as I have would conclude, he is simply not loyal to the Reagan economic policy.[63]

On whether Reagan should seek a second term:

You *should* run and you will win in 1984. Bush has been a fine companion and a good soldier—but only you can hold the party together and give the Reagan revolution a chance to be permanent rather than temporary.

Whatever your decision I strongly urge that you strengthen your team for a battle that will be more difficult and more important than 1980. I say more important because if we lose in '84 the cause of intelligent progressive conservatism will suffer a mortal blow.[64]

On shaking up the White House staff:

I do not know your people well—except for 3 or 4, but from all reports they are honest, competent, and personally loyal to you. However campaigning is just *not* their bag. You need at least two or three nut cutters who will take on the opposition so that you can take the high road.

I know that because of your innate decency and loyalty to your friends that you are repelled at the thought of dropping people who are loyal to you but who are not effective on the stump or on TV. But I urge you to bite the bullet and do what is necessary to field a tough, intelligent, hard-hitting team for the 1984 campaign…Shaking up a team at mid term is *not* a sign of weakness. Done the right way, as I'm sure you would, it increases your stature at home and abroad as a strong leader who will not tolerate ineffectiveness—let alone disloyalty or dishonesty. I speak from experience. Some charge me with being too tough on subordinates. In retrospect had I been tougher I might have avoided some of the problems which plagued me at the last.[65]

On the mounting pressures for a summit meeting with President Andropov of the Soviet Union:

> I strongly feel that you should avoid a quickie, get-acquainted meeting. Some well-intentioned advisors will urge you to agree to such a meeting because it will pull the teeth of the peace at any price groups and be reassuring to some of our jittery allies abroad. I will agree that this would be true—but only temporarily. Unless something substantive comes out, the effect of an atmospheric meeting wears off very quickly...I could not disagree more with those who say you should rush into a summit now because you need it politically in view of unfavourable polls. The polls will improve as the economy improves. And even assuming that does not happen, a non-substantive summit, as the Johnson experience demonstrated, would give you a big *temporary* lift and an even bigger *permanent* letdown.* [66]

On Reagan's first televised debate with his Democratic opponent Senator Mondale—widely reported as having swung the electorate in Mondale's favour:

> Even though you felt that you were not in top form for the first debate your performance on substance could not be faulted. In fact right after it ended Pat turned to me and said 'Mondale lost'. Only because he did better than expected and you did not knock him out of the ring did the media seize on the opportunity to make it appear as if he had won. The polls at the conclusion of the debate showed it very close. Only after a week of the media hammering home their prejudices on TV and in print did the perception shift decisively in Mondale's favour. This however is now an advantage to you. You go into the debate Sunday as an underdog...
>
> While the polls seem to be getting somewhat closer it is not because of the first debate. Its effect was minimal and temporary. What we are seeing is the predictable pattern of registered Democrats returning to their party as the election draws closer. But as your almost unanimous support among Republicans, overwhelming support among Independents and young voters, and a solid base

---

* The Reagan–Andropov summit did not take place.

among conservative Democrats who left their party permanently as you did thirty years ago can mean only one thing: you will win an overwhelming victory in the popular vote on Election Day and a decisive victory in the electoral vote approaching the one you achieved in 1980.[67]

Nixon was right in this prediction, not least because he knew something about bouncing back from the status of underdog. He was achieving just such a transformation for himself. While engaging in his extensive communications with the Reagan White House, he had also been burnishing his public image. He wrote two more books during Reagan's first term, *Real Peace*, a sequel to his best seller *The Real War* (1983) and *Leaders* (1982), which was his version of Churchill's *Great Contemporaries*, a series of profiles of world statesmen whom he had encountered in his career. The author's personal philosophy of leadership was carefully woven into every one of these pen-portraits. There was more than a touch of autobiographical feeling when he wrote that a leader must be 'willing to pay the price...the ruthless invasion of privacy, the grueling schedule, the sting of unfair and often vicious criticism the cruel caricatures'. Poignantly, Nixon quoted de Gaulle's opinion that 'a leader must choose between prominence and happiness because greatness and a vague sense of melancholy are indivisible'. In another passage, Nixon seemed to be describing his own withdrawal symptoms when he wrote of the 'aching', 'yearning' and 'almost physical pain' of the leader fallen from power who believes that his own judgment is best, even though fallible, 'and who chafes at seeing lesser men mishandle the reins'.

Nixon was an enormous success as an author. His books were all best sellers, and he used them as his calling card in the international arena. Over 3,000 copies of *The Real War* and 2,500 copies of *Leaders* were sent as personal gifts to opinion formers in every part of the world. In Britain alone, more than 750 signed copies of these volumes arrived on the desks of Ministers, Members of Parliament, journalists and academics. In other countries the mailing list stretched from Kings and Presidents to obscure writers whose books or articles Nixon had somehow noticed. This literary generosity, often accompanied by a flattering inscription ('To X, a leader of the future, with admiration from Richard M. Nixon') did no harm to the author's reputation. It was not only foreigners whose views were swayed in this way. Many American opinion-formers revised their judgement of the 37th President, among them *Time* magazine's influential White House correspondent Hugh Sidey, who after reading *The Real War* and *Real Peace* acclaimed

Nixon as a 'strategic genius', having written him off completely in 1974 for 'charting himself a course straight into the sloughs of history'.[68]

Such revisionism delighted the 'Sage of Saddle River', who stepped up both his foreign travels and his domestic speeches in a surge of energy that was linked to the rising tide of appreciation. There were times when he seemed to be almost in perpetual motion between 1981 and 1985. After attending President Sadat's funeral in Cairo in October 1981 as the senior figure in the US delegation consisting of Carter, Ford and Kissinger, Nixon set off on a Middle East tour of his own. He went to Saudi Arabia, Jordan, Tunisia, and Morocco and was royally received by the heads of state in all their national capitals. On his return he lobbied actively for the $8.5 billion sale of AWAC aircraft to Saudi Arabia in close consultation with the Saudi Ambassador Prince Bandar bin Sultan and was thought by the Saudis to have been responsible for shifting several key congressional votes to their side of the argument.

During the early 1980s Nixon made two more trips to China, two to the Far East and four visits to Europe, including one tour of Eastern Europe. Although travelling as a private citizen, his schedule usually included meetings with government leaders in every country. For example, during his visit to Britain in 1982 he had an hour long one-on-one meeting with Prime Minister Margaret Thatcher at 10 Downing Street. He also met five senior members of the Cabinet, three national newspaper editors, and addressed some fifty MPs and academics at a private meeting of the Conservative Philosophy Group. Such contacts provided him with fuel for his expanding journalistic output. He wrote columns and articles for the *New York Times*, the London *Sunday Times*, the *Wall Street Journal*, *Time*, and *Newsweek*. He gave briefings on foreign policy to think tanks, to academic seminars, and to the editorial boards of the national TV networks and newspapers. He was interviewed on television by star reporters and anchor men such as Peter Jennings, Tom Brokaw, Larry King, John Chancellor and Diane Sawyer. Most of these appearances were impressive and successful, but the Sawyer interview on CBS was in a different category, resulting in a permanent breach in her relations with Nixon. She needled him particularly harshly on Watergate, possibly because of a feeling on her part that she had to demonstrate her journalistic independence from her former boss. Nixon coped more than adequately with her tough questioning, but was inwardly hurt by it and felt he had been betrayed by an old friend.

Such reactions were rare. Nixon had a new life and plenty of new friends. However, there was still a consciousness on his part that 'Running for Ex-President' was a marathon that was not yet completed. Watergate was dead as an issue, but it could not be buried as an historical disgrace. That was why some prominent people still refused to meet Nixon; why Reagan could not publicly acknowledge his contribution to the Administration's foreign policy; and why the Republican National Committee did not invite him to, or even mention him, at the GOP's 1984 National Convention.

These gaps in Nixon's acceptability as a public figure were, however, far outweighed by the gains he had made. In the ten years since his resignation he had transformed his status from pariah to prophet; from indigent exile to influential ex-President. To his delight, even the *New York Times* acknowledged this transformation in a graceful tribute by John Herbers, published on the tenth anniversary of the resignation:

> A decade later he has emerged at 71 years of age as an elder statesman, commentator on foreign and domestic affairs, adviser to world leaders, a multi-millionaire and a successful author and lecturer honoured by audiences at home and abroad.[69]

Achieving such a recovery was the toughest personal endurance test of Nixon's career. It had required heroic qualities of moral courage, mental resilience, hard work and strong character. The private, spiritual dimension of his life—prayer, contemplation and a belief in redemption—had also played a crucially important part in making the comeback possible. Yet he himself was not yet satisfied. It was not in his nature to rest upon his laurels. He had, in the words he often used, 'a few more rounds to go'.

V. ELDER STATESMAN 1985–90

In his seventies, Nixon's life story began rounding off towards a happy ending. His tempestuous journey entered calmer waters, although there were no signs that he was slowing down. His working day began when he arrived in his New York office at 7.30 a.m. He would spend the first hour and a half clearing his correspondence, much of it with handwritten responses. Compassionate letters to the sick or the bereaved; quickie notes of appreciation to journalists whose articles he had enjoyed, or to young Congressmen whose speeches he had seen on television; and personal billets-doux to old friends and relatives were the staple diet of this large daily output. Then, at around 9 a.m. he would have a substantive meeting with his chief of staff John Taylor, whose creative intelligence had first impressed him when Taylor was working as a junior researcher on *Leaders*. 'Our house liberal', was Nixon's original description of his assistant, but gradually the chemistry between the thirty-one-year-old former Californian journalist and the seventy-one-year-old ex-President began to work so well that it became the best relationship he had enjoyed with an aide since his White House days with Henry Kissinger.

Nixon used Taylor as a daily intellectual sparring partner on whom to test his ideas about the morning's news stories, the latest political situation, or the overnight developments in foreign policy. From these dialectical discourses Nixon would move on to consider the possibilities for new articles or speaking engagements, debating each and every option with peculiar intensity.

'He never undertook any activity lightly,' recalled Taylor, 'because he doesn't know how to waste time. It pains him. He feels guilty. So a lot of our morning meetings were taken up with the question of whether such and such a project would be worth the effort. Above all, would it make an impact on the course of events? Every move he made had to be seen through that prism.'[70]

Nixon's efforts to exercise an influence on events remained prodigious. His private correspondence with the Reagan and Bush administrations continued. One of his habits was to write to senior new appointees, setting out his suggestions on how they should fulfil their new responsibilities. Among the most interesting of these unsolicited offerings was a ten-page letter on 28 January 1985 to Don Regan, the President's newly-appointed Chief of Staff, on how to run the White House (Nixon's basic message was: change the guard; tear up the pea patch; insist on staff loyalty; don't upstage the First Lady), and a seven-page letter to the new Defense Secretary Frank Carlucci on 6 November 1987, urging him to avoid 'the political firestorm developing on the right' by standing firm on the Strategic Defense Initiative.[71]

In his public statements on these and other issues, Nixon gave an impression of ubiquity by adroit use of selectivity. He seemed to be speaking out everywhere—on television; in the op-ed pages of the *New York Times* and the *Wall Street Journal*; in long interviews with magazines; and in speeches to prestigious audiences. In fact, this appearance of hyperactivity was an illusion. The record shows that he gave no more than three or four interviews a year and wrote a similarly restricted number of articles. However, since his pronouncements always made news and aroused much subsequent comment among columnists and chat-show performers, Nixon increasingly became respected as a powerful opinion former. He strengthened this reputation further with the publication of his sixth book, *No More Vietnams*, in 1985. Its theme was that the Vietnam conflict had been a just war in which the ultimate US victory had been needlessly thrown away by a defeatist Congress, aided and abetted by the liberal media. Predictably enough, the reviews in the *New York Times* and the *Washington Post* tore the book to shreds, while it was praised to the skies by conservative publications such as the *Chicago Tribune* and the *National Review*. All the attention put *No More Vietnams* on best-seller lists for eighteen weeks.

If one had to pinpoint the moment when Nixon was finally transformed in the public perception from controversial pundit to elder statesman, it would be April 1986, when *Newsweek* ran a flattering cover story on him under the banner headline 'HE'S BACK: THE REHABILITATION OF RICHARD NIXON'. Ironically, it was Katharine Graham, Chairman of the Washington Post Company (*Newsweek's* parent corporation) who played the role of the fairy godmother in bringing about this magical imprimatur. Graham had heard Nixon addressing the annual convention of the American Newspaper Publishers' Association the previous month, and was so impressed that she instructed her editors to write an upbeat story on his re-emergence. The piece would have appeared merely as an inside page feature, had it not been for Nixon's cunning as a journalistic negotiator. His opening gambit was to refuse all co-operation with *Newsweek*. Then, operating through one of his new young political friends, the Washington lobbyist Roger Stone, he let himself be persuaded to grant an interview and a photo-opportunity provided the article was upgraded into a cover story. After much huffing and puffing, *Newsweek* made the deal. The result was one of the most glowingly favourable profiles of Nixon's entire career.

If the Washington Post Company was prepared to make a 180° turn in its attitude to the 37th President, there was not much point in any other former adversaries continuing to fight the wars of Watergate. The walls of journalism's Jericho had fallen. Nixon had achieved media rehabilitation on his own terms, without having made any substantive concessions in the way of apologies or admissions. Even among the worst of his former enemies, he had now made an astonishing comeback.

Being Nixon, there was no question of resting upon his laurels. The late 1980s found him busier than ever. He made another trip around the world in 1986 and a few months later set off on a visit to Moscow to meet the new Soviet President, Mikhail Gorbachev. These private fact-finding missions resulted in several 'Eyes Only' memoranda to the White House, of which the most notable was a twenty-six-page briefing paper full of suggestions on how the President should negotiate with the Russian leader. Yet, for all his elaborate civility towards Reagan, Nixon was privately somewhat disenchanted with his successor's lack of grip on foreign policy. After a meeting to discuss Soviet arms control agreement possibilities in the White House on 28 April 1987, Nixon recorded some negative impressions in a private memcon.

Reagan, candidly, did not seem to be on top of the issues—certainly in no way as knowledgeable as Gorbachev...he was somewhat fuzzy...he looks far older, more tired, and less vigorous in person than in public. There is no way he can ever be allowed to participate in a private meeting with Gorbachev.[72]

With the election looming, Nixon paid less attention to Reagan, taking on a new role as a political fund raiser, forecaster, and sage. He made himself selectively available to special GOP events, and was such a major draw at them that he became legendary for some of his achievements, such as the evening when he helped to wipe out the whole of the New York State Republican Party's debts of over $800,000 with one speech.[73] As a commentator he wrote articles on the primaries for the London *Sunday Times*, and appeared on several domestic TV programmes. He could be brutal in his judgements.

'The best politics is poetry rather than prose', he said. 'Jesse Jackson's a poet. Cuomo is a poet. But Dukakis is a word processor.'[74]

In 1988, Nixon's own office word processors were working overtime as he wrote and published his seventh book, *1999—Victory Without War*. It was his attempt to influence the foreign policy debate in a presidential election year and it succeeded. He was critical of the 'superdoves' of the Carter years and the 'super-hawks' of the Reagan administration. Nixon the centrist wanted the United States to take up a new stance combining deterrence, negotiation, and competition. He made a prescient forecast about the coming clash between Eastern European nationalism and Soviet imperialism. 'These forces have produced tremors in the past but unprecedented pressures will build up along the fault line in the 1990s. Without genuine reform, a political earthquake in Eastern Europe is inevitable in the years before 1999.'[75]

The quotability and visibility of Nixon made him something of a cult figure among watchers of the political game, but he had deeper agendas of his own. At least a quarter of his day was devoted to serious reading. Each week he devoured a menu of heavy periodicals such as the *American Spectator*; the *New Republic*; *The Economist*; the *National Review*; the *Economist Foreign Report*; and the *Phillips American Political Report*, but books were his true passion. Paul Johnson's *Modern Times*; Will and Ariel Durant's *History of the World*; Judy Shelton's *The Coming Soviet Crash*; Robert Thompson's *Make for the Hills*; Zbigniew Brzezhinski's *The Grand Failure*; and Russell Braley's *Bad News: The Influence of the New York Times on American Foreign Policy* were among the new books he particularly enjoyed, but any attempt to compile such a list reveals only the tip of Nixon's reading iceberg. He was forever trying out new authors; dipping into fashionable best sellers and above all returning to his old favourites. In the winter of 1989/90 he read all eight volumes of Martin Gilbert's magisterial biography of Winston Churchill.

'Perhaps he had a fear that if he stopped working, his mind would atrophy,' observed John Taylor, 'but the more time I spent with him the more I realized that here was an extraordinarily powerful and unorthodox intellect which simply had to exercise itself.'[76]

This exercise took many forms. Every morning he received one or two visitors in his office for one-on-one dialogues about foreign policy. The schedule of these appointments read like an international *Who's Who*—senior administration figures past and present; experts from think-tanks; ambassadors ; foreign correspondents and overseas politicians. The most favoured of these visitors might be invited to one of his Saddle River dinner parties, which he elevated into something of an art form. The vintage wine would be chosen from a date which coincided with the principal guest's year of birth or some important milestone in his or her career. The menu would be likely to include regional or international dishes linked to other guests' home states or countries.

Gastronomically, perfection ruled. But the excellence of the cuisine was usually surpassed by the fascination of the guest list and the vitality of the conversation. Nixon took infinite pains as a host to bring interesting people together around his table. A typical evening would star a guest of honour such as Henry Kissinger; Bill Simon; Helmut Schmidt; Lee Kwan-Yew; Zbigniew Brzezhinski; or Senator Pat Moynihan. The co-stars might include one or two business tycoons like Rupert Murdoch; Malcolm Forbes; Sir James Goldsmith; Dwayne Andreas or Don Kendall. From the media Nixon had a penchant for inviting up-and-coming reporters such as Karen Elliott House of the *Wall Street Journal*; Howell Raines of the *New York Times*; or David Hoffman of the *Washington Post*. There might be a visiting British parliamentarian (Julian Amery, Christopher Soames); a Sovietologist (Dimitri Simes); a Middle East expert (Ardeshir Zahedi); or a bestselling author (Paul Johnson, Jean Smith). The mixture would be topped up by old friends or bright young advisers.

Nixon took great care at his dinner parties not to dominate the conversation himself, but he was a powerful conductor of the orchestra, changing the topics, calling the speakers and taking care to bring even the shyest guest into the spotlight. He claimed that his mentor for this conversational orchestration was the nineteenth-century British Prime Minister A.J. Balfour, of whom Churchill wrote in *Great Contemporaries* 'All who met him came away feeling that they had been at their very best.'[77] That was just the way it seemed in the warm glow of hospitality at Saddle River. The party usually ended over vintage port and cognac with the former President summarising the evening's discourses in an epilogue during which every guest's contribution was mentioned, all the threads were pulled together and eventually tied up in a neat and often brilliant bow of Nixonian strategic judgement.

Nixon as the political sage, the literary intellectual, the crowd-pulling fund raiser, the presidential adviser, and the genial host were roles in which he blossomed during his elder statesman years. Two other more private aspects of his nature that grew in this period were Nixon the family patriarch and Nixon the believer in spiritual values.

Ever since the resignation, the Nixon marriage had found strength in adversity. Fragile in appearance, Pat had a core of granite in her soul. In many ways she was the tougher of the two Nixons. She had pulled him through The Fund crisis of 1952, and dragged him back from the brink of death in October 1974. Her powerful solicitude during his convalescence, perhaps the most important single factor in his recovery, was reciprocated by her husband when she suffered a minor stroke in July 1976, allegedly as a consequence of reading *The Final Days*, a lurid and often unreliable account of the last weeks of the Presidency by the *Washington Post* journalists Woodward and Bernstein.

The stroke left Pat temporarily paralysed on one side, but after months of determined exercise therapy she recovered virtually 100 per cent of her mental and physical faculties. However, the scary intimations of mortality which they had both passed through bonded husband and wife together in a closer relationship than had existed since the early years of their marriage. They spent more time together; communicated better; and became more closely tuned to one another's emotions. 'Without question, the person whose company and opinion President Nixon valued most while I was his chief of staff was Mrs. Nixon's', observed John Taylor. 'His latter years have been characterized by the extreme attentiveness of his feelings towards her.'[78]

It was not always thus, but every member of the inner Nixon circle has noticed this mellowing of the marriage which has been further enhanced by their mutual enjoyment of their four grandchildren: Jennie Nixon Eisenhower, born 1978; Alexander Richard Nixon Eisenhower, born 1980; Melanie Nixon Eisenhower, born 1984; and Christopher Nixon Cox, born 1979.

Nixon has greatly enjoyed being a grandfather. Sensitive to each of his grandchildren's individual needs and interests, he often calls them, spends time with them, and takes them on expeditions. During the last three or four Christmases he has arranged a ritual of grandfatherly treats in New York, including trips to the circus, the Radio City pageant, and the Statue of Liberty. He gets totally absorbed in the relationships and is self-evidently comfortable in them. He likes to quote a remark made to him by the former Bulgarian President Todor Zhivkov in 1982: 'You are a very rich man. Having grandchildren is the greatest wealth a man can have.' Nixon takes the role seriously, recalling his own debt to his grandmother Almira Milhous: 'She was an inspiration to me and I hope that years later my four grandchildren will conclude that Mrs. Nixon, who is an excellent grandmother, and I have been an inspiration to them.'[79]

1990 was an *annus mirabilis* for Nixon. He celebrated his Golden Wedding; published a new best seller; was feted by politicians of all parties on a return visit to Congress; and presided over the dedication ceremony of his Presidential Library and Birthplace at Yorba Linda, California.

Much of this new-found happiness was reflected in his new book (the seventh he had published in twelve years) *In the Arena*. This was an uncharacteristically personalised volume of memoirs and advice, broken up into forty chapters with headings such as 'Family'; 'Religion'; 'Conversation'; 'Tension'; 'Privacy'; 'Pat'; 'Philosophy'; 'Decisions'; 'War'; and 'Peace'. The final section, entitled 'Twilight', is Nixon reflecting on old age. He quotes Sophocles: 'One must wait until the evening to see how splendid the day has been', and continues 'I can look back and say that the day has indeed been splendid. In view of the ordeals I have endured, this may strike some as being an incredible conclusion. I believe, however, that the richness of life is not measured by its length but by its breadth, its height, and its depth... I have been on the highest mountains and in the deepest valleys, but I have never lost sight of my destination—a world in which peace and freedom can live together. I have won some great victories and suffered some devastating defeats. But win or lose, I feel fortunate to have come to that time in life when I can finally enjoy what my Quaker grandmother would have called "peace at the center".'[80]

Grandmother Almira Milhous, who had urged the very young Richard to seek 'peace at the center' also inspired his childhood with the vision of a great man leaving behind him 'footprints in the sands of time'. She and all his family forbears would surely have been amazed by the footprint their descendant imprinted on the sands of Yorba Linda on 19 July 1990. It was the most important event in Nixon's life since he left the White House—the dedication of his $25 million Presidential Library and Birthplace.

The temperature that morning in southern California was in the mid-nineties, but the crowds that had been gathering since dawn seemed almost oblivious to the heat, perhaps because so many of them were proud to be participating in an historic spectacle. In the front rows of the audience were most of the major figures from the Nixon era, headed by four secretaries of state: William Rogers; Henry Kissinger; Alexander Haig; and George Schultz. Alongside were ten cabinet secretaries and forty-six White House aides, including Haldeman, Ziegler, Finch, Safire, Buchanan, Chapin, Stans and Klein. Over a thousand reporters were in attendance, headed by big names from the TV networks such as NBC's Tom Brokaw and ABC's Barbara Walters. Hollywood was represented by Gene Autry and Bob Hope. Religion by the Reverends Billy Graham and Norman Vincent Peale. Big business by Robert Abplanalp, Walter Annenberg, Max Fisher and Ross Perot. Diplomacy by a galaxy of international representatives led by the Ambassador of the People's Republic of China.

But it was not only the important and the famous who had made the journey to Yorba Linda that morning. Most of the 50,000-strong crowd were unknown young people from the surrounding area who had queued for admission, but there were also ordinary men and women from every chapter of the Nixon story who had come to pay their homage. Struggling in on crutches was seventy-eight-year-old Clint Harris, Dick Nixon's team-mate from the Whittier College freshman football squad of 1930. He and other classmates were outranked in age by ninety-four-year-old McIntyre Faries from Pasadena, a key figure on the 1946 selection committee which had picked the unknown Lieutenant Commander Nixon to be the Republican candidate in his first congressional race against Jerry Voorhis. Veteran voters and campaign workers from that election and all its successors were well represented. So were retired congressional colleagues, ex-staffers and former Secret Service agents from the vice-presidential years. One of the most moving groups was the gathering of young, middle-aged and elderly ladies who represented an unbroken, fifty-three-year line of Nixon secretaries. They included Evlyn Dorn, who had typed for the junior partner in the Whittier law office of Wingert, Bewley and Nixon in 1937; Dorothy Cox, who was Congressman-elect Nixon's first Washington secretary in 1946; Betty Lewis, who took down the shorthand notes of his cross-examination of Alger Hiss in 1948; Marje Acker, who was with him in his earliest days as a Senator in 1951; Loie Gaunt, another Senate office veteran still on his payroll, who has dedicated forty years of her life to 'The Boss'; Kathy O'Connor, his personal secretary since 1980, and her assistant, twenty-four-year-old Carmen Ballard. It says something about Nixon that he has remained a hero to this loyal sisterhood, especially to their doyenne, Rose Mary Woods, who was on cloud nine that morning. Resplendent in a green silk dress, she was meeting and greeting like a Hollywood hostess, even giving her old adversary Bob Haldeman a warm embrace after he whispered: 'I'm so sorry Rose, and for so many things.'[81] It was one of many hatchet-burying reunions, making it a day of reconciliation as well as dedication.

While everyone was getting settled, three brass bands, two drill teams and an *equipe* of Spanish dancers provided oompah and hooplah. Suddenly, 200 white doves of peace were spectacularly released with a fanfare of trumpets and then, to a football-stadium roar, there were the entrances of Presidents Bush, Reagan, Ford and Nixon with their wives. Standing in line on the platform they looked like Mount Rushmore come alive. It was the first time that four Presidents and their First Ladies had ever been assembled together in one group.

The feast of oratory that followed was magnificent, even if it did at times seem reminiscent of Dr. Samuel Johnson's dictum: 'Sir, in lapidary inscriptions a man is not upon oath.' The three Presidents who opened the proceedings had taken a great deal of advice from Nixon in private since his resignation, but this was the first occasion they had praised him in public. They seemed determined to make up for the sixteen-year gap. Gerald Ford produced some happy memories of working in Congress with Nixon in the 1940s, praised him for his courage, and for helping to bring about the collapse of Communism. Reagan began with one of his cornier jokes ('As Henry VIIIth said to each of his six wives, I won't be keeping you long'), and then swung into an encomium of Nixon the international states-man, calling him 'a man who understands the world. He understands politics, power, and the forces of history. Whether with Mao or Brezhnev, de Gaulle or Gandhi, President Nixon was the first among equals. A man whose foreign policy was universally acknowledged as brilliant. I do not think it is an exaggeration to say the world is a better place, a safer place, because of Richard Nixon.'

President Bush gave the longest and most reflective speech of the morning. He was graciousness personified, his gentlemanly character breathing through the sentences that had been honed for him by his speech writer Curt Smith, a long standing admirer of the 37th President. Noting that Nixon had come to power 'in times as tumultuous as any since Lincoln's'; that he had an 'intellectual's complex-ity'; and that he could be 'uncommonly sensitive to the feelings of ordinary people', Bush declared: 'He was the quintessence of Middle America who touched deep chords of response in millions of our fellow citizens. As President, uphold-ing what he termed the "silent majority" from Dallas to Davenport and Syracuse to Silver City, he loved America's good quiet decent people, and spoke for them.' After running through the highlights of the Nixon years, putting unusual empha-sis on the domestic achievements such as the ending of the draft, revenue sharing, and the setting up of the Environmental Protection Agency, Bush swung into his peroration: 'Richard Nixon helped change the course not only of America but of the entire world', he declared. 'Today, as the movement towards democracy sweeps our globe, you can take great personal pride that history will say of you: "Here was a true architect of peace."'

Nixon seemed somewhat overcome by the tumultuous ovation that he received, but speaking without notes he quickly produced some telling applause lines. 'We have been to Versailles, we've been to Westminster, to the Kremlin, to the Great Wall of China...but nothing, nothing we have ever seen matches this moment to be welcomed home again so warmly on this day by our friends.'

The theme of his twelve-minute address was that the individual should always be searching for new goals to achieve, new mountains to climb, and should never fear defeat. Delivering this familiar philosophical message with a particular direction to the young people in the audience, his backward glances at his own career were laconic. He referred to his past electoral dramas with the one liner, 'Won some, lost some, all interesting'. He said he had 'many memories, some of them good, some of them not so good', but that it had always been worthwhile to strive in the arena. 'We can't all be Governor—found that out here', he deadpanned to laughter. Recalling the days, seventy years before, when he used to lie awake in his Yorba Linda bedroom listening to the train whistle and dreaming of visiting far away places, Nixon gestured towards the small clapboard house his father had built, now standing in the garden of the Presidential Library. 'Let me tell you, it's a long way from Yorba Linda to the White House', he declared to cheers and even tears among his listeners. 'I believe in the American dream because I have seen it come true in my own life. I want your dreams to come true as well. You will suffer disappointments in life and sometimes you will be very discouraged. But the greatest sadness is to travel through life without knowing either victory or defeat.'[82]

Then, with a wave of his hand, the release of 50,000 balloons by his favourite advance man Ron Walker, and more tumultuous cheering from the crowd, well over half of whom had been too young ever to vote for him, Richard Nixon led the posse of Presidents off to a celebration lunch inside the Library. It had been a memorable morning.

Offstage, there were inevitably some discordant voices raised in criticism of this quasi-coronation ceremony. 'He ought to be living his life in private and in disgrace', wrote *Washington Post* columnist David Broder.[83] 'I hope the Library is more honest than his Presidency. All we get from him is the agonizing of a whiner who isn't man enough to say he was wrong', commented the liberal historian Arthur Schlesinger Jr.[84] 'He's shameless...and the worst thing is, he's busy rewriting the past', said Watergate author Stanley Kutler of the University of Wisconsin.[85] 'The cover-up continues', declared Nixon's leading American biographer, Stephen Ambrose.[86]

Such sniper fire did not diminish the continuing festivities. In the evening of the dedication day, another 1,500 Nixon well-wishers assembled for a banquet in his honour at the Century Plaza Hotel in Los Angeles. A series of celebrity speakers proclaimed their adoration for the guests of honour ('I not only admire him but I love him', Norman Vincent Peale; 'I can sum up all our feelings in one phrase. I hope President Nixon and Pat know how much they are loved', William E. Simon).

Nixon responded to this surging emotion like an old pro, with an address in which no helper went unthanked and few applause lines went unused. However, it was Pat who really stole the show. Unsteady on her feet from the lingering after-effects of her stroke and orthopaedic problems, she was sufficiently zestful at the microphone to deliver a charming and enthusiastic speech of appreciation. Pat had told many friends over the years that she never expected to live long enough to see her husband's reputation restored. Her joy at witnessing his life coming full circle shone on her face like a golden sunset. 'I'm tired but I'm happy tired', she said to the evening's organiser Loie Gaunt at the end of the long day.[87] Nixon was in a similar mood, with his feet up in his suite around midnight. 'I guess this is one of the happiest days of my life', he purred to Ron Walker.[88]

After such an event it would be tempting to close the chapter with the line, 'And he lived happily ever after.' But with Nixon nothing is ever that simple. The next day he was back to work, giving interviews, tiring out his secretaries with a cascade of thank-you letters, and making notes in preparation for his ninth book—on the Soviet Union. His restless energy is reminiscent of Tennyson's *Ulysses*, who thought in his old age:

> How dull it is to pause, to make an end,
> To rest unburnish'd, not to shine in use!
> As tho' to breathe were life. Life piled on life
> Were all too little, and of one to me
> Little remains.

Ulysses's remedy for this situation was to set off again for one last battle. Nixon, who had delivered his line at the banquet about life consisting of ninety-nine rounds and 'having a few more rounds to go' himself, shares a similar philosophy. Having found contentment and regained his honour, he is still ready to unsheathe his sword for one more fight—for the judgement of history.

THE VIEW FROM EAGLES NEST

The last time I saw Richard Nixon was at the end of a momentous week in which he had exerted more political influence than at any time since the zenith of his Presidency.

We met at his new home near Park Ridge, New Jersey, on 14 March 1992. He had spent much of the previous few days on centre stage in Washington and on prime-time television across the world. Later in our two-hour conversation we were to discuss the causes and consequences of his return to global prominence, but on this particular Saturday morning, Nixon was in an off-duty mood. He was laid-back, happy to enjoy several cups of coffee with Pat, and even to indulge in some rare moments of inconsequential small talk.

Our meeting did, however, begin with a revealing little pantomime of social embarrassment. Uncharacteristically, Nixon came downstairs some twenty minutes late for the appointment. This could not have mattered less, for nobody was in a hurry and Pat was the most welcoming of hostesses in his absence. However, Nixon made heavy weather out of his unpunctuality. His watch must have stopped (he held it to his ear); or perhaps it was slow? (visual watch inspection); or perhaps I had arrived early (enquiries about traffic conditions in New Jersey). Well then, the explanation must be that his secretary had told him the wrong time (compensatory praise for secretary's normal efficiency); but he was quite sure that

I had been expected at 10.30 not 10 a.m. (further puzzled inspection of watch). Eventually, Pat cut through these charades with a merry laugh. 'Oh come on Dick, you were just talking on the telephone',[1] at which point Nixon laughed too, and relaxed.

We began by talking about the house, which the Nixons had bought a year or so earlier after selling their fifteen-room home in Saddle River, New Jersey, to a Japanese businessman for $2.4 million. The new Nixon residence is a more modest establishment—a three-bedroom condominium unit at the end of a ter-raced row of mock Tudor townhouses. It is the smallest living space Richard and Pat Nixon have occupied for more than forty years, but it is bright, warm, com-fortable and well suited to the needs of a couple entering their eighties. Nixon said with a grin that the developers gave him a good deal (presumably a sizeable dis-count on the $649,000 asking price) and pointed out the additional facilities attached to his unit, such as the extra garden space, the bright yellow sun parlour, and the casement bow windows. For a few minutes the Nixons managed to sound like any house-proud suburban couple, but the tour entered a new dimension when we took the elevator to the third floor and reached what the former President calls 'Eagles Nest'.

Nixon says he loves Eagles Nest and it is easy to understand why. It is the sort of roof-top eyrie that can be found in the eaves of an Oxford College, crammed from floor to rafters with books and exuding a donnish ambience of scholarship. In one corner of this irregular shaped loft-library is a French writing table chosen by Nixon as his work desk because it resembles the one used by Charles de Gaulle. In another alcove stands a large globe and a glass case of memorabilia containing items such as an oriental silver jug given him by the Shah of Iran; a bust of Win-ston Churchill; and a knight in shining armour, which Pat bought as a fiftieth birthday present to him on a trip to Germany. Although Eagles Nest is very much Nixon's personal sanctuary, Pat's decorative touch is everywhere—in the warm red carpet, the Louis XIV chandelier and in the exotic armchair and sofa cover-ings which depict a colourful menagerie of giraffes, elephants, lions, and tigers. 'I was thinking of all Dick's world trips when I bought them,' she said.[2]

For all the eye-catching decor it is the books which dominate. For this is a true bibliophile's room, reflecting Nixon's lifelong thirst for serious reading. His intellectual penchant for multi-volume works of history, biography and philoso-phy features strongly. His political idols—Winston Churchill, Abraham Lincoln, Charles de Gaulle, Woodrow Wilson, Theodore Roosevelt and John Quincy Adams—have complete sections to themselves. But there are surprises too: John Galsworthy's novels; the writings of Carl Jung; a shelf of biographies of Napoleon;

Mark Twain's collected works; and a complete set of Tolstoy, not to mention the huge assembly of well thumbed and often annotated individual volumes, ranging from Clausewitz's *On War* to Paul Johnson's *Modern Times*, the latter being the contemporary history book which Nixon says he most admires.

Over coffee the conversation turns to health regimes and work routines. Pat, who is going to be eighty the following Monday, says how much she regrets not being able to go out and about with Dick more often because of her bronchial problem. Nixon, on the other hand, has the schedule of a man half his age. He rises at 5.30 a.m. every morning ('I'm more regular than any alarm clock'[3]); gets himself a spartan breakfast of grapefruit flakes and skimmed milk; then goes out for a two-mile walk at 6.30 a.m. Soon after 7 he is at his writing table for at least three hours of creative work—dictating, working on his thoughts for a new book, or drafting speeches and memoranda. He goes to his office in the nearby town of Woodcliff Lake at 10.30 a.m.; comes home for a cottage cheese and fruit lunch at 1 p.m.; naps for forty-five minutes ('My best sleep of the day'), reads in the afternoon for three or four hours, then watches the evening news with Pat. He dines lightly, respecting medical advice to eschew alcohol because of a recent heart fibrillation problem. ('When I told Bebe [Rebozo] about the doctor's veto he said, "My God, get a second opinion *at once!*"[4]) The day ends with another two or three hours of reading before switching off his light promptly at 11 p.m. Two days earlier, Tricia Nixon Cox told me that her father always kneels down and says his prayers before going to bed. When I asked Nixon about this he became pink cheeked with embarrassment, saying he did not want to discuss such personal matters.

So the talk switches to politics. Nixon is bubbling with ideas for reviving the Republicans' flagging fortunes in the election campaign, so much so that he has spent his early morning hours composing a private memorandum on the subject for George Bush. For some minutes the old pro, who had been a candidate in five presidential campaigns since 1952, sketches the game plans he thinks the White House should use for outflanking Pat Buchanan, Bill Clinton and other obstacles on the road to victory in 1992.

Nixon's conversation takes on a tone of ruthless cynicism as he discusses the Republican campaign's shortcomings. He sounds like a cross between a poker player discussing how to outwit his opponents despite a bad hand, and a sports coach urging an unsatisfactory athlete to become more competitive. Yet, despite all the veneer of exasperation, it is clear that the relationship between the 37th and 41st Presidents has at times been a strong one, notably during the Gulf War, when Nixon was the most stalwart of voices supporting Bush's leadership. The two men have been in close touch several times in the last few days, which for Nixon have been a seminal period—the week when he finally and definitively came in from the cold.

To some observers of Nixon's life story the celebrations at the Library and Birthplace Dedication ceremony, described in the last chapter, might well have seemed a suitably upbeat finale. Yet to the subject of the acclaim, the Yorba Linda festivities were not a case of *Finis coronat opus*. Nixon came to feel curiously unsatisfied by his California coronation of July 1990, later dismissing the event as 'playing before the home crowd'. Like the restless Ulysses of Tennyson's poem, he soon wanted to set off for another battlefield. This time his target was to be a group he had spent many years affecting to despise—the Washington establishment.

In Nixon's wandering years of post-Watergate rehabilitation, precious little has happened by chance. Thus the events of which he was the focal point during the week of 9–13 March 1992 were the culmination of a long-planned campaign, not a sudden lucky break. To the uninitiated, however, all that happened was that Nixon made a speech. How it came to be a speech that rang round the world is a tale from Eagles Nest worth telling.

Nixon's expertise in the field of superpower geopolitics has been tested to the full by the collapse of Communism in the 1990s. The unfolding drama inspired him to write what many consider to be the best of his nine books, *Seize the Moment*, but within weeks of completing the manuscript of this thoughtful foreign policy blueprint for America in the twenty-first century, he began to fret that he might have underestimated both the seriousness of the situation in the former Soviet Union and the paucity of the West's response to it. So, with characteristic thoroughness, Nixon re-evaluated his position, reading deeply, brainstorming with experts, and making a lengthy tour of the Commonwealth of Independent States with his favourite adviser on Russian affairs, Dimitri Simes. At the end of this period of research, Nixon decided he had something important to say. He made plans to deliver his message in a manner that would attract maximum attention, while simultaneously setting the seal on his post-Watergate quest for respect and honour as an elder statesman.

The first move in this double-barrelled strategy came from the Nixon Presidential Library which, in an unexpected leap of expansion from its base at Yorba Linda, suddenly convened a public conference at the Four Seasons Hotel in Georgetown under the title, 'America's role in the emerging world'. The second move, made in a letter to George Bush from Julie Nixon Eisenhower, was to secure the cooperation of the White House. Once it had been announced that the two keynote addresses on this theme would be delivered by Presidents Bush and Nixon, the Beltway's *corps d'élite* of security and foreign policy specialists fought for invitations. The third move was to line up an eminent cast of supporting speakers under the chairmanship of former Defense Secretary James R. Schlesinger, among them CIA Director Robert Gates; National Intelligence Council Chairman Fritz Ermath; Senators Daniel Patrick Moynihan and Warren Rudman; General Vernon Walters; US Trade Representative Carla Hills; Henry A. Kissinger; Zbigniew Brzezinski; Ambassadors Vladimir Lukin and Robert S. Strauss; plus several other top experts in their fields. Nixon had been the mastermind behind all these plans and invitations, carefully setting the stage for his personal synod of the foreign policy priesthood. His timing was also perfect in terms of presidential politics. The early primaries, in which Bush was doing badly, had been steadily degenerating into a vituperative slanging match in which international issues were noticeably neglected. The White House was thus persuaded to see the conference as an opportunity for a statesmanlike foreign policy speech from the President which would lift the election debate to a higher level. That might well have been a good strategy if the debate had been between Bush and any one of his numerous challengers. However, as things turned out, the real debate was to be between Bush and Nixon.

On the eve of the conference, extracts from a scathing private memorandum by Nixon appeared on the front page of the *New York Times*. The document had allegedly been intended for confidential circulation only to a handful of foreign policy specialists. Since Nixon has spent most of his career more leaked against than leaking, it might be charitable not to enquire too closely as to how the *New York Times* obtained this particular smoking gun. For the main thrust of the memo was the disclosure that Nixon was sharply critical of the Bush administration for its 'pathetically inadequate' response to events in the former Soviet Union. In a sentence which showed that the former President had lost none of his instinct for the political jugular he wrote, 'The hot-button issue in the 1950s was "Who lost China?" If Yeltsin goes down, the question "Who lost Russia?" will be an infinitely more devastating issue in the 1990s.'[5]

If Nixon had been intending to produce a titilating trailer for his conference, he could hardly have been more successful. The possibility of a split between President and former President on foreign policy at the same conference would have set the Democrats cheering and the Republicans reeling. So by the time Nixon strode to the microphone on the opening day, he had guaranteed himself maximum media attention, including live TV coverage of his entire speech by CNN and by several other national and international television channels.

Nixon addressed the conference for forty minutes without the support of a podium or the help of notes. Speaking in perfect rhetorical periods to pindrop silence from his audience, he warned of the dangers of giving inadequate American support to Yeltsin's Russia:

> What we have to realize is that the Cold War was not the traditional war over territory by great powers. It was a war of ideas, the ideas of Communism versus the ideas of freedom…But now, freedom is on trial, and if freedom does not work the Russian people are not going to return to Communism because it failed, but they will return, in my view, to what I would call a new despotism in which they trade freedom for security, and put their future in the hands of those who are going to make sure that they can have the necessities of life. This new despotism, which would have the overtones of imperialist Russian activities which have been traditional in Russian history, could be a far more dangerous threat to peace and freedom in the world, particularly to peace, than was the old Soviet totalitarianism.

After emphasising the dangers of American isolationism; praising Yeltsin as 'the most pro-Western leader in Russian history'; and making the point that foreign aid had been a political vote-winner during Harry Truman's Presidency, Nixon continued:

> Charity, it is said, begins at home, and I agree. But aid to Russia, just speaking of Russia specifically, is not charity. We have to realize that if Yeltsin fails the alternative is not going to be somebody better, it's going to be somebody infinitely worse. We have to realize that if Yeltsin fails, if freedom fails, the new despotism which will take its place will mean that the peace dividend is finished, we will have to rearm, and that's going to cost infinitely more than would the aid that we provide at the present time. It would also mean, if Yeltsin failed, if freedom fails in Russia, it means that a great wave of freedom that has been going on all over the world in these recent two or three years, that it will begin to ebb, and that dictatorship, rather than democracy, will be the wave of the future.

Nixon sat down to tumultuous applause from his audience, followed by ecstatic reviews from the media. There was a general consensus among the commentators and leader writers that the speech had been an important event, strengthening Yeltsin and discomforting the White House. As Peter Stothard, reporting for *The Times* of London put it: 'For those who like their politics as art the former President's attack on his inward looking successors was a rich, enduring moment. On the day that Mr. Nixon attacked the Administration's petty meanness to Boris Yeltsin, George Bush looked like Belshazzar at the feast.'[6]

Comparisons with Belshazzar aside, President Bush certainly found himself with a hard act to follow. In a lacklustre address to the conference later the same day, the best he could do was to praise Nixon, agree with his argument and promise future action along the lines requested in his predecessor's speech. Two weeks later, the White House announced the first of several new aid packages for Russia. The policy of the United States, perhaps the course of history, was being changed by the Phoenix of Watergate.

Talking to Nixon three days after his triumph, I had expected to find him savouring, if not seizing, the moment he had created. Yet almost the reverse was true. Sipping coffee in Eagles Nest, he was worrying whether his message had been strong enough. 'I'm always dissatisfied after every speech. As Lincoln used to say even after some of his best performances, "That speech didn't scour." I don't know whether mine scoured or not. I didn't deliver it as well as I would have liked. There were a couple of flubs. I missed out one of my best lines. I had intended to say: "The American people responded magnificently to the threat of war then. The question is: can we respond to the promise of peace now?"'

The recitation of the missing line set him off on a deeper train of thought. Had the effort of making the speech really been worthwhile? Time alone would tell. The editorials had been good, but by themselves they meant nothing. What mattered was the follow through. He was already following through with Speaker Tom Foley, who had promised support from the Democrats in Congress with an aid bill. Brent Scowcroft, the President's National Security Adviser, was also a strong supporter. The speech had won many friends on Capitol Hill. He knew that from participating in all the remaining sessions of the conference. But there could be a problem with Secretary of State James Baker, who was likely to be jealous of a new policy that involved criticism of his Department. Nixon thought he would have to work hard to keep the pressure up. He said he planned to dedicate most of his time to writing and speaking out on this theme, because he believed it was the best way to secure peace for the next generation. 'I know I've worried some of the nervous Nellies in the State Department, who say my plan is too expensive,' he said, 'but if Yeltsin goes down, and we see some new despot at the helm in Moscow, our rearmament program will become infinitely more expensive than the $20 billion a year Western aid programme I was advocating.'[7]

As Nixon talked there was a surge of adrenalin in his voice and body language. Becoming virtually oblivious of my presence, the words flowed out from him at a higher level of intensity. It was almost as though his thoughts and phrases were being dictated by some mystic inner force within. Totally shedding the carapace of cynicism that had characterised some of his earlier conversation on political and journalistic tactics, Nixon burned with a youthful idealism that belied his seventy-nine years. As he spoke of his plan to make another visit in a few weeks' time to Moscow, listing the recommendations he would make to Yeltsin, ticking off the counter-proposals he hoped to bring back to Bush, and re-emphasising his dream of bringing about a volte face in US aid policy for Russia, it was impossible not to be swept up and moved by the depth of his idealistic commitment to his latest and perhaps last crusade in the cause of peace.

The conversation that Saturday morning in Eagles Nest illustrated yet again the complexities and contradictions of Richard Nixon, providing glimpses of so many aspects of his multifaceted persona. His social insecurity; his industrious scholarship; his political cynicism; his intellectual realism; his hidden spirituality; and his iron determination to do great deeds in the search for a more peaceful world, were all on view. Twenty years earlier, when he was in the plenitude of his power, he might also have displayed his paranoia about the liberal media and his ruthlessness in the exercise of presidential prerogatives, but the Nixon character has mellowed since his tempestuous times in the White House. Longevity has brought him closer to serenity, perhaps even to that Quaker state of 'peace at the center'.

I asked Nixon about that particular phrase, which three-quarters of a century ago was used to describe those two great influences of his formative years, his mother and his grandmother. What did it mean, and did it now apply to him?

'Peace at the center means a private calm in the eye of the storm,' he replied. 'Stoicism isn't quite the right word for it, nor is serenity, nor is destiny, although they are all parts of it. It is more an acceptance of the belief that what will be, will be. Deep down I am basically a fatalist. You fight hard all the way but you never soar too high and you never allow yourself to sink too low... Even at the time of Watergate—incidentally, I can't think now how I lived through it; probably by not watching it on television!—and in that worse time after Watergate, I never gave up. I was always sure that the pendulum would swing. And it has. It has. So yes... I think that my fatalism did help me to weather the storms of the past... and yes, I do feel that "peace at the center" has come to me.'[8]

The atmosphere became charged with emotion as he spoke these words. Nixon turned away to look out of the window and there was a long silence in Eagles Nest as each of us sat alone with our thoughts. Mine were those of the biographer roaming across the landscapes of Nixon's career. From the hardships of Yorba Linda to the glories of the White House; from the private despair of two fraternal bereavements to the public triumph of two presidential election victories; from the bathos of the Checkers speech to the brilliance of the China initiative; from the lonely disgrace of resignation to the frequent homage now paid to him in his years of rehabilitation; from outer torment to inner peace. By any standards it has been an amazing journey by an extraordinary man.

Nixon's odyssey is central to his legacy. His life story bears comparison, in its resilience if not in its righteousness, to a modern political version of *Pilgrim's Progress*. For like John Bunyan's pilgrim, Nixon has spent much of the journey being scorned and rejected—principally by the East Coast media and liberal establishments. As a result of their unremitting hostility he was often down but never out. Invariably he fought back, sometimes against the longest of odds, consistently displaying a courageous tenacity that has made him a legend in the annals of 'impossible' comebacks and recoveries. Whether these qualities will one day cause the trumpets to sound for him on the other side is a matter for the celestial authorities, but on the earthly terrain of politics, Nixon's example of what determination and persistence can achieve will surely earn him a niche among the immortals. Indeed, one can imagine schoolteachers of the future giving pep talks to their charges with the cry, 'Fight back like Nixon did!'

Nixon, in his eightieth year, is still fighting. He cares deeply about his place in history, and understands that the reassessment of him has only just begun. So far he seems to be winning, for already there is a growing willingness to accept that his achievements as a peacemaker and international statesman give him a strong claim to be regarded as America's finest foreign policy President of the twentieth century. If he eventually achieves that historical honour, alongside the contemporary dishonour of being the first and only President to resign, the scales of judgement will at last be more evenly balanced. That is the least he deserves.

Sitting alone with him on that spring morning in Eagles Nest, I reflected on how my own respect for Nixon had increased during my four years of researching and writing this book. Unlike many politicians, he improves with intimacy. Getting to know him has been an utterly absorbing experience, in which familiarity bred not contempt but a considerable measure of affection and admiration.

My conclusion is that Richard Nixon, both as a man and statesman, has been excessively maligned for his faults and inadequately recognised for his virtues.

Yet even in a spirit of historical revisionism, no simple verdict is possible. Because of his Shakespearean complexity he will probably continue to polarise biographical opinion after his death, just as he has polarised political opinion throughout his career. His life has so far rolled for eighty years like a long and fascinating river, occasionally passing through strange ill-smelling pools, sometimes babbling along with the shallow currents of political expediency, yet most often flowing into mysteriously still waters in which there lie hidden depths of sensitivity, intellect, spirituality, foresight, originality, and wisdom. Moreover, he has consistently charted his course towards the horizons of high ideals and great achievements that have featured in his dreams since childhood. The river's route has been tortuous and tempestuous, but Richard Nixon has reached the estuary of old age secure in the knowledge that many of his dreams have come true.

PRINCIPAL SOURCES

NIXON'S PAPERS

National Archives, Laguna Niguel, California: Nixon Vice-Presidential Papers; Richard Nixon Library and Birthplace, Yorba Linda, California: Nixon's personal and family papers; Nixon's private archives in his office in Woodcliff Lake, New Jersey; National Archives, Alexandria, Virginia: Nixon Presidential Materials Project, containing Nixon's White House tapes and papers; Nixon's own dictated recollections of his childhood years, made in 1975.

THE AITKEN COLLECTION OF
TRANSCRIPTS AND INTERVIEWS

These consist of the 135 interviews the author conducted during his research for this book (see list below); memoranda and letters written to the author by Nixon; the Historic Video Transcripts, which are the unpublished transcripts of a video history series on Nixon's life co-produced by the author.

UNIVERSITIES AND LIBRARIES

University of California at Berkeley: the Oral History Project in the Bancroft Library; Duke University Archives: Richard Nixon Papers; California State University at Fullerton: Richard M. Nixon Project; Claremont College: H. Jeremiah

Voorhis Papers; Harry S. Truman Presidential Library, Independence, Missouri: George Elsey Papers; Princeton University; Dulles Oral History Collection in the Firestone Library; Dwight D. Eisenhower Library, Abilene, Kansas: Nixon Vice-Presidential Papers and the Fred Seaton Papers; Churchill College, Cambridge University: Selwyn Lloyd Papers; US Library of Congress; US Capitol Historical Society: Carl Albert Papers; Whittier College Library: the Nixon Collection.

PRIVATE COLLECTIONS OF LETTERS AND DOCUMENTS

Jonathan Aitken personal papers; Julian Amery personal papers; the David Bruce diaries; the Evlyn Dorn collection; the Helene Drown collection; the Ola Florence Jobe collection; Egil Krogh personal papers; Daniel P. Moynihan personal papers; the Hubert C. Perry collection; Sir Robert Thompson personal papers.

OTHER SOURCES

Hofstra University Presidential Conference, 19–21 November 1987; Public Records Office, Kew, Surrey: Foreign and Commonwealth Office files; 'Nixon: The Quest for Power', 1990, a WGBH and Thames Television documentary on Nixon; Alice Roosevelt Longworth, interview with author for ITV documentary 'The Reporters', 1969.

INTERVIEWS

Robert Abplanalp, Margery Peterson Acker, Frederick Albrink, Ray Arbuthnot, Boris Armanov, James Ash, David Astor, Howard Baker, Kenneth Ball, Dolores Latrup Ball, Carmen Ballard, Benjamin C. Bradlee, Jack Brennan, Edmund G. Brown, Herbert Brownell, Steven Bull, Dwight Chapin, William Clark, Ken Cole, Len Colodny, Charles E. Colson, John Connally, Curtis Counts, Virginia Counts, Edward Cox, Tricia Nixon Cox, John F. Cronin, Samuel Dash, Dorothy Cox Donnelly, Evlyn Dorn, Jack Dreyfus, Helene Drown, Jack Drown, Robert F. Durden, John Ehrlichman, David Eisenhower, Julie Nixon Eisenhower, Robert Ellsworth, Thomas W. Evans, McIntyre Faries, Robert Finch, Peter Flanigan, John Freeman, Frank Gannon, Leonard Garment, Loie Gaunt, Oleg Gordievsky, Eldon Griffiths, Alexander M. Haig, H.R. Haldeman, Clint Harris, Jerome Hellman, Richard Helms, Stephen Hess, Patrick J. Hillings, Patricia Hitt, Lord Home, Bob Huberty, James D. Hughes, James C. Humes, Allan Oakley Hunter, Arnold A. Hutschnecker, Gail Jobe, Ola Florence Jobe, Paul Johnson, Herbert Kalmbach, Howard Kaminsky, Donald Kendall, Paul W. Keyes, Kenneth

L. Khachigian, William E. King, Herbert G. Klein, Baruch Korff, S. Paul Kramer, Egil Krogh, Gerald C. Lasensky, Charles Lichenstein, G. Gordon Liddy, Howard Liebengood, Robert McFarlane, George McGovern, Mary McGrory, Jeb Magruder, Charles McWhorter, George Cranwell Montgomery, Richard Moore, Daniel Patrick Moynihan, Carlos Narváez, Clara Jane Nixon, Edward C. Nixon, Patricia Nixon, Richard Nixon, Kathy O'Connor, Robert C. Odle Jr., William Roger Perdue Jr., Hubert Perry, Raymond K. Price, William F. Price, Sandy Quinn, Charles G. Rebozo, Charles Rhyne, Elliot L. Richardson, Mary Roebling, William P. Rogers, Mary W. Roosevelt, James Roosevelt, Nicholas Ruwe, William Safire, Harrison Salisbury, Terry Sanford, Paul Sarbanes, Diane Sawyer, James Schlesinger, William Schultz, Rex Scouten, John Sears, Dimitri Simes, George Smathers, Paul Smith, James B. Stewart, Roger J. Stone Jr., William Stover, Marin Strmecki, John H. Taylor, Fred D. Thompson, Robert Thompson, Strom Thurmond, Ron Walker, Vernon Walters, Betty Walton, Dorothy Welch, Rose Mary Woods, David Young, Ardeshir Zahedi, Ronald L. Ziegler.

NEWSPAPERS AND MAGAZINES

Alhambra Post Advocate, Baltimore Sun, Congressional Record, London Daily Telegraph, Dallas Morning News, Fresno Bee, Kansas City Star, Los Angeles Daily News, Los Angeles Times, Manchester Guardian, Miami Herald, Monrovia News, Navy Magazine, New York Herald Tribune, New York Times, New Yorker, Newsweek, Quaker Campus, San Francisco Chronicle, South Pasadena Review, Time Magazine, Wall Street Journal, Washington Post, Washington Star, Whittier News.

NOTES

ABBREVIATIONS

ACTI The Aitken Collection of Transcripts and Interviews.

CSFP The Richard M. Nixon Project, California State University at Fullerton.

FCO Foreign and Commonwealth Office.

HVT The Historic Video Transcripts.

LN The Nixon Vice-Presidential Papers in the National Archives, Laguna Niguel, California.

NPMP The Nixon Presidential Materials Project in the National Archives, Alexandria, Virginia.

PRO Public Records Office, Kew, Surrey.

RND Nixon's own collection of dictated recollections of his childhood years, made in 1975.

UCBP The Oral History Project in the Bancroft Library, University of California at Berkeley.

WLP Nixon's private archives in his office in Woodcliff Lake, New Jersey.

YLP Nixon's personal and family papers in the Richard Nixon Library and Birthplace, Yorba Linda, California.

Prologue

1. Richard Nixon, *RN: The Memoirs of Richard Nixon* (Grosset & Dunlap Inc, 1978), p. 558.

Chapter 1: Background and Boyhood

1. RN's personal copy of *Disraeli* by Robert Blake can now be found in the replica of the Lincoln sitting room of the White House re-created in the Nixon Library and Birthplace at Yorba Linda, California.
2. Robert Blake, *Disraeli* (Eyre and Spottiswoode, 1966) p. 3.
3. These adjectives appear repeatedly in the adversarial and psychobiographies of Nixon, particularly Fawn Brodie, *Richard Nixon: The Shaping of His Character* (W.W. Norton & Company Inc, 1981) and David Abrahamsen, *Nixon vs. Nixon: An Emotional Tragedy* (Farrar, Straus and Giroux, 1977).
4. YLP, Box 1.
5. ACTI, RN memorandum to author, 8 August 1989.
6. Richard Gardner, *Richard Nixon: The Story of a Fighting Quaker,* unpublished manuscript, Whittier College Library, p. 8.
7. ACTI, Evlyn Dorn, interview with author, December 1989.
8. Roger Morris, *Richard Milhous Nixon: The Rise of an American Politician* (Henry Holt and Company Inc, 1990) Vol. I, p. 25.
9. Jessamyn West, *Hide and Seek: A Continuing Journey* (Harcourt Brace Jovanovich Inc, 1973) pp. 238–9.
10. Morris, *Richard Milhous Nixon,* Vol. I, p. 37.
11. ACTI, HVT, Folio 1, pp. 11–12.
12. ACTI, RN, memorandum to author, 8 August 1989.
13. ACTI, HVT, Folio 1, p. 10.
14. Ibid., p. 39.
15. YLP, Nixon essay 'Autobiography', East Whittier Grammar School, 20 October 1925.
16. West, *Hide and Seek,* p. 27.
17. YLP, Nixon tape recording, 1990.
18. RND, Folio B, p. 34.
19. Ibid., Folio A, p. 7.
20. Merle West, interview, CSFP.
21. Nixon, *Memoirs,* p. 6.
22. RND, Folio B, pp. 30–1.
23. Bela Kornitzer, *The Real Nixon: An Intimate Biography* (Rand McNally, 1960), p. 71.

24. ACTI, Edward C. Nixon, interview with author, July 1990.

25. ACTI, Helene Drown, Hubert Perry, Clint Harris, interviews with author, 1989.

26. ACTI, RN memorandum to author, 8 August 1989.

27. ACTI, Edward C. Nixon, interview with author, September 1991.

28. ACTI, RN memorandum to author, 8 August 1989.

29. Mary George Skidmore, interview CSFP.

30. Ibid.

31. ACTI, RN memorandum to author, 8 August 1989.

32. Virginia Shaw Critchfield, interview CSFP.

33. West, *Hide and Seek*, pp. 239–40.

34. Donald Jackson, 'The Young Nixon', *Life*, 6 November 1970.

35. Mary George Skidmore, interview, CSFP.

36. ACTI, RN Memorandum to author, 8 August 1989.

37. ACTI, Edward C. Nixon, interview with author, July 1990.

38. Kornitzer, *The Real Nixon*, p. 67.

39. ACTI, RN memorandum to author, 8 August 1989.

40. YLP, Box 1, taken from framed original.

41. ACTI, RN memorandum to author, 8 August 1989.

42. YLP, Box 1, from 'Work' by Angela Morgan, *Poems of Inspiration–An Anthology.*

43. ACTI, Edward C. Nixon, interview with author, September 1991.

44. Kornitzer, *The Real Nixon*, pp. 47–9.

45. ACTI, HVT, Folio 1, pp. 69–70.

46. RND, Folio A, pp. 16–17.

47. Ibid., p. 6.

48. ACTI, RN memorandum to author, 8 August 1989.

49. Ibid.

50. ACTI, HVT, Folio 1, p. 23.

51. RND, Folio C, p. 30.

52. Ibid., Folio A, pp. 33–4.

53. Ibid., p. 34.

54. Ibid., pp. 34–35.

55. R. Schreiber, 'Richard Nixon: A Mother's Story', *Good Housekeeping*, June 1960.

56. Nixon, *Memoirs*, p. 10.

57. ACTI, RN memorandum to author, 8 August 1989.

58. Harry Schuyler, interview CSFP.

59. YLP, Nixon essay 'Autobiography', East Whittier Grammar School, 20 October 1925.

60. RND, Folio C, p. 34.

61. Ibid., Folio J, p. 3.

62. ACTI, HVT, Folio 1, pp. 51–2.

63. RND, Folio B, p. 23.

64. Longfellow, 'The Ladder of St. Augustine', in *The Poetical Works of Longfellow* (Oxford University Press, 1904).

65. RND, Folio B, pp. 38–9.

66. Ken Clawson, 'A Loyalist's Memoir', *Washington Post*, Outlook section, 9 August 1979.

67. RND, Folio J, p. 9.

68. Elizabeth Glover, interview CSFP.

69. YLP, Nixon essay 'Autobiography', East Whittier Grammar School, 20 October 1925.

70. ACTI, HVT, Folio 1, p. 81; Nixon, *Memoirs*, p. 15.

Chapter 2: Whittier College

1. ACTI, Dolores Latrup Bell, interview with author, October 1991.

2. Paul Smith, interview CSFP.

3. ACTI, HVT, Folio 1, p. 85.

4. Stewart Alsop, 'Nixon on Nixon', *Saturday Evening Post*, 12 July 1958.

5. Nixon, *Memoirs*, pp. 19–20.

6. Merton Wray, interview, CSFP.

7. Earl Mazo, *Richard Nixon: A Political and Personal Portrait* (Harper and Bros., 1959), p. 33.

8. ACTI, Gail Jobe, interview with author, September 1991.

9. Garry Wills, *Nixon Agonistes: The Crisis of the Self-Made Man* (New American Library, 1970), p. 161.

10. ACTI, HVT, Folio 1, p. 94.

11. Ibid., p. 95.

12. Ibid., p. 97.

13. Ibid., pp. 86–7.

14. ACTI, Hubert Perry, interview with author, September 1991.

15. Lael Morgan, 'Whittier '34: Most likely to succeed', *Los Angeles Times*, 10 May 1970.

16. Paul Smith, interview CSFP.

17. RND, Folio F, p. 10.

18. Stewart Alsop, *Nixon and Rockefeller: A Double Portrait* (Doubleday, 1960), p. 222.
19. *Acropolis,* Whittier College Yearbook, 1934.
20. *Quaker Campus,* 18 November 1932.
21. Kornitzer, *The Real Nixon,* pp. 106–7.
22. ACTI, HVT, Folio 1, pp. 90–1.
23. Ibid., pp. 88–9.
24. ACTI, Paul Smith, interview with author, September 1989.
25. ACTI, RN, interview with author, October 1989.
26. Nixon, *Memoirs,* p. 15.
27. ACTI, HVT, Folio 1, p. 87.
28. WLP, Box 2.
29. ACTI, HVT, Folio i, p. 88.
30. WLP, Box 2.
31. YLP, Nixon college essay 'What Can I Believe ?', 9 October 1933.
32. Paul Smith, interview CSFP.
33. Gardner, *Richard Nixon,* p. 78.
34. ACTI, Ola Florence Jobe, interview with author, October 1991.
35. ACTI, Kenneth Ball, interview with author, July 1990.

Chapter 3: Spirituality, Sadness and Romance

1. ACTI, RN memorandum to author, 8 August 1989.
2. St. Matthew, 6:6.
3. Mary Elizabeth Guptill Rez, interview CSFP.
4. Tom Bewley, interview, CSFP.
5. Ibid.
6. YLP, Nixon college essay, 'What Can I Believe ?', 9 October 1933.
7. Nixon, *Memoirs,* p. 10.
8. *Decision* magazine, November 1962; *New York Times,* 26 January 1969.
9. Gardner, *Richard Nixon,* p. 23.
10. Kornitzer, *The Real Nixon,* pp. 65–6.
11. ACTI, HVT, Folio 1, p. 71.
12. Ibid., p. 72; RND, Folio A, p. 29.
13. Unattributable quote by Nixon staff member.
14. *New York Times,* 9 August 1974; Nixon, *Memoirs,* p. 1088.
15. ACTI, Ola Florence Jobe, interview with author, July 1990.
16. ACTI, RN memorandum to author, 8 August 1989.

17. Stephen E. Ambrose, *Nixon*, Vol. I, *The Education of a Politician 1913–1962* (Simon & Schuster, 1987), p. 52.

18. Henry Schuyler, interview CSFP.

19. RND, Folio A, pp. 30–1.

20. Ibid., p. 32.

21. ACTI, Edward C. Nixon, interview with author, July 1990.

22. Kornitzer, *The Real Nixon*, p. 92.

23. ACTI, RN memorandum to author, 8 August 1989.

24. Ibid.

25. YLP, Nixon college essay, 'What Can I Believe ?', 9 October 1933.

26. Ibid., 13 November 1933.

27. Ibid.

28. Ibid.

29. Ibid., 21 January 1934.

30. Ibid., undated essay believed to be April 1934.

31. Ibid., April 1934.

32. Richard Nixon, *In the Arena: A Memoir of Victory, Defeat and Renewal* (Simon & Schuster, 1990), p. 89.

33. Unattributable comment to the author from an Anglican archbishop who read the 'What Can I Believe ?' essays at Sandwich Bay near Canterbury while attending the Lambeth Conference in August 1988.

34. ACTI, Ola Florence Jobe, interview with author, July 1990.

35. Ibid.

36. Nixon, *Memoirs*, p. 14.

37. ACTI, Ola Florence Jobe, interview with author, July 1990.

38. Ola Florence Jobe collection, RN to Ola Florence Welch, undated but said to be 3 or 4 May 1929.

39. Morris, *Richard Milhous Nixon*, Vol. I, p. 143.

40. *Acropolis*, Whittier College Yearbook, 1934.

41. ACTI, Ola Florence Jobe, interview with author, July 1990.

42. ACTI, HVT, Folio 1, p. 56.

43. ACTI, Ola Florence Jobe, interview with author, July 1990.

44. ACTI, Dorothy Welch, interview with author, January 1992.

45. Ibid.

46. ACTI, Ola Florence Jobe, interview with author, August 1990.

47. Ibid.

48. Ibid.

49. Morris, *Richard Milhous Nixon*, Vol. I, p. 143.

50. Jackson, 'The Young Nixon', p. 56.

51. ACTI, Ola Florence Jobe, interview with author, July 1990.

52. Ibid.

53. Morgan, 'Whittier '34', *Los Angeles Times,* 10 May 1970.

54. ACTI, Ola Florence Jobe, interview with author, July 1990.

55. Ola Florence Jobe collection, RN to Ola Florence Welch, 15 January 1936.

56. Ibid.

57. ACTI, Ola Florence Jobe, interview with author, August 1990.

58. Unattributable comment to author by Nixon family member, July 1991.

59. Bryce Harlow, quoted in Hedley Donovan, *Roosevelt to Reagan: A Reporter's Encounters with Nine Presidents* (Harper and Row, 1987) p. 130; see also similar Bryce Harlow quotation in Tom Wicker, *One of Us: Richard Nixon and the American Dream* (Random House Inc, 1991), p. 652.

Chapter 4: Duke University

1. ACTI, Ola Florence Jobe, interview with author, July 1990.

2. ACTI, HVT, Folio 2, p. 104.

3. Ibid., p. 105.

4. Robert F. Durden, 'The Rebuilding of Duke University's School of Law', *North Carolina Historical Review,* Volume LXVI, No. 3, July 1989, p. 388.

5. RND, Folio C, p. 2.

6. Jackson, 'The Young Nixon', p. 56; Ambrose, *Nixon,* Vol. I, p. 77.

7. Ola Florence Jobe collection, RN to Ola Florence Welch, 14 January 1935.

8. ACTI, HVT, Folio 2, pp. 106–7.

9. ACTI, Frederick Albrink, interview with author, September 1990.

10. John Jolliffe, ed., *Life & Letters of Raymond Asquith* (Collins, 1980), p. 139.

11. Theodore H. White, *The Making of the President, 1972* (Atheneum, 1973), p. 355.

12. RND, Folio F, p. 20.

13. *Kansas City Star,* 4 November 1955.

14. RND, Folio B, p. 107.

15. ACTI, Frederick Albrink, interview with author, September 1990.

16. Ibid.

17. RND, Folio F, pp. 24–5.

18. Nixon, *In the Arena,* p. 130.

19. Ola Florence Jobe collection, RN to Ola Florence Welch, 5 January 1936.

20. ACTI, Bill Perdue, interview with author, September 1989.

21. ACTI, Frederick Albrink, interview with author, September 1990.

22. RND, Folio F, pp. 22–3.
23. Alsop, *Nixon and Rockefeller,* pp. 234–5.
24. ACTI, Frederick Albrink, interview with author, September 1990.
25. Ibid.
26. Nixon, *Memoirs,* p. 21.
27. Alsop, *Nixon and Rockefeller,* p. 233.
28. ACTI, HVT, Folio 2, p. 146.
29. Ibid., p. 147.
30. RND, Folio F, p. 2.
31. ACTI, Richard Moore, interview with author, July 1991.
32. RND, Folio F, pp. 30–2.
33. Ibid.
34. ACTI, HVT, Folio 2, p. 134.
35. WLP, Box 12, p. 23.
36. RND, Folio F, p. 33.
37. Jackson, 'The Young Nixon', p. 57.
38. Mazo, *Nixon,* p. 26.
39. Ibid.
40. ACTI, HVT, Folio 2, p. 109.
41. ACTI, Edward C. Nixon, interview with author, October 1991.
42. Gardner, *Richard Nixon,* p. 80.
43. John Morton Blum, *Woodrow Wilson and the Politics of Morality* (Little, Brown & Co., 1956) p. 13.

Chapter 5: Law, Love and Marriage

1. Duke University Archives, RN letter to Helen Kendall, 3 July 1937.
2. Duke University Archives, Dean Horack letter to RN, 10 August 1937.
3. ACTI, Evlyn Dorn, interview with author, 28 December 1989.
4. Ibid.
5. RND, Folio G, p. 4.
6. ACTI, Evlyn Dorn, interview with author, 28 December 1989.
7. Duke University Archives, RN letter to Dean Horack, 6 October 1937.
8. RND Folio G, pp. 36–7; ACTI, HVT, Folio 2, pp. 111–12.
9. Duke University Archives, RN letter to Dean Horack, 3 November 1937.
10. Fawn Brodie, *Richard Nixon: The Shaping of His Character* (W.W. Norton & Company Inc, 1981), p. 139.
11. Ibid.
12. WLP, Box 1, p. 17; Nixon, *Memoirs,* p. 22.

13. YLP, RN Income Tax Returns, 1938–40.
14. Unattributable comment to author, 30 December 1989.
15. Ibid.
16. Alsop, *Nixon and Rockefeller*, p. 195.
17. Lester David, *The Lonely Lady of San Clemente: The Story of Pat Nixon* (Crowell, 1978), p. 48.
18. RND, Folio G, pp. 7–8.
19. ACTI, Evlyn Dorn, interview with author, 28 December 1989.
20. Ibid.
21. Mazo, *Richard Nixon*, p. 33.
22. ACTI, Paul Smith, interview with author, September 1989.
23. ACTI, Hubert Perry, interview with author, September 1989.
24. Ibid.
25. Julie Nixon Eisenhower, *Pat Nixon: The Untold Story* (Simon & Schuster, 1986), p. 55.
26. Ibid.
27. Ibid.
28. Nixon, *Memoirs*, p. 23.
29. Elizabeth Cloes, interview CSFP.
30. ACTI, Virginia Counts, interview with author, October 1991.
31. Nixon Eisenhower, *Pat Nixon*, p. 21.
32. Marcia Wray, interview, CSFP.
33. Jessamyn West, 'The Real Pat Nixon', *Good Housekeeping*, February 1971, p. 124.
34. Nixon Eisenhower, *Pat Nixon*, p. 49.
35. Ibid., p. 44.
36. ACTI, HVT, Folio 2, pp. 115–16.
37. Nixon Eisenhower, *Pat Nixon*, p. 58.
38. Ibid., p. 59.
39. Ibid.
40. David, *The Lonely Lady of San Clemente*, p. 59.
41. RND, Folio G, p. 14.
42. Ibid., p. 17.
43. ACTI, Virginia and Curtis Counts, interview with author, October 1991.
44. ACTI, Kenneth Ball, interview with author, October 1989.
45. ACTI, Virginia and Curtis Counts, interview with author, October 1991.
46. ACTI, Curtis Counts, interview with author, September 1991.
47. ACTI, Edward C. Nixon, interview with author, September 1991.

48. Nixon Eisenhower, *Pat Nixon*, p. 64.
49. Ibid., p. 66.
50. Ibid.
51. Ibid., p. 67.
52. Judith Wingert, interview CSFP.
53. RND, Folio G, p. 18.
54. Nixon Eisenhower, *Pat Nixon*, p. 63.
55. ACTI, Virginia and Curtis Counts, interview with author, September 1991.
56. RND, Folio G, p. 19.
57. Ibid., p. 20; ACTI, HVT, Folio 2, p. 117.
58. Ibid.
59. RND, Folio G, pp. 20–1.
60. Ibid.
61. Ibid. pp. 21–2.
62. Nixon Eisenhower, *Pat Nixon*, p. 72.
63. Nixon, *Memoirs*, p. 26.
64. Ibid.
65. RND, Folio G, p. 34.
66. Morris, *Richard Milhous Nixon*, Vol. I, p. 239.
67. Ibid., p. 240.
68. Nixon, *Memoirs*, p. 26.
69. Ibid.
70. Milton Viorst, 'Nixon of the OPA', *New York Times* magazine, 3 October 1971.
71. RND, Folio G, pp. 35–6.
72. Kornitzer, *The Real Nixon*, pp. 139–40.
73. Nixon Eisenhower, *Pat Nixon*, p. 76.
74. Ibid., p. 77.
75. Ibid.
76. Ibid.

Chapter 6: War

1. ACTI, HVT, Folio 2, p. 120.
2. Ibid.
3. Evlyn Dorn collection, RN to Frank and Hannah Nixon, 1 November 1942.
4. ACTI, RN memorandum to author, 5 January 1990.
5. ACTI, HVT, Folio 2, pp. 181–2.
6. YLP, Harrison letter, 5 December 1942.

7. ACTI, HVT, Folio 2, p. 132.
8. ACTI, Evlyn Dorn, interview with author, 28 December 1990.
9. ACTI, HVT, Folio 2, p. 132.
10. *Navy* magazine, January 1969.
11. RND, Folio F, p. 19; see also YLP, Congressional Election Speech Notes 1946, Bougainville Speech.
12. ACTI, James Stewart, interview with author, January 1990.
13. RND, Folio F, p. 19; see also ACTI, HVT, Folio 2, p. 186.
14. Morris, *Richard Milhous Nixon;* Vol. I, p. 252.
15. ACTI, James Stewart, interview with author, January 1990.
16. YLP, RN reading notes.
17. Duke University Archives, RN letter to Dean Horack, 1 September 1943.
18. ACTI, Edward C. Nixon, interview with author, September 1991.
19. ACTI, HVT, Folio 2, p. 133.
20. Nixon Eisenhower, *Pat Nixon,* p. 81.
21. YLP, RN undated letter to Pat Nixon.
22. ACTI, HVT Folio 2, p. 133.
23. ACTI, James Stewart, interview with author, January 1990.
24. Ibid.
25. Ambrose, *Nixon,* Vol. I, p. 110.
26. Kornitzer, *The Real Nixon,* pp. 144–5.
27. ACTI, HVT, Folio 2, p. 133.
28. Ibid., pp. 126, 171.
29. Ibid., p. 127.
30. Kornitzer, *The Real Nixon,* p. 147.
31. Virginia Conn, 'Nixon, the Naval Officer', *Navy* magazine, January 1969.
32. RND, Folio E, p. 23.
33. YLP, South Pasadena speech, 13 September 1946.
34. ACTI, HVT, Folio 2, p. 187.
35. Kornitzer, *The Real Nixon,* p. 147.
36. RND, Folio E, p. 25.
37. Gardner, *Richard Nixon,* p. 108.
38. ACTI, HVT, Folio 2, p. 153.

Chapter 7: Election to Congress

1. YLP, Herman Perry, letter to RN, 3 October 1945; Nixon, *Memoirs,* p. 34.
2. Nixon Eisenhower, *Pat Nixon,* p. 86.
3. ACTI, James Stewart, interview with author, January 1990.

4. WLP, Box 4, p. 13.

5. YLP, RN, letter to Herman Perry, 6 October 1945.

6. WLP, Box 11, p. 17.

7. ACTI, McIntyre Faries, interview with author, July 1990.

8. Nixon, *Memoirs*, p. 35.

9. Roy Day, interview UCBP.

10. YLP, Roy Day, letter to RN, 12 November 1945.

11. ACTI, HVT, Folio 3, p. 194.

12. WLP, Box 1.

13. YLP, RN, letter to Herman Perry, 17 December 1945.

14. Morris, *Richard Milhous Nixon,* Vol. I., p. 261.

15. Drew Pearson, syndicated column, 27 July 1940.

16. ACTI, McIntyre Faries, interview with author, July 1990.

17. YLP, RN, letter to Herman Perry, 2 December 1945.

18. YLP, 'Challenge to Democracy' speech.

19. ACTI, Hubert Perry, interview with author, September 1989.

20. Nixon, *In the Arena,* p. 187.

21. WLP, Box 11, p. 17.

22. *Whittier News* et al., 6 March 1946.

23. H. J. Voorhis Papers, Voorhis, letter to RN, 16 April 1946.

24. Roy Day, interview, UCBP.

25. YLP, RN, letter to supporters, 12 July 1946.

26. YLP, RN, letter to Herman Perry, 6 October 1945.

27. Hubert C. Perry collection, Charles Cooper, memorandum to Herman Perry.

28. ACTI, RN interview with author, 5 January 1990; ACTI, HVT, Folio 3, pp. 204–6.

29. ACTI, RN interview with author, 5 January 1990.

30. Kornitzer, *The Real Nixon,* p. 160.

31. *Alhambra Post Advocate, South Pasadena Review,* et al., 5 September 1946.

32. *Monrovia News – Post,* 2 September 1946.

33. Paul Bullock, 'Rabbits and Radicals: Richard Nixon's 1947 Campaign Against Jerry Voorhis', *Southern California Quarterly,* Vol. LV, No. 3, Fall 1973, p. 338.

34. *Whittier News,* 24 October 1946.

35. Morris, *Richard Milhous Nixon,* Vol. I, p. 332.

36. ACTI, Helene Drown, interview with author, December 1989; Nixon Eisenhower, *Pat Nixon,* p. 402.

37. WLP, Box 2, p. 16.

38. *Time,* 18 November 1946.

39. Brodie, *Richard Nixon,* p. 189.

40. Herbert S. Parmet, *Richard Nixon and His America* (Little, Brown & Co., 1990), p. 97.

41. Morris, *Richard Milhous Nixon,* Vol. I, p. 336.

42. ACTI, HVT, Folio 3, p. 202.

43. Nixon, *Memoirs,* p. 42.

44. ACTI, Hubert Perry, interview with author, September and December 1989.

45. ACTI, HVT, Folio 3, p. 212.

46. ACTI, Hubert Perry, Clint Harris, Kenneth Ball and others, interviews with author, 1989–91.

47. Nixon, *Memoirs,* p. 39.

48. Nixon Eisenhower, *Pat Nixon,* pp. 89–90.

49. ACTI, HVT, Folio 3, p. 211.

50. Nixon, *Memoirs,* p. 40.

Chapter 8: Freshman Congressman

1. WLP, Box 2, Khachigian Folio, p. 19.

2. James Keogh, *This is Nixon* (G.P. Putnam's Sons, 1956), p. 119.

3. Congressional Record, 16 April 1947.

4. Paul Johnson, 'In Praise of Richard Nixon', *Commentary,* October 1988.

5. ACTI, HVT, Folio 4, pp. 221–2; Nixon, *Memoirs,* p. 43.

6. ACTI, HVT, Folio 4, pp. 221–2.

7. ACTI, Dorothy Cox Donnelly, interview with author, March 1990.

8. ACTI, Rex Scouten, interview with author, September 1990.

9. YLP, Jacqueline Kennedy, letter to RN, 5 December 1954.

10. YLP, RN, letter to John F. Kennedy, 5 February 1955.

11. Parmet, *Richard Nixon and His America,* p. 141.

12. Morris, *Richard Milhous Nixon,* Vol. I, p. 342.

13. Ruth Fischer, *Stalin and German Communism: A Study in the Origins of the State Party* (Oxford University Press, 1948).

14. Ralph de Toledano, *One Man Alone: Richard Nixon* (Funk & Wagnalls, 1969), pp. 64–5.

15. Congressional Record, 18 February 1947.

16. Ambrose, *Nixon,* Vol. I, p. 147; Brodie, *Richard Nixon,* p. 189.

17. Nixon, *Memoirs,* pp. 46–7.

18. Robert K. Carr, *House Committee on Un-American Activities 1945–1950* (Cornell University Press, 1952), pp. 48, 226–9.

19. Nixon, *Memoirs,* pp. 43–4.
20. WLP, RN, letter to Joseph C. Martin, 2 August 1947.
21. Stewart and Joseph Alsop, syndicated column, 4 August 1947.
22. Nixon, *Memoirs,* pp. 48–9.
23. WLP, Herter Committee Folio, p. 6.
24. Ibid.
25. Ibid.
26. Ibid.
27. Ibid.
28. Ibid.
29. Ibid.
30. Ibid.
31. Richard Nixon, *Six Crises* (W.H. Allen, 1962) p. 16.
32. ACTI, Hubert Perry, interview with author, September 1989.
33. ACTI, Patrick Hillings, interview with author, December 1989.

Chapter 9: The Hiss Case

1. WLP, Box 2, Folio 12, p. 3; Nixon, *Memoirs,* pp. 52–3.
2. Morris, *Richard Milhous Nixon,* Vol. I, p. 396.
3. Ibid., p. 397.
4. US House of Representatives, Committee on Un-American Activities, *Hearings Regarding Communist Espionage in the United States Government* (US Government Printing Office, 80th Congress, 2nd Session, 1948), p. 647 (Hereafter referred to as 'HUAC Espionage Hearings').
5. *Washington Post,* 6 August 1948.
6. Nixon, *Six Crises,* p. 10.
7. Ibid.
8. Ibid., pp. 10–11.
9. ACTI, HVT, Folio 3, p. 247.
10. ACTI, Dorothy Cox Donnelly, interview with author, March 1990.
11. Morris, *Richard Milhous Nixon,* Vol. I, p. 404.
12. HUAC Espionage Hearings, p. 647.
13. ACTI, S. Paul Kramer, interview with author, December 1989.
14. ACTI, RN, memorandum to author, 24 September 1990.
15. Nixon, *Six Crises,* p. 4.
16. ACTI, John Cronin, interview with author, September 1990.
17. ACTI, Dorothy Cox Donnelly, interview with author, March 1990.
18. HUAC Espionage Hearings, p. 671.

19. Robert E. Stripling, *The Red Plot Against America*, (Bell Publishing Company, 1949), p. 119.

20. WLP, Box 2, Folio 12, p. 15.

21. *Washington Post*, 7 August 1948.

22. ACTI, Dorothy Cox Donnelly, interview with author, March 1990.

23. Nixon, *Six Crises*, p. 22.

24. Ibid.

25. Ibid., p. 23.

26. Nixon, *Memoirs*, p. 57.

27. ACTI, William P. Rogers, interview with author, January 1991.

28. Ibid.

29. WLP, Box 2, Folio 12, p. 20.

30. Ibid., pp. 18–19.

31. Nixon, *Six Crises*, p. 21.

32. Ibid., p. 23.

33. Schreiber, 'Richard Nixon: A Mother's Story', p. 214.

34. ACTI, Dorothy Cox Donnelly, interview with author, March 1990.

35. HUAC Espionage Hearings, p. 945.

36. Ibid., pp. 961–2.

37. WLP, Box 2, Folio 12, p. 24.

38. HUAC Espionage Hearings, pp. 950–1.

39. Ibid., p. 955.

40. WLP, Box 2, Folio 12, p. 28.

41. Ibid., p. 30.

42. HUAC Espionage Hearings, p. 977.

43. Ibid., pp. 978–9.

44. Ibid., pp. 986–88.

45. Morris, *Richard Milhous Nixon*, Vol. I, p. 421; Allen Weinstein, *Perjury: The Hiss–Chambers Case* (Alfred A. Knopf Inc, 1978), p. 38.

46. Nixon, *Six Crises*, p. 37.

47. HUAC Espionage Hearings, p. 1001.

48. Nixon, *Six Crises*, p. 37.

49. Nixon Eisenhower, *Pat Nixon*, p. 100.

50. Robert Stripling, interview for WGBH/Thames Television series 'The Quest for Power', Episode One, 1991.

51. HUAC Espionage Hearings, pp. 1088–9.

52. Ibid., p. 1116.

53. Ibid., p. 1129.

54. Ibid.
55. Ibid., p. 1162.
56. Nixon, *Memoirs,* p. 65.
57. HUAC Espionage Hearings, p. 1191.
58. Nixon, *Memoirs,* p. 65.
59. *New York Times,* 30 August 1948.
60. George Elsey papers, George Elsey, memorandum to Clark Clifford, 27 August 1948.
61. Morton Levitt and Michael Levitt, *A Tissue of Lies: Nixon vs. Hiss* (McGraw Hill Book Company, 1979) p. 68.
62. Ibid.
63. WLP, Box 3, Folio 12, p. 5.
64. Ibid., pp. 53–4.
65. Morris, *Richard Milhous Nixon,* Vol. I, p. 461.
66. Weinstein, *Perjury,* p. 188.
67. Ibid.
68. Ibid., p. 189.
69. Whittaker Chambers, *Witness* (Andre Deutsch, 1953), p. 578.
70. Nixon, *Memoirs,* p. 68.
71. ACTI, HVT, Folio 3, p. 262.
72. Ibid.
73. Morris, *Richard Milhous Nixon,* Vol. I, p. 479.
74. Ambrose, *Nixon,* Vol. I, p. 193.
75. Nixon, *Six Crises,* p. 55.
76. Ambrose, *Nixon,* Vol. I, p. 193.
77. Morris, *Richard Milhous Nixon,* Vol. I, p. 477.
78. ACTI, HVT, Folio 3, p. 266.
79. Ibid., pp. 279–80.
80. Weinstein, *Perjury,* p. 300.
81. ACTI, Betty Lewis Walton, interview with author, June 1990.
82. ACTI, Robert Finch, interview with author, July 1990.
83. ACTI, RN memorandum to author, March 1989; HVT, Folio 3, pp. 268–9.
84. Christopher Andrew and Oleg Gordievsky, *KGB: The Inside Story of its Foreign Operations from Lenin to Gorbachev* (Hodder & Stoughton, 1990), pp. 227–33.
85. ACTI, Oleg Gordievsky, interview with author, February 1992.
86. ACTI, HVT, Folio 3, pp. 279–80.
87. Nixon, *Memoirs,* p. 81.

Chapter 10: The Senate Election

1.   Roy Day/Frank Jorgenson interviews, UCBP; Ambrose, *Nixon*, Vol. I, p. 199.
2.   Nixon Eisenhower, *Pat Nixon*, p. 104.
3.   Nixon, *Memoirs*, p. 72.
4.   WLP, Box 3, Folio 14, p. 3.
5.   Ebell Club announcement and speech, *Los Angeles Times*, 4 November 1949.
6.   Morris, *Richard Milhous Nixon*, Vol. I, p. 553.
7.   *Los Angeles Daily News*, 30 March 1949.
8.   Henry D. Spaulding, *The Nixon Nobody Knows* (Jonathan David, 1972), p. 268.
9.   *Los Angeles Times*, 30 March 1949.
10.   William Costello, *The Facts About Nixon: An Unauthorized Biography* (Viking Press, 1960), p. 263.
11.   These epithets are recorded in various news stories in the *Los Angeles Daily News* (a paper owned by Manchester Boddy) in the period April–June, 1950; *Los Angeles Times*, 3, 19, 26 May 1950.
12.   *Los Angeles Times*, 23 May 1950.
13.   Ibid.
14.   Morris, *Richard Milhous Nixon*, Vol. I, p. 543.
15.   Nixon, *Memoirs*, p. 75.
16.   ACTI, Pat Hillings, interview with author, 29 December 1989.
17.   Helen Gahagan Douglas, *A Full Life* (Doubleday, 1982), p. 339; Morris, *Richard Milhous Nixon*, Vol. I, p. 616.
18.   Jean Begeman, 'Million Dollar Senators', *New Republic*, 9 April 1951; Morris, *Richard Milhous Nixon*, Vol. I, p. 616.
19.   WLP, Box 3, Folio 14, p. 30.
20.   Nixon Eisenhower, *Pat Nixon*, p. 110.
21.   WLP, Box 3, Folio 14, p. 17.
22.   Morris, *Richard Milhous Nixon*, Vol. I, p. 542.
23.   WLP, Box 3, Folio 14, p. 17.
24.   *Los Angeles Times*, 3 November 1950.
25.   LN, Senate Campaign Material, 'Douglas-Marcantonio Voting Record'.
26.   Wicker, *One of Us*, p. 76; Mazo, *Richard Nixon*, p. 81.
27.   Nixon, *Memoirs*, p. 76.
28.   *San Francisco Chronicle*, 3 November 1950.
29.   WLP, Box 3, Folio 14, p. 34.
30.   Ibid. p. 35.

31. Nixon, *Memoirs*, p. 77, (reported from campaign despatch in *San Francisco Chronicle*).

32. Dan Rather and Gary Paul Gates, *The Palace Guard* (Harper & Row, 1974), p. 4.

33. Nixon campaign speech, 18 September 1950; see also Morris, *Richard Milhous Nixon*, Vol. I, p. 584.

34. *San Francisco Chronicle*, 6 May 1950.

35. Ibid.; Ingrid W. Scobie, 'Helen Gahagan Douglas and Her 1950 Senate Race with Richard M. Nixon', *Historical Society of Southern California Quarterly*, 58, Spring 1976, p. 116.

36. *San Francisco Chronicle*, 6 May 1950.

37. WLP, Box 3, Folio 14, p. 30.

38. Anne Edwards, *Early Reagan: The Rise to Power* (Hodder & Stoughton, 1987), pp. 417–18.

39. WLP, Box 3, Folio 14, p. 30.

40. Morris, *Richard Milhous Nixon*, Vol. I, p. 567.

41. *San Francisco Chronicle*, 31 October 1950.

42. ACTI, David Astor, interview with author, November 1991.

43. YLP, Sheridan Downey telegram to RN, 7 November 1950.

Chapter 11: Senator and Vice-Presidential Candidate

1. Ambrose, *Nixon*, Vol. I, p. 226.

2. Brodie, *Richard Nixon*, p. 244.

3. Parmet, *Richard Nixon and His America*, p. 232.

4. ACTI, Dorothy Cox Donnelly, interview with author, March 1990.

5. ACTI, Rose Mary Woods, interview with author, March 1990.

6. Ibid.

7. Nora Ephron, 'Rose Mary Woods, The Lady or The Tiger ?', *New York*, 18 March 1974.

8. Helene Drown collection, Pat Nixon, letter to Helene Drown, 22 May 1951.

9. Helene Drown collection, Pat Nixon, letter to Helene Drown, 4 September 1951.

10. ACTI, Arnold A. Hutschnecker, interview with author, September 1991.

11. Ibid.

12. Drew Pearson, Address to National Press Club, 14 November 1968; *New York Times*, 15 November 1968.

13. *New York Times*, 15 November 1968.

14. ACTI, Arnold A. Hutschnecker, interview with author, September 1991.

15. Helene Drown collection, Pat Nixon, letter to Helene Drown, 7 November 1951.

16. Morris, *Richard Milhous Nixon,* Vol. I, p. 655.

17. ACTI, George Smathers, interview with author, December 1992. Rebozo's original letter has been lost, but Smathers insists that this is a verbatim quote from it.

18. ACTI, Charles G. Rebozo, interview with author, October 1991.

19. Helene Drown collection, Pat Nixon to Helene Drown, 7 November 1951; RN to Jack Drown, 30 April 1952; RN to Richard Danner, 9 January 1952.

20. ACTI, RN, letter to author, March 1989.

21. Mazo, *Richard Nixon,* pp. 89–90.

22. Ibid.

23. Morris, *Richard Milhous Nixon,* Vol. I, p. 635.

24. Nixon, *Memoirs,* p. 92.

25. Ibid., p. 81.

26. Ibid.

27. Ibid., p. 376.

28. Ibid., p. 82.

29. ACTI, Herbert Brownell, interview with author, January 1991.

30. Ibid.

31. Ibid.

32. Mazo, *Richard Nixon,* p. 88.

33. Nixon, *Memoirs,* p. 86.

34. Sherman Adams, *Firsthand Report: The Story of the Eisenhower Administration* (Harper and Bros., 1961) p. 43.

35. ACTI, Herbert Brownell, interview with author, January 1991.

36. Nixon Eisenhower, *Pat Nixon,* p. 130.

37. ACTI, Herbert Brownell, interview with author, January 1991.

38. Nixon, *Memoirs,* p. 87.

39. Nixon Eisenhower, *Pat Nixon,* p. 116.

40. ACTI, Helene Drown, interview with author, September 1991.

41. Nixon Eisenhower, *Pat Nixon,* p. 115.

42. *New York Times,* 12 July 1952.

43. ACTI, Herbert Brownell, interview with author, January 1991.

44. YLP, John F. Kennedy, letter to RN, undated.

45. Nixon Eisenhower, *Pat Nixon,* p. 117.

46. Nixon, *Six Crises,* p. 76.

47. *Newsweek,* 15 September 1952.

48. Morris, *Richard Milhous Nixon,* Vol. I, p. 752.

49. *New York Times,* 3 September 1952.

50. LN Undeeded, Christian Herter letter to RN, 9 September 1952.

51. Brodie, *Richard Nixon,* p. 275.

52. Nixon, *Memoirs,* p. 92.

53. Mazo, *Richard Nixon,* p. 107.

54. Nixon, *Six Crises,* p. 80.

55. Stephen E. Ambrose, *Eisenhower,* Vol. I, *Soldier, General of the Army, President-Elect* (Simon & Schuster, 1984), p. 554.

56. Ibid., p. 557.

57. Nixon, *Six Crises,* p. 93.

58. *Fresno Bee,* 9 September 1952; ACTI, Oakley Hunter, interview with author, July 1991.

59. Morris, *Richard Milhous Nixon,* Vol. I, p. 852.

60. ACTI, Patrick Hillings, interview with author, January 1991.

61. Nixon, *Memoirs,* p. 96.

62. Ibid., pp. 97–8.

63. Kornitzer, *The Real Nixon,* pp. 197–8.

64. ACTI, Helene Drown, interview with author, September 1991.

65. Nixon Eisenhower, *Pat Nixon,* p. 120.

66. Nixon, *Six Crises,* p. 107.

67. Nixon, *Memoirs,* p. 103.

68. Ibid.

69. Ibid., p. 101.

70. Ibid., p. 103.

71. *New York Times,* 24 September 1952.

72. ACTI, William P. Rogers, interview with author, January 1991.

73. Morris, *Richard Milhous Nixon,* Vol. I, p. 836.

74. Emmet John Hughes, *The Ordeal of Power: A Political Memoir of the Eisenhower Years* (Atheneum, 1963), p. 40.

75. *Mazo, Richard Nixon,* p. 137.

76. ACTI, Herbert Brownell, interview with author, January 1991.

77. *New York Times,* 24 September 1952.

78. ACTI, Rose Mary Woods, interview with author, September 1990.

79. Nixon, *Memoirs,* p. 107.

80. Helene Drown collection, Richard Nixon, letter to Helene Drown, September 1952.

81. Nixon, *Memoirs,* p. 108.

82. Nixon Eisenhower, *Pat Nixon*, p. 126.
83. Kornitzer, *The Real Nixon*, p. 205.
84. Nixon, *Memoirs*, p. 109.
85. Robert Browning, 'The Lost Leader', *The Poetical Works of Robert Browning*, Vol. IV (Oxford University Press, 1991).
86. Costello, *The Facts about Nixon*, p. 117.
87. Nixon, *Memoirs*, p. 112.
88. *Los Angeles Times*, 31 October 1952.
89. Nixon, *Memoirs*, p. 113.
90. Morris, *Richard Milhous Nixon*, Vol. I, p. 855.
91. Ibid.
92. ACTI, Patrick Hillings, interview with author, January 1990.
93. YLP, Hannah Nixon, note to RN.

Chapter 12: The Vice-Presidential Years 1953–1956

1. Nixon, *Memoirs*, pp. 87–8.
2. RN interview, Dulles Oral History Project; Mazo, *Richard Nixon*, p. 203.
3. FCO telegrams, 4, 8, 11 September 1953, PRO file 371/106954.
4. FCO telegram FZ 10345, 3 October 1953, PRO file 371/106954.
5. Sir Gerald Templer to Anthony Eden, 27 October 1953, PRO file 371/106954.
6. FCO telegram, 3 November 1953, PRO file 371/106954.
7. Parmet, *Richard Nixon and His America*, p. 315.
8. Nixon Eisenhower, *Pat Nixon*, p. 139.
9. ACTI, Rex Scouten, interview with author, September 1990.
10. Nixon, *Memoirs*, p. 132.
11. Ibid., p. 127.
12. Eisenhower Library, Eisenhower Letter to Syngman Rhee, 2 January 1954.
13. ACTI, Pat Nixon, interview with author, March 1992.
14. YLP, Eisenhower, letter to RN, 15 December 1953.
15. de Toledano, *One Man Alone*, p. 163.
16. Nixon, *Memoirs*, p. 149.
17. WLP, Box 29, p. 769.
18. *New York Times*, 14 March 1954.
19. Ibid.
20. Ibid.
21. Nixon, *Memoirs*, p. 146.
22. Thomas C. Reeves, *The Life and Times of Joe McCarthy* (Stein & Day, 1982), p. 578.

23. Nixon, *Memoirs*, p. 147.

24. WLP, Box 28, p. 819.

25. Ibid., p. 9.

26. Parmet, *Richard Nixon and His America*, p. 262.

27. Nixon, *Memoirs*, p. 159.

28. Ibid., p. 161.

29. Parmet, *Richard Nixon and His America*, p. 262.

30. WLP, Box 28, pp. 4, 31.

31. Nixon, *Memoirs*, p. 163.

32. Thomas Babington Macaulay, 'Horatius', *Lays of Ancient Rome*, (Longman, 1849).

33. Nixon Eisenhower, *Pat Nixon*, p. 151.

34. Pat Nixon personal papers; Nixon Eisenhower, *Pat Nixon*, p. 152.

35. Nixon, *Six Crises*, p. 132.

36. Ibid.

37. ACTI, William P. Rogers, interview with author, January 1991.

38. Nixon, *Six Crises*, pp. 143–4.

39. Nixon, *Memoirs*, p. 167.

40. Ibid.

41. Hughes, *The Ordeal of Power*, p. 317.

42. Mazo, *Richard Nixon*, p. 157.

43. Nixon, *Six Crises*, p. 158.

44. Nixon, *Memoirs*, p. 167.

45. Ibid.

46. Nixon, *Six Crises*, p. 160.

47. Ibid.

48. *New York Times*, 27 February 1956.

49. ACTI, Dorothy Cox Donnelly, interview with author, March 1990.

50. Public Papers of the President, 1956 (US Government Printing Office, 1958), pp. 287–9.

51. ACTI, Helene Drown, interview with author, December 1989.

52. Parmet, *Richard Nixon and His America*, p. 271.

53. Nixon, *Memoirs*, p. 171.

54. Dwight D. Eisenhower, *Waging Peace, 1956–1961* (Doubleday, 1965), p. 9.

55. Nixon, *Memoirs*, p. 172.

56. Ambrose, *Nixon*, Vol. I, p. 398.

57. Parmet, *Richard Nixon and His America*, pp. 279–80.

58. Nixon, *Memoirs*, p. 176.

59. RN handwritten note to Frank Gannon, January 1977; see also ACTI, Edward C. Nixon, interview with author, July 1990.

60. Nixon, *Memoirs*, p. 178.

61. Brodie, *Richard Nixon*, p. 357.

62. ACTI, RN to author, 18 September 1990.

63. Julian Amery papers, RN, letter to Julian Amery MP, 21 January 1987.

Chapter 13: The Vice-Presidential Years 1956–1960

1. William V. Shannon, 'Eisenhower as President', *Commentary*, November 1958, p. 290.

2. Wicker, *One of Us*, p. 178.

3. ACTI, James. D. Hughes, interview with author, June 1990.

4. YLP, Martin Luther King, letter to RN, 30 August 1957.

5. Nixon, *Memoirs*, p. 184.

6. Ibid.

7. *New York Times*, 28 November 1957.

8. White House Press Conference, 27 November 1957.

9. Nixon, *Six Crises*, p. 173.

10. Ibid., p. 175.

11. WLP, Box 27, p. 11.

12. Ibid., p. 19.

13. Nixon, *Six Crises*, p. 198.

14. Vernon A. Walters, *Silent Missions* (Doubleday, 1978), p. 323.

15. *Los Angeles Times*, 8 May 1958.

16. Nixon, *Six Crises*, p. 204.

17. Mazo, *Richard Nixon*, p. 231.

18. WLP, Box 27, p. 55.

19. ACTI, Vernon Walters quoting the letter in an interview with the author, August 1991.

20. Nixon, *Six Crises*, p. 219.

21. Walters, *Silent Missions*, p. 331.

22. ACTI, James D. Hughes, interview with author, June 1990.

23. Ibid.

24. *Los Angeles Times*, 30 April 1958.

25. Nixon, *Memoirs*, p. 199.

26. WLP, Box 27, p. 149.

27. Ibid., Box 28, p. 156.

28. Ibid., p. 162.

29. Ibid.

30. Mazo, *Richard Nixon,* p. 267.

31. *New Yorker,* 3 December 1958.

32. *New York Times,* 30 November 1958.

33. LN, Foreign Trip files, transcript of RN Guildhall speech, 28 November 1958.

34. State Department Telegram No. 2972, 2 December 1958; AP wire service report, 30 November 1958.

35. Jonathan Aitken personal papers, Selwyn Lloyd autobiography file S'Agaro 1962.

36. ACTI, James D. Hughes, letter to author, June 1990.

37. LN, RN, letter to Pat Hillings, 9 December 1958.

38. ACTI, Robert Carvel, letter to author, October 1988.

39. *Manchester Guardian,* 29 November 1958.

40. *London Daily Telegraph,* 29 November 1958.

41. *New York Times,* 30 November 1958.

42. LN, RN, letter to William S. White, 2 January 1959.

43. WLP, Box 28, p. 131.

44. Ibid., p. 111

45. Nixon, *Memoirs,* p. 207.

46. Ibid.

47. Nixon, *Memoirs,* p. 208.

48. *New York Times,* 25 July 1958.

49. WLP, Box 28, p. 131.

50. Ibid., p. 137.

51. ACTI, Donald Kendall, interview with author, September 1990.

52. Ibid.

53. William Safire, *Before the Fall: An Insider's View of the Pre-Watergate White House* (Da Capo Press, 1975) pp. 4–5.

54. ACTI, Harrison Salisbury, interview with author, July 1991.

55. *New York Times,* 25 July 1959.

56. Mazo, *Richard Nixon,* p. 191.

57. WLP, Box 28, p. 147.

58. Ibid.

59. Nixon, *Six Crises,* p. 261.

60. Nixon, *Memoirs,* p. 213.

61. ACTI, Boris Armanov, interview with author, January 1990.

62. WLP, Box 28, p. 276.

63. Ibid., p. 281.

64. Ibid., p. 282.

65. Nixon, *Six Crises,* p. 201.

66. ACTI, Elliot Richardson, interview with author, July 1991.

67. Ibid.

68. ACTI, Charles McWhorter, interview with author, September 1990.

69. Theodore H. White, *The Making of the President, 1960* (Jonathan Cape, 1962), p. 71.

70. Robert Rhodes James, *Rosebery: A Biography of Archibald Philip, Fifth Earl of Rosebery* (Weidenfeld and Nicolson; 1963), p. 31.

71. ACTI, Robert Finch, interview with author, September 1990.

72. Theodore H. White, *The Making of the President, 1968* (Jonathan Cape, 1969), p. 76.

73. Ambrose, *Nixon,* Vol. I, p. 540.

74. Selwyn Lloyd papers, Box 308.

75. ACTI, HVT, Folio 9, p. 87.

76. Ibid.

77. Ibid., pp. 62–3.

78. Ibid., p. 62.

79. Ibid., pp. 62–3.

80. *Wall Street Journal,* 4 January 1960.

81. WLP, Box 38, p. 2.

82. Parmet, *Richard Nixon and His American,* p. 386.

83. ACTI, RN, interview with author, July 1989.

84. FCO Telegram No. 417, 6 August 1960, PRO file 371/148578.

85. White, *The Making of the President, 1960,* pp. 198–9.

86. WLP, Box 38, p. 3.

87. Barry Goldwater, *With No Apologies* (William Morrow & Company Inc, 1979), p. 119.

88. ACTI, RN, letter to author, April 1989.

89. Nixon, *Six Crises,* pp. 440–1.

90. British Ambassador Telegram No. 417, 4 August 1960, PRO file, 371/148578.

Chapter 14: A Tale of Two Defeats

1. Nixon, *Memoirs,* pp. 224–5.

2. Nixon, *Six Crises,* p. 326.

3. Ibid.

4. ACTI, HVT, Folio 8, p. 48.

5. White, *The Making of the President, 1960,* p. 286.

6. Ibid., p. 285.

7. C. David Heymann, *A Woman Named Jackie* (Heinemann, 1989), p. 242.

8. White, *The Making of the President, 1960*, p. 286.

9. FCO Telegram, British Embassy Washington, 29 September 1960, PRO file F0371/148588.

10. WLP, Box 8, p. 9, Note of conversation with Keith Funston and others.

11. FCO Telegram, British Embassy Washington, 29 September 1960, PRO file FO371/148583.

12. Brodie, *Richard Nixon*, p. 454.

13. *New York Times*, 12 September 1960.

14. ACTI, Peter Flanigan, interview with author, March 1991.

15. Ibid.

16. Ibid.

17. Safire, *Before the Fall*, p. 49.

18. WLP, Box 17, p. 30.

19. Brodie, *Richard Nixon*, p. 431.

20. Herbert S. Parmet, *JFK: The Presidency of John F. Kennedy* (Dial Press, 1983), p. 55.

21. ACTI, HVT, Folio 8, p. 60.

22. Seaton papers, transcript of Henry Cabot Lodge's TV remarks, 16 October 1960.

23. Seaton papers, Nixon statement, 13 September 1960.

24. ACTI, Margery Peterson Acker, interview with author, July 1990.

25. Nixon made this observation privately to many people, including the author.

26. ACTI, HVT, Folio 12, p. 4.

27. Stephen E. Ambrose, *Eisenhower*, Vol. II, *The President* (Simon & Schuster, 1984), p. 597.

28. Theodore Sorenson, *Kennedy* (Harper and Row, 1965) p. 217.

29. WLP, RN record of conversation with George Humphrey, 31 October 1962.

30. Ambrose, *Eisenhower*, Vol. II, pp. 600–1.

31. LN, Transcript of first Nixon/Kennedy television debate, 27 September 1960.

32. WLP, Box 8, p. 37.

33. Nixon, *Memoirs*, p. 221.

34. White, *The Making of the President, 1960*, p. 309.

35. Ibid.

36. WLP, Box 8, p. 37.

37. Nixon, *Memoirs*, p. 222.

38. Ibid.

39. F.E. Smith quoted in Lord Beaverbrook, *Men and Power, 1917–1918* (Hutchinson, 1956), p. 13.

40. ACTI, Clara Jane Nixon, interview with author, July 1990.

41. Brodie, *Richard Nixon*, pp. 436–7.

42. ACTI, Mary McGrory, interview with author, July 1991.

43. ACTI, Harrison Salisbury, interview with author, July 1991.

44. White, *The Making of The President, 1960*, p. 338.

45. LN, transcripts of election speeches.

46. ACTI, James D. Hughes, interview with author, March 1990.

47. Ibid.

48. Nixon, *Six Crises*, p. 385.

49. Ibid., p. 389.

50. Ibid., p. 392.

51. Earl Mazo and Stephen Hess, *Nixon: A Political Portrait* (Macdonald and Company, 1968), p. 248.

52. Nixon, *Memoirs*, p. 224.

53. Ben Bradlee, *Conversations with Kennedy* (W.W. Norton, 1975), p. 33.

54. Mazo and Hess, *Nixon*, p. 248.

55. ACTI, Robert Finch, interview with author, July 1990.

56. ACTI, HVT, Folio 8, pp. 65–6, 71.

57. Mazo and Hess, *Nixon*, p. 249.

58. Nixon, *Six Crises*, p. 407.

59. ACTI, HVT, Folio 8, p. 72.

60. Nixon, *Six Crises*, p. 416.

61. ACTI, Dorothy Cox Donnelly, interview with author, January 1990.

62. John F. Kennedy Inaugural Address, 20 January 1961.

63. ACTI, HVT, Folio 8, p. 74.

64. Nixon, *Memoirs*, pp. 227–8.

65. ACTI, Rose Mary Woods, interview with author, September 1990.

66. ACTI, HVT, Folio 12, p. 18.

67. WLP, Box 14, RN dictated notes, p. 2.

68. YLP, 20 April 1961.

69. WLP, Box 33, RN notes of conversation with President Kennedy, 20 April 1961.

70. Nixon, *Memoirs*, p. 234.

71. Ibid., p. 235.

72. Ibid.

73. Ibid., p. 221.

74. WLP, Box 33, RN notes of conversation with President Kennedy, 20 April 1961.

75. YLP, statement of net worth, June 1962.

76. Ibid.

77. ACTI, Richard Moore, interview with author, May 1991.

78. Eisenhower Library, RN, letter to Eisenhower, 20 February 1962.

79. ACTI, RN interview with author, March 1990.

80. Nixon, *Memoirs,* p. 237.

81. LN, RN, letter to MacKinnon, 8 August 1961.

82. Nixon, *In the Arena,* p. 44 and passim.

83. Adela St. Johns quoted in Brodie, *Nixon,* p. 451.

84. Nixon, *Memoirs,* p. 240.

85. Nixon Eisenhower, *Pat Nixon,* p. 208.

86. LN, RN, statement to Californian Republic Assembly, March 1962.

87. *New York Herald Tribune,* 26 October 1965.

88. WLP, Box 18.

89. Parmet, *Richard Nixon and His America,* p. 424.

90. ACTI, Edmund G. Brown, interview with author, September 1991.

91. Nixon, *Memoirs,* pp. 242–3.

92. Parmet, *Richard Nixon and His America,* pp. 407–8.

93. WLP, Box 18.

94. ACTI, H.R. Haldeman, interview with author, January 1990; transcript of Leone Baxter's Deposition to California Supreme Court, Case No. 526150.

95. ACTI, H.R. Haldeman, interview with author, January 1990.

96. Ibid.

97. Ibid.

98. Nixon Eisenhower, *Pat Nixon,* p. 211.

99. Herbert Klein, *Making It Perfectly Clear* (Doubleday, 1980), p. 55.

100. Nixon, *Memoirs,* p. 244.

101. *Los Angeles Times,* 8 November 1962.

102. Ibid.

103. *Washington Star,* 9 November 1962.

104. Nixon Eisenhower, *Pat Nixon,* p. 215.

105. *Time,* 16 November 1962.

Chapter 15: The Wilderness Years 1963–1967

1. Safire, *Before the Fall,* p. 21.

2. ACTI, Pat Hillings, interview with author, April 1991.

3. Tom Evans, *Nixon Mudge Rose,* unpublished ms, p. 119.

4. Ibid., p. 122.

5. ACTI, Thomas Evans, interview with author, October 1990.

6. Evans, *Nixon Mudge Rose,* p. 3.

7. Ibid., p. 121.

8. ACTI, Leonard Garment, interview with author, October 1990.

9. Evans, *Nixon Mudge Rose,* p. 122.

10. ACTI, Leonard Garment, interview with author, October 1990.

11. Ibid.

12. ACTI, Jerome Hellman, correspondence and interview with author, December 1990.

13. Evans, *Nixon Mudge Rose,* p. 130.

14. Leonard Garment, 'The Hill Case', *New Yorker,* 17 April 1989, p. 93.

15. *Washington Post,* 28 April 1966.

16. Garment, 'The Hill Case', p. 93.

17. Ibid.

18. Bruce Allen Murphy, *Fortas: The Rise and Ruin of a Supreme Court Justice* (William Morrow & Company Inc, 1988), p. 196.

19. Garment, 'The Hill Case' p. 93.

20. Ibid., p. 104.

21. Evans, *Nixon Mudge Rose,* p. 136.

22. Garment, 'The Hill Case', p. 94.

23. Ibid., pp. 94–5.

24. *Dallas Morning News,* 22 November 1963.

25. ACTI, RN interview with author, September 1990.

26. YLP, RN, letter to Jacqueline Kennedy, 23 November 1964.

27. ACTI, Patrick Hillings, interview with author, March 1991.

28. YLP, Jacqueline Kennedy, undated letter to RN.

29. ACTI, HVT, Folio 12, p. 96.

30. Ibid., p. 24.

31. Ibid.

32. Ibid., p. 97.

33. ACTI, Vernon Walters, interview with author, August 1991.

34. ACTI, RN memorandum to author, 24 September 1990.

35. Evans, *Nixon Mudge Rose,* pp. 138–9.

36. Nixon, *Memoirs,* p. 260.

37. ACTI, HVT, Folio 12, p. 40.

38. ACTI, Patrick Hillings, interview with author, March 1991.

39. White, *The Making of the President, 1968*, p. 48.

40. YLP, RN memorandum to H.R. Haldeman, 30 November 1970.

41. ACTI, HVT, Folio 12, p. 50.

42. Ibid., p. 51.

43. ACTI, John Sears, interview with author, September 1990.

44. *New York Times,* 7 November 1966.

45. Jules, Witcover, *The Resurrection of Richard Nixon* (G.P. Putnam's Sons, 1970), p. 131.

46. Stephen E. Ambrose, *Nixon*, Vol. II, *The Triumph of a Politician, 1962–1972* (Simon & Schuster, 1989), p. 86.

47. *New York Times,* 28 October 1966.

48. ACTI, Charles McWhorter, interview with author, September 1990.

49. *New York Times,* 7 November 1966.

50. White House Press Conference, 4 November 1966.

51. Safire, *Before the Fall*, p. 39 [emphasis in original].

52. *New York Times,* 7 November 1966.

53. ACTI, RN interview with author, 4 January 1991.

54. ACTI, Nicholas Ruwe, interview with author, December 1988.

55. ACTI, John Sears, interview with author, September 1990.

56. ACTI, HVT, Folio 12, p. 53.

57. ACTI, RN, interview with author, 4 January 1991.

58. ACTI, Robert Ellsworth, interview with author, January 1991.

59. *Newsweek,* 6 June 1967.

60. *New York Times,* 5 July 1967.

61. ACTI, Selwyn Lloyd in conversation with author, July 1967.

62. ACTI, RN, interview with author, 4 January 1991.

63. Richard Nixon, 'Asia After Viet Nam', *Foreign Affairs*, October 1967.

64. ACTI, RN, memorandum to author, 24 September 1990.

65. Ibid.

66. *New York Times,* 5 September 1967.

67. Nixon Eisenhower, *Pat Nixon*, p. 233.

68. ACTI, Charles E. Colson, interview with author, August 1991.

69. ACTI, Thomas Evans, interview with author, September 1990.

70. Unattributable comment to author, January 1991.

71. ACTI, William P. Rogers, interview with author, January 1991.

72. ACTI, RN memorandum to author, 29 May 1991.

73. Witcover, *The Resurrection of Richard Nixon*, p. 52.

74. Charles de Gaulle, *The Edge of the Sword*, (Faber & Faber, 1960) p. 34. RN's personal copy with these annotations can be found in the Richard Nixon Library and Birthplace, Yorba Linda, California.

75. Ibid., p. 53.

76. Ibid.

77. RN's copy of *Great Contemporaries* can be found in the replica of the Lincoln sitting room of the White House re-created in the Richard Nixon Library and Birthplace, Yorba Linda, California.

78. Nixon, *In the Arena*, p. 89.

79. ACTI, RN memorandum to author, 29 May 1991.

80. ACTI, Thomas Evans, interview with author, September 1990.

81. ACTI, RN memorandum to author, 29 May 1991.

82. Ibid.

83. Nixon, *Memoirs*, p. 288.

84. ACTI, HVT, Folio 12, p. 59.

85. Ibid., pp. 58–9.

86. ACTI, Robert Abplanalp, interview with author, March 1991.

87. Ibid.

88. ACTI, George Smathers, interview with author, December 1991.

89. Witcover, *The Resurrection of Richard Nixon*, p. 38.

90. ACTI, Robert Abplanalp, interview with author, March 1991.

91. ACTI, Patrick Hillings, interview with author, March 1991.

92. Wicker, *One of Us*, p. 392.

93. Ibid.

94. Ibid.

95. Ibid.

96. Ibid., p. 393.

97. ACTI, Jack Dreyfus, interview with author, December 1990.

98. Ibid.

99. Ibid.

100. Wicker, *One of Us*, p. 393.

101. Nixon, *In the Arena*, p. 128.

102. Henry Kissinger, *White House Years* (Little, Brown & Co., 1979), pp. 498, 1155, etc.

103. ACTI, HVT, Folio 12, pp. 148–9.

104. Ibid., p. 66.

105. Ibid.

106. Ibid., p. 68.

Chapter 16: 1968

1. Doris Kearns quoted in William H. Chafe, *The Unfinished Journey: America Since World War II* (Oxford University Press, 1985), p. 360; Wicker, *One of Us*, p. 316.
2. Wicker, *One of Us*, p. 317.
3. Ibid., p. 319.
4. Lewis Chester, Godfrey Hodgson and Bruce Page, *An American Melodrama* (Viking Press, 1969), p. 146.
5. Ibid.
6. ACTI, Robert Ellsworth, interview with author, January 1991. Also confirmed by Senator Strom Thurmond, ACTI, Strom Thurmond, interview with author, September 1992.
7. *New York Times*, 6 March 1968.
8. Parmet, *Richard Nixon and His America*, p. 508.
9. ACTI, Nicholas Ruwe, interview with author, September 1988.
10. White, *The Making of The President, 1968*, p. 134.
11. Evans, *Nixon, Mudge, Rose*, p. 155.
12. White, *The Making of The President, 1968*, p. 134.
13. ACTI, Dwight Chapin, interview with author, September 1988.
14. ACTI, H.R. Haldeman, interview with author, November 1991.
15. Satire, *Before The Fall*, p. 278.
16. Nixon, *Memoirs*, p. 309.
17. ACTI, Nicholas Ruwe, interview with author, May 1988.
18. ACTI, Robert Finch, interview with author, July 1990.
19. Nixon, *Memoirs*, p. 312.
20. Witcover, *The Resurrection of Richard Nixon*, p. 350.
21. ACTI, HVT, Folio 12, pp. 132–4.
22. Ibid.
23. ACTI, Alice Roosevelt Longworth, interview with author for ITV documentary 'The Reporters', 1969.
24. *New York Times*, 10 August 1968.
25. Ibid.
26. Chester, Hodgson and Page, *An American Melodrama*, p. 583.
27. Nixon, *Memoirs*, p. 317.
28. White, *The Making of The President, 1968*, p. 298.
29. *New York Times*, 10 August 1963.
30. Wills, *Nixon Agonistes*, p. 49.
31. Chester, Hodgson and Page, *An American Melodrama*, pp. 282–3.

32. Ibid., p. 283; Wills, *Nixon Agonistes,* pp. 50–1.

33. Wicker, *One of Us,* p. 362.

34. Witcover, *The Resurrection of Richard Nixon,* p. 414.

35. Ibid., p. 313.

36. ACTI, Harrison Salisbury, interview with author, July 1991.

37. Clark Clifford, *Counsel to the President: A Memoir* (Random House Inc, 1991), p. 574.

38. Ibid., pp. 575–6.

39. Ibid., p. 576.

40. Wicker, *One of Us,* p. 339.

41. ACTI, RN memorandum to author, 29 May 1991.

42. White, *The Making of The President, 1968,* p. 379.

43. *New York Times,* 3 November 1968.

44. Parmet, *Richard Nixon and His America,* p. 521.

45. ACTI, RN memorandum to author, 29 May 1991.

46. Ibid.

47. ACTI, Patrick Hillings, interview with author, March 1991.

48. White, *The Making of The President, 1968,* p. 379.

49. Ibid., p. 381.

50. *Washington Post,* 6 November 1968.

51. ACTI, RN memorandum to author, 29 May 1991.

52. ACTI, Dwight Chapin, interview with author, March 1991.

53. *New York Times,* 7 November 1968.

54. Safire, *Before The Fall,* pp. 93–4.

55. Wills, *Nixon Agonistes,* p. 54.

56. ACTI, Benjamin Bradlee, interview with author, July 1991.

57. ACTI, James Humes, interview with author, July 1991.

58. ACTI, John Freeman, interview with author, July 1991.

59. ACTI, James D. Hughes, interview with author, March 1990.

60. *New York Times,* 21 January 1969.

Chapter 17: The Peaks and Valleys of the Presidency

1. Machiavelli, 'A Prince's Personal Staff' *The Prince,* (Dent, 1908).

2. ACTI, Charles Lichenstein, interview with author, July 1991.

3. ACTI, John Ehrlichman, interview with author, January 1992.

4. Nixon, *Memoirs,* p. 342.

5. ACTI, Daniel P. Moynihan, interview with author, July 1991.

6. Wordsworth, 'The Revolution as it Appeared to Enthusiasts' in Thomas Hutchinson, ed., *Wordsworth's Poetical Works,* (Oxford University Press, 1904).

7. ACTI, Daniel P. Moynihan, interview with author, September 1991; Moynihan papers, memorandum to President Nixon, 4 December 1970.

8. Nixon, *Memoirs,* p. 425.

9. Daniel P. Moynihan, letter to Anthony Lewis, 10 June 1991.

10. NPMP, Moynihan, memorandum to the President, 30 November 1970.

11. Satire, *Before the Fall,* p. 342.

12. ACTI, H.R. Haldeman, interview with author, November 1991.

13. ACTI, Benjamin Bradlee, interview with author, July 1991.

14. Ibid.

15. Safire, *Before the Fall,* p. 341.

16. Martin Gilbert, *Winston S. Churchill,* Vol. VI: *Finest Hour* (Heinemann, 1983), p. 317.

17. Nixon, *Memoirs,* p. 341.

18. Kissinger, *White House Years,* p. 11.

19. Nixon, *Memoirs,* p. 341.

20. Kissinger, *White House Years,* p. 93.

21. ACTI, H.R. Haldeman, interview with author, November 1991.

22. Kissinger, *White House Years,* p. 95; Nixon, *Memoirs,* p. 371.

23. ACTI, John Ehrlichman, interview with author, January 1992.

24. ACTI, David Bruce, anecdote to author, *c.* 1975.

25. ACTI, Ron Walker, interview with author, September 1991.

26. Kissinger, *White House Years,* p. 95.

27. Nixon, *Memoirs,* p. 372.

28. ACTI, John Freeman, interview with author, July 1991.

29. ACTI, Elliot Richardson, interview with author, July 1991.

30. ACTI, unattributable interview with author, July 1991.

31. Wicker, *One of Us,* p. 432.

32. Ibid., pp. 431–2.

33. John Ehrlichman, *Witness to Power: The Nixon Years* (Simon & Schuster, 1982), pp. 209–10n.

34. Kissinger, *White House Years,* p. 12.

35. H.R. Haldeman, Hofstra Conference, 1987.

36. Nixon, *Memoirs,* p. 374.

37. Garment, 'The Hill Case', 17 April 1989.

38. Parmet, *Richard Nixon and His America,* p. 566.

39. Ibid.

40. Nixon, *Memoirs,* p. 392.

41. Ibid., p. 402.

42. *Washington Post,* 7 October 1969.

43. James Kilpatrick syndicated column, *Baltimore Sun* et al, 14 October 1969.

44. Nixon, *Memoirs,* p. 403.

45. ACTI, Robert Thompson, interview with author, May 1991; Nixon, *Memoirs,* p. 404.

46. ACTI, Robert Thompson, interview with author, May 1991.

47. Nixon, *Memoirs,* p. 405.

48. ACTI, Robert Thompson, interview with author, May 1991.

49. Public Papers of the President, 1969, pp. 901–3.

50. Ambrose, *Nixon,* Vol. II, p. 310.

51. Parmet, *Richard Nixon and His America,* pp. 581–2.

52. Nixon, *Memoirs,* p. 409.

53. Thompson papers, Robert Thompson, Report on Visit to Vietnam, 28 October 25–November 1969.

54. Parmet, *Richard Nixon and His America,* p. 606.

55. Ibid., p. 608.

56. Ehrlichman, *Witness to Power,* p. 122.

57. Ambrose, *Nixon,* Vol. II, p. 330.

58. Wicker, *One of Us,* p. 497.

59. Ehrlichman, *Witness to Power,* p. 126.

60. *New York Times,* 10 April 1970.

61. Ibid.

62. ACTI, John Ehrlichman, interview with author, January 1992.

63. Ibid.

64. Wicker, *One of Us,* p. 506.

65. Martin Anderson at the Hofstra Conference, 1987.

66. State of the Union Message, 1970.

67. John Whittaker at the Hofstra Conference, 1987.

68. Ibid.

69. ACTI, John Ehrlichman, interview with author, January 1992.

70. Ibid.

71. Nixon, *Memoirs,* p. 521.

72. Safire, *Before the Fall,* pp. 470–1.

73. Nixon, *Memoirs,* p. 448.

74. Ibid., p. 450.

75. Ibid., p. 449.

76. *New York Times,* 30 April 1970.

77. Ibid.

78. Nixon, *Memoirs,* p. 454.

79. Ibid., p. 457.

80. ACTI, Raymond Price, interview with author, September 1990.

81. ACTI, Arnold A. Hutschnecker, interview with author, September 1991.

82. Personal Papers of the President, 1970, p. 411.

83. Nixon, *Memoirs,* p. 457.

84. Ibid., p. 459.

85. NPMP, memorandum of events, 8–9 May 1970.

86. ACTI, HVT, Folio 23, p. 93.

87. ACTI, Egil Krogh, interview with author, September 1991.

88. NPMP, memorandum of events, 8–9 May 1970.

89. Ibid.

90. Safire, *Before the Fall,* p. 207.

91. ACTI, HVT, Folio 19, pp. 174–5; NPMP, memorandum of events, 8–9 May 1970.

92. NPMP, memorandum of events, 8–9 May 1970.

93. Safire, *Before The Fall,* pp. 209–10.

94. Parmet, *Richard Nixon and His America,* p. 13.

95. Safire, *Before the Fall,* pp. 210–11.

96. ACTI, Egil Krogh, interview with author, September 1991.

97. H.R. Haldeman, *The Ends of Power* (New York Times Books, 1978), p. 107.

98. Thompson papers, report to the President on South Vietnam by Sir Robert Thompson, 12 October 1970.

99. ACTI, H.R. Haldeman, interview with author, November 1991.

100. Stanley I. Kutler, *The Wars of Watergate: The Last Crisis of Richard Nixon* (Alfred A. Knopf Inc, 1990), pp. 123–25.

101. ACTI, H.R. Haldeman, interview with author, November 1991.

102. US House of Representatives, Committee on the Judiciary: Impeachment Hearings, Statement of Information Book VII, Part 4, p. 1754.

103. Haldeman, *The Ends of Power,* p. 107.

104. Nixon, *Memoirs,* p. 475.

105. NPMP, RN, memorandum to Haldeman, 16 June 1969.

106. ACTI, John Ehrlichman, interview with author, January 1992.

107. ACTI, Raymond Price, interview with author, January 1992.

108. Theodore H. White, *Breach of Faith: The Fall of Richard Nixon* (Atheneum, 1975), p. 142.

109. ACTI, Charles E. Colson, interview with author, September 1991.

110. Ibid.

111. Ibid.

112. Ibid.

113. ACTI, John Ehrlichman, interview with author, January 1992.

114. Ibid.

115. Len Colodny and Robert Gettlin, *Silent Coup: The Removal of a President* (Victor Gollancz, 1991), p. 97.

116. ACTI, G. Gordon Liddy, interview with author, January 1992.

117. ACTI, H.R. Haldeman, interview with author, May 1992.

118. Colodny and Gettlin, *Silent Coup,* p. 104.

119. ACTI, Charles E. Colson, interview with author, January 1990.

120. Nixon, *Memoirs,* p. 508.

121. ACTI, H.R. Haldeman, interview with author, January 1990.

122. Haldeman, *The Ends of Power,* p. 110.

123. NPMP, Ehrlichman's notes of meeting, 17 June 1971.

124. Seymour M. Hersch, *The Price of Power: Kissinger in the Nixon White House* (Summit Books, 1983) 5 PP- 384-5-

125. Haldeman, *The Ends of Power,* p. 112.

126. ACTI, Egil Krogh, interview with author, September 1991.

127. ACTI, David Young, interview with author, February 1992.

128. Ibid.

129. J. Anthony Lukas, *Nightmare: The Underside of the Nixon Years* (Viking Press, 1976), p. 94.

130. ACTI, Egil Krogh, interview with author, September 1991.

131. ACTI, David Young, interview with author, February 1992.

132. ACTI, Egil Krogh, interview with author, September 1991.

133. Ibid.

134. ACTI, David Young, interview with author, February 1992.

135. Nixon, *Memoirs,* p. 514.

136. ACTI, Benjamin Bradlee, interview with author, September 1991.

137. Nixon, *Memoirs,* p. 514.

Chapter 18: Peace Making and Election Winning

1. ACTI, RN, interview with author, July 1991.

2. ACTI, Alexander M. Haig, interview with author, January 1992.

3. Kissinger at the Hofstra Conference, 1987.
4. Raymond Price, *With Nixon* (Viking Press, 1977), p. 34.
5. ACTI, RN, interview with author, July 1991.
6. C.L. Sulzberger at the Hofstra Conference, 1987.
7. Kissinger, *White House Years*, p. 734.
8. ACTI, Donald Kendall, interview with author, November 1990.
9. White House Press Office transcript, 6 July 1971.
10. Ibid.
11. Nixon, *Memoirs*, p. 544.
12. Ibid., p. 554.
13. Jonathan Aitken personal papers, diary entry 1 July 1971, Harold Macmillan in conversation with author and other British Members of Parliament at The Carlton Club.
14. Nixon, *Memoirs*, p. 558.
15. Ibid., p. 559.
16. ACTI, Harrison Salisbury, interview with author, July 1991.
17. Nixon, *Memoirs*, p. 562.
18. Ibid.
19. Ibid., p. 579.
20. The Hofstra Conference, 1987.
21. Kissinger, *White House Years*, p. 129.
22. Nixon, *Memoirs*, pp. 369–70.
23. Ibid., pp. 406–7.
24. Ibid., p. 418.
25. Parmet, *Richard Nixon and His America*, p. 623.
26. Kissinger, *White House Years*, p. 737.
27. Ibid., p. 712.
28. Nixon, *Memoirs*, p. 601.
29. Kissinger, *White House Years*, p. 1185.
30. Public Papers of the President, 1972, pp. 583–7.
31. *New York Times*, 10 May 1972.
32. Nixon, *Memoirs*, p. 606.
33. ACTI, Dimitri Simes, interview with author July 1991 (Dimitri Simes was present at the Zakharov party and overheard Brezhnev's comment).
34. Nixon, *Memoirs*, p. 619.
35. ACTI, Dimitri Simes, interview with author, July 1991.
36. Nixon, *Memoirs*, p. 613.
37. Safire, *Before the Fall*, p. 448.

38. Ibid.

39. Kissinger, *White House Years,* p. 1227.

40. Safire, *Before the Fall,* p. 451.

41. Kissinger, *White House Years,* p. 1233.

42. The Hofstra Conference, 1987.

43. Nixon, *Memoirs,* pp. 588–9.

44. Ibid., p. 653.

45. Ehrlichman, *Witness to Power,* pp. 327–8.

46. White, *The Making of the President, 1972,* p. 279, attributed to Jesse Unruh of California.

47. ACTI, H.R. Haldeman, interview with author, November 1991.

48. ACTI, Robert Odle, interview with author, July 1991.

49. *Miami Herald,* 18 June 1972.

50. Nixon, *Memoirs,* p. 626.

51. Ibid., p. 646.

52. White, *The Making of the President, 1972,* p. 202.

53. WLP, RN letter to Terry Eagleton, 2 August 1972.

54. Nixon, *Memoirs,* p. 668.

55. *Washington Post,* 10 October 1972.

56. Nixon, *Memoirs,* p. 709.

57. ACTI, George McGovern, interview with author, January 1991.

58. Nixon, *Memoirs,* p. 710.

59. ACTI, HVT, Folio 8, p. 39.

60. NPMP, White House tape, 15 September 1972.

61. ACTI, H.R. Haldeman, interview with author, May 1992.

62. ACTI, H.R. Haldeman, interview with author, November 1991.

63. Ibid.

64. Charles Colson, *Born Again* (Chosen Books, 1976), p. 45.

65. Nixon, *Memoirs,* p. 689.

66. Kissinger, *White House Years,* p. 1351.

67. Nixon, *Memoirs,* p. 691.

68. Kissinger, *White House Years,* p. 1352.

69. Ibid., pp. 1345–6.

70. Nixon, *Memoirs,* p. 692.

71. Ibid., p. 691.

72. Kissinger, *White House Years,* p. 1368–9.

73. Nixon, *Memoirs,* p. 697.

74. Ibid., p. 705.

75.   Ibid., p. 707.

76.   Ambrose, *Nixon*, Vol. II, p. 631.

77.   Nixon, *Memoirs*, p. 718.

78.   Ibid., p. 733.

79.   Ibid., p. 734.

80.   Ibid., p. 736.

81.   Nixon, *Memoirs*, p. 734.

82.   Kissinger, *White House Years*, p. 1454.

83.   Ibid., p. 1464.

84.   Nixon, *Memoirs*, p. 747.

85.   Kissinger, *White House Years*, p. 1469.

86.   Ibid; Nixon, *Memoirs*, pp. 749–50.

87.   Safire, *Before the Fall*, p. 161.

88.   Ehrlichman, *Witness to Power*, p. 307.

89.   Oriana Fallaci, *La Stampa*, 16 November 1972.

90.   Ehrlichman, *Witness to Power*, p. 314.

91.   NPMP, White House tape, 5 January 1973.

92.   Colson, *Born Again*, p. 80.

93.   ACTI, RN, interview with author, July 1991.

94.   ACTI, RN, memorandum to author, 30 September, 1991.

95.   Ibid.

96.   Ibid.

97.   Ibid.

98.   Ibid.

Chapter 19: Watergate and Resignation

1.   Ambrose, *Nixon*, Vol. II, p. 562.

2.   ACTI, Robert Abplanalp, interview with author, March 1991.

3.   ACTI, Charles G. Rebozo, interview with author, September 1991.

4.   ACTI, Charles E. Colson, interview with author, January 1992.

5.   Bruce Oudes, *From the President: Richard Nixon's Secret Files* (Harper & Row, 1989), p. 202.

6.   Colodny and Gettlin, *Silent Coup*, p. 106.

7.   Ibid., pp. 106–7.

8.   Ibid., p. 124.

9.   Ibid., p. 125.

10.   Ibid., p. 159.

11.   ACTI, G. Gordon Liddy, interview with author, January 1992.

12. Nixon, *Memoirs*, p. 635.

13. Haldeman, *The Ends of Power*, p. 217.

14. NPMP, White House tape, 23 June 1972.

15. US Senate, Select Committee on Presidential Campaign Activities, Watergate Investigation, Hearings, Book 9 (Government Printing Office, 1974).

16. Haldeman, *The Ends of Power*, p. 30.

17. Ibid.

18. Ibid., p. 31.

19. Nixon, *Memoirs*, p. 6.

20. NPMP, White House tape, 23 June 1972.

21. Haldeman, *The Ends of Power*, p. 38.

22. White, *Breach of Faith*, p. 165.

23. Colodny and Gettlin, *Silent Coup*, p. 217.

24. NPMP, White House tape, 15 September 1972.

25. Ibid.

26. Kutler, *The Wars of Watergate*, p. 230.

27. John W. Dean III, *Blind Ambition: The White House Years* (Simon & Schuster, 1976), p. 142.

28. Speaker Carl Albert interview, US Capitol Historical Society, 5 October, 1976.

29. Nixon, *Memoirs*, p. 773.

30. ACTI, Howard Baker, interview with author, September 1991.

31. Ibid.

32. Kutler, *The Wars of Watergate*, p. 257.

33. ACTI, Howard Liebengood, interview with author, September 1991.

34. NPMP, White House tape, 28 February 1973.

35. Nixon, *Memoirs*, pp. 779–80.

36. NPMP, White House tape, 13 March 1973.

37. Nixon, *Memoirs*, p. 783 [emphasis in original].

38. ACTI, Egil Krogh, interview with author, September 1991.

39. Nixon, *Memoirs*, p. 789.

40. White, *Breach of Faith*, p. 199.

41. NPMP, White House tape, 21 March 1973.

42. Nixon, *Memoirs*, p. 793.

43. NPMP, White House tape, 21 March 1973.

44. ACTI, John Ehrlichman, interview with author, January 1992.

45. NPMP, White House tape, 22 March 1973.

46. Nixon, *Memoirs*, p. 806.

47.   Dean, *Blind Ambition,* p. 212.

48.   Nixon, *Memoirs,* p. 827.

49.   Ibid., p. 832.

50.   Haldeman, *The Ends of Power,* p. 293; Nixon, *Memoirs,* pp. 846–7.

51.   Ehrlichman, *Witness to Power,* p. 390.

52.   Nixon, *Memoirs,* p. 848.

53.   Public Papers of the President, 1973, pp. 328–33.

54.   Macaulay on John Bunyan, 1830.

55.   *Washington Post,* 17 May 1973.

56.   White, *Breach of Faith,* p. 234.

57.   *New York Times,* 26 June, 1973.

58.   ACTI, Howard Baker, interview with author, September 1991.

59.   ACTI, Howard Liebengood, interview with author, October 1991.

60.   Nixon, *Memoirs,* p. 893 [emphasis in original].

61.   ACTI, Rose Mary Woods, interview with author, January 1992.

62.   ACTI, Robert Finch, interview with author, July 1990.

63.   ACTI, H.R. Haldeman, interview with author, November 1991.

64.   Nixon, *Memoirs,* p. 755.

65.   ACTI, Donald Kendall, interview with author, September 1990.

66.   NPMP, Haldeman's notes, 9 February 1971.

67.   ACTI, Lord Home, interview with author, May 1989.

68.   Haldeman, *The Ends of Power,* pp. 203–5.

69.   ACTI, Richard Helms, interview with author, September 1991.

70.   ACTI, Samuel Dash, interview with author, January 1992.

71.   ACTI, Leonard Garment, interview with author, January 1992.

72.   ACTI, Alexander Haig, interview with author, January 1992.

73.   Ibid.

74.   ACTI, Leonard Garment, interview with author, January 1992.

75.   Nixon, *Memoirs,* p. 900.

76.   ACTI, Leonard Garment, interview with author, January 1992.

77.   Ibid.

78.   ACTI, Alexander Haig, interview with author, January 1992.

79.   Ibid.

80.   Nixon, *Memoirs,* p. 903.

81.   ACTI, Alexander Haig, interview with author, January 1992.

82.   ACTI, Elliot Richardson, interview with author, September 1991.

83.   Ibid.

84.   ACTI, HVT Folio 23, pp. 23–4.

85. Nixon, *Memoirs,* p. 904.
86. *New York Times,* 1 May 1973.
87. Nixon, *Memoirs,* p. 912.
88. ACTI, Elliot Richardson, interview with author, September 1991.
89. ACTI, HVT Folio 12, pp. 135–6.
90. ACTI, Herbert Brownell, interview with author, January 1991.
91. ACTI, Alexander Haig, interview with author, January 1992.
92. Nixon, *Memoirs,* p. 922.
93. Kissinger, *Years of Upheaval,* pp. 514–16.
94. Nixon, *Memoirs,* pp. 926–7 [emphasis in the original].
95. ACTI, HVT Folio 12, p. 31.
96. Stephen E. Ambrose, *Nixon,* Vol. III, *Ruin and Recovery, 1973–1990* (Simon & Schuster, 1991) p. 238.
97. Nixon, *Memoirs,* p. 929.
98. ACTI, Alexander Haig, interview with author, January 1992.
99. ACTI, Elliot Richardson, interview with author, September 1991.
100. Nixon, *Memoirs,* pp. 933–4.
101. Ibid., p. 934.
102. ACTI, Elliot Richardson, interview with author, September 1991.
103. Ibid.
104. Roger Morris, *Haig: The General's Progress* (Seaview Books, 1982), p. 251.
105. Nixon, *Memoirs,* p. 935.
106. Author's diary, 21 October 1973.
107. Nixon, *Memoirs,* p. 935.
108. Ibid., p. 945.
109. Ibid. p. 949.
110. *Washington Post,* 8 November 1973.
111. Bob Woodward and Carl Bernstein, *All the President's Men* (Quartet Books, 1974), p. 333.
112. ACTI, Charles S. Rhyne, interview with author, January 1992.
113. Ibid; ACTI, Rose Mary Woods, interview with author, January 1992.
114. Nixon, *Memoirs,* pp. 974–5.
115. *Washington Post,* 7 August 1973.
116. Nixon, *Memoirs,* p. 957.
117. Ambrose, *Nixon,* Vol. III, p. 329.
118. Ibid., p. 328–9.
119. Ibid., p. 329.
120. Nixon, *Memoirs,* p. 1044.

121. Ibid., p. 1050.

122. Ibid., p. 1051.

123. Ibid., p. 1056.

124. ACTI, Alexander Haig, interview with author, January 1992.

125. ACTI, HVT Folio 23, p. 69 and passim.

126. Ibid., p. 68.

127. Nixon, *Memoirs*, p. 1062.

128. ACTI, HVT Folio 23, p. 92.

129. ACTI, James Schlesinger, interview with author, October 1991.

130. ACTI, Alexander Haig, interview with author, January 1992.

131. ACTI, HVT Folio 23, p. 84.

132. Ibid., p. 78.

133. Ibid., p. 79.

134. Nixon, *Memoirs*, p. 1070.

135. Ibid., p. 1069.

136. Ibid., p. 1079.

137. ACTI, HVT Folio 23, p. 81.

138. Ibid., p. 93.

139. Ibid., p. 94.

140. Ibid.

141. Ibid., p. 83.

142. Ibid., pp. 98–9.

143. Ambrose, *Nixon*, Vol. III, p. 434.

144. Ibid.

145. Public Papers of the President, 1974, pp. 626–9.

146. Nixon, *Memoirs*, p. 1083.

147. Public Papers of the President, 1974, pp. 626–9.

148. Ibid.

149. ACTI, HVT Folio 23, p. 95.

150. Ibid., p. 104.

151. Ibid., p. 105.

152. Public Papers of the President, 1974, pp. 630–2.

153. ACTI, HVT Folio 23, p. 106.

154. Public Papers of the President, 1974, pp. 630–2.

155. Nixon, *Memoirs*, pp. 1089–90.

156. ACTI, HVT, Folio 23, p. 107.

157. ACTI, Howard Baker, interview with author, September 1991.

158. Suzanne Garment, *Scandal: The Culture of Mistrust in American Politics* (Random House Inc, 1991), pp. 14–15.

Chapter 20: Exile and Renewal

1.   Robert Sam Anson, *Exile: The Unquiet Oblivion of Richard M. Nixon* (Simon & Schuster, 1985), p. 30.
2.   ACTI, Egil Krogh, interview with author, September 1991.
3.   *New York Times*, 26 May 1977.
4.   Unattributable interview with author by Nixon staff member, July 1991.
5.   Anson, *Exile*, p. 55.
6.   ACTI, RN, letter to author, 27 January 1991.
7.   Anson, *Exile*, p. 54.
8.   Ibid., p. 57.
9.   *New York Times*, 9 September 1974.
10. *New York Times*, 4 October 1974.
11. ACTI, Howard Baker, interview with author, September 1991.
12. ACTI, RN, letter to author, 27 December 1991.
13. Anson, *Exile*, p. 77.
14. RN diary entry, 2 December 1974.
15. Nixon, *In the Arena*, p. 23.
16. ACTI, Frank Gannon, interview with author, September 1991.
17. RN diary entry, 18 November 1974.
18. Ibid.
19. Ibid.
20. Unattributable interview with author by Nixon staff member, September 1991.
21. Nixon Eisenhower, *Pat Nixon*, p. 434.
22. RN diary entry, 10 November 1974.
23. RN diary entry, 18 November 1974.
24. Ibid.
25. RN diary entry, 20 November 1974.
26. RN diary entry, 2 December 1974.
27. RN diary entry, 7 December 1974.
28. Kutler, *The Wars of Watergate*, p. 576.
29. Nixon Eisenhower, *Pat Nixon*, p. 437.
30. ACTI, Jack Brennan, interview with author, September 1991.
31. ACTI, Arnold A. Hutschnecker, interview with author, September 1991.
32. ACTI, Patrick Hillings, interview with author, April 1991.

33. ACTI, Frank Gannon, interview with author, September 1991.

34. Ibid.

35. Ibid.

36. Nixon, *In the Arena*, p. 19.

37. RN diary entry, 2 December 1974.

38. RN diary entry, 26 December 1974.

39. Anson, *Exile*, p. 92.

40. ACTI, RN interview with author, December 1989.

41. David Frost, 'I *Gave Them a Sword': Behind the Scenes of the Nixon Interviews* (William Morrow & Company Inc, 1978), p. 82.

42. Anson, *Exile*, p. 180.

43. Ibid., pp. 162–3.

44. Ibid., p. 167.

45. Ibid., p. 169.

46. Unattributable interview with author by Nixon staff member, September 1991.

47. Anson, *Exile*, p. 187.

48. ACTI, Jack Brennan, interview with author, September 1991.

49. Anson, *Exile*, p. 196.

50. *New York Times*, 14 November 1978.

51. All quotations not otherwise attributed in this section are from Jonathan Aitken personal papers, author's diaries for November 1978.

52. George Thomas, letter to Richard Nixon, 3 November 1978.

53. ACTI, Lord Blake, letter to author, 6 November 1990.

54. WLP, RN, letter to President Carter, 20 December 1978.

55. WLP, President Carter, letter to RN, 22 December 1978.

56. Anson, *Exile*, p. 207.

57. Nixon Eisenhower, *Pat Nixon*, p. 458.

58. ACTI, Jack Brennan, interview with author, July 1991.

59. WLP, RN memorandum to President-elect Reagan, 18 November 1980.

60. Ibid.

61. ACTI, William Clark, interview with author, September 1991.

62. ACTI, Robert C. McFarlane, interview with author, October 1991.

63. WLP, RN, letter to President Reagan, 14 January 1982.

64. WLP, RN, letter to President Reagan, 1 November 1982.

65. Ibid.

66. WLP, RN, letter to President Reagan, 25 February 1983.

67. WLP, RN, letter to President Reagan, 17 October 1984.

68. Anson, *Exile*, p. 235.
69. *New York Times*, 9 August 1984.
70. ACTI, John Taylor, interview with author, October 1991.
71. WLP, RN, letter to Frank Carlucci, 6 November 1987.
72. WLP, RN memcon to file dictated night of 28 April 1987.
73. ACTI, Roger Stone, interview with author, July 1991.
74. *New York Times*, 15 April 1988.
75. Richard Nixon, 1999: *Victory Without War,* (Simon & Schuster, 1988), p. 130.
76. ACTI, John Taylor, interview with author, October 1991.
77. Winston S. Churchill, *Great Contemporaries,* (Odhams 1947), p. 195; Nixon, *In the Arena*, p. 143.
78. ACTI, John Taylor, interview with author, October 1991.
79. ACTI, RN letter to author, 27 December 1991.
80. Nixon, *In the Arena*, pp. 368–9.
81. ACTI, Rose Mary Woods, interview with author, July 1990.
82. All extracts from presidential speeches taken from White House Press Office transcript issued 19 July 1990.
83. *Los Angeles Times,* 17 July 1990.
84. Ibid.
85. Ibid.
86. *New York Times,* 20 July 1990.
87. ACTI, Loie Gaunt to author, 21 July 1990.
88. ACTI, Ron Walker, interview with author, September 1991.

Epilogue

1. ACTI, Patricia Nixon, interview with author, 14 March 1992.
2. Ibid.
3. ACTI, RN, interview with author, 14 March 1992.
4. Ibid.
5. *New York Times* 11 March 1992.
6. *The Times* (London), 17 March 1992.
7. ACTI, RN, interview with author, 14 March 1992.
8. Ibid.

INDEX

'yellow' sheet, 220
Yeltsin, Boris, xix, 679–82
Yom Kippur War, 107, 550
Yorba Linda, Cal., 2, 5–9, 12, 14–16, 18, 78, 85,
    97, 301, 395. 618, 669–70, 672, 678, 683
    Elementary School, N. a pupil at, 13–15, 21
    Presidential Library and Birthplace, 399,
        669, 678
Young, David, 498–500

Z

Zahedi, Ardeshir, 638, 667
Zawawi, Omar, 638
Zelnick, Bob, 639
Zetterberg, Stephen, 173
Zhivkov, Todor, 669
Ziegler, Ron, x, 355, 483, 581, 602, 614, 626,
    628, 630–31, 633, 638, 670